# HISTORY OF TIPU SULTAN

# HISTORY OF TIPU SULTAN

Mohibbul Hasan

*History of Tipu Sultan*
Mohibbul Hasan



First Edition 1951
Second revised and enlarged edn 1971
Reprinted 2005, 2009, 2013, 2017, 2022
**Reprinted 2024**

ISBN 978-81-87879-58-9



*Published by*
**AAKAR BOOKS**
28 E Pocket IV, Mayur Vihar Phase I
Delhi 110 091, India
www.aakarbooks.com

*Printed at*
D.K. Fine Art Press, Delhi

*To*

*the Memory*

*of*

*Sabira Zaidi*

## PREFACE TO THE SECOND EDITION

The first edition of *History of Tipu Sultan*, published in 1951, has been out of print for many years. Although, in 1962, I was able to visit Britain and France and consult the private papers and records relating to the second half of eighteenth century India, I could not, on account of my preoccupations elsewhere, start work on the second edition of the book. Meanwhile, a number of studies on Tipu Sultan have come out. In 1962 Professor K. Antonova of the Oriental Institute, Moscow, brought out *The Struggle of Tipu Sultan against British Colonial Power*, containing six documents that throw light on Tipu's efforts from 1793 onwards to enter into an offensive and defensive alliance with the French. A short study of Tipu has been made by Subbaraya Gupta in his *New Light on Tipu Sultan* (1967). His account of the political and administrative history of Tipu's reign is very sketchy and superficial and is based on secondary sources. But his chapter on Tipu's Endowments to the Hindus and Hindu Institutions is valuable and contains new information. Mr. Denys Forrest's *Tiger of Mysore—The Life and Death of Tipu Sultan* (1970) is a substantial and, on the whole, an objective work. But unfortunately it is not well documented and is poor on Tipu's administration and religious policy and his industrial and commercial activities. Besides, it is mainly based on the English and French published works and some unpublished English records. The author has not consulted the private papers in Britain, the archival material in Paris, and the Persian, Marathi and Portuguese sources. Another work which is expected to be soon published, is Dr. C. K. Kareem's Ph.D. thesis entitled *Kerala under Haidar Ali and Tipu Sultan*. Dr. Kareem is the first person to have made an extensive use of the local records in Malayalam.

In this edition I have made a reassessment of the sources, and attempted, with the help of works, hitherto unutilised, to make a more detailed study of Tipu and fill in the gaps left out in my earlier work. I have, accordingly, rewritten a number of chapters, made alterations and additions in others, and corrected mis-statements and removed obscurities which occurred in the first edition.

It is evident from the French records and the Wellesley Papers that Tipu started negotiations with the French shortly after concluding the Treaty of Seringapatam in 1792, and that, in 1797, he sent an embassy to the Isle of France and obtained some troops. This, however, did not entitle Wellesley to invade Mysore. As an independent ruler Tipu was perfectly within his rights to align himself with any power he liked. Macpherson had, in February 1786, offered to send help to the Marathas and the Nizam in the Maratha-Mysore War, and, in October 1787, Cornwallis had tried to form a coalition of the Marathas, the Nizam and the English against Tipu. Again, on July 7, 1789, Cornwallis had given certain assurances to the Nizam which were of an offensive nature and were openly directed against the Sultan. Yet Tipu had not used these provocations as a *casus belli*.

Tipu reaped the fruits of his father's policy. He inherited the enmity of the English, the Marathas and the Nizam from Haidar Ali, who had earned it because of his repeated invasions of the Carnatic and his expansionist aims. Tipu could have won over his Indian rivals by surrendering the conquests which his father had made; and he could have gained the goodwill of the English by becoming their client. The first would have reduced him to a third rate power and the second to the status of the Nawabs of Oudh and the Carnatiç. To a man possessed of his ability, energy and ambition neither of these conditions could be acceptable.

In powers of organisation and administrative ability, Tipu was equal to his father. But he was more intrepid and a better soldier, though as a general and as a skilful politician he was inferior. He also did not show in his dealings with men and affairs the same tact and political judgement as Haidar did. His character, too, was more rigid and uncompromising. This explains why in his last war with the English he preferred death to submission. Haidar would have, in a similar situation, submitted to even the most humiliating terms and waited for an opportunity to retrieve his position.

Although Tipu did not understand the intricacies of European politics and the social and economic forces existing in England and France, he was in many respects modern in outlook. He was the first Indian prince to think of sending his son to Europe for education and to try to model his administration on that of the European Companies. He was also the first Indian ruler to establish trading factories in India and abroad, to realise the importance of western technological progress and employ European technicians to develop industries in his kingdom. He was in many respects much ahead of his time; but, owing to the social, economic and political conditions obtaining in India and Western Europe, his failure was inevitable. No one, not even Haidar Ali, would have been able to prevent the map of India from turning red.

Tipu has been regarded by some writers as the first Indian nationalist and a martyr for India's freedom. But this is a wrong view arrived at by projecting the present into the past. In the age in which Tipu lived and ruled there was no sense of nationalism or an awareness among Indians that they were a subject people. It will, therefore, be too much to say that Tipu waged war against the English for the sake of India's freedom. Actually he fought in order to preserve his own power and independence, although it is clear from his correspondence that he was, more than any other Indian prince, conscious of British designs on India, and accordingly warned the Nizam and the Marathas against the danger. He even tried to form a confederacy of Indian rulers to prevent the establishment of British rule.

It is my pleasant duty to express my gratitude to Dr. F. R. C. Robinson of Trinity College, Cambridge, for reading parts of the manuscript and giving useful suggestions. I am thankful to Dr. A. H. Morton of the British Institute of Persian Studies, Tehran, for providing me with valuable material on the relations between Tipu and Fath Ali Shah Qajar. My thanks are also due to Mr. Denys Forrest for his comments on the first edition of my book and for helpful information. Mr. Forrest and I have been debating Tipu for the last two years during which he was writing his *Tiger of Mysore* and I was preparing the second edition of my book. I am obliged to Dr. C. K. Kareem for sending me an English translation of the local records in Malayalam bearing on Tipu's rule in Kerala. I am thankful to my son Mr. Najmul Hasan of *the Hindustan Times* for going through the proofs and to Mr. Muhammad Qamaruddin of Calcutta University for help of various kinds. Last but not least, I am under deep obligation to the French Government and the British Council for a generous grant which enabled me to visit Britain and France and consult the records and private papers relating to Tipu Sultan.

*University of Kashmir,*
*Srinagar*

MOHIBBUL HASAN

## PREFACE TO THE FIRST EDITION

The story of Tipu Sultan's life has not before been told in any detail or fairness to him. Wilks's *History of Mysore* was published too soon after the fall of Seringapatam, and was obviously written without full knowledge of facts. Moreover, Wilks, as James Mill observed, "appears to have little pleasure in praising the Sultan, but great in imputing to him all the bad qualities which belong to the most despicable, as well as the most odious, of the human race". Bowring's *Haidar Ali and Tipu Sultan* is nothing else but a summary of Wilks's work. There are also brief references to the career of Tipu in the general histories of India, but in most of these he is the mark of passionate and most foul obloquy. On the other hand, his biographies in Urdu, published in recent years, have made him the subject of fulsome adulation. In the present work, however, an attempt has been made to give an accurate picture of Tipu Sultan by disengaging his personality from masses of fictions and distortions which have gathered round him. As practically the whole of Tipu's life was taken up with fighting, I have devoted considerable space to campaigns and battles. However, other aspects of his career have not been ignored. Sufficient attention has been paid to the causes and results of wars, while Tipu's relations with the English, the French, the Nizam, the Marathas and the Ottoman Sultan have been fully discussed. The last three chapters of the book have been devoted to a description of the Sultan's Government and army, his reforms and religious policy, his efforts at industrialisation and State Socialism, his character, his failures and achievements. It is hoped that this study will enable the reader to appraise the career and character of this extraordinary man.

I take this opportunity to record my indebtedness to my friend and colleague, Dr. N. K. Sinha, whose advice and assistance were of inestimable value throughout the course of my work. I owe him more than I can ever repay. I am grateful to Dr. A. B. M. Habibullah who read considerable parts of the book in manuscript and gave me valuable criticisms. My thanks are due to Professor Nilkantha Sastri of Madras for having translated for me into English the relevant portions of the Mackenzie Manuscripts. I am under deep obligation to Rev. Fr. C. Van Exem of St. Xavier's College, Calcutta, who, in spite of his official duties and manifold activities, not only translated the Dutch records for my use, but also cheerfully undertook the painful task of reading through the proof-sheets. I am grateful to the following for useful suggestions and help of various kinds: Dr. M. Z. Siddiqi, my uncle Shaikh Jawwad Ali Khan, Dr. Mahdi Husain, Mr. S. K. Roy, Mahmud Khan of Bangalore, Rev. Fr. V. Courtois of St. Xavier's College and Chevalier Panduranga S. S. Pissurlencar. I should like to acknowledge my gratitude to the Director of the Indian National Archives, Delhi; to the Curators of the Madras Record Office, and the Bibliotheque Publique, Pondicherry; and to the Librarians of Calcutta University and the Royal Asiatic Society of Bengal, for their unfailing courtesy and assistance. Finally, I would thank the authorities of the University of Calcutta for a grant which enabled me to visit Madras, Pondicherry and Mysore in order to collect material for this book.

*Calcutta University,*
*March,* 1951

# CONTENTS

## ILLUSTRATION



## MAPS

## ABBREVIATIONS[1]

| | |
|---|---|
| A.N. | Archives Nationales, Paris. |
| B.M. | British Museum. |
| Cal. Per. Cor. | Calendar of Persian Correspondence. |
| F.O. | Foreign Office Papers, Public Record Office, London. |
| I.H.C. | Proceedings of the Indian History Congress. |
| I.H.R.C. | Proceedings of the Indian Historical Records Commission. |
| I.O. | India Office Library, London. |
| J.I.H. | Journal of Indian History. |
| Mack. MSS. | Mackenzie Manuscripts. |
| M.A.R. | Reports of the Mysore Archœological Department. |
| M.R., Mly. Cons. | Madras Records, Military Consultations. |
| M.R., Mly. Count. Cor. | Madras Records, Military Country Correspondence. |
| M.R., Mly. Desp. | Madras Records, Military Despatches to Court. |
| N.A., O.R. | National Archives of India, 'Original Records in Persian. |
| N.A., Pol. Pro. | National Archives of India, Political Proceedings. |
| N.A., Sec. Pro. | National Archives of India, Secret Proceedings. |
| P.A. | Pondicherry Archives (these have now been removed to Paris). |
| P.R.C. | Poona Residency Correspondence. |
| W.P., B.M. | Wellesley Papers, British Museum. |

[1] For other abbreviations, see Bibliography.

Reproduced from the *Tarikh-i-Sultanat-i-Khudabad* with the kind permission of the author.

The original was in the Collection of the late Sri Ram of Delhi, author of the *K̇humkhana-i-Jawid*.

CHAPTER I

# ANCESTRY, EARLY LIFE AND ACCESSION

THE history of Tipu Sultan's family, until it was raised to prominence by his grandfather, Fath Muhammad, is for the most part obscure. But from some accounts it appears that Tipu was descended from the Quraish of Mecca;[1] and it was probably at the end of the sixteenth century that his ancestors arrived in India by sea[2], instead of following the usual land route from the north-west. Beyond these facts nothing is known about them before they emigrated to India.[3]

The first person of the family about whom some tradition has been preserved was Shaikh Wali Muhammad who, according to Kirmani, came to Gulbarga from Delhi with his son Muhammad Ali during the reign of Muhammad Adil Shah (1626-56) of Bijapur.[4] He was a religious man, and attached himself to the shrine of Sadr-ud-din Husaini, commonly known as Gisu Daraz,[5] and was given a monthly allowance for his subsistence. He married his son, Muhammad Ali, to the daughter of one of the servants of the *dargah*. When Wali

[1] Kirmani, p. 6; *Tarikh-i-Tipu*, f.61b; *Sultan-ut-Tawarikh*, f.80; *Haidar-namah*, p. 81.

[2] *Sultan-ut-Tawarikh*, f.80; *Tarikh-i-Tipu*, f.61; *Haidar-namah*, p. 81. From Kirmani's account it appears that Tipu's ancestors came at the end of the 16th century by the land route from the north-west.

[3] According to an anonymous version preserved in *Karnama-i-Haidari* (pp. 687-94), the origin of the family is traced to one Hasan b. Yahya (d. 874/1469), a Quraish, who was the Sharif of Mecca. His grandson, Ahmad, proceeded to Sana in Yemen, married the daughter of its chief, and after the latter's death became its ruler. But in a conspiracy organised by some of the nobles of Sana to depose him, he was assassinated. His thirteen-year-old son, Muhammad, however, succeeded in escaping to Baghdad where he started business and soon became a prosperous merchant. It was Hasan b. Ibrahim (d. 1075/1664), the sixth in descent from Yahya who, having lost all his money owing to the dishonesty of his father's employees, emigrated to India in search of a livelihood. Hasan began to live in Ajmere with the *mutawalli* of the shrine of Khwaja Muin-ud-din Chishti, and married his daughter. After his death a posthumous son was born to him and was named Wali Muhammad. When the latter grew up, he, with his son Muhammad Ali, proceeded to Shahjahanabad, and from there to Delhi. The rest of the family history is the same as given by Kirmani. The above account may be true; it is also possible that the pedigree was manufactured to bolster up the dynastic prestige of Haidar and Tipu. But I have not found it mentioned in any other source for the History of Haidar and Tipu.

[4] Kirmani, p. 6. Kirmani wrongly calls Muhammad Adil Shah as Ali Adil Shah.

[5] *Ibid.; Sultan-ut-Tawarikh*, f.81. But it does not give the name of the person who attached himself to the shrine. For a short account of the saint's life, see E.I. (New) s.v.

Muhammad died, Muhammad Ali proceeded to Bijapur and began to live with his seven brothers-in-law who were employed in the army of Ali Adil Shah II (1657-72).[1] Soon after, war broke out between the Mughals and the Bijapuris, and in the conflict all the seven brothers-in-law were killed. After this tragedy Muhammad Ali left Bijapur with his family for Kolar whose chief, Shah Muhammad, having some previous acquaintance with him, received him well, and put him in charge of his property. Besides acting as Shah Muhammad's agent, Muhammad Ali also did some farming and rented fields and gardens.[2]

*Fath Muhammad*

Muhammad Ali had four sons: Muhammad Ilyas, Shaikh Muhammad, Muhammad Imam and Fath Muhammad. When they grew up their father advised them to become devotees like their grandfather. But they preferred the profession of arms; so, after the death of Muhammad Ali in about 1697, his son Fath Muhammad left Kolar to enter the service of Nawab Saadatullah Khan of Arcot, who made him a *jamadar* and gave him the command of 200 foot and 50 horse. After some time Fath Muhammad sent for Sayyid Burhan-ud-din, a *pirzada* of Tanjore, and married his daughter. As he served the Nawab faithfully, he was raised to the command of 600 foot, 500 horse and 50 rocket men. It is not known why Fath Muhammad left Arcot.[3] However, he next took service with the Raja of Mysore probably through the recommendation of his nephew, Haidar Saheb, son of Shaikh Ilyas, who was already in the employment of the Raja. But Fath Muhammad did not stay long in Mysore. Although he was given the title of *naik*, yet, owing to the dissensions among the various chiefs in Mysore, he became disgusted and left the State. He then entered the service of Nawab Dargah Quli Khan of Sira,[4] who gave him the command of 400 foot and 200 horse and put him in charge of the fort of Dodballapur.[5] Here in 1721 a son was born to him and was named Haidar Ali. He had also another son called Shahbaz, born three years earlier.[6]

[1] From some accounts it appears that Muhammad Ali was also in the service of the Bijapur Government.

[2] Kirmani, pp. 6-7.

[3] *Ibid.*, pp. 7-10. Kirmani says that Fath Muhammad left Arcot because of the dissensions which followed the death of the Nawab. But the Nawab's death did not take place until 1732. There is some confusion regarding this period of Fath Muhammad's career.

[4] *Ibid.*, p. 10. *Tarikh-i-Tipu*, f.61b, and *Haidar-namah*, p. 81, wrongly give the name of the ruler of Arcot as Dil Dilair Khan. Sira is a town in Tumkur District, Mysore.

[5] It is situated on the right bank of the Arkavati, 27 miles north-west of Bangalore.

[6] Kirmani, p. 11.

*Haidar Ali*

After a few years Dargah Quli Khan died and was succeeded by his son Abdul Rasul Khan. Meanwhile Tahir Khan, through the influence of his patron, Saadatullah Khan, had secured his appointment to the *subedari* of Sira. But Abdul Rasul Khan, aided by Fath Muhammad, refused to give up Sira. This led to an armed conflict in which both Abdul Rasul Khan and Fath Muhammad were killed. Tahir Khan thus became the *subedar* of Sira.[1] Abbas Quli Khan, son of Abdul Rasul Khan, was, however, left in possession of his father's *jagir* of Dodballapur.[2] As Fath Muhammad had left some debts, Abbas Quli Khan began to persecute his family which was in the fort.[3] Although Haidar was at this time only about five and Shahbaz about eight years of age, they were tortured to discharge their father's debts. In this way Abbas Quli Khan seized whatever the family possessed. Plundered of all her property, and alarmed at the treatment meted out to her children, Fath Muhammad's widow informed Haidar Saheb, her husband's nephew, who was employed in Mysore,[4] about her distress. Haidar Saheb immediately appealed to Devraj, the *dalavayi* of the Raja of Mysore, for help. Devraj wrote to the *subedar* of Sira, who reprimanded Abbas Quli Khan for his high-handedness and ordered him to release the family.[5] After securing her freedom, Fath Muhammad's widow, accompanied by her children, proceeded to Bangalore and from there to Seringapatam.[6] Henceforth they began to live under the protection of Haidar Saheb, who brought up Haidar and Shahbaz as his own children and taught them the use of arms and horsemanship. But when they grew up they left him and entered the service of Abdul Wahhab Khan, younger brother of Nawab Muhammad Ali of Carnatic who held the *jagir* of Chittoor.[7] Meanwhile, as Haidar Saheb had become prosperous and influential in Mysore, he sent for his cousins. On their arrival he

[1] Kirmani, pp. 11-13; Wilks, i, pp. 267-8.

[2] *Ibid.*, p. 268. Kirmani wrongly says that Abbas Quli Khan was the son of Dargah Quli Khan.

[3] *Haidar-namah*, p. 81, and *Tarikh-i-Tipu*, f.62a, wrongly say that the family was persecuted by the Nawab of Sira. Thirty-two years later, when Haidar occupied Dodballapur, Abbas Quli Khan fled to Madras; and when Haidar invaded the Carnatic in 1767, he became so panicky that he embarked on a crazy vessel, and would not land until he was assured that Haidar had left the Carnatic. (Wilks, i, p. 493 footnote).

[4] Kirmani, p. 13; *Sultan-ut-Tawarikh*, f.83.

[5] *Ibid.*: *Haidar-namah*, p. 81; *Tarikh-i-Tipu*, f.62a. Except for minor differences the events related in the different works are substantially the same. Both *Haidar-namah* and *Tarikh-i-Tipu* say that the debt was paid by the *dalavayi* and in return Haidar and Shahbaz entered the Raja's service. But it must be remembered that the boys were too young at the time for any kind of employment.

[6] *Sultan-ut-Tawarikh*, f.83; Kirmani, p. 16.

[7] *Ibid.*

presented them to Nanjaraj, the Commander-in-Chief and younger brother of Devraj, who gave them the command of 300 foot and 50 horse.[1] On the death of Haidar Saheb, Shahbaz succeeded to the command of his detachment.[2] It appears that Haidar Ali at first did not possess any independent command but was attached to his elder brother. However, the dash and courage which he displayed in various engagements, and particularly in the siege of Devanhalli[3] (1749) held by Naraingauda, greatly impressed Nanjaraj who conferred on him the title of Khan and a separate command of 200 foot and 50 horse.[4] This was the beginning of his career. Henceforth the obscurity which surrounds his early life disappears and he stands in the full limelight of history.

The next great event in his life was when he accompanied the Mysore army which was despatched by Nanjaraj in 1749 to the assistance of Nasir Jung, Asif Jah Nizam-ul-Mulk's son, who was engaged in the struggle for the Nizamat with his nephew Muzaffar Jung. Nasir Jung at first overpowered his rival who surrendered to him, but on the night of December 16, 1750, he was himself treacherously assassinated by the Pathan Nawab of Cuddapah. Owing to the confusion which followed the incident, Nasir Jung's treasure fell into the hands of the French. But a portion of it was also seized by Haidar Ali with the help of his Bedar peons.[5] On his return to Mysore, with the wealth thus obtained, he augmented his troops and began to train them with the help of some French deserters.[6]

Meanwhile, the contest for the Nawabship of the Carnatic had been going on between Muhammad Ali and Chanda Saheb. Muhammad Ali, hard pressed by his rival, who was supported by the French, applied to Nanjaraj for assistance, and in return promised to cede Trichinopoly and its dependencies to Mysore.[7] Nanjaraj, dazzled by the prospect of acquiring fresh territory, at once proceeded to Trichinopoly to the help of Muhammad Ali. From February to December 1752, the Mysoreans, along with the English, fought Chanda Saheb and the French. And although in May Chanda Saheb was killed, Muhammad Ali did not cede Trichinopoly to Mysore, but ceded only the island of Srirangam.[8] Thereupon, Nanjaraj joined the French and tried his best to capture Trichinopoly from Muhammad Ali and the English. But he did not succeed, and had to return

[1] *Ibid.*, pp. 16-17.
[2] *Haidar-namah*, p. 81; Kirmani, p. 17.
[3] A town 23 miles north of Bangalore.
[4] *Haidar-namah*, p. 81; *Tarikh-i-Tipu*, ff.63b-64b.
[5] Kirmani, pp. 20-21; Wilks, i. p. 300.
[6] *Ibid.*, p. 311.
[7] Kirmani, p. 23; Wilks, i, p. 310.
[8] Kirmani, pp. 23-24; Wilks, i, p. 319. Srirangam is an island and town two miles north of Trichinopoly.

disappointed to Mysore.[1] But although the Trichinopoly campaign proved disastrous to Nanjaraj, it was a blessing in disguise for Haidar who was present throughout the war with the Mysore army along with his detachment. It provided Haidar with the first-hand knowledge of the European mode of warfare, and the courage and perseverance which he displayed in the campaign greatly impressed Nanjaraj and led to his further advancement, so that, when in 1755 he returned to Mysore from Trichinopoly, he was appointed *faujdar* of Dindigul, where a strong man was required to crush the refractory *poligars* of the district. Haidar punished the *poligars*, and succeeded in establishing law and order. During his stay at Dindigul, he also augmented his troops, organised his artillery, and established an arsenal under the supervision of French engineers.[2]

Meanwhile, conditions in the capital were becoming chaotic. The relations of the Raja of Mysore with Nanjaraj and Devraj, who had reduced him to a mere puppet, were very strained. There were even serious differences between the brothers relating to matters of state policy.[3] Moreover, owing to the cost of the expedition to Trichinopoly and the invasions and extortions of the Nizam and the Marathas, the Mysore Government was financially bankrupt. In consequence, the pay of the troops was several months in arrears. They were, therefore, discontented, and to get their grievances redressed sat in *dharna*, preventing water and provisions from being carried into the house of Nanjaraj.[4]

On hearing of the disturbed state of Seringapatam, Haidar immediately proceeded there, for he was regarded as the only man capable of restoring normal conditions. He reconciled Devraj to Nanjaraj, assured the Raja of his protection and succeeded in discharging the arrears of pay to the soldiery.[5] These measures enhanced his prestige so much that, when the Marathas invaded Mysore in 1758, he was appointed Commander-in-Chief, and was entrusted with the task of repelling the invaders.[6] Haidar, as usual, rose to the occasion and, by carrying on a successful struggle against the invaders, extorted favourable terms of peace.[7] He returned to Seringapatam in triumph, and was welcomed by the Raja and the people as the saviour of Mysore.

The State finances were, however, still disorganised, and the pay of the troops having again fallen into arrears, they once more sat in

[1] Kirmani, pp. 24-25.
[2] Sinha, *Haidar Ali*, pp. 14-7.
[3] Devraj retired from political life in Feb. 1757. (Wilks, i, p. 397).
[4] *Ibid.*, p. 405.
[5] *Ibid.*, pp. 406-7.
[6] Kirmani, p. 30.
[7] *Ibid.*, pp. 31-3; Wilks, i, p. 412

*dharna.* Nanjaraj, unable to cope with the problems which faced him, and having lost his prestige owing to his repeated military defeats, decided to retire from political life.[1] Haidar, who was only waiting for this opportunity, quietly slipped into his shoes. Soon, however, Haidar found his position threatened by a conspiracy organised by his *diwan*, Khande Rao, who wanted to oust him from power and take his place, and by the Raja who felt that the change had not improved his prospects. But Haidar, owing to his fertility of mind, strong determination and courage, succeeded in defeating his enemies. By 1761 he had become the undisputed ruler of Mysore.[2]

After this Haidar embarked upon his career of conquest; and although he suffered some setback because of the three Maratha invasions of Mysore (1764-72), he had, by 1778, succeeded in carving out for himself an extensive kingdom.

*Birth of Tipu*

Haidar's first wife was the daughter of Sayyid Shahbaz, commonly known as Shah Mian Saheb, a *pirzada* of Sira. She gave birth to a daughter but, while in child-birth, she was attacked with dropsy which made her paralytic for the rest of her life.[3] Haidar then married Fatima, also called Fakhr-un-Nissa, who was the daughter of Mir Muin-ud-din,[4] for some years the Governor of the fort of Cuddapah. When she became pregnant, she, with her husband, paid a visit to the tomb of Tipu Mastan Aulia in Arcot,[5] and prayed for her safe and easy delivery and for the birth of a son. Her prayers were answered and on Friday, the 20th Zil-Hijja, 1163 A.H. (November 20, 1750) a son was born to her at Devanhalli, where she had been living ever since its capture by the Mysoreans in 1749, and was named Tipu Sultan after the name of the saint. He was also called Fath Ali after his grandfather Fath Muhammad.[6]

It has been suggested by some writers that Sultan was the title

[1] *Ibid.*, pp. 415-6.

[2] *Ibid.*, p. 465 *seq.*

[3] Kirmani, p. 18.

[4] *Ibid.*, p. 19; *Karnama-i-Haidari*, p. 864. Mir Ali Raza Khan was her brother. He played a distinguished part in the reign of Haidar. He was killed in the battle of Porto Novo (July 1781). Miles in his translation of *Nishan-i-Haidari* (p. 26) says that Haidar married the sister-in-law of Ali Raza Khan. But this is an incorrect translation. (See Kirmani, R.A.S.B.MS. No. 200, f.10a).

[5] His tomb was built by Nawab Saadatullah Khan in about 1729. (See Bowring, *Haidar Ali and Tipu Sultan*, p. 118 footnote). When Haidar occupied Arcot in 1780 he paid a visit to the tomb and gave generous offerings. (Hamid Khan, ff. 30b-31a).

[6] Kirmani, pp. 19-20; *Karnama-i-Haidari*, p. 864. I have not been able to find out the meaning of the word 'Tipu'. Probably like many other names it is meaningless. It is commonly thought that Tipu means tiger in Kanarese, but the Kanarese word for a tiger is *huli* and for a lion *simha*. (For a fuller treatment of this point, see Bowring, *Haidar Ali and Tipu Sultan*, pp. 223-4).

adopted by Tipu when he succeeded his father. But it appears from most of the contemporary sources that Sultan was a part of Tipu's name and not a title.[1] It is true that in the English and French contemporary accounts, Tipu, as a prince, is called Tipu Saheb, and immediately after his father's death he is mentioned as Tipu Sultan and sometimes as Nawab Tipu Sultan. But, it must be remembered that Europeans in those days used oriental names in a very loose and inaccurate manner. Besides, there is no evidence to show that Tipu assumed the title of either Sultan or Nawab at the time of his accession. It was in 1787 that he adopted the title of Padshah after the conclusion of his war with the Marathas.

The information regarding the early years of Tipu's life is very scanty; only a few stray facts are known about it. When Khande Rao plotted the destruction of Haidar, Tipu was with his father at Seringapatam and was only ten years old. Haidar Ali, realising that his life was in danger, and that he would not be able to defend himself, escaped from the capital on the night of August 12, 1760, leaving behind Tipu with the rest of the family. Khande Rao removed them to a house near the mosque inside the fort of Seringapatam, and placed a guard outside; otherwise he treated them kindly.[2] On the reconquest of Seringapatam, Haidar removed his family to Bangalore which he regarded as safer than the capital. And when Bednur was conquered in 1763, Tipu was sent there.[3]

### *Education*

Although himself illiterate, Haidar appointed able teachers to give his son the usual scholastic education of a Muslim prince. Tipu was also taught riding, shooting and fencing, and attended his father in military reviews in order to acquire knowledge in discipline and the art of war, especially as practised by the Europeans. His military preceptor was Ghazi Khan who was the best partisan officer in Haidar's service.[4] The names of his teachers of Urdu, Persian, Arabic, Kannada, Quran, *Fiqh* and other subjects are not known.

When in 1766 Haidar invaded Malabar, Tipu, who was then only fifteen years of age, was ordered to accompany him in order to gain experience of actual warfare.[5] On one occasion, in the course of this campaign, Tipu displayed great dash and courage. Haidar attacked Balam, a hilly country lying to the south of Bednur. Its *poligar* was

[1] Kirmani says that he was named Tipu Sultan. Peixoto, Hamid Khan and *Tarikh-i-Tipu* also refer to him as Tipu Sultan both while he was a prince and a ruler. It must be remembered that Sultan was also a part of the name of Tipu's sons.

[2] Punganuri, p. 8; Wilks, i, p. 469.

[3] Punganuri, p. 33.

[4] *Ibid.*, Stewart, *Memoirs of Hyder and Tippoo*, p. 43; Wilks, ii, p. 300.

[5] Punganuri, p. 33

defeated, but he refused to surrender. Tipu, in the meantime, with only two or three thousand troops penetrated through thick, dark forests to the place where the *poligar's* family and dependants had taken refuge, and attacked them. He slew many and captured the rest. This obliged the *poligar* to surrender. His example was followed by other Malabar chiefs who hastened to acknowledge Haidar as their suzerain.[1] Haidar was so proud of his son's exploit that he conferred on him the command of 200 horse to act as his bodyguard. Soon after the number was raised to 500 and a suitable *jagir* consisting of the districts of Malvalli, Konanur, Dharmapuri, Pennagaram and Tenkarai-Kottai was assigned to him.[2]

### *The First Anglo-Mysore War*

When the First Anglo-Mysore War (1767-1769) broke out the English were supported by the Nizam and the Marathas. But Haidar succeeded in breaking up the coalition and isolating the English. He first detached the Marathas and made peace with them, and then tried to win over the Nizam who lay encamped at Chennapatna, about 37 miles south-west of Bangalore. On June 11, 1767, he sent Tipu, accompanied by Mahfuz Khan and Mir Ali Raza, to the Nizam with five elephants, ten beautiful horses and cash and jewels as presents for him.[3] Tipu was received with kindness by the Nizam who addressed him as Nasib-ud-daulah[4] (the fortune of the State), gave him gifts of robes and jewels and conferred upon him the title of Fath Ali Khan Bahadur.[5] The young prince carried on the negotiation with tact, and succeeded in persuading the Nizam to change sides and join Haidar in fighting the English.

On his return to Seringapatam on June 19, Tipu was given his first nominal command under his military preceptor Ghazi Khan, and was ordered to proceed towards Madras. Mir Ali Raza Khan, Makhdum Saheb and Muhammad Ali also accompanied him. But while the Mysore horse were engaged in plundering St. Thomé and the very country houses of the Madras councillors, and had thrown the inhabitants of the town into the greatest consternation, he received a letter from Haidar, who had been defeated by Smith at Tiruvannamalai,[6] ordering him to return immediately. He, therefore, at once retraced his steps.[7] Major Fitzgerald and Colonel Tod tried

[1] Kirmani, pp. 96-97.

[2] Punganuri, p. 33. Malvalli is in Mysore District, Mysore; Konanur is in Hassan District, Mysore; the other three places are in Salem District, Tamil Nadu (Madras).

[3] *Ibid.*, p. 16; Kirmani, pp. 128-29.

[4] *Ibid.*, p. 129.

[5] Hamid Khan, f. 21b.

[6] It is a small town in South Arcot District, Tamil Nadu (Madras).

[7] Kirmani, p. 132; Wilks, i, p. 587.

to intercept him, but Tipu was much too quick for them and succeeded in joining the main army which lay encamped about ten miles from Vaniyambadi.[1] He was received by his father like a youthful hero whose exploits offered the only consolation for his own defeats.[2] Tipu was at this time only 17 years old.

The defeat at Tiruvannamalai did not dishearten Haidar, and although the monsoon had started, he continued his preparations for the next campaign. Early in November he marched from Kaveripatnam[3] to attack Tiruppatur[4] and Vaniyambadi. Tipu accompanied his father and helped him in the conquest of the two forts. He was also present when, immediately after, Ambur was besieged. Haidar lay before the place for about four weeks, but failed to capture it owing to the gallant resistance offered by Captain Calvert, and on the approach of the English army under Colonel Smith, he withdrew. Smith reached Ambur on December 6, and the next morning he marched to attack Haidar who was encamped at Vaniyambadi. He took Haidar by surprise and succeeded in dislodging him from the place. Tipu, who commanded the Mysore cavalry, distinguished himself on this occasion, and by holding in check the English advance secured a safe retreat for the main army to Kaveripatnam.[5]

On December 14, 1767, Tipu, again accompanied by Ghazi Khan, was sent with a light corps to reinforce Lutf Ali Beg who was engaged with the English on the Malabar coast. He was at Bednur when he heard of the capture of Mangalore by Major Garvin and Captain Watson on March 1, 1768. He at once set out with 1,000 horse and 3,000 foot. On the 7th there was a skirmish, but Tipu avoided giving battle and retreated. He attacked the English on the 15th and the 16th, but was repulsed. On May 2, however, he succeeded in capturing the bazaar of Mangalore, but was defeated in the attempt to seize the fort. But the English failed to hold out much longer. On hearing that Tipu had been reinforced by an army of 4,000 foot and 2,000 horse and by a train of artillery, and that Haidar himself had come down to the coast to join him, they decided to evacuate the fort. Their retreat was so panicky that they left behind their sick and wounded consisting of 80 Europeans and 180 sepoys, and most of their arms and ammunition,[6] and "the sepoys were said in the confusion to have fired upon their European comrades."[7] After this Tipu

[1] Sinha, *Haidar Ali*, p. 75. Vaniyambadi is a town in Salem District, Tamil Nadu (Madras).
[2] Michaud, i, p. 51.
[3] It is a village in Salem District.
[4] It is a town in Salem District.
[5] Kirmani, pp. 133-34. According to Kirmani Haidar defeated Smith at Vaniyambadi.
[6] Sinha, *Haidar Ali*, p. 82.
[7] Cadell, *History of the Bombay Army*, p. 83.

occupied Mangalore, and Haidar on his arrival on the coast expelled the English from the rest of his Malabar possessions.[1] Tipu continued to fight side by side with his father until the end of March, 1769, when Haidar dictated peace terms to the English before the very gates of Madras.

*The Maratha-Mysore War* (1769-1772)

In November 1769 the Marathas invaded Mysore. Haidar wanted to avoid pitched battles; his policy was to harass the enemy and thus compel them to withdraw from his kingdom. Accordingly, Tipu was despatched to destroy forage, poison wells and tanks, and to persuade the people to retire from their villages into the neighbouring forts. He was then required to remain on the outskirts of Bednur to intercept the convoys coming from Poona. Tipu performed the duties entrusted to him with considerable success; but, in February 1770, he was recalled by his father to help him in resisting the Maratha advance.[2] Tipu obeyed the summons, and was present with him when the latter, against the advice of his commanders, decided to retreat from near Melukote[3] to Seringapatam on the night of March 5, 1771. Haidar Ali, according to Kirmani, "let go the thread or clue of care and caution, and after eating and drinking what was presented to him, he rose, and the troops forming by his directions, commenced the march."[4] It was, therefore, not surprising that the retreat was turned into a rout. Tipu, being in charge of the baggage, was in the rear of the army. Haidar sent him repeated messages to come to the front, but everything was in such a state of confusion that no word reached him until the next morning. Wilks states that when Tipu came in the morning, "Hyder not only accosted him in a strain of the lowest scurrility, but in a paroxysm of brutal drunken rage, seized a large cane from the hand of one of his attendants, and gave the heir apparent a most unroyal and literally most unmerciful beating." Tipu felt so angry and hurt at the humiliation to which he had been unjustly subjected by his father that, as soon as he withdrew from his presence, he dashed his turban and sword on the ground, and swore that he would not draw his sword that day, and he kept his word.[5]

Meanwhile, in the general panic when many important commanders of Haidar were either killed, escaped or taken prisoners, Tipu escaped in the garb of a mendicant, accompanied by Sayyid Muham-

[1] Sinha, *Haidar Ali*, p. 82-3.
[2] Peixoto, v, 163; Wilks, i, p. 685.
[3] It is a sacred town in Seringapatam *taluk*.
[4] Kirmani, p. 102.
[5] Wilks, i, pp. 695-6. This account by Wilks is not supported by any other contemporary evidence.

mad, and joined his father at Seringapatam. Haidar, overwhelmed with grief at the thought of the loss of Tipu, was praying for his safety at the tomb of the saint, Qadir Wali, situated north-east of the fort.[1]

Although the Marathas had defeated Haidar, they failed to follow up the victory. They remained so much occupied with plunder that it was not until ten days had passed that they appeared before Seringapatam. Meanwhile, Haidar had completed his preparations for the defence of the capital. When its siege began, Tipu played an important part in its defence. He led out sorties, and created disruption in the Maratha ranks.[2] After continuing the siege for about 33 days, Trimbak Rao withdrew from Seringapatam, and early in October with 35,000 men he marched to Tanjore. From there he set out to plunder the Baramahal and Coimbatore. Tipu was thereupon despatched to harass Trimbak Rao and frustrate his designs.[3] But he was not successful, because with only about 6,000 horse he could not hold his ground against the large Maratha army. He, therefore, decided to return to the capital. But on his way back, he succeeded in routing and plundering one of the Maratha detachments.[4]

During the early part of the war, Tipu had been stationed in the province of Bednur to disrupt the Maratha lines of communications. He had performed this task with a great deal of success. But after his recall the Maratha forces were able to receive their supplies from Poona without any great difficulty. Haidar, therefore, again sent Tipu, accompanied by Srinivas Barakki, a noted partisan, with about 4,000 horse to the skirts of Bednur. Haidar's plan was successful, for the young prince captured a huge convoy coming from Poona.[5] This, according to Grant Duff, was "the only success which attended his (Haidar's) arms during the whole season."[6] In July 1772 Haidar agreed to a humiliating peace with the Marathas.

In November 1772 the Peshwa Madhav Rao died. This was a signal for an outburst of dissensions at Poona, which Haidar, as a skilful politician, could not fail to turn to his advantage. He, therefore, sent Tipu to reoccupy the territory which the Marathas had wrested from him. Tipu first besieged Sira, and captured it after a three months' siege. He then attacked Maddagiri[7] which fell in four days. After this he occupied Gurramkonda and Chennarayadurga,[8]

[1] *Haidar-namah*, p. 92; Wilks, i, 698. Kirmani, p. 104, says that Tipu escaped in the garb of a Pindari.

[2] Kirmani, pp. 109-110.

[3] *Ibid.*, p. 111.

[4] *Ibid.*, p. 113; Sinha, *Haidar Ali*, p. 112.

[5] Wilks, i, p. 702. According to Kirmani, p. 118, the military stores and provisions captured were laden on 30 elephants, 100 camels and 50 mules.

[6] Duff, i, p. 569.

[7] It is a *taluk* in Tumkur District, Mysore.

[8] It is a hill fortress in Tumkur District, Mysore.

and helped Haidar in the reduction of Hoskote.[1] In 1775 Tipu again helped his father to conquer Bellary, a dependency of Basalat Jung. In 1778, with 10,000 selected horsemen, he attacked Dharwar which was garrisoned by 3,000 troops. He looted the town and the mint, but failed to capture the fort, and was forced to retreat. However, on his way back to the main army, he succeeded in occupying Hubli,[2] and in February 1779, when Haidar attacked Chitaldrug, he helped him in reducing the fort.[3] Thus between the years 1774 and 1778 Haidar had succeeded, with Tipu's assistance, in reconquering not only the territories up to the Tungabhadra which the Marathas had wrested from him in the previous wars, but also that part of their kingdom which lay between the Tungabhadra and the Krishna.

### *The Second Anglo-Mysore War*

On July 20, 1780, Haidar Ali with an army of 90,000 men swept through the pass of Changama into the Carnatic.[4] He sent his second son Karim to attack Porto Novo, while he himself, with his eldest son Tipu, proceeded to invest Arcot.

When the news of Haidar's invasion of the Carnatic reached Madras, the Governor and Council decided that the main army of the Company should be assembled and formed under Sir Hector Munro near Conjeeveram to be joined there by the troops from Guntur under Colonel Baillie, after which operations should commence against the Mysoreans. Munro left Madras on August 25 reaching Conjeeveram after four days, and there waited for Baillie. Hearing of these movements, Haidar despatched Tipu with 10,000 troops and 18 guns to cut off Baillie's detachment on its way to join the main army;[5] while he himself abandoned the siege of Arcot and marched towards Conjeeveram to keep watch on Munro.

### *Defeat of Baillie*

Baillie, with a corps consisting of 107 Europeans, 2,606 sepoys and 9 guns, reached the river Kortalaiyar on August 25. It was dry then, and he should have crossed it. Instead, he committed the grave mistake of encamping on the north bank. That same night the river became flooded, and as a result, it was not until September 3 that Baillie was able to cross it. On the 6th, he managed to reach Peram-

[1] Kirmani, p. 123; *Haidar-namah*, p. 94. Hoskote is a town in Bangalore District.

[2] N. A., Sec. Pro., Dec. 18, 1775, Nos. 13-15. Towards the close of 1778 Dharwar was also occupied.

[3] *Ibid.*, March 18, 1779; *Haidar-namah*, p. 95.

[4] Wilks, i, p. 812.

[5] Gleig, *Munro*, p. 23. According to a French version (See Pissurlencar, *Antigualhas*, I, fasc. ii, No. 67, p. 242), Tipu was sent with a division of Haidar Ali Beg and 5,000 horse.

bakkam, fifteen miles from Conjeeveram.[1] The same day he was attacked by Tipu who had been continuously harassing him from the time he had left the south bank of the river.

The English occupied a very advantageous position. Two tanks and some large marshes covered them at nearly all points. Nevertheless, Tipu's ardour was not restrained and he attacked. His infantry advanced in such good order that Baillie thought that Munro himself was coming to his assistance. But the discharge of rockets from Tipu's cavalry on their wings made the English quickly discover their mistake. They at once replied by a general discharge of their cannon. As a result Tipu's infantry had to bend. Tipu then led an attack of his cavalry. But now a winding stream came to the rescue of the English, for it prevented the Mysoreans from crossing over and reaching the enemy. After the action had lasted for three hours, Tipu withdrew, having suffered a loss of 900 men from the cannonade.[2] He reported to his father that without reinforcements he would not be able to achieve his object of routing Baillie. Haidar, therefore, sent a division under Muhammad Ali.[3] Baillie, who had lost about 250 killed and wounded,[4] likewise wrote to Munro that he could not force his way to Conjeeveram, and hoped that the Commander-in-Chief would join him at Perambakkam.[5] On the 9th morning he received reinforcements of 1,000 men under Colonel Fletcher detached by Munro. The same night he left Perambakkam, but he had not proceeded even half a mile when Tipu again began to harass him by gun and rocket fire upon the rear of the English force. Still, the latter continued to advance, but when Conjeeveram was only nine miles away, Baillie, against the advice of Fletcher, his second in command, decided to halt for the rest of the night. He adopted this measure partly because he wanted to give rest to his troops overpowered by fatigue, and partly because he thought that by morning Munro would come to his assistance.[6] But as Munro did not come, his halt proved fatal and unnecessary, and Tipu was not slow to take advantage of it. Tipu ordered his guns to be placed during the night in an advantageous position and at once wrote to his father to support the attack with the main army. Haidar Ali, having ascertained from his spies that Munro would not leave his position, sent away the bulk of his infantry and artillery in the evening to reinforce Tipu.[7]

[1] Fortescue, iii, p. 442. Perambakkam is a village in Chingleput District, Tamil Nadu (Madras).

[2] Pissurlencar, *Antigualhas*, i, fasc, ii, No. 67, p. 243.

[3] *Ibid.*

[4] *Ibid.* But according to the English accounts Baillie lost 100 killed and wounded.

[5] Fortescue, iii, p. 443.

[6] Kirmani, p. 196; Innes Munro, p. 150.

[7] Fortescue, iii, p. 444.

At 4 o'clock in the morning he himself set off to take part in the attack on Baillie. Munro's stupor remained unbroken. Accordingly, when the next morning at five the English force began its march and had not proceeded more than six miles, a heavy fire from Tipu's guns opened on their rear, while Haidar's cavalry appeared on their flanks. Baillie, nevertheless, continued to advance and bravely resisted the attacks of the enemy. But finding the fire unbearable, he halted near the village of Pollilore[1] and engaged the enemy's batteries with his own guns, at the same time ordering ten companies of sepoys under Captains Rumtry and Gowdie to storm Tipu's guns. They succeeded in taking three or four, but, having lost their order during the advance, they had to relinquish the prize; and during the confusion which followed, they were charged by a large body of Mysore cavalry which cut most of them to pieces.[2] An hour later, Haidar himself advanced to the attack. At first his troops were taken for Munro's by the English detachment, and a great shout of joy rose up from everyone. But when they found that the new troops were not Munro's but Haidar's, their joy was turned to dismay. Within a short time they were surrounded by Haidar's cavalry, while his artillery opened a cross-fire on them. The English, thereupon, formed themselves into a square and bravely resisted the attacks of the Mysoreans. But soon after, Lallée, perceiving that the English had placed their ammunition behind a small ravine, ordered his artillery to aim at it. They succeeded in blowing up three of the English tumbrils. This spread consternation in the English force. Taking advantage of this a fresh charge of cavalry was made. The Indian sepoys, who had to bear the chief brunt of the attack, became completely demoralised and they either fled or were killed. Baillie, however, rallied the Europeans who had also been thrown into confusion. But soon, finding that resistance was useless, he surrendered.[3] 200 Europeans, including 50 officers, most of them wounded, were taken prisoners.[4] These were the remnants of Baillie's total force of 3,853 men. The Mysorean losses amounted to about 2 or 3,000 men.[5] When the English prisoners were brought before Haidar he pitied their condition, treated them kindly and gave them each a piece of cloth and a rupee.[6] They were then sent off to Seringapatam. Wilks's account

[1] It is a village about 6 miles from Conjeeveram.

[2] Fortescue, iii, pp. 444-45. Wilks, ii, p. 20, says that the loss of the sepoys was slight, but he is always in the habit of minimising the English losses.

[3] Fortescue, iii, pp. 446-47; Pissurlencar, *Antigualhas*, i, fasc, ii, pp. 243-44; Kirmani, p. 198.

[4] Fortescue, iii, p. 447; Wilson, ii, p. 8.

[5] Kirmani, p. 198.

[6] Hamid Khan, ff. 30a-30b. Tipu also treated the prisoners with great humanity. (See Lawrence, *Captives of Tipu Sultan*, p. 130).

that the massacre of the English troops continued even after quarter was given, appears to be a fabrication.[1]

The disaster which befell Baillie's army was, according to Sir Thomas Munro, "the severest blow that the English ever sustained in India."[2] And for this the main responsibility rests with Munro, who refused to move from his camp in Conjeeveram for the sake of his stores and heavy guns. When at last he did move in the morning, his march was so aimless and tardy that he was too late to rescue Baillie, and on hearing the fate of the English detachment, returned to Conjeeveram. Demoralised by the defeat of Baillie, and finding himself without provisions—for the stock of provisions he now discovered was barely sufficient for one day's consumption—he decided to retreat to Madras. The heavy guns and all stores which could not be carried, were thrown into a large tank and the retreat commenced early on the morning of September 11.[3]

If after Baillie's retreat Haidar Ali had attacked Munro with his whole army, he would have not only destroyed his army but would have met with hardly any serious opposition up to the gates of Madras. "I am almost confident," wrote Sir Eyre Coote, "had Hyder Ali followed up his success at that time to the gates of Madras, he would have been in possession of that most important fortress."[4] But Haidar missed the opportunity and, instead of setting out with his whole force, he merely despatched Tipu with some cavalry in pursuit of Munro. Tipu harassed the English troops all the way to Chingleput, captured the whole of their baggage, and killed and wounded 500 men.[5] Munro, however, succeeded in reaching Chingleput on the morning of September 12, and after joining the detachment from the south under Colonel Cosby, resumed the march next day and arrived safely at Marmalong, about four miles south of Madras, on the 15th.

On the 19th Haidar left Conjeeveram, and proceeded to capture Arcot the siege of which had been postponed because of Munro's approach. The place had been strengthened under the supervision of a European engineer, but after six weeks two breaches having been effected, on October 31 Tipu and Maha Mirza Khan were ordered to carry out a simultaneous assault. Tipu failed in the attempt, but Maha Mirza Khan succeeded in entering the breach. Tipu, thereupon, rallied his men and made a fresh attack. This time he succeeded and easily occupied the town. The loss of the town disheartened the

[1] Wilks, ii, p. 22. The French accounts and Hamid Khan do not refer to any atrocities. Even Innes Munro does not say anything about them, although he mentions that 16 English officers and privates remained unhurt due to the clemency of the French hussars.

[2] Gleig, *Munro*, p. 25.

[3] Fortescue, iii, p. 448.

[4] N.A., Sec. Pro., Nov. 18, 1780, pp. 2137-8.

[5] Innes Munro, p. 172.

garrison who immediately after surrendered. They were given favourable terms which were strictly adhered to by Haidar.[1]

After the conquest of Arcot, Tipu was ordered to march against Satghur, Ambur and Tiagar.[2] Satghur was a strong fort with a garrison of 2,000 men and sufficient provisions and ammunition to withstand a long siege. But when Tipu surrounded the place, Wali Muhammad Khan, its Commandant, seeing the strength of the Mysore army, lost heart and capitulated on January 13, 1781.[3]

From Satghur Tipu proceeded to attack the fort of Ambur. It contained a garrison of brave soldiers commanded by an Englishman, named Captain Keating, who refused to surrender and bravely defended the place for over a month. But after the walls were breached, and his ammunition was exhausted, he capitulated on the 15th.[4]

During this period Tiagar was also reduced by Tipu. After cannonading the fort for about four weeks, its walls were breached and Tipu prepared to make an assault. But owing to the shortage of water, Roberts, its Commandant, agreed to surrender. Tipu thereupon ordered the firing to cease. However, as during the night there was a rainfall which temporarily relieved the garrison, and as Roberts heard that Sir Eyre Coote was hurrying up to his relief, instead of capitulating the next morning, as agreed upon, he opened fire from the guns of the fort. Hostilities therefore recommenced. But very soon the garrison was again driven to extremity, for Coote had been unable to render them any assistance. After making only a single march towards Tiagar he had become inactive owing to the lack of military supplies. The Commandant, therefore, again offered to capitulate. But this time Tipu refused to listen to him, and gave orders to assault the fort which, after severe fighting, was occupied on June 7. The Commandant and other officers were taken prisoners.[5] Tipu next marched against other forts in the locality and occupied them one by one without much difficulty. He then returned to his father, who was at Arcot with the main army, and was honoured with gifts.[6]

Shortly after Tipu was ordered by his father to resume the siege of Wandiwash, which had been abandoned in January 1781 on the approach of Sir Eyre Coote. Tipu invested the place on June 22 with thirteen pieces of battering train, supported by an "adequate force,"[7]

[1] Wilks, ii, pp. 34-35.

[2] Satghur and Ambur are in North Arcot District. Tiagar is a village in South Arcot District.

[3] Kirmani, pp. 205-6.

[4] N.A., Sec. Pro., April 27, 1781, p. 1050; Wilson, ii, p. 13; Kirmani, p. 206. Kirmani says that the Commandant held out for 15 days.

[5] Kirmani, pp. 210-11; Wilks, ii, p. 46.

[6] Innes Munro, p. 209.

[7] Wilks, ii, p. 63. According to N.A., Sec. Pro., Sept. 7, 1781, p. 2053, Tipu had 30,000 troops. But this is an overstatement.

and took possession of the *pettah*. He then made preparations for besieging the citadel and succeeded in completely surrounding it. But just when he was ready to open the batteries to cause a breach, he received an order from Haidar to capture it by an escalade and then to proceed to intercept the English detachment coming from Bengal by land. So Tipu changed his own plan of attack and made an attempt at escalade on the night of July 16, but was repulsed partly because Captain Flint had been informed of the impending attack and had accordingly prepared for it, and partly because the news of the defeat of Haidar by Coote at Porto Novo had damped the spirit of the assailants.[1] After this failure, Tipu, on hearing of the arrival of Coote at Karunguli[2] on his way to relieve Wandiwash, raised the siege and set off towards Conjeeveram to intercept the English forces sent from Bengal under Colonel Pearse. He assembled his forces at Gummadipundi, half-way on the high road from Madras to Nellore, expecting that the detachment would march along this ordinary road. But Pearse took the shorter route, although more difficult, which passed between the lake of Pulicat and the sea along the shore, and succeeded in joining Coote at Pulicat on August 2.[3] Having thus failed to intercept the English detachment, Tipu returned to his father at Arcot in the first week of August.

### *Defeat of Braithwaite*

From Arcot Tipu was sent to Tanjore where he inflicted a crushing defeat on Colonel Braithwaite on February 18, 1782. Braithwaite, who commanded the Company's forces in Tanjore with 100 Europeans, 1,500 Indian troops and 300 cavalry, lay encamped at the village of Kumbakonam on the banks of the Coleroon. He was in an open country but, being protected by large and deep rivers, he considered himself prefectly secure from any surprise attack. Tipu invaded Tanjore with 10,000 horse, an equal number of infantry, 20 pieces of cannon and 400 Europeans under Lallée, and after capturing a number of places attacked the English. He was so swift in his movements that the latter were completely taken by surprise. Colonel

[1] N.A., Sec. Pro., Sept. 7, 1781, p. 2053; Wilks, ii, p. 64. During the period that Tipu was operating in the North and South Arcot Districts, and against Wandiwash, Haidar was campaigning in Tanjore. On June 16, 1781, Coote proceeded from the neighbourhood of Cuddalore to expel the Mysoreans from there, and to give protection to Trichinopoly against which Haidar was preparing to march. Haidar decided to check the English advance, and even prepared to hazard a battle. "He was dissuaded, it is said, but in vain, from this rash design by the prudence of his eldest son." (Mill, iv, p. 147). The result was that Haidar was defeated by Coote on July 1, 1781, in the battle of Porto Novo, and sustained severe loss. (For this battle see Sec. Pro., Sept. 7, 1781, pp. 2037-52).

[2] It is a village with historic fort in Chingleput District, about 45 miles south of Madras.

[3] N.A., Sec. Pro., Sept. 7, 1781, p. 2071.

Braithwaite tried to retreat to Tanjore, but found it impossible as he was surrounded on all sides by the enemy. He, therefore, formed the army into a hollow square, with the artillery outside and cavalry in the centre, and prepared to resist. The incessant fire from the guns of the Mysoreans and the attacks of their cavalry inflicted great loss upon the English army. The latter, however, bravely held its ground for about twenty-six hours (from February 16 to 18), but they failed to withstand the last attack led by Lallée with his 400 Europeans, supported by the Mysore cavalry, and became panic-stricken.[1] So Braithwaite sued for protection, which was immediately given. It is wrong to say that, but for the mediation of Lallée, the English troops would have been brutally massacred. In reality, after Braithwaite had sent a flag of truce not a single person was killed, and although his troops were taken prisoners,[2] they were not badly treated. One of the prisoners himself testified that Tipu "paid them every attention that was necessary. He not only furnished them with clothes and money, but at the same time gave strict orders to all his keeladars to be attentive to them during their march to Haidar's army, who was then lying at Conjeeveram."[3]

The result of Tipu's victory over Braithwaite was that it totally upset Coote's plans, and enabled the Sultan to occupy a large part of Tanjore easily. Tipu continued to operate in the south until he was ordered by Haidar to join the French troops who had arrived under Duchemin at Porto Novo on February 25, 1782. Accordingly, he proceeded to Porto Novo where he joined the French, and at the end of March moved with them against Cuddalore which was invested on April 2. As it was poorly defended, it capitulated the next evening. It proved to be a convenient station, both naval and military, to the French. From Cuddalore Tipu, along with the French troops, proceeded on May 1 to effect a junction with his father. The united armies marched on Perumukkal, a hill fort situated about twenty miles north-west of Pondicherry, and appeared before it on May 11. As soon as Coote heard of this, he marched to its relief, but owing to a violent storm accompanied by rains his progress was arrested, so that when he reached Karunguli he heard that Perumukkal had capitulated on the 16th.[4] From Perumukkal the united forces marched to Wandiwash where they had not been more than four days when, on hearing of the approach of the English, they withdrew towards

[1] Mill, iv, pp. 172-73.

[2] N.A., Sec. Pro., March 11, 1782, p. 983. "Colonel Braithwaite, sometime after the engagement began, sent a flag of truce to the enemy, after which no person was killed, but the remainder of the garrison was taken prisoner." (*Ibid*).

[3] Lawrence, *Captives of Tipu Sultan*, p. 126. Mill also observes: "And it is but justice to add, that Tipu treated his prisoners, especially the officers and wounded men, with real attention and humanity." (Mill, iv, p. 173).

[4] N.A., Sec. Pro., June 6, 1782, pp. 1921-3, 1930.

Pondicherry. Coote, anxious to give battle to Haidar, followed him. The latter entrenched himself in a strong position near Kilyanur, fourteen miles north-west of Pondicherry. The English General, realising that it would be dangerous to fight on the ground chosen by the enemy, moved towards Arni on the 30th,[1] which, because of its central position, was Haidar's chief depot for storing military supplies. Coote calculated that a move to this place would oblige the Mysoreans to leave their strong position at Kilyanur. He was right in his judgment,[2] for as soon as Haidar heard of this advance, he detached Tipu the same evening with orders to proceed to Arni and reinforce it, following himself the next day without his French allies who refused to accompany him. Tipu by forced marches reached Arni accompanied by Lallée and occupied a commanding position on June 2. At 8 o'clock in the morning when the advance guard had reached the ground near the fort on which Coote intended to encamp, Haidar commenced a very brisk though distant cannonade in its rear, while Tipu opened a heavy fire from the front.[3] This was an embarrassing situation for the English army which was in a hollow with commanding ground all round.[4] However, by ten, Coote retrieved the situation and attacked Haidar who retreated across the river of Arni leaving a gun, five tumbrils full of ammunition, and two carts loaded with shot which had got stuck in the bed of the river.[5] This was probably only a tactical retreat,[6] because when Coote returned on June 4 to resume the siege of Arni, he found, to his despair, that Haidar was still present in the neighbourhood, and Tipu had not only reinforced the garrison but had also removed the treasure from Arni. In such a situation, there was nothing left for Coote to do except to march back to Madras.[7]

After this Tipu continued campaigning in Tanjore until November, when he was ordered by Haidar to proceed to the west coast for the protection of his Malabar possessions menaced by the Company's forces.

### *Tipu is Sent to Malabar*

On February 8, 1782, Sardar Khan, who had invested Tellicherry, was defeated by Major Abington. He lost all his military equipment

[1] N.A., Sec. Pro., July 4, 1782, pp. 2054-5.

[2] *Ibid.*, p. 2147.

[3] Wilks, ii, p. 137.

[4] N.A., Sec. Pro., July 4, 1782, p. 2055.

[5] *Ibid.*, p. 2062.

[6] *Haidar-namah*, p. 97, attributes the victory to Haidar. It is significant that Haidar's loss in the battle of Arni was slight. Coote observed: "I do not conceive it could have been considerable. We captured 30 or 40 horses of all kinds." The English casualties, on the other hand, were 74 men and 7 horses. (N.A., Sec. Pro., July 4, 1782, p. 2149.)

[7] *Ibid.*

and was taken prisoner with about 1,200 men.[1] But he felt so ashamed of his defeat that he committed suicide soon after.[2] The English followed up their victory by capturing the French fort of Mahé the next day, and Calicut on the 13th.[3]

Hearing of these losses, Haidar sent Makhdum Ali to the Malabar coast. But Makhdum also failed to make any progress, and on April 7 he was defeated and killed at Trikalur, about sixteen miles east of Calicut, by Colonel Humberstone who had been sent by the Bombay Government to act with Major Abington from Tellicherry against Haidar's kingdom on the Malabar coast.[4] After this victory Humberstone returned to Calicut in May because heavy rains and the stubborn resistance offered by the Mysoreans had prevented him from pushing his way to Palghat. But in the third week of May be again set out from Calicut, and after occupying Ramagiri Kota[5] on September 21, marched on Palghat. He made repeated attempts to capture it but it proved too formidable. Finally, on October 21, owing to a judicious and bold attack by the Mysoreans, he lost nearly all his provisions and ammuntion. He was, therefore, left with no alternative but to retreat to the coast as fast as he could. During the march his troops were constantly harassed by the Mysoreans who hung on their flanks and rear.[6] On November 18, when he reached Ramagiri Kota, he heard the news of Tipu's approach with a large army including the corps of Lallée.

The news of the disaster which befell Makhdum's army greatly perturbed Haidar. He, therefore, ordered Tipu to proceed to the west coast to retrieve the situation. Accordingly, as soon as the state of the season appeared favourable, Tipu hurried from the vicinity of Karur to the relief of Palghat and reached there on November 16. But finding that Humberstone had already left, he immediately set out in pursuit, and on the morning of the 19th his advanced parties succeeded in overtaking the English army which had marched but a few miles from Ramagiri. Humberstone was, thereupon, obliged to make "a very rapid retreat,"[7] followed by Tipu who continued to harass and connonade the English army throughout the day until he reached the river Ponnani towards dark. Tipu had so far conducted the expedition with great swiftness and ability, but now he neglected to keep watch over the movements of the English troops under the impression that, as the river was impassable, they were at his mercy

[1] Cadell, *History of the Bombay Army*, p. 100; Wilks, ii, p. 108.
[2] *Haidar-namah*, p. 97.
[3] Cadell, *History of the Bombay Army*, p. 100.
[4] N.A., Sec. Pro., May 23, 1782, p. 1684.
[5] It is a village situated about half-way between Calicut and Palghat.
[6] Mill, iv, p. 183.
[7] M. R., My. Cons., Jan., 1783, Macleod to Madras, Nov. 30, 1782, vol. 85, p. 94.

and were trapped. This lack of vigilance on his part was taken advantage of by the English troops who, after finding a ford, which was for an ordinary man chin-deep, crossed the river under cover of night. As soon as Tipu came to know of it he at once set out in pursuit of the English. But they had such a big start that Tipu, in spite of the rapidity of his movement, could not overtake them and they succeeded in reaching the town of Ponnani, leaving behind, however, their equipment.[1]

On reaching Ponnani, Tipu, with the assistance of Lallée, began operations against it. On the morning of November 29 he made a strong and well designed assault in four columns on the position of Colonel Macleod who had arrived from Calicut the previous evening to reinforce Humberstone. But he failed to achieve any success. The position occupied by Macleod was very strong. The sea was on one side, the river on the other, while the front was protected by a wood and a morass.[2] Tipu, nevertheless, continued to blockade the town, and would have occupied it if he had not received the news of his father's death and been compelled to leave.[3]

*Haidar's Death and his Will*

Haidar had been suffering from carbuncle since November 1782. But at first it was considered by his physicians to be an ordinary boil. Soon, however, the true nature of the disease was found out, and the Hindu, Muslim and French physicians tried their best to cure him, but in vain. His health continued to deteriorate and he died on the morning of December 7, 1782, at Narasingarayanpet near Chittoor at the age of 60.[4]

There were various rumours current at the time regarding Haidar's last advice to Tipu. Those that emanated from the English side suggested that a few days before his death Haidar had written to Tipu that his struggle with the English had been futile, for they were too powerful to be crushed, and had, therefore, advised him to make peace with them and not to trust the French any longer.[5] According to another English source, Tipu was supposed to have found, while performing the last rites to his father's body, a scrap of paper in Haidar's turban in which he was advised to make peace with the English.[6] According to Michaud, on the other hand, Haidar advised

[1] Wilks, ii, pp. 163-64; see also A.N., C[2] 141, Lallée to Minister, Aug. 31, 1783, f. 17b. Ponnani is a town and port in Palghat District, Kerala.

[2] *Memoir of John Campbell*, p. 34; M.R., Mly. Cons., Jan. 1783, vol. 85A, p. 144.

[3] A.N., C[2] 141, Lallée to Minister, Aug. 31, 1783, f. 17b.

[4] See A.N., C[2] 155, de Morlat to Minister, Feb. 6, 1783, ff. 203a-207a, for a good description of Haidar's illness and death.

[5] M. R., Mly Cons., Jan. 23, 1783, vol. 85A, pp. 427-28; M. R., Mly. Desp. to Court, vol. xviii, pp. 66-67.

[6] N.A., Sec. Pro., Feb. 10, 1783.

Tipu to ally himself with the French, for only with their help could the English, who were the strongest power in India, be driven out of the country.[1]

Both these accounts appear to be untrustworthy, since neither of them is corroborated by any reliable contemporary evidence. The English versions were merely wishful thinking, representing the desire of the Madras Government for a speedy end of the war. Moreover, they were intended to show the world that even a powerful ruler like Haidar was in the end obliged to recognise the invincible might of the English. The real fact, however, is that before he died Haidar sent for his secretary and ordered him to write to Tipu that he should immediately return to him after making suitable arrangements for the defence of his Malabar possessions.[2] Then, on the afternoon of the day he expired, he called his high officials like Purnaiya, Krishna Rao, Shamaiya, Abu Muhammad, Mir Sadiq, Muhammad Ali, Badr-uz-zaman Khan, Ghazi Khan and Maha Mirza Khan, and told them that he would soon die and requested them that, after he was no more, they should serve his son Tipu as faithfully as they had served him.[3]

As soon as Haidar died, his chief officers held a meeting and decided that his death must be kept a secret till the arrival of Tipu in order to prevent any possibility of rebellion. Surgeons continued to visit Haidar's camp twice daily. The chiefs also paid their regular visits. At the same time the army was kept in readiness, so that if there was any attempt at rebellion, it might be crushed. A careful watch was kept on letters sent and on people leaving.[4] At the same time Maha Mirza Khan was at once despatched to the Prince with the the news of Haidar's death. On the night of December 9 Haidar's body was deposited in a large chest and sent under an escort as if it were a valuable treasure being despatched to Seringapatam. At Kolar the body was for the time being deposited in the tomb of Fath Muhammad.[5] It was afterwards removed to Seringapatam and was buried in the grand mausoleum built by Tipu.[6]

In spite of every precaution the news of Haidar's death leaked out, and certain malcontents tried to exploit the situation. Muhammad Amin, who commanded 4,000 stable horse and was the cousin-german of Haidar, formed a conspiracy with Shams-ud-din, the Bakhshi, to overthrow the provisional Government and proclaim

[1] Michaud, i, p. 82.

[2] Kirmani, p. 248.

[3] *Haidar-namah*, p. 100. *Haidar-namah* does not mention the names of Badr-uz-zaman Khan, Maha Mirza, Ghazi Khan and Muhammad Ali. But Haidar must have invited them because they too enjoyed his confidence.

[4] A.N., C² 155, de Morlat to Minister, Feb. 6, 1783, ff. 208b-209a.

[5] Kirmani, pp. 249-50; *Haidar-namah*, p. 100.

[6] Kirmani, p. 262.

Abdul Karim, Haidar's second son, as ruler. They selected him as their candidate because he was a man of weak intellect and would permit them to rule in his name. But the plot was discovered. Bouthenot,[1] a French officer, who too was in the plot, confessed everything on being given assurance of personal security. Muhammad Amin and Shams-ud-din had therefore no other alternative but to confess their guilt. They were put in irons and sent to Seringapatam. Bouthenot was also sent as a prisoner to a fort lest he should correspond with Madras or incite Tipu's officers.[2] Similarly, some other mischievous elements also tried to raise their heads but they were suppressed by Poulet, the second Captain of the regiment *d'Austrasia*, who remained loyal to Tipu.[3]

Apart from these sporadic cases there was no serious rising and the business of the government continued to be carried on as usual. The reason was that the army was loyal to him[4] and, "in general, had the highest opinion of Tipu's humanity and abilities to command them, and were highly confident that they would succeed while he commanded them. Their idea of Karim Sahib was that he was of no experience and did not possess any good sense."[5]

On December 21, the army left Narasingarayanpet, and the next day encamped at Chuckmaloor to await the arrival of Tipu. The march was carried on in perfect order. Haidar's palanquin, which he was supposed to be occupying, was covered and was carried with all the honours of war.[6]

Tipu received his father's letter on the afternoon of December 11, 1782, and set out the next morning with great speed towards Chittoor. On reaching Coimbatore he appointed Sayyid Muhammad Mahdavi Commandant of Seringapatam in place of Muhammad Shitab,[7] and ordered Arshad Beg Khan, who had been appointed by Haidar to take charge of the Government of Malabar, to remain on the defensive at Palghat. Tipu's marches were at first the longest that his troops could bear, but they became shorter on receiving the information that the army and the chief officials were loyal to him. He reached the camp, which had been set up for him about two miles from the main army, on the evening of December 28.[8] He refused to be received with any display of pomp and show and entered

[1] The French officer was Bouthenot and not Boudelot as mentioned by Wilks.
[2] Wilks, ii, pp. 169-70; see also A.N., C[2] 115, de Morlat to Minister, Feb. 6, 1783, ff. 209a-10a.
[3] P.A.MS. No. 400, Bussy to de Castries, March 31, 1783.
[4] M.R., Mly. Cons., Feb. 1, 1783, Macleod to Stuart, Jan. 31, vol. 85 B. p. 512.
[5] N. A., Sec. Pro., Jan. 13, 1783. Letter from Geo. Taylor, Asst. Secretary to General Stuart, Dec. 11, 1782.
[6] A.N., C[2] 155, de Morlat to Minister, Feb. 6, 1783, f. 215b.
[7] *Tarikh-i-Tipu*, f. 95a.
[8] A.N., C[2] 155, f. 216a.

the camp after sunset in simple style, and when he gave audience to his principal officers he seated himself on a plain carpet as an expression of grief for his father.[1] The next morning he sent for his brother and the chiefs who had so well maintained law and order in his absence, and talked with them for a long time. After this all the army chiefs were allowed to come and pay their condolences and compliments. Then, at 9 o'clock in the night, he sat on the throne of his father with all pomp and ceremony, and assumed the title of Nawab Tipu Sultan Bahadur. His army saluted him with 121 guns and the French with 21.[2]

Tipu succeeded to a large kingdom which was bounded in the north by the river Krishna, in the south by the state of Travancore and the district of Tinnevelly, in the east by the Eastern Ghats and in the west by the Arabian Sea. He succeeded to a treasury at Seringapatam containing three crores of rupees, besides large quantities of jewels and valuables.[3] There was also a large treasury at Bednur, but soon after Haidar's death it was seized by Ayaz and Matthews. Moreover, he was left by his father an army of about 88,000 men, excluding garrisons and provincial troops,[4] which was at that time definitely the best fighting force in India.

The most pressing problem at the moment being the prosecution of the war, Tipu turned his attention to military matters. He ordered immediate payment of the arrears to the troops, and laid down that henceforth they would get their salaries regularly after thirty days. A French officer was employed to remodel the irregulars and organise the artillery, and arrangements were made to keep the army constantly supplied with provisions and other necessities. This was done by abolishing arbitrary control over prices in order to attract traders. The result of this measure, as testified by Stuart, was that supplies began to be available in plenty in Tipu's camp.[5] It was also at this time that the Sultan issued instructions to his officers to treat the prisoners of war generously. But while he was engaged in these reforms, he heard of the advance of the English army under General Stuart towards Wandiwash.

[1] Wilks, ii, pp. 171-72.
[2] C²155, ff. 216a-216b.
[3] Wilks, ii, p. 172.
[4] *Ibid.* According to Punganuri, pp. 34-35, Haidar's army at this time consisted of 12,000 regular cavalry, 2,000 irregular horse, 30,000 foot, 12,000 Carnatic militia, 5,000 infantry and some artillery.
[5] M. R., Mly. Cons., Jan. 18, 1783, General Stuart's Minute, vol. 85A, p. 287.

CHAPTER II

# THE WAR WITH THE ENGLISH (*Continued*)

## *Defeat of Stuart*

THE news of Haidar's death was received with great satisfaction by the English at Madras. The Governor pointed out that "we must derive as much advantage out of this as possible,"[1] and Coote wrote of "the many beneficial effects which may be expected to our general interests in India by the important event of Hyder Ali's death. It opens to us the fairest prospect of securing to the mother country the permanent and undisturbed possession of the eastern dominions."[2] Even Nawab Muhammad Ali waxed enthusiastic. "For God's sake," he requested the Governor of Madras, "use every exertion at this critical time."[3]

The English, however, failed to take advantage of Haidar's death. This was because the succession to the throne in Mysore was peaceful; the war of succession between Tipu and Karim, and the rebellion by important chieftains which the English expected did not take place.[4] In spite of this, if Stuart, who was acting Commander-in-Chief in place of Coote, had attacked the Mysoreans immediately on hearing the news of Haidar's death, he would have created a very embarrassing situation for Tipu who was then on the Malabar coast. In fact, Stuart was advised by the Governor of Madras to undertake the offensive as it was the most opportune moment. But he remained inert. At first he refused to believe the news of Haidar's death, but when he did believe it, he maintained that he could not undertake a campaign because his army was in a most deplorable state. There was no rice in stock with the result that the camp followers were dying in hundreds every day, and nearly half of the army was ill. Transport arrangements were very unsatisfactory because, for want of food and fodder, there were neither drivers nor bullocks. Moreover, the monsoon had covered the country with water, and the troops had no tents with which to protect themselves from the inclemencies of the weather.[5]

Stuart's contention that the army was in an unsatisfactory state

[1] N.A., Sec. Pro., Jan. 6, 1783, Macartney to Bengal, Dec. 13, 1782.
[2] *Ibid.*, Jan. 13, 1783.
[3] M.R., Mly. Cons., Dec. 14, 1782, Nawab to Macartney, Dec. 13, 1782, vol. 83A., p. 3905.
[4] *Ibid.*, pp. 3901-2.
[5] *Ibid.*, Jan. 18, 1783, vol. 85A, pp. 272-3.

was no doubt true. But it was he who was responsible for this. Only a month previously he had declared that his army would be in a position to move in any real emergency,[1] but when the time came for action he was caught unprepared. This was because, instead of organising his troops and preparing for war, he remained engaged in squabbles with and criticisms of every officer, civil, military or naval, from the Governor-General to Admiral Hughes.[2] In consequence, it was not until February 5, 1783, that he was able to move from Tirupachur[3] towards Wandiwash with a view to attacking Tipu. But by this time the Sultan was well-established on the throne of Mysore; and as soon as he heard of the movement of the English, he immediately set out with the French troops under Cossigny and encamped in the vicinity of Wandiwash. On the 13th the Mysoreans and the English, separated only by a tributary of the Palar, prepared for battle. Throughout the day there was a continual exchange of desultory firing, but early next morning the English retreated towards Wandiwash, closely pursued by the Mysoreans who killed and wounded nearly 200 of them.[4] Stuart had decided upon this course at the sight of "the order and discipline of the Sultan's army and the imposing appearance of the French battalions."[5] He was, in fact, so awed by Tipu that he withdrew the garrisons of Wandiwash and Karunguli, and blew up and destroyed their fortifications, thinking that they were sure to fall into the hands of the Mysoreans.[6] Tipu, however, could not follow up his victory and take advantage of Stuart's mistakes and fears, for he had to quit the Carnatic and proceed to the defence of his Malabar possessions which were invaded by the English forces under General Matthews.

*Matthews Occupies Bednur*

The Bombay Government had for long held the view that Haidar's Malabar possessions should be attacked in order to divert the whole or most of his forces from the Carnatic. The Madras Government was also of the same opinion, and regarded any other method of conducting the war as useless and a waste of time.[7] Humberstone had been accordingly sent to create such a diversion, but he had failed in the attempt and had been obliged to retreat to Ponnani where he was besieged by Tipu. On hearing this news, the Bombay Government at once sent their provincial Commander-in-Chief, General

[1] *Ibid.*, p. 272.

[2] Fortescue, iii, pp. 479-80.

[3] It is a village 5 miles south of Kortalaiyar river in Chingleput District, Tamil Nadu (Madras).

[4] Innes Munro, p. 308.

[5] Kirmani, pp. 260-1.

[6] *Hukm-namah*, R.A.S.B.MS. No. 1676, f. 8a; *Ibid.*, No. 1677, f. 26b.

[7] N.A., Sec. Pro., Jan. 20, 1783, Bombay to Bengal, Aug. 27, 1782.

Matthews, to the relief of Humberstone. But before Matthews could reach Ponnani, he heard that Tipu had left the west coast. He therefore did not proceed to Ponnani, as the English troops there were now out of danger, but landed at Rajamundroog, about eighty miles south of Goa, in the first week of January and carried it by assault. Onore, some fifteen miles southward, also soon fell with all its dependent posts.[1] But just when Macleod, who had arrived from Ponnani with reinforcements, was preparing to attack Mirjan[2] as the first step to an advance on Bednur, Matthews received instructions from the Bombay Government that, "if the intelligence (of the death of Haidar) were confirmed, he was to relinquish all operations whatever upon the sea-coast and make an immediate push to take possession of Bidnore."[3] The reason why the Bombay Government adopted this plan was that Bednur, a rich and fertile tract, could furnish supplies to the Company's armies, and since it was not far from the coast, it could easily support the operations of the English troops. Moreover, Bednur being one of Haidar's important provinces, the Bombay Government expected its invasion would compel him to make peace with the English.[4]

But Matthews did not approve of the scheme. Before invading Bednur, he wanted first of all to secure his rear and his line of communications. However, as ordered by his superiors, he gave up his old plan, cancelled the whole of his previous dispositions, and landed at Kundapur,[5] the nearest point on the coast from Bednur. In capturing the place he met with considerable resistance, not so much from the ordinary garrison as from the 500 horse and 2,500 infantry which were a part of the army sent by Haidar for the defence of his Malabar possessions.[6]

From Kundapur the English proceeded to Hosangadi, a small fort situated at the foot of the Ghats and commanding the pass of the same name which led to Bednur. During their advance they were constantly harassed, but when they decided to attack the fort it was found to have been abandoned, although it was well-built and supplied with fifteen pieces of excellent cannon. On January 25 the army entered the pass. The ascent consisted of a winding road of about seven miles in length defended by a number of redoubts well-supplied with cannon. But one by one all the redoubts were occupied and the English army succeeded in reaching Haidargarh, a very strong fort defended by 1,700 men and 25 cannon and situated at the

[1] Wilks, ii, p. 200.
[2] Mirjan is a village in North Kanara District, Mysore.
[3] M.R., Mly. Cons., Feb. 1783, vol. 86A, p. 719
[4] *Ibid.*, p. 716.
[5] It is a village in South Kanara District, Mysore.
[6] Wilks, ii, p. 202.

top of the Ghats. But like the others, this also was occupied without any difficulty.[1] From Haidargarh Matthews marched towards the town and fort of Bednur, still fourteen miles away. He possessed no more than six rounds of ammunition for each man, and if he had met with serious resistance his position would have been very precarious. But even this scanty ammunition remained unused, because Ayaz,[2] the Governor of the province of Bednur, sent an English prisoner, named Donald Campbell, with a proposal to surrender not only the town and fort of Bednur but the whole province, provided he was allowed to retain its governorship as before. Matthews having agreed to this, Ayaz surrendered Bednur on January 28. With the fall of the capital many other places in the province also submitted. Large quantities of treasure, stores and valuable effects were found in the fort of Bednur. All this treasure was appropriated by the officers, but no share was set aside for the Company.[3]

On hearing of the invasion of Bednur, Tipu had ordered Lutf Ali Beg to proceed to its defence. But when Lutf Ali reached Shimoga he found that the English were already in possession of a large part of the province, and were proceeding to occupy Anantapur in accordance with the agreement entered into with Ayaz.[4] Lutf Ali Beg at once sent a reliable officer with 300 Chitaldrug peons to surprise its Commandant, who at the orders of Ayaz had agreed to give up the place. The officer succeeded in his mission, and when the English troops appeared before Anantapur to occupy it, he refused to surrender. He made them repeated signs to withdraw, but when they persisted in their advance, the flag of truce was fired on.[5] Thereupon the English besieged the fort, and on February 14, 1783, succeeded in

[1] Innes Munro, p. 311.

[2] Ayaz was a Nair from Chirakkal who had been taken prisoner by Haidar during his Malabar campaign of 1766. He became a Muslim, and because of his abilities and handsome personality, he gained the confidence of Haidar who enlisted him in his *Asad-i-Ilahi* troops. In 1779 he was appointed Governor of Chitaldrug, and early in 1782 he was put in charge of the more important province of Bednur. (Cal. Per. Cor., vii, No. 953; Wilks, i, pp. 741-2). It was during this period that the English made overtures to him. At first Ayaz rejected them, but after Haidar's death he agreed to enter into an understanding with Matthews and hand over to him the whole province of Bednur. (Sec. Pro., May 12, 1783).

Miles in his translation of *Nishan-i-Haidari*, p. 8, refers to Ayaz as "Ayaz Khan, the adopted son of the late Nawab." But in the Bombay edition of the *Nishan-i-Haidari*, and in the R.A.S.B.MS.No. 200, and in other contemporary accounts he is only mentioned as Ayaz, the slave of the Nawab, or Ayaz Khan. The statement of Wilks, ii, p. 205, that Tipu was jealous of Ayaz, and treated him with gross indignity because he was a favourite of Haidar, and that the latter was accustomed publicly to contrast the qualities of his slave with that of his son, is not supported by any reliable evidence.

[3] N.A., Sec. Pro., May 12, 1783. Campbell to Hastings; *Ibid.*, May 26, 1783.

[4] Anantapur is a village in Shimoga District, Mysore.

[5] Wilks, ii, p. 207

carrying it. Luft Ali wanted to recapture it, and was only waiting for reinforcements when he was ordered by Tipu to proceed to the relief of Mangalore which was invested by the English. But before he could reach it, he heard that it had surrendered on March 9,[1] and the enemy had destroyed three men-of-war with fifty or sixty guns and several others of different sizes which were on the stocks.[2]

In the course of this campaign, particularly in the reduction of Anantapur and Onore, the English army perpetrated wanton cruelties. Mill tries to mitigate these by arguing that when quarter was asked for, it was not refused. But he is obliged to admit that "orders were given to shed the blood of every man who was taken under arms; and some of the officers were reprimanded for not seeing those orders rigidly executed."[3] The slaughter was so indiscriminate at Anantapur that all the inhabitants were wantonly and inhumanly put to death, and their bodies were thrown into the tanks in the fort.[4] Even women were not spared. "Four hundred beautiful women, all bleeding with wounds from the bayonet, and either dead or expiring in each other's arms, while the common soldiers casting off all obedience to their officers, were stripping them of their jewels and committing every outrage on their bodies. Many of the women, rather than be torn from their relatives, threw themselves into a large tank and were drowned."[5] The only crime for which the garrison of Anantapur was subjected to these atrocities was that they had offered resistance after the surrender of the fort had been promised by the former Commandant.[6] It is true that they had fired at the flag of truce, but this was done after making repeated signs to the English troops to withdraw. Even if we agree with Wilks that no such signs had been made, or with Scurry that two flags had been sent to the fort and both were detained, the fact remains that the punishments inflicted upon the garrison were out of proportion to their guilt.

### *Tipu Reoccupies Bednur and Besieges Mangalore*

Matthews's success in his invasion of Bednur was meteoric. But he was not allowed to enjoy it long, for Tipu's blow fell quickly on him. In the early part of April the Sultan appeared with a large army, including a French contingent, on the frontiers of Bednur. With 12,000 men he easily captured Haidargarh and Kavaledurga, and sent detachments to occupy the passes in the Ghats in order to cut off

[1] *Ibid.*, p. 208.
[2] *Memoir of John Campbell*, p. 49.
[3] Mill, iv, p. 188.
[4] *The Captivity...of James Scurry*, p. 98.
[5] *Authentic Memoirs of Tippoo Sultan*, p. 34.
[6] *The Captivity...of James Scurry*, p. 98.

the communications of the English army with the sea-coast.[1] Another force was sent to mask Anantapur, while Tipu himself with the rest of his army set out to invest Bednur. He first captured the town by a general assault and escalade, and then besieged the fort into which Matthews had been obliged to retreat with great loss.[2] He ordered the erection of thirteen batteries the regular heavy fire of which caused considerable damage to the buildings in the fort, and daily killed and wounded a large number of the garrison. The defenders, however, led out a number of sorties, but they were repulsed with considerable loss. Meanwhile, the Mysore detachments had occupied the passes in the Ghats, and had thus completely isolated Bednur from Mangalore. Owing to this blockade the garrison were soon reduced to a sad plight.[3] They began to suffer from a shortage of provisions, ammunition and water.[4] Moreover, a "putrid fever" raged in the fort, and 350 sick and wounded men lay exposed to the sun, because Tipu's guns had destroyed all places of shelter.[5] Under these conditions Matthews decided to surrender. He had held out for about eighteen days.[6]

Matthews sent a flag of truce, and informed the Sultan that he was prepared to surrender on the following terms: The English army would march out of the fort with the honours of war, and pile their arms on the glacis, leaving behind in the fort all the property which belonged to the Sultan. After being joined by the garrisons of Kaveledurga and Anantapur, they should be allowed to march unmolested with all their private property to Sadasivgarh, and thence to Bombay. They would not fight the Sultan for a stipulated period. Tipu should furnish them with a guard to protect them during their march which would remain under the orders of Matthews. Besides, a guard of a hundred sepoys from the garrison of Bednur with their accoutrements and thirty-six rounds of ammunition should also be allowed to attend Matthews as a bodyguard during the march to Sadasivgarh. Further, Tipu should furnish the English troops with sufficient provisions and proper conveyance for the sick. And lastly, for the per-

[1] N.A., Sec. Pro., June 23, 1783, Belcliffe to Macartney, May 20, 1783.
[2] Wilks, ii, p. 212.
[3] N.A., Sec., Pro., June 23, 1783, Belcliffe to Macartney, May 20, 1783.
[4] Kirmani, p. 265.
[5] *Sheen's letter in the Narrative of Captain Oakes*, pp. 83-84.
[6] Kirmani, p. 266. There is some difference of opinion regarding the duration of the siege. According to *Tarikh-i-Khudadadi*, p. 8 and *Sultan-ut-Tawarikh*, f. 18, it lasted ten days. Oakes states that it lasted seventeen days, and Sheen says that the cannonading continued for twenty days. According to Kirmani, it took the Sultan eighteen days to seize the fort. Different estimates have also been given of the number of troops which Matthews possessed. According to Wilks, Matthews had 1,200 sepoys and 400 Europeans. Sheen says that he had 1,200 men when he occupied Bednur. But from a letter of Belcliffe to Macartney (N.A., Sec. Pro., June 23, 1783) it appears that the number of the garrison was 2,500.

formance of the terms of the capitulation, Tipu should deliver two hostages before the garrison marched out of the fort.[1]

The Sultan was prepared to accept these terms with the alteration that, before setting out towards Bombay, the English troops should first march out and pile their arms not on the glacis, as proposed by Matthews, but in front of the Mysore army. The English considered this condition disgraceful and rejected it. Early next morning they sallied out in two divisions and stormed the Sultan's grand battery, killing a few of the French and about 100 irregulars. But on being surrounded by the main body of the Sultan's troops, they soon retreated precipitately into the fort.[2] A council of war was then held, and it was decided to accept the terms as altered by Tipu.[3]

But before leaving the fort Matthews ordered all the officers to draw from the Paymaster-General as much money as they wanted. Consequently "both officers and men drew as much as they should have occasion for, some officers taking two thousand and others one thousand pagodas." This was an open violation of an important term of the capitulation because, as Sheen testifies, "this money was all taken from the Sircar property, which by treaty was to belong to the captors. But the General, being apprehensive of so much money being discovered in possession of one man, ordered it to be distributed among the troops."[4]

When Tipu entered the fort after its evacuation by Matthews on the afternoon of April 28, 1783, he did not find there "a single rupee," for all the treasure had been appropriated by the English. This naturally aroused the Sultan's anger and they were harshly dealt with. He ordered them to be kept under a strict guard, deputed spies to watch their movements, and on the morning of May 1 had them searched. The result of the search was that "every knapsack was found to be lined with gold. While the search was going on, the English thrust pagodas down the throats of dogs and even fowls were crammed with precious morsels."[5] Tipu's officials, however, succeeded in securing the greater portion of this wealth which, in possession of the officers alone, amounted to about 40,000 pagodas.[6]

[1] *Sheen's letter in Narrative of Captain Oakes*, pp. 83-84; *Narrative of Captain Oakes*, pp. 1-2. But Oakes does not mention the second article.

[2] *Ibid.* Oakes does not mention this action. Nevertheless, its authenticity cannot be denied because it was in the course of this sortie that Sheen received a slight wound. It is probably to this action that Colonel Price, who was serving with a detachment of Matthews's army near the coast, refers in *Memoirs of a Field Officer*, p. 101.

[3] *Sheen's letter*, pp. 83-4.

[4] *Ibid.*, pp. 84-5, 87.

[5] *The Captivity...of James Scurry*, pp. 306-07.

[6] *Sheen's letter*, p. 88. According to *Tarikh-i-Khudadadi*, p. 12, jewels and money were concealed by the garrison in the cheeks of goats, in loaves of bread, and even in their own private parts. That was why the search had to be made "most minutely in every part, without the least regard to decency."

The appropriation of the Bednur treasure was not the only violation of the capitulation terms committed by the English, they also pillaged the public stores, burnt the Government records and failed to deliver all the Mysorean prisoners of war.[1] Tipu, therefore, put them in irons and marched them off to Chitaldrug.

It has been maintained by Wilks that Tipu had made up his mind to seek some pretext to infringe the terms of the capitulation, but "an empty treasury, together with the money found on searching the prisoners, exempted him from the necessity of recurring to fictitious pleas."[2] There is, however, no evidence to substantiate this view. It is certain that Tipu was glad to get this opportunity of punishing Matthews, whose cruelties towards the garrisons of Onore and Anantapur, and whose transactions with the traitor Ayaz were still fresh in his memory. But there is nothing to show that he had any preconceived plans, and that if Matthews had adhered to the terms of the capitulation, Tipu would still have imprisoned him for his past misdeeds.

After the capture of Bednur, Tipu marched towards Mangalore, the principal sea-port in South Kanara by which Haidar had maintained communications with the outside world. At the end of April Tipu had sent about 4,000 men under Husain Ali Khan against Mangalore. But they had been surprised by Campbell, twelve miles from Mangalore, early on the morning of May 7, and had retreated in confusion with the loss of 200 men. When, however, Tipu approached, Campbell was defeated and compelled to retreat into the fort.[3] Husain Ali Khan distinguished himself on this occasion, and in the attempt to retrieve his prestige was seriously wounded.[4]

Tipu arrived before Mangalore on May 20, 1783. The English still held an important height commanding the principal access to the town and situated over a mile from it. But after the town was invested, the sepoys who held the post had their retreat cut off. So when they were attacked on the 23rd, they became panic-stricken and fled in great disorder down the hill. The panic spread even among the troops which were sent to reinforce them. The English casualties on this occasion amounted to 4 officers, 10 European and 200 Indian soldiers, including 3 officers and two companies of sepoys whose retreat had been entirely cut off. After this defeat the English withdrew the remaining posts and shut themselves up into the fort. Tipu, thereupon, began preparations for a siege.[5]

[1] M.R., Mly. Sundry Book, 1784, vol. 61, pp. 885-94.
[2] Wilks, ii, p. 213.
[3] *Memoir of John Campbell*, p. 44; Kirmani, pp. 266-7.
[4] *Ibid.*, p. 267.
[5] *Memoir of John Campbell*, p. 49; Forrest, *Selections*, ii, Home Series, p. 288; Wilks, ii, pp. 214-5.

By May 27 he had completed eleven embrasures, and from batteries erected on the north, the east and the south a heavy fire was constantly maintained, while large stones, some of them weighing 150 pounds, were thrown into the fort, taking a heavy toll of human life and causing great damage to the buildings. The fortifications on the north side were entirely dismantled on June 4, and on the 7th a practical breach was effected in the wall. Approaches to the fort were continually pushed nearer. On July 4, and then again on the 6th, attempts were made to assault the fort but without any success. Meanwhile, as heavy rains had started, siege operations greatly suffered, although almost daily the Mysoreans tried to enter the fort.[1] By the end of July, however, preparations to assault the fort were completed. The fortifications were entirely destroyed on the three sides, and the approaches were carried on to the mouth of the ditch, which was beginning to be filled with coconut trees and the ruins of the fort walls. Only a few days were required to capture the fort.[2] But just at this time news reached Mangalore of the cessation of hostilities between the French and the English, and orders were received by Cossigny on July 22 to withdraw from the conflict.[3] This upset Tipu's plans, while it raised the drooping spirits of the English. Decimated by disease, weakened by desertions and suffering from the effects of a shortage of provisions, the garrison could not have held out longer. But with the withdrawal of the French their prospects became brighter, and so they girded themselves to fresh resistance. Soon however negotiations for a cessation of hostilities began. Tipu demanded as a condition of armistice that Campbell should evacuate Mangalore and retire to Tellicherry at the head of the garrison with all honours of war and all personal effects. But Campbell rejected this. However, owing to the efforts of de Morlat, an armistice was signed on August 2, 1783. In the course of the siege the English had lost 1,400 men, killed, wounded and missing, and between 30 and 40 officers killed and wounded.[4]

### *The Armistice is Signed*

By the terms of the Armistice, Campbell was to remain in possession of the fort of Mangalore, while Tipu was to remain in possession of the trenches and the batteries erected in front of the fort. There was to be no extension of lines by either party; the positions as occupied by

[1] See Forrest, *Selections*, Home Series, ii, pp. 287-92, for a detailed account of the siege.

[2] N.A., Sec. Pro., Nov. 10, 1783; M.R., Mly. Cons., Oct. 14, 1783, Macartney to Hastings, vol. 93A, p. 4448.

[3] N.A., Sec. Pro., Aug. 18, 1783.

[4] *Ibid.*, Nov. 10, 1783; A.N., C²155, de Morlat to Campbell, July 21, 1783, f. 313a.

them on the day of the armistice were to be maintained. Tipu was not to erect fresh batteries, while the English were neither to repair the breaches nor to receive any kind of help from the outside. But in order to guard his trenches and batteries, Tipu could keep 3,000 men along with the usual guards and he could send 100 armed sepoys inside the fort to be posted at various places to see that nothing was done against the articles of cessation. Similarly Campbell could place 1,000 men in the batteries and the trenches to see that no new preparations were made. Despatches were to pass along the sea-coast either way, but not inland through Tipu's country nor by sea. The prohibition regarding the conveyance by sea was later, however, taken away. Tipu was required to establish near the fort a bazaar where the garrison could buy its provisions at the same rate as the Mysoreans. But Campbell could not take into the fort at any one time more than 10 to 12 days' provisions. As regards those articles which were not obtainable in the bazaar, such as salted beef, salt and liquor, he could import them from other places, but they were not to exceed more than one month's ration. Major Campbell was to give two English officers as hostages to Tipu, and similarly the latter was to give hostages to Campbell. These terms were to apply to Onore and Karwar also, with the difference in the number of men allowed to remain in the trenches or to go into the fort. Tipu could retain 900 men in his lines and send 30 men into the fort. Similarly, the English could keep 30 men in the lines to see that no fresh preparations were made by Tipu.[1]

While Tipu was engaged in the operations on the Malabar coast, the Government of Madras had planned a diversion by sending a force under Captain Edmonds in the middle of May to attack his kingdom from the north-east. An adventurer, named Sayyid Muhammad,[2] who paraded under the title of "Nawab of Kurpa," was used as a pawn for this purpose, and with English support occupied Cuddapah which was a *jagir* of Mir Qamar-ud-din Khan, son of the late Mir Saheb. On hearing this, Tipu despatched Qamar-ud-din Khan towards Cuddapah. Qamar-ud-din first totally defeated Sayyid Muhammad, and then, on July 28, routed the English troops under Montgomery sent to support the pretender.[3] Thus the attempt

[1] N.A., Sec. Pro., Nov. 10, 1783; M.R., Mly. Sundry Book, 1784, vol. 61, pp. 885-94; see also A.N., C²155. Nos. 1-25, for details of negotiations for the armistice and for de Morlat's role in it.

[2] Sayyid Muhammad was the son of one of the religious persons attached to the tomb of Gisu Daraz at Gulbarga. He married the daughter of the former Nawab of Cuddapah, and by virtue of this alliance laid claims to Cuddapah and its dependencies. (Wilks, ii, p. 216).

[3] Wilson, ii, pp. 95-96. Wilson says that the attack was made by Qamar-ud-din Khan in the course of a parley for a cessation of hostilities pending the discussion for a treaty of peace. But it must be remembered that Qamar-ud-din could not have started any parley with the English without orders from Tipu.

of the Madras Government to create a diversion in the north-east in favour of the English armies, shut up in the province of Bednur, ended in a complete fiasco.

*Invasion of Mysore from the South*

Nor did the invasion of Tipu's kingdom from the south produce the expected results. Just before Haidar's death, John Sullivan, the Company's Resident at Tanjore, had devised a plan that the army in the south under Colonel Lang should penetrate into Tipu's kingdom from one side, while the army under Colonel Humberstone at Ponnani from the other. The two armies were to unite at Coimbatore and then proceed with further operations. But the plan fell through because, although the Madras Government approved of it, Sir Eyre Coote and the Government of Bombay opposed it on the ground that the Company's troops were not strong enough to overcome the resistance of the Mysoreans.

Sullivan, however, devised another plan for the invasion of Mysore. He entered into negotiations with a Brahmin named Tirumala Rao, who professed to be an agent of the Mysore Rani, Maharani Lakshmi Ammanni,[1] and concluded with him a treaty for restoring the imprisoned Raja to the throne. Tirumala Rao's reward, in case of success, was to be ten per cent of the revenues of the restored districts and the office of *pradhan* or Chief Minister to be held hereditarily in the family. The treaty was signed on October 28, 1782, subject to the confirmation by the Governor-General and Council.[2] Accordingly, Colonel Lang was despatched, accompanied by Tirumala Rao, to invade Mysore from the south. On April 2, 1783, the fort of Karur was captured; on the 16th Aravakurichi was assaulted, and Dindigul surrendered on May 4. Shortly after, owing to Lang's resignation, Fullarton succeeded to the command. The latter left Dindigul on May 25, and on June 2 occupied Dharapuram, where he obtained valuable supplies of ammunition, grain and cattle.[3] In spite of these successes, Fullarton was not in a position to realise any ambitious project, for, as he observed: "The southern army was not in sufficient strength to think of marching to Seringapatam, nor could we have opposed the whole power of Tipu Sultan."[4] In fact, the army was so weak that Fullarton could not even afford to garrison Dharapuram and had to destroy its fortifications.[5] Under the circumstance, the object of his operations was limited to drawing off the pressure on

[1] See *Mys. Gaz.*, ii, pp. 2558-60, and Wilks, ii, p. 240, for more information regarding Maharani Lakshmi Ammanni and Tirumala Rao.

[2] Aitchison, *Treaties*, ix, pp. 200-206.

[3] M.R., Mly. Sundry Book, 1785, vol. 66, pp. 35-37.

[4] *Ibid.*, p. 37.

[5] *Ibid.*, p. 39.

the English in the Bednur province. But with a weak army he could not have succeeded even in this, for the Mysore forces in the Coimbatore area were strong enough to resist the English invasion.

Meanwhile, on May 31, Fullarton received General Stuart's order to march with haste to Cuddalore. He, therefore, gave up the campaign and set out to relieve Stuart. But on arriving within three forced marches of General Stuart's camp, he received the intelligence of the cessation of hostilities between the English and the French. Since the danger to Stuart had now been removed, he returned southwards, his numbers nearly doubled by a reinforcement from the army set free at Cuddalore. He was preparing for a fresh invasion of Mysore when he received the intimation of an armistice between Tipu and the Company. In consequence, he postponed the enterprise, and busied himself in suppressing the refractory *poligars* of Tinnevelly and Madura.[1] But Fullarton did not cease making preparations for war and intriguing with the Rajas of Travancore and Calicut and other Malabar chieftains against Tipu, for the prospect of marching upon Seringapatam had captured his imagination. So, after having succeeded in reducing the *poligars* to obedience, he marched to Dharapuram in accordance with the Madras Government's instructions of August 18 to remain on the frontiers, ready to act offensively in case Tipu violated the terms of the armistice.[2]

### *Breaches of the Armistice by the English*

Meanwhile, Fullarton was finding his position very difficult. Although his army had swelled to 13,500, they were short of supplies and their pay was twelve months in arrears. Towards the end of September they were in such an "alarming situation" that he was obliged to solicit from the Madras Government "a latitude of purveyance, even in the enemy's country," because, owing to the ravages of war, the Company's southern provinces were not capable of supporting the English forces.[3] But on October 16, when the supplies of his troops were almost exhausted, he received news from Tellicherry that Tipu had recommenced hostilities against Mangalore.[4] Anxious to obtain some pretext for a renewal of war in order to relieve his immediate distress, Fullarton, without even trying to verify the news or waiting for orders from the Madras Government, decided to launch an offensive; and leaving Palni[5] on October 22, marched towards Palghat, which commanded the communications between the Malabar and Coromandel coasts and was situated in the midst of a very fertile

[1] *Ibid.*, p. 39.
[2] *Ibid.*, p. 85.
[3] *Ibid.*, p. 87.
[4] *Ibid.*, p. 93.
[5] Palni is a town in Madurai District, Tamil Nadu (Madras).

country.[1] Besides, Fullarton selected Palghat as his objective, because he believed that its reduction "could not fail to weigh essentially in the negotiations for peace then said to be in agitation".[2]

This invasion of Mysore territory was a distinct violation of the Armistice of Mangalore. Roshan Khan, Tipu's commander in the area, therefore strongly protested against it. But Fullarton totally disregarded his protests and continued to advance. He occupied a number of small intermediate posts; and, after a difficult and tedious march through thick teak forests, reached Palghat on November 5, and immediately began its siege.[3] On November 15 Roshan Khan forwarded to him a letter from the Governor of Madras ordering him to desist from all offensive operations, and return within the limits possessed by him on July 16, 1783. But Fullarton did not answer; he simply sent back the messenger who had carried the letter under the guard of two sepoys. The same day he stormed Palghat.[4] He obtained in the fort 50,000 pagodas, besides a number of guns and large quantities of provisions and military stores.[5] Although it was considered to be one of the strongest forts in India, it had been captured without much difficulty. The reason was that, because of the armistice, its commander had been lulled into a false sense of security and had not adopted sufficient measures of defence.[6] From Palghat Fullarton marched to Coimbatore which he reached on November 26. On the 28th it surrendered to him even before any breach was effected. The same day Roshan Khan sent a letter from the Commissioners to Fullarton ordering him to cease hostilities. But the letter was sent back unopened, and the messenger who carried it was threatened with punishment if he dared to show his face again.[7]

Although Fullarton repeatedly defied the orders of the Commissioners and the Governor of Madras, he was not even reprimanded for it.[8] This shows he had invaded Mysore with the consent of his superiors. The fact is that Macartney sent Fullarton two sets of contradictory orders. By those which were sent through Tipu's officers, Fullarton was required to abstain from hostilities; by those which were sent to him directly, aggression was not only connived at but even encouraged. Thus writing to Fullarton on December 13, 1783, Macartney observed: "We think the places should not be res-

[1] M.R., Mly. Sundry Book, 1785, vol. 66, p. 97.
[2] *Ibid.*
[3] *Ibid.*, p. 103.
[4] *Ibid.*, 1783, vol. 60A, pp. 107-08.
[5] *Ibid.*, 1784, vol. 61. p. 712.
[6] *Ibid.*, 1783, vol. 60A, pp. 107-08.
[7] *Ibid.*, pp. 245-46, Nov. 28, 1783, Roshan Khan to Mir Muin-ud-din; see also pp. 232-35.
[8] Again on Dec. 6, Roshan Khan forwarded the Commissioners' letter to Fullarton, but as before it was ignored. (*Ibid.*, vol. 60B, pp. 418-19).

tored till you hear further from us...the possession of Palagatcherry might be a security for the garrison of Mangalore, by affording the means of retaliation for any act of treachery or violence that he (Tipu) might attempt against the latter."[1] Besides, with the help of the new conquests, Macartney wanted to increase the Company's bargaining power in the negotiations for peace with Tipu. But in the end, realising that Fullarton's conduct was a great hindrance to the peace talks, and might lead to an open rupture with Tipu, he ordered the English troops to return within the limits occupied by them on July 26, 1783. Accordingly, they began evacuation on December 28, but not before they had inflicted considerable damage upon the Sultan's property. On quitting Coimbatore they plundered the surrounding districts and carried away from the fort a number of guns and considerable quantity of provisions and ammunition. They destroyed the town of Palghat and carried away 100,000 pagodas (60,000 from Palghat and 40,000 from Palicotah), besides large supplies of grain, military stores and a number of guns, and instead of delivering the fort to the Mysore officers they delivered it to its Raja.[2]

Soon after the armistice was signed, Campbell paid a visit to the Sultan on August 13, and informed him of the shortage of provisions in the fort. Tipu received him with due respect, gave him a *khilat* and a horse, and immediately ordered a bazaar to be set up for the garrison near the fort.[3] In spite of this, on August 20 General Macleod, who held the chief command of the Company's forces on the coasts of Malabar and Kanara, arrived before Mangalore with the object of reinforcing the fort with a detachment of the Hanoverians. Although this was an open violation of the fifth article of the armistice, according to which Major Campbell was not entitled to receive any help either by land or sea, Tipu not only allowed Macleod to land in Mangalore, but even ordered arrangements to be made for his stay in the town, and permitted him to visit the fort. And when the General visited Tipu, he was received cordially, and given a palanquin, a horse and a *khilat* as presents. He left the coast on August 23, fully satisfied with the Sultan's treatment of the garrison.[4] In the succeeding months also the bazaar near the fort continued to supply the garrison those articles which were mentioned in the third article of the armistice.

[1] *Ibid.*, p. 383, Macartney to Fullarton, Dec. 13, 1783. Macartney again wrote on Jan. 24, 1784, to Fullarton "to retain possession of Palagatcherry in case of any accident it should not have been restored." (*Ibid.*, 1785, vol. 66, p. 129).

[2] *Ibid.*, 1784, Tipu to Appa Saheb and Srinivas Rao, Jan. 26, 1784, vol. 61, p. 712.

[3] *Memoir of John Campbell*, p. 51; N.A., Sec. Pro., Nov. 10, 1783, Tipu to Macartney, Sept. 6, 1783.

[4] *Ibid.*

The English however were not satisfied with such arrangements. They were anxious to reinforce the fort with sufficient men and supplies so that, in case the peace talks failed and hostilities broke out, it might be able to withstand a long siege. Macleod, therefore, appeared before Mangalore early in October, and then again at the end of the month, and demanded Tipu's permission to revictual the fort. But Tipu refused on the ground that the quota of supplies fixed by the terms of the armistice had already been sent in.[1] The Bombay Government, anxious to retain Mangalore which it considered "a most desirable possession,"[2] thereupon ordered Macleod to forcibly relieve the garrison.[3] Accordingly, on November 22, the General arrived before Mangalore with a squadron and a large army, and insisted on sending 4,000 bales of rice into the fort. But Tipu rejected the demand as the amount was considerably more than what had been fixed by the armistice. His attitude all the more stiffened because of the insolent and threatening behaviour of Macleod who had appeared with men-of-war and troops before Mangalore in violation of the terms of the armistice, and because of the aggression committed by Fullarton in the Coimbatore province. A resumption of hostilities between Tipu and the English thus seemed inevitable. It was, however, averted by the efforts of Piveron de Morlat who was anxious to preserve peace. He proposed a compromise which was accepted by both parties. Considering Macleod's demand for 4,000 bales of rice as exorbitant, his proposal was that the garrison be immediately allowed to admit 1,000 bales of rice, and that after this had been consumed, a further 1,000 bales could be sent in. Besides, one month's supplies of salt, meat and liquor were also to be admitted. Onore was to be allowed 200 bales of rice and one month's supplies.[4] This agreement was very favourable to the garrison, for, according to the third article of the armistice, no more than ten or twelve days provisions were to be admitted into the fort.[5]

But, in spite of the agreement, Macleod did not give up his intrigues and aggressive designs. He advised Campbell "to put the garrison to half allowance of rice and bread and pay them the other half in money," and to "let the commissary buy as much as possible" so that

[1] M.R., Mly. Cons., Dec. 8, 1783, Tipu to Macleod, Oct. 24, vol. 94B, p. 5293. Intelligence received from Mangalore: The people from the fort visit the bazaar arranged by Tipu, and buy flour and provisions for the garrison. (*Ibid.*, Oct. 31, 1783, vol. 93B, p. 4775).

[2] *Ibid.*, Dec. 8, 1783, vol. 94B, p. 5308.

[3] *Ibid.*, Fullarton to Madras, Nov. 15, 1783, p. 5292; *Ibid.*, Dec. 3, 1783, vol. 94A, p. 5195.

[4] M.R., Mly. Sundry Book, 1784 de Morlat to Macleod, Nov. 27, vol. 61, pp. 910-11.

[5] *Ibid.*, p. 910; see also A.N., C[2] 155, ff. 335a-57b, Nos. 1-16, 43, 44, for the negotiations carried on by de Morlat about this question.

the garrison might be able to hold out for another two months. He further informed Campbell that, "if the Admiral arrives on the coast, I hope he will furnish us with the means to force the points of the river, if I find by your signals and by communication with you, it is necessary."[1]

Macleod sailed away on December 2. He returned on the 27th and was again permitted to land supplies for the garrison.[2] The supplies for another month reached Mangalore at the end of January, 1784, in two ships under Colonel Gordon, second in command to Macleod.[3] But they came too late, for, on January 26, Campbell had decided to capitulate, and on the 29th he delivered the fort to Tipu, to quote his own words, "under articles the most beneficial I could ask for the garrison, and which the Nawab has most honourably and strictly adhered to."[4] The terms were that the fort was to be delivered in exchange for any other fort in the Carnatic in possession of Tipu, to be stipulated in the treaty of peace. The garrison was to march out with all the honours of war. They were to be sent on boats furnished by Tipu, who was also to provide provisions for the journey. In case sufficient boats were not available, they were to be sent by land, and Tipu was to provide them with provisions and the means of transport as long as they were in his territory. The garrison was entitled to take with them whatever belonged to the Company; all that belonged to the Sultan was to be left behind.[5]

Campbell had held out with great courage and perseverance for more than eight months; he could not continue any longer for both he and his men had reached the end of their patience. The Europeans were on the verge of mutiny, while a number of Indian soldiers were daily going over to the enemy. Twelve to fifteen men were dying every day, scurvy was violently raging, hospitals were filled with nearly two-thirds of the garrison, and the rest had scarcely any strength left to hold their arms.[6] Campbell himself was in the last stage of consumption.[7]

It is wrong to blame Tipu for the sufferings of the garrison, for, although *dal* and *ghee* were lacking, there was no shortage of rice, and, up to the time of the surrender, the English continued to buy from the bazaar near the fort. Writing on December 19, 1783, to the Governor-General and Council, Macleod observed: "Tipu does not

[1] M.R., Mly. Cons., Jan. 6, 1784, Macleod to Campbell, vol. 96A, pp. 35-36.
[2] Wilks, ii, p. 228.
[3] *Ibid.*, p. 229.
[4] M.R., Mly. Cons., Feb. 20, 1784, Campbell to Madras, Feb. 6, vol. 97A. p. 531.
[5] M.R., Mly. Sundry Book, 1784, vol. 61, pp. 820-25.
[6] M.R., Mly. Cons., Feb. 20, 1784, Campbell to Madras, Feb. 6, vol. 97A p 533.
[7] *Memoir of John Campbell*, p. 57.

hinder our revictualizing Mangalore and Onore."[1] What Tipu really objected to was the bringing into the fort more provisions than stipulated in the terms of the armistice. It was in fact the shortage and poor quality of those articles which were brought from outside that caused the greatest privation to the garrison. And for this the Government of Bombay was mainly responsible. The Commandant of Onore, for example, admitted: "We are not at this period in absolute want of provisions—but of such as are wholesome—provisions are, however, the least of our wants."[2] The supply which Macleod brought on November 22, 1783, for the fort of Mangalore "was drawn from damaged stores bought of a navy agent, and of the beef and pork, not one in twenty pieces could be eaten, even by dogs."[3] The supply admitted into the fort on December 31 was also of a poor quality. Only a small part of the supply of "salt meat was eatable and the biscuit was full of vermin;" and although the same quantity of rice was admitted as before, there was less beef and arrack, while no refreshments were landed for the officers.[4] It appears that the garrison was neglected because Macleod had been able to capture on the Malabar coast "a fortress of still more importance, and consequently better worth preserving even than Mangalore."[5]

Foiled in his designs against Mangalore, Macleod directed his attention to the small Moplah settlement of Cannanore which he attacked early in December 1783. He justified his aggression on the ground that, in the beginning of November, 300 of his men who were coming from Karwar to join him at Tellicherry, were imprisoned by the Bibi of Cannanore and Tipu. The boat *Superb*, which was carrying them, having been destroyed in a storm, two officers and two hundred men who were driven ashore near Mangalore were detained by Tipu. About a hundred men were wrecked near Cannanore, and were imprisoned by the Bibi who put them in irons. Since both Tipu and the Bibi refused to release them, Macleod attacked Cannanore.[6]

In reality, the reasons for Macleod's aggression were quite different. In a letter to the Governor of Madras he wrote: "Finding my army at leisure I seized the opportunity of reducing the Mopla settlement which has been a most inveterate enemy with Tellicherry....This is one of the finest settlements in India and an acquisition of great value

[1] N.A., Sec. Pro., May 13, 1784, Macleod to Hastings, Dec. 29, 1783.

[2] Forrest, *Selections*, Home Series, ii, p. 309, Torrians to Macleod, March 27, 1784.

[3] Mill, iv, p. 201; *Memoir of John Campbell*, p. 51.

[4] Wilks, ii, p. 222.

[5] M.R., Mly. Sundry Book, 1784, vol. 61, p. 1145.

[6] N.A., Sec. Pro., May 13, 1784, Macleod to Macartney, Jan. 1; N.A., Sec. Pro., March 9, 1784. Macleod to Bengal, Jan. 8.

to Bombay."[1] In another letter he observed: "This is the strongest fort I have seen in India excepting our own Capital. It is much more valuable to us than Mangalore, because no enemy can step between it and the sea." Its possession was also coveted because it was a very good pepper settlement while "Tellicherry was dull and had no future."[2] Moreover, the army under General Macleod was "at that time so hard pressed for an existence as to be under the necessity (after having fruitlessly used every entreaty and made liberal offers of money for a supply of provision) of desperately attacking Cannanore."[3]

The campaign against Cannanore was a short one, lasting only for six days (December 9 to 14). Although the Moplahs fought with great courage, in the end they were defeated. The casualties on the English side amounted to 279 men and officers; the Bibi's losses were much heavier. Cannanore and its 42 dependent fortresses were occupied, and the English obtained four lakhs of pagodas and large quantities of provisions. The Bibi and her family were made prisoners, and were released only after she had agreed to sign a treaty as dictated by Macleod.[4] By this treaty her possessions were restored to her, but she was required to pay to the Company a tribute of three lakhs of pagodas annually. Her forts were to be at the disposal of the Company, and all the merchandise and other property in the town and in the forts were to be considered as lawful prize for the army. The Company was also given the monopoly to purchase all the pepper in the settlement.[5]

Macleod's high-handed behaviour was approved by the Madras Government.[6] But the Bombay Government disavowed and annulled the treaty on the ground that Macleod had no right to enter into any engagement without reference to the Company. Besides, since the Bibi was an ally of Tipu, they did not want "to retard the great work of peace." They, therefore, ordered the restoration of Cannanore to the Bibi.[7] It was, however, not until April 1784, after the Treaty of Mangalore had been signed, that it was evacuated by the English.

[1] M.R., Mly. Sundry Book, Macleod to Macartney, Jan. 17, 1784, vol. 61, pp. 766-67.

[2] *Ibid.*, Feb. 6, 1784, pp. 792-93; N.A., Sec. Pro., May 13, 1784, Macleod to Macartney, Jan. 1.

[3] Innes Munro, p. 349.

[4] N.A., Sec. Pro., April 13, 1784, Anderson to Hastings, Feb. 11.

[5] *Ibid.*, March 9, 1784.

[6] M.R., Mly. Sundry Book, Madras to Macleod, Feb. 6, 1784, vol. 61, p. 798. Macartney admitted that both Fullarton and Macleod had violated the terms of the Armistice. (Macartney Papers, Bodleian MS. Eng. hist. C. 79, f. 27a).

[7] N.A., Sec. Pro., May 13, 1784.

CHAPTER III

# THE FRENCH AND THE SECOND ANGLO-MYSORE WAR*

After the death of Haidar war against the English in the Carnatic was carried on mainly by the French. But before describing it, it would be useful to mention the part which the French had hitherto played in the Second Anglo-Mysore War. Before the war began, the French in India had promised to help Haidar against the English. But when he invaded the Carnatic in July 1780, and hostilities began, they did not render him any assistance beyond furnishing him with military stores. The reason was that, although they had been themselves at war with the English since 1778, they had not yet received any reinforcements from France.[1] It was exactly four years after the rupture of peace between England and France, and over a year and a half after the outbreak of the Anglo-Mysore War, that a small land army consisting of about 2,500 men under the command of Duchemin appeared on Indian soil. It was brought by the Bailli de Suffren and reached Porto Novo on February 25, 1782.[2] Its object was to reconquer the French possessions in India, and to assist Haidar who was to be the mainspring of a coalition of Indian rulers for the expulsion of the British from the country. Duchemin's appointment as commander was, however, only temporary; he was to be replaced by the Marquis de Bussy, who had for many years played a distinguished part in the affairs of South India, and who was shortly to arrive with a much larger army in India.

When Haidar heard of the arrival of this army he was overjoyed,[3] because with its help he hoped to crush the English. Very soon, however, he was disillusioned, for Duchemin refused to act according to his advice, and showed great lack of initiative and enterprise. Haidar proposed to him, and he was seconded in this by Suffren, to make an

*This is based on my article, *The French in the Second Anglo-Mysore War*, which appeared in *Bengal: Past and Present*, vol. lxv, Jan.-Dec., 1945.

[1] When Louis XVI declared war against England in Feb. 1778, hostilities between the French and the English began in India as well. Although grandiose schemes for the expulsion of the English from India had been worked out for a number of years, yet when the war came, the French were caught unprepared, and before the year was out, they had lost all their settlements in India to the English. (*Journal de Bussy*, pp. 152 *seq.*)

[2] *Ibid.*, Intro. p. vii. D'Orves was at first the commander, but after he died on Feb. 9, 1782, the Bailli de Suffren succeeded to the chief command of the French navy in the Indian waters.

[3] *Ibid.*, p. 114.

immediate attack on Nagapatam which, not being properly defended, was easy to capture, and which was the key to the rich province of Tanjore, from where the French could obtain supplies for their troops.[1] But Duchemin not only did not march on Nagapatam, he even refused to disembark unless and until Haidar agreed to enter into a treaty with the French, and sent Piveron de Morlat and two officers, MM. de Moissac and de Canaple to him with his proposals. But Haidar evaded the proposal for a treaty, although he assured the French agents that all the needs of the French troops would be looked after, and immediately ordered his treasurer to send to Porto Novo one lakh of rupees.[2]

Partially satisfied with this reply, Duchemin ordered the disembarkation of his army,[3] and by the end of March, reinforced by a Mysore force under Tipu, left Porto Novo. According to Haidar's instructions to his officers, he was well supplied with provisions and the means of transport. In fact, with the exception of bread there was nothing lacking.[4] Nevertheless, instead of proceeding towards Nagapatam, as Haidar desired, Duchemin marched on Cuddalore; but after occupying it on the morning of April 3, he remained inactive for nearly a month. He justified his inactivity on the ground that he lacked funds and was short of troops whose number was daily diminishing on account of sickness and disease.[5] He refused to undertake any campaign until the arrival of Bussy lest it should compromise the honour of France.[6]

After various evasions and dilatory tactics, on May 1, 1782, Duchemin, accompanied by Tipu, at last left Cuddalore, and advanced to join Haidar who was proceeding to besiege Perumukkal. The united armies of the French and Haidar appeared before it on May 11, and after occupying it on the 16th,[7] set out towards Wandiwash. Coote, anxious to save the place, marched to its relief. Haidar asked Duchemin to give battle to the English, but he refused on the ground that he had been ordered by Bussy and the Vicomte de Souillac, Governor-General of the French possessions in the East, not to risk any general action until the arrival of sufficient reinforcements from France, because a defeat would compromise the French prestige.[8] This

[1] Ch. Cunat, *Histoire du Bailli de Suffren*, p. 118.

[2] *Journal de Bussy*, pp. 114-15.

[3] *Ibid.*, p. 116.

[4] *Ibid.*, p. 107; see also *Memoirs du Chevalier de Mautort*, pp. 203-04. The shortage of bread was due to the fact that wheat is not much grown in the Carnatic, nor is it the staple food of the people.

[5] *Journal de Bussy*, p. 120.

[6] *Ibid.*, p. 288. Meanwhile Duchemin did not give up his efforts to conclude a treaty with Haidar. (For these negotiations, see *Journal de Bussy*, pp. 116-20).

[7] See p. 20 *supra*.

[8] *Journal de Bussy*, p. 288 footnote.

refusal to fight was Duchemin's great blunder, because the combined forces of the French and Haidar were far superior to the English army both in numbers and equipment, and would easily have defeated Coote.[1] Haidar was, therefore, very annoyed at the French commander and threatened to make a separate peace with the English. He even refused to supply him with money or provisions.[2] He had nothing but contempt for the French troops who were devoid of discipline, and whose officers spent their time in mutual bickerings and jealousies, and in shameful scramble for power and prestige.[3] He felt that the French were a nation "*très légère*", and without character, who never kept their engagements or their promises.[4]

The appointment of Duchemin as commander of the French forces in India had been, in fact, a mistake on the part of the French Government. As Malleson observes: "Duchemin was a sailor rather than a soldier. But he was strong neither on sea nor on land. He was as weak mentally as physically. A terrible fear of responsibility acted upon a constitution unable to bear the smallest fatigue."[5]

Duchemin died on August 12, 1782, and was provisionally succeeded by the Comte d'Hofflize, a man respected for his judgement and good sense. Nevertheless, Haidar's relations with the French did not improve; for the new commander, being "a prisoner of the situation created by his predecessor, hardly appeared to be better qualified to take up any initiative."[6] As de Launay observed: "Duchemin is dead, the State has lost nothing. M.le Comte d'Hofflize has succeeded him, the State has gained nothing. He is a very good man as an individual but very incompetent for the work he is assigned."[7] Owing to this Haidar felt so disgusted that he would have made a complete break with the French had it not been for de Launay and Suffren who continued to humour him and assure him that a large army under Bussy would shortly be arriving from France.[8] The memory of Bussy's exploits in the Deccan was still fresh in the mind of Haidar who, therefore, retained his friendship with the French, hoping that, on Bussy's arrival, he would be able to defeat the English. But he died on December 7, 1782, and Bussy reached India three months later.

[1] Malleson, *Final French Struggles in India*, p. 31.

[2] *Journal de Bussy*, p. 200; see also *Memoirs du Chevalier de Mautort*, p. 218. Haidar had promised the French to pay them one lakh of rupees every month and regularly paid the money for five months. He also gave Duchemin money to raise and equip two battalions of sepoys for the French army. But after he got disgusted with Duchemin he discontinued financial aid.

[3] *Journal de Bussy*, pp. 143, 287.

[4] A. N., C² 155, Launay to Bussy, Aug. 2, 1785, f. 265a.

[5] Malleson, *Final French Struggles in India*, p. 19.

[6] *Journal de Bussy*, Intro, p. xvii.

[7] A. N., C² 155, f. 286a.

[8] *Ibid.*, p. 97.

Hofflize, who had hitherto remained inactive, stirred himself on hearing the news of Haidar's death. At the invitation of Piveron de Morlat, he decided to set out and join the Mysore army. But its officers, not sure of his loyalty to Tipu, opposed his leaving Cuddalore. In spite of the assurances of de Morlat that Hofflize was loyal, and that his presence would help checkmate the activities of disloyal elements, Tipu's ministers remained adamant. However, with great reluctance they agreed to his remaining at Jinji until the arrival of Tipu.[1]

On hearing of Tipu's arrival in the Carnatic, Hofflize moved from Jinji and joined him at Chuckmaloor on January 10, 1783. Together they marched against Stuart and encamped in the vicinity of Wandiwash. But when, after the retreat of Stuart,[2] Tipu asked Hofflize to accompany him to the province of Bednur, the French commander refused on the plea that, since he was expecting the arrival of Bussy, he could not leave the Carnatic. In fact, he and Launay tried to dissuade Tipu from going to the west coast and pressed him to await Bussy's arrival. But Tipu refused the suggestion on the ground that his Malabar possessions were rich and important and, therefore, must be recovered, and he wanted Suffren to help him in this. But Suffren pointed out that it was winter and the season was not good for operation. Besides, he had to proceed to Trincomali to meet Bussy. Since Tipu was paying the French troops 40,000 pagodas per month, he was very angry at these refusals. Hofflize, thereupon, allowed the Sultan to take 600 French troops under Cossigny's command, but he himself remained in the Carnatic waiting for Bussy.[3]

Bussy left Cadiz on January 4, 1782, arriving at the Isle of France on May 31. Here he was detained by a prolonged illness, and a number of his troops were affected by scurvy. However, as Suffren was constantly urging him to hasten to India, he embarked on December 18 with about 2200 troops, although both he and his men were still convalescent.[4] Bussy wanted to disembark between Karikal and Nagapatam in order to seize the latter which was a better military base than Cuddalore. But the English, suspecting a possible attack, had strengthened it.[5] So he proceeded to Porto Novo, which he

[1] A. N., C[2] 155, Morlat to Minister of Marine, Feb. 6, 1783, f. 213 b. Letters of Hofflize sent to Madras were intercepted by Vennaji Pandit, the Mysore agent with the French army. Although Morlat pointed out that the letters were of a purely personal nature and were addressed by Hofflize to his relations in Madras, the suspicion of the ministers could not be dispelled, particularly after the experience of the machinations of Bouthenot. (See *ibid.*, ff. 213a-214a).

[2] See p. 28 *supra*.

[3] P.R.C., ii, No. 65. It was not Bussy, as mentioned in this document, but Hofflize who sent Cossigny with Tipu. Bussy had not yet arrived in India.

[4] *Journal de Bussy*, pp. 299-300.

[5] *Ibid.*, p. 320; see also P.A,M.S.. No. 398.

reached on March 16, 1783, and disembarked on the night of the 16th and 17th.

When Duchemin had been sent to India it was understood that this was a temporary arrangement, and that very shortly he would be replaced by Bussy who, because of his past exploits in the Deccan and his experience of India, was regarded as the best person to form a confederacy of the Indian princes to crush the English power in the country.[1] In reality, however, the appointment of Bussy like that of Duchemin was a mistake, for he was no longer the Bussy of twenty years before. He was an old man of sixty-two whose vigour of mind and body had been impaired, and who had lost his powers of self-confidence, initiative and enterprise.[2]

From the time Bussy landed in India, he estranged Tipu by his tactlessness, and by his policy of unenlightened national interest. He unjustly blamed Tipu for the lack of sufficient supplies for his troops, and wrongly complained of the Sultan's departure from the Carnatic before his arrival in India[3], and of the failure of Mir Muin-ud-din Khan, better known as Sayyid Saheb, Tipu's officer in the Carnatic, to wait on him when he had disembarked at Porto Novo. It was due to a feeling of frustration that nothing was done according to his liking that led Bussy to indulge in bitter invectives against Tipu. Even Haidar was not spared, for he had refused to be dominated by Duchemin. Bussy denounced both father and son as "brigands and tyrants" on whose words no reliance could be placed, and maintained that the French should not have established friendly relations with either Haidar or Tipu. Instead, they should have entered into an alliance with the Marathas and especially with the Nizam.[4] However, as the attempt to negotiate a treaty with them had failed, and as there was no prospect of its success in the near future, Bussy remained friendly with Tipu, realising that, if the Sultan left him and made peace with the English, the position of the French would become very embarrassing. But he hoped that, with the arrival of fresh troops from France under de Soullanges, he would be able to act effectively, declare his true intentions, and "give the law."[5]

These vituperations of Bussy against both Haidar and Tipu were quite unjustified. In reality, it was the French who had not fulfilled their part of the promise. In spite of their repeated declarations they had failed to render any effective help to the Mysoreans: Bussy had come nearly three years after the outbreak of the Second Anglo-

[1] *Journal de Bussy*, Intro. pp. vii-viii.
[2] A,N., C² 155, de Morlat to de Souillac, April, 1783-May 1, 1783, f. 251a.
[3] *Ibid.*, p. 339.
[4] *Ibid.*, pp. 339-40.
[5] *Ibid.*. p. 357.

Mysore War, and with a much smaller army than had been originally announced. Haidar had waited for him in vain, and Tipu had delayed his departure for the Malabar coast. The Sultan could not stay any longer in the Carnatic because his Malabar possessions had been seriously threatened by the English. However, on his departure for the west, he had left behind a large army under Sayyid Saheb with instructions to co-operate with the French and give every assistance to Bussy on his arrival in India.[1] Accordingly, when Bussy landed at Porto Novo he was given whatever help in provisions and the means of transport Sayyid Saheb was capable of giving.[2] Sayyid Saheb himself could not be present at the time of the disembarkation of the French troops, because he had to proceed to the relief of Karur, the Commandant of which had thrice asked for his help. The place had been attacked by Colonel Lang who, after destroying its fortifications, was preparing to effect a breach.[3]

From Porto Novo Bussy at once marched to Cuddalore. The total army under his command, including the troops under Hofflize, consisted of 3500 Europeans, 300 to 400 caffres and 4,000 sepoys.[4] Besides, he had also at his disposal the Mysore forces left by Tipu in the Carnatic. Nevertheless, Bussy remained inactive. Instead of undertaking a campaign, he spent his time in ease and comfort in the company of his admirers.[5] Even when he heard of Tipu's victories on the Malabar coast he did not move. His experienced officers advised him to take the offensive, and occupy Perumukkal which, because of its strategic importance, General Stuart was proceeding to occupy.[6] But Bussy refused to leave Cuddalore on the ground that he had no cavalry. He even forbade Houdelot, who had been left by Hofflize to watch the movements of the English army, to try

[1] P.A.MS. No. 495. Tipu informed Bussy that he had left behind in the Carnatic 35,000 men under Sayyid Saheb. But Bussy maintained that the troops under Sayyid Saheb numbered between 12 to 14,000 only.

[2] P.A.MS. Nos. 586, 603; see also *Journal de Bussy*, p. 350, and A.N., $C^2$ 233, Bussy to de Castries, March 21, 1783, No. 13; March 31, 1783, No. 14; and Sept. 9, 1783, No. 16, for Bussy's complaints that he lacked oxen and provisions. But it must be remembered that Sayyid Saheb was unable to place at Bussy's disposal unlimited supplies because the Carnatic, owing to the devastation caused by the war, was plunged in famine. Sayyid Saheb himself did not possess sufficient supplies for his troops.

[3] P.A.MS., No. 497.

[4] *Journal de Bussy*, p. 356.

[5] *Memoirs du Chevalier de Mautort*, p. 274; Ch. Cunat, *Histoire du Bailli de Suffren*, p. 281.

[6] *Ibid.*, The united forces of Haidar and the French had captured Perumukkal on May 16, 1782. Tipu at the time of his departure for the west had proposed to Hofflize to occupy it. But the latter had refused on the ground that his already small army would be further reduced if he had to garrison the place. So Tipu had ordered the demolition of its fortifications. But as the demolition had not been completed, it could have formed a useful military post for the French, if Bussy had occupied it.

prevent its advance.[1] The result was that Stuart, in spite of his dilatory movements, occupied Perumukkal on May 9, 1783, and after fortifying it, advanced on Cuddalore.

On realising that Cuddalore was in danger, Bussy wrote to Sayyid Saheb to hasten to his aid. Sayyid Saheb, in compliance with this request, immediately came, and placed his army numbering about 10,000 men at the disposal of Bussy.[2] But the latter, instead of undertaking an offensive, employed himself only in strengthening the defenses of Cuddalore, and again refused permission to Houdelot who, reinforced by some Mysore cavalry, was anxious to march against the English. Houdelot was ordered merely to watch the movements of the English army.[3] Owing to Bussy's defensive tactics, Stuart was able to march unopposed from Perumukkal and reach the river Pennar on the morning of June 5.[4] But as the French forces were strongly entrenched on the opposite bank near Cuddalore, and the crossing appeared difficult, Stuart marched to the west along the river. Bussy also made the same movement, but halted, for he did not want to be too far from Cuddalore. Stuart, on the other hand, moved further west, and the next morning succeeded in crossing the river without opposition[5] He then made a successful movement towards the south of Cuddalore, and reached the sea on June 7. He encamped two miles south of the fort, and employed himself until the 13th in making preparations for the siege of Cuddalore with the help of the naval forces under Sir Edward Hughes.[6]

On June 13 the operations commenced. Early in the morning Colonel Kelly attacked a post situated on a height and commanded by the Mysoreans. The latter, taken by surprise, fled without offering any resistance, and so the post was occupied. The second post to the right of this was next attacked, and although Colonel Blynth, who commanded it, put up a stiff resistance, it was also captured. After this, at 8-30 in the morning, a general attack on the main French position was made. But due to Hofflize's courage and skill, it was repulsed with great loss. Two more attacks were made, but they also met with the same fate.[7] Emboldened by these successes, the French emerged from their trenches and pursued the English to a considerable distance, inflicting upon them great loss. But they had to with-

[1] P.A.MS. No. 402.

[2] Martineau, *Bussy et l'Inde Francaise*, p. 354.

[3] *Ibid.*

[4] Innes Munro, p. 321.

[5] According to Mautort, Hofflize was prepared to march with his brigade and some pieces of cannon to the opposite bank of the river and prevent the English from crossing it. But he was not given permission by Bussy. (*Memoirs du Chevalier de Mautort*, pp. 281-82).

[6] Wilks, ii, pp. 185-86.

[7] *Ibid.*, pp. 186-87; P.A.MS. No. 402.

draw in consternation, since one of their positions had been dexterously occupied by an English detachment.[1] Nevertheless, Cuddalore had been saved. The bullocks and other military supplies provided by Sayyid Saheb had proved very helpful in its defence,[2] while the Mysore light troops had performed useful service outside the town.[3] The French also had fought with great valour, and Bussy, elated with victory, embraced Hofflize and Boissieux, and with tears of joy in his eyes cried out: "My friends, it is to you, it is to your brave regiment that I owe the success of this day."[4] The total English casualties during the day amounted to 1,116, while those of the French were only 450.[5] The number of troops on the French side consisted of 3,000 Europeans and 2,000 sepoys, besides about 10,000 Mysoreans.[6] The English army amounted to about 11,000 men: 1,660 Europeans, 8,340 sepoys and 1,000 cavalry.[7]

The French officers advised Bussy to follow up his victory and attack the English during the night while they were tired, demoralised, and short of ammunition. But in the words of Mill, because "the spirit of Bussy was chilled with age and infirmities," he "restrained the impetuousity of his officers who confidently predicted the destruction of the British army."[8] He even decided to withdraw the same night all his troops from positions outside Cuddalore, and to shut himself up in the town. This caused great consternation in the army. "The officers were furious and the soldiers swore vehemently. They said that the army had won the battle in spite of the General, but that today he has lost it in spite of the soldiers."[9] Taking advantage of Bussy's mistakes the English recovered from their defeat, and once again prepared to invest Cuddalore. Bussy, thereupon, immediately wrote to Suffren for help. The latter at once sailed for Cuddalore and reached there on June 15 just when Hughes was about to attack. By outmanoeuvring the English Admiral, Suffren succeeded in covering Cuddalore and occupying the position held by Hughes. And after he had completed his preparations by embarking 600 Europeans and 600 sepoys furnished by Bussy, he attacked the English squadron on the 20th. The fight lasted the whole day. The British admiral wanted to come to close quarters; the French admiral kept up a distant cannonade which cost the

[1] Mill. iv, p. 192.
[2] Martineau, *Bussy et l'Inde Francaise*, p. 296.
[3] Wilks, ii, p. 195.
[4] *Memoirs du Chevalier de Mautort*, p. 296.
[5] Wilks, ii, p. 189. According to Townshend Papers, B.M. 38507, f. 287 b, the English lost 1200 killed and wounded.
[6] P.A.MS. No. 599
[7] Innes Munro, p. **329.**
[8] Mill, iv. p. 192.
[9] *Memoirs du Chevalier de Mautort*, p. **298.**

enemy in the course of three hours 532 men. As the English vessels had suffered severely, Hughes sailed away the following morning to Madras in order to refit, leaving Stuart at the mercy of the French.[1] Suffren was quick to exploit the situation. He landed the 1,200 troops which had been supplied to him, together with 1,100 men from the fleet, and planned with Bussy an attack upon the English.[2] But Bussy did not attack, and let the opportunity slip. It was only after Stuart had recovered from the shock of Hughes's defeat and departure that Bussy decided to risk an action.

On June 25, at three in the morning, Bussy sent Chevalier de Dumas, an incompetent officer, with 800 Europeans and 500 sepoys, to lead a sortie, but as it was badly conducted, Dumas was defeated with great loss and taken prisoner.[3] But Stuart could not take advantage of the French setback because of the deplorable state of his army which was wasting away from sickness and casualties, and suffering from a great scarcity of provisions, with no prospect of relief either from the fleet or from Madras. As a matter of fact, if the French had made a resolute counter-attack at this time, the English army would certainly have been destroyed. But, as usual, Bussy showed a great lack of boldness and enterprise. Owing to the failure of the sortie he thought the English were still too strong to be attacked from the front. He, therefore, decided to wait until, after exhausting their strength, they should commence retreating.[4] But his opportunity never came, because within a few days he was obliged to cease hostilities. On June 23, 1783, news reached Madras that Preliminaries of Peace had been signed at Versailles on February 9, 1783, between England and France. This news was immediately communicated to Bussy. "Under different conditions," to quote the words of the French General, "the Madras Government would not have hesitated to conceal from us the news which they had received,"[5] but now, in order to save the English army before Cuddalore from destruction, it at once sent two Commissioners, Staunton and Sadlier, with letters to Bussy and Suffren, informing them that, since peace had been made between the French and the English in Europe, hostilities should cease between the two nations in India also. The Commissioners reached Cuddalore on June 30 in a frigate bearing a flag of truce, and after three days, during which the armistice terms were adjusted, hostilities ceased on July 2.[6]

To the Indian powers, who had been fed for a long time on pro-

[1] P.A.MS. No. 402; M.R., Mly. Cons., June 24, 1783, vol. 90A, pp. 2724-5.
[2] P.A.MS. No. 402.
[3] *Ibid.*, Wilson, ii, p. 81.
[4] P.A.MS. No. 402.
[5] *Ibid.*
[6] *Ibid.*, Wilks, ii, pp. 196-97.

mises and hopes of the arrival of a large army under Bussy to wage war on the English, the news of peace came as a great surprise; for hardly had they been informed of Bussy's arrival when they heard of the suspension of arms. In the words of Bussy himself: "Little is the advantage which this peace will procure for us, it will be difficult to preserve the reputation and glory of the nation."[1]

Immediately after the armistice, Bussy sent orders to the French troops, who were engaged along with the Mysoreans in prosecuting the siege of Mangalore, to cease fighting.[2] On receiving this order, Cossigny refused to continue to fight. Even Lallée and Boudelot, who were in Tipu's service, withdrew. This aroused the Sultan's indignation. He looked upon the conduct of the French as a stab in the back, for they had backed out just when Mangalore was about to fall, and had made their peace with the English without consulting him and without any regard to his interests.[3] He tried to compel them to fight, but they refused, and apprehending an attack from him, prepared to defend themselves. So Tipu offered them 50 pagodas each in order to win them over. In consequence 64 men joined him.[4] Cossigny left the camp after a few days, and stayed for sometime at the Jesuit seminary of Mount Marian.[5] He then left for the English possession of Tellicherry on the Malabar coast without even waiting for Bussy's instructions, and from there went to Pondicherry, while the remnants of his detachment proceeded to Mahé and thence to the Isle of France. Lallée and Boudelot, however, remained at Mangalore, but they held themselves aloof from military operations.[6]

On the same day that Bussy sent orders to the French troops at Mangalore to stop fighting, he also wrote to Tipu to make peace with the English, and promised him in this connection every help that was within his power. Two or three days later he sent a Brahmin, named

[1] P.A.MS. No. 403.

[2] N.A., Sec Pro., Aug. 18, 1783..

[3] *Ibid.*, Tipu to Muhammad Ismail, his agent with Bussy; Martineau, *Bussy et l'Inde Francaise*, p. 379.

[4] A.N., C[4] 66, Cossigny to de Castries, Sept. 3, 1784.

[5] Pissurlencar, *Antigualhas*, i, fasc. ii, No. 79.

[6] *Ibid.*, Martineau, *Bussy et l'Inde Francaise*, p. 385-86. Cossigny complained of lack of supplies and ill treatment. But Tipu refuted the charges. He pointed out that Cossigny had come with him from the Carnatic with 650 men, and he had given him for them Rs. 26,000 a month, in addition to 900 seers of rice per day, 105 seers of *ghee*, 20 sheep and 14 oxen. But Cossigny had given his troops only Rs. 5-2 fanams each per month and $1\frac{1}{3}$ seers of rice per day, having sold most of the rice, sheep and oxen in the market. In consequence his troops had been discontented and 80 of them had deserted. So Tipu had asked de Morlat to inquire into the matter. He had even suggested the appointment of an Inspector to be present at the time of the distribution of salary and ration. But Cossigny had opposed this. (See A.N., C[2] 155 Tipu to Sayyid Saheb, received Oct. 2, 1783, ff. 372a-b; *Ibid.*, Tipu to Appaji Ram & Srinivas Rao, Sept. 5, 1783, f. 373a; also *Ibid.*, Cossigny to Bussy, Aug. 5, 1783, f. 374a.

Kishen Rao, to the Sultan to explain to him the aims of French policy.[1] He also instructed Piveron de Morlat, the French agent with Tipu, and other French officers at Mangalore, to persuade the Sultan to cease hostilities.

Bussy was anxious to bring about peace between Tipu and the English in the first place, because, in accordance with the sixteenth article of the Treaty of Versailles, both the French and the English were required to ask their allies to participate in the general pacification. In the second place, because the evacuation of the Carnatic by the Mysoreans was also a condition of the treaty, and the Madras Government had written to Bussy that, "whilst Tipu will not recall the troops from the Carnatic, it cannot proceed to return the French territories."[2] Moreover, Bussy realised that, if war continued, Tipu was bound to succumb to the English-Maratha-Nizam coalition which the Bengal Government would sooner or later succeed in organising. Bussy did not want Tipu's defeat which he felt would lead to the strengthening of the British power in India.

At first Tipu refused to listen to Bussy's advice. In the end, however, better counsels prevailed. Deprived of his French allies, tired of a long war, and threatened by a confederacy of the English and the Marathas, he agreed to an armistice which was signed at Mangalore on August 2, 1783.[3]

After the conclusion of the armistice, Bussy tried to arbitrate a peace treaty.[4] But he was ignored both by Tipu and the English. The Madras Government had sought his assistance in securing a suspension of arms with Tipu, but now that fighting had stopped, it no longer wanted his interference[5] which would enhance French prestige in India. Tipu had, at first, asked Bussy to send a French agent to help in the peace talks, but now he did not desire French mediation. This was partly because he had not yet recovered from the shock of their betrayal, and partly because he was not sure if they would work in his interest. In one of the letters addressed by de Castries to Bussy, he had written that the English and their allies should be restored all the territory that Haidar had occupied before 1776. When Tipu came to know of this he was furious, and had recalled Muhammad Osman, his agent with Bussy.[6] And that is why Sayyid Saheb despatched the two Mysore *wakīls*, Appaji Ram and Srinivas Rao, to Madras in September without informing Bussy, although the latter had asked him to send them along with the

[1] P.A.MS. No. 532.
[2] P.A.MS. No. 704.
[3] N.A., Sec. Pro., Sept. 4, 1783.
[4] *Ibid.*, Aug. 18, 1783.
[5] *Ibid.*, Aug. 28, 1783.
[6] A.N., C[2] 233, Sept. 28, 1783, No. 19.

French agents.[1] This was a sufficient indication that Tipu did not want French interference in the peace negotiations. Nevertheless, Bussy persisted, and sent Paul Martin along with Kishen Rao to participate in the talks and keep watch over the French interests. But both Martin and Kishen Rao were ignored by Tipu's *wakils* who did not even care to meet them.[2] Kishen Rao was obliged to leave after some time. Martin remained till November, but his presence proved useless, since he was neither taken into confidence by Tipu's *wakils* nor by the Madras Government.[3] De Morlat, however, remained until the conclusion of the Treaty of Mangalore. And although Tipu directly negotiated with the English Commissioners without any French mediation, de Morlat proved himself useful to him, just as he had been useful at the time of the cessation of hostilities. After the conclusion of peace his mission came to an end and he left for Pondicherry.[4]

[1] P.A.MS., No. 541.

[2] Ibid., Nos. 678, 713. Kishen Rao wanted to see Tipu's deputies in Madras, but they informed him that Macartney's permission was necessary for this. Actually neither Tipu nor the English wanted French mediation. (See C² 233, Bussy to de Castries, Sept. 28, 1783, No. 19, and *Ibid.*, Martin to Bussy, Oct. 6 & 9, 1783, No. 3).

[3] Martineau, *Bussy et l'Inde Francaise*, p. 383.

[4] A.N., C² 234, de Morlat to de Castries, June 25, 1784.

CHAPTER IV

# THE TREATY OF MANGALORE AND ITS REACTIONS

### *Peace Negotiations Between Haidar and Coote*

PEACE negotiations between Haidar and the English began as early as February 1782. Annaji Pandit, who had been for several years Haidar's *wakil* at Madras, wrote to a servant of Sir Eyre Coote that his master wanted accommodation with the English, but desired that the latter "should make the first overtures."[1] To this Coote replied that first there should be an exchange of prisoners or a general release, and then he would persuade the Bengal Government to conclude a friendly alliance with Haidar. The Bengal Government was at first reluctant to enter into any direct talks with Haidar because of the Treaty of Salbai.[2] However, they maintained that, since negotiations had been opened, they were ready to make use of the opportunity. But Haidar must, as a condition of peace, "separate himself from his connection with the French, and dismiss the forces which they have sent to his assistance." In return for this the English would not exact any reparation from him for the losses they had sustained at his hands.[3]

Haidar considered the English proposal unsatisfactory, so the talks were discontinued. But they were again revived when, on June 19, Muhammad Osman, a messenger from Haidar, arrived at the English camp and informed Coote that his master was anxious to maintain friendly relations with the English, and wanted to know on what conditions they were prepared to make peace. Coote replied that the Treaty of Salbai "was to be considered as the ground basis of all negotiations," and that there were two points to which Haidar was required to conform. First, he must immediately withdraw from the Carnatic, and secondly, he must sever all connections with the French. Osman pointed out that the Nawab would accept these terms provided his claim to Trichinopoly was recognised. Coote was ready to accept Haidar's demand, and wrote to the Bengal Government recommending the surrender of Trichinopoly.[4] But the Governor-General and Council were not prepared to make this concession,

[1] N.A., Sec. Pro., March, 4 1782. pp. 701-02, Coote to Bengal.

[2] By this treaty the Peshwa undertook to compel Haidar to release the English prisoners of war, and to relinquish the territories conquered from the English and their allies. (For more details see Aitchison, *Treaties*, vi. p. 40).

[3] N.A., Sec. Pro., March 18, 1782, p. 1150, Bengal to Coote.

[4] *Ibid.*, July 8, 1782, Coote to Bengal, June 21, pp. 2215-17.

because "the cession of Trichinopoly and the consequent command which he would obtain of the south division of the Carnatic would, in that case, prove both an encouragement to him to renew the war and an advantage in prosecuting it."[1] Owing to this attitude of the Bengal Government the peace negotiations once again broke down.

However, soon after, Haidar and Coote once more got in touch with each other, and the Madras Government wrote to the Governor-General and Council for permission to make peace with Haidar on the basis of the Treaty of Salbai. In fact, even before any reply could be received from Calcutta, approaches were made through Colonel Braithwaite who had been taken prisoner by Tipu in Tanjore. But the Bengal Government, confident of military aid from Poona, refused to yield to Haidar's demands. It no longer desired to negotiate peace even on the basis of the Treaty of Salbai because it argued that, "until Hyder Ali shall be compelled to solicit peace or be disposed to move for an accommodation from some change in his affairs, every advance to a negotiation with him would be but an encouragement to him to persist in the war."[2]

### *Macartney Opens Peace Negotiations*

Haidar died in December 1782, and the English, at first, hoped that it was a favourable opportunity to strike a smashing blow at the power of Tipu, his successor. So they gave up the idea of making peace. But, as we have seen, they failed to achieve their object. The Madras Government, therefore, once again turned its attention to the termination of the war; and when, early in February 1783, Sambhaji, the agent of the Raja of Tanjore at Madras, was making a pilgrimage to Conjeeveram, Macartney, the Governor of Madras, asked him to find out Tipu's intentions regarding peace, to secure alleviation of the distress of the English prisoners of war, and to try to separate Tipu from the French.[3] Sambhaji met at Conjeeveram two of Tipu's chief confidants who explained to him what their master wanted. When he returned to Madras, he brought with him Srinivas Rao who was deputed by Tipu to treat with the Madras Government. Macartney, having first interviewed Sambhaji and then Srinivas Rao, was informed by them that the Sultan was ready to conclude peace and to evacuate the Carnatic provided he was given the districts of Pudukkottai and Polypady and some other small posts in the Carnatic bordering upon his kingdom. He was also willing to inquire into the

[1] *Ibid.*, Bengal to Coote, pp. 2265-68.
[2] M.R., Mly. Cons., March 5, 1783, Bengal to Madras, vol. 86B, pp. 1022-24.
[3] *Ibid.*, Feb. 11, 1783, President's Minute, vol. 86A, pp. 609-11; see also Select Committee's instructions to Sambhaji, pp. 635-36.

treatment of the English prisoners, and to give up his connections with the French who might later arrive in India, but as to those who had already joined him, "his honour would never permit him, either to deliver those troops or, by separating from them, to let them become a prey to the English," because like his father he was also pledged to protect them.[1] To this Macartney replied that Tipu could maintain his word by sending the French to their own country instead of delivering them over to the English. Srinivas Rao, thereupon, suggested that the Company should send an authorised person who should confer with Tipu and clarify matters.[2]

Lord Macartney conveyed Tipu's proposals to the Select Committee which received them favourably, and wrote to the Governor-General and Council for permission to conclude peace with Tipu on the basis of the Treaty of Salbai, adding that the Sultan may be permitted to retain "small posts and districts of Pudukkottai and Polypady and other small posts of little value but convenient to and bordering" upon his kingdom.[3]

Macartney was prepared to make these concessions, because he felt that the Company could not bear the strains of war any longer. The pay of the Madras army was several months in arrears, and there was an acute shortage of supplies, partly because the Carnatic was in ruins, and partly because, owing to the absence of the English fleet from the Coromandel coast, all supplies of money and provisions from Bengal were intercepted by the French squadrons.[4] Moreover, the dissensions between the civil and military authorities at Madras made effective prosecution of the war very difficult. The Court of Directors had also instructed the Madras Government that "a safe and speedy peace with all the Indian powers is our primary consideration. This must never be forgotten. Nor must any step be taken, but such as shall have a direct tendency to accomplish this desirable object."[5]

But the Governor-General thought Macartney's attitude humiliating and undignified, and he was so angry with him that he wanted him to be suspended. He argued that there was no urgent need of peace, for he had supplied Madras with three million sterling. He refused to empower the Madras Government to make a separate treaty with Tipu because that would be a breach of the Treaty of Salbai, and maintained that the Company's "policy consists in a vigorous prosecution of war, moderation amidst success, firmness in

[1] *Ibid.*, March 9, 1783. President's Minute, vol. 87A, pp. 1064-65; *Ibid.*, Feb. 1783, President's Minute, vol. 86B, pp. 904-05.

[2] *Ibid.*, March 9, 1783, President's Minute, vol. 87A, pp. 1064-65.

[3] *Ibid.*, Feb. 19, 1783, Madras to Bengal, vol 86B, pp. 792-94.

[4] *Ibid.*, Feb. 11, 1783, President's Minute, vol. 86A, p. 609-11.

[5] *Ibid.*, Desp. to Madras, No. 10, p. 146, cited in Das Gupta, *Studies in the History of the British in India*, p. 138.

every adverse change of fortune, but a guarded avoidance of the submission which in eagerly soliciting and courting pacific arrangements adds to the insolence, encourages the obstinacy, and justifies the perseverance of the enemy in war and in every case gives him the plea of dictating his conditions."[1] As regards the cession of "small posts and districts", Hastings observed that this would, in future, facilitate the invasion of the Carnatic. Moreover, if they were ceded on the ground that they bordered on Tipu's kingdom, it would then be a strong argument for the cession of the next small district and so *ad infinitum*.[2]

It was, thus, owing to the uncompromising temper of the Bengal Government that the negotiations between Srinivas Rao and Macartney broke down and the former left Madras. But they were again revived after the armistice was signed between Tipu and the Company on August 2, 1783. In September Tipu's agents, Appaji Ram and Srinivas Rao, arrived in Madras to "conclude peace on terms that will be consistent with the dignity of the Cirkar." In case of any difficulty they were required to refer to Mir Muin-ud-din, the Mysore commander in the Carnatic.[3] The terms which they put forward were that there should be mutual restitution of conquests, but Tipu should be given Tiagar, Vellore and other places in the Carnatic as a *jagir*. There should also be mutual release of prisoners, and Ayaz and those deserters who had taken up residence at Tellicherry and with the Raja of Travancore should be delivered to Tipu, and no protection should be offered to his rebel subjects by the Company in future. Lastly, an offensive and defensive alliance between Tipu and the English should be formed.[4]

The reply of the Madras Government to these proposals was that Tipu should entirely evacuate the Carnatic, including the possessions of the Rajas of Tanjore and Travancore, within four months of the cessation of hostilities, and that the Company could not grant any *jagir* to the Sultan. The Company was willing to restore all the Mysorean prisoners of war, but the case of Ayaz was of a different category. As he had not been taken prisoner, he was not in the Company's custody, nor were his whereabouts known. Besides, the Company had entered into an agreement with him for the security of his person, therefore it could not surrender him. Similarly, those persons who might have taken refuge in Tellicherry could not be sent back. Nor did the Company demand the return of its deserters who might be

[1] N.A., Sec. Pro., April 1, 1783, Hastings to Select Committee, March 24.
[2] Macartney Papers, Bodleian, MS. Eng. hist. c. 77 ff. 28b *seq.*
[3] M.R., Mly. Cons. Oct. 31, 1783., Tipu to his agents at Madras, Oct. 12, vol. 93B, pp. 4773-74.
[4] *Ibid.*, Dec. 10, 1783, vol. 94B, pp. 5378-80. See also A.N., C[2] 155, Tipu to Bussy, Aug. 14, 1783, ff. 367b-368a.

unwilling to return to its service. With regard to an offensive and defensive alliance, the Madras Government pointed out that it was not prepared to conclude any such engagement with Tipu, because the non-fulfilment of its terms would lead to war with him as it had done with Haidar. However, the Government was willing to stipulate that, "in case of the Company being at war with any Indian or European power in India, or if Tipu being at war with any power excepting the Rajas of Tanjore and Travancore and the Nawab of Arcot, who are under the immediate protection of the Company, no assistance whatsoever directly or indirectly shall be offered by the Company or by Tipu to their respective enemies."[1]

This convention of neutrality was suggested by the Madras Government as an alternative to the proposal of Srinivas Rao and Appaji Ram for an offensive and defensive alliance, lest Tipu should think that, after the restoration of places and prisoners and the evacuation of the Carnatic, the English intended to help the Marathas and the Nizam in the spoilation of his kingdom.[2] The Bengal Government was, however, opposed to the clause on the ground that "it would be offensive to the Marathas and other States who would consider themselves as the objects of it," and instead proposed that, "as long as Tipu abstains from hostilities against us and our allies, that is the Nizam-ul-mulk, the Nawab of Arcot, and the Rajas of Tanjore and Travancore, we shall also abstain from hostilities."[3] In reality, this clause would have given greater offence to the Marathas than that proposed by the Madras Government, because it especially mentioned the Nizam as a friend of the Company.

Since the counter-proposals put forward by the Company were not acceptable to Tipu's *wakils*, they departed from Madras. The failure of the negotiations was largely due to the intransigent attitude of Warren Hastings who refused to grant the Madras Government permission to negotiate a separate treaty on the ground that "every object of it was comprehended in that already concluded with the Marathas."[4] Moreover, he was confident that the Marathas would compel the Sultan to submit to the Treaty of Salbai.[5]

However, there were three factors which obliged him to agree to a separate peace with Tipu. First, the pressure from the Court of Directors who enjoined on him an early peace. Secondly, owing to the poor state of Bengal finances, and the prospect of a famine in Northern India which had compelled the Bengal Government to prohibit the export of grain from the province, the Governor-General and Council

[1] *Ibid.*, Oct. 6, 1783, President's Minute, vol. 93A, pp. 4329-32.
[2] *Ibid.*, Oct. 14, 1783, vol. 93A, p. 4448.
[3] *Ibid.*, Dec. 10, 1783, Hastings to Madras, Nov. 14, vol. 94B, p. 5352.
[4] *Ibid.*, June 3, 1784, Madras to Bengal, vol. 100A, p. 2218.
[5] N.A., Sec. Pro., Sept. 29, 1783, Anderson to Hastings, Sept. 13.

no longer entertained the idea of a renewal of hostilities. Lastly, the advice which he received from Anderson, the Company's agent with Sindhia, convinced him that it was futile to object to a separate peace with Tipu. Since the Marathas had considerable claims against Mysore, which they wanted to settle before peace was made between Tipu and the Company, their mediation would not only be not helpful; it would, in fact, complicate the negotiations and delay the peace. Nor was Anderson sure of the Maratha assistance in spite of the promises of Mahadji Sindhia and Nana Phadnavis; for, while Sindhia was too busy in Hindustan to come to the south, the forces of the Peshwa, being at the disposal of Haripant, Holkar and that faction which was opposed to Sindhia, it was difficult to say if they would ever agree to Nana's wishes. Moreover, Tipu was bitterly opposed to a peace on the basis of the Treaty of Salbai, because, to quote Anderson, "he has no assurance of our continuing at peace, since the very terms of that treaty admit of our resuming hostilities whenever a rupture shall happen between him and the Peshwa."[1] He wanted a direct peace, for, so long as the Maratha claims on him remained unsettled, he would always expect danger from them.

*The English Commissioners Proceed to Mangalore*

The above were the circumstances which induced Warren Hastings to grant the Madras Government permission to enter into a separate treaty with Tipu. However, even before this decision was taken, Macartney and his Council had, on the suggestion of Appaji Ram, appointed on October 31, 1783, Anthony Sadlier, Second in Council and Committee of the Presidency, and George Leonard Staunton, private secretary to Lord Macartney, to proceed to Mangalore in order to secure the release of the English prisoners of war, and to enter into a treaty with Tipu "as shall be agreeable to the preliminary articles of the peace concluded in Europe, and to the consequent instructions of the Court of Directors." They were also empowered to extend the period of the armistice which was to expire on December 2, 1783, to another date as they thought fit.[2] The Governor and Select Committee justified their action of appointing Commissioners to proceed to Mangalore and to conclude peace with Tipu, without obtaining the previous permission of the Supreme Government, by arguing that "our treasury is empty, our credit exhausted, no supply of money from Bengal. Add to this that there is a famine apprehended in Bengal from where we draw the greatest part of our supplies of rice and provisions, an embargo on all grains

[1] *Ibid.*, Nov. 10, 1783, Anderson to Hastings, Oct. 22.
[2] M.R., Mly. Sundry Book, vol. 60A, p. 3.

is laid on these, and our stores here are drained almost to the bottom."[1]

The Commissioners, accompanied by Tipu's *wakils*, set out from Madras on November 9, and reached Conjeeveram on the 11th. From here they proceeded to Arni to meet Sayyid Saheb who was empowered by Tipu to treat with the English. Owing to bad weather, heavy rains and swollen rivers, the progress of the Commissioners was so slow that it took them nine days to reach Arni.[2] Here they held a number of meetings with Sayyid Saheb in which they proposed that the Mysoreans should entirely evacuate the Carnatic, and after this had been completed, they would give orders to the English officers to evacuate those parts of Tipu's kingdom occupied since the commencement of the war. But Mangalore and other Malabar possessions of the Sultan would be restored only when all the prisoners had been released.[3]

Sayyid Saheb turned down these proposals. He was prepared to enter into reciprocal agreements, and reminded the Commissioners of the conference at Madras in which the mutual restitution of conquests had been agreed upon. He was ready to evacuate the Carnatic provided the Commissioners "put letters into his hands addressed to the officers commanding to the southward, northward and westward, including the officer commanding at Mangalore, to deliver up to the officers of Tipu the several places that had been conquered from him by the Company." He was also ready to release all the Company's prisoners of war after Mangalore had been evacuated by the English.[4]

The counter-proposals not being acceptable to the Commissioners, Appaji Ram suggested as a compromise that the Mysoreans should first evacuate the Carnatic and hand it over to the representatives of the Company. But the prisoners should be released only after the English had evacuated all the possessions of Tipu including those on the Malabar coast. The compromise was accepted by Sadlier,[5] but rejected by Staunton, who maintained that "the restoration to Tipu of the fortresses on the coast of Malabar should not take place till such absolute release of the said prisoners and people should be effected."[6] Tipu's *wakils* were ready to pledge themselves that the terms of the treaty would be carried out by the Sultan, and that all the prisoners would be released. They even proposed that, if Mangalore were

[1] Cited in Das Gupta, *Studies in the History of the British in India*, pp. 146-47, and footnote 30.

[2] M.R., Mly. Sundry Book, vol. 60A, pp. 32, 37. The Commissioners were accompanied by 1456 public followers, exclusive of public servants. (*Ibid.*, vol. 60B, p. 505.)

[3] *Ibid.*, Commissioners to Madras, Nov. 26, 1783, pp. 140 *seqq.*

[4] *Ibid.*, Nov. 21, 1783, pp. 88-9.

[5] *Ibid.*, pp. 104-06.

[6] *Ibid.*, pp. 106-07.

evacuated immediately, they would consent to all the places to the east of the Western Ghats, which the English had captured, being retained by them till the restoration of the prisoners. Sadlier was disposed to give up Mangalore and accept "the pledge" as sufficient security, but Staunton, in spite of the assurances of the *wakils*, refused to give in. He wanted the prisoners to be released before Mangalore was surrendered.[1] To this the *wakils* could not agree. They had yielded on many points. They had agreed to evacuate the Carnatic before the English evacuated Tipu's possessions, and they had given every possible assurance to the Commissioners regarding the release of the prisoners. On the question of Mangalore, however, they refused to compromise. They felt that, if all the prisoners were released, the English might not afterwards give up Tipu's Malabar possessions, particularly Mangalore which the Bombay Government was extremely anxious to retain. Hence they wanted "to retain something in their hands till the evacuation of Mangalore."[2]

There was, however, one point on which agreement was arrived at. It was decided to restore Cumbum and Settupattu to their previous rulers. Accordingly, letters were written to Major Lysaght by the Commissioners to deliver Cumbum over to Qamar-ud-din Khan, and similarly, orders were issued by the *wakils* to the latter to surrender Settupattu to the English.[3] But the main issues having remained undecided, the Commissioners set out for Mangalore to treat directly with Tipu.

They left Arni on November 25 and reached Malvalli on December 24. From here they wanted to proceed first to Seringapatam in order to meet the English prisoners of war who were confined there. But the *wakils* refused to accompany them by that route and advised them to proceed directly to Mangalore via Maddur as desired by the Sultan; for, if they went to Seringapatam, they would not be allowed to enter the fort and interview the prisoners.[4]

The Commissioners protested against this attitude of the *wakils* on the ground that it was a violation of the Madras agreement according to which they were entitled to visit Bangalore and Seringapatam.[5] The *wakils*, on the other hand, maintained that their action was perfectly consistent with the agreement which was that, if the negotia-

[1] *Ibid.*, pp. 130 *seq.* Staunton's opinion was upheld by the Madras Government when the matter was referred to it. And owing to the constant differences between Sadlier and Staunton, it appointed a third Commissioner, named Huddlestone, in order to facilitate decision by a majority. He joined his colleagues at Udayagiri in Nellore District, Andhra Pradesh, on December 27, 1783.

[2] Cumbum is in Kurnool District, Andhra Pradesh, and Settupattu is a small village in South Arcot District, Tamil Nadu (Madras).

[3] M.R., Mly. Sundry Book, vol. 60A, Commissioners to Madras, Nov. 25, 1783, pp. 120-23.

[4] *Ibid.*, vol. 60B, pp. 435, 472-78.

[5] *Ibid.*

tions between Sayyid Saheb and the Commissioners proved successful, the latter could at once proceed to Seringapatam where they could both settle the final terms of the treaty with Tipu and also meet the English prisoners. But as the negotiations at Arni had failed, the Commissioners were no longer entitled to go to Seringapatam where, owing to the same reason, Tipu would not be present to receive them.[1] But these arguments had no effect on the Commissioners who were determined to have their own way. Their plan was to start as soon as they had secured 25,000 maunds of rice which would be sufficient for their journey.[2] But as the plan leaked out, the *wakils* not only refused to give them more rice than was necessary for their normal requirements, but also prohibited the merchants from selling it to them. The Commissioners fretted and chafed and threatened to return to Madras if their demand for 25,000 maunds of rice was not complied with.[3] But, in the end, realising that the *wakils* would not give in and their journey to Seringapatam would be futile, they changed their attitude and agreed to proceed directly to Mangalore.

It was due to military reasons that Tipu did not want the Commissioners to visit Seringapatam. Although the armistice had been signed, still, owing to the breakdown of the Arni talks, and the atmosphere of suspicion and distrust which hung over the relations of the English and the Mysoreans, the prospects of a peace treaty were not bright. Under the circumstance, Tipu could not allow the Commissioners to meet the English prisoners, and thus obtain first-hand information regarding the fortifications of Seringapatam and other military secrets. It was also for military reasons that the Commissioners had not been allowed to visit Bangalore. Nevertheless, they were permitted to send to the prisoners at Bangalore and Seringapatam whatever articles they wished, and the parcels which they sent were safely delivered to the prisoners.[4]

The Commissioners left Malvalli on January 1, 1784, and reached Mangalore on February 4. Thus it had taken them nearly three months from Madras to reach their destination. Wilks suggests that it had taken them such a long time because they were deliberately made to proceed slow.[5] But in reality there is no truth whatsoever in this allegation. When the Commissioners set out from Madras on November 9, their progress was hampered by bad weather, heavy

[1] *Ibid.*, *Wakils* to Commissioners. Dec. 27, 1783, pp. 506-12.
[2] *Ibid.*, Dec. 29, 1783, pp. 472-78.
[3] *Ibid.*, The *wakils* told the Commissioners that they had no rice in stock, but humorously added that they could supply them plenty of horse grain instead. (*Ibid.*, p. 504).
[4] M.R., Mly. Desp. to England, Feb. 4, 1784, vol. 19, p. 136.
[5] Wilks, ii, p. 262. Wilks says: "They were permitted to proceed as fast and no faster than the progress of famine in Mangalore."

rains and swollen rivers, so that they reached Arni after nine days.[1] Here, and then at Malvalli, over a fortnight was wasted in fruitless discussions with Tipu's *wakils* and among themselves.[2] Sometimes, because of their inability to come to a decision, the Commissioners had to wait for days together for instructions from Madras.[3] Moreover, they travelled in a leisurely fashion, and it did not seem that they were in a hurry to reach Mangalore. It is true that they were made to proceed through circuitous and difficult routes, but that was not done with the intention of retarding their progress to Mangalore; it was done owing to military considerations.

*Peace Negotiations in Mangalore*

On February 13 the Commissioners presented a memorial to Tipu in which they demanded from him the fulfilment of the ninth article of the Treaty of Salbai by evacuating the Carnatic and releasing the English prisoners of war. The English were also prepared to cede those of Tipu's possessions which were in their hands, but "such a cession is not to be considered as being in return for the evacuation of the Carnatic or the release of the prisoners, as the same are already settled by the Maratha Treaties." Nevertheless, the Commissioners would give orders for the evacuation of Onore, Karwar and other places as soon as 100 English prisoners (one-half officers or persons in the rank of gentlemen) had been delivered. Dindigul, Karur and Dharapuram would be given up as soon as all the prisoners, native and European, had been released. If Tipu refused to accept these terms within a month, it would mean war, and the English would be joined by the Marathas, and together they would compel him to submit to the ninth article of the Treaty of Salbai in accordance with the agreement signed between the Peshwa and the Company on October 29, 1783.[4]

Tipu's reply to the memorandum was that, as soon as peace was made, he would evacuate the Carnatic, and would not merely release "100 prisoners" as a first instalment but the whole lot at once, and

[1] M.R., Mly. Sundry Book, 60A, Commissioners to Macartney, pp. 32, 37.

[2] *Ibid.*, vol. 61, Sadlier's Minute of Jan. 16, 1784. pp. 625-6. The differences between the Commissioners were very acute. Sadlier accused Staunton of "arbitrary and tyrannical conduct," while Staunton accused Sadlier of having "united with the deputies of Tipu." (p. 633) Even after Huddlestone joined them their differences remained. Sadlier and his servant were accused of being in secret communication with Tipu's *wakils*. (See for more details M.R., Mly. Sundry Book, vol. 61, pp. 1102-14, 1189-91).

[3] It took a long time for letters from Madras to reach the Commissioners because pagodas were sent along with them, and these could be carried only by reliable persons and not by ordinary couriers. (Macartney Papers, Bodleian, MS. Eng. hist. C. 92, Appaji Ram and Srinivas Rao to Macartney, Feb. 25, 1784).

[4] M.R., Mly Sundry Book, vol. 61, pp. 974-85.

they would be handed over to the Commissioners instead of being sent to any English fort or neutral settlement. As regards the Treaty of Salbai, Tipu argued that, as "none of my letters or *wakils* were sent to the English during the time of concluding the said treaty between them and the Maratha State, therefore, consider to what authority you had to mention it to me." His *wakils* also informed the Commissioners with whom they held a meeting on February 14 that, since the Sultan was an independent ruler, the Treaty of Salbai should not be referred to, and "the present negotiations were to be carried on unconnected with any other State."[1] As regards the English threat of war the *wakils* maintained that, if the Marathas joined the Company in the invasion of Mysore, Tipu would not be left without allies, for the French would immediately come to his assistance.[2]

The conditions on which Tipu was prepared to make peace were almost the same as had been proposed by his *wakils* at Madras. He demanded the cession of certain districts in the Carnatic, the surrender of Ayaz and an offensive and defensive alliance. He further maintained that "the Carnatic should be evacuated precisely at the time when the possessions taken from the Cirkar since the commencement of the present war should be evacuated, and that the prisoners of every denomination should be immediately delivered up to people who may be sent by the Commissioners to take charge of them at the different places where they are now confined."[3] However, in a memorandum sent to the Commissioners on February 19, 1784, Tipu stipulated that he was prepared to release all the prisoners and deliver them over to the English and also restore two, four or five places in the Carnatic as desired by the Commissioners, but in return the English should hand over Cannanore, Onore and Sadasivgarh. Besides, the English should also restore Dindigul and other places, and return the 55,000 pagodas which Fullarton had taken away from the fort of Palghat, and only then would he order the entire evacuation of the Carnatic.[4]

The Commissioners rejected these demands as they were determined not to compromise on the question of the release of the English prisoners and the evacuation of the Carnatic. They also refused to return the 55,000 pagodas on the ground that the Company itself was entitled to an indemnity from the Sultan for the great damage inflicted by the Mysore armies upon the Carnatic. However, the Commissioners were ready to waive aside the question of indemnity provided Tipu was willing to grant the Company commercial privileges in his kingdom.[5]

On February 22 the Commissioners placed before Tipu's ministers

[1] *Ibid.*, pp. 985-91.
[2] *Ibid.*, pp. 992-94.
[3] *Ibid.*, pp. 994-96.
[4] *Ibid.*, pp. 1013-14.
[5] *Ibid.*, pp. 1061-62.

a draft treaty which contained twenty-nine articles and was the most complete and detailed statement of the English demands so far formulated.[1] Although the Commissioners agreed not to make the Treaty of Salbai the basis of their negotiations, they refused to modify their attitude regarding the release of the English prisoners and the evacuation of the Carnatic. At the same time they demanded that Tipu should renounce all claims on the Nawab of Carnatic; that all the people belonging to the Venkatagiri Raja, who were taken prisoners while returning from Vellore, should be restored within one month of the conclusion of peace; that the Raja should be given the district of Kanigiri[2] on the usual annual rent; that Morari Rao should be set free and given a *jagir;* that Tipu should allow a representative of the Company to reside at his court along with two companies of sepoys; that *tappals* should be established from the pass of Changama via Seringapatam to Tellicherry; that the fort and district of Mount Delli, which were captured by Sardar Khan at the beginning of the war, should be restored to the factory of Tellicherry; that the Rajas of Coorg, Chirakkal, Kottayam and Kadattanad, who had been deposed for having sided with the English, should be reinstated in their respective countries and should not be molested for having helped the English against Mysore; and finally, that Tipu should grant commerical privileges to the Company in his kingdom.

Tipu turned down the terms of the draft treaty, and informed the Commissioners on February 22 that, as the talks had failed, he would leave for Seringapatam the next morning.[3] He did not approve of the clauses relating to the release of prisoners and the mutual restoration of territory, and regarded the demand for the release of Morari Rao and the reinstatement of the Malabar Rajas as an interference in his internal affairs. Nor was he prepared to establish *tappals* through his kingdom, or to allow a representative of the Company to reside at Seringapatam. He also rejected the article relating to commercial privileges, since its acceptance would give the English complete control over the economic life of his kingdom.[4]

The rejection of the proposals by Tipu and his announcement that he would leave for Seringapatam the next morning, greatly perturbed the Commissioners, for it meant a renewal of hostilities. So they changed their intransigent attitude, and after holding a number of meetings with Tipu's *wakils,* decided to give up the demand that a

[1] *Ibid.,* pp. 1064-77.

[2] It is a town in Nellore District, Andhra Pradesh.

[3] The clauses relating to commercial privileges in Mysore were included on the advice of the Bombay Government. In order to safeguard its commercial interests it had appointed Callander and Ravenscroft as Commissioners to proceed to Mangalore. (*Ibid.,* 867 *seq.*).

[4] *Ibid.,* pp. 1200-01.

Company's representative be permitted to reside at Seringapatam and that *tappals* be established through the Mysore Kingdom. They also dropped the proposal for the release of Morari Rao and for the reinstatement of the Rajas of Coorg, Chirakkal, Kottayam and Kadattanad in their respective kingdoms, and greatly modified the clauses relating to the grant of commercial privileges to the Company in Mysore.[1] Tipu on his side relinquished his claims upon the Carnatic, and agreed not to demand the surrender of Ayaz and the return of 55,000 pagodas taken away by Fullarton from the fort of Palghat. He also promised to send the English prisoners to the nearest English garrison, and to supply them during their march provisions to be paid for by the Company.[2]

Thus agreement was at last arrived at on a number of questions. But there were two which still remained unsettled, and on these Tipu refused to make any concession. The first was regarding an alliance with the Company. Although Tipu gave up the demand for an offensive and defensive alliance with the Company, he insisted upon the inclusion of the clause that the English and his Government should not help the enemies of each other either privately or publicly. Tipu was particularly anxious to include this article in the treaty because of the Maratha danger, and he informed the Commissioners that if it was not accepted he would march off to Seringapatam. This announcement placed the Commissioners in a very embarrassing situation. If they refused, it meant war; if they accepted, it would be against the instructions of the Governor-General who, regarding the proposal as offensive to the Marathas, Tipu's potential enemies, wanted to stipulate that the Company should abstain from hostilities against Tipu so long as he abstained from hostilities against the Nizam, the Nawab of Carnatic, and the Rajas of Tanjore and Travancore.[3]

In the end, however, the Commissioners accepted Tipu's proposal, with some alteration, in defiance of the orders of the Governor-General. There were two considerations which influenced their decision. First, they realised that if Tipu's demand was accepted, it would not give the Marathas as much offence as the clause proposed by the Governor-General which, while including the Nizam as a friend of the Company, did not refer to the Marathas as such.[4] Secondly, they felt that, since Tipu had given in to nearly all their important demands, it would be a mistake to break the negotiations on this point and thus precipitate war.[5]

The second question on which Tipu was uncompromising related

[1] *Ibid.*, pp. 1205-09.
[2] *Ibid.*, p. 1252.
[3] *Ibid.*, pp. 1252, 2156-61.
[4] *Ibid.*, p. 1162.
[5] *Ibid.*, p. 1164.

to the restoration of his territories by the English. From the beginning this question had been a stumbling block to the success of the negotiations. We have seen that both at Madras and at Arni the Commissioners had refused to surrender any part of Tipu's kingdom unless and until all the prisoners were released and the whole of the Carnatic evacuated. However, as the Sultan insisted that the evacuation of the Carnatic should take place simultaneously with the evacuation of his territories, the Commissioners, in their memorandum of February 12 submitted to the *wakils* at Mangalore, proposed as a compromise that the Company would cede Onore and Karwar after 100 Europeans including 50 officers or persons of the rank of gentlemen had been released; but Karur, Dharapuram and Aravakurichi would be ceded only after the entire evacuation of the Carnatic and the release of all the prisoners of war had taken place. But Tipu remained as adamant as ever. Thereupon, the Commissioners suggested that the Company would evacuate all the possessions of Tipu at the same time as the evacuation of the Carnatic; but it would retain Dindigul and Cannanore as a pledge for the release of the prisoners. Tipu also rejected this proposal, for just as the English did not trust him, he too was suspicious of their designs and was not sure that after the release of all their prisoners, they would withdraw their forces from Dindigul and Cannanore. He, therefore, proposed five articles[1] of which the Commissioners were required to accept any one: (1) The Commissioners shall remain with Tipu till the restoration of Dindigul and Cannanore and shall leave only after the treaty had been delivered to him duly signed by the Government of Madras; (2) In lieu of Dindigul, Tipu shall be allowed to garrison Tiagar and Nellore or else Ambur and Satghur; (3) Two of the three Commissioners or at least one shall stay back, empowered by the other two, to restore Tipu's possessions after the evacuation of the Carnatic and the release of the prisoners had taken place; (4) The Commissioner shall give the order for the restoration of Dindigul or Cannanore; (5) Cannanore shall be restored in the presence of Tipu's officers and at the same time as Onore and other places.

At first the Commissioners rejected all the proposals, and, on March 4, informed the Sultan of their decision. But realising that Tipu was not bluffing, and that he would break off negotiations and march off to Seringapatam if all his five demands were rejected, they yielded and accepted the second proposition with the alteration that Tipu's troops should keep possession of Satghur and Ambur in the Carnatic as long as the English remained in possession of Dindigul and Cannanore, and that orders should be given for their restoration to the respective parties immediately and reciprocally after the release of all the pri-

[1] *Ibid.*, pp. 1333-4.

soners.[1] Agreement having been arrived at on all points, the Treaty was signed on March 11, 1784.

*Reactions to the Peace and Tipu's Treatment of the Commissioners*

The Treaty of Mangalore[2] was a diplomatic victory for Tipu; for, on the whole, he had been able to secure favourable terms from the Commissioners. He had secured the undignified burial of the Treaty of Salbai, in so far as it referred to him, and he had made the Commissioners accept the condition that the signatories would not assist the enemies of each other, directly or indirectly, nor would they make war upon each other's friends or allies. Tipu had also succeeded in whittling down the demand of the Commissioners for commercial privileges in his kingdom; and he had made them agree in the end to the principle of simultaneous restoration of each other's possessions. It is true he had failed to obtain any district of the Carnatic, but he had recovered his own territory which the English had conquered in the course of the war.

For the English also the terms of the treaty were not unreasonable, considering some of the crushing defeats they had sustained in the war, and the economic and military situation they were faced with during the period of the negotiations. They got back those places in the Carnatic which were held by the Mysoreans; and, as a pledge of the release of their prisoners of war, they were allowed to retain Dindigul and Cannanore. They secured the renewal and confirmation of all commercial privileges given to the Company by Haidar by the treaty of 1770; and they further obtained Tipu's assurance to restore them Mount Delli and the privileges enjoyed by the Company at Calicut. Thus they were able to secure all their reasonable demands. They compromised only with regard to those demands which were either unimportant, or were too exorbitant to be acceded to by Tipu. "In short," as Dodwell observes, "much the same terms were obtained from Tipu as Hastings had managed to get from the Marathas.'[3] Warren Hastings, nevertheless, regarded it as a 'humiliating pacification,'[4] and the Board so much disapproved of it, that they were even prepared to cancel it. That they did not do so was because they thought "this would throw the affairs of the Company in confusion," and because, "already restoration of territories and exchange of prisoners had taken place."[5]

Warren Hastings had, in fact, never shared Macartney's desire for a speedy peace, for he expected to secure better terms by prolonging

[1] *Ibid.*, p. 1367.
[2] *Ibid.*, pp. 1377-85; see also Aitchison, *Treaties*, ix. pp. 207-11.
[3] *Cambridge History of India*, p. 288. [4] *Ibid.*, p. 333.
[5] N.A., Sec. Pro. April 20, 1784, Minute of the Board. (Hastings absent in Lucknow).

the war. Expecting the military assistance of the Marathas, he was even ready to renew hostilities although a cessation of hostilities had taken place and the negotiations between the Commissioners and Tipu were passing through their last stages. Macartney, on the other hand, was neither sure of Maratha assistance nor optimistic of the results of a renewal of hostilities. He knew that, owing to their internal troubles, the Marathas would not be able to render any support to the English for some time to come,[1] while the affairs of the Company were in such a state as could not justify a fresh war with Tipu. The Company was heavily in debt and its commercial credit was nearly gone. The army was nine months in arrears and the garrisons upwards of eleven months. The Bengal Government had not given any financial assistance since the death of Coote and, in consequence, the assigned revenues of an impoverished and ravaged Carnatic had been the only support of the Madras Government. Besides, there was no possibility of Bengal being able to spare any money for the war against Tipu in the near future, for its own army was six months in arrears and on the point of mutiny, while the danger of famine loomed large in the Presidency. The resources of both Calcutta and Madras were strained to their furthest limit.[2] That is why Macartney wrote: "Peace was necessary for us, for had war continued for a few months more, we must have inevitably sunk under the accumulated burden of our expenses."[3]

It is true that Fullarton had achieved a large measure of success, but this has been made much of. His victories were possible because no effective resistance was offered to him; owing to the cessation of hostilities Tipu's Commandants of Palghat and Coimbatore had relaxed their measures of defence. Fullarton had also not yet faced either Tipu or any of his important commanders. Further progress of his army towards Seringapatam appeared doubtful, for he would have had to contend with larger and stronger armies led by abler generals. Besides, Seringapatam was still 100 miles distant, while Fullarton was ignorant of the geography of the country, and his army, being twelve months in arrears, was discontented. Defeat would have proved disastrous to him and would have deprived the Madras Government of the principal army it possessed.[4] Tipu's

[1] M.R., Mly. Cons., Jan. 18, 1784. Madras to Bombay, Jan. 1, vol. 96A, pp. 208-9.

[2] *Ibid.*, Dec. 27, 1783, Minute of the Select Committee, vol. 95A, pp. 5600-03.

[3] N.A., Sec. Pro., Nov. 23, 1784. Madras to Bengal, Oct. 29.

[4] *Ibid.*, M.R., Mly. Cons., Dec. 8, 1783, 94B, pp. 5308-11. The Bombay Government was also solicitous for peace. It was indebted to the amount of two hundred and twenty lakhs of rupees. Its expenses were three times more than its income. The southern army was without military stores and cattle which the Bombay Government was not in a position to supply. (*Ibid.*, July 15, 1784. vol. 100C, p. 2669).

position, on the other hand, was much more favourable for the prosecution of the war. His armies were intact, he possessed a full treasury, his kingdom had suffered very little from the devastations of war, and, because of his victories, his prestige stood high. Although he was deprived of his French allies, he had nothing to fear from the English so long as they measured swords with him alone without the assistance of any of the Indian powers. That in spite of this Tipu made peace was because of his anxiety to consolidate his power and crush those refractory chiefs who, taking advantage of the war, had renounced his authority.

The advantages enjoyed by Tipu as against the military and financial difficulties of the English were completely ignored by the critics of the treaty who did not cease to denounce it. The reason was that "men's minds were irritable with defeat and the treaty became the object of a host of legends. Tipu was said to have treated the deputies with unparalleled indignity, erecting a gallows by their encampment and keeping them in such a state of panic that they contemplated flight to the English ships lying off the town."[1] But these legends were without any foundation whatsoever. As Dodwell observes: "They had their origin in the excitable imagination of Macleod. They seemed to have passed to Calcutta by way of Bombay, along with extraordinary versions of the ill-treatment accorded to the prisoners by Tipu."[2] According to the *Memoir of John Campbell* about seventy or eighty conspirators were hanged by the orders of Tipu on three gibbets. These gibbets were still standing when the Commissioners reached Mangalore, and led to the circulation of the story that they had been erected to intimidate the Commissioners in order to extort favourable terms of peace from them.[3] Lord Macartney also wrote: "No gibbets were erected before their tent doors or in their camps. None were erected even in their sight after they had encamped. There were several gibbets in the neighbourhood of Mangalore on which diverse persons who had plotted against Tippu recently had been executed. These gibbets being upon an elevated spot must be seen for several miles round Mangalore, even in sight of the forts and of Tippu's Camp, as well as that of our Commissioners whose encampment indeed was upon a spot of their own choice; and no gibbet was erected on it or even approached to it."[4] As regards the insults supposed to have been heaped on the Commissioners, Macartney wrote: "Our Commissioners complained of no

[1] *Cambridge History of India*, v, p. 288.

[2] *Ibid.*, p. 289. Dodwell also says: "Military officers, indignant at peace at the moment when success seemed possible, spread numerous stories about the conclusion of this peace." (*Shorter Cambridge History of India*, p. 592).

[3] *Memoir of John Campbell*, pp. 57-8.

[4] M.R., Mly. Cons., June 3, 1784, Madras to Bengal, vol. 100A, p. 2221.

inattention that could affect the Company or the negotiations; they frequently expostulated on the difficulty of communicating with the Company's vessels in the road of Mangalore. That difficulty produced a momentary attention to silly conjectures and low reports concerning the situation of the Commissioners. In this state of doubt the letters were written, which you received upon the subject, but after the Commissioners were free upon the conclusion of the treaty, the opportunity of genuine and full intelligence from the Commissioners themselves precludes all excuse of catching and spreading loose and improbable tales."[1]

Similarly, there is no truth whatsoever in the allegation that the Commissioners were treated with indignity and deliberately subjected to discomforts during their journey to Mangalore. As soon as Tipu came to know that the Commissioners intended to proceed to Mangalore, he sent instructions to his officers to welcome them in a manner befitting their status and to look after their welfare.[2] Accordingly, from the time they set foot on the Mysore soil, they were shown great consideration and hospitality. Writing from Callaway on November 14, 1783, the Commissioners observed that Tipu's *amildar* of the place had been attentive to them.[3] Similarly from Arni they wrote: "Our arrival was welcomed by all the appearance of gladness and refined expressions of Eastern politeness. Our colours were saluted by thirteen guns; visits were paid by the principal officers of Mir Muin-ud-din's camp, refreshments were immediately sent, among the rest, no less than 8,000 measures of rice."[4] Even though the conference at Arni had failed and the Commissioners had refused to accede to the terms of the Sultan, on leaving the place they and their secretary, Jackson, received from Sayyid Saheb presents of dresses, shawls, jewels and rings, besides 4,000 rupees in cash.[5] There is no doubt that from Malvalli they were made to proceed to Mangalore by a difficult and circuitous route, but this, as has been mentioned, was due to military reasons.[6] Tipu could not allow them to travel by the main roads because it was still possible that hostilities might be resumed. The Commissioners were, however, provided with every comfort during their journey, and allowed considerable freedom of movement. They travelled in a leisurely fashion, and rode and hunted

[1] *Ibid.*

[2] M.R., Mly. Sundry Book, Tipu to Sayyid Saheb, Nov. 19, 1783, vol. 60A, pp. 183-4.

[3] Macartney Papers, B.M. 22452, Commissioners to Macartney, Nov. 18, 1783, f. 46b.

[4] M. R., Mly Sundry Book, Commissioners to Macartney, Nov. 18, 1783, vol. 60A, p. 46; also Macartney Papers, B. M. 22452, f. 46b.

[5] *Ibid.*, vol. 61, pp. 1462-4.

[6] See pp. 71-2 *supra*.

almost every day.[1] When they reached Mangalore, a salute was fired, and they were treated with every consideration. And after the Treaty of Mangalore was signed, and the Commissioners prepared to leave the town, they and their secretary received presents of shawls, jewels, horses and cash from Tipu.[2]

But the generous treatment accorded to the Commissioners by the Sultan and his officers was not taken any notice of at the time. Instead, the stories fabricated by Macleod and others of the ill-treatment of the Commissioners and the English prisoners of war were taken to be true by Englishmen both in India and in England. The bitterness which they engendered together with the disappointments of an early peace which had failed to bring any territorial gains to the Company, and which had prevented many officers from seeking revenge for the losses they or their compatriots had suffered at the hands of Tipu, made it certain that the Treaty of Mangalore "was merely a truce which would not last very long."[3] Innes Munro was only voicing the sentiments of the Company's officers when he said: "It is to be hoped that the treaty of peace, which the Company has lately concluded with Tippu, is only meant to be temporary."[4]

[1] M.R., Mly. Sundry Book, *Wakils* to Commissioners, Dec. 29, 1783. vol. 60B, pp. 506-12; also M.R., Mly. Count Cor., *Wakils* to Macartney, Feb. 11, 1784, vol. 33A, No. 25.

[2] M.R., Mly. Sundry Book, vol. 61, pp. 1462-4.

[3] Cal. Per. Cor., vii, Intro. p. x.

[4] Innes Munro, p. 370.

## CHAPTER V

# CONSPIRACIES AND REBELLIONS

TIPU's succession to his father had been on the whole peaceful. Except for a feeble and ill-organised attempt to instal Abdul Karim, his younger brother, as ruler, no serious challenge was offered to his authority. But while he was fighting the English on the Malabar coast, a dangerous and well-laid conspiracy was organised at Seringapatam to capture it and restore the old Hindu dynasty. Singea, the head of Post and Police in the Coimbatore province, Ranga Iyenger, head of that department at Seringapatam, Narasinga Rao, the Muster-Master, the Pay-Master and Town-Major at the capital, and Subharaja Urs, a descendant of Devraj, were the chief leaders of the conspiracy. They were in constant touch with Ranga Iyenger's brother, Shama Iyenger, commonly called Shamaiya, Minister of Post and Police in Mysore, who was at Mangalore with Tipu. They were also in communication with Tirumala Rao, the Marathas and the English.[1] Negotiations with the latter were carried on through Singea who was at Coimbatore. July 24, 1783, being the pay-day of the troops, was fixed for the coup, for on that day, it was thought, they would be scattered in the *cutchehry* without arms, and so could be easily attacked and overpowered.[2]

The task of executing the conspiracy was entrusted to Narasinga Rao. The plan was to cut off Sayyid Muhammad Mahdavi, the Governor of Seringapatam, Asad Khan, the Commandant of the fort, and the loyal troops, and then seize the fort and treasury. The English prisoners of war at Seringapatam, who had been taken into confidence, were to be at once released and placed under the command of General Matthews. Fullarton was to advance on Seringapatam and to help in the restoration of the old dynasty. But the plan miscarried. While returning home from the office on the night of July 23, Sayyid Muhammad was secretly informed by a *subedar* about the plot. Sayyid Muhammad thereupon at once took action. He intercepted a despatch which was ready to be sent to the English, inviting them to march on Seringapatam, and seized the principal conspirators. Singea, who had arrived from Coimbatore to participate in the enterprise, was immediately executed along with many others. Narasinga Rao was hanged on the receipt of orders from

[1] Lawrence, *Captives of Tipu Sultan*, p. 140-6; also Wilks, ii, p. 248.
[2] *Ibid.*, ii, p. 248-9; Punganuri, p. 35.

Tipu. Shamaiya Iyenger, after his complicity in the plot had been proved, was put in irons and sent to Seringapatam, where he and his brother Ranga Iyenger were kept in separate cages. Muhammad Shitab, who was the Governor of Seringapatam at the time of Tipu's accession, but had been superseded by Sayyid Muhammad, was also imprisoned. He was later released when his innocence was proved.[1]

In November 1783, about four months after this event, another conspiracy came to light. Its leader was Muhammad Ali, a prominent officer of the Mysore infantry. Because of his courage, outspokenness and unbounded generosity to the poor, he had been a favourite of Haidar Ali. Nevertheless, he had plotted with Sir Eyre Coote against his master for a petty sum of 2000 huns. But his intrigues had been discovered and he had been deprived of his command. However, after the battle of Pollilure, in which he had distinguished himself, he was restored to his post.[2] After Haidar's death, he continued to enjoy the confidence and favours of Tipu. In spite of this, he did not cease his intrigues with the English. While the Mysoreans were encamped before Mangalore, Muhammad Ali was in charge of the coast and was required to ensure that no one entered the fort from the sea without Tipu's permission. But he allowed Macleod to visit the fort and concert with Campbell measures for its relief and defence. He entered into an agreement with Macleod by which he promised to help him in reinforcing the garrison of Mangalore and in attacking Tipu's army. In return for these services, Muhammad Ali was to be rewarded with twenty thousand rupees in cash and a *jagir* of fifteen thousand rupees. Qasim Ali, alias Rustam Ali Beg, who was Tipu's former Commandant of Mangalore and a protégé of Muhammad Ali, was to get Mangalore as a *jagir*.[3] Muhammad Ali even offered to deliver Tipu into the hands of Campbell, provided the latter was prepared to send two or three hundred men from the fort.[4] But Campbell, doubting the sincerity of Muhammad Ali, and realising that in the event of a miscarriage of the enterprise the loss of the detachment would prove fatal to the garrison, declined the proposal. Later, however, Campbell "regretted exceedingly that he had not

[1] Wilks, ii, pp. 249-50; Punganuri, p. 35. The account of the conspiracy as given by Kirmani, p. 246, is incorrect. He wrongly gives Muhammad Ali the credit for suppressing the conspiracy. Kirmani is also wrong in stating that the Commandant was in league with Shamaiya and that, after the failure of the plot, Sayyid Muhammad was appointed the Commandant. Actually Sayyid Muhammad was already in charge of the capital when the conspiracy was organised, and Asad Khan was not in any way connected with the plot. Similarly, Shamaiya was not at Seringapatam at this time, as stated by Kirmani, but was at Mangalore.

[2] Wilks, ii, pp. 231-32; *Tarikh-i-Khudadadi*, I.O.MS., p. 29.

[3] *Ibid.*, pp. 30-31.

[4] *Memoir of John Campbell*, p. 58. See also for a brief account of the correspondence between Muhammad Ali and Campbell, Rushbrook Williams, *Great Men of India*, chapter on *Tippu Sultan* by H. H. Dodwell, p. 214.

sooner known the full scope of his (Muhammad Ali's) views, and the real character of that intrepid personage."[1]

Macleod went away to bring troops from Tellicherry for the execution of the plan. But on his return to the coast he found that a few days before the date fixed for the coup, both Muhammad Ali and Qasim Ali had been arrested and the plot discovered.[2] The circumstances which led to the discovery of the plot were as follows: Tipu Sultan had ordered an inquiry to be made into the conduct of Qasim Ali Beg for having surrendered the fort of Mangalore to the English without any resistance. The inquiry commission having found him guilty of treason, the Sultan ordered that he should be hanged in the presence of Mysore troops in order that his death might be a warning to other mischievous persons. But before the sentence could be carried out, Muhammad Ali arrived at the place of execution, struck off Qasim Ali's shackles, and mounting him on an elephant, set out towards the fort. The chief officers of the army advised him against such a course, but he refused to listen to them and, brandishing his sword, called upon the assembled troops to follow him. A large number of men belonging to his regiment obeyed his summons. Tipu, hearing of these developments, immediately despatched Sayyid Ahmad and Ghazi Khan with some troops to pursue the rebels and bring them back, and then he himself set out after them. On the approach of the Sultan, most of the followers of Muhammad Ali fled, the rest were surrounded and captured. Qasim Ali and many of his accomplices were hanged, while Muhammad Ali was sent as a prisoner to Seringapatam.[3] But on the way he committed suicide by swallowing diamond powder. Among his articles was found a small box containing letters which revealed that he had been carrying on intrigues with the English against Haidar Ali and Tipu Sultan for a long time.[4]

*Rebellion in Balam*

After making peace with the English, Tipu directed his attention towards the Malabar Christians who had intrigued against him in the Second Anglo-Mysore War and, under Portuguese influence, had forcibly converted many Hindus and Muslims to Christianity.[5]

[1] *Memoir of John Campbell*, p. 57.

[2] *Tarikh-i-Khudadadi*, pp. 31, 33.

[3] *Ibid.*, pp. 33-6; Kirmani, pp. 269-70; and Pissurlencar, *Antigualhas*, fasc. ii, No. 79. According to Kirmani, Tipu personally tried to reason with Muhammad Ali. He even postponed the execution of Qasim Ali for a day. But Muhammad Ali remained adamant.

[4] Kirmani, p. 271; see also *Sultan-ut-Tawarikh*, ff. 33-6, for an account of the conspiracy. The statement of Wilks, ii, p. 233, that Tipu caused Muhammad Ali to be strangled is not supported by any reliable evidence.

[5] Tipu's policy towards the Malabar Christians will be discussed in the chapter on *Religious Policy*.

After punishing them, Tipu marched to suppress a rising in Balam.[1]

Balam had been occupied by Haidar in 1762, but had been left in the hands of its *poligar* on condition that he paid an annual tribute of 5,000 pagodas. But during the Second Anglo-Mysore War, Krishnappa Nayak, the Raja of Balam, rebelled against the Mysore Government and entered into league with the English. While Tipu was at Mangalore he tried to persuade Krishnappa Nayak to discharge the arrears of tribute and give up his refractory conduct, but without any result. When, therefore, Tipu's hands were free from his war with the English, he decided to chastise the Raja. Sayyid Hamid was ordered to attack the Raja's capital from the rear, while Tipu himself marched on it from the front. But when the two armies reached the place, it was found that the Raja had fled.[2] Tipu, nevertheless, recalled the Raja and, after making him promise to remain loyal and pay the usual tribute, restored to him his kingdom. During the Third Anglo-Mysore War, Krishnappa Nayak again rebelled and joined Parashuram Bhau's army when it advanced on Seringapatam in 1792. On the cessation of hostilities, afraid of being punished by Tipu for his disloyalty, he fled to Coorg. He was, however, again recalled and given a part of Balam by Tipu, while the rest was annexed.[3]

*Rebellion in Coorg*

From Balam Tipu marched to crush the Coorgs who had also rebelled against the Mysore Government. Coorg[4] had been invaded by Haidar in 1773 at the invitation of Linga Raja of Haleri who had espoused the cause of his nephew, Appaji Raja, to the throne of Coorg against Devappa Raja of Horamali. After occupying the country, Haidar gave it to Appaji Raja on condition that he paid him an annual tribute of 24,000 rupees.[5] On Appaji's death in 1776, Linga Raja succeeded him. But Linga Raja died soon after in 1780

[1] Balam was the name applied to a tract of country round about Belur, a *taluk* in the Hassan District of Mysore. It is now called Manjarabad. After 1792 Tipu ordered a fort to be built on an elevated spot in Balam. When it was completed he visited it, and finding the country covered by a fog, he called it Manjarabad, "the abode of fog" (*Manju*). *Mys. Gaz.*, v. pp. 948, 950; see also Rice. *Mysore and Coorg*, ii, pp. 299, 326. But according to Persian accounts, after the rebellion was suppressed, 'Bul' as they called Balam, was renamed Manzarabad signifying the date of its conquest (Kirmani, p. 299; *Tarikh-i-Khudadadi*, I.O.MS., p. 48).

[2] *Tarikh-i-Khudadadi*, I.O.MS., pp. 45-8.

[3] Rice, *Mysore and Coorg*, ii, p. 299.

[4] Coorg, situated on the summits and slopes of the Western Ghats, is now in Mysore State. It is bounded in the north and east by the Hassan and Mysore Districts of Mysore, and on the south and west by the Cannanore District, Kerala.

[5] *Tarikh-i-Coorg*, ff 20b-22b.

leaving behind two sons, Vira Rajendra Wodeyar and Linga Raja. As both were young, Haidar became their guardian and assumed the entire possession of Coorg until the princes should come of age, when it would be restored to them. A Brahmin named Subbarasaya, who was formerly one of the secretaries of the Coorg Raja, was entrusted with the government of the country.[1]

Enraged that Haidar Ali had appointed to the government of Coorg a Brahmin, instead of setting up one of the sons of Linga Raja as ruler, the Coorgs raised the banner of revolt in June 1782. Being shortly after engaged in war with the English, Haidar could not do anything about it, except to order Subbarasaya to remove the princes from Mercara, where they had been residing, to Goruru in Arkalgudu *taluk*, Hassan District, so that the rebels might be deprived of a rallying point.[2] When Tipu became ruler of Mysore, he also could not take any vigorous action against the Coorgs owing to his war with the English. But he ordered the princes to be removed to Periapatam, a stronger place and farther removed from the scene of action than Goruru,[3] and sent Haidar Ali Beg with a force to suppress the Coorgs. As Haidar Ali Beg failed in the expedition, Raja Kankeri was sent to his assistance. Together they at first achieved some success but, overwhelmed by the Coorgs who attacked them from all sides, they were routed in the end. Haidar Ali Beg fled, while the Raja, who held his ground for some time, was killed fighting.[4]

After making peace with the English and pacifying Balam, Tipu marched towards Coorg early in 1785. The rebels offered serious resistance but were defeated, and Tipu occupied Mercara which he renamed Zafarabad. Zain-ul-Abidin Mahdavi was appointed *faujdar* of Coorg, and after law and order was restored in the country, Tipu returned to Seringapatam where he occupied himself with matters relating to the administration and defence of his kingdom.[5]

But no sooner was Tipu's back turned than the Coorgs again revolted. This time they rebelled under the leadership of Munmate Nair and Ranga Nair who occupied nearly the whole of Coorg and prepared to besiege Mercara, its capital.[6] Finding his position untenable, the *faujdar* wrote to Tipu for assistance. The Sultan,

[1] *Ibid.*, ff. 23b-24b. Rice says Subbarasaya was a Treasurer of the Raja of Coorg.

[2] Rice, iii, p. 110, is wrong in saying that the princes were removed immediately after the death of their father. In fact they were allowed to remain at Mercara, Coorg's capital, and were removed only after the rising.

[3] *Tarikh-i-Coorg*, ff. 25a-b.

[4] In *Tarikh-i-Khudadadi* and *Sultan-ut-Tawarikh* the leader of the rebels is mentioned as Cooty. But *Tarikh-i-Coorg* does not mention any such person.

[5] *Tarikh-i-Khudadadi*, I.O.MS., pp. 51-4.

[6] Kirmani, p. 291.

thereupon, sent Zain-ul-Abidin Shushtary with some troops to his relief.[1] Shushtary entered Coorg at Ulagulli, and although he was opposed by four or five thousand Coorgs, who put up serious resistance, he managed to reach Mercara. But finding he could not hold out any longer, he retreated towards Bettadapur, a strong place on the western frontier of Mysore, pursued by the rebels who at Ulagulli captured his baggage and killed a number of his men. On hearing this news, Tipu himself decided to proceed to Coorg.[2] He left Seringapatam towards the end of October 1785, entered Coorg at Ulagulli, and without much difficulty reached the neighbourhood of Mercara, where he encamped in order to celebrate Muharram, but despatched troops and provisions to relieve the garrison of Mercara. After the Muharram ceremonies were over, Tipu proceeded to Mercara and sent out detachments under Lallée, Husain Ali Khan, Mir Mahmud and Imam Khan in different directions to crush the Coorgs.[3] The latter fought with great courage, but they were defeated and a large number of them were taken captive. To prevent future risings he transported the rebels to Mysore,[4] and in their place ordered new settlers to be brought from Adwani in the Bellary District. They were settled on farm lands and advanced loans. Some of these men returned to Mysore because the climate of Coorg did not suit them, while others remained there. Nagappaya, a nephew of Subbarasaya, was appointed *faujdar* of Coorg.[5] But these measures failed to crush the Coorgs, and it was not long before that they again broke out into open revolt against the Mysore Government.

[1] According to Kirmani, p. 292, Tipu sent Shushtary with 2,000 irregular infantry as an advance-guard of the main army. But according to *Tarikh-i-Coorg*, Shushtary was sent with 15,000 troops.

[2] *Tarikh-i-Coorg*, f. 26a.

[3] Kirmani, p. 297.

[4] It is difficult to estimate the number of men sent away by Tipu. Wilks, ii, p. 283, places the number at 70,000, and Rice, iii, p. 111, at 85,000. But this is preposterous, for the whole population of Coorg at that time did not amount to these figures. In 1836 the population of Coorg was returned at 65,437. (*Imp. Gaz.* (1885), iv, p. 33). According to Moegling, *Coorg Memoirs* p. 28, in former days the Coorgs seemed to have scarcely mustered more than 4,000 or 5,000 men. It was chiefly the men belonging to the fighting class who were deported to Mysore. But their number could not have been large, for sufficient men were left behind to cause another revolt soon after. The question of the conversion of Coorgs to Islam will be discussed in the chapter on *Religious Policy*.

[5] *Tarikh-i-Coorg*, f. 27a.

CHAPTER VI

# THE WAR WITH THE MARATHAS AND THE NIZAM

It was from the time of the Peshwa Balaji Baji Rao that Mysore began to be seriously subjected to the attacks of the Marathas; for he believed that the Maratha expansion should not only be directed northwards but also southwards. Accordingly, he invaded Mysore in 1753 and 1754, and in March 1757 he repeated the invasion and appeared before Seringapatam. In order to save the capital, Nanjaraj agreed to pay him thirty-two lakhs of rupees. Of this amount he paid six lakhs in cash, and for the rest ceded thirteen *taluks* as security. But on the advice of Haidar Ali, who returned soon after from Dindigul, where he was *faujdar*, the agreement was abrogated and the Maratha agents were expelled from the ceded districts.[1] This angered the Marathas who, towards the end of 1758, demanded payment of the arrears of tribute from the Raja, and threatened an invasion of his country if their demands were not acceded to within thirty-six hours. Haidar Ali counselled the rejection of the ultimatum and prepared to resist. And when the Marathas invaded Mysore, he pursued a successful struggle against them and in the end concluded the war by securing favourable terms of peace.[2]

The success achieved by Haidar Ali in the conflict served to rouse the jealousy and hostility of the Marathas who saw in him an obstacle to their expansionist aims. That was why they supported Khande Rao in 1760 when he planned the overthrow of Haidar. But owing to their preoccupations in northern India, their help was ineffective, and they retired from Mysore on receiving from Haidar five lakhs of rupees and the province of Baramahal.

The defeat which the Marathas sustained at the hands of Ahmad Shah Abdali at Panipat in January 1761, dealt a severe blow to their power. Madhav Rao, who succeeded his father, Balaji Rao, to the Peshwaship in September 1761, remained engaged for a few years in reorganising his forces and holding his own against the encroachments of the Nizam. It was therefore not until April 1764 that he was able to undertake an offensive against Haidar Ali who, meanwhile, had made himself powerful by consolidating his position in Mysore and by bringing new territories under his rule. Madhav Rao could not tolerate the existence of a strong kingdom in South

[1] Sinha, *Haidar Ali*, pp. 5, 20, 22.
[2] *Ibid.*, pp. 23-5; Wilks, i. pp. 410-13.

India which was not only a threat to his possessions but also an obstacle to his policy of expansion. He therefore undertook three campaigns (April 1764 to July 1772) to overthrow Haidar's power, and inflicted severe defeats on him. This was a critical period in Haidar's career. But he survived the ordeal through his diplomatic skill, great resourcefulness and strong determination, and by the opportune death of Madhav Rao on November 18, 1772.

Madhav Rao's death was a signal for an outbreak of dissensions at Poona which kept the Marathas occupied for a number of years. He was succeeded by his younger brother, Narayan Rao, who was murdered nine months after. Next his uncle, Raghunath Rao, became Peshwa, but very soon he, too, was ousted from power by the rival faction led by Nana Phadnavis who invested Madhav Rao Narayan, the posthumous son of Narayan Rao, as Peshwa. Raghunath Rao, thereupon, sought the alliance of the Bombay Government which, being anxious to secure possession of the island of Salsette, readily agreed to take up his cause. The result was that the war of succession to the Peshwaship became merged in the First Anglo-Maratha War.

Haidar Ali, who was closely watching the developments at Poona, was not slow to take advantage of the difficulties of the Marathas. He at once entered into a treaty (Treaty of Kalyandrug 1774) with Raghunath Rao by which the latter ceded to him the territory conquered by Madhav Rao in the three campaigns, and in return Haidar recognised him as Peshwa and promised to pay him an annual tribute of six lakhs.[1] In 1775, Raghunath Rao permitted Haidar to take possession of all the Maratha territory up to the right bank of the Krishna.[2] Armed with this sanction, Haidar Ali, between 1774 and 1778, not only reoccupied all the places he had lost to Madhav Rao in the three wars, but he also annexed the Maratha territory up to the right bank of the Krishna. Nana Phadnavis at first refused to recognise these conquests but, anxious to crush Raghunath Rao and the English, he relaxed his hostility towards Haidar. This led to an alliance between the latter and the Peshwa in February 1780. The Peshwa recognised Haidar's sovereignty over the Maratha territory south of the Krishna, and in return Haidar promised to pay him an annual tribute of twelve lakhs of rupees and to help him in the war against the English. Each also pledged himself not to make peace with the English without the consent of the other.[3]

So long as the Anglo-Maratha war was on, Nana remained friendly

[1] Wilks, i. pp. 714-15.
[2] *Ibid.*, p. 726.
[3] *Tarikh-i-Khudadadi*, I.O.MS., p. 24; Sardesai, *Marathi Riyasat*, uttarbhag, i, p. 217, cited in J.I.H., xi, p. 319; see also Sardesai, *New History of the Marathas*, iii, p. 173.

with Haidar, but after the conclusion of the Treaty of Salbai on May 17, 1782, his attitude changed, and in violation of the treaty of 1780, he began to demand the restoration of the territory south of the Krishna. He even threatened Haidar that he would enter into an offensive alliance with the English and the Nizam and enforce the Treaty of Salbai in case his demands were not complied with.[1] But if they were acceded to, he was prepared to scrap the Treaty of Salbai which had not yet been ratified, and to recommence hostilities against the English.[2] Haidar being engaged in hostilities against the English, his answer was such as to protract the negotiations.[3]

After the death of Haidar, Nana began to press the Maratha claims upon his son and successor, Tipu Sultan, and called upon him to abide by the Treaty of Salbai.[4] Tipu resented the Maratha attitude which he regarded as a gross betrayal of the Maratha-Mysore alliance of 1780.[5] He informed Nana through his *wakil*, Nur Muhammad Khan, that he had suffered great losses in men and money in his war with the English on account of the Marathas, and that they should not have concluded peace with the English without consulting him. However, Nana should not ratify the treaty, but should recommence hostilities against the English. He himself intended, after the capture of Mangalore, to invade the Carnatic and join Bussy who was very soon due to arrive from France.[6] But Nana, dissatisfied with Tipu's replies, and constantly pressed by the English for assistance, decided to impose his demands by force of arms, and informed Sindhia that, after the rains, he intended in conjunction with Holkar's troops to help the English to defeat Tipu.[7] Meanwhile, negotiations for an offensive alliance between the Marathas and the English which had been going on proved successful. And on October 28, 1783, a treaty was signed between Mahadji Sindhia, representing the Peshwa, and David Anderson, representing the English Company. By this treaty the Peshwa was to call upon Tipu to release the English prisoners of war and restore the Carnatic, otherwise he would "help the English and make war, in which case neither of the contracting parties will make peace with him without the consent of the other," and the

[1] To the English, on the other hand, Nana gave the impression that he was very friendly with Haidar, and had entered into a fresh treaty with him to which the French were also a party. By these tactics, Nana wanted to recover either Salsette from the Company or the Maratha territories from Haidar. (Khare, vii, Intro. p. 3656; Duff, ii, p. 153).

[2] Khare, vii, Intro. p. 3657

[3] Wilks, ii, p. 112.

[4] Khare, vii, No. 2677.

[5] N.A., Sec., Pro., April 13, 1784, Anderson to Hastings, Feb. 15

[6] Khare, vii, Nos. 2681, 2695.

[7] N.A., Sec. Pro., July 7, 1783.

territories of Tipu that would be conquered would equally be divided between the contracting parties.[1]

But this treaty did not lead to any result for, as Duff observes, "Nana's jealousy of Sindhia's assumption of authority, and his own projected alliance with Nizam Ally, impeded the scheme of this league, in which Sindhia and the English would have borne parts so prominent."[2] Besides, Nana could not help the English since the Peshwa's forces were at the disposal of Holkar who was against Sindhia. The latter himself would have liked to invade Tipu's kingdom, but he was too much preoccupied with his schemes of self-aggrandisement in northern India.[3]

Meanwhile, Tipu concluded the Treaty of Mangalore with the English. This filled Nana with anger and disappointment, because an army from Poona under Haripant was already on its way to invade Mysore.[4] He had expected to reduce Tipu's power and recover the Maratha territories south of the Krishna with the help of the English, but now that opportunity had passed. He had also regarded the Marathas as the 'patrons' of Tipu,[5] and had been anxious to mediate peace between him and the English in order to enhance his prestige both at Poona and outside. But Tipu had refused to be considered a client of the Marathas. He had openly defied the Treaty of Salbai, and had concluded peace with the English without the mediation of the Marathas. Besides, the termination of the Anglo-Mysore War had not meant any diminution of his strength. On the contrary, he had emerged from the war with enhanced prestige, and possessed a large kingdom, a full treasury and a well-disciplined army. Nana, therefore, began to make plans for the subversion of his power, and for this purpose sought the alliance of the Nizam.

The relations of Haidar with the Nizam had never really been cordial. He had always aroused in him feelings of fear and jealousy. That was why the Nizam had been won over by the English and the Marathas in their wars against Haidar. It was true that in August 1767 the Nizam had allied himself with Haidar to fight the English, but this friendship had been only short-lived, and by February 1768 he had left his ally and gone over to the English. In February 1780 he had again joined Haidar, along with the Marathas, against the English. But beyond paying lip service to the cause of the confederacy, he had not rendered any assistance to his allies, and had subsequently detached himself from them.

The chief cause of the Nizam's hostility towards Haidar was that

[1] *Ibid.*, July 21, 1784.
[2] Duff, ii. pp. 154-55.
[3] N.A., Sec., Pro., Nov. 10, 1783, Anderson to Hastings, Oct. 22.
[4] Sardesai, *New History of the Marathas*, iii, p. 176.
[5] N.A., Sec. Pro., Nov. 10, 1783, Anderson to Hastings, Oct. 22.

he claimed Mysore as his tributary; but Haidar had asserted his independence and refused to acknowledge him as his overlord. Besides, not content with this, Haidar had brought Kurnool, Cuddapah and other places, which had been subject to Hyderabad, under his control, and had extended his ambitions even to other parts of the Nizam's kingdom. After his death his son, Tipu, aroused in the Nizam feelings of even greater fear and jealousy. The Nizam therefore welcomed Nana's proposal for the invasion of Mysore which would enable him to humble Tipu, recover his lost territories, and remove a permanent threat to the security of his kingdom.

The first step which Nana took against Tipu was to demand the arrears of tribute for four years. Tipu admitted the justice of the demand, but 'politely' expressed his inability to pay immediately on the ground that he had greatly suffered in the war against the English, and informed Nana through his *wakil*, Nur Muhammad Khan, that he would discharge the dues after the conclusion of peace.[1] At the same time that Nana made the demand on Tipu, he sent his *wakil*, Krishna Rao Ballal, to the Nizam ostensibly to ask for the arrears of *chauth* and *sardeshmukhi*, but in reality to propose an offensive alliance against him. The proposal was received favourably by the Nizam, who agreed to meet Nana at a conference in which they might settle their mutual differences and concert plans for the invasion of Mysore. Accordingly, they set out from their capitals with great pomp and show, attended by a large army, and in June 1784 met at Yadgir, situated near the confluence of the Bhima and the Krishna.[2]

The Nizam demanded as a preliminary article of the agreement the restoration of Bijapur and Ahmadnagar. There was a prolonged discussion over the point, but since Nana was reluctant to cede the places to the Nizam, only a general agreement was arrived at between the parties. It was decided that the Marathas and the Nizam should jointly make war on Tipu the following year, and after recovering the districts which both of them had lost by the encroachments of Haidar Ali, they should occupy the rest of Tipu's kingdom which should be equally divided between them.[3] After this settlement the conference, which had lasted from June 7 to 25, terminated, and the parties returned to their respective capitals early in July 1784.[4]

Meanwhile, the Nizam had been demanding the *peshkush* for the *diwani* of the Carnatic Balaghat from Tipu. The latter, being informed of the agreements concluded at Yadgir, retorted by asserting his

[1] *Hadiqat*, pp. 354-55; Khare, viii, pp. 3840-41.

[2] *Hadiqat*, pp. 355-56; Khare, viii, p. 3841; Duff, ii, p. 156. The Nizam, according to *Hadiqat*, set out from Hyderabad on February 6, 1784, and met Nana on June 6. He left Yadgir on about June 25.

[3] *Hadiqat*, p. 357. Khate, viii, p. 3841.

[4] *Hadiqat*, p. 358. Duff, ii, p. 157.

claims to the *subedari* of Bijapur.[1] This made the Nizam imagine that Tipu intended to attack his kingdom. He therefore wrote to Nana for help, and at the same time sent an envoy to Tipu to placate him.[2] It was fortunate for the Nizam that the Sultan had no intention of attacking him—such rumours having been spread by war-mongers and alarmists—for Nana was not at this time in a position to send him any help. This was partly because he was unprepared for war, but chiefly because he had to deal with a conspiracy whose object was the deposition of Madhav Rao Narayan and the elevation of Baji Rao, the son of Raghunath Rao, to the Peshwaship.[3] Nana was nevertheless hustled into a conflict with Tipu owing to the Nargund affair.

*The Mysoreans Attack Nargund**

When Haidar Ali had in 1778 occupied Nargund,[4] which was a petty state under the Peshwa's protection, he had left it to its chief, Venkat Rao Bhave, a Brahmin Desai, on condition that the latter acknowledged his supremacy and paid him an annual tribute.[5] This arrangement was confirmed by Nana in February 1780 when he entered into an alliance with Haidar and recognised his suzerainty over all the Maratha territories south of the river Krishna.[6]

In spite of this, Venkat Rao and his able minister, Kalopant Pethe, who wielded real power in Nargund, continued to look upon the Peshwa as their real overlord and maintained secret correspondence with the influential men at Poona. On January 8, 1783, Kalopant wrote to Bara Saheb that the Marathas must take advantage of Haidar's death and recover all the lands which the Mysoreans had taken from them between the years 1774 and 1778.[7] But as they were involved in their own internal dissensions, they failed to avail themselves of this opportunity. Disappointed with the Poona Government, the Desai of Nargund endeavoured to form a union with the English. He applied to the Bombay Government through an Englishman in his service, named Yoon, for some troops, claiming that he was an independent prince and was ready to co-operate with the Company in the invasion of Mysore.[8] But these overtures were ignored since negotiations for a peace with Tipu Sultan were in progress.

[1] N.A., Sec. Pro., Sept. 2, 1784, Resident at Hyderabad to Hastings, Aug. 3.
[2] Wilks, ii, p. 284.
[3] Duff, ii, p. 158.
* This is mainly based on my article *Tipu's Attack on Nargund* published in *Bengal: Past and Present*, vol. lxiv, Jan.-Dec., 1944.
[4] Nargund is in Dharwar District, Mysore.
[5] Sinha, *Haidar Ali*, p. 134.
[6] See p. 81, *supra*.
[7] Khare, vii, No. 2668. Chintaman Rao, being the senior chief of the Patwardhans, was addressed as Bara Saheb. (Parasnis, *The Sangli State*, pp. 15-16).
[8] Duff, ii, p. 107.

Besides the secret intrigues which Venkat Rao carried on with the Marathas and the English, he also openly defied the Sultan's authority and was joined by the *poligar* of Madanapalli. He attacked the fort of Sudum, and plundered the surrounding country, killing a number of Tipu's peaceful subjects.[1] He gave the Peshwa every information regarding Tipu, and confident of Maratha support, since he was related to the powerful Brahmin family of Patwardhan, he evaded Tipu's demands for tribute.[2]

So long as Tipu was engaged in the war against the English, he left the Desai to his devices. But as soon as the Treaty of Mangalore was signed, and his hands were free, he decided to punish the chief. He first of all demanded the tribute which Venkat Rao had not paid for the last two years, and simultaneously sent his two *wakils*, Muhammad Ghiyas Khan and Nur Muhammad Khan, to Poona to induce Nana not to take sides with the Desai.[3] But Nana could not afford to hold himself aloof, for Venkat Rao was related to the Patwardhan family and claimed the Peshwa's protection. So he intervened on the ground that the tribute demanded was more than what the Marathas and Haidar used to realise, and declared that Tipu had no right to exact more than the ordinary tribute; that "jagirdars, on the transfer of districts, were liable to no additional payments; and that the rights of Suwusthanees, who had been guilty of no treason against the State to which they owed allegiance, had been invariably respected."[4] Tipu's reply was that he had a right to levy what he chose from his own subjects, and that the Poona Government had no right to interfere in his internal affairs. Besides, Tipu argued that the chief of Nargund had actually been guilty of treason, and therefore he was not bound to respect the "rights of Suwusthanees." Writing to his *wakil*, Muhammad Ghiyas Khan, he observed: "If a petty zamindar, and a subject of our Government like this, may not be punished, how shall our authority be maintained." In spite of this, Tipu was prepared to forgive Venkat Rao provided he agreed to compensate for the ravages he had committed in Mysore and to discharge the arrears of tribute. But Nana rejected these terms.[5]

While these discussions were going on between the *wakils* and Nana, Tipu sent Sayyid Ghaffar towards Nargund to inquire into the conduct of its chief. Sayyid Ghaffar reported that the Desai was

[1] Kirmani, p. 283.
[2] Khare, viii, p. 3893.
[3] *Ibid.*, pp. 3893-4. The *wakils* were also sent to discuss the question of the tribute which the Mysore Government had not paid to the Peshwa for the last three years. But the real object of their visit was to keep Nana in good humour in order to prevent him from helping the Desai.
[4] Duff, ii, p. 167. *Savasthanis* were the Brahmins possessing old hereditary *jagirs*.
[5] Kirkpatrick, *Letters of Tippoo Sultan*, Nos. 3, 27.

hostile to the Sultan and was being instigated in his refractory conduct by Parashuram Bhau, his friend and relation. Hearing this, Tipu sent his brother-in-law, Burhan-ud-din, with 5,000 cavalry and 3 *cushoons* of infantry to Nargund.[1] Burhan marched via Chitaldrug and Savanur, and after joining Sayyid Ghaffar in the vicinity of Dharwar, proceeded to Nargund which he reached in January 1785. He sent a message to Venkat Rao that if he surrendered and gave up his hostile attitude, his life would be spared and his *jagir* restored to him.[2] But Kalopant, expecting Maratha aid, refused these offers, and with 2,000 cavalry, 2,000 infantry and some guns advanced to meet Burhan outside the walls of Nargund. But he was defeated and compelled to retreat into the town. Burhan, thereupon, turned his artillery against the town. Kalopant led out a number of sorties, and on one occasion made a surprise attack upon the Mysoreans, destroying two of their batteries and killing several of their men.[3] Still he was unable to maintain his position long. In the beginning of February Burhan attacked the town and succeeded in gaining a strong foothold there. A few days later he again attacked and occupied the whole town. Kalopant fought bravely, but was, in the end, compelled to take refuge in the fort which was then besieged by Burhan-ud-din.[4]

Kalopant had been all this time expecting help from Poona. In fact, it was because he had been sure of Maratha assistance that he had openly defied Tipu. When Parashuram Bhau heard of Burhan's attack on Nargund, he wrote to Nana that troops should immediately be sent to its relief.[5] Nana was anxious to help Venkat Rao, but owing to the distracted state of the Poona Government he did not consider himself strong enough to fight Tipu. He, therefore, tried to come to a settlement of the Nargund affair with the *wakils* of Tipu who were still at Poona and were constantly telling Nana that their master had no intention of occupying Nargund, and that the siege would soon be raised.[6] When, however, Nana came to know that Burhan had seized the town of Nargund, he could no longer continue his

[1] Kirmani, p. 283. A *cushoon* comprised from 600 to 1,500 men, and possessed from 1 to 5 guns. (M.R., Mly. Sund. Book, No. 101 (1792-95), pp. 101-03. If we take a *cushoon* as consisting of about 1000 men and 2 to 3 guns on an average, then it would mean that Burhan had about 3000 infantry and 6 to 9 guns, besides 5,000 cavalry and the troops under the command of Sayyid Ghaffar. Khare, viii, p. 3894, says that Burhan had an army of 10,000 cavalry, 15,000 infantry and 17 guns.

[2] Kirmani, pp. 286-87.

[3] Khare, viii, No. 2811.

[4] *Ibid.*, No. 2812. In some of the letters the word 'bazaar' has been very often used. This is probably because the bazaar or the market-place of Nargund occupied a strategic position and covered a large space.

[5] *Ibid.*, p. 3894.

[6] *Ibid.* No. 2813.

dilatory policy and had to act. He ordered Parashuram Bhau to hasten to the relief of Venkat Rao, and despatched Ganesh Pant Behre with 5,000 troops to join him,[1] Parashuram Bhau, who was sick of Nana's policy of appeasement, was glad to receive this order, although it was qualified by the instruction that hostilities should be avoided if Burhan-ud-din raised the siege of the fort. He immediately collected men for the campaign and divided them into three armies: 5,000 cavalry under Janoba Subedar were to protect the communications through Manoli; 10,000 cavalry under Raghunath Rao Kurundwarkar were to proceed to Nargund via Ramdurg; while Parashuram Bhau himself, with 7,000 troops, decided to remain at Mudhol ready to help the besieged in case his services were required.[2]

Hearing of these Maratha preparations, Burhan tried to reduce the fort before the relieving forces arrived. The fort of Nargund had a garrison 2,000 strong, possessed ammunition and provisions sufficient for about six months and, being situated on a steep hill, was capable of making strong resistance.[3] Burhan made two attempts to assault it, but was repulsed with loss. The garrison used their guns with effect, and by rolling down large stones killed many of the assailants. Emboldened by this success, and expecting to be relieved soon, they made a sortie, attacked the batteries and killed some of the Mysoreans.[4] Burhan would have continued the siege, but due to the approach of the Maratha armies with whom he wanted to avoid a clash, he withdrew from Nargund. He sent his camp followers and big guns to Dharwar, and with only his light troops encamped near a stream called Bennihalla.[5] Grant Duff thinks that "Tipu's officers had been compelled, from want of water, to raise the siege."[6] There is no doubt that, owing to the hot weather, the Mysoreans did experience a shortage of water, and that was why after leaving Nargund they encamped near a stream; but the shortage was not so acute as to have compelled Burhan to raise the siege, for water was being brought on camel-back and in bullock-carts from the river near which the army was encamped.[7] In reality, the siege had been raised by the orders of Tipu who was anxious to maintain friendly relations with the Marathas. It is this which the *wakils* tried to impress upon Nana. Nana, on the other hand, contended that Burhan had withdrawn from Nargund because he was not strong enough to prosecute

[1] *Ibid.*

[2] *Ibid.*, Nos. 2815, 2824 and p. 3897. Manoli is a town in Belgaum District. Ramdurg and Mudhol are also in Belgaum District.

[3] *Ibid.*, pp. 3895-6.

[4] *Ibid.*, Nos. 2816, 2817.

[5] *Ibid.*, No. 2825.

[6] Duff, ii, p. 167. Bennihalla or Butter-Stream is a stream which passes through Dharwar District, Mysore.

[7] Kirmani, p. 287.

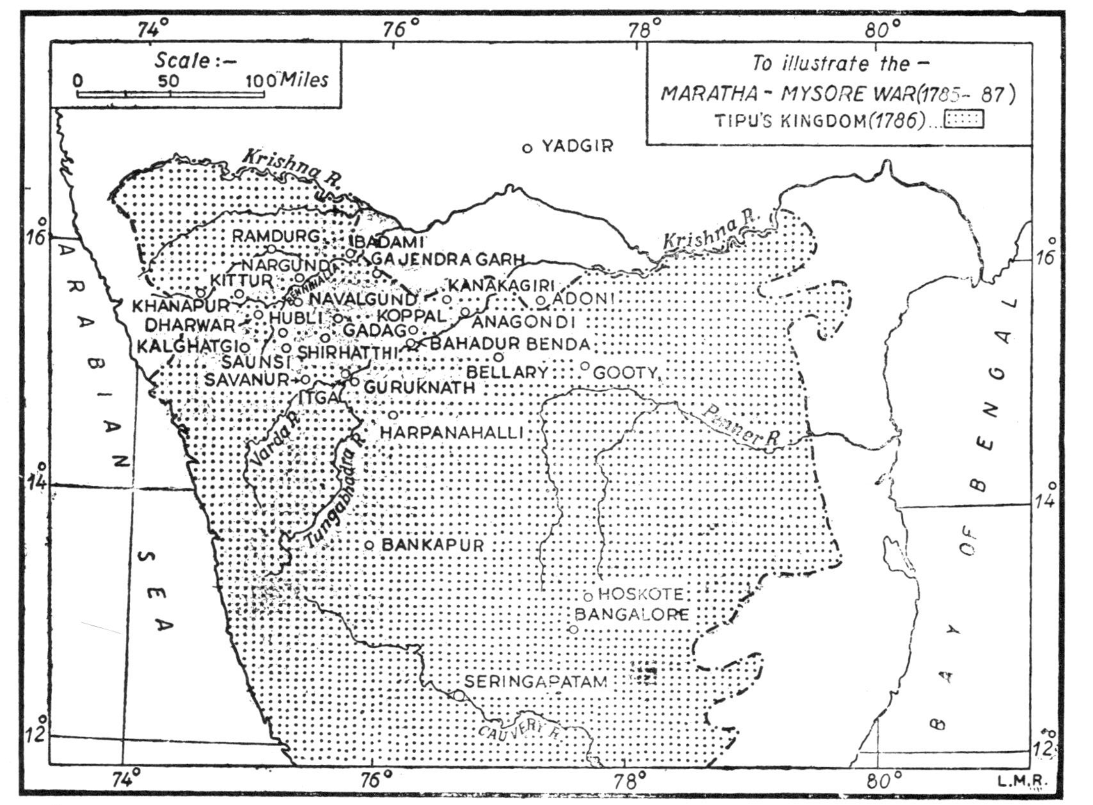

Scale :-
0 50 100 Miles
To illustrate the -
MARATHA - MYSORE WAR (1785 - 87)
TIPU'S KINGDOM (1786) ...
YADGIR
Krishna R.
RAMDURG
BADAMI
NARGUND
GAJENDRA GARH
KITTUR
KANAKAGIRI
ADONI
KHANAPUR
NAVALGUND
KOPPAL
HUBLI
DHARWAR
GADAG
ANAGONDI
KALGHATGI
SHIRHATTHI
BAHADUR BENDA
SAUNSI
BELLARY
GOOTY
SAVANUR
GURUKNATH
ITGA
HARPANAHALLI
Varda R.
Tungabhadra R.
Penner R.
BANKAPUR
HOSKOTE
BANGALORE
SERINGAPATAM
CAUVERY R.
ARABIAN SEA
BAY OF BENGAL
74°
76°
78°
80°
16°
14°
12°
L.M.R.

the siege of the fort and at the same time to fight the Maratha armies advancing towards his rear.[1] However, as the siege had been raised, and negotiations with Tipu were in progress, he wrote to Bhau not to provoke hostilities with the Mysoreans till the end of the rains, and to remain at Ramdurg after evacuating Venkat Rao and Kalopant along with their families from the fort, which was to be left with a garrison under the command of an experienced officer.[2] But Kalopant refused to be evacuated. He maintained that, if he left, the garrison would become demoralised. He was, therefore, determined to stay and hold out till the end of the rains. Besides, if a settlement with Tipu was going to be made, there was no need for him to leave the fort.[3] Parashuram Bhau agreed with Kalopant and disagreed with Nana. Being suspicious of Tipu's intentions,[4] both he and Ganesh Pant Behre in their zeal to help the Desai, and "hoping to acquire fame and establish their credit at Poona," ignored Nana's orders and attacked the Mysoreans. But they were repulsed with a loss of twenty men and one elephant. When Nana heard of this he reprimanded Bhau for disobeying his orders. At the same time, in order to repair the disgrace of defeat, he sent Tukoji Holkar with a large force to Bhau's assistance, and began preparations for war.[5]

Meanwhile, negotiations between Nana and Tipu's *wakils* were going on. Proposals and counterproposals were being put forward. At length the *wakils* proposed that Tipu Sultan would immediately pay the Peshwa the tribute due for two years on condition "of being left to do what he pleases with the fort without interruption." As a temporary expedient Nana agreed to this, and allowed twenty-seven days for obtaining the necessary answers from the Sultan regarding the payment of the money.[6] In spite of this, the talks proved abortive and did not lead to any understanding. The reason was that Tipu, having seen through Nana's real design, refused to bind himself by an agreement which would fill the coffers of the Marathas and would remain in force for a few months only. Nana's policy was to get the money from Tipu and to drag things on till the end of the rains, when it would be possible for him to undertake a campaign, and recover all the Maratha territories south of the river Krishna which Haidar had conquered.[7] So Nana continued to humour the *wakils*, and to be gracious and accommodating towards them. But while professing peaceful intentions, he prepared for war, and tried to organise a

[1] Khare, viii, No. 2830, Nana to Bhau, April 7, 1785.
[2] *Ibid.*, Nos. 2820, 2828, Nana to Bhau, March 13, April 6, 1785.
[3] *Ibid.*, No. 2838; see also p. 3901.
[4] *Ibid.*
[5] Forrest, *Selections*, Maratha Series, i, p. 518.
[6] *Ibid.*
[7] *Ibid.*

confederacy of the Marathas, the Nizam and the English against Tipu Sultan.[1]

Tipu, on the other hand, wanted to maintain friendly relations with the Marathas. But he was not prepared to relinquish his claims to the territories his father had conquered, and was determined to punish the Desai of Nargund for his insolent and refractory conduct. That was why, when Nana took up the cause of Venkat Rao, Tipu was indignant, for it implied interference in his internal affairs. That he did not make a break with the Poona Government and his *wakils* continued to negotiate with Nana, was because he also, like Nana, was trying to gain time. But while the latter's aim was to prevent the fall of Nargund till the end of the rains, the former wanted to occupy it before the Marathas might be in a position to act effectively against him. For Tipu the capture of Nargund had become necessary not only for subduing and chastising its chief by way of example, but also because it was a strong fort, and, being situated near his northern frontier, it was of strategic importance in view of the imminence of a conflict with the Marathas.

Parashuram Bhau's unprovoked attack on the Mysore army gave the Sultan his pretext to commence operations against Nargund which had been suspended on the approach of the Maratha forces. On April 12 Burhan was joined by Qamar-ud-din Khan who had been ordered by the Sultan to proceed to his help from Cuddapah.[2] Thus reinforced, Burhan sent one part of his army towards Nargund and another towards Manoli with the object of isolating Nargund. The Marathas offered only a feeble resistance and continued to retreat until they reached the river Krishna. The result was that on May 5 Ramdurg was captured by the Mysoreans, who, soon after, also occupied Manoli.[3] Having thus completely cut off Nargund from any possibility of outside assistance, Burhan advanced to invest it early in May. At first, owing to the constant bickerings between him and Qamar-ud-din Khan, the progress of the siege was greatly retarded. Tipu, therefore, exhorted them to be good friends, and assigned to them a military council of three experienced officers whose advice they were required to follow.[4] In June, Burhan sent a message to Kalopant through Haidar, the Commandant of Badami,[5] that if he capitulated, the life and property of the garrison would be guaranteed, and they would be allowed to go wherever they pleased. But Kalopant refused the offer, and replied that he had written to Poona and would act as ordered from there.[6] His object was to hold on till

[1] *Ibid.*, Khare, viii, No. 2818
[2] Kirmani, p. 288; Wilks, ii, p. 285.
[3] Khare, viii, p. 3902; Wilks, ii, p. 286.
[4] *Ibid.* [5] Badami is a village in Bijapur District, Mysore.
[6] Khare, viii, No. 2856.

the end of the rains when he was certain to be relieved by the Peshwa's armies. Accordingly, he carried on the struggle wth great courage. But due to the ceaseless cannonading and the successful blockade of the fort, the garrison was reduced by the end of July to a sad plight. Ammunition and provisions ran short, lack of water was desperately felt, and many of the garrison were sick. So Kalopant, finding it impossible to resist any longer, finally agreed to surrender.[1] And on being promised security of life and property, and permission to depart, the garrison consisting of about 1,650 men marched out of the fort on July 29.[2] At first they were detained by Burhan-ud-din pending orders from the Sultan. But on receiving his instructions, Burhan gradually released them in batches, so that by the end of September all of them had been set free, except Kalopant and Venkat Rao who were sent in chains to the fort of Kabbaldurga[3] along with their families.[4] The reason why the capitulation terms were not observed in the case of these two men was that they had given the Sultan considerable trouble; so he did not want to let them go unpunished. But it is incorrect to say that the Desai's "daughter was reserved for the Sultan's seraglio,[5]" for there is no reference to this in the Maratha records. Similarly, the story mentioned in one of the news-letters that Burhan sent for the pretty daughter of Kalopant to see her and to select her for Tipu's harem,[6] is nothing but a pure fabrication, for this too is not supported by any reliable evidence. The news-letter report cannot be regarded as authentic, because the information contained in such letters was generally based on hearsay and bazaar gossip.

After occupying Nargund, Burhan-ud-din marched on Kittur[7] whose ruler, Mallasayja, had also revolted against the Sultan. When he appeared before the place, the Desai, realising that resistance would be futile, capitulated. In spite of this, he and his family, along with his minister Gurupant, were imprisoned by Venkat Rangayya, who had been deputed by Tipu to realise five and a half lakhs of rupees as arrears of tribute from Kittur. Venkat Rangayya also began to harass the people of the state and forcibly extorted from them large sums of money. When Burhan-ud-din came to know of this he intervened. He secured the release of the chief and Gurupant,

[1] *Ibid.*, No. 2869; P.A. MS., No. 5356, Montigny to Souillac, Nov. 30, 1785.

[2] Khare, viii, No. 2861.

[3] It is a fortified conical hill in Malvalli *taluk*, Mysore District. It was used by Haidar and Tipu as a prison for political prisoners.

[4] Khare, Nos. 2869, 2870. Venkat Rao and Kalopant were first sent to Seringapatam, and from there to the fort of Kabbaldurga. They were released in 1787 at the conclusion of the Maratha-Mysore War.

[5] Duff. ii, p. 168. But Khare regards it as a fiction. (Khare, viii p. 3905).

[6] Khare, viii, No. 2867.

[7] It is a village in Belgaum District, Mysore.

assured them of their safety and remonstrated with Venkat Rangayya for his oppressive measures.[1] As Venkat Rangayya did not like Burhan's interference, he left for Dharwar in a fit of anger. Kittur was annexed by Tipu, but he set apart a sum of money for the support of its chief.[2]

From Kittur Burhan-ud-din marched towards other Maratha states which were subject to Mysore, and within the two months of November and December he succeeded in occupying Dodvad, Khanapur, Sada, Hoskote, Padshapur and Jamboti.[3] The rulers of these places, like those of Nargund and Kittur, had also been guilty of treason, and therefore their states were likewise annexed to Mysore.

### *Nana Forms a Coalition Against Tipu*

The news of the successes achieved by Burhan-ud-din came as a great blow to Nana, for it meant the failure of his policy. Nana would have undertaken a campaign against Tipu immediately on hearing of the fall of Nargund, but he had not been able to do so owing to the unstable conditions at Poona.[4] Moreover, Parashuram Bhau, disgusted with Nana's policy, which he regarded as one of procrastination and appeasement, had dismissed his troops and returned to his *jagir* of Tasgaon. It is true that Ganesh Pant Behre still lay encamped on the banks of the Krishna, but owing to the rains and the unprepared state of his army, he was not in a position to move.[5] Nana was, therefore, left with no alternative but to wait till the monsoon was over. Meanwhile he busied himself with diplomatic and military preparations. He endeavoured to induce the English to join the coalition against Tipu, called upon the Maratha chieftains to rally around the Peshwa, and once again despatched Krishna Rao Ballal to the Nizam with an invitation to meet him in order to discuss plans for the invasion of Mysore. Although Tipu had not committed any act of aggression—he had only punished his refractory vassals—yet Nana was determined to use it as a pretext of war against the Sultan in order to redeem his prestige, and recover the territories which Haidar Ali had conquered from the Marathas between the years 1774 and 1778.

The response from the Maratha chieftains was very favourable. Mudhoji Bhonsle, who had come to Poona to be reconciled to Nana,[6] promised to help the Peshwa against Tipu. But owing to his illness he

[1] Khare, viii, No. 2897.
[2] Stokes, Belgaum, cited in *Belgaum Gazetteer, Bombay*, p. 386.
[3] Khare, viii, Nos. 2879, 2884. All these places are in Belgaum District, Mysore.
[4] P.R.C., ii, No. 17.
[5] Khare, viii, p. 3902.
[6] Nana was angry with Mudhoji for having helped the English against the Peshwa in the First Anglo-Maratha War. (Duff, ii. pp. 141-2.)

had to leave for Nagpur in September. However, he left behind his son Manyaba with 2,000 men, assuring Nana that he would send more troops on reaching Nagpur, and that as soon as he got better he would himself return with an army of 10,000 men.[1] Holkar was also ready to march against Tipu with 20,000 troops, 10,000 pindaris and some artillery;[2] and although Bhau, disagreeing with Nana's policy towards the Nargund question, refused to visit Poona, he was willing to participate in the campaign as soon as it started.[3]

The Nizam's reply to Krishna Rao Ballal was that he was prepared to join the confederacy provided he was given twenty-five lakhs of rupees for war expenses, and the province of Bijapur and the fort of Ahmadnagar were restored to him. Realising that if he referred the matter to Poona it might cause considerable delay, and afraid lest Nana should not accept the terms of the Nizam, Krishna Rao assured the latter on his own responsibility that the conditions would be favourably considered and requested him to proceed to Yadgir. The Nizam was satisfied with this reply and set out at the end of November 1785.[4] In order to effect a junction with the Nizam's army, Nana sent Haripant on December 1, 1785, towards Yadgir. He himself set out from Poona on December 12, and overtook Haripant at Pandharpur.[5] Here he was joined by Parashuram Bhau and Raghunath Rao Kurundwarkar, and together they proceeded to Yadgir where the Nizam was waiting to meet them.[6]

The talks between Nana and the Nizam lasted for about a month and a half. According to the news-writer at the court of the Nizam, the differences between the parties were very great. "The whole of their proceedings," he reported, "are in a most confused state, and what they determine one day is objected to on the next."[7] But at length agreement was reached, which was not very different from that concluded between them at that very spot in June 1784. An offensive alliance was formed, and the invasion of Mysore was to be carried out immediately. After recovering their respective territories in possession of Tipu, the Nizam and the Marathas were to divide the rest of their conquests equally among themselves.[8] It was, however, decided that the allies should first direct their efforts to the conquest of the Maratha

[1] Khare, viii, No. 2919.
[2] *Ibid.*, No. 2959.
[3] *Ibid.*, No. 2923.
[4] *Hadiqat*, pp. 362-3.
[5] It is a sacred town in Sholapur District. Bombay.
[6] Khare, viii, pp. 3996-7; Duff, ii, p. 172.
[7] N.A., Sec. Pro., April 4, 1786.
[8] Khare, viii, No. 2966; *Hadiqat*, p. 365. Duff, ii, p. 172, is wrong in saying that the Nizam was to get one-third of the conquests made by the allies. He would never have agreed to this particularly after Nana had virtually refused to restore Bijapur to him. Besides, already a year ago an equal division of conquests had been agreed upon between him and Nana,

districts between the Tungabhadra and the Krishna. As regards the cession of Bijapur and Ahmadnagar to the Nizam, Nana's answer was unsatisfactory.[1]

After the negotiations were over, Nana expressed his desire to return to Poona about the middle of April, partly because he felt indisposed,[2] but chiefly because he did not want to leave the young Peshwa alone for long. He wanted the Nizam and Haripant to take charge of the campaign. This attitude of Nana evoked loud protests from the confederates, who took his intention to return to Poona for lack of enthusiasm about the war. The Nizam pointed out that he had joined the campaign because of his friendship for the Marathas although he was on good terms with Tipu. If, therefore, Nana did not stay, he would also leave.[3] Similarly Mudhoji Bhonsle, who had arrived on January 16, 1786, and Bhau also prepared to leave. Alarmed at these developments, which threatened to break up the confederacy, Nana postponed his departure.[4] The Nizam, however, in spite of the efforts of Nana and Haripant to dissuade him, departed for Hyderabad on April 25, 1786, leaving behind 25,000 troops under the command of Tahawwar Jung.[5] Duff says that the Nizam left because he did not relish the prospect of a monsoon campaign,[6] but in reality he left because of his disappointment with Nana who refused to cede Bijapur to him[7] in spite of the promises made by the Maratha *wakil*, Krishna Rao Ballal.[8] Nana, on the other hand, disavowed having ever granted powers to the *wakil* for making any such promises; so he was very displeased with the Nizam for returning to Hyderabad at a time when his presence was urgently required.[9]

*The Invasion of Mysore*

When the Nizam left for Hyderabad, the allied armies advanced towards Badami and began operations against it on May 1, 1786. It was a well-fortified town built on the plain near Tipu's northern frontier, and had a garrison of about 3,000 men.[10] It contained a small citadel and was further protected by two hill forts on each flank.[11] For nearly three weeks the confederates tried their best to effect a breach in the walls but did not succeed. So they decided to capture

[1] *Hadiqat*, p. 365; P.R.C. ii, No. 9; Duff, ii, p. 172.
[2] *Hadiqat*, p. 365; P. R. C., ii, No. 5.
[3] Khare, viii, No. 2966.
[4] *Ibid.*, pp. 3998-9; P.R.C., ii, No. 5.
[5] Khare, viii, No. 2975. But according to Malet (P.R.C., ii, No. 5) the Nizam left behind 15,000 horse and 20,000 foot.
[6] Duff, ii, p. 173
[7] P.R.C., ii, No. 9; *Hadiqat*, p. 365.
[8] *Hadiqat*, p. 362.
[9] P.R.C. ii, No. 9.
[10] *Ibid.;* Mir Alam (*Hadiqat*, p. 367) says it had 2,000 men.
[11] P.R.C., ii, No. 9; Duff, ii, p. 173.

it by assault; and on the morning of May 20, with 20,000 infantry, they marched to the attack. But as they advanced, the mines filled with gunpowder, laid by the Mysoreans in the ditch and the covert way, were made to explode, thus causing great loss of life among them. This, however, did not damp their spirits, and with great courage and determination they rushed forward and climbed the walls by means of ladders. The garrison offered resistance but were defeated and fled to the fort, pursued by the confederate troops who tried to enter it with the fugitives. In this the assailants were not successful.[1] The huge stones which were rolled down from the fort, and the heavy fire of musketry which was opened upon them by the garrison, proved exceedingly destructive, killing 800 Marathas and an equal number of the Nizam's troops. The Mysorean loss amounted to only about 400 men.[2]

Although the fort was saved for the time being, Haidar Bakhsh, its Commandant, realised that he would not be able to hold out much longer, for as the town was in the hands of the enemy, the fort would be cut off from the water supply which it drew mainly from a large tank situated in the town. He, therefore, made overtures of capitulation. But Nana, who felt very much chagrined at the losses he had sustained in the siege, rejected the proposal and insisted on his surrendering unconditionally. The Commandant at first refused to agree but, owing to the acute shortage of water which had caused a number of deaths, and seeing the determined attitude of the besiegers, he surrendered unconditionally on May 21 on being assured that the lives of the garrison would be spared.[3] Parashuram Bhau suggested that Haidar Bakhsh and others who had behaved treacherously in the Nargund affair should be imprisoned. But Nana and Haripant did not accept his advice because they thought it would be a violation of the assurance given to the garrison.[4]

After the capture of Badami, Nana set off for Poona on May 26, leaving Haripant in command of the army. Mudhoji Bhonsle went back to Nagpur leaving the greater part of his troops with his second son Khanduji under the command of Haripant, and promising to return with a reinforcement after the Dussehra festival. Similarly Parashuram Bhau left for Tasgaon, assuring Nana, who was opposed to his departure, that he would return after his son's thread ceremony was over.[5]

Haripant, who was now in charge of the campaign, marched on

[1] Khare, viii, Nos. 2979, 2981; Duff, ii, p. 174.
[2] P.R.C., ii, No. 9.
[3] *Ibid.*
[4] Khare, viii, No. 2981. According to *Hadiqat*, p. 367, the garrison was imprisoned for a few days and then released.
[5] Khare, viii, p. 4007.

Gajendragarh[1] in June 1786. Rajjab Khan, its Commandant, at first refused to surrender, but as no help reached him—the troops sent to relieve him having been intercepted—he surrendered on June 19 after taking a bribe; and on being assured that the garrison would be allowed to go freely to their homes.[2]

Meanwhile, the Maratha forces were operating in other theatres of war. The victories achieved by Burhan-ud-din having greatly alarmed Nana, he sent Tukoji Holkar at the end of February to the help of Ganesh Pant Behre who was finding it difficult to hold his own against the Mysoreans in the Kittur area. Burhan-ud-din, hearing of the advance of Holkar and realising that with the arrival of the latter his troops would be greatly outnumbered by the Marathas, decided to give up offensive operations and to remain on the defensive. He sent away his heavy guns and camp followers to Dharwar and Mishrikot;[3] and after garrisoning Kittur with 3,000 infantry and a few guns, occupied with some light troops a strategic position in a hilly area close by and waited for the Marathas. But Holkar did not think it profitable to attack Burhan-ud-din. Instead, he directed his attention towards the Kittur district, of which he succeeded in occupying every part except the fort of the same name. This was also invested, but could not be captured. Holkar, then, accompanied by Ganesh Pant Behre, marched to Savanur whose Nawab had asked his help against the Mysoreans.[4]

Savanur had been captured by Haidar in 1776, but he had restored it to its Pathan ruler, Abdul Hakim Khan, on an annual tribute of four lakhs of rupees. In order to consolidate and strengthen his new conquests between the Tungabhadra and the Krishna, Haidar had, in 1779, entered into a marriage alliance with the Nawab by giving his daughter to the latter's eldest son, Abdul Karim Khan, and taking the Nawab's daughter for his eldest son, Karim Saheb. On that occasion Haidar gave back to Abdul Hakim the remaining half of the territory which the Marathas had taken from him and also reduced his tribute to one-half. But in return Abdul Hakim was required to maintain for Haidar's service 2,000 select Pathan horse to be commanded by two of his sons.[5] At first the Nawab maintained the corps, but as the horsemen who were killed during the Second Anglo-Mysore War were not replaced, it was found that after the Treaty of Mangalore their number had dwindled to 500. Tipu Sultan, therefore, ordered the Nawab to send his representatives to Seringapatam to settle accounts for his failure to maintain the

[1] It is a town in Dharwar District, Mysore.
[2] Khare, viii, No. 2986; Kirmani, p. 301.
[3] It is a large village in Dharwar District, Mysore.
[4] Khare, viii, p. 4009; Duff, ii, p. 174.
[5] Wilks, i, p. 759.

required number of horsemen. He also demanded the tribute which had not been paid for a number of years. And when the Nawab's ministers visited Seringapatam, he placed before them a bill for twenty-one lakhs of rupees which the Nawab was required to pay. This included the arrears of tribute and the amount which the Nawab had saved by not maintaining the required number of horsemen.[1]

The Nawab paid about one-half the amount and expressed his inability to pay the rest.[2] In reality the chief reason why he was evading Tipu's demand was that the Marathas had dissuaded him against payment, and had warned him that in case of compliance they would make a break with him. If, on the other hand, he persisted in his refusal and was attacked by Tipu, they promised to come to his assistance.[3]

The Nawab listened to the Maratha advice and did not discharge his arrears of tribute. Tipu, therefore, sent Raghavendra Naik, one of his principal bankers, with some troops to realise the amount from him. Hearing of this Holkar and Behre hastened to Savanur with a view to seizing Raghavendra Naik. But the latter managed to escape across the Tungabhadra,[4] and only two or three inferior bankers fell into Holkar's hands, from whom he exacted a ransom of two lakhs of rupees. Burhan-ud-din, who had been watching Holkar's movements and had followed him, attacked him near Savanur, but was repulsed by the combined forces of the Marathas and the Nawab. So he retreated to Jerianvatti on the Varda, thirty miles above Savanur.[5]

After this success Tukoji Holkar, with 15,000 troops, marched towards Kittur, leaving 15,000 men under Ganesh Pant at Bankapur to protect the Nawab of Savanur and to capture Tipu's territory in the Lakshmeshwar area which originally belonged to the Patwardhan family. Holkar also left 15,000 men under Bapu Holkar at Bayahatti[6] to establish Maratha power in the Dharwar area. Ganesh Pant captured nearly all the posts in the Lakshmeshwar area, and similarly Bapu Holkar succeeded in occupying Saunsi, Navalgund, Gadag, Shirhatti and New Hubli in Dharwar district.[7] Bapu Holkar then proceeded to occupy Old Hubli whose ruler, Kenchengauda, had agreed to surrender it. But, as Tipu's Commandant of Dharwar informed Kenchengauda that, if he proved treacherous, his son, who was a hostage with him, would be put to death, he refused to

[1] *Ibid.*, ii, p. 302; see also *Bombay Gaz.*, *Dharwar*, xxii, pp. 798-800, for the Nawab's relations with Haidar and Tipu.
[2] Wilks, ii, p. 303.
[3] Khare, viii, p. 4010.
[4] *Ibid.*
[5] Duff, ii, p. 176.
[6] It is a large village in Dharwar District, Mysore.
[7] Khare, viii, p. 4010.

give up the place. Bapu, therefore, invested Old Hubli, but on Burhan-ud-din's approach he raised the siege and retired to Bayahatti, where he was joined by Tukoji Holkar who had arrived from Kittur after having failed to capture it. Together the Maratha chieftains marched against Old Hubli and occupied it towards the end of June. Burhan-ud-din could not again come to its relief as he had to proceed to Mishrikot.[1]

The cause of Burhan-ud-din's failure against the Maratha offensive of March to June, led by Tukoji Holkar and Ganesh Pant Behre, lay in the insufficient forces at his disposal. Even after he had been reinforced by the troops from Bednur under Budr-uz-zaman Khan, his father-in-law, his army was greatly outnumbered by the Marathas and was not strong enough to undertake offensive operations.[2] He, therefore, adopted defensive tactics, moving with light troops from place to place in an effort to relieve the various garrisons beleaguered by the Marathas. But owing to the disloyal conduct of the Desais, who were in league with Holkar and Behre, he failed to prevent the Marathas from conquering one by one almost all the places in the districts of Kittur, Dharwar and Lakshmeshwar. Of the important forts only Kittur and Dharwar remained in possession of the Mysoreans. They had defied every effort of the Marathas to reduce them.

Tipu Sultan was in Coorg when he was informed by Nur Muhammad Khan, his *wakil* at Poona, that the Marathas and the Nizam were planning to invade Mysore. He immediately returned to Seringapatam in January 1786, and set himself to the task of dissolving the confederacy. A *wakil* was sent to Hyderabad to dissuade the Nizam from joining the coalition, a secret agent was despatched to Tukoji Holkar with five lakhs of rupees for him to secure his friendship and neutrality in the war,[3] and Muhammad Ghiyas was sent to Poona with twelve elephants and jewels worth three lakhs of rupees as presents for Nana to prevail on him not to open hostilities. Muhammad Ghiyas and Nur Muhammad Khan, the Mysore agents at Poona, obtained an interview with Nana through the help of Lakshman Rao Raste. Muhammad Ghiyas inquired from Nana the cause of his hostility towards Tipu Sultan. Haidar Ali had stood by the young Peshwa at a critical time when he was in danger of being ousted by the English and Raghunath Rao. Tipu had also followed the policy of his father by remaining friendly with the Marathas. Nevertheless, they had violated the treaty of alliance concluded between the Peshwa and his father in 1780 by making peace with the English without consulting him, by refusing assist-

[1] *Ibid.*, Nos. 2990, 2993.
[2] Wilks, ii, p. 295.
[3] *Hadiqat*, p. 361.

ance against the English in the Second Anglo-Mysore War and by planning to invade his kingdom.[1] Nana's reply was that the Sultan had not paid his tribute for a number of years, and that as soon as it was discharged hostilities would be suspended. But Muhammad Ghiyas insisted that Nana should first stop hostilities, and then the money would be paid. But Nana would not agree to this.[2] Tipu's *wakils*, however, did not give up the attempt to secure peace and followed Nana to Yadgir. It was only when the allied armies were about eight miles away from Badami that the *wakils* departed after being dismissed by Nana who, for militay reasons, and because there was no chance of extorting any money from them, did not consider their presence any longer desirable.[3]

Having failed in his negotiations with the Poona Government to avert war, Tipu set out towards Bangalore at the end of March 1786[4] in defence of his kingdom. On arriving there, he again made an effort to secure a peaceful settlement of his differences with the Poona Government by sending his agents to Mudhoji Bhonsle and Haripant; but as before, he failed to achieve any result.[5] He, therefore, left Bangalore, where he had stayed for about twenty days,[6] with about 1,200 regular infantry, 30,000 horse, 10,000 regular foot and 22 guns, besides the contingents sent by his *poligars* and his tributaries.[7] His progress was at first slow because he wanted his troops to join him from different parts of his kingdom, and to gain time for the rains to swell the Tungabhadra, which would prevent the Marathas from sending any relief to the south of that river.[8]

### *Tipu Attacks Adoni*

The allies expected that Tipu would march from Bangalore to the relief of Burhan-ud-din. Instead, he proceeded to relieve Gooty which was being besieged by the Marathas. The latter, hearing of this, withdrew to Badami. Tipu, thereupon, to their surprise suddenly appeared before Adoni which was held by Mahabat Jung, Basalat Jung's son and nephew of the Nizam.[9] Tipu's object in directing his arms against Adoni was to create a diversion in favour of Burhan-ud-din, who was hard pressed by the Marathas, and to prevent any further

[1] *Ibid.*, pp. 361-2; *Tarikh-i-Khudadadi,* I.O.MS., pp. 24, 25, 64; *Sultan-ut-Tawarikh,* ff. 31, 52.

[2] *Hadiqat,* p. 362.

[3] *Ibid.*, p. 366-7.

[4] P.R.C., ii. No. 11.

[5] *Tarikh-i-Khudadadi,* I.O.MS., pp. 65-66; *Sultan-ut-Tawarikh,* f. 53.

[6] P.R.C., ii, No. 11.

[7] Kirmani, p. 301. According to Cossigny Tipu entered the war with 50,000 cavalry, 112 pieces of cannon and 12 howitzers (A.N., $C^2$ 172, Cossigny to de Castries, May 4, 1786, No. 33).

[8] P.R.C., ii. No. 11.

[9] A.N., $C^2$ 172 Lallée to Cossigny, June 23, 1786, f. 65a.

advance of the enemy into his kingdom. For he knew that an attack on Adoni, which was a strong frontier post of the Nizam south of the Tungabhadra and contained the family of his brother and nephew, could not be ignored.

Alarmed and taken by surprise at Tipu's approach, Mahabat Jung at once wrote to the Nizam and the Marathas for help, calling upon them to save the honour of his family which would otherwise fall into the hands of the enemy.[1] At the same time he sent Asad Ali Khan, his minister, to persuade Tipu not to attack Adoni, and offered him a large sum of money. But the Sultan rejected these overtures since Mahabat Jung refused to visit him and join him against the Marathas.[2]

Haripant had hardly occupied Gajendragarh when he heard of Tipu's attack on Adoni. This news came as a great surprise to him for, according to the intelligence received from the Maratha spies, he expected the Sultan to march to the assistance of Burhan-ud-din. Still he at once ordered the Nizam's troops serving under him and the 20,000 Marathas under Appa Bulwant and Raghunath Rao to hasten to the relief of Adoni.[3] The Nizam, too, on receiving Mahabat Jung's letter, immediately despatched his younger brother, Mughal Ali Khan, with 25,000 men to the help of his nephew, and wrote to Haripant and to Tahawwar Jung to march at once to Adoni.[4] All these forces met at Bunnoor and, after crossing the Tungabhadra with some difficulty, moved towards Adoni with an army of nearly sixty thousand men.[5]

Tipu tried to capture Adoni before the arrival of the relieving forces. He succeeded in occupying the town, and on June 24 besieged the fort. But its walls were so strongly built that his guns failed to effect a breach. He, therefore, made two attempts at assault, but owing to the gallant resistance offered by the garrison and the absence of ladders high enough for the walls, he was repulsed with great loss. He was also foiled in the attempt to enter the fort by digging a tunnel[6] and, on the approach of the allied armies, he raised the siege and encamped a few miles to the south in a commanding position.[7] On June 22 Haidar Husain Bakhshi, with about 700 horse, which formed part of the Sultan's advanced troops, attacked a very large body of Maratha horse without the permission of his chief, Ghazi Khan. He

[1] Khare, viii, p. 4013.
[2] Kirmani, p. 302; Wilks, ii, p. 296.
[3] Duff, ii, p. 175, says that Haripant sent Krist Rao Bulwant, but from letter No. 2991 (Khare, viii) it appears that it was Appa Bulwant who was sent,
[4] Khare, viii, No. 2987; Cal. Per. Cor., vii. No. 604.
[5] Duff, ii, p. 175.
[6] Mack MS. Mad. 15-4-13 (Adoni).; A.N., C² 172, Lallée to Cossigny, June 23, 1786, f. 65a.
[7] Kirmani, p. 302; Khare, viii, No. 2987.

was defeated with considerable loss. On hearing this Tipu hastened to his relief. As a result a severe engagement took place which lasted for several hours. But it was indecisive although each party claimed a victory. The 50,000 Mughal troops for the most part remained as passive spectators.[1]

Tipu Sultan, by attacking Adoni at the end of the season, had created great problems for the allies. Although they had succeeded in relieving the place, their success was only short-lived, because, owing to the difficulty of supplies, they felt they could not long hold their ground at Adoni. They had not established any depots south of the Tungabhadra, while they could not depend upon the resources of the tract between the Tungabhadra and the Krishna of which a large part was still in the hands of Tipu. Besides, there was the difficulty of communication, for the Tungabhadra had already started to swell and would soon be flooded. Afraid lest the allied armies be isolated, Haripant wrote to Appa Bulwant to evacuate Mahabat Jung and his family before the crossing of the river became difficult.[2] Mughal Ali Khan also agreed to this plan, and accordingly, on the early morning of July 2, the allies evacuated Adoni.[3] As soon as Tipu came to know of this, he set out to pursue them, but they succeeded in recrossing the Tungabhadra, and he was able to capture only a few stragglers and some baggage.[4] He could not follow them across the river because, in the meantime, it had become flooded.

The evacuation of Adoni was disapproved by Parashuram Bhau;[5] and Malet, the British agent at the Court of Poona, regarded the conduct of the allied commanders as extremely pusillanimous in having left such a strong and strategically important place at the mercy of Tipu.[6] But owing to the difficulty of supplies, combined with the half-hearted way in which the Nizam's troops were participating in the war, the evacuation of Adoni was the only correct strategy followed by the allied commanders; for, as the subsequent events of the war showed, their presence south of the Tungabhadra in face of an army like that of Tipu's would have proved disastrous to them.

### *Tipu Crosses the Tungabhadra*

After making good their retreat, Mahabat Jung proceeded to Raichur and Mughal Ali Khan returned to Hyderabad, while the

[1] Kirmani, p. 306; Khare viii, No. 2991. Mir Alam does not mention this action. Malet derived his information from Maratha news-service.
[2] *Ibid.*, p. 4015.
[3] *Ibid.*, No. 2996
[4] Kirmani, p. 306.
[5] Khare, viii, No. 3000.
[6] P.R.C., ii, No. 14.

Marathas and the rest of the Mughal troops under Tahawwar Jung marched to join Haripant at Gajendragarh. Tipu Sultan, on the other hand, returned to Adoni and occupied the fort, taking possession of the guns and ammunition which the allies in their haste had failed to destroy.[1] He destroyed its fortifications and removed the guns and stores to Gooty and Bellary,[2] and placed Adoni in charge of Qutub-ud-din Khan.[3] He then proceeded against some of his refractory *poligars*,[4] and after reducing them approached the Tungabhadra, which contrary to the advice of his generals he decided to cross.[5] About the middle of August a vanguard of his troops crossed in the night at the ford of Guruknath,[6] and seized a small village fort which commanded the passage. By August 20 the whole of the Mysore army, along with its equipment, had crossed the ford in small basket boats and rafts, mostly obtained from Bednur, in spite of the opposition of the Maratha forces sent by Haripant. Tipu encamped at Itga at the confluence of the Tungabhadra and the Varda at a strategic position, with the Tungabhadra in his rear, the Vala, a small rivulet, on his front, and commanding ground on either flank.[7]

Haripant had been quite certain that Tipu would not undertake the daring and dangerous enterprise of crossing the Tungabhadra while it was flooded. Although he had been warned by the Nawab of Savanur that Tipu was massing troops on the south bank of the river and intended to cross it, he had disregarded these warnings and had turned his attention to occupying all the Mysore territory in the Dharwar district.[8] After capturing Gajendragarh he had proceeded against the strong fort of Bahadur Benda. But before he was able to occupy it, he received the distressing news that some of Tipu Sultan's troops had crossed the Tungabhadra. He, therefore, sent a large body on August 15 to oppose and harass the Mysoreans. After

[1] Duff, ii, p. 176; Khare, viii, p. 4016.

[2] Wilks, ii, p. 298.

[3] Kirmani, p. 307.

[4] *Ibid.*, pp. 307-8.

[5] Kirkpatrick, *Select Letters of Tippoo Sultan*, p. 387; *Tarikh-i- Khudadadi.* I.O.MS., p. 70.

[6] The fords across the Tungabhadra are numerous, and hence the difficulty of identifying it. Duff, ii, p. 176 footnote, calls the ford Gurhghaut, but cannot state its situation. Wilks, ii, p. 299, calls it Kurrucknaut. According to Khare, viii, p. 4017, the ford is called Ghagnath, and is situated in the Haveri subdivision of Dharwar Dist. But these accounts do not seem to be correct. Actually the ford must be the one near Bellahuse, about ten miles from Hospet in Bellary Dist., and is called by Kirmani as Guruknath. (*Nishan-i-Haidari*, f. 123; see also Wilks, ii, p. 299 footnote). Besides, Itga where Tipu encamped after crossing the Tungabhadra (Khare, viii, No. 3013) is also in Bellary Dist, about 27 miles south of Savanur.

[7] Khare, viii, No. 3013; P.R.C., ii, No. 23; A.N., $C^2$ 172, Lallée to Cossigny, Oct. 9, 1786, ff. 71a-b.

[8] Khare, viii, pp. 4016-7.

occupying Bahadur Benda on August 17, which was treacherously surrendered to him, he himself moved the next day with his whole force, having already detached the van of his army consisting of about 20,000 men under Bajipant Anna. Raghunath Rao Patwardhan was left with 10,000 men to prosecute the siege of Koppal, a strong fort about four miles from Bahadur Benda.[1] But, as we have seen, the troops sent by Haripant could not prevent Tipu from crossing the Tungabhadra, and by the time he arrived there, the Sultan had completed the crossing and was encamped on a commanding position to the north of the river.

Haripant encamped at Kalkeri about eight miles from Tipu's camp.[2] For a number of days only minor skirmishes took place between the two armies. For, although Haripant tried to inveigle Tipu out of his camp in order to give him battle, he refused to move out and remained occupied in strengthening his position.[3] At last on the night of August 28 he marched out with some troops to make a surprise attack on the Marathas, but finding that they had been informed of his design and were on the alert, he returned to his camp. Four days later Tipu again set out to surprise the enemy, but could not achieve his object.[4]

Meanwhile, Haripant, whose army had swelled to about 100,000 men by the arrival of Tukoji Holkar from Hubli and Raghunath Rao Patwardhan from Koppal, was finding it difficult to remain in the neighbourhood of Itga owing to the shortage of supplies and the spread of sickness in his camp. He, therefore, proceeded to Savanur.[5] He was followed by Tipu who marched along the banks of the Tungabhadra, and on approaching Savanur made two night attacks early in September, but neither proved decisive. On the 15th Tipu encamped in a strong position about five miles from Savanur, where he was joined soon after by Burhan-ud-din from Kalghatgi[6] and by Badr-uz-zaman Khan who arrived with a large convoy of provisions from Bednur.[7]

For a few days, every afternoon, Tipu made demonstrations of a serious attack, but after driving back the outposts returned to his camp.[8] On October 1 again he made a similar demonstration, and hoping that he had deluded the Marathas into thinking that as

[1] P.R.C., ii, Nos. 20, 23; Khare viii, No. 3013.

[2] Khare, viii, No. 3013; P.R.C., ii, No. 23.

[3] Khare, viii, No. 3015.

[4] *Ibid,*, p. 4022.

[5] *Ibid.*, p. 4023; Duff, ii, p. 177. Wheat was 6 seers a rupee; gram 8 seers a rupee; and ghee 1¼ seers a rupee. (See P.R.C., ii, No. 21).

[6] Wilks, ii, p. 300; Khare viii, p. 4024. Kalghatgi is a *taluk* in Dharwar Dist., Mysore.

[7] Kirmani, p. 314.

[8] Wilks, ii, p. 300.

before he did not intend any serious attack, he decided to surprise them during the night. He divided his army into four columns, of which the left centre was commanded by himself, the right centre by Mirza Khan, the left by Burhan-ud-din, and the right by Mir Muin-ud-din. It was agreed that on reaching the pre-arranged point of attack, Tipu would fire a signal gun which was to be at once answered by the heads of other columns, so that each might know the position of the others and immediately commence the attack. The troops moved off soon after the evening meal, but, owing to the darkness of the night and the heavy rains, the heads of all columns except his own lost their way. As a result, when Tipu approached the enemy's camp and fired the signal there was no response. After a long delay a second signal was fired, but this was replied to by only one commander. It was a little before dawn that he entered the Maratha Camp, but found himself accompanied by only 300 men. With daybreak, however, he was able to assemble and organise his forces, but the camp was found empty; the Marathas, warned by their spies of the impending attack, had evacuated their ground and occupied a commanding position on a height near by from which they started cannonading. Tipu ordered his troops not to return the fire in order to deceive the Marathas into thinking that he did not possess long range guns, and thus be tempted to advance towards him. The ruse succeeded, and the enemy forces advanced. As they approached, he let loose a heavy fire which was continued for about seven hours. This spread consternation in their ranks, and they were compelled to fall back with considerable loss to a position to the left of the town of Savanur.[1] The next day being Id-uz-Zuha, Tipu suspended military operations, but on the third day he again attacked and succeeded in dislodging the Marathas from their position.[2] Owing to the repeated losses sustained at the hands of the Mysoreans and the difficulties of obtaining forage and provisions, Haripant quitted Savanur and moved eastward. The Nawab also, realising that he would not be able to resist the Sultan alone, evacuated his capital on October 2, and with his family joined the allies.[3] The troops which were left for its defence being unable to hold it, Tipu entered Savanur with the support of its inhabitants.[4]

[1] *Tarikh-i-Khudadadi*, I.O.MS., pp. 74-77; *Sultan-ut-Tawarikh*, ff. 57-59; Khare, viii, No. 3020. But Khare does not mention the defeat of the Marathas. There is, however, no doubt that the Marathas suffered a reverse. (See P.R.C., ii. No. 26.)

[2] *Sultan-ut-Tawarikh*, f. 59.

[3] *Ibid.*, f. 60; *Tarikh-i-Khudadadi*, I.O.MS., p. 78; Khare, viii, Nos. 3034, 3040.

[4] *Ibid.*, No. 3043; see also for a good description of the capture of Savanur, A.N.,C² 172, Lallée to Cossigny, Oct. 9, 1786, ff. 71a-b. Lallée says that the Nawab and his eldest son escaped, but his whole family was seized and sent to Seringapatam on October 8.

Tipu remained in Savanur until the first of Muharram 1201 A.H. (October 24, 1786), when he proceeded to the vicinity of Bankapur to celebrate that festival.[1] Haripant tried to lure him into the plains, but he refused to give up the strategic position he occupied. He did not move even when Haripant besieged and then on November 14 stormed Shirhatti,[2] a fortified town about 20 miles north-east of Savanur. It was on November 30 that, having deposited his heavy baggage at Bankapur,[3] Tipu left the place, and moving along the river Varda, encamped not far from the Maratha camp on the banks of a rivulet about four miles north of Itga. Haripant, finding the enemy too near, decided to fall back on Kalkeri.[4] On December 2, with probably the knowledge and connivance of Holkar,[5] Tipu made a serious night attack on the allies who were proceeding towards Kalkeri, and threw their forces into great confusion. As Malet wrote: "This has been a severe blow to the Mahrattas and will, I apprehend, be found so in its consequences." Haripant's losses, however, were slight; Tahawwar Jung and Bhonsle, on the other hand, suffered heavily for, besides large casualties, they lost all their baggage and military stores. This was because Haripant, suspecting the danger of a night attack, had sent away his camp followers and was thus able to retreat without much loss, while Tahawwar Jung and Bhonsle were entrapped by Tipu because of their heavy baggage which, in spite of the advice of Haripant, they were carrying with them.[6] Tipu also captured a large number of women, 2000 camels and 2000 horses. He restored the prisoners, men and women, to the confederates, after giving each two rupees and a sheet of cloth,[7] but retained the rest of the booty.

After this victory Tipu moved on the broken ground along the banks of the Varda and the Tungabhadra, and encamped between Koppal and Bahadur Benda.[8] On January 3 he began the siege of Bahadur Benda, and up to the 8th made three attempts to storm it, but was repulsed with great loss. Hostilities then ceased for a few days and negotiations for peace began. But since the talks proved abortive, again firing commenced; and on the 13th an attempt at an escalade was made.[9] The garrison put up a stiff resistance but,

[1] *Sultan-ut-Tawarikh*, f. 60; *Tarikh-i-Khudadadi*, I.O.MS., p. 79; Duff, ii, p. 177. Bankapur is a town in Dharwar Dist., Mysore.

[2] Khare, viii, No. 3052.

[3] *Ibid.*, No. 3065; Duff, ii, p. 177.

[4] *Khare*, viii, No. 3065.

[5] Malet says that there was a rumour current at Poona that the attack was made with the knowledge and connivance of Holkar. Holkar's troops consequently did not suffer in this action at all. He was against Nana, and so did not want Tipu's defeat which would increase Nana's prestige. (See P.R.C., ii, No. 41.)

[6] *Ibid.*, No. 40; Khare, viii, No. 3065.

[7] Kirmani, p. 322.

[8] Duff, ii, p. 177.

[9] P.R.C., ii, No. 49; Khare, viii, No. 3076.

finding there was no hope of relief and losing heart after their Commandant was shot by Tipu, they capitulated on condition of security of life and freedom to return to the Maratha army.[1] Bahadur Benda was a formidable fort and inaccessible to the enemy, still Tipu had captured it. "It is amazing," wrote Yoon, Malet's news-agent, "that such a strong fort as this was taken in seven or eight days and the Maratha army between four or five leagues distance."[2]

After occupying Bahadur Benda, Tipu renewed his attempts to surprise the allied forces, and inflicted severe loss on them. The Nizam's troops being ill-organised, less vigilant, and encumbered with heavy baggage suffered the most.[3] These attacks continued until February 10, when a cessation of hostilities took place.

*Peace is Signed*

The Maratha-Mysore War had been provoked by the Marathas and the Nizam who were anxious to reduce Tipu's power and take back the territories which his father had conquered from them. Tipu, on the other hand, wanted to live on amicable terms with them provided there was no interference in his internal affairs, and he was left in the enjoyment of the possessions which he had inherited from his father. That was why he did his best to dissuade Nana from helping the chief of Nargund who was his tributary, and from invading Badami which was part of his kingdom. But in face of the Maratha obduracy and aggressiveness his efforts failed, and he was left with no alternative but to draw his sword in defence of his kingdom. However, alarmed by the intrigues of Malet at Poona and by the military preparations of Lord Cornwallis, in September 1786 Tipu sent a letter to Haripant through his *wakil*, Nur Muhammad, informing him that the war had been caused by the Peshwa's interference in the Nargund affair, but that was a minor issue on which they should not fight. The Maratha chief should, therefore, send two *wakils* to settle the terms of peace, for it was in the interest of both the Mysore and Maratha Governments that they should remain united.[4] A similar letter was sent to Poona. Again in November Tipu made approaches. This time it was done through Gangadhar Raste and Tukoji Holkar.[5] Nana had hitherto rejected all overtures from Tipu because he was certain of English military aid.[6] He also did not want any kind of settlement with Tipu until he had obtained

[1] *Tarikh-i-Khudadadi*, I.O.MS., p. 85; *Sultan-ut-Tawarikh*, f. 64.
[2] P.R.C., ii, No. 49.
[3] Wilks ii p. 306.
[4] Khare, viii, No. 3027.
[5] P.R.C., ii, No. 35.
[6] *a*. See *infra*, p. 146. According to Cossigny Muhammad Ali promised 30,000 troops to the Nizam on condition that he was given a share in the conquests (A.N., C[2] 179, ff. 301 *seq*).

possession of those lands which Haidar had captured from the Marathas. It was only after Cornwallis had expressed his inability to help the Peshwa that Nana allowed Haripant to receive peace proposals from Tipu. The latter, therefore, sent Badr-uz-zaman Khan and Ali Raza Khan to the Maratha camp, while Haripant appointed Tukoji Holkar and Gangadhar Rao Raste to treat with them.

The terms proposed by Tipu were that the Marathas should recognise his sovereignty over the territory between the Tungabhadra and the Krishna and restore to him the places conquered in the course of the war. In return he would discharge forty-eight lakhs of rupees as arrears of tribute, thirty-two lakhs immediately and sixteen lakhs after six months, and would in future regularly pay twelve lakhs of rupees annually as laid down in the treaty of 1780.[1] But Haripant rejected these proposals, and replied that peace was only possible if Tipu was willing to restore Adoni to Mahabat Jung and cede to the Marathas the territory which was in their possession at the time of the Peshwa Madhav Rao.[2] Tipu refused to accept these terms, for he considered the demand for the surrender of conquests made by his father and already recognised by the Peshwa as extremely unjust. Haripant, thereupon, proposed that Tipu should release Kalopant, return Adoni, Kittur, Nargund and Savanur to their respective rulers and cede Badami and Gajendragarh to the Peshwa. He should discharge the arrears of tribute to the Peshwa and pledge himself to pay twelve lakhs of rupees annually in future. This draft was acceptable to Tipu with some alterations.[3] He was prepared to release Kalopant and restore Adoni, Nargund and Kittur to their respective chiefs. But he could not return Savanur to Abdul Hakim Khan who was his tributary and owed him a large sum of money. The demand for its restoration could only be made when the Nawab had settled all his dues. However, Tipu would cede Badami to the Peshwa, discharge all arrears of tribute and pay in future twelve lakhs annually. In return the Marathas should give him back all the places they had captured in the war, including Gajendragarh and Dharwar, enter into an offensive and defensive alliance with him and address him in future by the title of Padshah.[4]

The Marathas had hitherto suffered heavily in the war which had been one of attrition for them; and as the English had refused to help them, there was no possibility of the tide of war turning in their favour. Haripant, therefore, accepted all the proposals except the one

[1] Khare, viii, No. 3071.
[2] *Ibid.*, No. 3073.
[3] *Ibid.*, No. 3074; *Hadiqat*, pp. 371-2.
[4] *Ibid.*, p. 372.

which required that Tipu was to be addressed in future as Padshah, instead of merely as Tipu or Fath Ali Khan. However, due to the intervention of Tukoji Holkar, who pointed out that it was a trifling matter, a compromise was arrived at, and Haripant agreed that in future Tipu would be addressed as "Nabob Tippoo Sultan, Futeh Ally Khan."[1] As all the controversial points had been settled, the Treaty of Peace between Tipu and the Peshwa was signed in April 1787.[2] But although the name of Mahabat Jung was mentioned in the treaty, the Nizam was not made a party to it. This was due to the Maratha dissatisfaction with the Nizam on account of the feeble support which he had given in the war. However, after the Nizam had complained to the Maratha Government about this exclusion, he was included in the treaty and Tipu agreed to return to him those of his frontier posts which the Mysoreans had captured in the course of the war.[3]

*Criticism of the Peace*

Although Tipu had won the war, he lost the peace. While the treaty was for him a diplomatic defeat, it was a victory for the Marathas who had been defeated on the battlefield and yet had secured advantageous terms. Tipu, on the other hand, had neither obtained any accession of territory nor any indemnity. On the contrary, he had to cede Raichur and Adoni to the Nizam, pay the Marathas a large sum as arrears of tribute and surrender to them Kittur, Nargund and Badami, the very places in whose defence he had waged the war. It is true that he did not suffer any loss of revenue for he annexed Kanakagiri, Anagondi and Savanur by removing their rulers.[4] But the loss of the territory which he ceded to the Marathas meant a reduction in the extent of his kingdom. Besides, Kittur, Nargund and Badami, being situated on his frontiers, were of considerable strategic importance, and would be in the Maratha hands spring-boards for the invasion of Mysore. The reason why Tipu granted such lenient terms to the Marathas was that he wanted to establish close ties of friendship with them in view of Lord Cornwallis's military and diplomatic preparations against him. At first it appeared that the concessions he had made were compensated

[1] *Hadiqat*, pp. 372-3. Mir Alam says that Tipu wanted to be addressed as Sultan, and this demand was acceded to through the mediation of Holkar. But this is incorrect for Sultan was part of Tipu's name. (See p. 9, *supra*.)

[2] Haripant, Raste and Holkar received an elephant and a *khilat* each from Tipu. (Khare, viii, No. 3083.) But Holkar also obtained 4 lakhs of rupees in cash and 2 lakhs of rupees worth of jewels, besides the sum of 10 lakhs which Tipu had promised to pay him at the commencement of the war. (*Hadiqat*, p. 373.)

[3] I.O., Mack, MS., No. 46, p. 51.

[4] P.R.C., ii, No. 68.

by his obtaining an offensive and defensive alliance with the Marathas and the Nizam. But in reality the concessions proved to be in vain, for it was not long before that the Peshwa violated the peace treaty and joined the coalition formed by the English to overthrow his power.

*Causes of Tipu's Success in the War*

Tipu displayed considerable military skill in this war. He crossed the Tungabhadra while it was flooded, and inflicted severe defeats upon the confederates in a series of night attacks which wore them down and obliged them to listen to overtures of peace.

Tipu also showed great ability as a strategist. He kept close to the river banks which were steep and rocky. It was difficult ground for the movements of the Maratha cavalry, but was favourable to the operations of his infantry, and this proved decisive in this war. Haripant tried his best to inveigle Tipu out, but he refused to give up his position. He always selected his own ground, and throughout the campaign the initiative remained in his hands.

Besides, by marching along the banks of the river Tipu was enabled to draw his supplies with facility from his kingdom south of the Tungabhadra. The Marathas, on the other hand, had to bring their supplies from a long distance, a difficult undertaking in face of the flooded streams and rivers and Tipu's efficient intelligence service, which enabled his irregular horse to intercept the Maratha convoys. The shortage of supplies was in no small measure responsible for the Maratha reverses in this war.

Furthermore, the confederate armies were ill-organised and ill-disciplined, and because of their pay being in arrears were discontented. The Nizam's troops were only half-heartedly participating in the war, for they did not expect to reap much benefit from it. Holkar was supposed to be in the pay of Tipu, and several times his pindaris looted the baggage of the Maratha army.[1] Similarly, the other members of the confederacy were also more busy in promoting their own interests and in finding fault with each other than in prosecuting the war with earnestness. Tipu, on the other hand, enjoyed the great advantage of an undivided command; and owing to his personal direction of the campaign his commanders could not give expression to their mutual jealousies. His forces were well-disciplined and their morale was high, and although numerically smaller than the armies of the confederates, this inferiority was more than balanced by their superiority in infantry and artillery.[2] His

[1] Khare, viii, Nos. 3065, 3068. Mir Alam also says that Holkar was bribed by Tipu. On one occasion he had advised the Sultan to make a night attack on Haripant's army. He now advised Tipu to conclude peace. (*Hadiqat*, p. 271.)

[2] Khare, viii, No. 3030.

cavalry too was less numerous, but his irregular horse under Ghazi Khan, Wali Muhammad, and Ibrahim Khan proved very effective in harassing the enemy and cutting off their supplies.

*Annexation of Rayadrug and Harpanahalli*

After the conclusion of peace with the Marathas, Tipu set out to punish Venkatapati, the *poligar* of Rayadrug, and Basappa Naik, the *poligar* of Harpanahalli,[1] for their treacherous conduct during the Maratha-Mysore War. Haidar Ali had once pardoned them for carrying on intrigues with the Marathas and the Nizam after they had pledged themselves to remain loyal to him.[2] However, when the Maratha-Mysore war broke out they entered into communication with Tipu's enemies. Being in attendance on Tipu during the war, the *poligars* sent secret information to the Marathas regarding his movements, and while he was at Savanur, they bribed two Muslims to assassinate him. The plot was, however, discovered. As Tipu was at the time engaged in the war, he did not take any action against the conspirators. But after the termination of hostilities he decided to punish them.[3]

On approaching Rayadrug and Harpanahalli, Tipu sent about two thousand men to surprise the forts, and at the same time imprisoned the *poligars*, who were with him, along with their two Muslim accomplices. The next day the conspirators were court-martialed, and on conviction were sentenced to death. The two Muslims were immediately executed, but the death sentence on the *poligars* was commuted to imprisonment, and they were sent as prisoners to Bangalore.[4] Rayadrug and Harpanahalli were annexed.

*Tipu Adopts the Title of Padshah*

From Harpanahalli and Rayadrug Tipu marched back to Bangalore, where he stayed for about fifteen days, and then returned to Seringapatam.[5] On arriving there, after a few days, he adopted the title of Padshah. The celebrations to commemorate this event took place on a Friday. Several lakhs of rupees were distributed among the poor on this occasion, and the *khutba* was recited in the name of

[1] *Madras Dist. Gaz.*, *Bellary*, pp. 251, 299.

[2] *Sultan-ut-Tawarikh*, f. 69.

[3] *Ibid.*, f. 70. Kirmani, p. 324, says that besides being in secret communication with the Marathas, the *poligars* were also guilty of not waiting upon the Sultan when summoned by him. But from *Sultan-ut-Tawarikh*, it appears that the *poligars* were present with the Sultan's army. Miles in his translation of *Nishan-i-Haidari* (p. 137) omits the passage which refers to the intrigues of the *poligars* with Tipu's enemies.

[4] *Sultan-ut-Tawarikh*, ff. 70-71; Kirmani, p. 324.

[5] *Sultan-ut-Tawarikh*, f. 71.

Tipu Sultan Padshah instead of that of the effete Mughal Emperor.[1] It was also about this time that Tipu struck new rupees and called them *Imami*,[2] introduced the Muhammadi era which began about thirteen years prior to the *Hijra*,[3] and gave orders for the construction of a throne of gold, ornamented with precious jewels in the shape of a tiger.[4]

[1] *Tarikh-i-Tipu*, f. 5. Wilks ii, p. 294, wrongly says that the event took place in Jan. 1786 after Tipu's return from Coorg.

[2] Kirmani, p. 327. On one side was written: "The religion of Ahmad was illumined in the world by the victories of Haidar," and on the other, "He is the only just King."

[3] *Ibid.* For a discussion of Tipu's new era, see Islamic Culture, xiv, April 1940, pp. 161 *seq.*

[4] Kirmani, p. 328.

CHAPTER VII

# TIPU AND THE FRENCH 1784-89

TIPU SULTAN had been greatly disappointed and embittered by the conduct of the French during the Second Anglo-Mysore War. He had called them false and perfidious, because they had not helped him in proportion to the hopes they had raised and the promises they had made, and because in the end they had betrayed him by making, behind his back, a separate peace with the English.[1] That he did not completely break his relations with them was because he cherished the hope that they might yet prove useful allies in any future war against the English or any of the country powers.

The French authorities, admitting their past mistakes, tried to make amends by wooing Tipu. Vicomte de Souillac, the Governor-General of the French establishments in the East, wrote to him to forget the last war and plan for the next one, for which large land and sea forces would be sent from France for driving out the English from India.[2] De Souillac also sent his agent, Rama Rao, with instructions to tell him that a French alliance was necessary for his survival and for overthrowing English power, and that the French were trying their best to counteract English intrigues against him both at Poona and Hyderabad. Rama Rao was also to suggest that the Sultan should increase the number of troops in the French detachment that was with him, and replace Sieur Morampont by M. de Couffreville, who was not only more competent but could also act as French Resident. Furthermore, Rama Rao was to request for a larger establishment on the Malabar coast, from where military help could be more easily rendered to the Sultan than from the tiny port of Mahé. But Tipu's response to these proposals was vague and evasive. He showed the same indifference to de Morlat who wrote to him that he had been deputed by Souillac to negotiate an alliance with him against the English.[3] Tipu's indifference to the French

[1] See p. 52, *supra*,

[2] A.N., C[2] 169, de Souillac to Tipu, August 19, 1785, ff. 179a *seq.*; *Ibid.*, de Morlat to Tipu, Sept. 14, 1785, f. 149b.

[3] *Ibid.*, de Souillac to Rama Rao, June 9, 1785, ff. 156a *seq.*; also Tipu to de Morlat, undated, ff. 154b-55a and Tipu to de Souillac, Sept. 21, 1785. De Souillac wanted the cession of Onore with the surrounding territory, because Mahé's fortifications had been destroyed by the English in the last war and the construction of new defences would be very expensive. De Souillac would have preferred Mangalore, but he knew Tipu would never give it. (C[2] 169, f. 22b.)

approaches was due not to his victories over the English in the last war which might have turned his head, but to his disappointments with the French in the Second Anglo-Mysore War about which he never ceased harping in his letters to them. At the same time, knowing that nothing could be gained by responding to the advances of the French authorities in India, he expected to gain his object by negotiating directly with Louis XVI and his ministers.[1]

De Souillac's attempt to gain the friendship of Tipu was not intended to be directed against the Nizam or the Marathas. On the contrary, he wanted to remain friendly with all the Indian powers, and for this reason he avoided a meeting with Tipu, which would have aroused the suspicions of the Nizam and the Marathas.[2] What the French really desired at this time was to prevent the Indian powers from fighting with each other and to unite them under their own leadership in a confederacy against the English.[3] This is evident from a letter which Bussy wrote to Comte de Vergennes. He observed: "The Marathas and the Nizam have made an alliance to destroy Tipu Sultan. This plan marvellously suits the English. I have laboured and still labour to break it, and at the same time to unite the three Indian powers against the English without compromising ourselves."[4] It was in accordance with this policy that de Souillac advised Nana, the Nizam and Tipu to forget their differences and become friends,[5] and Cossigny, Governor of Pondicherry, warned Nana that if the Peshwa, the Nizam and Tipu did not unite and remained attached to their narrow selfish interests, the English would profit by this and reduce them to the position of the Nawabs of Oudh and Carnatic.[6]

But the attempt of the French to prevent war was not successful, and hostilities broke out between Tipu and the Marathas who were allied with the Nizam. The French thereupon became active in mediating peace between them. Cossigny appealed to the Nizam to make sacrifices as a Muslim and as an Indian and make peace with Tipu, who was the only Muslim prince in the country capable of challenging British power. Cossigny assured the Nizam that he would do his best to restore the glory which the Muslims had lost.[7] Cossigny also called upon Nana to be ready to make sacrifices in order to save the country from English domination, and asked him for the conditions upon which he would be willing to conclude

[1] *Ibid.*, Tipu to de Souillac, August 3, 1785, f. 63b; also *ibid.*, Tipu to Louis XVI, 3 Zilhijja, 1199 A.H./Oct. 7, 1785, ff. 163a-64b.
[2] *Ibid.*, from de Souillac, Sept. 15, 1785, No. 15.
[3] P.A.MS. No. 442, Bussy to de Castries, Oct. 20, 1784.
[4] *Ibid.*, No. 437, Bussy to Vergennes, Aug. 4, 1784.
[5] *Ibid.*, No. 894, Cossigny to Montigny, March 8, 1786.
[6] *Ibid.;* also A.N., C² 172, Cossigny to Nana, undated, ff. 181 a-b.
[7] A.N., C² 237, Cossigny to Nizam, Aug. 3, 1787, No. 132.

peace, so that Tipu might be persuaded to end hostilities.[1] Montigny, the French representative at Poona, even gave the assurance that, in case persuasion failed, Tipu would be forced to come to terms.[2] But Nana gave only vague replies. The French were no longer considered strong enough to have any weight in the counsels of either the Hyderabad or Poona Government.[3]

The French policy in this war was also determined by the sixteenth article of the Tready of Versailles (1783), which forbade the English and the French from participating in the wars of the Indian powers. That was why the French did not render military assistance to Tipu when he was attacked by the Marathas. Cossigny, however, informed Tipu that if the English joined the Marathas and attacked him, the French would come to his help.[4] In fact, Cossigny favoured an alliance with Tipu whether the English helped the Marathas or not, and was prepared to supply him 8000 rifles, which he had demanded. Cossigny maintained that it was only with Tipu's help that the English power in India could be overthrown.[5] Tipu was very powerful and was certain to defeat the Maratha-Nizam coalition.[6] But in case he was defeated it would be most unfortunate.[7]

De Souillac, however, did not agree with Cossigny, and instructed him not to enter into any treaty with Tipu, because that would antagonise the Marathas.[8] He regarded Tipu as proud, vain, imperious and undependable, and felt that it would be a good thing if he were beaten and humiliated, for then he would throw himself into the arms of the French.[9] De Souillac, in fact, preferred an alliance with the Marathas thinking that Tipu's power was ephemeral and likely to be sooner or later overwhelmed by the combined forces of the English, the Nizam and the Marathas. Even Marechal de Castries, Minister of Marine, had written to Bussy as early as November 1, 1783, that an alliance with the Marathas would be more useful to the Company than one with Tipu whose "power was new and had not the time to acquire real stability." "The Marathas," on the other hand, according to him, "had a stability, more strong and proper to create a revolution in India."[10] But the Marathas did not favourably respond to the overtures of the French whom they

[1] P.A.MS. No. 944, Cossigny to Montigny, Dec. 27, 1786.
[2] P.R.C., ii, No. 17.
[3] *Ibid.*
[4] A.N., C² 172, Cossigny to Tipu, undated, f. 30b.
[5] *Ibid.*, Cossigny to de Castries, Jan. 20, 1786, f. 22b.
[6] *Ibid.*, Feb. 22, 1786, ff. 28a-b.
[7] *Ibid.*, Jan. 20, 1786, f. 23a.
[8] *Ibid.*, f. 22b.
[9] A.N., C² 169, from de Souillac, Sept. 15, 1785, f. 22a; also C⁴ 67, de Souillac to de Castries, Nov. 25, 1785, No. 51.
[10] P.A.MS. No. 550.

regarded as Tipu's friends and having a secret alliance with him. Montigny, the French agent, tried his best to assure Nana that there was no compact between the French and Tipu, and that they would not help him in his wars against the Marathas.[1] It would be only if the English broke the sixteenth article of the Treaty of Versailles and went to the assistance of the Marathas, that they would be obliged to give up their neutrality and join Tipu Sultan.[2] But in spite of these assurances, Nana ignored the French. He preferred the friendship of the English whom he regarded as more powerful and dependable allies. A special agent, named Gudar, arrived in Poona early in August 1786 from Pondicherry to establish friendly relations with the Peshwa. But his efforts bore no fruit either. Malet succeeded in counteracting the intrigues of both Gudar and Montigny.[3] Nor were the French successful with the Nizam. Aumont, who was sent to negotiate an alliance with him, proved ineffective. Cossigny's letters also had no effect on the Nizam, who observed that "the English invasion of India has not given me the same pain as the usurpation of Tipu."[4]

The failure of the French to win over the Nizam and the Marathas ultimately brought about a change in de Souillac's policy. Moreover, he was greatly impressed by Tipu's victories against the Maratha-Nizam coalition and became inclined to agree with Cossigny, Governor of Pondicherry, that it was in French interest to form an alliance with Tipu, with whose help alone the English could be driven from India, and that the Marathas could not be effective against the English, partly because they were disunited and could be bought off, and partly because their army was entirely composed of cavalry.[5]

De Souillac was also convinced of Tipu's sincere desire for French friendship by his refusal to accept the seventeen lakhs of rupees which his father had advanced to the French during the Second Anglo-Mysore War and which they were now prepared to pay back. Influenced by these considerations, de Souillac welcomed Tipu's idea to send an embassy to the court of Louis XVI in order to negotiate directly an alliance with the French Government and secure its military assistance against his enemies.[6] But Tipu at first did not

[1] *Ibid.*, No. 894.

[2] *Ibid.*, No. 952, Cossigny to Nana, Jan. 5, 1787. The French position was that if the English helped Tipu or the Nizam or the Marathas, they would then come to the assistance of the other power.

[3] P.R.C., ii, No. 17.

[4] A.N., C² 180, Conway to de Castries, Oct. 12, 1787, ff. 127 *seq.*

[5] *Ibid.*, C² 237, Cossigny to de Castries, July 19, 1787, No. 132.

[6] Tipu had been telling the French authorities in India that he wanted to send an embassy to Louis XVI (see A.N., C² 169, Tipu to de Souillac, Aug. 3, 1785, f. 63b); also P.R.C., ii, No. 17.

send any separate mission. The ambassadors despatched to the Ottoman Sultan at the end of 1785 were also ordered to proceed to Paris after completing their work at Constantinople. From Paris they were required to go to London.[1]

The ambassadors were to inform Louis XVI of how the English had established their power in India and the atrocities they were committing upon the Muslims, Hindus and French. They were to recount the history of the Second Anglo-Mysore War in which the French had played such an inglorious part. Tipu would have won a total victory over the English, and would have expelled them if it had not been for the French who had withdrawn from the conflict and made a separate peace with them without consulting him. He and his father had made great sacrifices for them, but they had betrayed him at a critical moment.[2]

After making these statements, the ambassadors were to submit to Louis XVI proposals for a Treaty of Perpetual Alliance between him and their master. The French king was to send 10,000 troops under able commanders who would be under Tipu's direct orders, and if they and their soldiers committed any crime they would be tried according to Mysore laws. In the event of war with the English, no peace would be made with them either by Tipu or the French for ten years. If, in the meantime, the English desired peace, it would not be concluded unless they were deprived of all their possessions, which would then be divided between Tipu and the French. The ambassadors were further to request Louis XVI to send to Mysore artificers and workmen who could make guns, watches, china and glassware and other articles.[3]

But the embassy could not proceed beyond Constantinople,[4] having been recalled from there by Tipu. Meanwhile, alarmed at the English intrigues at Poona, Tipu had decided to send a separate embassy to France. De Souillac, and in particular Cossigny, encouraged him and aroused great hopes in his mind in regard to the outcome of the mission. As a gesture of French goodwill, it was decided that all expenses of the embassy from Mysore to Paris and back would be borne by the French government. In addition, de Souillac purchased a boat, *Roi l' aurore*, which was to carry the

[1] *Hukm-namah* No. 1677 (R.A.S.B.), f. 5b. The sending of ambassadors to Europe by Indian rulers was not Tipu's innovation. The Peshwa Raghunath Rao had sent Maniar Parsi to England to secure the friendship of the British Government; and Nana for a long time entertained the idea of sending his agent to England with a view to obtaining the support of the English Company for reducing Tipu's power. (See P.R.C., ii, Nos. 42, 54, 70, 77, 88.)

[2] *Hukm-namah* No. 1677 (R.A.S.B.), ff. 22a-26a; *Hukm-namah* No. 1676, ff. 4a-13a.

[3] *Ibid.*, f. 13b; *Hukm-namah* No. 1677, ff. 7b-8b.

[4] See next chapter.

envoys to France, and gave it as a present to Tipu. In order to create an impression, both in India and Europe, he wanted the boat to fly Tipu Sultan's flag, to have an Indian crew, and a Muslim captain, though the real captain would be Pierre Monneron, who was a native of France but a subject of the king of Portugal.[1] He had visited the Sultan in the middle of 1786 to enter into a commercial treaty with him on behalf of the French Government, and had promised to conduct the envoys to France and bring them back safely to India.[2]

De Souillac's plan was that *l' aurore* should directly proceed to Mangalore and reach there by the 15th January, 1787, and the envoys should sail from there by the end of the month or early in February. But Monneron was not able to leave the Isle of France for Mangalore until early January; and when he reached Cochin on the 19th March, he received information from Cossigny that the envoys had arrived in Pondicherry at the end of January. It seems that, at Tipu's request, Cossigny had changed de Souillac's plan of disembarking at Pondicherry instead of at Mangalore. However, Monneron continued his journey to Mangalore in order to deliver some war material, which Tipu had asked him to purchase, and to fill his boat with spices. He reached Mangalore on the 28th March and left on the 7th April, reaching Pondicherry on the 5th May.[3]

The embassy consisted of Muhammad Darwesh Khan, Akbar Ali Khan and Osman Khan. Akbar Ali Khan was accompanied by his son and Osman Khan by his nephew.[4] Besides, the envoys were attended by their footmen, butlers, cooks and bodyguards. In all there were eighty persons ready to embark. But Monneron considered

[1] A.N., C² 179, de Souillac to Cossigny, Nov. 22, 1786, ff. 9a-b. Although *l'aurore* was presented to Tipu and he was permitted to hoist his flag all along the way, yet when it approached the French coast, the French flag was to be hoisted. (C² 179, Cossigny's instructions to Monneron, July 21, 1787, ff. 43a *seq.*)

[2] P.A.MS., No. 1036; P.R.C., ii, No. 45; Tantet, *L'Ambassade de Tippou*, pp. 1, *seq.*

[3] A.N., C⁴ 73, de Souillac to Cossigny, Nov. 22, 1786, No. 41; C² 174, Monneron to de la Luzerne, April 28, ff. 111a *seq.*; and C² 179, de Souillac to Cossigny, March 25, 1787, ff. 29a *seq.* According to Conway it was Monneron who suggested to Tipu the idea of sending the envoys to Pondicherry, but he concealed this from de Souillac. He went to Mangalore to fill the boat with spices; and although de Souillac had instructed him to proceed direct to the Cape of Good Hope, he stopped at both the Isle of France and the Isle of Bourbon to discharge his cargo. It seems Monneron was more interested in his commercial profits than in the embassy. (C²180, Conway to de la Luzerne, No. 16.)

[4] Wilks, ii, p. 361, says that Osman Khan was at one time Tipu's valet. But this is incorrect. He had been a great confidant of Haidar, who had sent him on a number of missions. He had also been the Superintendent of the Surgeons and Physicians of the Household and of the Medicines. He was between 50 and 60 years of age when he was sent to Paris by Tipu. (Sec P.R.C., ii, No. 45; Sec. Pro., July 8, 1782). Darwesh Khan was the youngest of the ambassadors, being about 45 (C²187, f. 45a).

this number too large and reduced them to forty-five.[1] Owing to the bad weather, the Ramazan and the Id festival, it was not until the 22nd July that he was able to sail from Pondicherry.[2]

De Soulliac's original instructions were that *l'aurore* should proceed directly to the Cape of Good Hope without stopping at the Isle of France or the Isle of Bourbon. But Monneron stopped at the Isle of Bourbon for re-provisioning; and as the boat developed a leak which could not be repaired there, the journey was continued to the Isle of France. Meanwhile the rudder had also been damaged. The repair of the ship, the Muharram celebrations and the good climate of the Isle prolonged the stay until the 4th December. The ship reached the Cape on January 3, 1788. But here again it was delayed owing to unfavourable winds, and it was not until the 11th February that *l'aurore* was able to leave. She next had to put in at the Isle of Ascension in order to obtain fresh water, because the 200 barrels of fresh water which she had at the time of leaving the Cape had been exhausted by the envoys and their staff who refused to economise. The boat again stopped at the Isle of Goru for obtaining supplies. She would have left on April 18, but Darwesh Khan fell ill, and it was only when he had recovered that she was able to sail on the night of the 28th. Meanwhile, most of the members of the mission were suffering from scurvy, and three of them died. It was, therefore, decided to stop at the port of Malaga and obtain enough supplies of fresh vegetables and provisions. The journey from Malaga to France was uneventful.[3]

The Vicomte de Souillac had instructed Monneron to land at Brest in order to impress the envoys by the size of the French navy, and, accordingly, preparations on a grand scale had been made there to receive them.[4] But as Brest was not considered warm enough for persons accustomed to a tropical climate, *l'aurore* made for Toulon, where it reached on the afternoon of June 9, 1788, ten months and seventeen days after its departure from Pondicherry. It bore Tipu's flag which had been hoisted as it approached the French coast.[5]

According to the instructions of the French Government, receptions were given and fireworks displayed in their honour, and they were taken to the theatre and military reviews. They left Toulon on

[1] Tantet, *L'ambassade de Tippou*, p. 138.

[2] A.N., C²174, Monneron to de la Luzerne, April 28, 1788, ff. 111a *seq.* The date of the departure of the embassy given by Wilks is wrong.

[3] *Ibid.*

[4] *Ibid.*, de Morlat to de la Luzerne, March 26, 1788, ff. 100a *seq.* Piveron de Morlat had made preparations to receive the envoys at Brest.

[5] Tantet, *L'ambassade de Tippou*, p. 9; P.A. MS., No. 996; Michaud, i, p. 138. It seems it was decided at Monneron's suggestion that *l'aurore* should proceed to Toulon and not to Brest, where it would be too cold for the envoys and their staff. (See A.N., C² 174, Monneron to de la Luzerne, April 28, 1788.

June 21, arriving in Paris on the evening of July 16. Marseilles, Grenoble, Dijon, Lyons, La Palisse, Moulins, Nevers, Montargis, and Fontainebleau, through which they passed, gave them an enthusiastic welcome. Paris also received them with great honour. They were led in a carriage drawn by six horses and escorted by cavalry, and crowds came out to see and greet the visitors from a strange and far off land.[1]

The envoys were lodged in a house, formerly occupied by Necker, in the Rue Bergère. It was refurnished and its garden improved. Every effort was made on the part of the French authorities to make the envoys comfortable. As they were fond of rice, several varieties of it were obtained from Toulon, and they were supplied with live sheep, goat, game and poultry, because they did not take meat except of the animal slaughtered in their own way. Each envoy was separately provided with a carriage and six horses.[2]

Arrangements were made to prepare dresses for the envoys by the French government so that they should be properly and decently clad when they appeared before Louis XVI. Clothes were also made for their staff who were scantily dressed according to European standards, and whose thin muslin dresses would, it was felt, cause their death during winter.[3]

The envoys were not happy at first, thinking that not enough attention was being paid to them. They were not satisfied with their accomodation, which they felt was insufficient. What they desired was a separate building for each of them, and suggested that Louis XVI, who possessed a number of palaces, should place one at their disposal. To provide them with more room, it was decided to remove their large boxes and bundles to another building, and place instead cupboards and wardrobes, where they could place their things. But they refused to part with their baggage. Similarly, they rejected the idea of their servants staying in an adjacent building or even on the second floor of their own building, because they wanted them to be near them, so that they could yell and shout for them whenever they required them. Hearing of their dissatisfaction with their lodgings, the French authorities showed them l'École Militaire, a very spacious royal edifice, but as by this time they had settled down, they did not like to move.[4]

[1] Tantet, pp. 9-10,; also F.O. 27/28, Dorset to Carmathian, June 19 & 26, 1788, Nos. 43, 44; A.N., C² 174, Extract from the *Register of the Controle de la Marine*, Toulon, June 17, 18, 1788, ff. 141a *seq.*, Marseilles, June 26, 1788, ff. 179a *seq.*

[2] *Ibid.*, Launay to de la Luzerne, July 18, 1788, f. 269a; *Ibid.*, July 23, 1788, f. 274b; *Journal de Paris*, June 30, 1788, pp. 794-95.

[3] A.N., C² 174, Launay to de la Luzerne, July 23., 1788, f. 274a; *ibid.*, from de la Luzerne, July 26, 1788, f. 238a.

[4] *Ibid.*, July 18, 1788, ff. 268a-b; July 23, 1788, ff. 275a-b; July 26, 1788, f. 280a.

Another cause of their dissatisfaction was that not many people called on them.[1] Besides, they were getting impatient at the delay in meeting the French ministers and in having an audience with Louis XVI. However, on July 31 Comte de la Luzerne, Minister of Marine, invited them to dinner to meet M. Montmorin, Secretary for Foreign Affairs, and thc audience with the French king was fixed for August 10.[2] Since the king desired that the envoys should find a large crowd on their arrival at Versailles, a notice was inserted in the *Journal de Paris*.[3] M. de Breze, Grand Master of Ceremonies, was invited from Paris to discuss the ceremonies to be observed at the reception.[4] The envoys wanted to make their bows to the king while sitting, but they were told that they would have to stand before him.[5] They also wished that the presents they had brought be publicly carried, but it was decided that, since they were of low value and their display would cause ridicule in the French and particularly in the English papers, they were to be carried privately.[6] Since the audience was to be public, certain changes were made in the address of the envoys by Ruffin, the official interpreter, to avoid causing offence to the English.[7]

On the 10th August, Louis XVI received the envoys with great pomp. The principal apartments of the Versailles palace were filled with spectators, and the salon d'Hercules, where the audience was to take place, was occupied by persons of rank of both sexes. The Dauphin, being unwell, could not come. But the Queen, Marie Antoinette, was seated in a private box on the side of the throne—the envoys were required neither to look at her nor to salute her—while the Duke of Normandy, his wife and daughter, the Comtesse d'Artois and Madame Elizabeth, the king's sister, were in a box on the other side. Three envoys approached the king with great dignity, and Darwesh Khan, the leader, after presenting the king with some pieces of gold, diamonds and pearls and a few muslins, that were recieved by de la Luzerne and placed on the table near the throne, delivered his address in low tones which was translated into English

[1] It was the policy of the French authorities to discourage people, particularly foreigners, from meeting them in order to prevent them from becoming victims of intrigues. (C[2] 187, f. 45b.)

[2] F.O. 27/28, Dorset to Carmathian, July 24 & 31, 1788, Nos. 52, 54. The envoys ate only nuts and vegetables because the meat served was not of the animal ceremoniously killed.

[3] A.N., C[2] 189, to Lt. General of Police, Versailles, Aug. 4, 1788, f. 8a.

[4] *Ibid.*, to M. de Breze, f. 9a.

[5] *Ibid.*, to the ambassadors, Aug. 10, 1788, f. 43a.

[6] *Ibid.*, *Memoire*, f. 52a. According to an intelligence received by Malet, the embassy carried very costly presents said to amount to 300,000 pounds sterling, besides the cancelled bonds of nineteen lakhs of rupees which the French owed Tipu. (See P.R.C., iii, No. 9,)

[7] A.N., C[2] 189, to M. Ruffin, Versailles, Aug. 7, 1788, f. 29a.

by Ruffin.[1] He recounted the history of English aggression, high-handedness and tyranny which had caused suffering to both the Indians and the French. He then described the mistakes of the French authorities in India, particularly of Duchemin and Bussy, and complained of the withdrawal of Cossigny from his army and the conclusion of peace with the English without his knowledge, thus leaving him alone to continue the war. In the end he made a request for seeds of flowers and plants of various kinds, and for technicians, workers and doctors to be taken with them to Mysore, and pointed out that other matters would be communicated later, because their mention in public would not be proper.[2]

After the audience, the envoys dined with de la Luzerne. The next day they dined with the principal ministers and on the 12th with Montmorin. They had their last meeting with de la Luzerne on September 2, when they presented a draft of an offensive and defensive alliance. Its terms were: The war against the English was to be prosecuted for a period of ten years. Tipu was to be assisted with ten thousand French troops, who would be under his command and whose expenses would be borne by him. After the conquest of the Carnatic, the French were to be given a territory attached to Pondicherry and Madras along with the surrounding area. Similarly Bengal, Bihar and other English possessions, after their occupation, would be handed over to the French.[3]

When the ambassadors had left India, Marechal de Castries was the Minister of Marine, and they had brought letters from Tipu addressed to him. But by the time they arrived in France, he had relinquished his office and had been replaced by Comte de la Luzerne. Castries had favoured the continuance of intrigues with the Indian princes against the English, and believed that it was still possible to revive French power in India. But de la Luzerne held the view that, owing to the greater resources of the English and their military superiority in the country, French influence could no longer be reasserted; nor was there any likelihood of the Indian powers uniting against the English. It was, therefore, decided to withdraw French troops from India and to concentrate them in the Isle of France, for only in this way could France maintain her position in the East.[4]

Owing to this new orientation of French policy along with the French government's assurance to the English that no negotiations

[1] *Ibid.*, ff. 35a-b; C[2] 174, ff. 246a-247b; F.O. 27/29, Dorset to Carmathian, Aug. 11, 1789, No. 57.

[2] A.N., C[2] 174, Address presented by the envoys, ff. 250a (in Persian with a French trans.)

[3] A.N., C[2] 189, f. 149a. (Copy of a letter in Persian presented by envoys to de la Luzerne on Sept. 2, 1788).

[4] Holden Furber, *John Company at Work*, pp. 73-4.

would be carried on with Tipu's envoys hostile to English interests, the failure of the embassy was a foregone conclusion.[1] Moreover, as France was at this time in the grip of social and economic crisis, which very soon led to the Revolution, she was not prepared to undertake any fresh commitments. The envoys were, therefore, informed that Louis XVI could not enter into any alliance with Tipu owing to the Treaty of Versailles (1783). In case, however, war broke out between the French and the English, and Tipu also entered it, the French would send troops to help him. These would be under Tipu's orders, and no peace would be made without his consent. The French king would not claim any conquest made in India, because he wanted only factories and trade.[2]

As regards the French policy in the Second Anglo-Mysore War, the king regretted the role of Bussy, and pointed out that it was a mistake on his part to have separated himself from his ally. To Tipu's request for craftsmen and technicians, who could improve the manufacture of arms and introduce new industries in his kingdom, the envoys were told that such persons could be arranged for. Some of them could go with them, while others would be sent later by a route other than via Mangalore to avoid giving the English any cause of complaint. French seeds and plants would also be made available, but spice and camphor trees did not grow in France and could be obtained from Moluccus island.[3]

Although the envoys had completed their mission, they were not anxious to leave. However, having run out of money, for they had not only spent Rs. 100,000 (250,000) livres which Tipu had given them for their expenses,[4] they had got into a debt of 49,414 livres for making various purchases.[5] Moreover, the French authorities were getting tired of the stay of "the expensive excellencies". De la Luzerne, therefore, wrote to the envoys on behalf of Louis XVI requesting them to leave because the cold weather was fast approaching. He also informed them that Tipu had written to Louis XVI to arrange for their departure as soon as possible.[6] So, ulti-

[1] I.O., Sec. despatches to Bengal (1788-1803), Sec. letter to Governor-General in Council, July. 15, 1788, p. 2; also F.O. 27/29, Dorset to Carmathian, 7& 14 Aug., 1788, Nos. 55, 58.

[2] A.N., C² 187, Louis XVI to Tipu, Aug. 16, 1788, f. 56a.

[3] A.N., C² 189, *Covnseil d'etat*, Aug. 7, 1789 ff. 37a-38a.

[4] A.N., C² 187, f. 54a. Tipu also wrote to the ministers in Paris to advance money to the ambassadors, if they required it.

[5] *Ibid.*, *Memoire*, Nov. 2, 1788, ff. 5a-b. The money was finally paid by the French Government to the merchants.

[6] A.N., C² 189, Launay to de la Luzerne, Sept. 21, 1788, f. 197a; *Ibid.*, de la Luzerne to Ruffin, Sept. 22, 1788, f. 199a. The stay of the envoys in Paris cost the French Government 2,63,122 livres. But the total expenditure on the embassy from the time it arrived in Pondicherry at the end of January 1787 to its return from France in May 1789 was 8,19,284 livres. (C² 187, ff. 319a *seq.*). In addition to

mately, the envoys left Paris for Brest on October 9, accompanied by Captain Macnamara, who was deputed to reach them safely to India and to act as the envoy of Louis XVI to Tipu Sultan. They were given rich presents for themselves and for their Sultan. On their way to Brest they passed through Orleans, Tours, Nantes and l' Orient, where they visited various factories. In Brest they visited some men-of-war, and were shown the naval monoeuvres.[1]

The envoys left Brest in the *Thytes* on November 17,1788. Captain Macnamara wanted to land at Mahé, but the boat having lost her passage owing to bad weather, made for Pondicherry, where it reached on May 11, 1789.[2] Tipu had made preparations on a grand scale to receive Macnamara with honours due to an envoy, and sent Zain ul-Abidin with horses and elephants to the frontier to recieve him.[3] But Macnamara remained behind to execute orders for the evacuation of Pondicherry in accordance with the new change in French policy,[4] and informed Tipu that he would visit Mangalore next November and bring with him the presents from Louis XVI which, being heavy, could not be sent by land with the ambassadors.[5] However, the ambassadors having secured permits from the Nawab of Arcot, proceeded after fifteen days by the land route to Coimbatore, where the Sultan then lay encamped.[6] Tipu was glad that they had brought with them "artists and workmen",[7] who would help

---

this, many articles of porcelain worth 24,000 livres were presented to Tipu (this does not include the value of other articles presented to him); and the articles of porcelain presented to the envoys were worth 6,000 livres. (*Ibid.*, f. 337a). One livre was equivalent to one British pound.

[1] A.N., C² 187, de Morlat to de la Luzerne, Nov. 3, 1788, ff. 10a-b; ambassadors to de la Luzerne, Nov. 17, 1788, ff. 24a-b.

[2] Tantet, *L'ambassade de Tippou*, pp. 28-9; A.N., C² 187, Macnamara to de la Luzerne, June 12, 1789, f. 83a.

[3] *Ibid.*, ff. 76a *seq.*

[4] Tantet, *L'ambassade de Tippou*, pp. 28-9. But in a letter to Tipu, Macnamara wrote that he had to stay back in Pondicherry in command of a man-of-war, because an English squadron had arrived in Madras. (A.N., C²187, Macnamara to Tipu, June 23, 1789, f. 79b.)

[5] *Ibid.*

[6] *Ibid.*, Macnamara to de la Luzerne, June 12, 1789, ff. 83a-b; Tantet, *L'ambassade de Tippou*, pp. 28-9.

[7] Ray, *Some India Office Letters of Tipu*, No. IV. Tipu had demanded 10 masters for casting cannon; 10 gunsmiths; 10 foremen for casting incendiary bombs; 10 workers of Seve porcelain; 10 glass-workers; 10 wool-carders; 10 watch-makers; 10 textile-makers; 10 printers of Oriental languages; 10 weavers; one skilful doctor and one surgeon; one engineer; one caster of bullets; clove plants; camphor trees; fruit trees of Europe; seeds of flowers of various kinds; seeds of linseed and 10 workers necessary for their cultivation, (C² 174, Address presented by the envoys to Louis XVI in Persian, ff. 250a-b, 257a-258b; French trans. ff. 251a *seq.* Shawwal 28, 1202 A.H./Aug. 1, 1788), However, the number of persons who agreed to enter Tipu's service were: 10 casters of cannon; 10 gunsmiths; 10 casters of bullets; 10 porcelain-workers; 10 glass-makers; 10 weavers of cloth; 10 tapestry-makers; 10 watch-makers; 10 farmers and workers of hemp;

introduce such industries in Mysore as were not known in the East: but he was disappointed at their failure to secure an offensive and defensive alliance with France.[1]

*The French Propose a Commercial Treaty with Tipu*

Meanwhile for various reasons, Tipu's relations with the French in India remained estranged. In September 1787 he occupied the territory of Kurangod Nair on the ground that the latter was in league with the Raja of Travancore and his other enemies. But the French regarded the territory under their protection. Besides, being situated on the banks of the river Mahi, it was of great importance to the trade of their port of Mahé; so they requested the Sultan to restore it to Kurangod Nair.[2] Tipu at first refused to recognise the claims of the French, but when the Raja of Colastri, whom he had appointed as an arbiter in the dispute, decided in their favour, he issued instructions to his officers on the Malabar coast to return the territory to them. But because of its lucrative spice trade it was not restored, and the Mysore officers began to collect duties on the imports and exports of Mahé which passed through the country of Kurangod Nair.[3] It seems that Tipu had issued secret orders not to cede the territory to the French, otherwise his officers would not have repeatedly ignored his orders.[4] His attitude in the affair was partly determined by the commercial importance of the territory, and partly by its strategic importance, but most of all by the unfriendly behaviour of the French on several occasions.

The French had been trying for a long time to dominate North Malabar in order to gain control over its spice trade. In 1774 Duprat, the French Commandant of Mahé, had monopolised the pepper trade of Kadattanad, and had informed the officers of Haidar that if they wished to buy pepper they could do so only through Mahé and not directly from Kadattanad. In 1773 he had helped the Zamorin to reoccupy Calicut, brought it under French suzerainty,

2 printers of Oriental languages; one physician; one surgeon; 2 engineers; 2 gardeners. Contracts with these persons were signed by the envoys. A watch-maker was to get Rs. 100 a month and an advance of Rs. 1,200. The doctor and surgeon were to get Rs. 200 a month each and an advance of Rs. 600. A gardener was to get Rs. 67 a month and an advance of Rs. 600. An engineer was to get Rs. 2000 a year. The lowest paid was the weaver and his wife. The former was to get Rs. 720 a year and the latter Rs. 380 a year. (A.N., $C^2$ 187, ff. 13a-16a; $C^2$ 189, ff. 256a-62a).

[1] Wilks, ii, p. 361, and Michaud, i, p. 140, say that the ambassadors remained in disgrace for some time.

[2] P.A.MS., Nos. 1089, 4565, 1199. Mahé being situated south of the mouth of the river Mahi, was very close to the territory of Kurangod Nair, which lay on the banks of the same river.

[3] *Ibid.*, Nos. 4571-4.

[4] A.N., $C^2$ 191, Canaple to Conway, March 29, 1789, No. 16.

and secured exclusive commercial privileges for the French, although it had been captured by Haidar.[1] During the American War of Independence they had been obliged to suspend their activities on the Malabar coast, but after the Treaty of Versailles (1783) they again revived the policy of inciting the Malabar chiefs against Tipu by giving them arms and protection in Mahé in order to secure commercial concessions from them. Thus they helped the ruler of Kadattanad in his revolt against Tipu, and obtained from him the complete monopoly of the spice trade in his kingdom.[2] Tipu resented the French intrigues and their attempts to interfere in Malabar affairs. He regarded the Malabar chiefs as his tributaries and was himself interested in the spice trade of the west coast. This explains the high-handed behaviour of his officers. They placed restrictions on Mahé's trade; they entered the town in pursuit of the Nairs, pillaged houses and carried away families. On one occasion even the French flag was torn[3]. When Tipu was informed by Conway about this, he ordered that those who had torn the French flag be punished and the inhabitants of Mahé were not be molested. Tipu also sent warnings to his *amildar*.[4] But in spite of this, conditions in Mahé did not improve.[5]

Tipu had of late become anxious at the intrigues of the English agents at the courts of Hyderabad, Poona, Gwalior and Nagpur against him. Still regarding the French as his friends, he requested them in November 1, 1788, through Lallée to inquire from the English the object of the treaty which they had made with the Nizam, for he suspected it to be specially directed against him. At the same time he proposed an alliance with the French. But the French authorities at Pondicherry replied that they could not enter into any agreement with him, and that they had no right to ask the English why they had made an alliance with the Nizam, since none of its clauses was directed against the French.[6]

The French had been complaining for some time that Tipu had placed restrictions upon their exporting sandalwood, pepper, cardamom and rice from his kingdom.[7] The reason why the Sultan had banned the export of rice from Mangalore to Mahé was that he believed that it was from the latter place that the English settlement

---

[1] Law de Lauristan, *Etat Politique de l'Inde en* 1777, Intro. pp. 22-4.

[2] P.A.MS., Nos. 4592, 4624.

[3] A.N., C[2] 191, Canaple to Conway, March 29, 1789, No. 16.

[4] *Ibid.*, Tipu to Conway, June 15, 1789, No. 16.

[5] But we should not take the French accounts of the high-handedness of Tipu's officers for granted. De Fresne himself admitted that he exaggerated these accounts in order to impress Tipu and thereby control the activities of his officers. (A.N., C[2]291, de Fresne to de la Luzerne, Aug. 7, 1790, No. 13.

[6] P.A.MS., Nos. 1006.

[7] *Ibid.*, No. 894.

of Tellicherry obtained its rice.[1] As regards the spice trade, the Sultan himself was interested in it and wanted to establish a state monopoly. Nevertheless, he was ready to grant concessions to the French in return for military aid against his enemies.

In the middle of 1786 Monneron was sent by the Pondicherry Government to Mysore with three urns of porcelain and 500 rifles as presents from Louis XVI. His object was first, to settle the mode of payment of the nineteen lakhs of rupees which Tipu had advanced to the French in the Second Anglo-Mysore War; secondly, to give permission for exporting goods worth three or four lakhs from Mysore which had been purchased; and thirdly, to enter into a commercial treaty for the exclusive purchase of pepper, sandalwood and cardamom.[2] To the first question Tipu pointed out that he did not want the money back. What he most valued was French friendship. As regards Monneron's second demand, the Sultan replied that he had banned exports from Mysore by way of the Carnatic because the English benefited from this trade. However, now he would give orders to his *amildars* that linen be sold to merchants who held letters from Cossigny. The Sultan also promised to give permission to buy spices from his possessions[3]. But as no treaty was entered into, the French were skeptic about the Sultan's verbal promises in view of his open policy to preserve his own monopoly of the Malabar trade.[4]

Early in October 1788, the French sent the following proposals to the Sultan for a commercial treaty: They promised neither to give help to his enemies nor to form any connections with the rulers on the Malabar coast without his consent. The French Company's vessels and those of Tipu were to help each other if they were attacked by the country powers. The Company was to be given facilities to purchase the annual produce of pepper in his kingdom and of a quantity, which would be stipulated, of sandalwood, cardamom, cotton yarn, wool, cotton cloth, gum, ivory and other goods. The prices and conditions of purchase would be settled by mutual arrangement. These exports would be paid for in cannon, muskets, ammunition, men-of-war, silk, woollen goods or other articles from Europe,

[1] *Ibid.*, Nos. 4631-32. Goa also obtained its rice from Mangalore and supplied it to Tellicherry. Actually there was a great deal of smuggling in rice, and Tipu's officers participated in it. To prevent this the Sultan decided to purchase all the rice of the coast and sell it himself. (A.N., C²191, Canaple to Conway, May 12, 1789, No. 16.)

[2] A.N., C²172, Cossigny's instructions to Monneron, envoy to Tipu Sultan, Feb. 2, 1786, ff. 197a-198b.

[3] *Ibid.*, Monneron to Cossigny, Sept. 14, 1786, ff. 201a *seq.*

[4] *Ibid.*, But Cossigny states that owing to the removal of restrictions Pondicherry's trade improved, and daily goods from Mysore began to enter the town. (*Ibid.*, Cossigny to de Castries, July 6, 1786, ff. 45a *seq.*)

as demanded by Tipu. In case there was a balance, it would be paid for in bullion or silver.[1]

If Tipu Sultan was not prepared to agree to these proposals, the French Company instead asked to be given facilities for buying the articles produced in Mysore from the merchants of the country without any competition, at prices to be fixed annually, with the joint approval of Tipu, the Company's agents and four principal merchants of the kingdom.[2] The French further proposed that the French Company should be allowed to build factories and warehouses on the coast or in places suitable for its trade. Tipu should give land necessary for the purpose and permission to enclose it with suitable walls. The Company should also be allowed to move its goods inside the kingdom either by land or water without paying any duties. The duties on the European goods which had been sold and those on the Indian goods to be exported would be paid only once a year. But in case the European goods were not sold and the Company wanted to export them, it would not be required to pay duty a second time. The Company would be permitted to export annually a certain quantity of rice from Mangalore, or from other ports of Mysore, without paying duty. The Company would also not pay any duty on gold and silver, or on those articles meant for the use of its employees. All the servants of the Company, both European and Indian, would be subject to its civil jurisdiction.[3]

These proposals were rejected by the Sultan for the very good reason that their acceptance would give the French complete monopoly over the trade and commerce of his kingdom—a thing he could not tolerate. Besides, what he desired was not so much a commercial treaty as an offensive and defensive alliance. However, as the war with the English became imminent, Tipu, in order to secure the friendship of the French, gave them permission to export sandalwood, spices and rice from Mangalore. But this did not please them, for the concession fell far short of their proposals, and the prices demanded for the articles exceeded the market rates.[4] Tipu was, however, not prepared to grant them any further concessions unless and until they agreed to render him military assistance against his enemies.

[1] P.A.MS., No. 1089.
[2] *Ibid.*
[3] *Ibid.*
[4] *Ibid.*, No. 4609.

CHAPTER VIII

# EMBASSY TO CONSTANTINOPLE

In 1784 Tipu Sultan sent Osman Khan to Constantinople to find out whether an embassy to the Ottoman Government would be fruitful. On receiving a favourable reply, he deputed Ghulam Ali Khan, Nurullah Khan, Lutf Ali Khan and Jafar Khan, with Sayyid Jafar and Khwaja Abdul Qadir as Secretaries, to proceed to Constantinople.[1] From there they were required to go first to Paris and then to London to dissuade the kings of France and England from giving assistance to the Nizam and the Marathas in the Maratha-Mysore War.[2] But as they were recalled from Constantinople, they could not fulfil this part of their mission. Meanwhile, Tipu had despatched a special embassy to the Court of Versailles.[3]

Tipu decided to send an embassy to Constantinople in order to secure confirmation of his title to the throne of Mysore from the Ottoman Caliph.[4] The idea of securing an investiture from the Caliph was no innovation on the part of Tipu. With the exception of the Mughal Emperors who regarded themselves as Caliphs in their kingdom in their own right, a number of Muslim rulers of India had secured confirmation of their title to the throne from the then ruling Caliphs. Thus Iltutmush and Mahmud of Ghazna had obtained their investiture from the Abbasid Caliphs of Baghdad, while Muhammad b. Tughlaq, Firoz Shah Tughlaq and Mahmud of Malwa had secured it from the Abbasid Caliphs of Egypt. Now that the Caliphate had become vested in the Ottoman dynasty, Tipu wanted to obtain his investiture from the Ottoman ruler in order to legalise his status which appeared to be anomalous. The Nizam, the Nawab of Carnatic, and the Marathas possessed legal titles to their territories. Even Haidar Ali, Tipu's father, had a legal position: He had been a *dalavayi* of the Raja of Mysore, and had procured, through the good offices of Basalat Jung, the Government of the Subah of Sira from the Mughal Emperor.[5] Tipu, on the other hand, was regarded as a usurper, for he had dethroned the Raja of Mysore who was a tributary of the Mughals. This was very embarrassing to the Sultan who,

[1] Wilks, ii, p. 361.
[2] N.A., Sec. Pro., Jan. 5, 1787, No. 3.
[3] See p. 116, *supra*.
[4] For a further discussion of this point, see Dr. I. H. Qureshi's article, "*The Purpose of Tipu Sultan's Embassy to Constantinople*" in J.I.H., xxiv, 1945, pp. 77-84.
[5] *Ibid.*, pp. 81, 83; also Wilks, i, 491-92

therefore, decided to send envoys to the Caliph to secure confirmation of his position.[1]

He would have liked to get such a confirmation from the Mughal Emperor, but he knew he would not succeed. In 1783 he had tried to obtain the *sanad* of Arcot and a rank of 7,000 through Mukand Rao, his *wakil* in Delhi. He had offered to pay the *peshkush* and a large sum of money to the Emperor. Montigny, the French representative in Delhi, had also canvassed on his behalf, and had won over Nawab Amir-ul-umara (Muhammad Shafi Khan) and other nobles to his side.[2] At first the Emperor Shah Alam was inclined to the French, and was ready to form an alliance with them with a view to expelling the British from India.[3] But Major Brown, the English Company's representative in Delhi, and Majdud-ud-daulah, the favourite minister of Shah Alam who was a great supporter of the English, defeated the schemes of Tipu's *wakils* and the French.[4] The result was that Tipu not only failed to obtain the grant of Arcot, he did not even get any *khilat*.[5] Thus, having failed to secure sanction for his authority from Delhi, Tipu decided to obtain it from Constantinople, realising that any recognition from the Ottoman Caliph would be of far greater value than that from the effete Mughal Emperor.[6]

Besides desiring to legalise his position, Tipu wanted to obtain the Caliph's military assistance against the English who were his most formidable enemies and were bent upon his destruction. His father, Haidar Ali, had obtained in 1775 a body of 1000 men from Shiraz in Persia;[7] there was no reason why, similarly, he should not get some troops from Turkey. And to secure the success of his mission and emphasise the urgency of his demand, he tried to stir up the religious passions of the Caliph by informing him that the English had possessed themselves of Bengal, the Carnatic, and other parts of India which belonged to the Mughals, and that they were oppressing the Muslims, forcibly converting them to Christianity, and turning mosques into churches.[8]

Tipu, it must be remembered, was eager to promote the trade,

[1] Tipu's anxiety in this matter is evident from the fact that at the time of negotiating peace with the Marathas in 1787, he insisted that the Peshwa should in future address him as Padshah. (See pp. 107-08, *supra*).

[2] N.A., O.R. 91, Enclosure from Major Brown, Sept. 18, 1783.

[3] N.A., O.R. 88, Bussy to Shah Alam, Sept. 10, 1785.

[4] Cal. Per. Cor., vii, No. 315; O.R. 84.

[5] N.A., O.R. 91. The *wakil* was told to make a *khilat* for Tipu at his own expense and present it as a gift from the Emperor. As regards the *sanad* for Arcot, he was informed that it was being prepared. He was then dismissed.

[6] N.A., Sec. Pro., Nov. 12, 1787, Nizam to Cossigny, Cons. No. 10.

[7] Rice, *Mysore and Coorg*, i, p. 268. Haidar sent another embassy for more troops, but it was lost in the Gulf of Cutch.

[8] *Hukm-namah*, MS. No. 1677, ff. 14a-15b.

commerce and industry of his kingdom, for he held the view that the political decline of the Muslims was the result of their indifference to trade and industry, and that it was because the Europeans were seriously applying themselves to these that they were bringing Muslim countries under their domination.[1] The ambassadors were, therefore, required to obtain commercial privileges in the Ottoman Empire and technicians from Constantinople who would introduce various industries into Mysore.[2] As the English agent from Basra reported: "We have reasons to believe that the embassy to the Porte is for the purpose of obtaining *firmaunds* to establish factories in the Turkish dominions...."[3] The ambassadors were also instructed to land at Masqat in order to strengthen the trade and friendly relations which already existed with Oman, and on their way up the Persian Gulf to touch Bushire and obtain commercial concessions from the Shah of Persia. They were further instructed to make a marine survey of the Persian Gulf and to study the geography, the social, political and economic conditions of the important places visited by them in the course of their journey, and to keep a record of their experiences.[4]

Ghulam Ali Khan, the leader of the delegation, was instructed to enter into a treaty with the Ottoman Government on the following basis: First, the Mysore and Ottoman Governments should always remain on friendly terms with each other. Secondly, the Ottoman Government should send Tipu a body of troops whose expenses would be borne by him, and they would be sent back to Constantinople at his expense, whenever they would be required by the Caliph. Thirdly, the Caliph should send Tipu technicians who should be able to make muskets, guns, glass, chinaware and other things. In return Tipu would send such workmen as were available in his dominion and required by the Caliph. And lastly, Tipu should be given trade facilities in the Ottoman Empire. In return, he would give similar facilities and privileges to the Ottoman Government in the Mysore kingdom, Tipu, in addition, proposed that he should be given the port of Basra, and in return he would present the Caliph the port of Mangalor.[5]

The ambassadors left Seringapatam on November 17, 1785, and sailed from Tadri, a small port on the Malabar coast, on the night of Wednesday, March 9, 1786, in four ships named *Ghurab-i-Surati*,

[1] *Ibid.*, f. 16b.
[2] *Ibid.*
[3] N.A., Sec. Pro., Jan. 5, 1787, from Basra, Sept. 24, 1786, No. 3. *firmaunds* is a corruption of *farman* (pl. *faramin*).
[4] In accordance with Tipu's instructions the envoys kept a diary of the journey entitled *Waqai-i Manazil-i Rum*, ed. Mohibbul Hasan. For Tipu's relations with the Imam of Oman and Karim Khan see *infra*, pp. 131-32.
[5] *Hukm-namah*, ff. 10b-11b; 15b-16a; also *Waqai*, p. 150.

*Fakhr-ul-Marakib*, *Fath-i-Shahi Muazi* and *Nabi Bakhsh*. They were accompanied by a large staff of about 900, comprising secretaries, interpreters, attendants, sweepers, cooks and soldiers, and carried with them considerable quantities of cloth, sandalwood products, spices, gold and silver coins of Mysore, rich dresses, jewellery and four elephants.[1] Some of these articles were to serve as advertisements for the products of Tipu's kingdom and were to be sold at various ports of call. The remaining articles were intended as presents to the nobles, high officials and rulers of Oman, Persia and Turkey. As regards the elephants, one was to be presented to the Ottoman Sultan, and the other was to be sold to realise the expenses of the journey, while the other two were meant for the kings of France and England, where the envoys were required to proceed after fulfilling their assignment in Constantinople.[2]

On leaving Tadri, the ships headed straight for the Arabian coast and reached Masqat on April 8. The envoys were received by Khalfan b. Muhammad, Governor of Masqat, and his two sons. Later, Nurullah called on the Khalfan and gave him two letters, one of which was addressed to him and the other to the Imam of Oman. Since the latter was at Rustaq, his capital, the letter was sent to him. On the 26th the Imam himself arrived in Masqat. He inquired from Nurullah about the position of the English in India, and instructed the Khalfan to take a personal interest in the affairs of Tipu.[3]

Meanwhile, the envoys had been able to dispose of some of the goods. Different varieties of cloth and shawls were sold to Maoji Seth, an Indian broker at Masqat. Sandalwood was sold through him at 57 *hun haidari* per candy, and cardamoms weighing $4\frac{1}{2}$ candies were sold at the rate of 15 *huns* per *ratl*.[4]

On the 25th June the envoys left Masqat, and visited a number of ports and islands before reaching Bushire on the 23rd July. Shaikh Nasir, Governor of Bushire, sent his son with a message of welcome. He himself could not come as he had to proceed on a campaign. The envoys were informed that Shaikh Nasir intended to send a mission to Mysore in order to seek Tipu's permission for establishing a factory at Mangalore, and in return to allow him to build one at Bushire. They were requested to recommend his proposals to the Sultan. The envoys, accordingly, gave letters to the representative of Shaikh Nasir, addressed to their master, endorsing the proposals.[5]

[1] *Waqai*, pp. 1-2.

[2] *Hukm-namah*, ff. 2b-3a, 4a. The elephants died before they reached Basra.

[3] *Waqai*, pp. 3-6.

[4] *Ibid.*, p. 6. According to Manesty, 200 candies of pepper and some piece-goods were sold at Masqat. (I.O. Factory Records, Manesty to Court of Directors, Sept. 5, 1786, f. 348b.)

[5] *Waqai*, pp. 24-5.

On reaching Basra, they sent a letter to Jafar Khan, king of Persia, that Tipu was anxious to promote trade relations with Persia, and desired that Persian merchants should come to his ports for the purpose of trade.[1]

On July 28, the envoys left Bushire, reaching the island of Kharag on the 30th night. On the night of August 7, the dhow and *Fath-i-Shahi*, along with 17 other vessels, all sailed together from Kharag island for fear of the Kaab pirates, who infected the route to Basra. They anchored off the island of Khargu, which they left on the 11th, touching the next day the ports of Dilum, Bung and Bahragan. They then entered the Khor Musa.[2]

The progress of the ships up the Shatt-ul-Arab was very slow owing to bad weather and the *shamal*. On the morning of the 17th they entered the Khor Basra. The envoys had already sent a messenger to Ibrahim Agha, the *Mutesellim* of Basra, informing him of their arrival; so after they had passed the villages of Muhammareh, Derbend and other villages, situated on either side of the Shatt-ul-Arab, they were received by Haji Muhammad Effendi Defterdar and Haji Jawwad, the Kaptan Pasha, who had come with eight boats to meet them and escort them to Basra owing to the danger from the Kaab pirates. The Turkish officers left two of their officers for the protection of the *dao saif*, and set out with the rest to protect the other ships that were following behind.[3] Meanwhile, news arrived that on the night of August 18, the *Nabi Bakhsh* had caught fire and sunk, causing the death of 50 persons, including women and children. The remaining persons were saved by the efforts and timely help of Jafar Khan, one of the envoys.[4]

On the arrival of the *Fath-i-Shahi* and the *Ghurab-i-Surati*, the *dao saif* raised anchor, and together they reached Basra on August 22.[5] A few days after they wrote to Sulaiman Pasha that they had arrived at Basra, and that they would set out as soon as they received his reply. On October 3 the letters came from Ahmad Agha, the *Kahya*[6] of Sulaiman Pasha[7], informing him that he was glad to hear of their

[1] *Ibid.*, p. 47.

[2] *Ibid.*, pp. 25 *seq.*

[3] *Ibid.*, pp. 36-9.

[4] *Ibid.*, pp. 40-1. Manesty says between 40 and 50 persons perished. In addition, 400 candies of pepper, a small quantity of sandalwood and other articles were also lost. The articles that remained with the envoys were 600 candies of pepper, 50 candies of sandalwood and 15 candies of cardamom. (I.O. Factory Records, Manesty to Court of Directors, Sept. 5, 1786, f. 248b.)

[5] *Waqai*, p. 42.

[6] *Kahya* is the Turkish version of the Persian *Kat-Khuda*, literally "lord of the house" or Major-domo. Here it means the chief minister in a provincial government under the Pasha. (Longrigg, *Four Centuries of Modern Iraq*, p. 354; Gibb, *Islamic Society and the West*, vol. i, part 2, p. 200.)

[7] Sulaiman Pasha was a Georgian freedman of Hasan Pasha, Viceroy of Baghdad. Owing to his abilities he became the *Mutesellim* of Basra in 1765. When the Persians under Sadiq Khan invaded Basra he defended it with courage. But

arrival, and that the Governor had issued orders to the *Mutesellim* to send them with an escort to Samawah, where troops would be waiting to bring them to Baghdad. On being told of this, the *Mutesellim* assured the envoys that they would be able to set out by October 25. But for various reasons their departure had to be postponed again and again. In the first place, the boats in which they were to sail could not be arranged by the Basra authorities. In the second, it was found that the Euphrates route was unsafe because of the refractory conduct of the Khazail tribe.[1] The envoys felt disappointed and angry, blaming the Basra Government for placing obstacles in their way, and threatened to leave for Constantinople by another route. Luckily, however, news came from Sulaiman Pasha that the Euphrates route was now safe, and that the envoys should be allowed to proceed.[2] Accordingly, they sailed with a retinue of 300 men on December 8 in four boats.[3] But on reaching Qurnah on the 15th, they were informed by Shaikh Suwaini, the chief of the Muntafiq tribe, then virtually in possession of Basra and the neighbouring areas, to return to Basra at once.[4] It appears that the Shaikh wanted the envoys to pay him duty on the goods they were carrying, and that unless this was done he would not allow them to proceed.[5] Moreover, it was not known for certain as to who was the Governor of Baghbad at this time; for rumours were afoot that Sulaiman Pasha had been deposed and in his place Sulaiman al-Shawi, chief of the Ubaid and head of the Shawi family, had been appointed Pasha of Baghdad.[6] Owing to these unsettled conditions

Basra was captured and he was sent as prisoner to Shiraz. He was released after four years. In July 1780 he was appointed Pasha of Baghdad and held that office until his death in 1802 at the age of 82. (Longrigg, *Four Centuries of Modern Iraq*, pp. 187-220.)

[1] Khazail, a large tribe which occupied an area extending from Kufa to Samawah and a portion of the adjoining Shamiya desert, are strong and warlike and are all Shiites. They were a great source of trouble to the Turkish Government, because they interrupted communications between Basra and Baghdad by the Euphrates river. [*Description du pachalik de Baghdad*, p. 59; *Bombay Selections* (1600-1800), p. 324.]

[2] *Waqai*, pp. 97-8.

[3] *Ibid.*, p. 103. Manesty says that the envoys left with 300 men, and gives the date of their departure as Dec. 7 (I.O. Factory Records, Manesty to Court of Directors, Dec. 20, 1786, f. 266a.)

[4] *Waqai*, pp. 116-17. Suwaini al-Abdullah was at first loyal to the Turkish Government, but later revolted, and in 1785 occupied Basra. Early in July 1787, however, he was assassinated by a negro slave. (Longrigg, *Four Centuries of Modern Iraq*, pp. 195 *seq.*)

[5] *Waqai*, p. 114.

[6] *Ibid.*, pp. 116 *seq.* Sulaiman al-Shawi was at first friendly with Sulaiman Pasha. But later on, jealous at the advancement of Ahmad Agha, a Georgian, whom Sulaiman Pasha made his *Kahya*, he revolted. He defeated the Turkish troops and hovered round Baghdad ready to attack it. Meanwhile, a sudden rumour spread that he had been appointed Pasha of Baghdad. For a time Sulaiman Pasha himself believed it. (Longrigg, *Four Centuries of Modern Iraq*, pp. 203-4.)

the *Mutesellim* advised the envoys to return to Basra. Accordingly, they sailed back, reaching Basra on the night of December 24. It was not until the *Mutesellim* was assured that the rumours regarding the dismissal of Sulaiman Pasha were baseless, and received a letter from the latter ordering him to send the envoys immediately to Qurnah, where 500 horsemen would be waiting to escort them to Baghdad, that he advised them to set out again. Meanwhile, the Ottoman Sultan also wrote to Sulaiman Pasha that Tipu's ambassadors, who had come to discuss matters relating to trade, should be at once sent to him.[1]

In the course of their stay in Basra the envoys disposed of various articles through Abdullah Yahudi. Sewa and Prem, the two agents of Maoji Seth, also helped the envoys in their transactions. There was, of course, a great deal of haggling, and instances were not wanting of customers getting the feeling of being cheated. Abdullah, for example, had purchased some bales of cloth. When he took them to his house, he found them to be defective. So he wanted to return them, but Nurullah refused to take them back.[2]

The rates at Masqat and at Kharag had been favourable, yet goods had not been sold there, because it was expected that at Basra the rates would be higher. However, since the rates were found to be lower, Nurullah had to fix the prices so that the sale could be effected. Black pepper was to be sold at 30 *huns* per candy; black cloth at Rs. 1-12 as. per *anga*. But, since even at these rates it was difficult to find customers, a further reduction of prices was made. Thus black pepper was sold at 39 *huns* per candy.[3]

On their return to Basra, they received a message from Ibrahim Agha to remain on their boats for a few days longer, during which Suwaini would arrive, and then they could leave.[4] Nurullah agreed, but soon, realising that the Turkish officers were not helpful, he informed Ibrahim Agha that if his departure did not take place within a few days, he would hire a small boat, and leave with Jafar Khan for Baghdad, and from there arrange the recall of the others.[5] The *Mutesellim* tried to dissuade him from taking this step, telling him that Suwaini would soon be coming to Basra, and the matter would be discussed with him. Besides, favourable reports had already arrived from Baghdad. Sulaiman Pasha had been confirmed in his office, and had sent 500 horsemen to escort them to Baghdad. The Turkish Sultan had issued a *farman* that Tipu's *wakils* were respectable and trustworthy and, having come to discuss the question of

[1] *Waqai*, pp. 117 *seq*.
[2] *Ibid*., p. 82.
[3] *Ibid*., pp. 64-5,69.
[4] *Ibid*., p. 122.
[5] *Ibid*., p. 130.

exchange of Mangalore with Basra and other matters, should be at once sent to Constantinople.[1] In spite of all this, Nurullah remained distrustful of the Basra authorities. But in the end, after strong assurances were given and promises made by the *Mutesellim* that the envoys would soon be able to leave, Nurullah gave up his plan of setting out without the help of the Basra Government. But now there was the difficulty of transport, for the ambassadors had still a large number of men with them. Moreover, differences had arisen between Ghulam Ali Khan and Nurullah Khan on account of mutual jealousies and rivalries. In consequence, Ghulam Ali refused to travel in the company of Nurullah, and began to make arrangements to proceed alone. Owing to all this much time was wasted. In the end, after much persuasion, Ghulam Ali changed his mind and agreed to travel together with other members of the embassy.[2]

The envoys left Basra by the Tigris route on February 10, 1787,[3] with a retinue of 400 men, including 200 sepoys trained in the European fashion. The three hundred thousand rupees and the rich presents which they carried had created a sensation in the country. When they reached Baghdad on April 25, escorted by 500 horsemen who had been sent to meet them at Samawah, they were received by Sulaiman Pasha with great honour. From Baghdad they went to pay visits to Najaf and Karbala, and returned after 20 days.[4] They set out from Baghdad on May 29, escorted by the *qapiji bashi* sent by the Sultan from Constantinople. They travelled overland via Mosul and Diarbeker, and reached Scutari on the 1st September. They entered Constantinople on the 25th, and were lodged in one of the palaces of the city. On the 1st October, the Grand Wazir granted them a public audience, but received them without any extraordinary ceremony. They presented to him rich dresses, jewellery and 70,000 Venetian sequins. In return they received robes of honour.[5] Later, the Grand Wazir gave a magnificent fête in their honour at the village of Kelhana, where first the Turkish soldiers performed their exercises, and then "the Indian sepoys went through the European exercises with great regularity and quickness." All the high officials were present at the function, and the Sultan, Abdul Hamid 1, himself was there incognito.[6]

On November 5 the Sultan received the envoys with honour and invested them with sable furs and the two secretaries with ermine

[1] *Ibid.*, pp. 125, 133, 150. [2] *Ibid.*, pp. 134 *seq.*

[3] I.O. *Factory Records, Persia and the Persian Gulf*, No. 18, Manesty to Court of Directors, March 15, 1787, f. 286.

[4] Affaires Étrangères Bl 107 (Archives Nationales, Paris), Rousseau to de Castries, April 25, 1787, No. 39; also F.O. 78/8-1787, Robert Ainslie to Carmathian, June 9, 1787, f. 96b.

[5] *Ibid.*, Oct. 20, 1787, ff. 216 b-17a.

[6] *Ibid.*, Oct. 25, 1787, f. 235a.

furs.[1] Meanwhile plague had broken out in Constantinople, and many persons belonging to the embassy died. The severe cold weather, to which the Mysoreans were not accustomed, also took a heavy toll of their lives. So that by the end of January 1788, out of their retinue of 400 men, only 70 had survived. Ghulam Ali Khan was dangerously ill. For a change of climate, therefore, the envoys moved to Scutari on the Asian coast.[2]

It has been mentioned above that the envoys were required to proceed from Constantinople to France and thence to England. Accordingly, after their arrival at the Ottoman capital, they began to press the French ambassador to make arrangements for their journey to France. Meanwhile, Tipu had sent a mission directly to France.[3] It had stayed there for over five months and cost the French exchequer a large sum of money. The French Government was therefore not prepared to receive another mission, particularly in view of the worsening economic situation in the country. Moreover, the French Government had changed its policy in India, and it looked upon a second embassy from Tipu not only serving no purpose, but likely to involve it in an embarrassing position *vis-à-vis* England, whom it had promised not to give any cause of provocation.[4] That is why the Comte de Montmorin, advised the French ambassador in Constantinople to dissuade Tipu's envoys from proceeding to Paris. But if they insisted on coming, they were to be informed that they would be treated like the envoys of any other foreign power, and that no special treatment would be shown to them as had been done in the case of the first embassy.[5] Owing to these reasons the envoys gave up the idea of going to France and decided to return to India. Meanwhile, Tipu had also sent instructions to them to return.

On March 4 the envoys had a farewell audience with the Sultan,[6] and at the end of the month they sailed for Alexandria. From there they proceeded up the Nile to Cairo, and thence crossed to Suez. From Suez they sailed to Jeddah, and then went to Mecca and Medina to make the pilgrimage according to the instructions of Tipu Sultan.[7] After this they set out on their homeward journey from Medina via Jeddah and reached Calicut on December 29, 1789. They arrived at Tipu's camp in the neighbourhood of the Travancore Lines early in January 1790.

[1] *Ibid.*, Nov. 10, 1787, f. 241a.

[2] *Ibid.*, 78/9-1788, ff. 22a-b.

[3] *Affaires Étrangères*, Bl 448, *Correspondance Consulaire—Constantinople*—1787-90 (Archives Nationales, Paris), Choiseul-gouffier to de la Luzerne, Oct. 30, 1788.

[4] F. O. 27/29, Dorset to Carmathian, Aug. 7, 1788, No. 55.

[5] *Affaires Étrangères—Turquie* (Archives Nationales, Paris), Montmorin to Choiseul-gouffier, Aug. 22, 1788, vol. 178, f. 44a.

[6] F.O. 78/9-1788, March 8, 1788, f. 63b.

[7] *Ibid.*, March 25, 1788, ff. 68a, 76b.

The embassy had cost the Mysore Government a large sum of money, and, in addition, the envoys had suffered all kinds of privations in the course of the journey. Three of the four boats in which they had travelled to Basra had been wrecked, causing great loss of life and property. Many of their retinue had died of dysentery, fever, cold and plague. Out of about 900 men who had left the shores of Malabar, only a handful returned to their homes.

In spite of the enormous expense, great suffering and loss of life, the embassy was able to secure from the Ottoman Sultan only the letters patent, which gave Tipu permission to assume the title of an independent king, and the right to strike coins and to have the *khutba* read in his name. The envoys were also given for Tipu friendly letters, *khilats,* a sword and a shield studded with precious stones by the Caliph and his Grand Wazir.[1] But the embassy failed to obtain either any commercial concessions or military help.

It must be remembered that at this period the very existence of Turkey was threatened by Catherine II, Empress of Russia, and Joseph II, Emperor of Austria, who had entered into an agreement in 1787 to partition the European provinces of the Ottoman Empire, and to set on the throne of Constantinople Catherine's grandson, Constantine. Faced with these dangers, Turkey was provoked into declaring war against Russia on August 15, 1787. From February of the following year she had to fight Austria also, which, as Russia's ally, had declared war against her. Turkey could not expect any assistance from France, her traditional ally, which was occupied with ever-increasing troubles at home. But she could count upon the support of England which had entered the lists in alliance with Prussia and Holland in 1788 in order to restore and maintain the balance of power in south-eastern Europe in favour of Turkey. In fact, the Younger Pitt was actually trying to mediate peace between Turkey and her enemies, Austria and Russia. Under these circumstances, the Ottoman Sultan could not afford to antagonise Britain by entering into an alliance with Tipu. The contemporary sources do not throw much light on the British attitude towards this embassy. But judging from their relations with Tipu Sultan, it could not have been anything but hostile. Manesty, the English agent at Basra, writing to the Court of Directors on September 5, 1786, observed; "The *Wakils* want to obtain *firmaunds* to establish factories in Turkish dominions for selling the produce of his kingdom. We think this is a circumstance very material for the Honourable Court of Directors to be acquainted with, as we apprehend it precludes all hopes of your servants at Tellicherry being able to provide pepper for your

[1] *Waqai*, p. 155; Kirmani, p. 328; J.I.H., vol. xxiv, April and Aug. 1945, p. 84, n. 28.

homeward ships."[1] It is obvious from this statement that the British could not have watched with complacence the activities and plans of the ambassadors. On the contrary, they must have done their best to frustrate them with the help of the great influence which they commanded both at Baghdad and Constantinople.

[1] I.O. *Factory Records*, Manesty to Court of Directors, Sept., 5, 1786, No. 18, f. 249a

CHAPTER IX

# REBELLION IN COORG AND MALABAR

EARLY in 1789 the Coorgs again broke out into open revolt against the Mysore Government. Vir Raja, who had been in confinement in the fort of Periapatam for the last four years, escaped with his family at midnight about the middle of December 1788, and took refuge at Kurchi in Kiggatnad.[1] But soon after he fell into the hands of the Kottayam Raja who compelled him to cede three of the valuable districts belonging to Coorg. After purchasing his freedom, the Raja returned to Coorg, and with the assistance of his followers surrounded the camp of the Kottayam Raja, who had ascended the Ghats to take possession of the districts ceded to him, and compelled him not only to return the document extorted from him but also to renounce all claims to the Wynaad country.[2]

After this, Vir Raja turned his attention to the Mysoreans who were in occupation of Coorg. In a short time he succeeded in expelling them, including the new settlers who had been settled in the country by Tipu's orders. He then established his camp at Siddesvara, and from there carried on raids into Mysore, seizing large numbers of cattle and considerable supplies of grain. Hearing of this, Tipu sent a large force under Ghulam Ali, Ghazi Khan and Dil Delair Khan to crush Vir Raja. They entered by way of Siddesvara. The Coorgs disputed every inch of ground, but were defeated, and Ghulam Ali captured large supplies of grain and many prisoners. But he could not complete his task of crushing the Coorgs, for at this time revolt broke out in Malabar and he was ordered by Tipu to proceed there. On the march, he was attacked by the Coorgs in the Kodantura pass, but he defeated them and reached Payavur safely. Owing to the unsettled state in Coorg and the west coast, Tipu despatched Muhammad Raza, Azam Ali Khan, Fazal Khan and Jean Castorez to the help of Ghulam Ali. This reinforcement took the Heggalaghat route. Vir Raja took up his post at the entrance of the pass, made a surprise attack on the Mysoreans and dispersed them, capturing their baggage and killing and wounding a number of them.[3]

Alarmed at this news, Tipu sent his brother-in-law, Burhan-ud-din, to Coorg. Burhan was required to suppress the Coorgs by strengthening the four forts of Kushalnagar (Fraserpet), Mercara, Beppunad and

[1] *Tarikh-i-Coorg*, f. 27b.
[2] *Ibid.*, f. 32b.
[3] *Ibid.*, ff. 32a-35a.

Bhagamandala. But while he was proceeding to Mercara, he was attacked by Vir Raja and sustained considerable loss. So he returned to Seringapatam, and after informing Tipu of the situation in Coorg,[1] concerted with him another campaign. Burhan set out with a large army, and Tipu himself left the capital early in September 1789. But Burhan did not succeed in defeating Vir Raja who captured the three Mysore forts. Mercara still remained in the hands of the Mysoreans, but it was isolated and liable to fall at any moment.[2] Tipu himself could not visit Coorg because he had to proceed to Malabar which was blazing up in revolt, and as soon as he had suppressed the rising in Malabar, war broke out with the English. Coorg thus remained unsubdued.

*Rebellion in Malabar*

Haidar first came in contact with Malabar in 1757 when he sent his brother-in-law, Makhdum Ali, with some troops to the assistance of the Raja of Palghat who was at war with the Zamorin of Calicut. Makhdum Ali advanced to the sea coast, and compelled the Zamorin not only to restore to the Raja of Palghat his territory, but also to make a military contribution of twelve lakhs of rupees to be paid in instalments. The money was never paid, but it was not until 1766 that Haidar was able to turn his thoughts to Malabar.

Malabar was at that time divided into a number of petty states constantly fighting with each other. North Malabar consisted of the Nair principalities of Chirakkal, Kadattanad, Kottayam, Kurangod Nair and the Moplah principality of Cannanore which owed nominal allegiance to Chirakkal. South Malabar was divided between the Zamorin of Calicut and the Raja of Cochin, who had been for some time past the victim of the aggression of both the Zamorin and the Raja of Travancore.

Haidar invaded Malabar in January 1766, and by about the middle of April succeeded in subduing its chiefs. He then returned to Coimbatore. But he had not been there long when he heard of a revolt in Malabar. He, therefore, marched back, and with great ruthlessness suppressed the rising. The Nairs, however, were not crushed, and soon they again raised the banner of revolt. During the Second Anglo-Mysore War, Malabar became the battleground for the Mysore and English armies, and a large portion of it was occupied by the latter. But after the conclusion of the Treaty of Mangalore, Tipu recovered possession of it. Tipu was anxious to strengthen his hold over Malabar because of its spice trade, and because, as the Second Anglo-Mysore War had taught him, of its strategic importance for the safety

[1] *Tarikh-i-Coorg*, ff. 35b-36a.
[2] Rice, *Mysore and Coorg*, iii, p. 113.

of Mysore. But the exactions of his revenue collectors, combined with the independent spirit of the inhabitants and the English instigations to the Rajas to shake off Tipu's authority, had caused rebellion in the province. Owing to misgovernment, the Moplahs of Ernad and Walavanad were also discontented. The Nairs were led by Ravi Varma belonging to the house of Zamorin, while the leader of the Moplahs was Goorkul of Manjeri (a sub-division of Ernad, south of Calicut). To keep Ravi Varma quiet Tipu had granted him a *jagir* in 1784, and in order to establish good government he had separated the civil from the military authority. Arshad Beg, who was in charge of the government of Malabar since Haidar's death, retained only the military command, while the civil administration was entrusted to Mir Ibrahim and Mir Ghulam Husain who were appointed first and second *diwans* respectively. The new officers were instructed by Tipu to establish law and order and to promote the welfare of the province.[1]

But these reforms did not improve matters. In 1786 Goorkul Moplah of Manjeri rose in rebellion.[2] Owing to the unsettled state of the province, Tipu decided to visit it. He arrived in Calicut early in April 1788 by the way of the Tamarassheri pass, without any army or train of artillery.[3] He had only such troops as generally accompanied him.[4] He dismissed both Arshad Beg and Ibrahim. The former was suspected of disloyalty and of carrying on intrigues with the Nairs and the Moplahs,[5] and the latter of dishonesty and rapacity. In their place Husain Ali Khan was appointed to the command of the army, and Sher Khan as first *diwan*.[6] Tipu left Calicut on May 9[7] and proceeded to the south bank of Beypore river, where he laid the foundation of his new capital of Malabar and named it Farokhabad or Farrookhia. Here he ordered a fort to be built since the fort of Calicut was no longer tenable. The capital was also made the coverging point of new roads. It was better situated to become a port than any other place on the sea coast. Many persons from Calicut were compelled to settle there; but during the Third Anglo-Mysore War, after Malabar was occupied by the English, they returned to Calicut, and very soon hardly any trace of the new capital was left.[8]

[1] *Report of Joint Commissioners*, p. 35; Logan, *Malabar*, vol. i, part ii, p. 448.

[2] *Report of Joint Commissioners*, p. 36.

[3] Logan, *Malabar*, vol. i, part ii, p. 449; P.A.MS., No. 4577.

[4] N.A., Sec. Pro., May 27, 1788, Capt. Kyd from Tellicherry, April 14.

[5] Kirmani, pp. 331-2; Punganuri, p. 39. Arshad Beg returned to Seringapatam and died of grief. He was buried by Tipu's orders in the Lal Bagh.

[6] *Report of Joint Commissioners*, p. 37; Kirmani, p. 332, says that Mahtab Khan Bakhshi was appointed in pl ce of Arshad Beg.

[7] P.A.MS., No. 4583.

[8] *Report of Joint Commissioners*, p. 37. Tipu's capital is now a small village called Ferokh (*Imp. Gaz.*, xii, p. 88). Punganuri, p. 39, and *Sultan-ut-Tawarikh*, f. 74, call it Farrokhi; *Report of Joint Commissioners*, p. 37, calls it Farokhabad.

Owing to the approach of the rainy season, Tipu returned to Coimbatore towards the end of May. From Coimbatore he proceeded to Dindigul, the *jagir* of his relation Sayyid Saheb, who entertained him sumptuously. Both in the Coimbatore and Dindigul districts the refractory *poligars* were punished. In the month of August he returned to Seringapatam by the route of Gajalhatti.[1]

Tipu had not been long at his capital before he heard the news of a serious outbreak in Malabar. The leader of the revolt was Ravi Varma on whom a *jagir* had been conferred to keep him quiet.[2] Besides the Nairs who followed him, he was also joined by the Moplahs and the Coorgs. From July to November 1788, Ravi Varma made himself master of the open country and then invested Calicut.[3] Alarmed at the news, Tipu sent Lallée and Qamar-ud-din Khan with 6,000 Mysoreans and 170 Europeans in December 1788.[4] As many of the Rajas had been given protection by the factors of Tellicherry, Tipu sent a formal request to them on February 15 not to give them any further protection.[5] At the same time he sent detachments of his troops under Lallée, Omar Beg, Sayyid Saheb and Bakaji Rao in various directions to suppress the rising. The Raja of Cochin also helped the Mysoreans.[6] As a result the insurgents were defeated. Many of them were captured and the rest escaped to the jungles. In January 1789 Tipu again entered Malabar through the Tamarassheri pass. Leaving a force at Calicut to complete the subjugation of the Nairs, at the end of February he directed his steps northwards.[7] Hearing of this the Rajas of Kottayam and Kadattanad escaped to Tellicherry and thence to Travancore. But the Raja of Chirakkal paid a visit to the Sultan who received him with distinction and dismissed him with costly presents. But soon after, on discovering that the Raja was carrying on intrigues against him with his enemies, he sent troops to bring him back. The Raja's fortified palace at Kuttipuram was surrounded, but his men offered resistance and in the skirmish the Raja was killed.[8] Thereupon, his kingdom was annexed by the Sultan.

Tipu then proceeded to Cannanore at the invitation of the Bibi. He gave her a portion of the territory of Chirakkal, and solemnised the preliminary ceremonies of the marriage between his son Abdul Khaliq and her daughter. By these measures Tipu wanted to pacify the

[1] Wilks, ii, p. 321; Punganuri, pp. 39-40.
[2] Logan, *Malabar*, vol. i, part ii, p. 452.
[3] P.A.MS., Nos. 4592, 4597; Logan, *Malabar*, vol. i, part ii, p. 452.
[4] *Ibid.* According to Mack. MS., I.O. No. 46, the army was sent in Jan. 1789.
[5] Logan, *Malabar*, vol. i, part ii, p. 453.
[6] I.O.Mack. MS. No. 46, pp. 89, 98.
[7] Logan, *Malabar*, vol. i, part ii, p. 453.
[8] *Ibid.; Report of Joint Commissioners*, p. 46. But according to *Tarikh-i-Coorg*, the Raja, afraid of being punished by Tipu, committed suicide.

Moplahs of South Malabar, and in this he was successful. He left North Malabar on April 22, 1789, and proceeded to Coimbatore.[1]

Although Tipu had succeeded in pacifying the Moplahs, the Nairs remained as turbulent as before, and as soon as Tipu's back was turned, they returned from the jungles and began to harass the Mysore forces stationed in the province and to carry on depredations all round. On April 22, 1789, they even killed Tipu's *amil* of Irvernad with some of his troops.[2]

The cause of Tipu's failure to crush the Nairs lay in the terrain of Malabar which is extremely hilly and thickly wooded. There were no roads, and owing to the rains, which fell from June to September and then again from October to December, the campaigning season was very short. All this greatly hampered the movements of the Mysore army, while it was very favourable to the rebels who retired into the jungles on the arrival of Tipu in Malabar, and returned to the open country on his departure. Moreover, they were given every assistance by the English and the Raja of Travancore.

Tipu wanted to establish peace in Malabar by giving it good government, by winning the goodwill of its people, and by constructing new roads which would enable him to put down the Nair risings. But unfortunately the Third Anglo-Mysore War broke out and Tipu had to devote all his energies to it. Meanwhile, the Malabar chiefs, who had already been for some time past in correspondence with the English, entered into treaties with them whereby they agreed to become tributaries of the Company, provided their territories, from which they had been expelled by the Sultan, were restored to them. The English campaign on the Malabar coast was successful, and so, according to the agreement, the different chiefs were reinstated in their petty states. The Treaty of Seringapatam (1792) legalised their new status, and henceforth they became vassals of the English Company.

[1] Logan, *Malabar*, vol. i, part ii, pp. 453, 456; Wilks, ii, p. 332.
[2] P.A.MS., No. 4629.

## CHAPTER X

# TIPU AND THE ENGLISH 1784-88

The Treaty of Mangalore, as we have seen, was not approved of by the Bengal Government and by many of the Company's military officers. Warren Hastings had called it a "humiliating peace,"[1] and Innes Munro had "hoped that the treaty of peace, which the Company has lately concluded with Tippoo Sahib, is only meant to be temporary."[2] The result of this attitude was that, while officially the English were at peace with Tipu, their relations with him remained strained, and cases of infractions of the treaty by them were not infrequent.

It was stipulated in the Treaty of Mangalore that Cannanore should be restored to the Bibi in the presence of an officer deputed by Tipu. But, instead, the place was evacuated by the English without waiting for the arrival of the Sultan's representative. And before quitting it, they laid waste the adjacent country, plundered the inhabitants, blew up the magazine of the fort and threw the guns into the sea.[3] They committed similar depredations during their evacuation of Onore, Karwar and Sadasivgarh.[4] When Lord Macartney heard of this he greatly disapproved of the conduct of the English officers. He regarded it as a violation of the fourth article of the treaty, and was prepared "to rectify the mistakes in any manner that Tippoo points out."[5]

But these were not the only instances of the violations of the treaty by the English. They plundered Dindigul, and started collecting revenues from the district which, by the treaty, they were not entitled to do.[6] Moreover, they began to incite revolts in Tipu's kingdom and to give refuge to his refractory subjects. A large number of Nairs fled to Tellicherry, where they received protection from the English and from where they carried on raids into Tipu's territory.[7] Tipu wrote to the chief of Tellicherry about this, but his complaints fell on deaf ears. This made the Sultan so indignant that he informed the chief not to

[1] *Camb. Hist. India,* v, p. 333.

[2] Innes Munro, p. 370

[3] M.R., Mly. Cons., May 23, 1784, Tipu to Macartney, vol. 99B, p. 2050.

[4] *Ibid.*, May 28, 1784, Tipu to Macartney, pp. 2127-8.

[5] *Ibid.*, May 23, 1784, Select Committee's Minute, p. 2050; Mly. Desp. to England, June 8, 1784, vol. 19, p. 156.

[6] M.R., Mly. Cons., July 15, 1784, vol. 100C, pp. 2683-4.

[7] P.R.C., iii, No. 37A.

address him any longer;[1] and although he restored to the English their factory at Calicut, he postponed the restitution of Mount Delli to them. Furthermore, he imposed an embargo on pepper, cardamoms and sandalwood, and instigated the Chirakkal Raja to occupy the island of Dharmapattanam which was the key to Tellicherry. The island was, accordingly, seized by the Raja in June 1788.[2]

*The English and the Maratha-Mysore War*

When war between Tipu and the Peshwa became imminent, Sindhia sent a message to Anderson, the English agent at his court, through Appaji Pundit that, as Tipu was assembling troops near the Maratha frontier, the English Company should help the Poona Government in accordance with the Treaty of Salbai, and should enter into an offensive and defensive alliance with the Peshwa and the Nizam against him.[3] The request for help and the proposal for an alliance was conveyed by Anderson to Macpherson, the Governor-General, who replied that the Treaty of Salbai did not stipulate "that the friends and enemies of the Company and the Maratha State are mutual." Its thirteenth article only laid down that the Company would not afford help to any nation against the Peshwa, and accordingly the Company would not help Tipu. But at the same time it would not assist the Marathas either, for, according to the Treaty of Mangalore, it was bound not to assist the enemies of Tipu Sultan.[4]

Macpherson would have very much liked to help the Marathas immediately, for he regarded their requests as "fair and reasonable."[5] That he did not do so was partly due to Pitt's India Act, which forbade the Governor-General and Council from entering into any alliances which might lead to war with the country powers, and partly due to the sixteenth article of the Treaty of Versailles, but chiefly because the finances and army of the Company were in a deplorable state.[6] Macpherson, however, very soon gave up this policy of neutrality. He had already declared that, "though we wish not to be parties in their own disputes, we are determined to maintain a decisive influence in whatever scale we may think it just and political to throw the force of our aid....for there is certainly a point beyond which a pacific system, however desirable, cannot be pursued to the

[1] *Ibid.*

[2] M.R., Mly. Cons., Jan. 25, 1788, vol. 120A, p. 50x; P.R.C., iii, No. 37; Logan, Malabar, vol. i, part ii, p. 453.

[3] M.R., Mly. Cons., July 1, 1786, Anderson to Macpherson, May 10, vol. 108A, pp. 1815-6.

[4] *Ibid.*, Macpherson to Anderson, May 26, p. 1818.

[5] N.A., Sec., Pro., March 28, 1787, Macpherson to Carnac, Company's Agent with Tipu, Dec. 20, 1785, cons. No. 8.

[6] *Ibid.; Ibid.*, Dec. 7, 1785, cons. No. 7a.

attainment of any permanent tranquility."[1] When, therefore, war broke out between Tipu and the Marathas, and Nana pressed the English for assistance, Macpherson offered to send five battalions to the help of the Nizam.[2] He even went to the extent of assuring Nana that the battalions would be ready to accompany the Maratha armies to the Carnatic Balaghat, Lahore or wherever their services would be required.[3] But this was an open violation of the Treaty of Mangalore which had laid down that Tipu and the Company "will not directly or indirectly assist the enemies of each other."

The reason why Macpherson violated the treaty with Tipu and offered help to the Marathas was that, in the first place, he was anxious to counteract the French intrigues at Poona and to prevent the Peshwa from coming under the influence of the French by calling in the aid of their troops. In the second place, he wanted to prevent the overthrow of the Marathas and thus maintain the balance of power in the country, being convinced that, in case the Maratha power suffered an eclipse, Tipu would become very dangerous to the English.[4] Moreover, Macpherson agreed to render help to the Marathas so that they might continue the war against Tipu instead of making peace with him; for, as Cossigny observed, it was in the English interest to see the Indian powers fighting with each other and weakening themselves.[5]

But the offer of help given by Macpherson to the Nizam and the Marathas was disapproved by the Home Government, who wanted the Company to remain neutral whether the Marathas were defeated or victorious in the war against Tipu, and to interfere and take sides only in case of French interference, or if its possessions were threatened by any power.[6] Accordingly, they pointed out that the Governor-General should have informed the Marathas that the Company would help them only in case Tipu were helped by the French. If, on the other hand, the Marathas secured French assistance, the Company would be obliged to help Tipu. But contrary to this, the Governor-General had promised assistance to the Peshwa without

[1] *Ibid.*
[2] *Ibid.*, Feb. 14, 1786, cons. No. 4.
[3] Khare, viii, No. 3004, Sindhia to Nana, July 26, 1786. This assurance was given in a letter written in Persian by Macpherson. Afterwards, Malet interpreted it in a different way, and informed Nana that the battalions could be employed to defend the Peshwa's territory and not to invade Tipu's kingdom. But Nana regarded this as a breach of the assurances given by Macpherson in his previous letters. Besides, Nana maintained that the question of aggression did not arise, for Nargund, Kittur and other places were parts of the Maratha kingdom. Macpherson, in fact, not only violated the Treaty of Mangalore, he also opened himself to the charge of duplicity made by Nana.
[4] N.A., Sec. Pro., Feb. 14, 1786, cons. No. 3.
[5] P.A.MS., No. 894.
[6] N.A., Sec. desp. from England, July 21, 1786, vol. 1, pp. 32-35.

any certainty that the French meant to offer help to Tipu. Such a policy, the authorities in London thought, "results in the first place in throwing Tippoo into the arms of the French, and in the second place, it makes Tippoo hostile to us."[1]

When, therefore, Lord Cornwallis was appointed Governor-General in place of Macpherson, he was advised by the Board of Control "to adopt a pacific and defensive system" based on "the universal principle... that we are completely satisfied with the possessions we already have." At the same time he was instructed that if the French took one side in the war, the Company was automatically to take the other.[2] Cornwallis found on taking office: "We are got into a very awkward foolish scrape by offering assistance to the Marathas; how we shall get out of it with honour, God knows, but out of it we must get somehow, and give no troops."[3] He, accordingly, repudiated his predecessor's engagements, and withdrew the offer of help to the Nizam and the Peshwa, while assuring them that, in case the French helped Tipu, the Company would immediately come to their assistance.[4]

But it must not be thought that Cornwallis took this step because he was wedded to a pacific policy, or because he believed that even Tipu was entitled to 'a square deal.'[5] In reality he would have liked to help the Marathas, but adopted a neutral attitude as a matter of expediency. He feared that, if aid were given to the Marathas, it would lead to war with Tipu and the French in close alliance with each other; but for such a war the English Company was not prepared at the time, because its army was in an unspeakable state, and its finances, excepting in Bengal, were in an alarming condition. Besides, he did not wish to be drawn into a war in which the French would be inevitably arrayed on the side of Tipu against the English, for this would not only create diplomatic complications in Europe, it would also make the defeat of Tipu a very difficult task. Furthermore, the offer of help had been made to the Marathas in order to prevent them from securing the assistance of the French, and also "on the assumption of the ascendancy of Tippoo's power and on the possibility that it might be rendered still more formidable by an introduction of a French force." But as "these suppositions no longer existed," there was no need to send troops to the help of the Nizam or the Marathas.[6]

[1] N.A., Sec. Pro., Feb. 26, 1787, Sec. Commit. of E.I.C. to Bengal, Sept. 22, 1786, cons. No. 8.

[2] Board's Secret Letters, i, March 8, July 19, Sept. 20, 1786, cited in Philips, *The East India Company*, p. 66, footnote 1.

[3] P.R.O., 30/11/134, Cornwallis to Dundas, Sept. 17, 1786, f. 3a.

[4] P.R.C., ii, No. 37.

[5] Thompson and Garratt, *Rise and Fulfilment of British Rule in India*, p. 174.

[6] P.R.C., ii, No. 37.

Cornwallis, nevertheless, believed that if the English wished to establish their supremacy in India they would have to fight Tipu sooner or later, for the balance of power in the country had become heavily tilted in favour of Mysore. Of all the Indian states, the kingdom of Mysore was the strongest, the best governed and the most prosperous. Its ruler had defeated the combined forces of the Nizam and the Marathas, and the friendships which he was trying to form with the king of France and the Sultan of Turkey by sending his ambassadors to them appeared to Cornwallis to be fraught with great danger to the English interests in India. He was convinced that Tipu was "a prince of very uncommon ability and of boundless ambition, who had acquired a degree of power in extent of territory, in wealth, and in forces that threatened the Company's possessions in the Carnatic and those of all his other neighbours with imminent danger."[1] He, therefore, considered it necessary to reduce Tipu's power. Besides, he felt that time had come to set the stage for a second expansion of the English possessions in India. For this he turned his covetous eyes towards Tipu's kingdom, and particularly towards his Malabar possessions, which were rich in spices, sandalwood and pine trees and possessed a number of fine ports like Calicut and Cannanore. Their acquisition, he thought, would at least be a partial compensation for the loss of the thirteen North American Colonies.

Henry Dundas, the President of the Board of Control, also urged Cornwallis to embark on a policy of expansion. He wanted Bombay to be enlarged so that it might become self-supporting. He believed that "a chain of military posts along the western coast of India must add great security to our Indian Empire," and these posts were to be obtained either "by negotiation or otherwise."[2] Later, Dundas favoured the use of force to negotiation, and advised Cornwallis to destroy Tipu "that restless and perfidious tyrant", set up the old Raja in his place and reduce Mysore to the status of Travancore, Tanjore and Oudh. He did not think that, if Tipu was overthrown, the balance of power would be upset and the Marathas would become strong. There was no danger of this because they were disunited.[3]

[1] P.R.O., 30/11/152, Cornwallis to Grenville, April 24, 1791, f. 24a. See also Campbell's estimate of Tipu as "an active, ambitious and enterprising prince, whose troops are in higher order than the force of any Asiatic state we are acquainted with." (*Ibid.*, 30/11/118, Campbell to Cornwallis, May 1, 1787, f. 88b.)

[2] Melville Papers, MSS. No. 3387, Dundas to Cornwallis, April 3, 1789, No. 3, pp. 65, 67.

[3] *Ibid.*, Nov. 13, 1790, No. 54, p. 157; also P.R.O. 30/11/116, Dundas to Cornwallis, Nos. 53, 54 Nov. and Dec. 1790.

*Aggressive Designs of Cornwallis*

To achieve these objects Lord Cornwallis first of all directed his attention to the reorganisation of the Company's army and finances; and owing to the zeal and effort with which he undertook this task, he was able to inform Malet towards the end of December, 1787, that "the Company's armies are ready in all the provinces."[1] Finding himself thus prepared, he started negotiations for an alliance with the Marathas and the Nizam against Tipu Sultan. Ostensibly the alliance was to be defensive, but in reality it was to be offensive. Writing on October 23, 1787, to Forster, who was the Company's agent at Nagpur, Cornwallis observed: "We want to form an alliance with the Mahrattas against Tippoo, our common enemy," and asked him to request Mudhoji Bhonsle "to induce the Poona Government to take the lead in a general confederacy of the Mahrattas for renewing the war against Tippoo," and to give a free passage through Cuttack to the troops sent from Bengal to fight him.[2] In a letter directly addressed to Mudhoji, Cornwallis reminded him of the great injuries suffered by the Marathas at the hands of Haidar and Tipu, and called on him to avenge himself. Mudhoji was assured that no peace would be made with Tipu without mutual consent, and until all the territory between the Krishna and Tungabhadra rivers had been recovered by the Marathas.[3] Similarly Cornwallis wrote to Palmer at Gwalior: "If Sindhia could be persuaded not only to use his influence with the Poona Government to take the lead in a general confederacy of the Mahrattas to renew the war against Tippoo, but to take a personal share in it himself, I should consider it a mark of friendship, well deserving of some splendid service in return from our Government."[4] Letters were also sent to the authorities at Poona; and Malet, the Company's agent there, submitted proposals to Nana for an alliance with the Peshwa's Government.

It has been maintained that Cornwallis made advances to the Marathas thinking that Tipu intended to invade the Carnatic. In reality, however, Tipu was not in a position to wage war with the Company, partly because he was not prepared for it, and partly because he could not expect any help from the French who were at peace with the English.[5] It is true that rumours of Tipu's invasion of the

[1] N.A., Sec. Pro., Dec. 14, 1787, Cornwallis to Malet. Similarly Campbell observed to Stuart: "I have great pleasure in acquainting you that we are in great forwardness in our preparations for Tippoo; and that there seems to be a cheerful spirit in the army to meet him, which I shall try to alleviate to the best advantage." (P.R.O., 30/11/134, Campbell to Stuart, Oct. 6, 1787, f. 12a.)

[2] N.A., Sec. Pro., Nov. 8, 1787, Cornwallis to Foster, Oct. 23.

[3] *Ibid.*, Cornwallis to Bhonsle, Oct. 23, 1787.

[4] N.A., Pol. Pro., April 7, 1794, cons. No. 1, Cornwallis to Palmer, Oct. 20, 1787. (Made from the original found in possession of Palmer.)

[5] N.A., Sec. Pro., May 7, 1788, Governor-General's Minute of April 14; M.R., Mly. Sec. Cons., Oct. 9, 1787, Cornwallis to Madras, vol. 119B, p. 467.

Carnatic were current at the time, but they were without any foundation whatsoever, having been fabricated by the Raja of Travancore and the Nawab of Carnatic and other persons who were anxious to embroil the Company in a war with Tipu.[1] In fact, Cornwallis himself did not believe in such rumours, and wrote to the Madras Government: "He (Tipu) will not undertake hostilities against us."[2] That in spite of this Cornwallis made approaches to the Marathas clearly shows that he had aggressive designs on Tipu.

However, because of the Treaty of Versailles and the instructions of the Court of Directors, and because Tipu had not given any provocation to the English, Cornwallis could not propose an offensive alliance. He, therefore, proposed to Nana that if Tipu invaded the Carnatic or attacked any of the allies of the Company with or without French assistance, the Marathas would immediately create a diversion by attacking the northern frontier of Mysore with the support of a battalion of Europeans, a brigade of sepoys, and a good field of battering train supplied by the Company, but paid for by the Marathas. If, on the other hand, the Marathas were attacked by Tipu alone, the Company would remain neutral. It would only help them in case they were attacked by Tipu with the aid of French troops.[3]

These proposals were not acceptable to Nana who regarded them heavily weighted in favour of the English. He wanted equality in commitments, and in addition, was in favour of both an offensive and defensive alliance. Malet did his best to explain to Nana the implications of the Treaty of Versailles (1783) and of the Parliamentary Act of 1784, according to which the Company could not help the Marathas if Tipu attacked them alone; nor could it enter into an offensive alliance with them.[4] But these explanations proved futile, for Nana was not interested in the niceties of European politics or Acts of British Parliament. The talks therefore broke down. This however did not come as a surprise to the English, for Malet had been from the beginning pessimistic about the success of the negotiations, and had informed Cornwallis that the Marathas would not accept the proposals because "they are already chagrined on our refusal of aid in the last war with

[1] Campbell's letters to Cornwallis showed that the rumours had no foundation, and that Tipu was inclined to listen to reason because of English military preparations, Maratha hostility and Conway's coldness to his approaches. (P.R.O., 30/11/118, Campbell to Cornwallis, Oct. 9, 1787, f. 178b.)

[2] M.R., Mly. Sec. Cons., Oct. 9, 1787, Cornwallis to Madras, vol. 119B, p. 467. It was because there was no danger from Tipu that Cornwallis pressed the demand for Guntur on the Nizam; also P.R.O., 30/11/150, Cornwallis to Dundas, December, 5. 1789, f. 161.

[3] M.R., Mly. Sec. Cons., Oct. 5, 1787, vol. 119B, pp. 428-30; N.A., Sec. Pro., Dec. 14., 1787, Malet to Cornwallis, Oct. 28.

[4] *Ibid.*, Cornwallis to Malet Dec. 14, 1787.

Tipu. They would reply that our own treaties become inviolable when it suits your convenience, yet when the same convenience urges, you scruple not to abide by your treaties. They will say that now you require our aid with a reservation that we should pay your troops in fighting your battles and you make a merit of relinquishing imaginary conquests as a compensation for the sacrifice of our late pledged faith. Yours will be the real advantage while we will only incur the expenses of war."[1]

But the failure of the talks did not mean a break in the relations between the English and the Marathas, for Cornwallis continued to humour Nana, knowing that sooner or later he would be able to find some pretext for a conflict with Tipu, when limitations over his powers would be removed and it would be possible to agree with Nana's views. Meanwhile, Cornwallis wanted "to keep up the most friendly intercourse" between the English and the Marathas, and "a free communication of sentiments on the views and interests of both nations."[2]

Just as Cornwallis incited the Marathas against Tipu, he similarly stirred up the feelings of the Nizam by dangling before him the prospect of recovering those of his territories which Haidar Ali had forcibly occupied. But as the Company itself was demanding the Guntur Sarkar from the Nizam, the English intrigues at Hyderabad did not lead to any result. In fact, owing to the Guntur controversy,[3] the relations between the Nizam and the English became so strained for a time that it seemed he would throw in his lot with Tipu.

But after the Nizam had agreed to surrender the Guntur Sarkar to the Company in September in accordance with the treaty of 1768, he demanded the fulfilment of another article of the same treaty which pledged the Company to help him in the recovery of his ancestral dominion from Haidar, and sent his minister, Mir Abul Qasim, better known as Mir Alam, to Calcutta to enter into a new agreement with the English. Cornwallis informed the Nizam that he could not enter into any treaty as it would be against the Act of Parliament, and would arouse the jealousy of the Marathas whose friendship he was anxious to cultivate. But he wrote him a letter on July 7, 1789, which was explanatory to the treaty of 1768 and was, therefore, equally binding upon the English as a regular treaty. The letter explained

[1] *Ibid.*, Malet to Cornwallis, Oct. 28, 1787.

[2] P.R.C., iii, No. 24.

[3] According to the treaty of alliance concluded between the Nizam and the Company in 1766, in return for the 5 Sarkars, including the Sarkar of Guntur, the Company had agreed to furnish the Nizam with a subsidiary force when required, and to pay 9 lakhs a year when the assistance of its troops was not required. The Guntur Sarkar which the Nizam had given in *jagir* to his brother Basalat Jung, was not to be taken possession of till the latter's death. (Aitchison, *Treaties*, ix, pp. 22-25). In 1782 Basalat Jung died and the Guntur Sarkar was retained by the Nizam. In 1788 the Company revived its claim to the Sarkar. (*Ibid.*, p. 3.)

that in the sixth article of that treaty it was stipulated that the English troops should be lent to the Nizam "wherever the necessity of the Company's affairs would permit," but now it was to mean that the Nizam could employ the Company's troops against any one except those in alliance with the Company, that is, the Peshwa, Sindhia and other Maratha chiefs, the Nawabs of Carnatic and Oudh and the Rajas of Tanjore and Travancore.[1] As Tipu's name was not included in the list, the implication was that the Nizam was entitled to employ the Company's troops against him, since he was not considered to be one of the powers in alliance with the Company. Further, the letter declared that circumstances prevented the execution of those articles of the treaty of 1768 which go to vest the Company with the *diwani* of the Carnatic Balaghat, yet, "should it hereafter happen, that the Company should obtain possession of the country mentioned in those articles with your Highness's assistance, they (the Company) will strictly perform the stipulations in favour of your Highness and the Mahrattas."[2]

The Company had concluded two treaties with Haidar subsequently to the treaty of 1768. It had also concluded a treaty with Tipu in 1784 by which it had recognised his sovereignty over the territories he possessed. The Governor-General's letter was, therefore, a violation of the Treaty of Mangalore. It was also "a violation of the spirit of the India Act,"[3] for it was of an offensive nature, and was more calculated to bring about war with Tipu than being "an avowed contract of defensive arrangement."[4] The letter was thus one more instance which showed that Cornwallis was determined to wage war on Tipu, and that he was only waiting to manufacture some incident for a *casus belli*.

[1] *Ibid.*, pp. 43-5.
[2] *Ibid.*, p. 44. The Treaty of 1768 contemplated the conquest of the Carnatic Balaghat which was in possession of Haidar. The *diwani* of this territory was to be granted to the Company who engaged to pay the Nizam seven lakhs of rupees annually, and to the Marathas their *chauth*. (*Ibid.*, p. 33.)
[3] *Short. Camb. Hist. of India*, p. 600.
[4] Malcolm, *Political History of India*, i, p. 57.

CHAPTER XI

# THE WAR WITH THE RAJA OF TRAVANCORE

Travancore was a small, weak state until the thirties of the eighteenth century. But Martanda Varma, during his reign of twenty-nine years (1729-1758), succeeded in transforming it into the most powerful kingdom in Malabar. Rama Varma, who ascended the throne in 1758, continued his uncle's ambitious policy,[1] and taking advantage of the decline of the Dutch power in India and the internecine wars among the Malabar chiefs, he gradually conquered the whole country from Cranganur to Cape Comorin "partly by guile and in an unlawful manner, and partly by force of arms."[2] In consequence, many small kingdoms were swept away, while the Raja of Cochin lost the best part of his kingdom and became a mere puppet in Rama Varma's hands.[3] But Rama Varma was not content with these acquisitions; his ultimate object was the "unification of Malabar under one flag."[4] He was, however, compelled to cry a halt to his career of conquest owing to Haidar Ali's invasion of Malabar in January 1766, which not only threatened his ambitious schemes but even the integrity of his kingdom.

When Haidar was the *faujdar* of Dindigul, Martanda Varma, the then Raja of Travancore, being hard pressed by his refractory chiefs, had asked for his assistance. Haidar had readily offered it. But meanwhile, the chiefs had submitted. The Raja, therefore, informed Haidar that he no longer required his services. Haidar, nevertheless, demanded compensation; but it was refused.[5] Martanda Varma having died in 1758, Haidar claimed payment from his successor, Rama Varma, and at the same time called on him to become his tributary. Rama Varma was prepared to pay the money, but he refused to become Haidar's vassal, since he was already a vassal of Muhammad Ali of Carnatic.[6] And knowing that this answer would not satisfy Haidar who would sooner or later attack Travancore, he prepared for resistance by strengthening the Travancore lines and by establishing closer ties of friendship with the English.[7] Moreover,

[1] Pannikar, *Malabar and the Dutch*, p. 95.
[2] Dutch Records, No. 13, p. 107.
[3] *Ibid.*, p. 108.
[4] Pannikar, *Malabar and the Dutch*, p. 95.
[5] Menon, *History of Travancore*, p. 159.
[6] Francis Day, *The Land of the Permauls*, p. 144.
[7] *Ibid.*

with the object of weakening the position of Haidar in Malabar, he began to stir up rebellions against him, and to give refuge to the rebels in Travancore.[1] Incensed at the insolent and hostile conduct of Rama Varma, and convinced that as long as he remained unsubdued, the hold of Mysore over Malabar would remain precarious, Haidar Ali decided to invade Travancore. But owing to his wars with the Marathas and the English, which kept him engaged till the end of his days, he could not undertake any large-scale and systematic military operations. Meanwhile, Rama Varma kept up his intrigues and acts of hostility against Haidar. He continued to incite rebellions in his kingdom; he gave free passage to the English troops through his country in 1778 for attacking the French port of Mahé which was under Haidar's protection; and when the Second Anglo-Mysore War broke out, he gave military aid to the English.

Like his father, Tipu also remained preoccupied for a number of years with very important matters. At first he had to fight the English, and after the Treaty of Mangalore he was kept busy pacifying Coorg and his Malabar possessions. He was then called upon to face the Maratha menace. It was, thus, not until the middle of 1787 that he found himself free to turn his attention to the Raja of Travancore who, during all these years, had been pursuing a hostile policy towards him. The Raja had rendered useful assistance to the English in the Second Anglo-Mysore War, and even after the Treaty of Mangalore, to which he was bound to adhere having been mentioned as an ally of the Company, he did not desist from stirring up rebellions in Malabar and from giving refuge to the rebels in Travancore. Tipu repeatedly warned the Raja to refrain from acts of hostility, but confident of English support, he ignored the warnings. In 1788, under the pretext that his kingdom was threatened by Tipu, he secured the services of two battalions of the Company's native infantry to be stationed on his frontiers at his expense, and was promised further assistance, if required, of 'Europeans and natives' to be maintained at the expense of the Company and employed "against the designs of the enemy."[2] Thus assured of English support, he laid claim to the territory belonging to Kolut Nair, who was a tributary of Tipu, on the ground that he was related to one of his intimate friends and descended from a common ancestor. He also asked the Governor of Madras to help the Malabar chiefs in recovering their kingdoms from Tipu.[3] Moreover, he refused to demolish that part of the Travancore lines which, the Sultan maintained, were built upon the territory of the Raja of Cochin who was a tributary of Mysore. And further, he purchased

[1] MR., Tellicherry Factory Records, April 2, 1780.
[2] Menon, *History of Travancore*, p. 239.
[3] M.R., Mly. Count. Cor., Raja to Madras Governor, June 10, 1789, vol. 38, No. 59.

Ayicotta and Cranganur from the Dutch knowing fully well that Tipu was also anxious to buy them.

The kingdom of Travancore occupied the southern extremity of the Indian peninsula. It began near the island of Vypin at the Chimmamanglum river, about twenty miles north of Cochin, and ended a little to the east of Cape Comorin. On the east it was bounded by the lofty escarpments of the Western Ghats which terminated near the southern Cape, and on the west and south it was washed by the ocean. It was thus secure against a land attack on all sides except the north where, though partially protected by the Ghats, it lay open towards Cochin. To make up for the want of a natural barrier on that side, Rama Varma, on the advice of his Dutch Commander-in-Chief, General Eustachio De Lannoy,[1] ordered in 1764 the construction of a series of defensive works known as the Travancore lines. The following is their description given by Pawney, the Company's agent with the Raja, in a letter to the Government of Madras: "They run from west to east, commencing at the sea on the island of Vipeen, and continue to a broad river called Chinamungulum, on the opposite side of which they begin again and extend to the Elephant mountains, where they terminate upon the top of one of them from which run a chain of mountains to a high northern latitude, and as low south as the extreme point of the peninsula or Cape Comorin; so that the eastern boundary of the State is protected by them. From the sea to Chinamungulum river the lines are four or five miles; from the opposite bank to the extremity at the mountains they are twenty-four or twenty-five miles. They consist of a ditch sixteen feet broad and twenty feet deep with a thick bamboo hedge, a slight parapet and good rampart and bastions on rising ground almost flanking each other from one extreme of the lines to the other. They are only assailable by regular approaches from the north."[2]

As soon as Tipu found his hands free after his peace with the Marathas, he asked Rama Varma to demolish that portion of the lines which was erected on the territory of the Cochin Raja, partly because the latter was his tributary,[3] and partly because they cut him off from about two-thirds of the kingdom of Cochin which was to their

[1] De Lannoy was taken prisoner by the Travancoreans when they totally defeated the Dutch at Colachel on Aug. 10, 1741. He was appointed by Martanda Varma to discipline a few companies of sepoys which formed his body-guard battalion. He constructed many new forts in the State and repaired old ones. He helped the Raja in suppressing rebellions and in his schemes of conquest. Because of his ability and services he was raised to the rank of a General, and appointed Commander-in-Chief of the Travancore army. (Menon, *History of Travancore*, pp. 136-7, 164.)

[2] M.R., Mly. Cons., Feb. 16, 1790, Pawney to Hollond, Feb. 1, vol. 133C, p. 415.

[3] *Ibid.*, Jan. 1, 1790, Pawney to Hollond, Dec. 18, 1789, vol. 133A, p. 5.

south.[1] But Rama Varma turned down the demand. He maintained that the land on which the lines were built had been lawfully acquired from the Raja of Cochin in return for the assistance which he had rendered him against the Zamorin of Calicut, and that there had been no extension of the lines since they were erected twenty-five years ago before the Raja of Cochin became Mysore's tributary.[2]

But these claims of Rama Varma were quite unfounded. It was in 1764 that the lines began to be constructed under the supervision of De Lannoy, and they were completed in 1777 when he died while giving his finishing touches to them.[3] During this period the lines continued to be extended whenever it was regarded strategically necessary. Thus, for instance, in July 1766 Rama Varma began to extend the lines to near Cranganur fort and on the territory of the Cranganur Raja. Thereupon the Dutch protested because they feared that this might offend Haidar Ali.[4] The portion of the lines across the island of Vypin, a breadth of about 1,500 yards, was erected in 1775.[5] Since the possessions of Cochin and Travancore were intermixed at places and the lines intersected the Cochin country[6], it is not a matter of surprise that Rama Varma should have encroached upon the territory of the Cochin Raja and built the lines on it, for the forcible acquisition of land was quite in keeping with his policy of expansion in Malabar. Even Captain Bannerman, Commander of the Company's detachment in Travancore, admitted that "the Raja of Travancore finds himself much embarassed with regard to the defence of the lines across the island of Vypin, for they were constructed on the king of Cochin's territory."[7] As regards the contention of Rama Varma that he had lawfully acquired land from the Raja of Cochin, it must be remembered that the different Malabar princes "always had claims, often of great obscurity, to places in one another's territories."[8]

Besides refusing to demolish the lines, Rama Varma further provoked Tipu by purchasing from the Dutch the islands and forts of Ayicotta and Cranganur which the Sultan himself was anxious to acquire. By these actions the Raja virtually threw a challenge to Tipu Sultan.

[1] Francis Day, *The Land of the Permauls*, p. 52; Wilks, ii, pp. 340-1.
[2] M.R., Mly. Cons., Jan. 1, 1790, 133A, p. 5; *Ibid.*, Feb. 16, 1790, vol. 133C, pp. 414, 416.
[3] Dutch Records, No. 13, p. 25.
[4] Francis Day, *The Land of the Permauls*, p. 144.
[5] Wilks, ii, p. 341.
[6] M.R., Mly. Cons., Feb. 16, 1790, Pawney to Hollond, Feb. 1, vol. 133C, p. 416; Menon, *History of Travancore*, p. 155.
[7] I.O., Home Misc. Series, Bannerman to Campbell, May 16, 1788, vol. 85, pp. 8-9.
[8] Dutch Records, No. 13, p. 19.

Ayicotta is situated on the northern extremity of the island of Vypin on the Malabar coast; two and a half miles to the north-east of Ayicotta lies Cranganur, and close to these are the islands. Soon after Tipu made peace with the Marathas, he started negotiations with the Dutch for the purchase of these forts. He wanted to acquire them, first, because of his policy of expansion in Malabar which he had inherited from his father. Already Chetvai and Paponetty had been occupied by Haidar, and now Tipu wanted to extend the boundaries of his kingdom further. Secondly, Tipu's experience of the Second Anglo-Mysore War had taught him that, in case of another conflict with the English, Palghat would again be one of their first objects of attack, because, apart from other advantages, it offered them the only means of establishing an easy and practical communication between the Malabar and Coromandel coasts.[1] Tipu, therefore, wanted access to this pass both from the east and the west to be carefully guarded, and for this purpose he was desirous of possessing himself of Cranganur, distant only twenty miles from Ponnani which had formed the base of Humberstone's operations against Palghat in the Second Anglo-Mysore War. In fact, Tipu did not want any place on that side of the coast to remain in the hands of an unfriendly power which might allow the English to use it as a spring-board for an invasion of his kingdom. At the same time it would not be correct to say that Tipu wanted Ayicotta and Cranganur for an invasion of Travancore, for such an invasion was strategically unsound—to approach the lines from Cranganur a river had to be crossed. It was easier to attack the lines from positions eastwards along an extent of about twenty miles; and subsequent events showed that it was the lines that Tipu first attacked and not Travancore. In fact, once the lines were carried, the forts fell almost without any resistance.

In 1776, Sardar Khan, Haidar's Governor at Calicut, had attempted to take the Cranganur fort by surprise, but had failed.[2] Soon after Tipu made peace with the Marathas, there were rumours that he would demand the fort of Cranganur and the Dutch islands near it. In September 1787 Mysore troops appeared near Cranganur, but they soon withdrew.[3] Meanwhile negotiations were going on between Rama Varma regarding the disposal of Cranganur and of the islands, which had formerly belonged to the Zamorin. In August 1788, Tipu's commander of Chetvai, having come to know of it, wrote to Angelbeek, the Dutch commander at Cochin, that if the Dutch were intending to sell the islands, he would be compelled to inform Tipu. Angelbeek became alarmed at this, and at once handed

[1] M.R., Mly. Sundry Book, 1785, vol. 66, p. 97.
[2] Van Lohuizen, *The Dutch E.I.C. and Mysore*, pp. 95-6.
[3] *Ibid.*, p. 144.

over the islands to the Raja.[1] Convinced that Cranganur would, similarly, be transferred to Rama Varma, the Mysoreans, in May 1789, appeared before the fort and summoned it, but met with refusal. As they had not brought with them heavy artillery they did not lay siege to the place.[2] In July 1789 information reached Cochin that Tipu intended to attack the Dutch. To Angelbeek the situation appeared desperate, for he was short of money, and he could get help neither from the Dutch possession of Ceylon nor from the English.[3] Of course Rama Varma was prepared to help, but this would be ineffective unless the English also became involved in the war. But this seemed unlikely. On May 14, 1789, Pawney, the English Company's Resident with the Raja, had informed the Governor of Madras that Tipu intended to attack Cranganur, and had asked for his instructions as to the course he should follow on the occasion and the advice he should give Rama Varma.[4] Hollond, who had replaced Campbell as Governor of Madras, replied that "the Company's troops are only to be employed in defence of the Rajah's own country, and that you must urge the Rajah to be extremely cautious in his conduct during the present critical situation, and on no account afford Tippoo Sultan pretext for invading the Travancore country."[5] When again in July 1789, an attack on Cranganur by Tipu was expected and the Raja was eager to help the Dutch, Hollond warned him against such a step.[6] Owing to this attitude of the Madras Government, the Raja expressed his inability to help the Dutch. The latter, thereupon, sold the forts to him, realising that they would not be able to protect them alone, but that if they were in the hands of the Raja, the English would help to defend them. In this way they contrived to raise a barrier against Tipu's attack on Cochin, which was their only remaining possession left in India and, in effect, threw themselves under the protection of the English Company, which was pledged to support Rama Varma if his kingdom was invaded by Tipu Sultan.[7]

The transaction entered into by the Raja with the Dutch was contrary to the advice given by the Company's Government. The

[1] *Ibid.*, p. 147.
[2] *Ibid.*, p. 148.
[3] *Ibid.*, p. 149.
[4] M.R., Mly. Cons., May 26, 1789, Pawney to Hollond, May 14, vol. 129C, p. 1447.
[5] *Ibid.*, pp. 1447-8.
[6] M.R., Mly. Count. Cor., Hollond to Raja, Aug. 17, 1789, vol. 38, No. 70, pp. 121-22; also N.A., Sec. Pro., Sept. 9, 1789, Madras to Bengal, Aug. 16, Cons. No. 1.
[7] Auber, *Rise and Progress of British Power in India*, p. 104. It is true that both Madras and Calcutta had expressed themselves against the purchase of the forts, but the Raja was certain that in the end he would secure the Company's help on account of the Tipuphobe elements both in India and in England.

Raja had first asked through Captain Bannerman the advice of Archibald Campbell, the Governor of Madras, regarding the matter, but the latter had dissuaded the Raja from entering into any transaction.[1] In spite of this the Raja continued his negotiations with the Dutch for the purchase of the forts. When Hollond, Campbell's successor, came to know of this he immediately instructed the Resident to dissuade the Raja from "making purchases from the Dutch of lands and forts which they hold under the Rajah of Cochin, a tributary of Tippoo, as likely to have the appearance in the eyes of the chief, of collusive transaction." Pawney was further informed that "the Government of Madras would not support him (the Rajah) in any contest in which he might engage, beyond the limits of his own possessions."[2] But this letter, which was sent on August 17, 1789, reached Pawney too late to be effective. The Raja had already purchased the forts from the Dutch on July 31. Pawney knew all the time about the negotiations which the Raja was carrying on with the Dutch; in fact he was privy to them. But knowing the sentiments of Hollond in the matter, he kept them a secret, and informed him on August 4 after the transaction had been carried out, and it was too late to prevent it.

On hearing the news of the purchase of Cranganur and Ayicotta, Hollond was very annoyed with the Raja who had entered into the transaction without his permission, and wrote to him that by his act he had forfeited the Company's protection, and that he should immediately give back the forts to the Dutch so that things might be re-established where they stood before.[3] Lord Cornwallis also disapproved of the conduct of the Raja, and informed Hollond that the latter should return the forts to the Dutch, and refrain from entering into any connections with them which might be offensive to Tipu. The Raja would be helped only if Tipu attacked him without provocation, but, "should he provoke Tipu by making collusive purchases of forts or places in the territories of one of his tributaries,......he will justly draw Tipu's resentment upon himself and at the same time forfeit all right to the Company's friendship or interference in his favour." Cornwallis even condemned the conduct of Pawney "in having adopted the ideas of the Rajah in the matter of the purchase of the places."[4]

The Raja was upset by these admonitions and, fearing lest he should forfeit the Company's support, tried to justify his action. He maintained that he had secured the approval of the preceding Governor of Madras, Sir Archibald Campbell, for the purchase of

[1] *Memoirs of Tippoo Sultaun by an Officer in East India Service*, p. 44.
[2] M.R., Mly. Cons., Aug. 28, 1789, Madras to Bengal, vol. 131A, pp. 2374-5.
[3] *Ibid.*, Aug. 30, 1789, Madras to Pawney, pp. 2386-7.
[4] *Ibid.*, Sept. 29, 1789, Cornwallis's letter, Sept. 9, vol. 131B; pp. 2659-61.

the forts; that they were situated only a gunshot from the boundary of his country, and were, in consequence, important to its security; that the Dutch never paid any tribute to the Raja of Cochin and had an independent right to dispose of them.[1]

The Raja's contentions, however, were not based on facts. His assertion that before purchasing Ayicotta and Cranganur he had obtained the permission of Archibald Campbell was entirely false, because, when the latter was questioned about it, he informed the Court of Directors in a letter of September 20, 1790, that "he neither countenanced nor advised the Rajah in the purchase of Cranganur and Ayicotta." The Court of Directors also pointed out that "nothing appeared on the Madras records to corroborate the assertion of the Rajah relative to those places having been purchased by him in consequence of Sir Archibald Campbell's advice."[2] Hollond, too, stated that the Raja had purchased the forts without the consent of the Madras Government.[3] Similarly, Cornwallis did not believe the Raja, and pointed out that Campbell never made any communication about the purchases either to him or to his Council.[4] It is only much later, when the war was half way through, that in order to justify the war and the Raja's actions that led to it, he informed Dundas of having seen the correspondence between Campbell and Bannerman which showed that the Raja had entered into negotiations with the Dutch not only with the sanction but the advice of Campbell, and that, owing to the latter's poor health, the whole episode must have escaped his memory.[5]

The second statement of the Raja is also not borne out by facts. Cranganur was some miles away and not within gunshot of the Travancore lines;[6] nor was it true that the forts in question were necessary for the defence of a country so strong and difficult of access as Travancore.[7] The Madras Government believed that "Cranganore and Jaicottah are Dutch places of no strength."[8] Lord Cornwallis also thought that "the forts, if they deserve that name, were after all of

[1] *Ibid.*, Pawney to Hollond, Sept. 9, p. 2663; Mly. Count. Cor., Raja to Hollond, July 2, 1789, vol. 38, No. 54, pp. 87-9.

[2] *Cobbett's Parl. Hist.*, xxviii, pp. 1302-3; M.R., Mly. Count. Cor., Hollond to Raja, Nov. 16, 1789, vol. 38, No. 106. Hollond also maintained that the Raja had not obtained the permission of Campbell to purchase the forts, for if Campbell had given the permission he would have informed him according to "established custom." As already mentioned, Campbell had refused permission to the Raja (see *supra*, p. 159 and footnote).

[3] N.A., Sec. Pro., Jan. 27, 1790, Hollond to Cornwallis, Jan. 3, Cons. No. 1.

[4] P.R.O., 30/11/51, Cornwallis to Dundas, Dec. 5, 1789, ff. 161a-b.

[5] *Ibid.*, Sept. 3, 1791, f. 87a. It is strange that such an important matter should have been forgotten by Campbell.

[6] *Cobbett's Parl. Hist.*, xxviii, p. 1289.

[7] Governor-General's letter of Dec. 15, 1789, cited in *Cobbett's Parl. Hist.* xxviii, p. 1289.

[8] N.A., Sec. Pro., Sept. 9, 1789, Madras to Bengal, Aug. 16. Cons. No. 1.

very little consequence, and if I had been informed of what was going forward, I should have advised the Rajah not to purchase them."[1] Pawney, too, observed: "Cranganore and Jaicottah will be found upon examination to be very inconsiderable and not acquisitions worthy of serious competition."[2] Even the Raja acknowledged that "there is not the slightest benefit or advantage accruing to me from the possession of Jaicottah and Cranganore."[3] That in spite of this he purchased them was because their acquisition fitted in with his general policy of expansion in Malabar. Moreover, he was afraid that, if he rejected the offer of the Dutch, "Tippoo should of a sudden possess himself of them,"[4] and he could not tolerate that a fort, however unimportant, close to the lines should be in the hands of his enemy.

The last argument of the Raja, however, that the Dutch were free to sell the forts to whomsoever they liked, appears to be sound. The Dutch, no doubt, used to pay the Cochin Raja annually half the income of the import and export duties—"a revenue which he enjoyed in the time of the Portuguese and which was left to him afterwards by treaty,"[5] and which was "the only remnant of his former greatness."[6] When the Raja became the tributary of Mysore, all the privileges enjoyed by him passed on to Tipu, who now began to receive his share of the taxes.[7] Similarly, the Dutch Company paid twelve pagodas annually as rent to Tipu's land-lessor.[8] But the rent or taxes that Tipu or his subject received, were not tribute as he interpreted, and did not give him the right to claim sovereignty over the forts which the Dutch had conquered from the Portuguese. (It seems that the Sultan identified rent with tribute, using the words interchangeably in his letters to the Governor of Madras). Even if we accept that the Dutch paid him tribute, this did not, according to the political usage of 18th century India, restrict their freedom to dispose of their possessions.[9] In fact, later on, Tipu did not speak of his right, but pointed out that it was unkind of the Dutch to have

[1] Ross, *Cornwallis*, ii, p. 126.
[2] *Cobbett's Parl. Hist.*, xviii, p. 1292.
[3] *Ibid.*, p. 1289.
[4] *Ibid.*
[5] Dutch Records, No. 13, pp. 125, 228.
[6] *Ibid.*
[7] See M.R., Mly. Cons., Jan. 5, 1790, Tipu to Raja, undated, p. 47 (Tipu uses the word tribute); M.R., Mly. Count. Cor. Tipu to Hollond, Sept. 12, 1789, vol. 38, No. 92, pp. 169-71 (Here the word rent is used); *Ibid.*, Feb. 22, 1790, vol. 39, No. 59, pp. 125-26. Tipu sent all the papers to Hollond about his dispute with the Raja and the Dutch.
[8] Van Lohuizen, *The Dutch E.I.C. and Mysore*, pp. 155-56.
[9] Haidar, and later Tipu, paid tribute to the Poona Govt., but this did not imply any restriction on their sovereignty, and they never tolerated interference in their internal affairs.

sold the forts to his enemy instead of to him.[1] Tipu's real grievance appears to be that, although he received rent and taxes from the Dutch, he had not been given preferential treatment; instead, he had been ignored in favour of a petty prince with whom he was on inimical terms. Moreover, he had shown his interest in the forts before the Raja did;[2] and while he was trying to acquire them, the Raja had come forward and purchased them. All this hurt Tipu's pride, and he felt cheated and insulted. Pannikar is not wrong in accusing the Dutch of double-dealing[3]—Van Lohuizen's attempt to whitewash their conduct is not convincing.[4] But the Raja of Travancore should also share the blame with them. He took advantage of the rivalry between Tipu and the English to extend his territory.[5] He did not purchase Cranganur and Ayicotta because he regarded them strategically important for the defence of his kingdom; he acquired them for self-aggrandisement and in order to abet the Dutch in their schemes.

However, even after the forts had passed into the hands of Rama Varma, Tipu continued his efforts to acquire them. He asked Hollond, the Governor of Madras, to persuade the Raja to return the places to the Dutch.[6] He tried to prevail upon the Dutch through the Raja of Cochin to demand them back, and offered to pay for them six lakhs of rupees, which was twice the amount they had obtained from the Raja.[7] He also directly wrote to the Raja to cancel the transaction with the Dutch.[8] But his efforts failed; neither the Dutch wanted to regain possession of Cranganur and Ayicotta nor was the Raja prepared to relinquish his hold over them.[9]

Towards the end of October 1789, Tipu encamped in the neighbourhood of Palghat. From here he invited the Raja of Cochin to visit him. But the latter, on the advice of the Raja of Travancore, feigned illness, shut himself up in a room and refused to see Abdul

[1] P.R.O., 30/11/151, Cornwallis to Dundas, Jan. 2, 1790, f. 3a.

[2] See p. 157, *supra*,

[3] Pannikar, *Malabar and the Dutch*, p. 110.

[4] Van Lohuizen, *The Dutch E.I.C. and Mysore*, pp. 151 *seq.*

[5] P.A.MS., No. 1337.

[6] M.R., Mly. Count. Cor., Tipu to Hollond, Sept. 12, 1789, vol. 38, No. 92, pp. 169-71.

[7] M.R., Mly. Cons., Nov. 1789, Pawney to Hollond, Oct. 20, vol. 131C, p. 2911.

[8] *Ibid.*, Jan. 1, 1790, vol., 133A. Before this Tipu had written several times to the Raja.

[9] Soon after the transaction, the Raja thought of restoring the forts to the Dutch, because from the letters of Cornwallis and Hollond it appeared that the Company would not help him to defend them. The Dutch, too, were alarmed for they realised that if Tipu attacked the forts, Rama Varma would not be able to hold them long, and the Mysoreans, after occupying them, would advance against Cochin without setting foot on Travancore's original territory. The Dutch therefore prepared for the defence of Cochin. But the skirmish of Dec. 29 dispelled the fears. (Van Lohuizen, *The Dutch E.I.C. and Mysore*, pp. 157-59.)

Qadir, Tipu Sultan's *wakil*.[1] On December 14 Tipu arrived at a place about twenty-five miles distant from the lines. On the following day he sent a *wakil* to Rama Varma with a letter demanding, first, that Rama Varma should deliver up the rulers of Calicut, Chirakkal, Kadattanad and other refractory subjects of the Mysore Government, and should, in future, abstain from harbouring them; secondly, that he should give up Cranganur and Ayicotta; and lastly, that he should demolish that portion of the lines which crossed the territory of the Cochin Raja.[2]

Rama Varma's reply to these demands was highly unsatisfactory. He flatly refused to demolish the lines and restore Cranganur and Ayicotta to the Dutch; and as to the demand for the surrender of the rebels, he maintained that he never gave protection to them, and that they had entered his kingdom without his knowledge. The Rajas of Chirakkal, Calicut and Kadattanad, however, had been given asylum because they were his relations. No demand for their repatriation had ever been made by Tipu before, but since it had now been made they would be asked to depart from Travancore.[3]

The justification of the Raja of Travancore for the presence of rebels in his kingdom was very inadequate. He gave refuge to the rulers of Chirakkal, Calicut and Kadattanad not because they were his relations, but because he wanted to use them as pawns in the game of Malabar politics. His statement that rebels entered his kingdom without his knowledge was also quite false, for the complaint of the Mysore Government that the Raja harboured its rebels went back to the time of Haidar.[4] After Haidar's death, Tipu also had the same grievance and complained about it not only to the Raja but also to the Government of Madras. The latter had, thereupon, warned the Raja not to "give assistance or encouragement to any of the *poligars* or others on the Malabar coast with whom Tipu may have disputes."[5] But this had no effect upon the Raja, who did not give up his policy of inciting rebellions in Malabar and extending protection to the rebels in his kingdom.

Having failed to secure the acceptance of his demands, Tipu marched towards the lines so that by his presence near the boundaries of Travancore, Rama Varma might be induced to change his hostile attitude. On December 24 he encamped about four miles from the

[1] Menon, *History of Travancore*, pp. 219-20.

[2] M.R., Mly. Cons., Jan. 1, 1790, vol. 133A.

[3] *Ibid*

[4] Sinha, *Haidar Ali*, p. 154.

[5] M.R., Mly. Count. Cor., Governor to Raja, April 17, 1788, vol. 37, No. 36. Later, Cornwallis also advised the Raja not to meddle in the disputes between Tipu and the Raja of Cochin, and warned him that, if he did this and it led to a conflict with Tipu, the English would not help him. (I.O. Pol. & Sec. Dept. Records, Cornwallis to Sec. Committee, Nov. 5, 1789).

lines, and again sent his emissary to the Raja with his demands.[1] But, as before, the Raja's reply was unsatisfactory.

Meanwhile, Tipu sent his troops to seize a number of rebels who had taken refuge in the jungles and hills adjoining the Travancore State. They were rounded up, but while they were being escorted to the camp, the Travancoreans fired upon their guards. This provoked the Mysore troops who retaliated[2] by attacking the weakest part of the lines at the eastern extremity, to which they had been conducted on the night of December 28, 1789, by some of the inhabitants of the country.[3] The Travancoreans were taken by surprise and fled. The result was that, soon after daylight, the Mysoreans succeeded in seizing a considerable extent of the rampart and in introducing a large number of their troops within the wall. After this they marched along the rampart to capture the gate, and thereby admit the rest of the army within the lines. At first the resistance was feeble, and the Travancoreans fled from one post to another; but across one square enclosure used as a magazine and barrack, along which the Mysoreans had to pass, about 800 Nairs, with the help of a six pounder-gun, managed to check their advance, and with the aid of further reinforcements, inflicted great loss on them. The conflict lasted nearly four hours. Being exposed to the attacks of the Raja's forces coming both from the right and the left, the Mysoreans were completely demoralised and fled in panic.[4]

It has been taken for granted by some historians that Tipu was present with his troops during the engagement, and that, although he escaped with his life, he was wounded by a musket ball, and his palanquin, his seals, his sword, his pistol and a silver box containing his diamond rings and jewels fell as trophies into the hands of the enemy.[5] In reality, no reliable evidence exists to prove that Tipu was personally present during the attack by his troops upon the lines. He himself denied it; he even maintained that the engagement had taken place without his knowledge, and that as soon as he heard of it he at once recalled his troops and sent back the Travancore prisoners of war to the Raja.[6] It appears that the rumour of Tipu's narrow escape and his being wounded was spread by some *harcarahs* who claimed to have returned from Tipu's camp. But their reports cannot be taken

[1] P.R.C., iii, No. 53.
[2] N.A., Pol. Pro., Feb. 10, 1790, Tipu to Hollond, Jan. 1, Cons. No. 9.
[3] *Ibid.*, Feb. 3, 1790, Pawney to Hollond, Jan. 4, Cons. No. 5.
[4] *Ibid.;* Mackenzie, p. 16. Wilks, ii, pp. 357-8, is wrong in saying that only 20 men turned the fortune of the day. Regarding the number of Mysoreans killed and wounded, there are different versions. The Raja says they lost 1000, while according to Mackenzie their casualties amounted to 1,500.
[5] Wilks, ii, p. 358; N.A., Pol. Pro., Feb. 10, 1790, Pawney to Cornwallis, Jan. 10, Cons. No. 1.
[6] *Ibid.*, Tipu to Hollond, Jan. 1, 1790, Cons. No. 9.

seriously. They also informed Pawney that Qamar-ud-din Khan had been killed in the course of the attack, and because of this there was general mourning in the Sultan's Camp.[1] But this was obviously a lie because Qamar-ud-din Khan survived even the Fourth Anglo-Mysore War. Similar false reports were spread by a certain *mutasaddi* who was taken prisoner, and who claimed to have been a commander of 10,000 in the Mysore army. Wilks chiefly based his account of "the attack on the lines" upon the report of this *mutasaddi* about whom even Pawney said: "I do not place much confidence in what he has related."[2] With regard to the statement that the Travancoreans secured the Sultan's palanquin, sword and other articles, this also appears to be based on hearsay. Tipu, it must be remembered, never used a palanquin. As Wilks observes: "He was usually mounted and attached great importance to horsemanship, in which he was considered to excel. The conveyance in a palanquin he derided, and in a great degree prohibited, even to the aged and infirm."[3] Moreover, in none of the letters addressed by the Raja of Travancore to the Governor of Madras and the Governor-General is there any mention that his troops had secured Tipu's palanquin and sword, although he was the first person to have referred to them. He only mentioned that four horses, two stands of colours and two drums fell into the hands of his troops.[4]

From the above analysis it is obvious that the evidence in favour of Tipu's presence with his troops during their attack on the lines is not conclusive. Tipu, as already mentioned, maintained that he was not only not present during the attack, but was even ignorant of it; and his statement was corroborated by the Governor of Madras who wrote to Kennaway that the attack was made by accident and without any order from Tipu.[5] Even General Medows, who was very hostile to Tipu, regarded it as "a minor affair and not regular hostilities."[6] And in reality this so-called "attack on the lines" was nothing more than a frontier incident. But Rama Varma magnified it into a premeditated and planned act of aggression on the part of Tipu with the object of embroiling the Company in a war with the latter. That the Sultan had no intention of commencing hostilities against Travancore at this time is evident from the fact that he had not come prepared for it. He was

[1] *Ibid.*, Pawney to Cornwallis, Feb. 10, 1790, Cons. No. 1. Malet stated that Tipu had not been wounded. (P.R.C., iii, Nos. 81 and 88.)

[2] *Ibid.*, Feb. 3, 1790, Pawney to Hollond, Jan. 4, Cons. No. 5.

[3] Wilks, ii, p. 761.

[4] Raja to Medows, May 1, 1790, cited in Mackenzie, p. 17, footnote; Raja to Hollond, Jan. 1, 1790, cited in Mackenzie, p. 18, footnote; I.H.R.C., xix, p. 145. According to the record No. 1 the Raja's troops took a flag and its staff as trophies from Tipu's army.

[5] N.A., Pol. Pro., April 2, 1790, Cons. No. 1.

[6] M.R., Mly. Desp. to Court, Sept. 16, 1790, vol. 20, p. 69.

"ill provided both with guns and ammunition,"[1] and the number of troops which accompanied him were not sufficient to undertake any large scale enterprise in which they would have to face an army of 100,000 including about 8,000 men dressed and equipped like the sepoys of the Company.[2] Moreover, he not only disavowed the "act of hostility" which took place on December 29, 1789, but subsequently for two months, his conduct remained conformable to such a disavowal.[3] He returned the Raja's prisoners of war, and wrote to the Governor of Madras that he desired the Company's mediation.[4] He again wrote to him on February 7 that he was ready to receive the Commissioners. He repeated the offer on February 22, and sent the papers in order to justify his stand in regard to the forts.[5]

On March 1 about 1,000 Travancore troops advanced from their lines into the Mysore territory under the plea that they wanted to reconnoitre and clear a thick jungle which grew in front of them, and where it was apprehended the enemy designed to erect a battery. But before they could advance about 400 yards, they were attacked by the Mysoreans, and although they were supported by a heavy fire from the ramparts, they were driven back with considerable loss. After this Tipu erected a number of batteries which soon put nearly all the guns of the lines out of action. On April 9 two parties of the Travancoreans consisting of 1,500 men each sallied forth from the lines to attack the Mysoreans. But like the attempt of March 1, it also ended in a fiasco, and the Raja's troops were driven back with loss.[6]

Meanwhile, Tipu tried his best to secure a settlement of his dispute with the Raja by negotiations. He wrote to the Governor of Madras to mediate in the matter,[7] and invited Pawney to visit his camp along with some other confidential persons in order to settle his differences with the Raja.[8] But his efforts proved futile, and in the face of repeated provocations from the Raja and the determination of the English to make war on him, Tipu resolved to invade Travancore.

From the morning of April 12, 1790, the Mysoreans began a regular cannonade which, within a few days, made a practical breach of at least three quarters of a mile. On April 15, at day-break, Tipu

[1] Pawney to Hollond, Jan. 17, 1790, cited in Mackenzie, p. 28 footnote., It is difficult to estimate the number of troops present with Tipu at this time. The English accounts give exaggerated estimates. According to *Tarikh-i-Tipu*. f. 98b, Tipu had only 2 *cushoons* which means about 2,000 men.

[2] Mackenzie, i, p. 29 footnote.

[3] N.A., Pol. Pro., March 3, 1790, Cons. No. I.

[4] N.A., Pol. Pro., Feb. 10, 1790, Tipu to Hollond, received Jan. 21, 1790, Cons. No. 9.

[5] M.R., Mly. Count. Cor., Tipu to Hollond, Feb. 22, 1790, Vol. 39, No. 59, pp. 125-26.

[6] Mackenzie, i, pp. 29-31.

[7] N.A., Pol. Pro., Feb. 10, 1790, Tipu to Hollond, Jan. 1, Cons. No. 9.

[8] *Ibid.*, Feb. 17, 1790, Tipu to Pawney, received on Jan. 26, Cons. No. 7.

attacked the lines with only about 6,000 men, and although 30,000 foot and 800 horse were ready to defend the breach, he planted his colours and advanced to the assault.[1] The resistance was inconsiderable, and the lines were carried more easily than was expected. The Raja's troops became panic-stricken and fled.[2] In fact they were so terrified that attempts to rally them proved unsuccessful; and as Pawney observed: "Never was there such a shameful flight."[3] The two English battalions, with three more which had been sent under Colonel Hartley from Bombay, retired to Ayicotta, finding themselves too weak to hold their position. The result was that Tipu took possession of the lines from the hills to the Chimmamanglum river with all their cannon and ammunition.[4]

After this Tipu marched towards Cranganur, and on April 18 arrived within one mile of the place. By April 26 he had completed the erection of batteries which by May 7 had demolished the defences of the fort and silenced all its guns.[5] Tipu was contemplating to storm Cranganur when Colonel Hartley withdrew the garrison from the fort on the night of May 7, realising that he was not strong enough to hold his ground any longer. Thereupon, the next morning Cranganur was occupied by the Mysoreans.[6] Ayicotta, Parur and other forts also surrendered soon after without any opposition. Tipu demolished the lines and the whole of Travancore lay open to him. He had, however, reached as far as Verapoly when he received the news of English preparations for the invasion of his kingdom. On March 24, therefore, he marched back. But for this English threat, which compelled him to withdraw, Tipu would have occupied the whole country with the greatest ease, for there was no organised force left to oppose him.[7]

We have seen that Cornwallis had made up his mind to fight Tipu and reduce his power, and that he was only waiting to find a pretext. The incident of December 29 furnished him with one. As soon, therefore, as he heard of "the attack on the lines," he at once declared war on Tipu without even caring to inquire whether it was a genuine act of aggression or merely a frontier incident. He implicitly believed the reports of Pawney regarding the attack, although only a few months back he had suspected him of suppressing the truth and had condemned his conduct "in having adopted the ideas of the Rajah in the matter of the purchase of the places."[8] He also rejected the Sultan's

[1] *Ibid.*, May 14, 1790, Cons. No. 11.
[2] *Ibid.*, Cons. No. 15.
[3] *Ibid.*, Cons. No. 8.
[4] Mackenzie, i, p. 31.
[5] *Ibid.*, p. 36.
[6] N.A., Pol. Pro., June 2, 1790, Pawney to Madras, May 7, Cons. No. 10.
[7] *Ibid.*, May 14, 1790, Pawney to Cornwallis, April 18, Cons. No. 8.
[8] M.R., Mly. Cons., Sept. 29, 1789.

proposals to avert war and settle his dispute with the Raja by peaceful methods. his change in his attitude is due to the fact that by this time he had completed his military preparations.

Tipu's differences with the Raja were of long standing, some of them going back to the lifetime of Haidar Ali. He had written about them to the Governor of Madras several times, but the Company's authorities had not done anything beyond expressing pious hopes and wishes that the dispute between Tipu and the Raja should be settled by negotiations instead of by an armed conflict. It was not until January 1, 1790, that at last the Madras Government, in accordance with the instructions of Lord Cornwallis, informed Tipu that his differences with the Raja should be settled by the appointment of Commissioners.[1] Tipu did not reject the suggestion; he only pointed out that it would be better if the Commissioners were sent to him. The Governor of Madras in his letter of February 2, 1790, agreed to this.[2] But Medows, who assumed office as Governor of Madras on February 20, thought that if the Commissioners were sent to the camp of Tipu, it would be "highly improper" and "tend to lessen the consequences of the Company's Government in the eyes of the princes of the country." Lord Cornwallis also regarded the act of sending Commissioners as a "humiliating step.[3]" In reality, however, there was nothing derogatory to the honour of the Company in taking such a step. In fact, that was the only way to avert war, for, as Hippisley observed in the House of Commons: "Tippoo was there on the very spot fittest to have the preference for the examination of the facts in dispute."[4] Moreover, it was and remained an invariable practice of the Company's Government to secure the settlement of disputes and negotiate alliances or treaties by sending its agents to the Indian rulers. If, therefore, the Company could send its representatives to the Indian princes to discuss matters in which, being a principal, its honour was directly involved, surely it could afford to send them to Tipu when it was only required to act in the capacity of a mediator on behalf of one of its allies. Nevertheless, Lord Cornwallis rejected Tipu's proposal. He even went a step further: He refused to give the Sultan another chance to accept the original proposal of the Madras Government according to which he had been invited to send his agent. For, when on May 22, 1790, Tipu wrote to Medows that he wished to send his *wakils* to him,[5] he was informed that negotia-

[1] *Ibid.*, Jan. 1, 1790, President's Minute, Vol. 133A, pp. 21-3.

[2] M.R., Mly. Count Cor., Tipu to Madras Governor, Feb. 22, 1790, No. 59, Vol. 39, pp. 125-6.

[3] N.A., Pol. Pro., March 17, 1790, Medows to Cornwallis, and Cornwallis's reply, Cons. No. 5.

[4] *Cobbett's Parl. Hist.*, xxviii, p. 1338.

[5] P.R.C., iii, No. 111.

tions were no longer possible, but that, if he desired peace, he should pay reparations. This was such an unjust condition that Tipu had no other alternative but to reject it.

The refusal of Cornwallis either to despatch Commissioners to Tipu, or to receive them from him for the settlement of the disputed points, and then to crown it by a demand for reparations, show that he did not desire the maintenance of peace. It is true that in November 1789 he had instructed the Madras Government to ask Tipu to appoint Commissioners for the settlement of his dispute with the Raja.[1] But Tipu received the proposal after a delay of nearly two months when the incident of December 29 had already taken place. This delay was through no fault of his. He should not, therefore, have been denied another opportunity for a settlement which would have been very likely reached. While criticising Hollond's attitude in having delayed sending the proposal regarding the appointment of Commissioners to Tipu, Cornwallis himself confessed that if the letter suggesting the appointment of Commissioners had reached Tipu before December 29, 1789, "it is not absolutely impossible that the reasonable propositions contained in it might have induced him to open a negotiation for settling the points in dispute."[2] But if Tipu was willing to listen to the proposals of the Madras Government before December 29, there was no reason to suppose that he would have rejected its proposals after that date. In fact, from his letters addressed to the Governor of Madras and the Governor-General, it is evident that he was ready to settle his dispute with the Raja by peaceful methods. But Cornwallis wanted war and not peace because, as he informed the Secret Committee: "We can never hope to see our armies better disciplined than they are at present."[3] Similarly, he wrote to Medows, the Governor of Madras: "At present we have every prospect of aid from the country powers, while he (Tipu) can expect no assistance from France."[4] To the Governor-General this was the most favourable opportunity for enhancing his country's 'honour' and promoting its 'interests'.[5]

[1] N.A., Sec. Pro., Nov. 13, 1789, Cons. No. 1.
[2] N.A., Pol. Pro., April 2, 1790, Cons. No. 1.
[3] I.O., Bengal Secret Letters, Vol. 1 (first series) Cornwallis to Secret Committee, April 12, 1790, No. 17.
[4] N.A., Pol. Pro., March 10, 1790, Cons. No. 4.
[5] *Ibid.*

CHAPTER XII

# THE COALITION AGAINST TIPU

Lord Cornwallis could not enter into an offensive and defensive alliance with the Marathas in 1787 because, in the absence of any provocation from Tipu, that would have been a violation of the India Act of 1784. But the so-called attack on the Travancore lines having freed the Governor-General from the restraints imposed by the Act, he immediately set himself to the task of organising a confederacy against Tipu. He was anxious to obtain the support of the Indian princes, and particularly of the Peshwa, in order that "the war should be speedily terminated not only from the point of view of the Company's finances, but also in order to preclude the coming of help from France."[1] To achieve the success of his negotiations, he used cajolery and inducements. He even employed threats, and appealed to the religious sentiments of the Hindu rulers.

Malet, the Company's agent at Poona, was instructed to inform the Peshwa about Tipu's aggression against an ally of the Company, and to "excite him to embrace this favourable opportunity to revenge the injuries that the Mahrattas have suffered from Tipu and his father by engaging heartily and vigorously with us in carrying on the war against him."[2] In case Nana refused the alliance, Cornwallis asked Malet to warn him that "we have no doubt of our own strength being sufficient to bring the war to an honourable issue, but that if the burden of it shall be left entirely upon ourselves, we shall probably not think it incumbent upon us in the course of future negotiations to attend to the interests of those of our friends who have contented themselves with looking on a scene."[3] In a letter to Raghuji Bhonsle,[4] Cornwallis wrote: "By the blessing of God this faithless conduct (of Tipu) will afford me an opportunity of proving my attention to treaties and my determination to protect my friends against an enemy whose ambition is known to the world, and whose injuries to the Mahratta State have been very great, and I have no doubt but the Mahratta chiefs will consider it to be their duty, as well as their interest, to take this opportunity to obtain reparation

[1] N.A., Sec. Pro., March 3, 1790, Cons. No. 1.

[2] *Ibid.*, Jan. 28, 1790, Cons. No. 1.

[3] P.R.C., iii, No. 60.

[4] Raghuji was the eldest son of Mudhoji, and became Raja of Nagpur after the death of his father in 1788 (Duff, ii, p. 230-1).

and recover their territories that were unjustly seized by his late father, and will join in punishing a man who is the enemy of all mankind, and whose heart is bent on the destruction of every sect as well Hindoo as every other."[1] Similar letters were sent to Mahadji Sindhia and Tukoji Holkar, who were requested to use their influence at Poona to bring about an alliance between the Peshwa and the Company.

The response of Holkar to the advances of Cornwallis was disappointing; for he not only himself refused to join the English, but advised the Nizam and the Peshwa to do the same. He was in favour of an alliance with Tipu. And when they ignored his advice, he remonstrated with them for having entered into a coalition with the English.[2]

Sindhia, on the other hand, was willing to offer his personal services in the war against Tipu, and was ready to proceed to Poona in order to obviate any delay in the negotiations for a union between the Peshwa and the English. But his condition was that, during his absence, the English should protect his kingdom in Hindustan, and Cornwallis should persuade the Rajas of Jaipur and Jodhpur to return to the dependence of the Marathas. But Cornwallis refused these conditions on the ground that their acceptance would involve the Company into a labyrinth of difficulties.[3]

Moreover, Cornwallis did not require Sindhia's mediation, for his proposal for an alliance was favourably received by the Poona Government which, on February 7, 1790, officially declared to Malet that it was ready to take part with the Company in hostilities against Tipu.[4] Nevertheless, it was not without some difficulty that the final terms of the treaty were adjusted; for Nana, taking advantage of the English desire for a union with the Marathas, wanted to extort favourable terms from them before joining the coalition against Tipu.

After holding a number of meetings with Malet, Nana, on February 23, sent to him through Behro Pant, both in the name of the Peshwa and the Nizam, the preliminaries consisting of ten articles. These formed the basis of the negotiations, and were subsequently agreed upon with some modifications. Their chief provisions were: That the ancient possessions of the Peshwa, now held by Tipu, shall be restored to the Peshwa, and the principality of Cuddapah shall be restored to the Nizam; that the ancient *zamindars* and *poligars* of different districts shall be reinstated therein; that the *nazrana* on such reinstatement shall be equally divided between the three contracting

[1] N.A., Pol. Pro., March 10, 1790, Cons. No. 5.
[2] N.A., Sec. Pro., May 21, 1790, Cons. No. 4; N.A., Pol. Pro., Oct. 22, 1790, Cons. No. 10.
[3] N.A., Sec. Pro., March 24, 1790, Cons. Nos. 1, 2.
[4] P.R.C., iii, No. 65.

parties—the Company, the Peshwa and the Nizam; that the Peshwa's ancient *peshkush* or tribute shall be assigned to him; that Tipu's *khalsa* possessions (crown lands) shall be equally divided between the contracting parties; that the Peshwa shall make peace with the consent of other parties; and that if, after the conclusion of peace, Tipu attacked any of the parties, the others shall be bound to assist the party attacked, if called upon.[1]

Although Malet expressed satisfaction with the draft, he regarded it as incomplete and criticised some of its clauses with the object of rendering "the terms as advantageous as possible" to the Company.[2] He was opposed to the article which laid down that Tipu's *khalsa* possessions should be equally divided between the contracting parties, and proposed instead that the Treaty of Partition should be equal and reciprocal only if each party entered the war at the same time. But in case the English should first commence hostilities and conquer any part of Tipu's country, such part should not be included in the partition, but should remain exclusively with the English Company. From the time, however, that the armies of the Peshwa and the Nizam should enter the enemy's country, all conquests should be equally divided without any exclusive claim of the Peshwa to ancient possessions.[3]

At first Nana rejected this amendment, but accepted it after the proviso was added that, in the general partition of territory, due attention would be paid to the wishes and convenience of the parties relatively to their respective frontiers.[4]

Malet also objected to another stipulation of the preliminaries that the military quotas of the contracting parties should be equal, and proposed instead that "each party shall employ a force adequate to the occasion, and to the extent of its power, with good faith. It would be impracticable for either party to ascertain the numbers of others. Good faith must, therefore, be the rule of action."[5] But in the end on this point also a compromise was arrived at, which was that, while the allies should enter the war with all their powers, they should not bring in less than 25,000 men.[6]

As decisions had been reached on most of the controversial issues, Malet entered into a Preliminary Agreement with the Poona Government on March 29. But before it could be reduced to its final form and ratified, there were still many questions to be settled and difficulties to be overcome. What, for example, were the powers of the

[1] N.A., Sec. Pro., March 24, 1790, Malet to Cornwallis, Feb. 24, Cons. No. 3.
[2] *Ibid.*
[3] *Ibid.*, April 7, 1790, Malet to Cornwallis, March 12, Cons. No. 1.
[4] *Ibid.*, April 23, 1790, Cons. No. 2.
[5] *Ibid.*, April 7, 1790, Cons. No. 1.
[6] *Ibid.*, April 23, 1790, Cons. No. 2.

Peshwa to act for the Nizam? What was the definition of ancient *poligars* and *zamindars*? And what was the correct interpretation of the word "district?" Besides, there was the question of Tipu's agents at Poona who were trying their best to prevent the formation of an alliance between the Company and the Peshwa.

Besides demanding one-third share for the Peshwa in Tipu's ancient possessions, Nana wanted, in addition, the tribute from the *zamindars* and *poligars* dependent upon the Mysore Government. Lord Cornwallis at first objected to this demand, and made it clear that the Marathas would not get the tribute from the *zamindars* and *poligars* in addition to the third share of the conquests; but that this tribute would be allotted as part of the third share to which they were entitled.[1] However, as Nana refused to forego his demand, Lord Cornwallis had to give in. The reason why the Governor-General yielded was expressed by him in a letter to Kennaway: "Though it would be desirable to obtain terms of precise equality in our treaty with the Marathas, yet as their hearty and early co-operation with us in the present war is of the utmost importance to our interests, I would designedly give them some advantage rather than retard the commencement of the operation of their forces."[2]

We have seen that Nana had agreed in the draft treaty of March 29 that he would employ a body of the Company's troops in the campaign, but now he maintained that, since he would employ a much larger body of Maratha troops, the Company's troops were no longer required. This change in his attitude was due to several reasons. In the first place, he felt that the payment of the Company's detachment would fall on the Peshwa, though its services would equally benefit the Peshwa and the Company. In the second place, he thought that, since the rainy season, during which military operations would have to be suspended, was very near, the services rendered by the detachment would not be in proportion to the expenses incurred by the Peshwa's Government. Finally, he did not wish to receive aid from the English in order to give Tipu the impression of his neutrality and thus obtain money from him. But Malet argued that the expenses would not be great, and that by declining the help of the Company's detachment not only would the military operations suffer, but it would also imply a failure on the part of the Peshwa in the discharge of the spirit of the treaty. The result of these discussions was that, ultimately, by his diplomatic tact, Malet was able to persuade Nana to adhere to the terms of the draft agreement and receive the detachment.[3]

By the middle of May almost all the controversial points had been

[1] *Ibid.*, April 30, 1790, Cons. No. 5, Cornwallis to Malet, April 26.
[2] *Ibid.*, Cornwallis to Malet, April 26, Cons. No. 4.
[3] *Ibid.*, May 12, 1790, Malet to Cornwallis, April 19, Cons. No. 12.

settled to the satisfaction of both parties. Nevertheless, Nana delayed the execution of the treaty because of the presence at Poona of Tipu's *wakils* who were doing their best to prevent its ratification by the Peshwa.[1] They had arrived at Poona on May 19 with Lakshman Rao Raste, bringing large sums of money, supported by liberal offers of territory to secure the assistance of the Peshwa in the war against the English, and if that was not possible, his neutrality.[2] The *wakils* were publicly received and, on June 8, Nana gave them an interview. He had made up his mind to join the English, but in order to secure the arrears of tribute from the *wakils* he treated them kindly, and tried to give them the impression that he would not enter into a union with the English.[3] Cornwallis, on the other hand, while certain that "notwithstanding the present doubtful appearance, the Mahrattas will ultimately perform their engagements,"[4] felt that the presence of the *wakils* at Poona was fraught with dangerous possibilities. Moreover, in order that the war might be vigorously prosecuted, Cornwallis did not want any further delay in the execution of the treaty. On his instructions, therefore, Malet strongly protested to Nana against the presence of Tipu's *wakils* at Poona and the friendliness shown to them, and pressed Nana to dismiss them and execute the treaty with the Company. In consequence, on June 1, 1790, a Treaty of an Offensive and Defensive Alliance was concluded between Malet, representing the English Company, and Nana, representing the Peshwa and the Nizam.

Malet had succeeded in outwitting the *wakils* by securing the ratification of the treaty by the Peshwa. Nevertheless, the *wakils* stayed on, still hoping to torpedo the alliance. Nana tolerated their stay because he wanted to secure from them the money they had brought from Seringapatam. But after he had extorted from them fifteen lakhs of rupees besides the durbar charges, he gave them audience of leave on August 4, and they left Poona on about August 17.[5]

[1] P.R.C., iii, No. 108.

Read wrote on Sept. 17, 1789, to the Governor of Madras that Sivaji Rao, the Maratha *wakil*, was in Tipu's camp, and it was reported that the Marathas had promised to help Tipu against the English. Again Read wrote on Jan. 4, 1790, that the Nawab of Arcot had sent an agent to Poona to persuade the Marathas to invade Mysore. But the Peshwa had replied that that was not possible because he had entered into a treaty with Tipu for 3 years and 3 months. (Mack. MSS.I.O., No. 46, p. 19.) It is quite likely that Nana promised Tipu help against the English. His policy at that time was to remain at peace with Tipu, as he had to deal with the intrigues of Holkar and Sindhia. Subsequently, by pretending to be on friendly terms with Tipu, he wanted to secure better terms of alliance from the English. But there is no reliable evidence to show that the Marathas had made any treaty with Tipu.

[2] P.R.C., iii, No. 110.

[3] *Ibid.*, No. 123.

[4] *Ibid.*, No. 113.

[5] *Ibid.*, Nos. 145, 147.

By this treaty the Marathas and the Nizam were required immediately to attack Tipu's northern possessions with an army of not less than 25,000 each, and reduce as much of his territory as possible before and during the rains. But after the rains, they were to prosecute the war against Tipu more vigorously, and in case the Governor-General required the aid of their cavalry, they were to furnish him 10,000 horse within one month from the time of his demand. This force was to act with the English army, and to be maintained at the expense of the English Company. Both the Nizam and the Marathas were to be allowed two battalions, and their expenses were to be borne by the Peshwa and the Nizam at the same rate as they cost the Company. All conquests were to be equally divided, unless the English, by being first in the field, had reduced any part of the enemy's territory before the allied forces entered on the campaign, in which case the allies were to have no claim to any part of such acquisitions. The *poligars* and *zamindars*, formerly dependent on the Peshwa and the Nizam, or those who had been unjustly deprived of their lands by Haidar Ali and Tipu Sultan, were to be reinstated on paying a *nazar*, which was to be equally divided among the three powers, but afterwards they were to become the vassals of the Peshwa or the Nizam. The names of these *poligars* and *zamindars* were specified. It was also stipulated that peace should be concluded by mutual consent, and that if, after the conclusion of peace, Tipu should attack any of the contracting parties, the others were bound to unite against him.[1]

Meanwhile, Kennaway, the Company's agent at the court of Hyderabad, was engaged in enlisting the support of the Nizam. Since the Poona Government claimed the power to conclude terms on behalf of the Nizam "on the strength of his being included in the Treaty of Salbai,"[2] the draft treaty of March 29, negotiated between Malet and Nana, was sent to him for acceptance. But the Nizam refused to recognise the claim of the Poona Government to treat on his behalf. Anxious "to emancipate himself from the power of the Mahrattas," he wanted to enter into a separate treaty with the English. Moreover, although he agreed to the substance of the draft treaty, he objected to its terms. He disapproved of the mode of partition as laid down in the tenth article of the draft, according to which the Peshwa was to get a tribute of about fifty or sixty lakhs of rupees from the *zamindars* and *poligars*, in addition to the third share of the conquests that may be made by the confederates.[3] "Since the expenses and hardships of war would fall equally on the three parties,"

[1] Aitchison, *Treaties*, vi, pp. 48-51.
[2] N.A., Sec Pro., March 31, 1790, Cons. No. 5.
[3] *Ibid.*, April 30, 1790, Cons. No. 12, Kennaway to Malet, April 9.

the Nizam regarded this clause as extremely unjust both to himself and to the English Company. He, therefore, proposed that "the acquisition of territory and property" should be equally divided between the confederates.[1]

The Nizam further wanted the defensive alliance against Tipu to be made general.[2] That is to say, the English Company and the Hyderabad Government should help each other not merely if they were attacked by Tipu, but also if they were attacked by any other power. The Nizam insisted on the inclusion of this article because of the apprehension that the Marathas might overrun his kingdom while his armies were away fighting Tipu. This had happened three years before, during the Maratha-Mysore War, when Tukoji Holkar had treacherously raided his territory in collusion with Tipu while the Hyderabad army had been engaged against the Mysoreans. The Nizam feared that what Holkar did then, Haripant might do now. That was why he was anxious for a separate article in the treaty which should guarantee the integrity of his kingdom.[3]

Some of the objections raised by the Nizam were admitted by Cornwallis, and the Preliminaries of March 29 were altered accordingly. Like the Peshwa, the Nizam was also given the right to the tribute of certain districts, in addition to a third share of the conquests that might be made by the allies.[4] Still the Nizam did not feel satisfied and objected to the surrender of districts yielding twelve lakhs of rupees to the Peshwa from the general partition. Malet, on the other hand, did not consider the claim of the Peshwa to that amount unreasonable, particularly when, after the overthrow of Tipu's power and the partition of the Mysore kingdom, he would be deprived of the tribute paid to him.[5] Besides, Malet argued that, even after the exclusion of the territory to be given to the Peshwa, the general partition was infinitely more advantageous to the Nizam than separate resumption. The Marathas had insisted upon the latter, and if that had been acceded to, the Nizam would not have obtained anything except Cuddapah, for the Maratha claims extended to almost every part of South India.[6] But even if the Peshwa's demands were unreasonable, Cornwallis was prepared "to make almost any sacrifice for the purpose of obtaining an immediate and vigorous co-operation of the Peswa's Government in the present war."[7] Kennaway was, therefore, asked by Malet to explain the position to the Nizam, but

[1] *Ibid.*, April 16, 1790, Cons. No. 4.
[2] *Ibid.*, March 31, 1790, Cons. No. 5, Kennaway to Malet, March 12.
[3] P.R.C., iii, Nos. 194, 199.
[4] Aitchison, *Treaties*, vi, Art. 7, p. 48.
[5] N.A., Sec. Pro., May 12, 1790, Malet to Kennaway, April 16, Cons. No. 4.
[6] *Ibid.*
[7] *Ibid.*, Cornwallis to Malet and Kennaway, May 10, Cons. No. 5.

in case he remained adamant, he was to be told that the Company "will give him out of its own share of partition four lakhs of rupees as Nizam's third of what the Peshwa will receive by the concession."[1]

With regard to the Nizam's demand that a separate article should be inserted in the treaty guaranteeing the integrity of his territory, Cornwallis argued that, since the Marathas had acceded heartily and cordially to the confederacy, it would be "improper to make any declaration in writing which contained suppositions that might give just cause of offence to the Peshwa's ministers."[2] He was, however, willing, provided the Marathas did not object, to include an additional article that, "should differences arise between any two of the confederates, the third party shall be bound to interpose his good offices and to take every means in his power to bring those differences to a just and amicable settlement."[3] But since the apprehensions of the Nizam could not be removed by the inclusion of this article, Cornwallis was obliged to give him definite assurances in private of the Company's assistance in case of Maratha aggression. Kennaway was instructed to tell the Nizam that the Marathas would never behave with such high-handedness towards one of their allies as to invade his territories, but, "if contrary to all probabilities the Mahrattas or any other power should attempt to injure or disturb his dominions while he is engaged in conjunction with us in the present war, I shall look upon the Company as bound by the strictest ties of honour to employ their whole force if necessary to obtain from him the most ample reparation."[4]

Even these assurances did not at first satisfy the Nizam, whose fears of a Maratha invasion were constantly being strengthened and kept alive by the Tipuphile party headed by Shams-ul-umara, who was opposed to the Nizam's entering the war as an ally of the English. But at length, Kennaway, by his tact and diplomatic skill, succeeded in removing the Nizam's fears and in persuading him to give up the demand for a separate article of guarantee in the treaty.

Similarly, Kennaway also secured the settlement of the question of a separate treaty demanded by the Nizam. The reason why the latter wanted a separate treaty with the English has already been referred to. But Cornwallis was opposed to it because separate articles were liable to cause complications at the time of the peace treaty. Besides, it was unnecessary to have separate articles when they were similar in substance to those proposed by the Peshwa. The Nizam had himself stated that he only objected to the terms of the

[1] *Ibid.*, Malet to Kennaway, April 16, Cons. No. 4.
[2] *Ibid.*, April 16, 1790, Cornwallis to Kennaway, April 12, Cons. No. 9.
[3] *Ibid.*
[4] *Ibid.*, April 30, 1790, Cons. No. 4.

draft treaty of March 29, but that he agreed to its essence, and as his objections had been met, and the treaty had been altered accordingly by Cornwallis, there was no necessity for a separate engagement. The Governor-General maintained that, "as the substance of the agreements is precisely the same, it would be most regular that a treaty of confidence should be formed for the three parties in one instrument."[1] But the Nizam was not prepared to accede to this proposition. Cornwallis therefore wrote to Kennaway that, "although in my opinion it would be most desirable that the three confederates should execute this treaty of confederacy in one instrument, yet you may assure His Highness that, if contrary to my wishes he should think it worth-while to require it, I shall not only sign a separate instrument, but also readily confirm and include in it the small deviation from some of the articles of the treaty concluded by Mr. Malet, to which you have already agreed."[2] On July 6, 1790, after protracted negotiations, a compromise was finally arrived at, and the Nizam signed another treaty of which the conditions were nearly the same as those of the treaty signed by the Peshwa on June 1.[3]

While engaged in forming a coalition of the English, the Marathas and the Nizam, Cornwallis also opened negotiations for obtaining the support of the tributaries and the refractory subjects of Tipu. He wrote to the Bombay Government to encourage the Malabar chieftains to rebel against the Sultan, and promised them his support in the undertaking. They were to be assured that their territories would be restored to them provided they agreed to become dependants of the Company, pay it "a very moderate tribute" and give it "advantageous privileges for carrying on commerce in the valuable products of their country."[4]

On August 8, 1790, Robert Taylor, the English chief of Tellicherry, managed to obtain the signature of the Bibi of Cannanore to the following terms as a preliminary to a future treaty of firm alliance: First, the Bibi agreed to admit the Company's troops to garrison her fortress of Cannanore during the present war, and to give her daughter's husband and one of her ministers as hostages, one day before the English troops set out, as a security for their admission into the fort. Secondly, she accepted the principle of free trade with the Company, and promised to supply it annually, at a favourable price, such quality of pepper and other articles as her country produced.[5]

Robert Taylor also entered into a treaty with the Raja of Coorg

[1] *Ibid.*, April 16, 1790, Cornwallis to Kennaway, April 12, Cons. No. 9.
[2] P.R.C., iii, No. 132.
[3] Aitchison, *Treaties*, ix, pp. 46-9.
[4] N.A., Pol. Pro., June 2, 1790, Cons. No. 4.
[5] *Ibid.*, Oct. 20, 1790, Cons. No. 33.

on October 26, 1790, by which the Raja agreed to treat Tipu and his allies as enemies, to furnish the English with supplies, to give them commercial privileges in his kingdom, to give the English troops a passage through Coorg and to have no connection with any other European nation; while the Company on its side guaranteed the independence of Coorg and the maintenance of the Raja's interests at the time of the termination of hostilities with Tipu.[1]

Similarly Pawney signed a treaty with Rama Varman, the Raja of Cochin, by which the Company agreed to assist him in recovering his possessions from Tipu, after which he would become the Company's tributary and pay an annual tribute according to the following scale: In the first year 70,000 rupees, in the second year 80,000 rupees, in the third year 90,000 rupees and thereafter 100,000 rupees.[2] Similar treaties were concluded with other Malabar chieftains like the Rajas of Chirakkal, Kadattanad and Kottayam.[3] Negotiations were also started with Rani Lakshmi Ammani of Mysore, and in 1790 General Medows informed her that if the allies proved victorious in the war, the English would gladly restore the kingdom of Mysore to its rightful rulers, but the question of the division of territories could only be considered later.[4]

### *Tipu and the Nizam*

Meanwhile Tipu Sultan was not inactive. As we have seen, he tried his best to counter the intrigues of Malet at Poona and to prevent the Marathas from joining the English against him. Similarly, he left no stone unturned to induce the Nizam to join him instead of joining the English. But just as his efforts failed at Poona, so at Hyderabad too they did not bear any fruit.

It was, however, the Nizam who, dissatisfied with the English attitude during the Maratha-Mysore War, and chagrined at the "Brahmins of Poona," who had concluded peace with Tipu without consulting him and caring for his interests, first made overtures to Tipu in August 1787. This was done through his nephew, Imtiaz-ud-daulah, and Shams-ul-umara, the Commander of his Household troops, and the principal *jagirdar* of the kingdom. As Tipu's response to the overtures was encouraging, the Nizam sent Hafiz Farid-ud-din and Bahadur Khan to Seringapatam in October 1787 with letters and presents for the Sultan. Ostensibly the ambassadors were despatched by Imtiaz-ud-daulah.[5]

[1] Aitchison, *Treaties*, ix, p. 279.
[2] N.A., Pol. Pro., Oct. 22, 1790, Cons. No. 2.
[3] P.R.C., iii, No. 109.
[4] Shama Rao, *Modern Mysore* (*Beginning to 1868*), p. 271.
[5] Mack. Mss.I.O., No. 46, pp. 53, 54. The Nizam also wrote to Cossigny to mediate between him and Tipu. (N.A., Sec. Pro., Nov. 12, 1787, Cons. No. 10).

The ambassadors reached Seringapatam in November. Tipu received the proposal for a treaty favourably, and wrote to the Nizam that he was ready to forget the wrongs he had suffered at his hands, "both on account of the union that as true Mussulmans ought to subsist between us and of the last advice given me by the Nawab," and requested him to appoint a time and a place where they could hold a conference and conclude a treaty.[1] Tipu further informed him that he was prepared to restore to him all the territory that appertained to the Deccan in the time of Nizam-ul-mulk; and, in order that the bonds of friendship might be further strengthened between the two families, he proposed the marriage of his son with the daughter of the Nizam.[2] The ambassadors returned to Hyderabad in February 1788 with these proposals.[3] But, although the Nizam had himself initiated negotiations, his replies to the proposals were only vague. In consequence, the exchange of embassies and friendly letters did not lead to any result.

After surrendering the Guntur Sarkar to the English in September 1788, the Nizam again made overtures to Tipu. He sent Farid-ud-din and Ramchandra during the last week of November 1788 to the Sultan who was then at Coimbatore.[4] He wrote to him that, as both of them were Muslims, they should forget their differences and become friends; and to give the impression of his sincerity, he sent him a splendid copy of the Quran.[5] Besides appealing to the religious sentiments of Tipu, the Nizam also tried to arouse his fears by warning him that the English intended to enforce the terms of the Treaty of 1768, which aimed at depriving him of a large part of his kingdom.[6]

As before, Tipu reacted favourably to the Nizam's advances. He informed Farid-ud-din that he was prepared to restore to the Nizam all the territory that appertained to the Deccan in the time of Nizam-ul-mulk. But in return the Nizam should make over to him the Guntur Sarkar for the same rent as paid by the English. Tipu further proposed a marriage between his son and the daughter of the Nizam, and stipulated that the latter should engage himself to help him in case of a war with the English and the Marathas. With these proposals, and accompanied by Tipu's *wakils*, Qutub-ud-din Khan and Ali Raza Khan, Farid-ud-din returned to Hyderabad on February 1, 1789, with costly presents for the Nizam.[7]

[1] *Ibid.*, p. 53.

[2] *Ibid.*, p. 55. Read at some places says that Tipu himself wanted to marry in the family of the Nizam. But this is incorrect.

[3] *Ibid.*, p. 54. Mir Alam does not always give correct dates. According to him the embassy returned on Jan. 27, 1789. (*Hadiqat*, p. 375.)

[4] Mack. Mss. I.O., No. 46, p. 86.

[5] Wilks, ii, p. 335.

[6] Aitchison, *Treaties*, ix, pp. 32-3.

[7] Mack. Mss.I.O., No. 46, p. 86; *Hadiqat*, p. 377.

At the same time that the Nizam sent Farid-ud-din to the Sultan, he sent Mir Alam to Calcutta. Mir Alam left Hyderabad on November 10, 1788, with a numerous retinue and presents for Cornwallis. He was instructed to demand from the Governor-General the fulfilment of other stipulations of the Treaty of 1768, since the Nizam had already given effect to the article that related to the Guntur Sarkar. After some difficulty he was able to secure from Cornwallis a respectable rent for the Sarkar and a promise of two battalions of sepoys and six pieces of cannon manned by Europeans, whenever the Nizam wanted to employ them against Tipu Sultan. These terms were regarded with satisfaction by the Nizam, for they gave him not only an immediate accession of revenue but also hope for acquiring territory in future.[1] Besides, the terms relieved him from all fears with regard to his southern frontiers. As a result, his replies to the proposals of Tipu were vague, and his reception of the Mysore agents, who were given their first audience on January 2, 1790, was rather cold. The marriage proposal was not accepted on the ground of the disparity of birth between the two families. The proposal for the recovery of Guntur was rejected because, as the Nizam maintained, he had himself voluntarily surrendered it to the English. With regard to the Carnatic, he pointed out that he was himself anxious to conquer it, but in the undertaking he did not need Tipu's assistance.[2] In spite of this, the Nizam did not break off negotiations with Tipu immediately after securing the assurance from Cornwallis, for he did not wish to antagonise him until he had concluded a treaty with the English for which talks had already commenced in January 1790. He, therefore, informed Tipu that the question of an alliance with him could be further discussed if he was willing to discharge the arrears of tribute on the basis of eight lakhs of rupees yearly which Haidar Ali had promised to pay him in 1766.[3] Meanwhile he kept Tipu's *wakils* under strict guard and surveillance. But on April 14 he broke off negotiations and dismissed them. He had by this time made up his mind to join the English.[4]

It has been suggested by Wilks that the negotiations broke down because the Nizam, considering himself of better lineage, refused to give the hand of his daughter in marriage to Tipu's son.[5] But this does not appear to be a correct explanation. In fact, it seems absurd that Tipu should have forfeited the friendship of the Nizam at such a critical time merely on sentimental grounds. The whole thing appears to be very frivolous. In reality, the reason why the talks failed was that the agents

[1] See pp. 151-2, *supra*.
[2] N.A., Pol. Pro., March 3, 1790, Cons. No. 4.
[3] *Ibid.*
[4] Mack. Mss.I.O., No. 46, p. 144.
[5] Wilks, ii, 335.

whom Tipu sent to Hyderabad were outwitted by Kennaway. They were unable to convince the Nizam that it was in his interest to ally himself with Tipu instead of with the English. Kennaway, on the other hand, succeeded in impressing upon the mind of the Nizam that his true interest lay in establishing a permanent and firm alliance with the English. The bait of territorial acquisition dangled by Kennaway dazzled his covetous imagination. Besides, Kennaway was enthusiastically supported by Mushir-ul-mulk, the Prime Minister, and Mir Alam, who were more skilful intriguers than Imtiaz-ud-daulah and Shams-ul-umara who favoured an alliance with Tipu. The death of Shams-ul-umara on January 11, 1790,[1] dashed to the ground any faint hope there still existed in the mind of those who favoured a union between Tipu and the Nizam.

There was yet another reason why the talks failed. The Nizam never really desired friendship with Tipu. He had made overtures to him only to excite the jealousy of the English, and thereby obtain better terms from them. He had at one time even gone to the extent of sponsoring a coalition of the Marathas, the French, Tipu and himself against the English; and for this purpose had despatched Suryaji Pundit, the Peshwa's *wakil* at Hyderabad, to Poona.[2] But these demonstrations of hostility were more pretended than real. It is true he was not enamoured of the English and looked upon them with suspicion, but he regarded Tipu as more dangerous. In fact, both to the Nizam and to the Marathas Tipu was a bugbear. That was why Cornwallis was able to say with confidence that he could not bring himself to imagining that "either the Mahrattas or the Nizam could be persuaded to take an active part against us in conjunction with Tippoo."[3] Cornwallis was certain that at any time he could secure their alliance by giving them some bones to gnaw.

### *Tipu and the French*

We have seen that Tipu sent an embassy to Paris in 1787 with a view to obtaining the aid of French troops in a war against the English or against any of the Indian powers. But the answer of Louis XVI, though sympathetic, was unsatisfactory. France was too deeply involved in her own internal troubles to undertake any fresh commitments.

Meanwhile, Tipu had also made approaches to the French in India. He informed them that the English-Maratha-Nizam coalition was not only directed against him but also against them, and suggested that they should create a diversion by entering the war.[4]

[1] *Hadiqat*, p. 379.
[2] Mack. Mss.I.O., No. 46, p. 56.
[3] P.R.C., iii, No. 72.
[4] A.N., C²191, Conway to de la Luzerne, Jan. 7, 1789, No. 16.

But Conway, the Governor of Pondicherry, unlike Cossigny, was hostile to Tipu, and wrote to de la Luzerne not to render him any help.[1] He was determined "to adhere strictly to the articles of the last treaty" and observed: "I will write civil letters to Tipu, but I will not supply him with a single man without orders, and such orders I will not receive."[2]

We have seen that Macnamara was sent with Tipu's ambassadors as an envoy of Louis XVI to Mysore. He had been unable to proceed from Pondicherry to Mangalore partly because of bad weather and partly because he had to execute orders for the evacuation of Pondichery. He finally arrived at Mangalore in February 1790, and delivered the presents from the French king and queen which could not be sent overland. In order to lull the suspicions of the English, he informed them that he was meeting Tipu in order to secure the release of the English prisoners of war. He landed at Chetona, nine leagues from where Tipu lay encamped. Tipu sent palanquins, horses and elephants to bring him, and on his arrival received him with honour. Macnamara had frank and friendly talks with the Sultan, and reviewed his troops by whom he was favourably impressed. To please Macnamara, Tipu issued instructions to his officers to hand over the territory of Kurangod Nair to the French and to place no restrictions on their purchase of spices, sandalwood and rice. In the course of the talks, he expressed his desire that the French join him in a war against the English. Macnamara was personally convinced of Tipu's sincerity towards the French and would have liked France to enter into an alliance with him, but he told the Sultan that, since his country was at peace with the English, she could not involve herself in a conflict by breaking the Treaty of Versailles. Macnamara left with letters and presents for the French king and queen and for de la Luzerne.[3] In these letters Tipu expressed his disappointment at the withdrawal of French troops from Pondicherry. This, he pointed out, would result in further strengthening the English, their common enemy. He requested Louis XVI to order the commander of the French forces at Pondicherry to send him 2,000 French troops without delay. All their expenses would be

[1] *Ibid.*, C²239, June 7, 1788, No. 6.

[2] National Library of Scotland, MS. No. 3837, Conway to Hippesley, Aug. 8, 1787, p. 219. Apart from his hostility to Tipu, Conway was not in a position to help him, even if he had wanted to, because of the French dependence on English financial aid. Writing to Dundas, Cornwallis informed him that he had given Conway a loan of one lakh and ten thousand rupees (*Ibid.*, MS. No. 3385, Cornwallis to Dundas, Aug. 9, 1790, p. 388). Realising that Pondicherry was subsisting on English economic aid, Conway wrote to Montigny, Commandant at Chandernagar, to pay all possible attention to Cornwallis and not to give him any cause of complaint. (*Ibid.*, March 8, 1789, p. 204.)

[3] A.N., C⁴102, Macnamara to de la Luzerne, 18 and 19 Sept., 1790.

borne by the Mysore Government and, on the termination of the war, they would be returned with honour.[1] But Macnamara was killed in the isle of France,[2] and the letters he was carrying did not reach their destination.

Soon after Macnamara's departure from the Mysore camp, Tipu addressed two more letters to Louis XVI, which were sent to de Fresne, the Governor of Pondicherry, to be despatched to France. Tipu also requested de Fresne for military aid, and in return promised help in case the English attacked Pondicherry. He expressed disappointment at the withdrawal of French troops from Pondicherry, and informed the Governor that, if the withdrawal was due to lack of funds, he was prepared to finance him.[3]

But as soon as hostilities between Tipu and the English broke out, de Fresne sent instructions to the commandants of various French factories in India to remain neutral.[4] This was not only due to the policy as laid down by the home authorities, but also due to conditions in Pondicherry. In the first place, Pondicherry had no troops to offer, and in the second, for some years past the French in Pondicherry were subsisting on English financial assistance, for money sent from Paris was not only insufficient, but never reached in time. When, therefore, Tipu demanded arms to be sent to the Malabar coast through some merchants, de Fresne did not accede to it. However, anxious not to displease one who regarded the French as his friends, he informed him that he had received the letter very late, that no vessels were available, and that soon the monsoon would not permit the vessels to proceed to the west coast.[5]

When in November 1790 Tipu invaded the Carnatic, he again tried to secure French assistance. On December 20, 1790, he sent Zain-ul-Abidin from Tiagarh along with an officer belonging to Vigie's detachment, which was formerly under Lallée, to de Fresne. He was publicly received on December 21. He gave the Governor a letter to be sent to Louis XVI whom he declared as a friend and an ally. De Fresne objected to this statement, because he was sure it would be reported to Madras, and he did not want to antagonise the English. He spoke to Zain-ul-Abidin that he had no troops to help the Sultan and, besides, it would compromise the position of the French

[1] Ray, *Some India Office Letters of the Reign of Tipu Sultan*, Nos. IV & V. Tipu addresses the minister as "Vizier of the Emperor of France".

[2] P.A., MS., Nos. 1323, 1479.

[3] *Ibid.*, 1263, 5300. At this time Tipu wrote several letters to Louis XVI and one to Marie Antoinette. He mentioned in these letters that he required only 2,000 men and no cavalry, infantry or arms and ammunition. (See A.N., C²295, Tipu to Louis XVI, Safar 8; Rabi ii 2,; Shawwal 13, 1206. Tipu to Marie Antoinette, Shawwal, 13 1206 A.H.).

[4] A.N., C⁴103, Cossigny to de la Luzerne, Nov. 1, 1790, No. 12.

[5] *Ibid.*, C²240, de Fresne to de la Luzerne, Feb. 20, 1790, No. 5.

who were on friendly terms with the English. De Fresne also refused a request for 100 men to increase Vigie's corps.[1]

Zain-ul-Abidin was, on his return, accompanied by M. Leger, Civil Administrator of French India, who was conversant with the Persian language. He acted as Tipu's envoy to Louis XVI, and proceeded to Paris with letters and presents from the Mysore ruler to the French king. Tipu requested for 6,000 troops, and offered to pay the expenses for their transportation, clothing and maintenance.[2] But owing to the unsettled conditions in France he was not able to receive any help. Thus, unlike the Second Anglo-Mysore War, Tipu had to fight this war single-handed against a combination of the English, the Marathas and the Nizam.

[1] *Ibid.*, C²295, Feb. 16, 1791, No. 31.

[2] *Ibid.*, C²299, Leger to Bertrand de Moleville, Minister of Marine, Oct. 10, 1792; also C²299, *Rapport*, Nov. 16, 1792.

CHAPTER XIII

## THE WAR: FIRST PHASE

Owing to his dissatisfaction with the Madras Government, Cornwallis had at first decided to proceed to Madras and take charge of the war against Tipu in person. But on learning that Medows, the Governor of Bombay, had been appointed the Governor and Commander-in-Chief at Madras, he changed his mind. Since he regarded Medows as "a man of acknowledged ability and character," he entrusted him with the responsibility of directing the war.[1]

The English plan of campaign was that General Medows with the main army should first take possession of the Coimbatore province and the bordering districts below the Ghats, and having secured this rich country as a base of supply, he should ascend into Mysore through the Gajalhatti pass. General Abercromby, the Governor of Bombay, on the other hand, was to reduce Tipu's possessions on the Malabar coast, and if circumstances permitted, to effect a junction with Medows; while Colonel Kelly was to penetrate from the centre of Coromandel into Baramahal for the defence of the Carnatic against the invasion of Tipu.

On May 24, 1790, Medows took the command of the principal force assembled near Trichinopoly, and on the 26th made his first march with an army of about 15,000 men. But so much time was lost in making commissariat arrangements, that it was not until June 15 that he was able to reach the frontier post of Karur, only fifty miles distant from Trichinopoly. Karur, found abandoned by the Mysoreans, was occupied the same day. Medows then, on July 3, advanced on Aravakurichi, a weak fort, which fell without resistance. After delivering it to its old Raja, he pushed on to Dharapuram, another weak fort which was also secured without opposition. Leaving there a large garrison, he proceeded to the town of Coimbatore, which having been found evacuated, he entered on July 21.

So far the English had not met with any opposition except from some bodies of irregular horse which had tried to harass them by hanging on their rear, carrying away a large number of cattle and wounding many of their followers. But on the day after the capture of Coimbatore, Medows learnt that Sayyid Saheb had arrived at

[1] Beveridge, *History of India*, ii, p. 587.

Danayakkankottai, about forty miles from Coimbatore, with about 4,000 cavalry "of very little merit."[1] He had been ordered by Tipu to hang upon the English army and disturb its communications. Medows, therefore, sent a large force under Colonel Floyd to surprise the Mysoreans. By a series of clever movements, Floyd not only drove Sayyid Saheb across the Bhavani, a tributary of the Cauvery, but pressed him so hard as to compel him to decamp towards the Gajalhatti pass. Sayyid Saheb's retreat was very injudicious, for it left the whole country to the south open to the English troops who, in consequence, easily seized Dindigul and other places.[2] For his mistakes, he was severely reprimanded by the Sultan.[3]

On August 5 Colonel Stuart was despatched with a strong force to reduce Dindigul, about 112 miles away. He arrived before it on the 16th. The fort of Dindigul was erected on the summit of a smooth granite rock nearly perpendicular on three sides, and accessible only on the east by a flight of steps. It had undergone considerable improvement within the last six years, and it possessed sufficient cannon, ammunition and provisions. The garrison, which consisted of about 800 men, was summoned with a declaration that, if they surrendered, they would be allowed to go to any part of Mysore with their personal belongings; but if they resisted they would all be put to the sword. The reply of the Commandant, Haidar Abbas, to the person who had brought this message was: "Tell your Commander, that it is not possible to account to my Prince for the surrender of a fort like Dindigul; therefore, if any other person comes on that errand, I will blow him from a cannon." On receipt of this answer, Stuart let loose his artillery which, after two days of cannonading, effected an imperfect breach. But as the ammunition was nearly exhausted, and no fresh supply could be expected before a week, he decided upon an assault, and ordered Major Skelly to lead it. The British troops attacked the fort with great vigour and resoluteness and, on the evening of August 21, made repeated efforts to penetrate; but owing to the strength of the fortifications, combined with the valour of the Commandant who headed his best troops at the breach, they were repulsed with loss. It was, therefore, a matter of surprise to the English to see, early next morning, a white flag displayed on the breach. What had happened was that the garrison, ignorant of the real strength of their opponents, were afraid to meet another assault, and had deserted their commander during the night. Haidar Abbas had, therefore, decided to capitulate. He surrendered the fort on August 22 after he had secured honourable terms. Colonel Stuart

[1] Mackenzie, i. p. 116 footnote, Floyd to Stuart, Sept. 21, 1790.
[2] Wilks, ii, pp. 385-6; Fortescue, iii, p. 560.
[3] Wilks, ii, p. 386.

next proceeded to Palghat which capitulated on the morning of September 22.[1]

Meanwhile Colonel Odham had captured Erode on August 7, and Colonel Floyd had seized Satyamangalam on August 26. The latter, situated on the north bank of the river Bhavani, was of considerable importance because of its proximity to the Gajalhatti pass through which the English troops were to enter into the heart of Tipu's kingdom.

The first part of the operations was thus successfully completed. The province of Coimbatore was occupied to provide supplies for the troops, and a line of posts was established leading directly from Karur to the Gajalhatti pass. But just when everything was ready for the invasion of Mysore, Tipu suddenly appeared in the neighbourhood of Floyd's detachment, which was stationed south of the Bhavani, opposite to the advanced post of Satyamangalam.

Tipu had withdrawn from Travancore on hearing of the English preparations for the invasion of his kingdom. He arrived at Coimbatore on May 24, and remained there throughout the month of June, watching the movements of Medows and intending to march against him. But as the movements of the English army were very slow, he did not think it worth-while to waste his time any longer. Leaving, therefore, Sayyid Saheb with some cavalry to impede the advance of Medows, who had by then only reduced the frontier post of Karur, Tipu set out for Seringapatam on July 1. He arrived there on the 12th, and remained busy for nearly two months in making preparations.[2] He then left Seringapatam on September 2 with 40,000 men and a large train of artillery. He reached the head of the Gajalhatti pass on the 9th, and immediately after, leaving his heavy stores and baggage at the summit of the Ghats under Purnaiya, began to descend the pass, the most difficult in all the eastern ranges.[3]

According to Wilks, Floyd had early intelligence of Tipu's movements, and he forwarded the information to General Medows with a suggestion that, considering the dispersed state of the English forces, he should be allowed to fall back upon army headquarters. But the intelligence was disbelieved, and Floyd was ordered to maintain his advanced position.[4] Medows, however, stated that "notwithstanding our vigilance the enemy came down quicker than our intelligence."[5] According to Munro and Mackenzie also the descent of the Sultan through the Gajalhatti pass into the Coimbatore province was so sudden, so silent, and so skilful that it came as a surprise to every one.[6]

[1] Mackenzie, i. pp. 74-8. [2] Mack. Mss. I.O. No. 46, p. 146.
[3] Fortescue, iii, p. 561; Wilson, ii, p. 194.
[4] Wilks, ii, pp. 391-2.
[5] N.A., Pol Pro., Oct. 13, 1790, Cons. No. 9.
[6] Mackenzie, i, p. 103; Gleig, *Munro*, i, p. 95.

Wilk's statement is thus incorrect, for Floyd became aware of Tipu's approach when it was too late for him to inform Medows and receive his instructions as to the course he was to follow. Floyd's patrol had observed Tipu's cavalry only on September 10, and Floyd sent a message to Medows on the 12th that the Sultan had arrived in person.[1]

On September 12 Tipu crossed the river Bhavani at the ford of Poongar, and encamped with a large portion of his army some miles to the south, while the remainder was ordered to proceed along the north bank in order to capture Satyamangalam and then cross the river.[2]

On the morning of the 13th, a large body of Mysore horse fell in with some English cavalry under Major Darby who had been sent to reconnoitre the ford of Poongar. The English were surrounded and hard pressed on all sides but, as they had seized a favourable post, they were able to carry on the conflict until the arrival of fresh reinforcements under Floyd. This not only saved them from destruction and secured an orderly retreat, but also compelled the enemy to retire with loss. The Mysoreans showed great courage, but they failed because of the nature of the country which was intersected by high and impenetrable enclosures of prickly hedges which greatly hampered the movements of Tipu's cavalry, while to the English, who were on the defensive, the terrain was very useful.[3]

Soon after this skirmish, Tipu himself advanced from the west to attack Colonel Floyd who was encamped south of the Bhavani; while, to distract the attention of the English, he ordered three of his guns to open upon them from the north bank. But as the English commander had managed to secure a strong position, Tipu could not approach; he only carried on a distant cannonade, which lasted the whole day and resulted in heavy English casualties and the disabling of three of their guns. But, at nightfall, Tipu retired to his camp.[4]

Owing to the heavy loss sustained by the cannonade, and finding themselves not strong enough to resist the Mysoreans, the English held a council of war in the night, and decided to abandon Satyamangalam and to retreat to Coimbatore. Accordingly, early in the morning, the troops commenced their march, leaving behind three guns and provisions in the fort of Satyamangalam. As soon as Tipu heard of this, he at once began preparations to pursue the English; but owing to the heavy rains which had fallen during the previous night, the troops had become scattered over the country; and when the order for march was given, they were busy preparing food, having fasted the previous day

[1] Fortescue, iii, p. 561 [2] Wilson, ii. p. 194

[3] *Ibid.*, pp. 194-5; Wilks, ii, pp. 392-3; A. N., C²240, de Fresne to de Vaivre, 27 July, 1790, No. 15

[4] Wilson, ii, p. 195; Fortescue, iii, p. 562.

and night. He, therefore, found considerable difficulty in getting his army ready for the pursuit, and in the end had to march with only a part of it, leaving orders for the rest to follow him.[1] At about ten in the morning his cavalry and light artillery overtook Floyd's rear and captured nearly the whole of his baggage.[2] Meanwhile, Tipu's main army also continued to grain ground, and was able by 2 o'clock to bombard the rear and flanks of the retreating English army. It succeeded in catching up with the English force at about 5 o'clock at the village of Cheyur, nineteen miles south of Satyamangalam. Floyd was obliged to halt and face the Mysoreans.[3] Tipu made a spirited attack, and in spite of the strong hedges which obstructed the ground, he had victory in his grasp, when Burhan-ud-din was killed. This made the Mysoreans lose heart. On top of that it was reported that Medows had come to Floyd's assistance. Tipu therefore drew off at nightfall.[4] Floyd's losses on September 13 and 14 had been very heavy. They amounted to 556 men killed and wounded. Besides, he also lost most of his baggage, his guns and draught oxen.[5]

During the battle Floyd had received a despatch informing him that Medows would march for Velladi on March 14. Realising that the only chance of saving his army was to force the junction with Medows, he set out at two in the morning, and reached Velladi at eight at night. But he was disappointed in not finding the General there. Medows had marched from Coimbatore to the relief of Floyd, but thinking that the latter had not yet left Satyamangalam, he had passed ten miles beyond of Velladi. Medows's northward move convinced Tipu that the General was manoeuvring to get between him and Seringapatam. He, therefore, fell back, and having recrossed the Bhavani, took up a strong position on the opposite bank, and waited for Medows. Tipu's front was protected by the river, while his two flanks were protected by the forts of Danayakkankottai and Satyamangalam. The Sultan also took great care to guard the fords of Satyamangalam and Poongar by which it was expected that Medows would try to cross the river.[6] But the English General, informed of Floyd's whereabouts, and realising that the invasion of Mysore was for the present no longer possible, avoided giving battle to Tipu and marched back to Velladi where he joined Floyd. From Velladi the two armies proceeded to Coimbatore, where they were joined by Colonel Stuart's division from Palghat on September 25.[7]

[1] Wilks, ii pp. 394-6.
[2] Fortescue, iii, p. 563; Gleig, *Munro*, i, p. 98.
[3] Wilks, ii, pp. 396-7.
[4] *Tarikh-i-Tipu*, ff. 100b-101a; Hamid Khan, f. 68b.
[5] Mackenzie, i, p. 119 footnote; Wilson, ii, p. 196.
[6] Mackenzie, i, pp. 120-1.
[7] Wilks, ii, p. 400.

Tipu had thus failed to cut off Floyd's army. This was partly due to Floyd's courage and perseverance, but chiefly because of the nature of the country which hampered the movements of the Mysore cavalry. Nevertheless, if Tipu had "followed up Floyd on the 15th, and condemned his troops to a third day of fighting, after two days had already passed without food or rest, he could hardly have failed to annihilate them."[1] But, although Tipu had failed to destroy Floyd's detachment, he had succeeded in the main object of his enterprise: He had checked the English invasion of Mysore through the Gajalhatti pass, and had converted a defensive into an offensive war.

Tipu now decided to reconquer the posts in the Coimbatore province occupied by the English. After ten days, during which he celebrated the Muharram, he set out towards Erode. The place "shamefully surrendered" on September 25 to a party of horse sent by him.[2] The terms of capitulation were observed, and the Company's troops were allowed to march to Karur.[3] From Erode, where valuable stores were obtained, he proceeded southward, and halted at a place about sixteen miles distant from where he could either attack the convoy advancing from Karur, or move towards Dharapuram or Coimbatore. As soon as Medows advanced from Coimbatore on September 29 to protect the convoy from Karur, Tipu quickly took advantage of the English General's preoccupation and proceeded southward with the object of seizing Coimbatore, which contained the English field hospital, stores and the battering train. His march was very rapid, and was continued in spite of severe rain throughout the night. But, hearing that Coimbatore had been reinforced by the troops sent by Colonel Hartley, who had arrived at Palghat from the Malabar coast, he rapidly marched to Dharapuram, which he besieged on October 6. On the 8th it surrendered on a capitulation, and the garrison was allowed to go free on condition that it would not serve again during the war.[4] But in spite of these successes, he had to give up his operations in the Coimbatore province and to march northward for the defence of Baramahal which had been invaded by the English.

According to the original plan of campaign, Colonel Kelly was to invade Baramahal on receiving reinforcements from Bengal. The troops sent from Calcutta arrived at Conjeeveram on August 1, 1790, but before Kelly could undertake the enterprise, he died on September 24. He was succeeded by Colonel Maxwell who, according to Medows's instructions, entered Baramahal with a strong army of

[1] Fortescue, iii, p. 564; Gleig, *Munro*, i, p. 99.
[2] Mackenzie, i, p. 124.
[3] Wilks, ii, p. 402.
[4] Wilks, ii, pp. 402-3; Wilson, ii, pp. 197-8.

9,500 men, excluding the troops of some of the *poligars* of the district who had joined him.[1] He encamped near the fort of Vaniyambadi and soon gained possession of it, for the Mysoreans had evacuated it.[2] On November 1 Maxwell approached Krishnagiri, the capital and the strongest fort of the district. But, finding that he would not be able to capture it by a regular siege, he established his headquarters near the central position of Kaveripatnam, intending to return and capture Krishnagiri by a surprise attack. But he was foiled in his movements by Tipu who had suddenly appeared in his neighbourhood.[3] Leaving behind a part of his army under Qamar-ud-din Khan in Coimbatore to watch the movements of Medows, Tipu had marched with the rest towards Baramahal with astonishing rapidity and secrecy. He had crossed the Cauvery on November 1 and 2, and reached the neighbourhood of Maxwell's army on the 9th.

On the 11th one regiment of English cavalry, while pursuing a party of irregular horse through a narrow pass, was suddenly attacked by about 2,000 Mysore horse and driven back with the loss of 70 men and 50 horses.[4] The next day Tipu himself appeared with his army to attack Maxwell. But as the latter, having crossed the Pennar river, was occupying a very strong position, Tipu did not think it advantageous to attack him. He tried his best to inveigle him into changing his position, but Maxwell remained on the defensive and awaited the arrival of Medows. So Tipu retired after sunset. On November 14 he appeared again, but as Maxwell refused to change his position, he withdrew on receiving the news of Medows's approach.[5]

General Medows, joined by the convoy from Karur, had returned to Coimbatore, and after strengthening the place, had set out to pursue Tipu. But the Sultan's march was so rapid and secret that the English followed him in vain, and it was only several days after he had crossed the Cauvery that Medows came to know of it. Anxious for the safety of Maxwell, whose cavalry was inferior to Tipu's, Medows decided to march to Baramahal. He crossed the Cauvery and reached the southern extremity of the Thopur pass on November 14.[6] Tipu did not want to be caught between the two English armies, so on receiving the intelligence of Medows's approach, he withdrew on the night of November 14 from the position he occupied. He encountered Medows the following day at noon at about twenty-nine miles from Colonel Maxwell's position at Kaveripatnam, but anxious to avoid battle, marched westward towards the Palakad pass

[1] *Ibid.*, pp. 199-200.
[2] P.R.C., iii, No. 164.
[3] Wilks, ii, p. 407.
[4] Gleig, *Munro*, i, p. 103.
[5] Wilks, ii, pp. 407-8.
[6] *Ibid.*, pp. 404, 408.

and encamped there. He had marched about forty-five miles in about twenty-four hours, notwithstanding the fact that he was encumbered with provisions, cannon and other necessary equipment. The ground on which he encamped at Palakad was well calculated to secure, if need arose, a safe retreat from Baramahal into Mysore by a pass very easy of access. Besides, the ground was also well suited to watch the movements of the English army.[1]

Meanwhile, Medows had effected a junction with Maxwell near Kaveripatnam. Tipu, realising that he would not be able to attack the united forces with advantage, changed the plan of his operations, and decided to attack the Carnatic in order to draw off the English from Mysore to the defence of their own possessions.[2] Accordingly, on November 18, he set out towards the Thopur pass. Medows, on the other hand, resolved to invade Mysore, because now he had at his disposal a force "far superior in number and equipments to any that Great Britain had assembled in India at a former period."[3] He moved southward on the same day as Tipu towards the pass of Thopur, and both reached the head of the pass almost at the same time. Tipu was attacked by the English with great vigour, but they failed to gain any advantage over him, for he succeeded in passing through before them without any loss. His cavalry covered the march of his infantry with great courage and skill.[4] He was personally present with the cavalry, and remained till the end, returning with a small escort only after the rest of his troops had passed.[5]

On emerging from the pass, Tipu struck off southward towards Trichinopoly, and did not halt until he had reached the north bank of the Coleroon, opposite the island of Srirangam, on November 28; but finding the river too swollen to cross, and also anxious to enter into the heart of the Carnatic, he contented himself with plundering the island of Srirangam. And on the approach of Medows, he made for Tiagar on December 6, which was eighty miles north of Trichinopoly. He remained before Tiagar from December 11 to 28. The place was defended by Captain Flint, who had distinguished himself in the defence of Wandiwash during the Second Anglo-Mysore War. Tipu made two attempts to capture the fort, but without success. As he did not think it worth-while to spend his time in a tedious siege, he withdrew and proceeded towards Tiruvannamalai, 35 miles north, which he occupied without any difficulty. He next captured Perumukkal on January 23 after a siege of only two days, and then marched to Pondicherry, expecting to obtain a promise of assistance

[1] Mackenzie, i, pp. 173-4.
[2] *Ibid.*, p. 175.
[3] *Ibid.*, p. 174.
[4] *Ibid.*, pp. 176-8.
[5] Wilks, ii, p. 411.

from the French.[1] Here he wasted valuable time. He should have attacked Madras before the junction of Medows with Cornwallis, and thus disturbed the latter's military preparations. He should have also attempted to destroy the military establishments of the English at Conjeeveram.[2]

General Medows, like Tipu, had also marched southward from the Palakad pass. He had reached the banks of the Cauvery opposite Karur on November 27, but while he was planning to invade Mysore, he was summoned to the relief of Trichinopoly. He was therefore obliged to give up his plan. He arrived at Trichinopoly on December 14, and then set out in pursuit of the Sultan who was always several marches ahead of him. He followed him as far as Tiruvannamalai when he received orders from Cornwallis, who had arrived in Madras on December 12, to return to the Presidency. In consequence, Medows marched towards Madras. He reached Vellout on January 27, where Cornwallis assumed command. This concluded the first part of the campaign against Tipu Sultan.

While Tipu had achieved great successes against the English in the south and the east, his troops had not fared well in the west. On December 10, 1790, his commander Husain Ali Khan was badly defeated by Colonel Hartley at Tirungadi, in the vicinity of Calicut, with a loss of 1,000 killed and wounded and 900 prisoners. The English lost only 50 men. The fugitives were pursued to the unfinished fort of Ferokh, where, two days after, about 1,500 men laid down their arms. But the Commandant succeeded in making good his retreat with the public treasure through the pass of Tamarassheri.[3]

Meanwhile, General Abercromby, the Governor of Bombay, had arrived at Tellicherry with a large force a few days before this action. From there he marched to Cannanore. The English had entered into a treaty with the Bibi by which they were entitled to send troops into her fort of Cannanore. But since she had signed the treaty under pressure, she instead admitted Tipu's troops into her fort when they approached Cannanore. This was regarded by the English as a breach of the treaty by the Bibi.[4] So Abercromby decided to reduce Cannanore. He appeared before it on December 14, and took it on the 17th, the 5,000 men in the fort surrendering to him. These defeats of the Mysore forces and their allies led to the establishment of British supremacy in Malabar.[5]

In spite of the defeat of the Mysoreans in Malabar, the first phase of the war had ended in favour of Tipu in the main theatre of war.

[1] *Ibid.*, pp. 411, 414-5; Fortescue, iii, pp. 567-8.
[2] A. N., C²295, de Fresne to Minister, Feb. 16, 1791, No. 31.
[3] *Ibid.*, p. 418; Cadell, *History of the Bombay Army*, p. 119.
[4] Pol. Pro., Dec. 24, 1790 Cons. Nos. 22, 23.
[5] Cadell, *History of the Bombay Army*, p. 120.

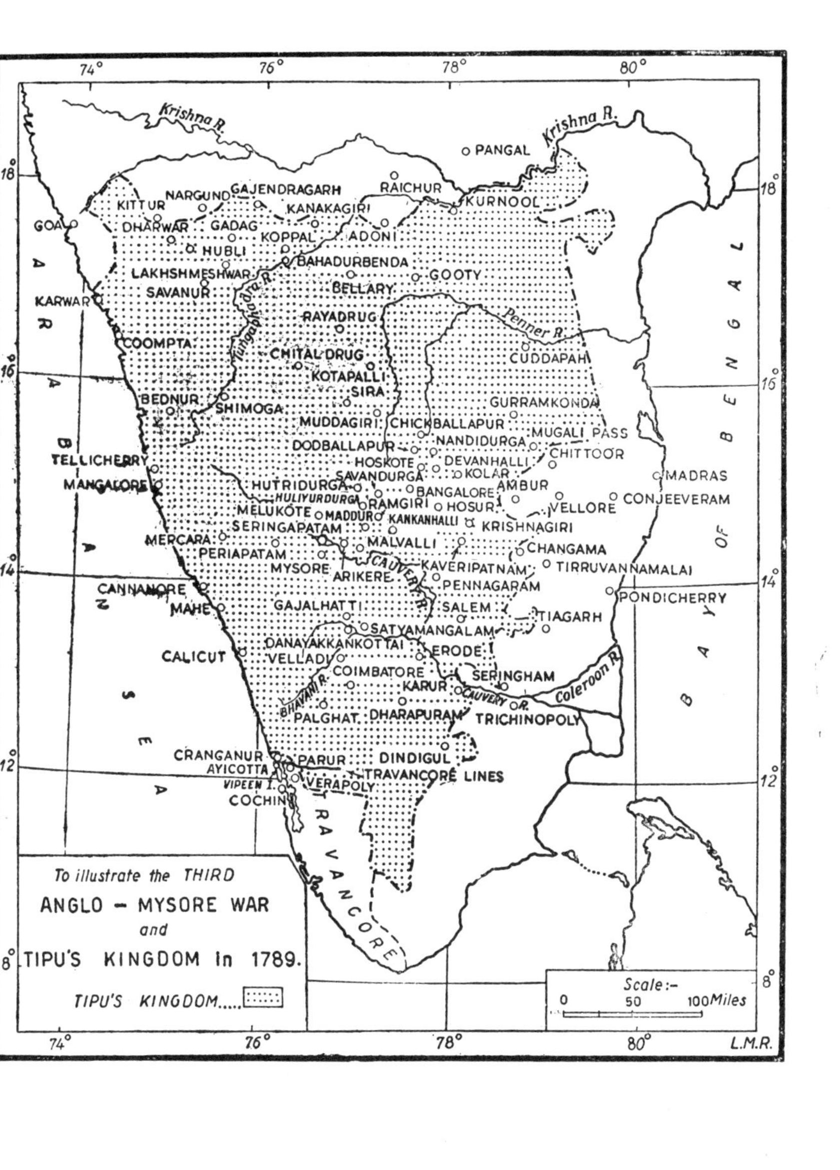

To illustrate the THIRD
ANGLO - MYSORE WAR
and
TIPU'S KINGDOM in 1789.
TIPU'S KINGDOM.....
Scale:-
0 50 100 Miles
L.M.R.
Krishna R.
Tungabhadra R.
Penner R.
Cauvery R.
Bhavani R.
Coleroon R.
ARABIAN SEA
BAY OF BENGAL
TRAVANCORE
PANGAL
RAICHUR
KURNOOL
KITTUR
NARGUND
GAJENDRAGARH
KANAKAGIRI
GOA
DHARWAR
GADAG
KOPPAL
ADONI
HUBLI
BAHADURBENDA
LAKHSHMESHWAR
GOOTY
SAVANUR
BELLARY
KARWAR
RAYADRUG
COOMPTA
CHITAL DRUG
CUDDAPAH
KOTAPALLI
SIRA
BEDNUR
SHIMOGA
GURRAMKONDA
MUDDAGIRI
CHICKBALLAPUR
MUGALI PASS
DODBALLAPUR
NANDIDURGA
CHITTOOR
TELLICHERRY
HOSKOTE
DEVANHALLI
MADRAS
MANGALORE
SAVANDURGA
KOLAR
HUTRIDURGA
BANGALORE
AMBUR
HULIYURDURGA
RAMGIRI
HOSUR
VELLORE
CONJEEVERAM
MELUKOTE
MADDUR
KANKANHALLI
KRISHNAGIRI
SERINGAPATAM
MERCARA
MALVALLI
CHANGAMA
PERIAPATAM
MYSORE
ARIKERE
KAVERIPATNAM
TIRRUVANNAMALAI
CANNANORE
PENNAGARAM
PONDICHERRY
MAHE
GAJALHATTI
SALEM
TIAGARH
SATYAMANGALAM
DANAYAKKANKOTTAI
ERODE
CALICUT
VELLADI
COIMBATORE
SERINGHAM
KARUR
PALGHAT
DHARAPURAM
TRICHINOPOLY
CRANGANUR
PARUR
DINDIGUL
AYICOTTA
TRAVANCORE LINES
VIPEEN I.
VERAPOLY
COCHIN

This was due to various reasons. In the first place, Tipu's cavalry was superior to that of the English; and although his artillery was not better served than that of his enemies, it was superior in numbers. In the second, he enjoyed superiority in the means of transport, having 140,000 oxen and 1200 mules at his disposal. It is true his infantry was not strong enough to face the English, but he avoided pitched battles.[1] By his swift marches and counter-marches he had baffled the English commanders who had toiled in vain to catch up with him. He had inflicted great loss on the English armies both in men and in material, and had not only foiled the plans of Medows for the invasion of Mysore, but had invaded the Carnatic, thus converting a defensive into an offensive war. He had definitely proved his superiority as a skilful general and as a tactician of the first rank. Even Cornwallis, who did not like to admit the defeats which the English armies had sustained during this period, acknowledged: "We have lost time and our adversary has gained reputation, which are two most valuable things in war."[2]

[1] A. N., C[2]240, de Fresne to Minister, July, 27, 1790, No. 12.
[2] Ross, *Cornwallis*, ii, p. 51.

CHAPTER XIV

# THE WAR: SECOND PHASE

*The Invasion of Mysore*

The failure of the Company's plan of campaign, and the losses which the English army, "the finest and best appointed that ever took the field in India,"[1] had sustained, greatly alarmed Lord Cornwallis. Medows was defeated, and the Carnatic lay at the mercy of Tipu. Besides, there was the danger that the Marathas and the Nizam, who were very unfavourably impressed by the military operations of the Company's forces, might leave the confederacy and make a separate peace with the Mysoreans. Cornwallis saw that "Tipu's efforts have been of late so vigorous and in some degrees so successful against our army...that our whole strength is to be utilised to reduce the power of so dangerous a neighbour."[2] He therefore reverted to his previous decision of personally conducting the war, thinking that his presence in the field would not only put fresh vigour in the ranks of the British army, but would also stir the Nizam and the Marathas into activity.

Cornwallis had not favoured Medows's plan for the invasion of Mysore. He held the opinion that Madras should be the actual base of operations, and that the invasion of Mysore should take place from the north-east instead of from the south.[3] He marched from Vellout on February 5, reaching Vellore on the 11th. From there he suddenly struck to the right, and on reaching Chittoor, turned westward and entered Mysore on the 19th, without having even fired a shot. The next day he encamped at Palmaneer.[4]

The success of this enterprise was due to the secrecy which Cornwallis had maintained regarding his movements. Besides, "Tipu's long inactivity before Pondicherry and his confidence that the British would never invade Mysore while he lay in the Carnatic, had enabled Cornwallis to steal a march on him."[5] When, however, Tipu became convinced that Cornwallis intended to invade Mysore, he thought that the invasion would take place through the easier passes of either Ambur or Baramahal, and the demonstrations which some

[1] Ross, *Cornwallis*, ii, p. 52.

[2] Fortescue, iii, p. 570.

[3] Hamid Khan (ff. 71b-73b) gives a very detailed and graphic account of the march of the English army from Madras to Bangalore.

[4] Fortescue, iii, p. 572.

[5] P.R.O., 30/11/152, Cornwallis to Grenville, Nov. 15, 1790, ff. 12a-b.

of the Company's forces sent towards the passes were ordered to make, also pointed to the same conclusion. That was why, as soon as he heard of Cornwallis's march towards Vellore, he quitted Pondicherry, and hastily returned to Mysore through the passes of Changama and Palakad to oppose the English forces. But Cornwallis, by contriving the appearance of a march towards Ambur, succeeded in deceiving him, and entered Mysore by the Mugali pass, although it was a much longer and more difficult route. By the time Tipu discovered the deception, the English were already well established on the soil of Mysore.[1] Expecting that Cornwallis would march against Bangalore, Tipu immediately proceeded there to make arrangements for its defence before the English could arrive. On reaching Bangalore on March 3, he imprisoned Sayyid Pir, its Commandant, and another officer, Raja Ramchandra, on a charge of intrigue, and appointed Bahadur Khan, the *faujdar* of Krishnagiri, as Commandant of the fort, while Muhammad Khan Bakhshi and Sayyid Hamid were appointed to assist him in its defence. After making these arrangements, he set out to check the advance of the enemy.[2]

Meanwhile, Cornwallis continued to advance in the direction of Bangalore. He took possession of Kolar on February 28, and of Hoskote on March 2. These places had practically no garrisons except a few matchlockmen, so they surrendered at the first summons.

Till now the English had not met with any resistance except from the irregular horse who harassed their flanks and rear by carrying away bullocks, and attacking the baggage and stragglers, and who, by destroying the crops of the areas through which the enemy passed, made the problem of supplies very acute for them.[3] When, however, Cornwallis arrived within ten miles of Bangalore, Tipu's cavalry appeared in some force, and on the morning of march 5 offered some resistance by cannonading the English army and by

[1] Hamid Khan, ff. 72a-b.

[2] *Tarikh-i-Tipu*, ff. 101b-102a; Kirmani, P. 345; *A Persian MS. History of Mysore*, Journal of Mysore Univ., Sept. 1944, Chap. xx. Wilks, ii, p. 430 footnote, says that Sayyid Pir was removed because he "had expressed doubts regarding the ultimate result of the siege." But this does not seem to be true. The chief cause why he was removed was that Tipu suspected him of disloyalty. Besides, it was necessary that Bangalore should have at this time a very able and courageous Commandant. And who could be better fitted for this post than Bahadur Khan? Wilks (p. 424) is also wrong in stating that Tipu had marched to Bangalore because he felt alarmed for the safety of his harem. In reality the Sultan had proceeded there to make arrangements for its defence which were not satisfactory. He would not have marched to Bangalore just to remove his family, because that task could have been performed by one of his officers. Besides, Bangalore being a very strong fort, Tipu did not think the English would be able to capture it.

[3] Hamid Khan, ff. 73a-b.

making an attack on its baggage. But this could not check its advance, and it succeeded in reaching Bangalore in the afternoon with the loss of about ten men.[1]

On the evening of March 6, Floyd, while carrying on the reconnaissance to the east of the fort[2] with his whole cavalry, fell in with about 1000 Mysore horse under Balaji Rao sent by Tipu against him. The Mysoreans at first held their ground, but, being greatly outnumbered, finally gave way. While pursuing them, Floyd saw from a height the rear of Tipu's army, which had just arrived and was setting up camp to the south-west of the fort. Although Floyd had been ordered by Cornwallis not to undertake any enterprise, he was tempted by the flattering prospect of striking a blow at the enemy.[3] At first he was successful, and the Mysoreans, who were either cooking their food or relaxing, were thrown into confusion. But very soon they rallied and counter-attacked the English. Floyd received a wound in the face and fell from the horse, but was carried away by his men who retreated in precipitation with the loss of 400 men.[4] About 100 prisoners were also taken, but they were sent back by Tipu after he had ordered their wounds to be dressed and given to each person a piece of cloth and a rupee.[5] The English losses would have been much heavier had it not been for the darkness of the night which helped the soldiers to escape.[6] The wound which Floyd received also proved a blessing in disguise, for as Munro observed: "Had it not happened, he would probably have pushed so far on, that he never could have extricated himself, for the enemy was strongly posted, and the flower of their cavalry, which was at some distance, was coming on, led by Tippoo."[7]

Although Tipu had gained a victory in the engagement against Floyd, he did not think it proper to remain on the same ground for fear of a night attack. So he moved to Kengeri, nine miles south-west of Bangalore, leaving 2,000 men for the defence of the town.[8] Cornwallis, on the other hand, owing to the loss which his troops had sustained and the shortage of grain and fodder which they were experiencing, decided not to waste any more time but to attack Bangalore, whose capture would not only furnish him with supplies,

[1] Gleig, *Munro*, i, p. 108.
[2] *Ibid.;* Rennell, *Marches of British Armies*, p. 60; Wilks, ii, p. 427, wrongly says that Floyd was sent to reconnoitre the south-west side of the fort.
[3] Wilks, ii, pp. 427-8.
[4] Hamid Khan, f. 74a.
[5] Gleig, *Munro*, p. 109. Munro says that in this action about 250 horses and about 100 men were taken; nearly 200 were wounded and 15 or 20 killed. But this is an understatement.
[6] Hamid Khan, f. 74b.
[7] Gleig, *Munro*, i, p. 109.
[8] *Ibid.*, p. 110.

but would also give him an excellent cover for carrying on the siege of the fort.[1]

The town of Bangalore was situated to the north of the fort. It was circular in form and about three miles in circumference. Its streets were wide and properly laid out, and few towns in India could boast of better houses and richer inhabitants. All round, except where it was defended by the fort, it had a dry ditch, twenty-five feet deep. A thick, broad jungle of trees, bamboos and thorny bushes extended along the ditch. There were four entrances to the town and all were well defended.[2]

The fort of Bangalore, constructed in the sixteenth century by its 'red chief', Kempe Gaude, was originally of mud, but it had been entirely rebuilt by Haidar and Tipu in stone. It was oval with a circumference of more than a mile. It possessed a strong lofty rampart, twenty-six bastions mounting three guns a piece, five cavaliers and a deep ditch, which at the time of the siege contained very little water. It had two gateways: One named Mysore, and the other the Delhi Gate, opposite the town.[3]

Cornwallis encamped to the north-east of Bangalore, and early on the morning of March 7 gave orders for an assault on the town. A gateway on the north side was the first point of the attack. It was carried without much difficulty, and the British troops pushed forward. But they met with great resistance at the inner gate which was barricaded with stones. Heavy guns were, therefore, brought up and the gate was at last forced. The assailants also scaled the rampart. The garrison put up an obstinate resistance, but in the end dispersed, and made for the fort as fast as they could.[4]

When the Mysoreans withdrew into the fort, the town was given over to plunder by the English troops in which women were outraged and considerable property was looted. Although a large number of people had fled with their belongings during the siege, there was hardly a soldier who did not secure a few ornaments of gold and silver and new clothes.[5] The English also obtained large quantities of grain and military stores and 125 pieces of cannon of which 85 were fit for immediate use. In the town there was a big gun-powder factory, a foundry for cannon, a workshop for making accoutrements and a machine copied from a French Encyclopaedia for producing different kinds of carabines. All these fell into the hands of the English.[6]

[1] Hamid Khan, f. 76a; Fortescue, iii, p. 575.
[2] Mackenzie, ii, p. 31.
[3] Wilks, ii, pp. 430-1.
[4] Mackenzie, ii, pp. 29-30.
[5] Hamid Khan, f. 77a.
[6] Mackenzie, ii. p. 46.

They, however, could secure only a small quantity of fodder, for the magazine of forage had been set fire to by the Mysoreans.[1]

Tipu was both astonished and grieved at the loss of the town, and moved out from Kengeri to try and recover it. Early on the afternoon of March 7, a part of his army made a demonstration to engage the attention of the English, while about 6,000 infantry under Qamar-ud-din Khan entered the town by a concealed movement. But Cornwallis understood the strategem and reinforced the town. Tipu's troops, nevertheless, fought with great courage and stubbornness, disputing every inch of ground. But finally they gave way and retreated to their camp. They lost from three to four hundred men. The English loss during the day amounted to 131 men.[2]

After the capture of the town, the siege of the fort commenced, and batteries were opened to breach the walls. A breach was effected on March 18, and the fire on the 20th widened it. Meanwhile, the condition of the English army was becoming serious. Owing to a great shortage of supplies—the forage found in the town having been consumed by the middle of the month—bullocks were dying daily by hundreds. Besides, two of the guns were completely disabled and the ammunition was running short. Cornwallis therefore decided to storm the fort, realising that any further delay would prove fatal.[3] There was also another reason which induced him to attack the fort immediately. The English forces, though besiegers, were actually themselves besieged, exposed as they were to the attacks both of the garrison and of Tipu's army, whose manoeuvres were becoming more threatening every day. Early on March 21, Tipu massed his army on the heights, to the south-west of the fort, to protect the guns which had been brought to cannonade the works of the English. Cornwallis therefore moved out as if to attack Tipu. Thereupon the latter withdrew the guns. They were, however, brought back in the evening. This greatly alarmed Cornwallis, for the position which the Sultan occupied commanded the breach.[4] Besides, he was informed by Krishna Rao, who was in Tipu's confidence, that the Mysoreans were preparing to attack the English. This made him decide to assault the fort on the night of March 21 before Tipu's plan materialised. The preparations for the attack were made so secretly that even the English troops were not aware of it. The exact time of the assault was fixed with the advice of Krishna Rao who, when the appointed hour approached, got the number of guards at

[1] Gleig, *Munro*, i, p. 110.

[2] Mackenzie, ii, pp. 32-3. Wilks, ii, p. 433, is wrong in saying that the Mysoreans lost over 2,000 killed and wounded in the assault.

[3] Mackenzie, ii, pp. 34, 49; Gleig, *Munro*, i, p. 115.

[4] Mackenzie, ii, pp. 37-8; Fortescue, iii, p. 577.

the breach reduced.[1] In consequence, when the assault took place, the Mysoreans were completely taken by surprise.[2] Meanwhile, the English found a circuitous way which enabled a few men to climb the main rampart where no opposition was expected. They were joined by others, and together they attacked the garrison. In spite of this, the latter put up a vigorous defence. The Commandant also fought valiantly, but after he was killed, the resistance ceased. Tipu had sent 2000 chosen troops with a view to reinforce the garrison, but they reached too late and were driven back with loss.[3] The English casualties on this day amounted to 131 killed and wounded, while the Mysoreans lost over 1000 men.[4] Shaikh Ansar and Sivaji along with about 300 men, who were mostly wounded, were taken prisoners. The rest escaped.[5]

The fall of Bangalore came as a great blow to Tipu, for it was the second town of his kingdom and was regarded by him as invulnerable. Its loss, together with the death of Bahadur Khan, one of his most faithful officers, affected him so much that he wept.[6] Bahadur Khan "was a tall robust man of about seventy years of age, with a white beard descending to his middle, and he was altogether one of those majestic figures which bring to the mind the idea of a prophet."[7] Cornwallis, greatly impressed by his nobleness of appearance and his gallantry, offered to send his remains to the Sultan for interment. But the latter, while expressing his admiration for the gesture of the Governor-General, suggested that Bahadur Khan's body should be handed over to the Muslims of Bangalore who would bury him according to the Muslim rites in one of the shrines of the saints.[8]

Tipu's strategy during the siege of Bangalore had been to avoid a general action, and to attack the English only when their resistance weakened. This was to be effected by cutting off their communica-

[1] Kirmani, p. 347.

[2] Gleig, *Munro*, i, p. 115; Rennell, *Marches of British Armies*, p. 64: Mackenzie, ii, pp. 38-9. Wilks, ii, p. 437, is wrong in saying that Tipu and the garrison knew that the assault would take place that night. For if they had known they would have taken precautions which, to quote Mackenzie, "if reasonably applied, would in all probability, have rendered success doubtful." (Mackenzie, ii, p. 40).

[3] *Ibid.*, pp. 40-42; Wilks, ii, pp. 435-6.

[4] Wilson, ii, p. 206.

[5] Hamid Khan, f. 78a; Kirmani, p. 347; Rennell, *Marches of British Armies*, p. 65. Hamid Khan says that Sivaji held a command of 3,000 horse and foot. But his statement that Krishna Rao was also taken prisoner along with Sivaji is incorrect. According to de Fresne and other accounts, which seem to be spurious, Bahadur Khan was in league with the English, otherwise how could Cornwallis have decided upon the assault of a fort which possessed a garrison of 4,200 men, whose walls were not breached and whose ditches were dry and deep. (A. N., C[2]295, de Fresne to Minister, Aug. 1, 1791, No. 34.).

[6] Mackenzie, ii, p. 45.

[7] Gleig, *Munro*, i, p. 114.

[8] N.A., O.R. 78, Rajab 16, 1205 A.H./March 21, 1791.

tions with their allies and the Carnatic, by destroying the neighbouring villages to prevent them from getting any fresh supplies, by constant cannonading and throwing of rockets, and by striking at the baggage and stores in order to harass them and create confusion in their ranks. These tactics had achieved a large measure of success. The English army was completely isolated from the Carnatic and its allies; there was a great shortage of forage, grain and ammunition, and cattle were dying daily by hundreds. The English cavalry dared not move outside the circle of picquets in the face of swarms of Mysore horse. After the fall of Bangalore Cornwallis wrote: "The army has sustained great fatigue and hardship in carrying on a siege in the face of an active and powerful enemy, and our distress for forage nearly occasioned a failure of the undertaking and is but relieved after the capture of the place."[1] From this it is clear that the condition of the English had become so precarious that if Krishna Rao had not come to their rescue, they would have been sooner or later overwhelmed by the Mysoreans.

It appears from contemporary accounts that Krishna Rao had been carrying on intrigues against the Sultan for some time past, and was in close touch with the party of Tirumula Rao, which wanted the restoration of the old dynasty to the throne of Mysore. After the fall of Bangalore a letter was intercepted which proved that Krishna Rao was in league with the English and the Marathas against Tipu. Sayyid Saheb was, therefore, sent to Seringapatam to punish Krishna Rao who happened to be there. On reaching the capital, Sayyid Saheb put to death Krishna Rao and his three brothers who were also in the plot.[2]

After repairing the breaches, and securing the place against a possible *coup-de-main*, Cornwallis moved from Bangalore on March 28 in a northerly direction with the object of forming a junction with the Nizam's cavalry which was bringing men, money and provisions for his army. The same day Tipu marched westward towards Dodballapur. About eight miles from Bangalore the two armies crossed each other, Tipu's rear falling on the English advance guard. But the English could not gain any advantage, and the Sultan successfully retreated, leaving one brass gun which he could not carry because its carriage broke down. He organised his forces near Dodballapur, and then proceeded towards Sivaganga with a view to intercepting the Nizam's cavalry, which was coming to join Cornwallis.[3]

[1] M.R., Mly. Cons., April 23, 1791, vol. 147B, p. 1898.

[2] *Tarikh-i-Tipu*, f. 102a; *A Persian MS. History of Mysore*, ch. xx; Kirmani, pp. 351-2; Wilks, ii, p. 450; Punganuri, p. 45. Different versions of the conspiracy are given in these works, but they all agree that Krishna Rao was in league with Tipu's enemies.

[3] Mackenzie, ii, pp. 54-5.

Meanwhile, Cornwallis continued his march, and on the way occupied the small forts of Devanhulli and Chickballapur, which surrendered without opposition. The latter was handed over to its former *poligar*. But it was soon retaken by surprise and escalade by a detachment sent by Tipu, and many of the *poligars* were put to the sword on a charge of treason.[1]

Although Cornwallis had by April 5 reached about seventy miles north of Bangalore, there was no trace of the Nizam's army. This was due to the efficient espionage service of Tipu which disseminated false intelligence and prevented communication between the allied forces. Cornwallis remained stationary for five days, and then, abandoning the hope of forming a junction with the Nizam's troops, moved southward to meet the English convoy coming from the Carnatic by way of the Ambur pass under Colonel Oldham. But after marching a day in this retrogade direction, he received fresh information which induced him to retrace his steps and again move northward. After two days march he joined the Nizam's force on April 13 at Kotapalli, eighty-four miles north of Bangalore. The Nizam's contingent was nominally 15,000, but in reality it consisted of 10,000 well-mounted horsemen. On the 14th the united armies moved from Kotapalli in the direction of the English convoy, with which the junction was effected on the 19th at Venkatagiri. The convoy had brought a large supply of provisions and stores, and a reinforcement of 700 Europeans and 4500 Indian troops, including 450 cavalry. Tipu had tried to strike at the convoy, but had been unsuccessful. The united armies then returned to Bangalore to make preparations for an advance on Seringapatam.[2]

### *Operations of the Nizam's and Maratha Armies*

While the English forces were engaged in the Coimbatore, Baramahal and Bangalore districts, the armies of the Nizam and the Marathas were operating in other parts of the Mysore kingdom. Their movements were at first slow because, while the Nizam's war preparations had not yet been completed,[3] the Marathas were busy extorting money from Tipu's *wakils* at Poona. Besides, the English campaign under General Medows had created an unfavourable impression on the minds of the Nizam and the Peshwa. In fact, the check which the English had received had greatly alarmed them. They were consequently delaying and procrastinating in order, as Lankhul wrote to Kennaway, "to benefit by our success and at the same time so far avoid extremities with Tippoo as to preserve an

[1] Rennell, *Marches of British Armies*, p. 73.
[2] Mackenzie, ii, pp. 56-8; Wilks, ii, pp. 443-4.
[3] N.A., Pol. Pro., Dec. 17, 1790, Cons. No. 3, Nizam to Nana.

opening for reconciliation."[1] Their plan was to watch the result of Lord Cornwallis's campaign against Bangalore before plunging themselves wholeheartedly into the war. Moreover, they were anxious to conserve their strength, while the English and Tipu exhausted themselves by fighting each other. In this way they expected they might be able to hold the balance and step in at the end.[2] However, as a result of Cornwallis's repeated appeals and remonstrances, they began to prosecute the war with greater earnestness. They were stirred into activity owing to the fear that the English might, on "the plea of want of exertion and earnestness on the part of their allies, at length come to an understanding with the enemy" without consulting them.[3] Such a contingency would be fraught with grave consequences for them, because it would leave them at the mercy of Tipu. They also began to fear that, if they did not exert themselves wholeheartedly in the war, the union with the English, as the Nizam wrote to Nana, "which the wheel of fortune has luckily thrown in our way is likely to be dissolved without our reaping advantage from it." The Nizam, therefore, suggested to Nana that they should wage war with greater zeal; and in order to give greater solidarity to the alliance and remove the apprehensions of the English, advised him that the Peshwa should himself move from Poona and take charge of the campaign.[4] To discuss these matters, Haripant, representing the Peshwa, met the Nizam at Pangal about the middle of March 1791, and decided that "both the Nizam and the Peshwa should abide by the terms of the treaty with the English, but only so far as might humble Tipu, without absolutely annihilating his power."[5] The Nizam and the Marathas regarded Tipu's power as a bulwark against the ambitious designs of the English, and wanted it to be weakened but not destroyed.

The Nizam's army began to assemble in the neighbourhood of Hyderabad in May 1790, and was joined early in June, in accordance with the terms of alliance, by an English detachment under Major Montgomery. But the detachment, according to Cornwallis's own admission, "reflects discredit upon our own military establishments," and "from its defects in numbers, discipline and equipment, it is incapable of rendering the services to the Nizam to which he is entitled by his treaty with the Company."[6] However, the combined forces moved south-west towards Pangal which was made the headquarters. Here the Nizam encamped in order to direct the campaign,

[1] *Ibid.*, Nov. 24, 1790, Cons. No. 24, Lankhul to Kennaway.
[2] *Ibid.*, P.R.C., iii, No. 168.
[3] N.A., Pol. Pro., Dec. 17, 1790, Cons. No. 3, Nizam to Nama.
[4] *Ibid.*
[5] Duff, ii, p. 202; P.R.C., iii, No. 254.
[6] *Ibid.*, No. 132.

while his army under Mahabat Jung after some delay crossed the Krishna on about July 13, and proceeded to Raichur. There it remained for six weeks until information was received that Tipu had marched to Coimbatore early in September. With no fear of further interception it then entered Tipu's kingdom, and after occupying various barrier fortresses, which surrendered without much resistance, the main army sat down to the siege of Koppal on October 28, 1790,[1] while the rest proceeded to the capture of Ganjikota, Sidhout, Cumbum and other places.

The plan of campaign pursued by the Hyderabad army was not in accordance with the wishes of the English and the Marathas. Anxious to obtain a speedy possession of the Cumbum and Cuddapah countries, the Nizam preferred the "Cumbum-Cuddapah" route. His allies, on the other hand, particularly the Marathas, wanted him to follow a more "centrical route" for invading Mysore, in order that his armies might be in a position to co-operate with and receive assistance from the Maratha forces.[2] Owing to the order and equipment of Tipu's army, and owing to his rapid and sudden movements, it was considered necessary that the Marathas and the Nizam should act together, as "neither of their armies acting separately would be a match for the enemy, should he advance in force against them."[3] But the Nizam was against following the "centrical route." This was because that route was covered by the strong forts of Gooty, Bellary and Sira, whose reduction appeared difficult.[4] Besides, he was suspicious of Haripant who might stab him in the back, just as Holkar had done during the last Maratha-Mysore War.[5] But the chief reason why he did not wish his armies to proceed direct from Adoni and operate in the neighbourhood of the Maratha forces, was that he was afraid lest the Marathas should interfere with and claim the conquests made by his troops.[6]

The Nizam's army, which was engaged in the siege of Koppal, very soon occupied the town; but its efforts to capture the fort, which was commanded by a brave officer, Nanaji Rao Salonkhe,[7] and was built on a lofty and precipitous rock and possessed strong fortifications, were not successful. The cannonade was at first so ineffective that it could not even effect a breach. This was due to bad artillery and a shortage of ammunition.[8] In fact, the guns were of such poor quality that in one week they were disabled by their own fire; and as there was a

[1] Wilks, ii, pp. 481-2.
[2] N.A., Pol. Pro., Nov. 3, 1790, Cons. No. 18.
[3] P.R.C., iii, No. 199.
[4] N.A., Pol. Pro., Nov. 10, 1790, Cons. No. 21.
[5] P.R.C., iii, No. 199
[6] N.A., Pol. Pro., Nov., 3, 1790, Cons. No. 18
[7] P.R.C., iii, No. 251.
[8] N.A., Pol. Pro., Dec. 9, 1790, Cons. No. 9.

dearth of materials to repair them, they could not be used again.[1] However, in the middle of January 1791, a new battering train arrived from Raichur and Pangal, and at length a breach was effected; but it did not prove useful to the besiegers, since a steep rock of considerable height rendered access to the wall of the fort very difficult. The morale of the garrison also remained very high. They led out frequent sallies and continued to harass their enemies. Their resistance was so stubborn that Kennaway informed Cornwallis on March 8, 1791: "I am afraid the chance of carrying Koppal by force is against us";[2] and Mushir-ul-mulk, the prime minister, several times thought of raising the siege, but was prevented from doing it by the Nizam.[3] Nevertheless, on April 18, the place surrendered by capitulation after five months of resistance, and the garrison were allowed to carry away their personal property. A week later, Bahadur Benda, another strong fort about three miles north, also surrendered on the same terms. Both places had been well garrisoned, and provided with sufficient military stores and provisions and could have prolonged their resistance. But the news of the fall of Bangalore had demoralised the garrison and led to their surrender. The Nizam's army found in the forts more than fifty pieces of cannon, and a considerable quantity of provisions and ammunition.[4]

Meanwhile, detachments of the Nizam's troops were engaged in occupying minor places, many of which fell without much resistance. The fort of Cumbum was reduced on November 16, 1790, by Farid-ud-din, and Sidhout surrendered to Muhammad Amin Arab on February 28, 1791.

The main army left Koppal on May 1, and directed its march towards Cuddapah. But on reaching Canool it received the news confirming the surrender of Ganjikota to Hafiz Farid-ud-din, who had once been sent by the Nizam as an ambassador to Seringapatam. The garrison of Ganjikota had resisted with great courage, but had been obliged to capitulate owing to a great shortage of supplies. The main army, thereupon, changed its route and marched to Ganjikota to join the detachment under Farid-ud-din. After halting there for a month, it proceeded to Gurramkonda, which was besieged on September 19, while various detachments were sent to besiege Gooty, Cuddapah and other places.[5]

The Marathas began preparations for war several months before the Treaty of Poona was signed with the English. Towards the end of March, 1790, Parashuram Bhau visited Poona at Nana's invitation

[1] P.R.C., iii, No. 203.
[2] *Ibid.*, No. 241.
[3] *Ibid.*, Nos. 218, 220; N.A., Pol. Pro., Jan. 13, 1791, Cons. No 13.
[4] Mackenzie, ii, p. 63; Wilks, ii, p. 482.
[5] *Ibid.*, P.R.C., iii, Nos. 309, 331.

and was entrusted by him with the command of the army[1] and given money to enlist soldiers.[2] Bhau returned to Tasgaon, his head-quarters, and began preparations. About June 20, his army consisting of about four or five thousand men was joined by the English detachment under Captain Little at Coompta not far from Tasgaon. The combined forces moved from Coompta on August 3 and crossed the Krishna by August 15.[3] Bhau's army had by this time increased to about 12,000 horse and 5,000 infantry;[4] and with this, after capturing Hubli, Mishrikot, Dodwad and other places, which surrendered without serious resistance, he arrived before Dharwar on September 18, 1790. Meanwhile, he had sent in various directions detachments which, between October 1790 and February 1791, succeeded in occupying Gajendragarh, Savanur and Lakhshmeshwar.[5]

Dharwar being the capital of the province between the Krishna and the Tungabhadra, which Haidar Ali had conquered from the Marathas, Bhau directed his arms to reduce it. It was commanded by Badr-uz-zaman Khan, a very brave officer, and possessed a garrison of 10,000 men and 15 guns. Owing to the Maratha danger, Tipu had recently sent 4,000 more men under Sher Khan to reinforce the place.[6] The defences of the fort were chiefly of mud, but were very strong. The town, however, was protected only by a low wall and a ditch which were not strong enough to withstand an attack.

The Maratha army took up its ground near Narendra, a village five miles north-west of Dharwar. From there every day some guns were dragged to the neighbouring hill from which they fired until the evening, when they were again dragged back to the camp.[7] On September 25, a party of the garrison sallied from the town, and attacked a Maratha detachment, and after killing four or five and wounding about twenty made good their retreat.[8]

On October 30, the army and the English detachment encamped about two miles south of the fort. Badr-uz-zaman the next day moved out of the town with 2,000 men and 4 guns to dislodge the enemy. But this time he was driven back by the English detachment supported by about 300 Maratha infantry, and left behind three

[1] Khare, viii, p. 4238.

[2] *Ibid.*, Nos. 3188, 3191.

[3] P.R.C., iii, Nos. 128, 129, 147. Khare, viii, p. 4289, says that during the months of June and July Bhau tried his best to increase the number of his troops, but they did not exceed 5000 cavalry and 2000 infantry.

[4] Khare, viii, p. 4291. According to Parasnis, *The Sangli State*, p. 18, Bhau's force in Sept., when nearing Dharwar, was 15,000 horse, and 3000 foot. But Bhau's target was 25,000 horse and 10,000 infantry. (Khare, viii, No. 3197).

[5] Khare, viii, p. 4292.

[6] *Ibid.*, No. 3218, Bhau to Bara Saheb, Aug. 31, 1790; Moor, p. 38; P.R.C., iii, No. 149. But Mackenzie, ii, p. 68, says that Dharwar had 7,000 men.

[7] Moor, p. 3.

[8] P.R.C., iii, No. 158.

guns.[1] On December 13 an attack by escalade was made on the town, headed by an English detachment and a body of Maratha infantry. The garrison put up a strong fight, but were compelled to evacuate the town and retreat into the fort. Captain Little and Lieutenant Foster, who had been the first to climb the wall, were wounded, the former severely, the latter mortally. As soon, however, as the Marathas entered the town, they began plundering and setting fire to it. Badr-uz-zaman Khan, taking advantage of the consequent confusion, sallied from the fort and drove out the Marathas from the town, killing about 500 of them; his own casualties being much smaller. But after a truce of about four days, during which each party burnt and buried their dead, the Marathas alone attacked the town and retook it on December 18. Having once thrown away the fruits of victory, they felt too ashamed to call in the aid of the English detachment.[2]

After the capture of the town, whose walls were levelled to the ground, the Marathas began the siege of the fort. But it was carried on in such an inefficient and dilatory manner that Lieutenant Moor, who was an eye-witness of the scene, thought that the Marathas "would not, with twenty guns against the present garrison, approach and breach Dharwar in twenty years." The following is a vivid account given by him of the way in which the firing was carried on by the Marathas: "A gun is loaded, and the whole of the people in the battery sit down, talk, and smoke for half an hour, when it is fired, and if it knocks up a great dust, it is thought sufficient; it is reloaded, and the parties resume their smoking and conversation. During two hours in the middle of the day, generally from one to three, a gun is seldom fired on either side, that time being, as it would appear by mutual consent, set apart for meals. In the night the fire from guns is slackened, but musketry is increased on both sides, and shells are sparingly thrown into the fort with tolerable precision."[3] Besides, while trying to breach the walls, the Marathas aimed at no particular spot, but fired at random all over the wall. They also followed the absurd practice of dragging the guns back to the camp at night, and as a result the Mysoreans were able to repair the slight damage which was caused by the irregular and ineffective cannonade. Furthermore, the Maratha guns were so old and of such poor quality that many times they burst from their own fire. There was also a great shortage of ammunition. The supply from Poona was so scanty and irregular that the guns had to remain silent for days together. Nor did the English detachment possess an efficient battering train.

[1] Moor, pp. 4-5; Khare, viii, No. 3237.
[2] Moor, pp. 6-7; Duff, ii, pp. 199-200.
[3] Moor, p. 30.

Captain Little had written to the Bombay Government asking for heavy guns and ammunition. But although one regiment of European infantry, one battalion of sepoys and a number of European artillerymen under Colonel Frederick reached Dharwar on December 28, no cannon or stores came along with them.[1]

In spite of these drawbacks, Colonel Frederick, who had assumed command of the English detachment, wearying of the length of the siege, decided to assault the fort even before the breach had become practicable. He was so confident of success that he did not even seek the assistance of the Marathas. But Bhau was opposed to his plan, and thought it would end in fiasco. Besides, he apprehended that if the English succeeded in capturing the fort their prestige would increase, while that of the Marathas would suffer.[2] However, owing to Frederick's enthusiasm and insistence, Bhau allowed him to have his own way. Frederick first sent a threatening letter to Badr-uz-zaman calling upon him to surrender or see his garrison massacred. The reply of the Commandant was that he could not surrender the fort for two days which were inauspicious, but that he would send his final reply on the third day.[3] Convinced that Badr-uz-zaman was only procrastinating, Frederick decided upon an assault; and early on the morning of February 27, 1791, his troops advanced to the attack. But just when they were about to cross the ditch, they had to give up the attempt, because the dry fascines with which the ditch had been filled were set fire to by the Mysoreans. The English again attempted to cross the ditch by filling it up with fascines, but, as before, these were set fire to by the garrison. As a result the English were obliged to retire to their trenches. Their casualties amounted to about 40 killed and over 100 wounded.[4] During the contest the Marathas had for the most part held aloof, but after the withdrawal of the English, they had a severe engagement with the garrison, who led out a sally, and lost about 100 men.[5] The disappointment caused by his failure to seize Dharwar greatly affected Frederick's already weak health, and he died on March 13. He was succeeded by Major Sartorius, and when after the fall of Dharwar the latter returned to Bombay, Captain Little again took charge of the detachment.[6]

At last on March 1 the expected supply of ammunition arrived from Bombay. About the same time Bhau also received a few addi-

[1] Duff, ii, p. 200.
[2] Khare, viii, No. 3277.
[3] *Ibid.*, No. 3279.
[4] *Ibid.*, Nos. 3284, 3285.
[5] Moor, p. 26.
[6] Duff, ii, pp. 201, 203. Frederick had a very poor opinion of Captain Little's military abilities, and during his discussions with Bhau never brought him along. (Khare, viii, No. 3279).

tional guns from Poona. With these fresh supplies, after a siege of twenty-nine weeks, a lodgement was at length effected on the crest of the glacis. This, however, did not bring the fall of the fort any nearer. The garrison continued to put up stiff resistance, and led out sallies which inflicted great loss on the Marathas.[1]

Meanwhile, conditions in the fort were becoming hopeless. There was a great shortage of water, provisions and shot.[2] Attempts made to secure supplies from the outside met with no success. Those caught in the act of carrying anything into the fort had their arms, feet and even noses cut off by the Marathas.[3] As a result the garrison became demoralised and began to desert. The news of the capture of Bangalore by Cornwallis further damped their spirits. Besides, the original garrison of 10,000 had fallen to 3,000 men owing to desertions and casualties. Badr-uz-zaman, therefore, with no hope of relief, and realising that owing to the conditions prevalent in the fort he would not be able to hold out much longer, agreed to surrender on March 30, and the last of the garrison evacuated the fort on April 4, at five in the evening.[4] The terms of surrender secured were highly honourable to the Khan. He was assured security of personal property, and was given the promise of a passport for his garrison, their fire-arms and public treasure to Shimoga which was still held by the Sultan. It was also agreed that the fort would not be taken possession of by the Marathas until three days after its evacuation, during which time Tipu's flag was to remain flying.[5]

Badr-uz-zaman Khan had put up a gallant resistance against the united efforts of the Marathas and the English for nearly twenty-nine weeks. He had surrendered only on obtaining an honourable capitulation, and when it was evident that further resistance was futile. By prolonging the defence of Dharwar, he had kept the principal Maratha army engaged for over six and a half months, and had thus prevented it from ravaging the Mysore territories and cutting off Tipu's supplies from his possessions to the north of Seringapatam.[6]

After evacuating the fort, while the Khan was proceeding to his camp, the Marathas made fun of him, and threw dust in his palanquin.[7] Parashuram Bhau advised Badr-uz-zaman Khan to pitch his

[1] Moor, pp. 32 f; Duff, ii, p. 201.

[2] Khare, viii, Nos. 3291, 3294, Nilkanth Appaji to Bara Saheb, March 4 and 8 respectively. Moor, p. 42, says that the garrison were straightened for provisions and shot, but they had plenty of water and powder. Bhau in his letter (Khare, ix, No. 3330) says that there was no shortage of either water or provisions. Bhau evidently wanted to give credit and importance to his capture of Dharwar by making these statements.

[3] Khare, viii, Nos, 3233, 3234.

[4] Moor, pp. 37-8.

[5] *Ibid.*, Mackenzie, ii, p. 70.

[6] Moor, p. 38.

[7] Khare, ix, No. 3323.

camp near him so that it might not be looted by the Marathas.[1] But the Khan, owing to the latter's insolent and provocative attitude, decided to encamp two miles away on the road to Shimoga, and was provided with an escort of 2000 Maratha horse. Nevertheless, on April 8, his party was attacked and plundered by the Marathas in violation of the terms of the capitulation. The Khan himself received severe wounds and several of his men lost their lives. He and his followers were robbed of everything including the seven guns which they had brought from Dharwar.[2]

The chief motive behind the attack on Badr-uz-zaman was to plunder him of his wealth and the Sultan's treasure which he was carrying. Grant Duff, however, says that the Marathas accused Haidar, Tipu and Badr-uz-zaman of habitual violations of their engagements. Thereupon, the Khan became enraged, and drew his sword, his troops following his example. It was this which caused the Marathas to attack the garrison.[3] But this account does not seem to be correct. It appears improbable that a man so shrewd and cool-headed as Badr-uz-zaman should have become aggressive, knowing that he was virtually a prisoner, and the odds were against him. As a matter of fact, the attack on him was made all of a sudden, so that he was taken by surprise. Although Moor does not mention the real cause of "this disgraceful transaction ,"[4] it is evident from his narrative that it was not the Khan but the Marathas who were responsible for this "villainous proceeding."[5] Mackenzie also observed: "Reports generally believed say that the articles of this capitulation were shamefully violated by the Bhow's troops."[6]

When Bhau heard of the incident he felt sorry. He received the Khan kindly and appointed an English surgeon to take care of his wounds. He punished many of those concerned in the affray, and restored to the Mysoreans the articles which could be recovered.[7] However, immediately after, on the pretext that the Khan had violated the terms of the capitulation, Bhau had him with several others imprisoned, and sent in irons to the fort of Nargund.[8] The Marathas maintained that Badr-uz-zaman had agreed to surrender the fort with its guns and stores in their actual condition, but that, instead, he had caused the powder in the magazine to be ruined by water and the stores to be destroyed.[9] Besides, 2,000 of the rifles in

[1] *Ibid.*, No. 3327.
[2] *Ibid.*, Nos. 3327, 3330 Moor, p. 43; Mackenzie, ii, p. 70.
[3] Duff, ii, p. 201.
[4] Moor, p. 43.
[5] *Ibid.*,
[6] Mackenzie, ii, p. 70.
[7] P.R.C., iii, No. 297.
[8] Kirmani, p. 354.
[9] Wilks, ii, p. 487.

the fort had also been either broken or buried underground.[1] But Badr-uz-zaman denied the charge and it does not appear from Moor's account that he broke any article of the capitulation. Moor says that when the Marathas entered the fort they found there a good stock of powder in the magazine. He does not mention that the powder had been ruined by water.[2] As regards the guns having been broken up, it appears from Moor's narrative that this had been done by Badr-uz-zaman before he had agreed to capitulate[3] in order to hammer them into shots owing to a shortage of ammunition. Probably it was the sight of these guns which led Bhau to accuse Badr-uz-zaman of the breach of the capitulation. Although it is possible that Bhau had no hand in the attack and plunder of the Khan, yet, as Duff observes, "the subsequent confinement of Badr-uz-zaman Khan and several other prisoners reflects discredit on the conduct of Pureshram Bhow,"[4] who had grossly violated the terms of the capitulation.

The capture of Dharwar facilitated the conquest of all the territory north of the Tungabhadra, there being no longer any Mysore force left in that area. Bhau crossed the river towards the end of April 1791 and marched southward. As he intended to proceed to Seringapatam, he wanted to occupy the intermediate posts in order to ensure supplies from the north.[5] He, therefore, himself marched against Ramagiri, while he sent detachments in other directions. Ramagiri, along with other forts, surrendered without resistance,[6] and Raghunath Rao Kurundwarkar succeeded in capturing Sante-Bednur, Mayakonda and Chengeri.[7] But Ganpat Rao Mahendale, who had been despatched towards Bednur, met with stiff resistance from the Mysoreans; and although he at first made some conquests, Tipu's forces which were stationed in Shimoga recaptured all he had taken. However, with the arrival of fresh reinforcements from Bhau, Ganpat Rao once again succeeded in recovering the posts and driving out the Mysoreans.[8] In the Karwar district the Maratha navy occupied many of the ports belonging to the Sultan. But owing to the monsoon, the navy sailed away leaving Babu Rao Salonkhe with only some infantry and small ships. The result was that Tipu's forces recovered the ports lost to the Marathas and expelled Salonkhe from the area.[9]

The movements of Bhau after the fall of Dharwar had been very

[1] Khare, ix, No. 3330.
[2] Moor, p. 42.
[3] *Ibid.*, p. 40.
[4] Duff, ii, p. 201.
[5] Khare, ix, p. 4476.
[6] Moor, p. 72.
[7] Khare, ix, No. 3341.
[8] *Ibid.*, No. 3354 and p. 4478.
[9] *Ibid.*, No. 3342.

rapid, but after capturing Ramagiri his progress slackened. He was urged by the English to strike a junction with Major Abercromby, who was advancing from Malabar through Coorg, and then together proceed to Seringapatam. But Bhau regarded the route as unsafe and ignored the advise. He remained busy completing the conquest of the districts of Bednur and Chitaldrug, and collecting revenues from his new acquisitions, until he was summoned by Haripant to accompany him to Seringapatam.[1]

Haripant set out from Poona on January 1, 1790, with less than 10,000 horse, and after fording the Krishna advanced to Gadwal,[2] from where he ordered the main body of his troops to march to Kurnool, while he himself proceeded to Pangal to consult with the Nizam regarding the conduct of the war. After spending over two weeks there, he joined his main army at Kurnool, where, owing to a shortage of troops, he stayed on instead of proceeding to Ganjikota as arranged with the English.[3] It was by about the middle of April that he despatched 10,000 horse under his son Lakshman Rao by way of Ganjikota to join Cornwallis. But the Maratha movements were so slow that they failed to join Cornwallis who had already advanced towards Seringapatam. Haripant, whose forces were now swelled by the addition of fresh contingents from the Maratha chieftains, immediately set out from Kurnool, and ordered Lakshman Rao to join him. The whole army then moved to Sira. The place was strong and had abundant supplies, but it surrendered without any resistance. After this Bulwant Suba Rao was despatched with an army to besiege Maddagiri, twenty miles east of Sira, while Haripant himself, after leaving a strong garrison at Sira, marched south-west to join the English army at Seringapatam. Bhau was ordered to march south-east, and the two Maratha armies were united at Nagamangala on May 24. The next day they advanced on Melukote, where they joined Cornwallis on May 28, 1791.[4]

### *Cornwallis's march on Seringapatam*

After striking a junction with the Nizam's cavalry and the convoy from the Carnatic, Lord Cornwallis returned to Bangalore where he began preparations for advancing on Seringapatam. He was anxious to end the war as speedily as possible, not only from considerations of economy, but also because of the precarious state of European and

[1] Duff, ii, p. 203.

[2] Gadwal is a town in Raichur District, Andhra Pradesh

[3] P.R.C., iii, Nos 234, 304; Duff, ii, p. 202. But Duff is wrong in saying that Haripant set out with 30,000 men from Poona. He had only 13,000 troops with him, although according to the terms of alliance he was expected to have 25,000 men.

[4] P.R.C., iii, No. 353; Duff, ii, p. 202-3.

Indian politics.[1] So far the French had abstained from helping Tipu, while the Marathas and the Nizam had promised whole-hearted co-operation to the English in the war, but there was no guarantee that such favourable conditions would last indefinitely.

Lord Cornwallis left Bangalore on May 4, 1791. Thinking that the Governor-General would march on Seringapatam by the main road, called Chennapatna, Tipu destroyed all grain and forage on that route, and took up a strong position supported by the hill forts of Ramgiri and Sivangiri, twenty-four miles south-west of Bangalore, determined to make a serious stand. Cornwallis therefore adopted the more difficult and circuitous route by Kankanhalli and Sultanpettah. But as he advanced, he found that on this route also all the neighbouring villages had been reduced to ashes, so that no vestige of forage or grain could be found. Nor was it possible to find a single person who was prepared to give intelligence regarding the enemy, or to act as a guide, or to inform where the grain had been concealed. In addition to these difficulties, owing to heavy rains, the unevenness of the roads, which were intersected by rivulets and ravines,[2] and the booby traps, which the Mysoreans had constructed, the English army had to undergo great privations. Conditions were made worse by the continued harassment to which it was subjected by the Mysore horse.[3] Moreover, owing to the shortage of forage and grain hundreds of cattle began to die. This caused a breakdown of the transport arrangements, and as a result large quantities of stores had to be destroyed. Even when the fort of Malvalli was reduced on May 10, and a considerable amount of grain was found there, it did not relieve the difficulties of the English. The loss on the march had been so great that the issue of rice to the troops had to be reduced to one-half of the normal allowance.[4]

In spite of these difficulties, Cornwallis continued to advance and reached Arikere, about nine miles east of Seringapatam, on May 13, 1791. There he intended to cross the Cauvery and proceed against Tipu's capital. But the river being in flood, he decided to proceed westward to the ford of Kannambadi, about eight miles above Seringapatam.[5]

Meanwhile, Tipu Sultan had not been inactive. Although he had avoided any general action, he had inflicted considerable suffering on the English army by hanging on to its rear, by digging booby traps, and by destroying grain and forage on the route. But as this could not prevent the advance of Cornwallis, he proceeded to his capital

[1] Forrest, *Selections*, *Cornwallis*, i, pp. 81-2.
[2] Mackenzie, ii, pp. 90-1; Wilks, ii, pp. 451-2.
[3] Hamid Khan, ff. 73a-b.
[4] Mackenzie, ii, p. 92.
[5] Wilks, ii, p. 453.

on May 9 to make arrangements for its defence. On the 13th he marched out with 3,000 cavalry[1] and some infantry, and took up a strong position about six miles in front of the English army, determined to give battle if Cornwallis attempted to approach Seringapatam. His right was on the river, and his left was protected by a rugged and an almost inaccessible height. This position was further strengthened by batteries above and a swampy and narrow ravine below. Finding that direct approach to the position which Tipu occupied was difficult, Cornwallis decided to conduct his army during the night of May 14 by a circuitous route which lay through a ridge of hills on the enemy's right and was easy to cross. By this means he expected to get to the rear of Tipu's army, and cut off its retreat to Seringapatam. Cornwallis observed utmost secrecy regarding his plans, and the army was ordered to move at 11 o'clock at night. But a heavy thunderstorm disconcerted the enterprise, and day broke before the force had proceeded four miles. Realising that he would not be able to carry out his original plan of which Tipu had become aware, Cornwallis tried to secure some advantage by forcing him to an action on ground other than that which he was occupying.[2] The Sultan did not decline the meeting and, according to Munro, "showed much judgement and decision in taking up his positions."[3] The skill which he displayed in his movements on this occasion even drew praise from Wilks who observed: "The praise cannot in justice be denied to him (Tipu) on this occasion, of seeing his ground, and executing his movements with a degree of promptitude and judgement which would have been creditable to any officer."[4]

The object of the English was to occupy a strong rocky ridge which was a continuation of the Karighatta hill, and was situated two or three miles to Tipu's left. But the Sultan saw through the English design, and before they could reach there, he sent a body of his troops under Qamar-ud-din Khan who occupied it and from there opened on the English a heavy fire which disconcerted them and caused considerable loss of life.[5] However, under the cover of rocks and broken ground, which offered some protection, the English army formed itself, and Colonel Maxwell was appointed to dislodge the Mysoreans from the ridge. Maxwell advanced with such courage and swiftness that he succeeded in capturing the height. Tipu's infantry, taken by surprise, withdrew leaving three guns. The success of this enterprise was the signal for the advance of the rest of the English army. In consequence, the action became general.[6] The Mysore infantry fought with great valour, defending every post and standing

[1] Gleig, *Munro*, i, p. 118.
[2] Wilks, ii, pp. 454-6.
[3] Gleig, *Munro*, i, p. 118.
[4] Wilks, ii, p. 456.
[5] Gleig, *Munro*, i. p. 118.
[6] Wilks, ii, pp. 457-8.

up to the fire of the musketry till the English troops were within a few yards of them.[1] But while the English and the Mysoreans were engaged in a fierce fight, the Nizam's cavalry under Asad Ali Khan, which had hitherto remained inactive, suddenly rushed to the aid of their ally. This proved decisive, and the Mysoreans retreated towards their capital, pursued by the enemy who wanted to seize the Karighatta hill.[2] But the batteries on the island commanded by Sayyid Hamid poured forth such heavy fire as compelled the English to give up the pursuit and retire.[3] The day thus ended definitely in a victory for Tipu. It is true, he had to retire to his capital, but not before he had succeeded in frustrating the designs of the English who, according to Munro, had gained nothing except "the liberty of looking at the island."[4] The English loss on the day was very heavy: It amounted to about 600 killed and wounded. The casualties on the Mysore side were about the same.[5]

After this action Lord Cornwallis halted until May 18, when he moved towards the ford of Kannambadi to force a passage over the Cauvery into Seringapatam. But on reaching the ford on the 20th, he found that he was not in a position to prosecute his plans. He had expected to be joined by Abercromby, and particularly by the Marathas without whose support he knew he had no chance of success against Seringapatam. But owing to the admirable vigilance of Tipu's scouting parties, he had no knowledge of their whereabouts. Moreover, the English army was in a wretched state. It "had suffered exceedingly from the inclemency of the weather, from wounds, and from extreme fatigue in bringing on the battering train and stores, which had to be dragged by hand from Seringapatam to Kannambadi. The season of the year was unfavourable to the cattle; they were infected with an epidemic, which killed them in vast numbers and rendered the greater part of what remained of little service. The scarcity of grain was such that the menial camp followers were reduced to the necessity of subsisting chiefly on the putrid flesh of the dead bullocks; and to add to the distress, small-pox raged in the camp."[6] Owing to these conditions, Cornwallis decided upon retreat in order to save his army from destruction. After a great part of the horses had been shot, and the whole of the siege train and heavy equipments destroyed, he began his melancholy and mortifying march from Seringapatam on May 20. "The ground at Caniambaddy", says Major Dirom, "where the army had encamped but six days, was covered, in a circuit of several miles, with the carcasses of cattle and horses; and the last of the gun-carriages, carts, and stores of the

[1] Gleig, *Munro,* i, p. 118.
[2] Hamid Khan, ff. 84b-85a.
[3] *Tarikh-i-Tipu,* f. 103.
[4] Gleig, *Munro,* i, p. 119.
[5] *Ibid.*
[6] Dirom, p. 2.

battering train, left in flames, was a meloncholy spectacle, which the troops passed as they quitted the deadly camp."[1] Seeing the desperate condition of the English army, Tipu's officers advised him to attack the enemy. But he did not follow their advice.

On deciding upon retreat, Cornwallis also sent orders to General Abercromby on May 21 to return to Malabar. Abercromby had entered Mysore with the object of co-operating with the main army under Cornwallis proceeding to invest Seringapatam. He had then advanced to Periapatam, distant about thirty-three miles from Seringapatam, according to the instructions of the Governor-General. But the latter, owing to the great efficiency of Tipu's light troops, was completely ignorant of his movements. This, as we have seen, was one of the reasons which had caused his retreat. Orders were, therefore, issued to Abercromby to return to Malabar.

Meanwhile, Abercromby had been attacked by Qamar-ud-din Khan and Sayyid Saheb who destroyed and seized his baggage.[2] He did not offer any resistance, but, according to Munro, "on a detachment of Tippoo's marching towards him without even seeing them, with an army superior to Sir Eyre Coote's, at Porto Novo, shamefully ran away, leaving his camp and his hospital behind."[3] On receiving Cornwallis's orders for retreat, Abercromby destroyed his heavy guns and equipment which, like the Governor-General, he could not carry with him owing to the difficulty of transport. During the retreat almost all the cattle perished, while the men were worn out by sickness and fatigue, and exposed to the incessant rains of the west coast.[4]

Hardly had the English army under Cornwallis covered six miles when a body of horse were seen approaching at a distance. They were taken to be Mysoreans, and appeared to attack the stores and baggage. Colonel Stuart, who brought up the rear, was ordered to oppose their advance. But soon it was discovered that they were the advance guard of the Maratha forces under Haripant and Parashuram Bhau which were proceeding to Seringapatam to the assistance of Cornwallis.[5] The Marathas had sent repeated messages regarding their movements, but owing to the vigilance of Tipu's scouts, Cornwallis had not received any. Ramchandra Pant, Bhau's son, had therefore been despatched with 5,000 men to obtain some news of the English army. It was this force which met the English, and brought the good news that the main Maratha army was very near.[6]

[1] *Ibid.*, pp. 3-4. Hamid Khan, f. 85a, gives a very vivid account of the condition of the English army at this time. He says rice was 6 rupees a seer, dal 4 rupees a seer, ghee 16 rupees a seer, and flour 3 rupees a seer.

[2] *Tarikh-i-Tipu*, ff. 103a-b.

[3] Gleig, *Munro*, i, p. 132.

[4] Dirom, p. 2.

[5] Wilks ii, pp. 464-5.

[6] Khare, ix, No. 3346.

The arrival of the Marathas was a great event for the English troops and was greeted with joy by them. For, if the Marathas had delayed any longer, the English army would have perished from starvation and from the attacks of Tipu, who would not have missed this opportunity.[1] The Marathas brought with them abundant provisions and supplies of every description which were placed at the disposal of the English, although this caused scarcity in the Maratha camp.[2] But while showing this generosity, the Marathas did not hesitate to take advantage of the desperate situation of their allies, and charged them exorbitant prices for every article which they supplied.[3]

The Maratha chiefs were anxious to proceed against Seringapatam, and pressed Cornwallis not to retreat, promising to supply him with grain and bullocks which he stood in need of. But Cornwallis did not accept their proposal which would keep the English for a long time "in a state of wretched dependence on the Maratha bazar" where they would "not only be obliged to pay an immense price for a scanty subsistance, but be exposed at times to the risk of a total failure."[4] Moreover, it was also due to the exhaustion of his troops, the loss of battering train and stores, the return of Abercromby, and the advanced state of the season, that Cornwallis thought it inadvisable to accept the Maratha suggestion, and decided to march back to Bangalore. But the failure to achieve success in this campaign greatly affected him, and he wrote to the Bishop of Lichfield and Coventry: "My spirits are almost worn out, and if I cannot soon overcome Tippoo, I think the plagues and mortifications of this most difficult war will overcome me."[5]

The Maratha chiefs, in the end, acquiesced in the decision of Cornwallis to postpone operations against Seringapatam till the next season, and the allied forces set out on June 6, 1791, from the neighbourhood of Melukote, where they had been encamped. They moved slowly towards Bangalore, occasionally diverging from the direct route as suited their convenience. Moving to the north-east, the English army arrived near the fort of Huliyurdurga on June 19. The place was strong, and at first its Commandant decided to defend it, but after the town was carried, he took fright, and on condition that

[1] Gleig, *Munro*, i, p. 120.

[2] Khare ix, No. 3346. The prices in the Maratha camp were: Rice 1¼ seers a rupee, gram 2 seers a rupee, flour 2 seers a rupee, and ghee 4 rupees a seer. But according to Hamid Khan, ff. 86a-b, the prices were: Rice 2 seers a rupee wheat flour 2½ seers a rupee, dal 4 seers a rupee, raggy 5 seers a rupee and ghee 1½ seers a rupee, According to Dirom, 3 seers of rice, 6 of raggy or gram for a rupee, was the common, and, in general, the lowest price. From these accounts it appears that the prices were not fixed, but varied according to the demands of the troops.

[3] Dirom, pp. 9-10; Mackenzie, ii, p. 108.

[4] M.R., Mly. Cons., June 17, 1791, vol. 149B, p. 2986.

[5] Ross, *Cornwallis*, ii, p. 98.

the private property of the garrison would be secure, and that they would be sent away with a safe escort, capitulated. At first the terms of the capitulation were observed, but after the escort left, the garrison, which was proceeding towards Maddur, was plundered by the Marathas of everything they possessed "down to the nearest article of wearing apparel." The fort of Huliyurdurga possessed a good supply of sheep, cattle and grain, and it proved to be of great relief to the English army. The fort was destroyed since neither the English nor the Marathas thought it worth retaining.[1]

The English army continued its march northward, and on arriving near Hutridurga summoned it. But the Commandant returned the answer that he had eaten "Tippoo's salt for twenty years," and was resolved not to surrender till Seringapatam itself was captured. Next Savandurga was summoned, but with no result. As Cornwallis was not in a position to undertake any siege for the present, he passed both the forts by.[2] The allied armies arrived in the neighbourhood of Bangalore on July 11, 1791.

Since the junction of the English and Maratha armies at Melukote, a number of conferences had taken place between the allied commanders to discuss the future plan of campaign. Parashuram Bhau and Haripant wanted the allied forces to march to Sira and occupy all the territory between it and the Krishna in order to open communications with the Maratha country, and he was supported in his proposal by the Nizam's commanders. Cornwallis, on the other hand, was opposed to this plan. He regarded the establishment of a free communication with the Carnatic equally important. Besides, his army was not in a position to accompany the Marathas. The clothes of the European troops were worn out, there was a great shortage of war material, and scarcity of rice and wheat in the Maratha bazaars, and the raggy food on which the troops fed was causing great sickness and discontentment among them. So Cornwallis thought it necessary to proceed to Bangalore, and refit his army for effective operations against Seringapatam in the next season. After a number of meetings it was eventually decided by the allied commanders that, as it would be impossible for the combined armies to subsist for long in the same place, the English should devote themselves to establishing communications with the Carnatic, while the Marathas should try to open communications with the Maratha country via Sira.[3] Accordingly, Bhau, accompanied by the Bombay detachment, proceeded towards Sira, while Haripant remained with Cornwallis as the representative of the Peshwa. Since Asad Ali Khan had already marched towards

[1] Wilks, ii, pp. 468-9.
[2] Dirom, pp. 21 *seq.*
[3] P.R.C., iii, Nos. 328, 332, 348; Cornwallis's letter to Court of Directors, Sept. 7, 1791; Duff, ii p. 205.

the north-east with most of the Nizam's cavalry, Raja Tejwant was left as commander, but was relieved of his diplomatic trust by Mir Alam,[1] who had reached the English camp near Hosur on August 16.[2]

[1] Wilks, ii, pp. 469-70.
[2] P.R.C., iii, No. 361.

## CHAPTER XV

# THE WAR: LAST PHASE

On reaching Bangalore, Lord Cornwallis at once began preparations for the next campaign against Seringapatam. He devoted himself during the rainy season to the task of establishing an uninterrupted communication with the Carnatic and with the Nizam's possessions, so that supplies could be easily available to the allied armies when they invested the Sultan's capital.

Of all the passes which led from the Carnatic into the table-land of Mysore, the Palakad Pass formed the most easy route. It was nearer Bangalore, and it was by this pass that the Mysore armies had always invaded the Carnatic.[1] It was commanded by several forts of which Hosur and Rayakottai were the most important. Cornwallis, therefore, first turned his attention to their conquest, which would not only open a free communication with the Carnatic, but would also protect it from the incursions of Tipu's horse.

On July 15 Cornwallis marched towards Hosur, situated about 28 miles south-east of Bangalore. The Sultan had tried to improve the defences of the place, but they had been left incomplete. On the approach of Major Gowdie's detachment, which had been sent in advance, it was evacuated. The garrison tried to blow up the fort, but the Major's advance was so sudden that they failed in the attempt. The fort was occupied on July 15. The hill forts of Anchetnidurga, Neelgiri and Rutlengiri surrendered a few days later.[2]

Major Gowdie was next sent to Rayakottai which was garrisoned by 800 men. It consisted of two forts, one at the bottom, the other at the top of a huge rock. On July 20 Gowdie succeeded in seizing the lower fort by an assault. He then made an attempt to capture the main fort. The garrison put up a stiff resistance, but on the approach of the main army under Cornwallis, the Commandant lost heart. He accepted a bribe from the English, and on July 22, on condition of security of private property and permission to reside with his family in the Carnatic, surrendered the "lofty and spacious fort, so strong and complete in all respects, that it ought to have yielded only to famine and a tedious blockade."[3] Kenchillydrug, Oodiadrug and other small forts also submitted at the same time. Rayakottai, Anchetnidurga and Oodia-

[1] Dirom, p. 29.
[2] *Ibid.*, pp. 31 *seq.*
[3] Dirom, pp. 34-5 Kirmani, p. 362.

drug were garrisoned; the others were dismantled.[1] Thus, with the exception of Krishnagiri, the capital of Baramahal, all the posts necessary to establish an easy communication with the Carnatic had been secured.

For some time Cornwallis remained in the neighbourhood of Hosur to cover a convoy which was coming from the Carnatic. On August 10 it arrived safely. It consisted of 100 elephants, all loaded with treasure, 6,000 bullocks with rice, 100 carts with arrack, and several hundreds of coolies carrying other supplies. It was, as Mill observed, "a convoy to which nothing similar had ever joined a British army on Indian ground."[2]

Lord Cornwallis next turned his attention to the forts situated to the north and east of Bangalore, which not only prevented the English from securing a complete command over the resources of the surrounding country, but also interrupted communications with the Nizam's army which was near Gurramkonda. He, therefore, sent Major Gowdie to reduce them. The Major easily reduced a number of forts of minor importance, but the strong fort of Nandidrug offered considerable resistance. It was perched on the summit of a huge rock of granite, about 1700 feet in height, inaccessible on all sides except by one steep and rugged passage which was fortified by two strong walls and an outwork which covered the gateway. Tipu wanted to erect a third wall to give added strength to the fort. He had dug its foundations, but owing to the sudden outbreak of war he could not build it. Nevertheless, in point of strength, the fort of Nandidrug ranked only second to Savandurga, Chitaldrug and Krishnagiri in the Mysore kingdom.[3]

Major Gowdie first attacked and carried the *pettah* about daybreak on September 22. He then began the siege of the fort on the 27th. It took twenty-one days to effect two breaches. On October 18 Cornwallis himself with the whole army encamped within a few miles of the fort with a view to intimidating the garrison; and having reconnoitred the breaches, directed that the assault should commence that night as soon as the moon should rise. Accordingly, the storming party under General Medows moved off shortly after midnight. The garrison put up a stubborn resistance both by heavy cannon and musketry fire, and by rolling boulders down the hill with tremendous effect. The storming party, however, succeeded in mounting the breaches, forcing open the gate of the inner wall, and finally in occupying the fort.[4] After this the place was given over to the plunder and rapine of the English army. Women were violated and sacred

[1] Dirom, p. 36.
[2] Mill, v. p.238.
[3] Dirom, p. 43; Mackenzie, ii, p. 151.
[4] Dirom, pp. 43-6.

places looted. Large quantities of valuables were obtained by the English soldiers by looting the temple in the fort which had an idol cut out of stone, and to which pilgrims came with gifts from all parts of India. Some of the men belonging to the garrison were put in chains, and with their women brought before Cornwallis.[1] Lutf Ali Beg, the Bakhshi, and Sultan Khan, the Commandant of the fort, and the fighting men were sent as prisoners to Vellore; the women, Brahmins and others were conducted to a fort six miles away.[2]

The capture of Nandidrug led to the immediate surrender of the neighbouring fort of Cumuldrug. It also disheartened the garrison of Gurramkonda and strengthened the confidence of the besiegers. Besides, it enabled the English armies to establish an easy communication with the Nizam's possessions.

During these operations of the English armies, Tipu Sultan was not sitting idle. While his Commandants were engaged in defending the forts scattered in different parts of his kingdom, he made a bold effort to recover the territories lost to the allies. Having with the exception of Bednur no place left from which he could draw any large supplies, he despatched, early in June, 2000 regular infantry with 8 guns and a large body of irregulars under Baqar Saheb, son of Badr-uz-zaman Khan, to capture Coimbatore.[3] It was commanded by Lieutenant Chalmers who possessed a small force consisting of a company of Indian Christians, and a battalion of Travancore sepoys under Migot de la Combe, a French officer in the service of the Raja of Travancore. It had only a few guns of inferior quality and some ammunition. As it was not considered strong enough to stand a siege, all the heavy guns and stores had been removed to Palghat which was commanded by Major Cuppage.[4]

On June 13, 1791, Baqar Saheb invested Coimbatore, and captured the *pettah* on the 16th. He then summoned Chalmers, threatening to put the whole garrison to the sword if he did not surrender the place. But as Chalmers rejected the summons, the siege of the fort commenced. The batteries opened fire on the evening of June 20, but it was not until August 7 that a breach was effected. On the morning of the 11th a general assault was made. The conflict lasted for two hours, and in the end the Mysoreans were repulsed with the loss of 200 men. Their defeat was rendered all the more complete by the approach of Major Cuppage who, on hearing of the desperate condition of the

[1] Hamid Khan, ff. 88b-89a; Kirmani, pp. 359-60.

[2] Dirom, p. 49.

[3] Mackenzie, ii, p. 126 says that Coimbatore was attacked by Shadavad Ali Khan. But according to Wilks and Dirom it was Baqar Saheb who was sent against Coimbatore. I have not come across anyone called Shadavad Ali Khan in the Persian accounts to have been in the service of Tipu.

[4] Dirom, p. 51; Wilks, ii, p. 502.

garrison, had hastened to their relief. The Major dislodged the enemy from all the positions they occupied, and pursued them till they had crossed the Bhavani. Having raised the garrison of Coimbatore to about 700 men under Lieutenant Nash and a body of Travancore sepoys, Cuppage returned to Palghat.[1]

While a strong detachment was engaged in recovering the province of Coimbatore, Tipu himself with the main army made a movement towards the north. This so alarmed Cornwallis, who thought that the Sultan was proceeding against Parashuram Bhau in the province of Chitaldrug, that he postponed his project of besieging Krishnagiri, and made a few marches in the same direction. But Tipu had no intention of distancing himself from his capital; his movement was only directed to cover a convoy which he expected from Bednur. And after this was accomplished, and a detachment sent by him under Qamar-ud-din Khan had cut off a corps under Bulwant Rao left by Haripant to mask Maddagiri, and had put to flight the garrison thrown by the Marathas into Dodballapur, the Sultan returned to the neighbourhood of his capital.[2] From there he despatched Qamar-ud-din Khan to try once more to seize Coimbatore.

Qamar-ud-din arrived before Coimbatore on October 5, and captured the *pettah* the same day. On the 8th he attacked a small party which occupied the embankment of a tank near the fort. Lieutenant Nash was at once sent to their relief. A severe struggle took place, but the English were repulsed and were obliged to withdraw into the fort. After this the Mysoreans erected batteries to breach the walls, and at the same time kept on steadily advancing their approaches.[3]

Lieutenant Chalmers continued to hold the place, expecting to be again relieved by Major Cuppage. Although the latter sent supplies of ammunition several times to Chalmers through sepoys who managed to get into the fort by night, he himself was unable to advance immediately. It was not until October 22 that he could set out from Palghat. Hearing of this, Qamar-ud-din Khan left part of his troops in the trenches and with the rest, on October 23, marched to Maddagiri, about seven miles westward, where the Major had arrived on his way to the relief of Coimbatore. Qamar-ud-din declined battle, and instead made a dexterous movement to the right of the English detachment with the object of cutting it off

[1] Mackenzie, ii, pp. 126-33.

[2] Dirom, p. 51; P.R.C., iii, No. 370.

[3] Mackenzie, ii, pp. 136-7. Wilks and Dirom do not mention the capture of the town by the Mysoreans. As regards the number of troops at the disposal of Qamar-ud-din Khan, Wilks, ii, p. 507, says that he had 8,000 regular infantry, 500 horse and 14 guns. But Mill, v, p. 207, regards this estimate as 'overcharged'. According to Mackenzie, Qamar-ud-din had 6,000 infantry, 500 stable horse in low condition, and 14 guns and a number of irregular troops.

from Palghat. This greatly alarmed Major Cuppage who became anxious for the safety not only of the more important post of Palghat, but also of a large convoy expected there from Dindigul on its way to join Abercromby. So he decided to retreat leaving Coimbatore at the mercy of the Mysoreans. But as soon as he set out, he was vigorously attacked by the Khan, who inflicted a severe defeat on him. His losses were heavy. But he succeeded in retreating and thus saving his army from destruction. Qamar-ud-din Khan returned to Coimbatore which he had now isolated.[1]

The siege of Coimbatore was resumed with fresh vigour and great skill. A practical breach was made; and the ammunition of the garrison having been nearly exhausted, and there being no hope of relief, Lieutenant Chalmers surrendered on November 2. The garrison was detained in the *pettah*, and then, in accordance with Tipu's instructions, sent as prisoners to Seringapatam. This was regarded by the English as a violation of the terms of the capitulation which according to them were: That the garrison should march out of the fort with their private property unmolested, and be immediately escorted to Palghat to proceed from thence to the coast; but that they were not to serve against Tipu and his allies during the war; and that all public property, all the guns, ammunition and stores were to be delivered to Qamar-ud-din Khan.[2] Chalmers maintained that this capitulation had been drawn both in Hindustani and English, and that there was no condition attached regarding the release of the garrison. The other capitulation had been drawn by Qamar-ud-din Khan in Persian,[3] which he (Chalmers) did not understand, and in which the release of the garrison and security of private property was made dependent upon the pleasure of the Sultan. The English and Hindustani versions, Chalmers pointed out, were taken away from him a few days before his release in February, 1792, but he was allowed to retain the Persian version. It was according to this that the question of the release of the garrison had been referred to the Sultan; and as the latter had refused to give his assent, they had been sent off to Seringapatam.[4]

Qamar-ud-din Khan, on the other hand, argued that no business had been transacted in English or Hindustani, and that the terms had been drawn up only in Persian. He was supported by Ali Raza Khan,

[1] Dirom, pp. 62-4; Mackenzie, ii, pp. 137-8. The English lost 78 killed and wounded; the loss of the Mysoreans is not known.

[2] N.A., Pol. Pro., Feb. 29, 1792, Cons. No. 4, Cornwallis to Tipu.

[3] N.A., O.R., 89. Qamar-ud-din Khan to Chalmers. No date. Bears a seal of Qamar-ud-din Khan. The terms of the capitulation are the same as mentioned above, except that the release of the garrison is made conditional upon the pleasure of the Sultan.

[4] N.A., Pol. Pro., March 9, 1792, Cons. No. 8, Cornwallis to Tipu; M. R., Mly. Sundry Book, vol 106, p. 3.

who stated that the business at Coimbatore had been transacted through him, and that no such Hindustani or English paper as suggested by Chalmers had any existence.[1] Chalmers's contention that the capitulation had been drawn in Hindustani does not seem to be correct. All such transactions took place either in Persian or English or in both. Hindustani was not given any official recognition. With regard to the other statement of Chalmers that he did not understand Persian, it must be remembered that there must have been some persons in the garrison who could read that language. Moreover, if the garrison had been granted the terms as suggested by Chalmers, there was no reason why they should not have been implemented by Tipu. On a previous occasion the garrison of Dharapuram had surrendered by capitulation to the Sultan and they had been immediately furnished with an escort and sent to the English army.[2]

While Qamar-ud-din Khan had proceeded against Coimbatore, a detachment of his army, chiefly horse, was sent under Baqar Saheb to reinforce the garrison of Krishnagiri and to cut off the communications of the English army in Mysore with the Carnatic. Baqar Saheb marched through the Thopur pass with great rapidity and secrecy, and succeeded in reinforcing Krishnagiri. Part of his detachment returned with a sum of money which had been collected in the district, while the rest remained in Baramahal with the object of interrupting English convoys. The appearance of this force having alarmed Cornwallis, he sent Maxwell in the direction of Pennagaram, a mud fort, not far from the entrance at Thopur, which had been occupied by a portion of Baqar Saheb's force and formed the base of his operations. Maxwell appeared before the place on October 31, and summoned the garrison, but they fired upon the flag. Thereupon, the fort was assaulted and carried by an escalade. The defenders demanded quarter, but it was refused, and 200 men were put to the sword before the anger of the English troops could be controlled.[3]

Owing to the loss of Pennagaram and other important places in Baramahal, Baqar Saheb felt that he could not successfully carry on operations in the district, so he descended by the pass of Changama into the Carnatic. But finding that Floyd was present there with his cavalry to oppose his advance, and that any enterprise towards Madras would be hazardous, he turned southward, and re-entered Mysore by the pass of Atur, thirty miles east of Salem.[4] Early in January 1791, however, a body of horse belonging to his division succeeded in penetrating into the heart of the Carnatic which they began to ravage. They even reached almost to the gates of Fort

[1] *Ibid.*
[2] See p. 191, *supra*.
[3] Mackenzie, ii, pp. 153-4.
[4] Wilks, ii, p. 501.

St. George, burning several of the adjacent villages, and carrying off large quantities of plunder. But they did not stay there long; they disappeared as quickly as they came.[1]

After the capture of Pennagaram, which he dismantled, Maxwell proceeded against Krishnagiri, the only important place which Tipu still held in Baramahal. Maxwell encamped on November 7 within a few miles of it, and the same night he carried the lower fort by an escalade without meeting much resistance, the garrison having been taken by surprise. He tried to follow up this success and attempted to gain the upper fort as well. For two hours the struggle continued. But the Mysoreans rolled down enormous stones which crushed at once both the ladders brought to climb the walls and the men. Owing to the heavy loss which the English sustained, Maxwell had to give up the siege. After destroying the lower fort and setting fire to the town, he proceeded to reduce several small forts which were still in the hands of the Mysoreans, and then rejoined the main army.[2]

After establishing his communications with the Carnatic and the Nizam's territory, Cornwallis decided to reduce the formidable forts lying between Bangalore and Seringapatam in order to prevent the possibility of a second retreat from a deficiency of supplies. He directed his efforts first to the capture of the strong fort of Savandurga, which offered great advantage to the Sultan for interrupting communications between Bangalore and his capital.

Savandurga, about twenty miles west of Bangalore, is a huge rock of granite, 4000 feet above sea level. The mountain from which it rises is about eight miles in circumference, and was surrounded by a thick belt of bamboo and thorny bushes of several miles in depth. The summit of the rock is split by a great chasm into two peaks, one called the black, and the other the white peak; and each was crowned with a citadel, so that in case one was taken by the enemy, the other might offer a safe retreat. The fort was further strengthened by the erection of high walls and barriers which defended every accessible point. The atmosphere of the surrounding country was considered very unhealthy, owing to which it derived the name of Savandurga or the Rock of Death. The fort was supposed to possess a garrison of 1,500 men.[3]

Lieutenant Colonel Stuart was entrusted with the conduct of operations against Savandurga, and he encamped on December 10 about three miles to the north, the only side which was to some extent accessible. Cornwallis also encamped about five miles in his rear to support him, and posted detachments on all strategic points in order

[1] Mackenzie, ii, pp. 174-5.
[2] *Ibid.*, pp. 154-5; Dirom, pp. 57-9.
[3] Mackenzie, ii, p. 162; Dirom, pp. 66-7, 69.

to prevent any kind of help reaching the garrison. The batteries were opened on December 17, and they effected a breach within three days. On the 21st the order for an assault was given. The forest now proved very useful owing to the cover it afforded the English as they advanced to the attack, while its trees and the rugged rocks enabled them to climb up the walls unseen. The assault took place at 11 o'clock. The Mysoreans tried to defend the breach, but were repulsed, and the eastern citadel was carried. They then endeavoured to return to the western citadel in order to put up a defence there, but the chasm which separated the two works retarded their progress, and the English troops who were pursuing them not only managed to enter the western citadel with them, they also succeeded in capturing it without any loss to themselves. But the Mysoreans lost 200 men including the Commandant who was killed fighting. The resistance offered by the Mysoreans had been very weak; they had trusted more to the natural strength of the fort than to their own efforts. Nevertheless, the fall of Savandurga greatly impressed the allies of the English, especially because the Marathas had once besieged it for about three years without any success.[1]

On December 23 Colonel Stuart was sent against Hutridurga, situated about twelve miles west of Savandurga. Its Commandant, as on a former occasion, treated with contempt a summons sent by Stuart, and threatened to fire on the flag if it were not taken away. The next morning, however, when the lower works were taken by assault, he requested a parley. But while the negotiations were in progress, the English, under the pretext that the garrison were making preparations for resistance, rushed to the assault. They broke some of the gateways, escaladed the rest, and soon became masters of the fort. The English did not lose a man; only a few were wounded. The Mysoreans lost 110. The Commandant with many others was taken prisoner, but the principal part of the garrison succeeded in making good their escape. The English obtained in the fort twenty pieces of cannon and a large quantity of grain.[2]

On December 22 the hill forts of Ramgiri and Sivangiri capitulated to Captain Welsh.[3] Huliyurdurga, which Cornwallis had captured during his retreat from Seringapatam, had been reoccupied by Tipu and repaired. Maxwell was now sent against it. The Commandant of the place instead of offering any resistance took fright and surrendered it on December 27.[4]

As a result of these successes, the line of communications for undertaking the siege of Seringapatam was made secure. On January

[1] *Ibid.*, pp. 67-72; Mackenzie, ii, pp. 162-8.
[2] *Ibid.*, pp. 169-71; Dirom, pp. 74-5; Hamid Khan, f. 90b.
[3] Mackenzie, ii, p. 168.
[4] Dirom, p. 116.

2, 1792, the last great convoy from Madras consisting of 50,000 bullocks carrying grain arrived at Bangalore. And after the arrival of the Nizam's army under Sikandar Jah in the neighbourhood of Hutridurga, Cornwallis set out towards Seringapatam.

*Operations of the Nizam's Army*

During these operations of the English, the Nizam's main army had been chiefly engaged in the fruitless attempt to capture Gurramkonda. The place was very strong. It consisted of a hill fort almost inaccessible and of two lines of fortifications surrounding the foot of the hill, both of considerable strength, and known as the outer and inner forts.[1] The garrison in Gurramkonda did not exceed 700 men,[2] and was commanded by Muhammad Mehdi, a brave officer.[3]

The siege of Gurramkonda began on September 15, 1791, under the directions of Hafiz Farid-ud-din. Since the Nizam's artillery failed to breach the walls, early in November Cornwallis sent a supply of ammunition, a detachment of sepoys, and the battering guns which had been employed at Nandidrug. Captain Andrew Read was given the entire direction of the operations against the fort. He made an effective breach, and, on the night of November 6, captured the lower fort by assault. Many of the garrison were taken prisoners, and several were killed, including Muhammad Mehdi, the Commandant, while the rest escaped to the upper fort. The latter being regarded as too strong to be stormed, no effort was made to pursue the fugitives and follow up the victory. The lower fort was handed over to Farid-ud-din by Captain Read.[4]

Soon after, a large reinforcement, consisting of 25,000 men under the Nizam's second son, Sikandar Jah, attended by Mushir-ul-mulk and Kennaway arrived from Pangal. The prince and his minister, thinking that the upper fort was too strong to be assaulted, although it had only a garrison of about four to five hundred men,[5] left Farid-ud-din with 5,000 men and 900 horse to reduce it by a blockade, while he himself with the main force and the English detachment marched towards Kolar in order to cover, in concert with Cornwallis, a convoy which was expected from the Carnatic. After this he intended to march towards Seringapatam. But before he had proceeded thirty miles from Gurramkonda, he received the news of the disaster which had befallen Hafiz Farid-ud-din; so he was compelled to retrace his steps.[6]

[1] Wilson, ii, p. 221.
[2] P.R.C., iii, No. 387.
[3] *Tarikh-i-Tipu*, f. 104a.
[4] Mackenzie, ii, p. 64; Wilks, ii, p. 514; P.R.C., iii, No. 389.
[5] *Ibid.*, No. 388A.
[6] Mackenzie, ii, p. 65.

Tipu Sultan, whose efficient intelligence service kept him in touch with the movements of the Nizam's army, had despatched Fath Haidar, his eldest son, with 10,000 men, mainly cavalry, to the relief of Gurramkonda.[1] The prince was only eighteen, and was assisted by Ali Raza Khan and by Ghazi Khan, Tipu's early military preceptor.[2] Fath Haidar appeared before Gurramkonda on December 21. Farid-ud-din advanced to meet him in order to avoid being exposed from the attack both in front and in the rear. But although Farid-ud-din had been warned by Mushir-ul-mulk of the approach of the Mysoreans, he, as Mir Alam says, on account of his overconfidence and pride, made the mistake of setting out to face the enemy with only a small force.[3] The result was that, being outnumbered, the greater part of his detachment was cut to pieces and he himself was killed. The young prince of Canool, supported by Raja Joth Singh, maintained an unequal struggle for some time; but after the Raja was severely wounded, the prince withdrew to join Sikandar Jah. Thereupon Fath Haidar marched upon the lower fort, the Mysoreans in the upper fort sallying at the same time. The Nizam's troops became panic-stricken and fled; but few escaped death at the hands of the enemy. Fath Haidar occupied the lower fort and captured a large quantity of treasure, besides a considerable supply of provisions and stores.[4]

It was expected that Fath Haidar would next march to intercept the convoy coming from the Carnatic in order to disrupt the allied plan of advancing on Seringapatam. And in view of the fact that the Nizam's army had been recalled owing to the disaster at Gurramkonda, the convoy, which had ascended the Ghats and had arrived at Venkatagiri, was exposed to great danger. But as Fath Haidar did not possess a sufficiently strong force, he reinforced the garrison of Gurramkonda, and after removing Qamar-ud-din Khan's family from the upper fort, returned to Seringapatam.[5]

On December 25 the English detachment under captain Read, supported by Sikandar Jah, again attacked Gurramkonda. But they succeeded in taking only the lower fort. As Sikandar Jah wanted to proceed to the assistance of Cornwallis, who was anxious to advance on Seringapatam, he left under Asad Ali Khan a force superior to that which had been lately destroyed, while he himself with the main army of 18,000 men, accompanied by the two Madras battalions

[1] Mackenzie, ii, p. 65, wrongly calls Fath Haidar as Hyder Saheb.

[2] Wilks, ii, p. 515.

[3] *Hadiqat*, pp. 383-4. Mir Alam says that Farid-ud-din set out with a small force. The statement of Wilks, ii, p. 515, that he advanced with 20 horsemen is ridiculous. Dirom, p. 84, says he had 200 horse. The statement of Mackenzie, ii, p. 65, that Farid-ud-din set out with his horse, which was 900, seems to be correct.

[4] *Hadiqat*, p. 384; Mackenzie, ii, pp. 65-6. The account given by Wilks of this event is not supported by any reliable evidence.

[5] Dirom, p. 85.

under Captain Read, marched southward, and joined Cornwallis at the village of Magadi near Hutridurga.[1]

*Operations of the Maratha Army*

We have seen that the Maratha forces under Parashuram Bhau separated from the English army in the neighbourhood of Bangalore, and set out towards Sira to establish communications with the Maratha states, to obtain subsistance for his troops, and to deprive Tipu of the resources of one of the most fertile parts of his kingdom.[2] Being short of money, Haripant also wanted to proceed in the same direction. But after Cornwallis had paid him twelve lakhs of rupees, which removed his present needs, he decided to remain with the English army as the political representative of the Peshwa.[3]

On the way to Sira, Nijagal surrendered to Bhau. But on approaching the hill fort of Devarayadurga[4] he found that, although the Mysoreans had evacuated the *pettah*, they refused to surrender the fort. Twice the Marathas and the English detachment attempted to capture it, but failed. In anger and revenge for the failure, Bhau burnt the *pettah*, and proceeded towards Sira which had been occupied by Haripant during his march to Seringapatam.[5] From Sira Bhau marched to Erode which, by paying a considerable sum, obtained Bhau's promise of protection from his irregular horse. In spite of this, the Marathas climbed the walls of the town and seized it, plundering the prosperous inhabitants of everything they possessed.[6]

On August 21 Bhau halted before Tulkh, situated twenty-five miles north-east of Chitaldrug and of no great strength. It was stormed by a party of Maratha infantry who burnt and plundered the town, and obtained some grain and cattle in the fort. About this time Bhau's cavalry surprised and cut off a body of Mysore horse and foot, which had molested his foraging parties and carried away many horses and camels. On August 31 the army moved to Kunkoopy which refused Bhau's summons, but capitulated the next day to the English detachment.[7]

Early in September the army moved to the vicinity of Chitaldrug which was regarded as one of the strongest forts in India. It was well provisioned, and had a garrison of 10,000 infantry and 1000 cavalry. It was enclosed by several walls, and on the north-west possessed a formidable ditch. A large town was at the foot of the hill on the

[1] Mackenzie, ii, p. 66-7; Wilson, ii, p. 222.
[2] See p. 219, *supra*.
[3] Khare, ix, No. 3366.
[4] Nijagal and Devarayadurga are in Tumkur Dist., Mysore.
[5] Moor, pp. 100-3; Duff, ii, p. 205. Duff says that the Commandant of Devarayadurga had promised to give up the fort, but on the approach of the Marathas, he fired upon them. But this is not supported by Moor.
[6] Moor, pp. 104-5. [7] *Ibid.*, pp. 127-8.

north side, enclosed by a wall and flanked by towers and a ditch. Bhau tried to secure possession of Chitaldrug by means of bribery, but Daulat Khan, its Commandant, remained loyal to the Sultan and rejected all his offers.[1] Finding the fort too strong to be reduced by a regular siege, Bhau moved off on November 2 to Chandgiri, thirty miles north-east of Chitaldrug, which he reached on the 21st. But owing to his illness he remained inactive until December 15, when he marched towards Bednur.[2]

The operations of Bhau till now had been very slow. He had made but few marches, and these had been confined mostly to foraging expeditions in the neighbourhood of Chitaldrug. The monsoon was the cause of his procrastination, and then after September, it was his prolonged illness.[3] Besides, he wanted to give his troops rest and food before beginning the campaign. Nevertheless, even during this period of inactivity the Marathas caused so much ruin and devastation that, according to Lieutenant Moor, "the curse of God could not have fallen on Egypt in a more destructive manner."[4]

At Melukote, Cornwallis and the Maratha commanders had agreed upon the plan of campaign which they were to pursue; and they had further decided that no desultory object should engage the attention of the confederates. Bhau was required to operate between Sira and Sivaganga, and to remain in the vicinity of the English army so that easy communications might be maintained with it. He was then to strike a junction with Abercromby and proceed to Seringapatam.[5] But owing to the prospect of plundering and conquering a province which had largely remained unaffected by the ravages of war, Bhau was tempted to exceed these limits and march to the west. This greatly alarmed Cornwallis, for it would expose the English supplies to great danger, and make it uncertain whether Abercromby would be able to move forward. Cornwallis even thought that the plan of campaign might fail and he might once again, owing to the want of supplies, be obliged to return without reducing Seringapatam.[6]

On December 18 the Maratha army reached Hole Honnur, a small town in Shimoga district, which had a garrison of 250 men. The next day it was besieged by Captain Little who stormed it at three in the morning of the 21st. The place was mercilessly plundered both by the English and Maratha troops, and the houses in different parts of the town were set on fire.[7] From Hole Honnur the army marched to

[1] *Ibid.*, pp. 128-9.
[2] *Ibid.*, pp. 135, 141.
[3] Khare, ix, p. 4492.
[4] Moor, p. 141.
[5] P.R.C., iii, No. 406.
[6] *Ibid.*, No. 409.
[7] *Ibid.*, No. 400; Moor, pp. 143-5. But Moor, p. 146, is wrong in saying that Hole Honnur had a garrison of 500 men.

Benkipur[1] whose garrison, demoralised by the fall of Hole Honnur, surrendered at the first summons. The army then proceeded to Shimoga, situated on the left bank of the Tunga.[2]

We have seen that Ganpat Rao Mahendale had been despatched by Bhau with 5,000 horse. After some initial successes he had been defeated by the Mysoreans. However, with the help of 4,000 horse sent by Bhau, he had recovered his conquests. But his further progress having been checked by the strong Mysore forces in the province, he withdrew, and joined the main army on December 24.[3]

Tipu had stationed at Shimoga, besides its garrison, a force of about 7,000 infantry, 800 horse and 10 guns under the command of his cousin, Muhammad Raza.[4] Hearing of the approach of the Marathas, Raza Saheb quitted his entrenchments close to the walls of the fort, and took his post in a thick jungle, a few miles to the south-west, with a view to attacking Bhau as soon as he began the siege of Shimoga. His position was judiciously chosen and was very strong. The river Tunga was on his right, an impenetrable jungle of bamboo covered his left, and a jungle and deep ravine protected and concealed his front. Owing, however, to lack of time, Raza Saheb had not been able to complete his defences, which would have rendered an attack on him almost impracticable.[5]

On the morning of December 29 Bhau approached the fort, but he did not commence the siege, realising that so long as Raza Saheb was in the neighbourhood he would not succeed in the enterprise. He, therefore, decided to dislodge him from his position.[6] He made a long circuit and encamped near the enemy with a view to attacking them. He sent 10,000 horse under his son, Appa Saheb, and Raghunath Rao Kurundwarkar to attack the Mysoreans. But as the Maratha cavalry proved ineffective in the jungle, Captain Little with 1,000 Bombay sepoys and 4 guns, supported by 500 Maratha infantry and 3,000 horse under Appa Saheb, was ordered to march against Raza Saheb. Captain Little entered the jungle at about ten in the morning. His advance was stubbornly opposed by the enemy who opened a heavy discharge of guns, musketry and rockets, and several times repulsed the English battalions and the Maratha infantry with considerable loss. At last, after the repulse of several parties, Captain

[1] It is called Bhadravati and is in Shimoga District, Mysore.

[2] Moor, p. 152; Mackenzie, ii, p. 178.

[3] See p. 212, *supra;* also Moor, pp. 88, 132, 152. Moor refers to Ganpat Rao Mahendale as Banna Bappoo Mendla.

[4] Dirom, p. 102. Mackenzie's estimate (ii, p. 178) that Raza Saheb had 3,000 men is rather low. On the other hand, Malet, on the basis of the information sent from the camp, put the number at 10,000. (P.R.C., iii, No. 407). But this also is an exaggerated figure.

[5] Moor, pp. 154, 158; Mackenzie, ii, p. 178.

[6] Dirom, pp. 102-3; Mackenzie, ii, p. 178.

Little decided to attack with his whole force, and himself headed his troops, attacking the posts on the enemy's right which appeared to be poorly defended. The Mysoreans fought with great courage, but towards evening they began to show signs of weakness. Thereupon, Captain Little ordered the cavalry under Appa Saheb to press forward. The force under Raghunath Rao Kurundwarkar also rallied to his support. This proved decisive, and Raza Saheb had to retreat, pursued by Captain Little who captured all his ten guns. Meanwhile, the Marathas engaged themselves in plundering the Mysoreans. They seized their camp and baggage, and such a quantity of arms that good muskets were sold in the bazaar at two rupees each.[1] Raza escaped to the hill fort of Kaveledurga with 400 horse and 1,500 foot. Thirteen loaded elephants, which he had sent away on the morning of the action, was all that he could save of his baggage.[2] The Marathas lost 500; the English losses were also very heavy. The loss of the Mysoreans, according to Moor, did not exceed 200.[3]

Raza Saheb had occupied a very strong position, and his troops had fought with great stubborness. That in spite of this he was defeated was because he had committed the grave mistake of drawing off the guns from the centre during the engagement, and of sending away the elephants and valuables. This was an injudicious action which betrayed a want of confidence in the infantry, and led to the demoralisation of his troops.[4] The defeat sustained by the Mysoreans was due to the great military skill displayed by Captain Little which was reminiscent of Lawrence and Clive; and had it not been for his leadership and the courage of his detachment, it is doubtful if the Marathas would have won the battle.[5]

After this victory the siege of Shimoga commenced under the sole direction of Captain Little. Shimoga possessed sufficient garrison, and was well supplied with cannon and military stores. But the defeat of Raza Saheb had demoralised the garrison, a greater part of which had consequently deserted. Muin-ud-din Khan, its Commandant, could not, therefore, hold out long; and after a breach was effected in the noon of January 3, 1792, and preparations for an assault were made, he agreed to give up the place. But remembering the breach of the capitulation of Dharwar, he stipulated that the life and property of the garrison should be guaranteed by Captain Little. As this condition was accepted, he evacuated the fort, and was accommodated in the

[1] Khare, ix, No. 3411; Moor, pp. 154-7; Dirom, pp. 103-4.

[2] Dirom, pp. 104-5; Moor, p. 157.

[3] Khare, ix, No. 3411; Duff, ii, p. 211; Moor, p. 157. The English accounts place the loss of the Company's detachment in killed and wounded at about 60. But this is an underestimate. According to Maratha accounts the English lost heavily.

[4] Moor, pp. 189-190.

[5] Duff, ii, p. 210; Moor, p. 190.

British camp. Bhau, however, managed to secure the Commandant and other principal officers of the fort, and contrary to the terms of the capitulation, deprived them of whatever valuables they possessed and detained them.[1] Duff says that Captain Little "was compelled to place the principal officers at the disposal of Pureshram Bhow, who, contrary to the terms of the capitulation, detained them in the same manner as he had kept Budr-uz-zaman Khan."[2] But if Captain Little had asserted himself, and had refused to deliver them over to Bhau, he would have had his way in the end. Captain Little, therefore, should also share the blame for the violation of the capitulation, because he had pledged himself to the safety of the garrison until they were escorted to a fort which was in Tipu's possession.

For over a week after the capture of Shimoga, Bhau remained engaged in sending detachments in different directions to reduce the small forts in the neighbourhood. About the middle of January he broke camp. But instead of proceeding to join the Bombay army according to the plan agreed upon, he set out towards the town of Bednur. On January 28, 1792, he reached within a few miles of it, and was preparing to invest it, when suddenly he started retreating. During his countermarch he reduced Kumsi and Anantapur and other small forts, and after leaving garrisons in Hole Honnur and Shimoga and a large army in the neighbourhood, he marched to Seringapatam on about February 10, 1792, reaching there on March 10.[3]

There were several reasons which caused Bhau's sudden retreat from Bednur. According to the plan of campaign agreed upon between the allied commanders, Bhau was required to operate between Sira and Sivaganga. Instead he had exceeded those limits and had started campaigning towards the west. He had occupied Benkipur and Shimoga and other places; but not satisfied with these conquests, he had moved further west towards Bednur. This meant that he would not only be unable to join Abercromby, he would also be delayed in reaching Seringapatam in time to assist Cornwallis in its siege. The Governor-General had strongly protested to the Poona Government against the high-handed behaviour of Bhau, and Malet had repeatedly urged Nana to expedite Bhau's advance to the Mysore capital. Nana and Haripant had, therefore, written to Bhau to give up operations, and at once proceed to Seringapatam. They tried to impress upon him that, if he did not reach the capital in time to participate in its capture, the Marathas, owing to their unequal war effort, might get less than their due share of Tipu's territory. So Bhau gave up the campaign in Bednur, realising that, if he got too deeply

[1] Moor, pp. 160-1, 187.
[2] Duff, ii, p. 211.
[3] Moor, pp. 169-73.

involved in it, it would be impossible to extricate himself for a long time.[1]

There was also another cause which obliged Bhau to quit Bednur. This was the news of the approach of Qamar-ud-din Khan. The Maratha invasion of Bednur had greatly alarmed Tipu, because it was the only province left in his possession and the source of most of his supplies. He had, therefore, despatched Qamar-ud-din Khan with a strong force of infantry to entrap Bhau in the woods. It was the news of the approach of the Mysore commander which induced Bhau to retreat, for he realised that his army, which consisted mostly of cavalry, would not be able to hold its own in a confined country against an efficient force of infantry.[2]

Although Bhau had not been able to occupy the whole province of Bednur, still, wherever his army went, it left nothing but a trail of destruction and desolation. Bednur was in a very flourishing state, but "the Maratha locusts," according to Khare, burnt and ravaged it so mercilessly and completely that it was reduced to extreme poverty, and it took over fifty years before it could recover its former prosperity.[3]

The allied armies marched from the neighbourhood of Hutridurga towards Seringapatam on February 1, 1792, taking the more northern route by Huliyurdurga. This passed through a country fertile and amply provided with water, and was in every way better than the central and shortest route by Chennapatna and the southernmost route by Kankanhalli, which Cornwallis had used in his first advance on Seringapatam in May 1791.[4]

On the way the allied forces met with no resistance. The irregular horse offered some harassment, but it was not effective enough to impede their advance. It appears that Tipu considered it wrong strategy to take the field in person or despatch a strong force against the enemies advancing on his capital. He had, it is true, destroyed all forage, but he rested his hopes mainly on the fortifications of Seringapatam, convinced that by protracting its siege his enemies would be compelled to withdraw once again owing to the approach of the monsoon and the shortage of supplies. This plan of defence had not only been successful in the last campaign against the English, but his father had also employed similar tactics in 1767 with success against the Marathas. So he was indifferent to the approach of the allied armies. He remained encamped to the north of the river Cauvery, employing his time in fortifying his camp, and strengthening the defences of the fort and island of Seringapatam.[5]

[1] P.R.C., iii, No. 439; Khare, ix, Nos. 3410, 3413.
[2] Moor, p. 170.
[3] Khare, ix, p. 4494.
[4] Wilks, ii, p. 709.
[5] Mackenzie, ii, p. 188; Dirom, pp. 131-2.

The result of Tipu's wrong strategy was that the allied armies reached Melukote on February 5 without even firing a shot. The next day they encamped behind the French Rocks,[1] situated about four miles north of Seringapatam. The English army was in the front, while the armies of the Marathas and the Nizam remained in the rear, at some distance, to prevent interference with the English camp. "The encampment of the confederate armies," Dirom wrote, "was judiciously pitched at such a distance from Seringapatam, and so covered by the French Rocks in front of its right, as to prevent immediate alarm to the enemy, either from its proximity or apparent magnitude."[2] The English army consisted of 22,000 men, 44 field guns and a battering train of 42 pieces. The Nizam's army under Prince Sikandar Jah had about 18,000 horse with two battalions under Captain Andrew Read. The Maratha army under Haripant possessed 12,000 horse.[3]

The island of Seringapatam, formed by the two branches of the Cauvery which after separating again reunite, is three and a half miles in length from east to west and one and a half miles in breadth at its widest point. In the western angle of the island was situated the strong fort of Seringapatam. Next to the fort at a distance of about 500 yards was the palace of Daulat Bagh. In the centre of the island, at a distance of about 1000 yards from the fort, was situated the *pettah*, surrounded by a lofty mud wall. Towards the eastern part of the island there stood the rich garden of Lal Bagh which was fortified towards the river by redoubts, batteries and a deep ditch. Batteries were also erected along the river on different parts of the island to give added strength to the defences of the place. The guns in the fort and other parts of the island were estimated at 300.[4] Around the island ran a bound hedge composed of bamboos and other thorny plants. This marked the limits of the capital, and formed an exterior line of defence. The bound hedge on the north side of the river enclosed an oblong space of about three miles in length and half a mile in breadth. It was in this space that Tipu was encamped with 40,000 infantry and 100 guns in front, and 5,000 cavalry in the rear. He occupied a commanding position which, besides the hedge, was guarded in the front by a large canal, rice fields and the windings of the Lokapavani river. The right of Tipu's position was not only covered by that river, but beyond it by the Karighatta hill, which he had lately fortified more strongly. It was commanded by Shaikh Ansar, a brave officer. The left of Tipu's encampment was protected by a redoubt, which stood

[1] It is called French because the French in the service of Haidar and Tipu were cantoned here.
[2] Dirom, p. 128.
[3] Wilson, ii, p. 224.
[4] *Ibid.*, p. 225; Mackenzie, ii, p. 185.

on an eminence at an Id-gah at the north-west angle close to the hedge and was commanded by Sayyid Hamid. Two redoubts were in the centre, also near the hedge, with about 600 yards between them. A second line of redoubts named Lally's, Muhammad's and Sultan's lay behind, nearly equidistant from the bound hedge and the river. The Sultan's redoubt was under the immediate command of Tipu, and his camp was pitched near it. His camp and the redoubts formed the first line of defence; the second line consisted of the defences of the island and the fort.[1]

The position Tipu occupied was so strong and the valour his troops had displayed on a previous occasion before Seringapatam had been so noteworthy, that Lord Cornwallis was deterred from attacking him in the daytime. Convinced that the result of such an enterprise would be doubtful, and would lead to a considerable loss of English lives, he decided to make a surprise night attack on the Mysoreans without any delay in order to ensure success.[2] Tipu did not suspect any attack thinking that so long as Parashuram Bhau and Abercromby did not arrive with their forces, Cornwallis would not undertake any important enterprise.[3] On the night of February 6, at half past eight, Cornwallis issued orders to march. The decision to attack the enemy had been kept a secret. With the exception of the chief officers, the soldiers were kept completely in the dark. The allies were informed at about 12 o'clock, only after the English army had marched, and advised by Cornwallis not to stir from their encampment until the next morning when the result of the night attack would be known.[4] When Haripant and Sikandar Jah heard of the march of Cornwallis they expressed great surprise that he had proceeded without guns and cavalry, and felt rather pessimistic about the outcome of the enterprise.[5]

Lord Cornwallis formed his army into three divisions. The right consisting of 900 Europeans and 2,400 Indians was under the command of General Medows; the centre consisting of 1,400 Europeans and 2,300 Indians was under himself with Stuart as his second in command; and the left consisting of 500 Europeans and 1,200 Indians was under Maxwell. The total forces thus amounted to about 2,800

[1] Dirom, pp. 130-1; Mackenzie, ii, p. 185.

[2] Forrest, *Selections*, *Cornwallis*, i, p. 130, Cornwallis to Court of Directors March, 4, 1792; N. A., Pol. Pro., March 2, 1792, Cornwallis to Charles Oakeley, Cons. No. 2.

[3] Wilks, ii, p. 527.

[4] Hamid Khan, ff. 95b-96a. Two sealed letters were left by Cornwallis for Haripant and Mushir-ul-mulk which were to be despatched after the English army had marched and the firing commenced. See also Khare, ix, No. 3414, Haripant to Nana, Feb. 11, 1792. In this letter Haripant describes the battle before Seringapatam.

[5] Dirom, pp. 141-2.

Europeans and 5,900 Indians.[1] Cavalry and guns did not accompany the English army because, owing to the night and the nature of the country, they were not expected to serve any useful purpose.[2]

The following was to be the plan of attack: "The officers commanding the leading corps in the right and centre divisions were directed, after driving the enemy from their camp, to endeavour to pursue them through the river and establish themselves on the island, and it was recommended to Lieutenant Colonel Maxwell to attempt to pass the river if, after having possessed himself of the heights, he saw that our attack on the camp was successful."[3]

At about 8-30, on a moonlit night, the three divisions moved. The right division under Medows entered the bound hedge at about 11-30, and turning to the right advanced rapidly against the Id-gah redoubt. It was not Cornwallis's intention to have this redoubt attacked as it was considered to be very strong, and stood at a considerable distance from Tipu's main front. It was thought that once the enemy's camp was forced, the redoubt would of itself fall into the hands of the English. However, "by some accidents to which all night operations must be liable," Medows approached the Id-gah redoubt and decided to seize it.[4]

The redoubt was commanded by Sayyid Hamid. It possessed eleven guns and was well fortified, but the Sultan had not been able to construct a drawbridge, so that a narrow pathway had been left for communication. A fierce struggle took place for the capture of the redoubt. The Mysoreans displayed great courage, and at first repulsed the English, inflicting on them considerable loss. But in the second attack, although some of the garrison defended themselves to the last, the redoubt was taken. Sayyid Hamid and nearly 400 of his men fell in its defence. But Monsieur Vigie and his 360 Europeans belonging to the corps of Lallée, who were stationed in the angle of the hedge in front of the redoubt, managed to escape. The English lost 80 men and 11 officers.[5] Their victory was dearly bought.

There were still other redoubts to the left of Tipu's camp to be occupied. But the stiff resistance which had been put up by the Id-gah redoubt, deterred Medows from making attempts against the others. Moreover, at that moment firing ceased both towards the centre and towards the left, and Medows, thinking that this signified either total victory or complete defeat, in either of which case it was necessary to proceed to the help of Cornwallis, countermarched and recrossed the bound hedge, leaving a strong force for the defence of

[1] *Ibid.*, p. 140.
[2] Forrest, *Selections*, *Cornwallis*, i, p. 139.
[3] N.A., Pol. Pro., March 2, 1792, Cons. No. 2.
[4] *Ibid.*
[5] Mackenzie, ii, pp. 207-8; Dirom, pp. 144-9; Wilks, ii, 530-1.

the Id-gah redoubt. In order to avoid the paddy fields and ravines, he made a detour, but by doing so lost his way, and got to the Karighatta hill without finding any trace of Cornwallis. Medows, thereupon, countermarched. But as he advanced the day broke, and he found it was unnecessary to proceed. He had met Cornwallis at the foot of the hill.[1]

*Operations of the Centre Division*

The centre division[2] was formed into three corps. The front corps was under Knox; the centre corps was under Stuart; and the rear corps, which formed a reserve, was under Cornwallis in a position to support the other corps of his division and wait for the co-operation of Medows and Maxwell. Between 10 and 11 o'clock, in the course of the march of the centre division, the front corps came into contact with a body of Tipu's cavalry escorting a party of rocket men who were on their way to disturb the English camp. The horsemen immediately galloped back to their camp to inform the Sultan of the impending attack, leaving behind the rocket men to impede the march of the English. The rocket men threw a number of rockets, but seeing that the enemy continued to advance, fell back with regularity and discipline. The front corps pushed on briskly, and entered the hedge at about 11 o'clock under a heavy but ill-directed fire from cannon and musketry. But due to the badness of the ground and the darkness of the night, and because each commander was required to pay more attention to speed than to the solidity of movement, the advanced companies split into two bodies. The party which first reached the river was under Captain Monson. It crossed without opposition under the very walls of the fort. Captain Lindsay even attempted to enter the gate of the fort with the fugitives, but it had been shut immediately before. The party now marched across the island through the bazaar, and took up post on the southern side.

The second party to reach the river was under Knox. It also crossed over without opposition. Knox then proceeded towards Daulat Bagh, Tipu's palace, and from there, with the help of two captured Frenchmen, marched to the eastern part of the island, to the town of Shahr Ganjam. Here he experienced much opposition from both the Sultan's cavalry and his infantry. Realising that he could not hold out long against his adversaries, he took post at the gate. Meanwhile, he heard the firing from the batteries which lined the river towards the eastern side of the island. This indicated that the English

[1] Dirom, pp. 150-1.

[2] The account of the operations of the centre and left division is based on Dirom, Mackenzie, Wilks, Fortescue, Hamid Khan, ff, 96b-99a, and Khare, ix, No. 3414. Haripant kept Nana regularly informed about the events connected with the war. See also Parasnis, *Itihas Sangraha*, ii, for these letters.

troops had penetrated the right of the enemy's camp, and were probably trying to force their way into the island. Knox, therefore, immediately despatched the greater part of his force to take the batteries. As they were all open to the rear they were carried at once without loss. The enemy taken by surprise dispersed. After this Knox occupied the town. The Mysoreans were so panic-stricken by these sudden and unexpected attacks from different directions that for the time being, they did not make any attempt to recover the town.

Monson and Knox were soon followed by a party under Captain Hunter who took post in Daulat Bagh. Very soon, however, Captain Hunter found himself in a difficult position. He realised that he had been discovered by the enemy who began to make preparations to dislodge him. He also perceived that his post would not remain tenable after daylight, when he would be exposed to the guns of the fort. He tried to inform Cornwallis about his position, but in vain; and not knowing that other English troops, who might come to his assistance had also passed into the island, he decided to quit the island. He succeeded in repassing the river, but not without loss from a heavy fire both of musketry and of cannon. He then joined Cornwallis at a critical moment, just when the latter was attacked by a superior force of Mysoreans.

The centre corps was under the command of Colonel Stuart. He marched against the Sultan's redoubt, but finding it abandoned, left some troops for its defence. He then proceeded to the eastern boundary of the bound hedge and met the division under Maxwell which had just defeated Tipu's right wing. Stuart and Maxwell after this crossed into the island.

The rear corps of the centre division was under the command of Cornwallis who had halted behind the Sultan's redoubt in expectation of being joined by Medows. About two hours before daylight, a large body of Mysoreans, part of Tipu's centre and left, who had recovered from the panic of the night, advanced and attacked the rear corps with great resolution. But fortunately for Cornwallis, just at this moment, he was joined by Captain Hunter who had returned from Daulat Bagh. A very severe struggle ensued. The Mysoreans fought with great valour and discipline, but were repulsed. After this Cornwallis drew off towards the Karighatta hill so that he might not be exposed to the fire of the fort, nor be surrounded by the Mysoreans during daylight. On approaching the foot of the hill he met Medows who was coming to his aid.

*Operations of the Left Division*

The left division under Maxwell directed its course towards the Karighatta hill which was an important post for Tipu, since it commanded one of the fords and the eastern part of the island, and protected the right wing of the Sultan's camp. Maxwell ascended the hill at about 11 o'clock just when the rocketting had commenced on the centre division. He made a vigorous attack and occupied the redoubt. The garrison, taken by surprise, made only a slight resistance. After this the Karighatta Pagoda was also occupied. Its defences were weak, because its wall had been lately levelled by Tipu who relied more on the works of the Karighatta hill, and believed that the batteries of the island would render a lodgement on the Pagoda hill by the enemy a dangerous attempt.

From the Karighatta Pagoda, Maxwell moved towards the enemy's camp. He crossed the Lokapavani river which covered a great part of the enemy's right wing and the hedge. But while trying to enter the right of Tipu's encampment, his division suffered severe loss, exposed as it was not only to the fire of Tipu's right, but also to the fire of some of the Sultan's troops who were posted behind the bank of a canal running round the bottom of the hill. Maxwell, nevertheless, broke through Tipu's right wing and formed a junction with Stuart, who then assumed command and advanced to cross the Cauvery into the island. But the depth of the river, the rocky bottom and a heavy fire from the lines and batteries appeared to make the crossing hazardous. The first attempt made where the river was not fordable, was beaten back with great loss. Attempts were then made to find a practicable ford. At last Colonel Baird found one, and crossed into the island. But he found himself in danger for the ammunition of his men had been damaged while crossing the river. Fortunately for him, at this very time, the batteries were taken by the party sent by Colonel Knox. In consequence not only was Baird saved, but Stuart and Maxwell were enabled to cross into the island, although, while wading across, a number of their men were drowned. Stuart then joined Knox in the town, and as senior officer took command of all the English forces on the island.

Thus, on the whole, the night attack of the English had succeeded. They had established themselves on the eastern side of the island, while to the north of the river they held the Id-gah and Sultan's redoubts and the Karighatta hill. The centre division under Cornwallis and the left under Maxwell had executed the duties allotted to them; and although Medows had failed in the task entrusted to him, he had by taking the Id-gah at least gained an important post.

The cause of the English success lay in their discipline and perseverance, and in the rapidity of their movements which had taken the Mysoreans completely by surprise. Tipu Sultan did not expect any attack until the arrival of Parashuram Bhau and General Abercromby. Meanwhile, he hoped to finish the works on the Karighatta hill and the Id-gah redoubt, and to improve the fortifications of the fort of Seringapatam. His tent was pitched near the Sultan's redoubt of which he held the command. He had just finished his evening meal when he heard of the attack on his camp. He immediately mounted, and gave orders to his troops to prepare for resistance. But before they could get ready, the mass of fugitives apprised him that the enemy had penetrated his centre, and that a column was advancing to the main ford. As this threatened his retreat, and as there was no time to organise resistance for the present to the north of the Cauvery, he decided to proceed to the fort, which he felt was in danger. He moved quickly, and crossed the ford just before the head of the English division reached it. Having entered the fort, he took his station at its north-east angle from where he could watch the operations and issue orders to his commanders.

When day dawned, Tipu found that his position was not hopeless, and that it could still be retrieved. He still possessed a number of redoubts within the enclosure, and several posts on the island; and what was most important, he held the fort. It is true, his forces, taken by surprise, had suffered heavily; nevertheless they had fought with great courage, and having by now recovered from the panic of the night, were prepared for further resistance. During the night, owing to darkness and confusion, the guns of the fort had been kept silent, lest the Mysoreans themselves should become targets. But as soon as it was daylight, the fire was opened, and the Mysoreans began to collect in order to expel the English from the positions they occupied.

The first attack was made against Stuart who occupied a position in front of the Lal Bagh facing the *pettah* of Shahr Ganjam and covered by the river on each flank. Shortly after day-break, Tipu's infantry approached under cover of old houses and walls and began firing on the English. The latter could only feebly return the fire, since their ammunition had been nearly exhausted during the night or damaged while they were crossing the river. But Cornwallis, who had taken his station on the Karighatta hill, whence he could watch every operation, immediately sent a force to the support of Stuart. On the arrival of this reinforcement, the Mysoreans withdrew.

The next attack that was directed against the English had as its object the recovery of the Sultan's redoubt. Tipu was anxious to take it because it had been lost without resistance, and because it commanded the communications between the island and the northern side of the Cauvery. At first, the Mysoreans surrounded the redoubt and kept up a constant fire against it. As its gorge was open towards the fort and the island, the English tried to barricade it. The barricade, however, was cleared by the fire of the fort, and at 10 o'clock the Mysoreans made an assault, but were repulsed with loss. At 1 o'clock in the afternoon, a second attack was made by about 300 mounted cavalry who with drawn sabres rushed towards the gorge. But the fire of the redoubt killed many of them and the rest retired. About an hour later, a third attempt was made by the Europeans, commanded by Monsieur Vigie. This attack, contrary to expectation, was the least formidable of the three; for, having advanced but a little way, and losing a few men, the Europeans fell back in disorder. This was the last attempt of the Sultan to recover the redoubt, and at about 4 o'clock in the afternoon, his troops quitted their post and retreated into the island.

About an hour later the Sultan directed his efforts to dislodging the English from the island. Two columns of infantry entered the *pettah*, and after driving in the outposts, advanced with great confidence to attack the main position of Colonel Stuart. But they were repulsed and compelled to retire.

In the course of these struggles, the Mysoreans had fought bravely, and several times repulsed the English,[1] but they failed to dislodge them from the Sultan's redoubt and the island. So Tipu ordered the evacuation of the redoubts between the Sultan's and Id-gah redoubts. Accordingly, during the night the Mysoreans quitted all the posts to the north of the Cauvery.

The English loss till now amounted to over 1,500 killed and wounded; the loss of the Mysoreans was over 2,000.[2] During the struggles for the redoubts and on the island, the 57 Europeans who were in Tipu's service, seeing the fortunes of their master at the lowest ebb, deserted to the English. Among them were Monsieur Blevette, an old man who was his chief engineer, and Monsieur Lefolu, his French interpreter, both of whom had been long in his and his father's service. Thirty of these Europeans, headed by Joseph Pedro, a Portuguese, who held the rank of Captain in Tipu's service, were immediately employed by the Marathas.[3] Besides these desertions, a large number of Coorgs, who had been brought by the Sultan from Coorg after their rebellion had been suppressed in 1785, also succeeded in escaping.[4]

With the withdrawal of the Mysoreans from the north of the Cauvery all the forage was now available to the English. In the *pettah* also the English obtained large quantities of grain for their troops and horses. Besides, the *pettah*, which had good houses and was surrounded

[1] A.N., C²242, de Fresne to Minister, March 5, 1792, No. 68.

[2] Parasnis, *Itihas Sangraha*, ii. According to one of Haripant's letters to Nana, the English army lost 1,500 (500 English and 1,000 Indians), while Tipu lost 3,000. According to another letter the English army lost 1,700 (700 English and 1000 Indians), while Tipu lost 2,000. The English estimates are unreliable. They overestimate Tipu's losses, and underestimate those of Cornwallis.

[3] Dirom, p. 183.

[4] *Tarikh-i-Coorg*, f. 64.

by a strong wall, afforded excellent protection to the English troops. Tipu's beautiful garden, the Lal Bāgh, was destroyed to furnish materials for the siege, while the gorgeous palace adjoining it was converted into a hospital. Thus, the position of the English forces was very strong both on the island and to the north of the Cauvery. On February 9 Cornwallis changed ground, and took up his final position for the siege.

But while preparations for the siege were in progress, a body of Tipu's cavalry made a daring attack upon the English magazine soon after daybreak on the 11th. They crossed the Cauvery in the neighbourhood of Arikere, and made a circuit around the north-east extremity of the Karighatta Pagoda to reach the English camp. They were taken for a part of the confederate forces, and were allowed to pass through the English picquets. Soon, however, it was discovered that they were Mysoreans. A party of sepoys opened fire on them and dispersed them. They escaped with little loss across the hills. As it was suspected that they intended to make an attempt on the life of Lord Cornwallis, he was persuaded to keep a guard of Europeans over his tent.[1]

So far all the fighting had taken place to the north of the Cauvery and on the island. The operations to the south of Seringapatam were to be carried out by Abercromby and Parashuram Bhau, who were soon expected to arrive. Abercromby set out from Cannanore on December 5, and with great labour ascended the Ghats and penetrated the Coorg country. He passed Periapatam on the 10th and crossed the Cauvery at Yedatore on the 11th. Informed by his spies of Abercromby's movements, Tipu despatched some of his cavalry under Fath Haidar to intercept him. Accordingly, on the 13th Abercromby was attacked by the Mysoreans who captured a great part of his baggage, and harassed his troops the whole day.[2] On the morning of the 14th, the Mysoreans attacked an allied detachment belonging to the troops sent by Cornwallis under Colonel Floyd to protect the Bombay army in its advance on Seringapatam, and compelled it to retreat.[3] But fortunately Colonel Floyd came to its rescue, as he also rescued Abercromby with whom a junction was effected the same day at Kannambadi. Together they marched and joined the main army on the 16th. Abercromby had brought with him 2,000 Europeans and 4,000 Indians.[4] Owing to this the siege operations

[1] Mackenzie, ii, pp. 219-20; Dirom, p. 192. Mackenzie says that the cavalry wanted to attack the magazine. But Dirom thinks that the horsemen had set out with the object of making an attempt on the life of Cornwallis.

[2] Gleig, *Munro*, i, p. 133.

[3] Hamid Khan, f. 99b; *Hadiqat*, p. 387. Mir Alam says the defeat was due to the cowardly behaviour of the Maratha troops who were busy eating and drinking.

[4] Dirom, pp. 193-4.

were pressed more vigorously, for now Cornwallis was in a position to invest the fort from the south as well.

The fort of Seringapatam, situated on the west end of the island, was triangular. Two of its sides were defended by the Cauvery, but the third side, situated towards the island, did not have any natural obstacle to oppose an attack. It was, therefore, at first decided to carry the main attack from the island on the north-east angle. But as this side was very strongly fortified, it was decided on the advice of Colonel Ross, the chief engineer, and on the information supplied by Monsieur Blevette and other Europeans who had deserted to the English, to make the principal attack across the river against the north face, whose defences were considered less formidable than those towards the island. The walls on the north side were not as thick as on the other; they had no outworks, while the flank defences were few and unimportant. The ditch was dry and inferior in width and depth, and the stone glacis built into the river was incomplete. Besides, the natural advantages of the ground were also favourable to an attack on this side. For, as Mackenzie observed: "From a gradual rise in the country, not only the buildings within, but the walls of the fort, were exposed to the very foundations." It is true that the river offered an obstacle to an attack from the north, but it was neither deep nor impassable. On the other hand, it offered security to the besiegers against sallies.[1]

On February 18, soon after it was dark, a detachment under Major Dalrymple crossed the south branch of the Cauvery, and approached the camp of the Mysoreans unperceived before midnight. The main body halted about a mile from the camp, while a party under Captain Robertson marched on to the attack. They entered the camp undiscovered, and after killing a number of troopers and horses retreated on the alarm becoming general. The object of the night attack was to divert the attention of the Mysoreans from the north of the fort where the English wanted to form during the night a channel, which was situated within 800 yards of the fort, into a parallel for an attack. When in the morning Tipu discovered that the English had been engaged during the night in constructing an important work, he ordered it to be severely bombarded, and despatched parties of infantry across the river to harass the English working on the parallel. The Sultan also tried to divert the stream, which supplied water to the enemy camp, into the Cauvery. In this way he wanted not only to deprive the English of water, but also to increase water in the bed of the river and make the approach to the fort difficult. But he failed to achieve his object because the embankment was very massive, and his troops were soon dislodged from the bank of the stream.

[1] Mackenzie, ii, p. 222; Dirom, pp. 195-6.

On February 19 Abercromby crossed the river to invest the fort from the south side, and took post on an adjacent height. Tipu opened fire upon the height, and at the same time endeavoured to recover a village up there which the English had occupied. But he did not succeed, and drew off to the fort at nightfall. The redoubt, which was within reach of the guns of the fort, was also evacuated by his troops. It was thereupon occupied by the English. The latter, however, quitted it the next morning for it was exposed to the guns of the fort. But, being situated close to the fort, its possession was considered necessary to begin the enfilading attack against that face of the fort. The redoubt was therefore reoccupied on the night of February 21 without any difficulty, for the Mysoreans, having once evacuated it, had not cared to garrison it. The next morning the English also seized the tope which was situated between the redoubt and the fort. This victory was, however, achieved only after a severe struggle. At first the Mysoreans drove the English troops from the tope, but soon after they were themselves dislodged and pursued. The Mysoreans again advanced with rapidity and courage, and again the English troops had to retire. But on the arrival of fresh reinforcement of men and ammunition, the English were finally able to drive back the enemy and establish themselves firmly in the tope. The action lasted from morning until sunset. The English loss during this engagement amounted to 104 men, killed and wounded. The loss of the Mysoreans is not known.[1]

By this time the second parallel had been completed and the batteries set up in positions advantageous for breaching the walls of the fort, when, on the morning of February 24, it was announced that Preliminaries of Peace had been settled, and that hostilities should cease.

[1] Mackenzie, ii, pp. 225-7; Dirom, pp. 208-9, 215-5; N.A., Pol. Pro., March 21, 1792, Cons. No. 2.

CHAPTER XVI

# THE TREATY OF SERINGAPATAM AND ITS CONSEQUENCES: CAUSES OF TIPU'S DEFEAT

We have seen that Tipu tried his best to avert war with the English, but did not succeed, and hostilities broke out. He, thereupon, directed his efforts to the conclusion of peace, and wrote to Cornwallis to send him a person of rank in order to adjust the existing differences and to remove misunderstandings between himself and the English Company. In case the Governor-General could not send any one, he was himself willing to send one of his representatives to him.[1] Cornwallis replied that he regarded him as an aggressor, and therefore he would neither receive his agent nor send his own to him. He was, however, prepared to open negotiations for the re-establishment of peace provided Tipu was ready to pay reparations to all the members of the confederacy, and to submit in writing his peace proposals.[2] Tipu refuted the charge that he was an aggressor, and maintained that it was in reality the Raja of Travancore who had been guilty of breaking the peace. He explained the causes of his conflict with the Raja, and informed Cornwallis that he had sent two of his confidential servants to the Raja in order to arrive at some settlement with him, but had not succeeded in the attempt. He was, however, anxious for peace, and therefore wanted to send a *wakil* to Cornwallis.[3] This letter remained unanswered.

The refusal of Cornwallis to respond favourably to Tipu's peace overtures was due to the fact that he wanted war and not peace. Owing to the same reason he had put forth such harsh terms as he knew Tipu would never accept. The war, it must be remembered, was extremely popular amongst Englishmen in India because it meant profits, and because, as Richard Johnson, a Calcutta resident, wrote to Dundas, the war was "under the present circumstances the most fortunate thing that could happen for the British interests in India."[4]

On March 25, after the loss of Bangalore, Tipu again wrote to Cornwallis pointing out that important matters could not be put in

[1] M.R., Mly. Cons., March 1, 1791, Tipu to Cornwallis, Feb. 13, vol. 145B, pp. 965-7.

[2] *Ibid.*, answer to above, Feb. 23, 1791, p. 969.

[3] N.A., O.R., No. 63, Tipu to Cornwallis, received on March 3, 1791.

[4] Home Miscellaneous Series, 435, Richard Johnson to Dundas, May 11, 1791, cited in Furber, *John Company at work*, p. 248.

writing, but could only be conveyed through some confidential person. But Cornwallis's reply was the same as before.[1]

While addressing Cornwallis directly, Tipu also wrote to de Fresne, the Governor of Pondicherry, to intercede on his behalf with the English authorities. De Fresne accordingly wrote to Cornwallis that Tipu earnestly desired peace, and asked him on what conditions would he be prepared to make it.[2] The Governor-General's reply to de Fresne was the same as he had repeatedly given to Tipu: That Tipu should pay reparations to the allies, and submit in writing the proposals on the basis of which negotiations could be opened. These proposals would then be communicated to the Nizam and the Marathas, and after consulting them, he would inform Tipu of his decision.[3]

On May 17 Cornwallis proposed an exchange of wounded prisoners of the battle that had taken place before Seringapatam on May 15, 1791. Tipu accepted the proposal, and at the same time took the opportunity of expressing his wish to send a confidential person to Cornwallis.[4] But the latter, not being in a mood to compromise, made his conditions even harsher, for, besides reparations, he demanded hostages as a security that Tipu would not in future break the peace. Tipu was, however, assured that in case the negotiations failed, the hostages would be returned to him.[5] Tipu replied on May 21 refuting the charge that he was an aggressor, and refusing to give any hostages on the ground that once an agreement was concluded, he would honour it, and so there was no reason why he should give any hostage.[6]

Meanwhile, the condition of the English forces retreating from Seringapatam was steadily deteriorating. While Cornwallis had not heard anything from Abercromby, and the Marathas had not yet arrived, his army was dwindling because of sickness and starvation. He, therefore, showed a disposition to come to terms. He no longer insisted that Tipu should submit proposals in writing, but informed him on May 24 to send his representative to Bangalore, where peace terms could be discussed with the representatives of the allies.[7] Tipu, glad at this change of attitude in Cornwallis, accepted his proposal, and on May 27 sent out a flag of truce, followed by a number of servants carrying

[1] N.A., O.R., No. 85, Tipu to Cornwallis, March 27, 1791; N.A., Pol. Pro., April 29, 1791, Cons. No. 7, Tipu to Cornwallis and reply of Cornwallis.

[2] *Ibid.*, Feb. 23, 1791, Cons. No. 10, de Fresne to Cornwallis.

[3] *Ibid.*, No. 11, Cornwallis to de Fresne. See also A.N., C[2]295, Nos. 10-19, for the efforts of Tipu and de Fresne to bring about peace.

[4] N.A., O.R., No. 203, May 17, 1791.

[5] M.R., Mly. Cons., June 17, 1791, Cornwallis to Tipu, May 19, vol. 149B, pp. 3027-31.

[6] *Ibid.*, pp. 3019-21.

[7] *Ibid.*, pp. 3032-3.

baskets of fruits for him. Meanwhile, however, the position of the English army had considerably improved owing to the arrival of the Marathas who placed abundant supplies at its disposal. So the next morning (May 28) the flag and the fruits were returned by Cornwallis with an answer that he could not enter into any truce without the consent of his allies, and that Tipu should first release all the prisoners of war, and agree to a truce until his proposals were accepted and the terms of the treaty adjusted.[1] Evidently Cornwallis, conscious of an accession of strength owing to the arrival of the Marathas, had gone back on his words, and had put forth a new set of terms.

While trying to conclude peace with the English, Tipu also made advances to the Nizam and the Peshwa, even after they had invaded his kingdom and dismissed his *wakils* from their courts.

On April 15, 1791, Tipu wrote to Muhammad Amin Arab that he wished to send a confidential person to the Nizam in order to remove misunderstandings and establish friendly relations with him. He desired the end of hostilities because it was causing useless destruction of human beings. Besides, as Muslims, he and the Nizam should not fight each other.[2] Since Muhammad Amin's reply to this letter was very insolent, Tipu wrote directly to the Nizam and to the Nizam's principal wife, Bakhshi Begum. Tipu requested her "to make use of your friendly interposition so that His Highness's gracious favour may be manifested towards me, the enemies of true religion be overthrown, and the troops which are supposed to have been sent to their assistance may be recalled."[3] In the letter to the Nizam Tipu wrote: "The advantages and benefits of unity and harmony among the followers of Islam are certainly exposed to your full view. . . I am sure that your blessed mind is ever engaged in adopting measures to increase the power of Islam and the splendour of the faith of Muhammad as indeed befits the world of leadership and your good name. You will please suggest the ways and means for affording protection to the honour, life and property of the people who are dependent on Muhammadan chiefs, and who in fact constitute a unique trust held for God, the Real Master."[4] But these appeals to the Nizam's humanity and religion fell on deaf ears. Both he and Bakhshi Begum upbraided Tipu for having committed aggression and brought unhappiness upon Hindus and Muslims alike, and informed him that if he wanted peace he should compensate the allied powers and write to them jointly. The Nizam could not receive any confidential person, or make a separate peace with him because that would be a violation of the treaty of alliance with the English.[5]

[1] Dirom, p. 5.
[2] P.R.C., iii, No. 292.
[3] N.A., O.R., No. 379.
[4] *Ibid.*, No. 16.
[5] *Ibid.*, No. 381, Bakhshi Begum to Tipu.

Tipu's negotiations with the Peshwa's Government were carried on through the Raste family. Tipu was anxious that one of his agents should be allowed to reside with the Peshwa, and requested him that necessary *parvanas* should be sent so that Ali Raza Khan might be able to proceed to Poona without any difficulty.[1] Ali Raza Khan and Srinivas Rao, Tipu's agents, even reached Chitaldrug and there waited for a passport from the Peshwa. But no such passport was sent, for Nana refused to treat with the Sultan separately. Ali Raza was informed that Tipu must first pay reparations, agree to restore the territories belonging to the allies occupied by Haidar Ali, put his proposals in writing, and then a reply would be given to him in consultation with the allies.[2] But the progress of the English arms after Cornwallis took charge of the campaign greatly alarmed the Marathas who wanted Tipu's power to be weakened but not destroyed. In consequence, when Tipu repeated his request to send his *wakils* to discuss the terms of peace, Haripant accepted it. In fact, the Nizam and the Marathas were even ready to make a separate peace with Tipu in case Cornwallis refused to terminate the war.[3] The Governor-General had, as we have seen, agreed to receive Tipu's *wakils* while his fortunes were at the lowest ebb, but as soon as they had improved, he had changed his attitude, and put forth harsher conditions for a settlement with Tipu. Early in August 1791, however, "at the warm instances of Haripant," he again agreed to receive Tipu's deputies.[4] Tipu accordingly sent Appaji Ram to Bangalore. He arrived in the neighbourhood of the English camp, which was situated seven miles south of Hosur, on August 6, and expressed his desire to meet Cornwallis and Haripant in order to treat with them directly. But although Haripant was agreeable to it, Cornwallis, who regarded himself as a principal in the war, refused to meet Appaji Ram, a mere agent of Tipu. He was, however, ready to appoint deputies who could hold talks with Appaji on his behalf, and informed Appaji to proceed to Hosur and meet the representatives of the allies. But since Appaji's instructions were to meet only Cornwallis and Haripant, he refused the offer and left on August 23.[5] Haripant and Mir Alam who desired peace had been evidently outmanoeuvred by Cornwallis. Tipu had also committed a great mistake in having insisted on a minor point of procedure and prestige, for by so doing he had virtually played into the hands of Cornwallis who wanted a pretext to sabotage the

[1] N.A., Pol. Pro., Nov. 24, 1790, Tipu to Anand Rao Raste, Cons. No. 15.

[2] *Ibid.*, Feb. 23, 1791, Cons. No. 13, Nana to Ali Raza Khan.

[3] P.A.MS., No. 1563, Raymond to de Fresne, Dec. 29, 1791; N.A., O.R., No. 246, Tipu also wrote to the English and the Nizam.

[4] Ross, *Cornwallis*, ii, p. 103.

[5] *Ibid.*, pp. 107-8, 119-20; M. R., Pol. Desp. to England, Sept. 19, 1790, vol. 1, pp. 326-7.

negotiations. It appears that owing to the disastrous retreat of the English from Seringapatam, Tipu thought himself out of danger and in a stronger position, and so was not ready to submit to any indignities. In reality, however, he had missed a great opportunity, with the result that in the course of his negotiations at Seringapatam he had to submit not only to the procedure he had now rejected, but also to peace terms which were much harsher than those he might have been able to obtain at Hosur.

When Cornwallis was once more preparing to march on Seringapatam, Tipu again wrote to him on January 7 that he wanted to send his *wakil* to negotiate peace.[1] Similarly he made approaches to the Nizam and the Peshwa. Cornwallis replied on the 16th after consulting Haripant and Mir Alam that the allies were ready to make peace, but, before the talks could be opened, Tipu should first pay reparations and release the garrison of Coimbatore.[2] To this Tipu replied on the 19th that he was not in the habit of breaking engagements, and that the fort of Coimbatore had not capitulated, but had been captured by Qamar-ud-din Khan, who had agreed to release the garrison only after his permission had been obtained.[3] Cornwallis's answer was that a capitulation had been signed between Qamar-ud-din Khan and Chalmers, but that it had been violated by the former. However, if Tipu wanted to disprove this, he should send either both Chalmers and Nash or one of them so that the real facts might be known.[4] Cornwallis no longer insisted upon the release of the whole garrison because, owing to the insistence of the Marathas for peace and the heavy loss which the Enslish army had sustained on the night of February 6, he had decided to bring the war to a conclusion.

Tipu had hitherto rejected the terms offered by Cornwallis for the cessation of hostilities because he had regarded them as unjust, and had hoped to obtain better terms either by breaking up the coalition against him, or by a military decision. But he had succeeded in neither. He had tried his best to disrupt the coalition by treating separately with its members, but his overtures had been spurned. Nor had he been successful on the battlefield. He had lost a major part of his kingdom, and his resources both in men and money were dwindling day by day, while those at the disposal of his adversaries were still vast. If he had measured swords only with Cornwallis or with any of the country powers, he would have been more than a match for them, but he was not strong enough to hold his own against the Anglo-

[1] N.A., O.R., No. 19; M. R., Mly. Cons., Jan. 24, 1792, Tipu to Cornwallis, Jan. 7 vol. 158B, pp. 429-30.

[2] *Ibid.*, Cornwallis to Tipu, pp. 431-2.

[3] N.A., O.R., No. 46, Tipu to Cornwallis. A similar letter was sent to the Peshwa by Tipu in Marathi. (O.R., No. 48).

[4] P.R.C., iii, No. 424.

Maratha-Nizam coalition. Although he had regarded his position before Seringapatam and the defences of the island as impregnable, he had been defeated. This had shaken his self-confidence. It is true that the fort was still in his possession, but it was invested on all sides, and on the arrival of Parashuram Bhau it was likely to be more effectively isolated. Thus, as no gleam of hope appeared to brighten his prospects, and as there was no likelihood of the tide of war turning in his favour, he agreed to accept the armistice terms proposed by the allies, and on the morning of February 8, released Chalmers and Nash along with five others belonging to the garrison of Coimbatore. They were accompanied by Muhammad Ali, one of Tipu's confidants, who was required to explain certain important matters to Cornwallis.[1] The release of Chalmers and Nash satisfied the Governor-General who intimated Tipu on the 11th to send his *wakils* to the allied camp to discuss the Preliminaries of Peace.[2]

On February 13 Ghulam Ali Khan and Ali Raza Khan left the fort, and proceeded to the camp pitched for the conference near the Id-gah, where they met Kennaway representating the English, Mir Alam representing the Nizam, and Govind Rao Kale and Bachaji Mahendale representing the Peshwa. After some formal ceremonies had been performed and methods of procedure regarding future meetings settled, the conference adjourned. The next day Tipu's *wakils* were asked by the allied representatives the concessions and compensation their master was prepared to give in order to secure peace. They replied that the Sultan only desired peace, but that if the allies demanded anything from him, he would be informed.[3] The allied deputies, thereupon, proposed that Tipu should, first, cede a territory yielding an annual revenue of three crores of rupees; secondly, he should pay eight crores of rupees towards defraying the expenses of the war; and lastly, he should give two of his sons as hostages, until the first two conditions, if agreed upon, had been carried out. These terms were regarded by the *wakils* as exorbitant, and they pointed out that the payment of such a huge sum was beyond the means of the Sultan who had himself suffered great losses in the war.[4] On Febuary 17, therefore, the allied proposals were modified. Tipu was now required to cede half of his kingdom to the allies, "adjacent to their kingdoms and at their option," give an indemnity of six crores of rupees, release all the prisoners of war since the time of Haidar Ali, and lastly, give two of his sons as hostages.

[1] *Ibid.*, No. 433; N.A., O.R., No. 88, Tipu to Cornwallis, Feb. 8, 1792.

[2] P.R.C., iii, No. 436.

[3] M.R., Mly. Sundries, vol. 106, p. 1. This is a journal of the conference held from Feb. 14 to April 10, 1792, to settle terms of peace between Tipu and the allies. It was written by Kennaway.

[4] *Ibid.*, p. 2; Parasnis, *Itihas Sangraha*, ii, Haripant to Nana, Feb. 25, 1792.

Kennaway informed the *wakils* that these were the final terms and needed no discussion.[1] Carrying these demands the *wakils* returned to the fort in order to place them before the Sultan and seek his opinion. The next day at 5 p.m. the conference again took place. The *wakils* informed the allied deputies that the Sultan considered the terms very harsh, and that instead he would be prepared to cede one-fourth of his kingdom, and pay two crores of rupees in ready money. But these terms were rejected by Kennaway who threatened the *wakils* with a renewal of hostilities if his demands were not complied with, and told them to quit the camp and immediately return to the fort. This attitude of Kennaway embarrassed Ghulam Ali Khan and Ali Raza Khan, so they consulted each other and proposed that Tipu would cede one-third of his kingdom and pay two crores and fifty lakhs of rupees. But as these terms too were unacceptable to Kennaway they finally proposed to cede one-half of the Mysore kingdom and pay three crores of rupees. They pointed out that that was the limit to which Tipu could go. But Kennaway rejected even these conditions. When, however, they were referred to Cornwallis he expressed his satisfaction, and maintained that it was beyond the capacity of Tipu to surrender more than what he had offered. Haripant also agreed with Cornwallis, although he demanded a further sum of sixty lakhs of rupees as "durbar charges" which was to be a gratuity to the chief officers of the allied powers who had served in the war. The *wakils* considered the sum very large, and after a great deal of haggling got it reduced to thirty lakhs.[2] During these discussions Mushir-ul-mulk had been of the opinion that Tipu should be left with just enough territory to yield an income of one crore of rupees, while the rest of his kingdom should be annexed by the allies; and in addition, that he should be required to pay fifteen crores as indemnity. But both Cornwallis and Haripant had regarded these conditions as extremely harsh, and had them dropped.[3]

Although agreement had been arrived at on two points, there were still others to be settled before the preliminaries could be signed. Tipu objected to the phrase "at their discretion" which implied that the allies could take any part of his kingdom which they desired, even parts of his "ancient possessions."[4] But after Kennaway had assured the *wakils* that "none of Tippoo's ancient possessions were to be required by the allies," he agreed to the retention of the phrase "at their discretion."[5]

[1] *Ibid.,;* M.R., Mly. Sundries, vol. 106, p. 5.
[2] *Ibid.*, pp. 6-11; Parasnis, *Itihas Sangraha*, ii, Haripant to Nana, Feb. 25, 1792.
[3] *Ibid.*,
[4] M.R., Mly. Sundries, vol. 106, p. 12.
[5] *Ibid.*, p. 19.

With regard to the amount of money to be paid, the *wakils* pointed out that the Sultan would pay one and a half crores of rupees, of which fifty lakhs would be in ready money, and the rest in jewellery, elephants and horses. To this form of payment the allied deputies objected, arguing that it would be difficult to dispose of these things and to fix their prices in terms of money. In the end, however, it was agreed that Tipu should pay one crore and sixty five lakhs of rupees in money and bullion and the remainder in instalments within twelve months.[1]

The question of hostages appeared to be the greatest stumbling block in the negotiations. Tipu at first did not want to give any hostages at all, but when the allies refused to compromise on this point, he agreed to send one of his sons, and instead of the other son two or three of his officers. This suggestion was also rejected, and the allied deputies refused to listen to Tipu's objections to send his children on grounds that they were too young and he was very fond of them, and that they would be denied proper attention and education. So Tipu was left with no alternative, short of war, except to yield. His eldest son, Fath Haidar, who was about eighteen years of age, was absent with the troops; and being very promising was regarded as heir to the throne. Abdul Khaliq, aged eight, and Muiz-ud-din, aged five, were therefore selected as hostages, for the others were so young as to be out of the question.[2]

As agreement had been arrived at on all points, Tipu signed the Preliminaries on February 23, and on the morning of the 24th hostilities ceased. The Preliminary Treaty consisted of the following articles:

1. One-half of the kingdom, which was in Tipu Sultan's possession before the war, was to be ceded to the allies from the countries adjacent to their respective boundaries, according to their discretion.
2. Three crores and thirty lakhs of rupees were to be paid by Tipu Sultan either in gold mohurs, pagodas or bullion. One crore and sixty five lakhs to be paid immediately and the rest in three instalments, of not exceeding four months each.
3. All prisoners belonging to the four powers and held since the time of Haidar Ali were to be released.
4. Two of the three eldest sons of Tipu Sultan were to be given as hostages for the due performance of the treaty.[3]

On February 26, about noon, the princes left the fort under the salute of its guns. The Sultan himself was present on the rampart over the gateway to see them depart. They were each seated on a silver

[1] *Ibid.*, pp. 14-6.
[2] *Ibid.*, pp. 5, 14, 16. Cornwallis gives the ages of Abdul Khaliq and Muiz-ud-din as ten and eight respectively. (Ross, ii, p. 152).
[3] Aitchison, *Treaties*, ix, pp. 210-11.

haudah on a richly caparisoned elephant and attended by the *wakils* who were also on elephants. The procession was led by a number of camel *harcarahs* and seven standard-bearers carrying green flags, and followed by pikemen with spears inlaid with silver. A guard of two hundred sepoys and a party of horse brought up the rear. On approaching the English camp, they were received by a salute of twenty-one guns. At their own tents, which were pitched near the mosque redoubt, they were met by the allied deputies. They were then escorted to the camp of Cornwallis who, attended by his staff and some of the principal officers of the army, received them at the door of his tent as they dismounted from their elephants. He embraced them and led them in; and when they were seated, one on each side, Ghulam Ali Khan addressed him in these words: "These children were this morning the sons of the Sultan, my master; their situation is now changed and they must now look up to your Lordship as their father." Lord Cornwallis assured the *wakils* and the princes that they should not feel the loss of a father's care, and that every attention would be shown to them. He presented each of them with a gold watch which gave them great satisfaction. The princes were well bred and every one was greatly impressed by their politeness, dignity and reserve.[1]

The next day Cornwallis paid them a return visit accompanied by Kennaway, Mir Alam and the Maratha *wakils*. Each of the princes presented him with a fine Persian sword; in return he made them a present of some elegant fire-arms. Meetings and exchange of presents also took place with Haripant and Sikandar Jah.[2] "There was," observed Major Dirom, "a degree of state, order, and magnificence in everything much superior to what we had seen amongst our allies. The guard of sepoys, drawn up without, were clothed in uniform; and not only regularly and well armed, but compared to the rabble of infantry in the service of the other native powers, appeared well disciplined, and in high order."[3] On the morning of February 28 a royal salute was fired from the fort to signify that the Sultan was satisfied with the reception given to his sons. On the night of the 29th and the next morning he sent one crore nine lakhs and a half of rupees to the allied camp.[4]

The adjustment of the articles of the definitive treaty presented considerable difficulties. Kennaway demanded from the *wakils* the revenue papers of the Mysore kingdom. They returned from the fort

[1] Dirom, pp. 226-30.

[2] *Ibid.*, p. 23; *Hadiqat*, pp. 230-1; Parasnis, *Itihas Sangraha*, ii, Haripant to Nana. Some of the letters written by Haripant to Nana during the period do not bear any date.

[3] Dirom, p. 230.

[4] *Ibid.*, p. 233.

on March 3 accompanied by Suba Rao, Tipu's chief *peshkar*, who brought some revenue papers belonging to the period just before the war, and regarding some of the districts, such as Coorg, were as old as seven years. They were not only incomplete, but were also regarded by the allies as incorrect, for they did not bear the seal or signatures of *qanungos* and *sarishtadars*. Kennaway's view was that Tipu had given a decreased estimate of the ancient districts "which he knew would not be taken from him, while he had given an increased estimate of the frontier districts, which he expected the allies would want to annex." Mushir-ul-mulk, on the other hand, thought that the revenues stated by Tipu, regarding the districts he wished to surrender, did not much exceed what these were worth, but that the accounts of the districts which he had included in his "ancient possessions" and which he wished to retain were set down at not even half their real value. On March 4, therefore, Kennaway asked for correct and complete papers from the *wakils*, and informed them that if the papers were not forthcoming within two days the allies would proceed with the work of territorial division from their own estimates. He was informed that the official papers of Bednur, Coimbatore, Calicut, Dharwar, Bangalore and many other places had been destroyed by the allied troops. Many had also been lost during the English attack on the Sultan's camp on the night of February 6, 1792. However, whatever remained would be produced, but it would take some time. The allies considering this reply unsatisfactory, decided to partition according to the accounts which they themselves could procure. Kennaway, having drawn out a draft of the definitive treaty conformable to the preliminaries and containing a specification of the countries to be ceded, sent it on the evening of March 9 to Tipu's *wakils*.[1]

At the conference, which was held the next morning, the *wakils* and Suba Rao began criticising the draft treaty. The *wakils* wanted the allied deputies to examine the terms of partition in the light of some of the papers which Suba Rao had brought with him. But Kennaway replied that the time for examining new papers was past, and that neither fresh accounts would be examined nor would the terms of the division as specified in the draft be relaxed. In spite of this discouraging reply, Suba Rao did not cease from criticising the draft proposals. He objected to the inclusion of Coorg, which was one of the doors of Seringapatam, and pointed out that Danayakkankottai,[2] which the English wanted to annex, was distant from their frontiers while it was close to Bangalore. Similarly, Bellary, Gooty

[1] M.R., Mly. Sundries, vol. 106, pp. 24-8.
[2] It is about 30 miles south of Bangalore and in Salem Dist., Tamil Nadu (Madras).

and Salem were also far away from the frontiers of the allies. But these objections were waived aside by Kennaway. The conference therefore adjourned and the *wakils* returned to the fort with the draft treaty.[1] When the Sultan saw it he was filled with anger and astonishment, and exclaimed: "To which of the English possessions is Coorg adjacent? Why do they not ask for the key of Seringapatam? They knew that I would have died in the breach sooner than consent to such a cession, and durst not bring it forward until they had treacherously obtained possession of my children and my treasure."[2]

On March 12 the *wakils* returned and informed Kennaway that their master was ready to sign the draft treaty provided the allies relaxed on certain points. Tipu was willing to cede half of his kingdom according to the valuation of his own papers, and the other half as valued by the allies. The objections raised by the *wakils* against the draft treaty on the 9th were repeated, but their main criticism was directed against the inclusion of Coorg in the schedules as part of the Company's share. Coorg, they maintained, was one of the gates of Seringapatam from which it was only about a day's march. It also commanded the best approach to Seringapatam from the sea. Besides, the English were not entitled to demand Coorg on the basis of the preliminaries, for it did not lie "adjacent" to the English possessions.[3] Further, since Kennaway had given assurance to the *wakils* that none of Tipu's "ancient possessions" would be demanded,[4] the English had no right to include Coorg as part of their share, for, according to the list forwarded by the Sultan to the allies, it formed part of his ancient possessions.[5] It might be argued that Calicut had also been included by Tipu in this list, and yet Cornwallis had demanded it. To this the answer was that the question of Calicut had already been raised before signing the preliminaries,[6] but no such reference to Coorg had been made at that time.

Thus the demanding of Coorg was an open infringement of the preliminaries. Nevertheless, Cornwallis refused to make any alterations in the draft. Kennaway was not even prepared to enter into a critical examination of the term "adjacent," but when pressed by the *wakils* gave the strange interpretation that in matters of business it signified "not far removed."[7] Kennaway also justified the inclusion of Coorg in the Company's share on the ground that the Company had entered into a treaty with the Raja of Coorg. But to this the

[1] M.R., Mly. Sundries, vol. 106, pp. 30-3.
[2] Wilks, ii, p. 553.
[3] M.R., Mly. Sundries, vol. 106, p. 35.
[4] See p. 259 *supra*.
[5] M.R., Mly., Sundries, vol. 106, Appendix 12, pp. 51 *seq*.
[6] *Ibid*., pp. 12, 16.
[7] *Ibid*., p. 35.

*wakils* replied that that treaty could not be binding on the Sultan. As these discussions led to no result, the *wakils* demanded their dismissal. But Kennaway suggested that they should return to the fort and bring back the Sultan's final answer by sunset the next day. To this they replied that it was useless to refer the matter to the Sultan for he was adamant on the issue of Coorg. However, they insisted that, before they left, Cornwallis should be informed of the talks that had taken place between them and the allied deputies so that they might know his final opinion as well.[1]

Since it was expected that Cornwallis would give a favourable reply, the next evening there was a meeting between the *wakils* and the allied deputies with a view to arriving at some compromise. Kennaway informed the *wakils* that Cornwallis, in order to avoid extremities, had consented to a deduction of 4,50,000 pagodas from the calculations made by the allies of 43,19,694 pagodas as the revenue-value of the country to be ceded to the allies. But he was not prepared to listen to any objections regarding the countries included in the schedules, and particularly regarding Coorg. But this concession did not satisfy the *wakils*, and they repeated their former objections against the draft treaty. As Kennaway refused to listen to their arguments, the conference terminated.[2]

Owing to the breakdown of the talks Cornwallis issued orders to resume the siege of the fort with a view to coerce Tipu into accepting the draft treaty. Accordingly, guns were sent back to the island and the redoubts, and the working parties resumed their labour. Parashuram Bhau, who had arrived on February 24, was ordered to cross the river and be in readiness to invest the south side of the fort. Bhau of course, as usual, exceeded the orders by ravaging the country as soon as he had crossed the river, and capturing a number of cattle and camels belonging to the Sultan's army. The princes were also told to be ready to proceed to the Carnatic. Their Mysore guard was disarmed and treated as prisoners of war. On the morning of March 14, the princes were actually on the march to Bangalore, guarded by Captain Welsh's detachment. However, at the request of the *wakils*, Cornwallis suspended their departure for one day. They were allowed to halt, and encamped on the road to Bangalore in the rear of the English army.[3]

The detention of the princes and their guard was a distinct breach

[1] *Ibid.*, p. 36.

[2] *Ibid.*, pp. 81-2. It was not only the value of Tipu's countries but also the value of his money which was in dispute. In the end, however, Cornwallis decided to fix up the value of Tipu's coins as a mean between the rate at which he desired to pay them, and that at which the allies insisted to have them. On this basis the difference was to be divided with Tipu. (Dirom, p. 238).

[3] Dirom, pp. 234, 244-5.

of trust on Cornwallis's part. In a letter of May 19, 1791, Cornwallis had informed Tipu that, if the negotiations broke down, the hostages would be returned;[1] and since the negotiations had failed, he ought to have restored not only the princes and their guard but also the money which he had received from Tipu. But in spite of this he detained the princes and refused to return the money on the ground that Tipu had violated the preliminaries by declining to abide by the partition award, by using evasions in submitting accounts and settling the rate of exchange of the money agreed to be paid, and, lastly, by continuing even after the signature of the preliminaries the repairs and works in the fort.[2]

In reality, however, it was the allies who had broken the preliminaries of peace. As Mill observed: Tipu "complained, not without reason," that to demand from him a territory "which approached to his very capital, and was not contiguous to the country of any of the allies, was a real infringement of the preliminary articles."[3] Besides, there was no mention of Coorg in the preliminaries. In fact, at the time of signing the armistice it did not occur to Cornwallis to include Coorg in the territories to be ceded to the English. It was later that this idea was suggested to him. On finding that Coorg was going to be left into the hands of Tipu, Abercromby visited Cornwallis and pleaded on behalf of the Raja of Coorg. He reminded Cornwallis of the treaty which the English Company had entered into with the Raja and according to which it was pledged to restore to him his estate. It was the result of this meeting that Coorg was included in the list of the districts to be annexed by the English.[4] However, as it was a new demand, Cornwallis had no right to present it to the Sultan as a *fait accompli*. But he did so believing that "after giving up his two sons as hostages and paying even by our account above eleven hundred thousand pounds, it is not easy to suppose that he (Tipu) can have an idea of renewing hostilities."[5] The Bengal Government subsequently admitted that Tipu's claim to Coorg "was justified" and pointed out that it "would have been returned to him but for the treaty with the Raja."[6] However, it must be remembered that Tipu was not bound by any treaty which the Company might have concluded with the Raja or with any other ruler. His claim to Coorg, therefore, remained unaffected.

The second charge against Tipu that he had used evasions in submitting accounts and settling the rate of exchange of money agreed

[1] M.R., Mly. Cons. June 17,1791, Cornwallis to Tipu, May 19, vol. 149B, pp. 3027-31.

[2] M.R., Mly., Sundries, vol. 106, p. 37.

[3] Mill, v, p. 321.

[4] *Tarikh-i-Coorg*, ff. 66a-67b.

[5] N.A., Pol. Pro., April 4, 1792, Cons. No. 2, Cornwallis to Oakeley.

[6] *Ibid.*, June 20, 1798, Cons. No. 83, Bengal to Bombay, June 14, 1798.

to be paid by him was equally false. Tipu had to face real difficulty in preparing the accounts owing to the destruction caused by the war. But whatever papers he had submitted to the allies were perfectly genuine. As Wilks observed: "No doubt remains in my mind that the accounts furnished to Lord Cornwallis, (on which were founded the schedules of 1792, and subsequently those of 1799), were actually extracted from the records of the revenue, and exhibited the most correct account that Tippoo Sultan was capable of giving of the gross revenue of his country."[1] The allies, on the other hand, tried to impose their terms in an arbitrary manner, and the accounts which they had prepared were not correct. Since their object was to secure as much territory and money from Tipu as they could, they employed the services of such people to prepare accounts as were either deserters or under their influence.

With regard to the last accusation that Tipu continued the repairs and works in the fort even after the armistice, he denied the charge and maintained that "His Lordship has been misinformed; but for his satisfaction, if he desired it, he would throw down one of the bastions that he might see into the fort."[2] In fact, it was the allies who had been guilty of violating the armistice. After the preliminaries had been signed the English troops under Stuart continued depredations in the Lal Bagh and in the Ganjam suburbs, while Abercromby's army ravaged the villages south of the Cauvery, and Asad Ali Khan continued hostilities in the neighbourhood of Gurramkonda. It was only after the *wakils* had repeatedly protested to Cornwallis that he sent orders to Abercromby to change ground to Kannambadi, and to Stuart not to cut trees in the Lal Bagh nor to destroy houses in the Ganjam.[3] Bhau, however, continued his depredations. He stopped Tipu's supplies, and massacred a number of his troops.[4] Incensed by Bhau's activities, Tipu requested Cornwallis either to recall him from across the river and bring him to account for his atrocities, or "he (Tipu) should consider it as a still greater favour, if His Lordship would be pleased to permit him to go out and punish Bhow himself."[5] But Tipu's remonstrances did not have any effect on the conduct of Bhau, who, even after the treaty was signed, did not desist from his plundering raids. Regarding Bhau's march from Seringapatam after the ratification of the treaty, Cornwallis observed: "I cannot help apprehending that he will commit many irregularities upon his

[1] Wilks, *Report on the Interior Administration of Mysore*, Art. 146.
[2] Dirom, p. 236.
[3] M.R., Mly. Sundries, vol. 106, pp. 21, 24-5.
[4] Khare, ix, p. 4478.
[5] Dirom, p. 246. Khare, ix, p. 4498, says that Bhau was ready to take up the challenge, but since peace was about to be concluded, this could not be allowed.

march, for his corps has hitherto paid very little respect to the treaty."[1]

Nor did the allies fulfil their part of the contract in the matter of the release of the prisoners of war. Cornwallis had accused Tipu of violating the capitulation of Coimbatore and refused to open any kind of negotiations with him until the garrison had been released. But he had nothing to say regarding the violations of the capitulations of Dharwar and Shimoga by Parashuram Bhau. Badr-uz-zaman Khan, it must be noted, was released by Bhau after repeated protests by Tipu only in August 1792, five months after the signature of the treaty. But Haridas Pant, Tipu's *diwan* of Dharwar, was not released on the ground that he was a deserter, and that he did not wish to return to Mysore. In reality Haridas was not a deserter, but had been taken prisoner along with Badr-uz-zaman Khan on the fall of Dharwar. Govind Rao Kale, the Maratha *wakil*, informed Cornwallis that Haripant had no objection to Haridas's going to Tipu if he so desired. But Cornwallis ignored the suggestion.[2] Besides Haridas, there were many other prisoners of war and Mysore subjects who had been forcibly carried away during the war by the allied forces and had not been released. The English, on the other hand, were very keen on the restoration of each and every Englishman in Mysore irrespective of whether he was a deserter, a prisoner of war, or in Tipu's service.

While Cornwallis issued orders for resuming the siege of the fort, Tipu began preparations for its defence, and his prospects at the moment appeared to be much brighter than they had been at the time of the armistice, for, in the meantime, Qamar-ud-din Khan had managed to throw himself into the fort with his division and the supplies which he had brought from Bednur. On the other hand, the position of the English had in many respects deteriorated. A great part of the materials prepared for the siege was formed of the cypress trees brought from the Lal Bagh. This had become so dry, brittle and inflammable as to be unfit for use. As the garden had been almost cut down, the new stock would have to be brought from a considerable distance. Besides, the English camp by remaining fixed at the same place for about six weeks had become filthy.[3] A number of soldiers were already sick, and it was feared that, after some time, their number might grow so large as to reduce the strength of the effective men laying the siege. That is why Mackenzie remarked that if Tipu had held out for a few months more, his enemies would not have been able to stand against the approaching monsoon.[4] Similarly, Raymond, the commander of the European

[1] P.R.C., iii, No. 449.
[2] Malcolm, *Political History of India*, ii, pp. xli-xlii.
[3] Dirom, p. 240.
[4] Mackenzie, ii, pp. 235-36.

troops in the Nizam's army, wrote: "If he (Tipu) had known like me the state of his enemies he would have saved his money and his beautiful provinces."[1] It is certain that, owing to his efficient intelligence service, Tipu knew the condition of his enemies, and he was also in a position to hold out for a few months more. That in spite of this he gave up the idea of resuming hostilities was because he felt alarmed for the safety of his sons who were with the English as hostages, and whom Cornwallis refused to send back to the fort. On March 18, therefore, he sent the *wakils* to the English camp with the treaty duly signed, which the next morning was formally delivered to Cornwallis by the princes. But Haripant and Sikandar Jah absented themselves from the ceremony.[2] On the morning of the 22nd, Cornwallis, accompanied by Kennaway and the deputies of the Nizam and the Marathas, proceeded to the princes' tent and delivered to them the ratified counterparts of the definitive treaty.[3] By the end of March the allied commanders put their forces in motion towards their respective frontiers. As a gesture of magnanimity and humanity, Tipu amply supplied them with *doolies* and bearers for the transport of the sick whose number had greatly increased during the stay of the allied armies before Seringapatam.[4] Before Haripant left, Tipu paid him a visit and warned him in prophetic words: "You must realise I am not at all your enemy. Your real enemy is the Englishman of whom you must beware."[5]

The war was supposed to have been fought for the defence of the Raja of Travancore. Yet in the peace treaty his interests were completely ignored. He was the first to have borne the brunt of Tipu's invasion, and had suffered severe losses. He had paid twenty-five lakhs of rupees (ten lakhs annually, nearly half of his total annual revenues) towards the war expenses to the English, besides supplying them with troops and provisions.[6] In spite of this he did not obtain any indemnity either in cash or in territory. In fact, he was so completely ignored by his allies that even his name was not mentioned in the treaty. For this the Raja felt greatly disillusioned and observed: "The Company cares more for money than for their friends."[7] He had expected that by bringing about a conflict between Tipu and the English, he would eliminate the former and thus establish his hegemony over Malabar. But to his utter disappointment he watched the English power rapidly spread over the

[1] P.A.Ms., No. 5303, Raymond to de Fresne, May 26, 1792.
[2] Dirom, pp. 246-7.
[3] Malcolm, *Political History of India*, ii, p. xli.
[4] *Ibid.*, p. xliii.
[5] Cited in Sardesai, *New History of the Marathas*, iii, p. 192.
[6] N.A., Pol. Pro., July 13, 1791, Cons. Nos. 11, 12; I.H.R.C., xix, record No. 4, p. 146; Menon, *History of Travancore*, pp. 239-40.
[7] Menon, *History of Travancore*, p. 240.

Malabar coast and monopolize the market for pepper which was the main source of his profit.[1] He was not even allowed to retain possession of Cranganur, which was handed over to the Raja of Cochin.

The revenue of Tipu's kingdom, according to the schedule prepared by the allies, amounted to about two crores and thirty-seven lakhs of rupees. Thus, the revenue of the territory ceded was estimated at 1,18,50,294 rupees, and each share amounted to about thirty-nine and a half lakhs of rupees. The boundaries of the Maratha kingdom again extended to the river Krishna. The Nizam's acquisitions consisted of Cumbum, Cuddapah, Ganjikota and the districts between the lower Tungabhadra and the Krishna. The Nizam had also obtained Gooty, but on the insistence of Tipu to retain it, it was relinquished by Mir Alam at the suggestion of Cornwallis. The English obtained the districts of Baramahal and Dindigul, a large extent of the Malabar coast, including the ports of Calicut and Cannanore, and the whole territory of the Raja of Coorg. In extent they secured as much territory as their allies did, but while the Nizam and the Marathas got back what had once belonged to them, the English acquired new and more valuable territories. The province of Malabar because of its spices, and its good ports like Calicut and Cannanore, and because of its strategic importance was particularly a very valuable gain.[2] They had been coveting it for a long time, and had at last secured it.

The Treaty of Seringapatam, on the other hand, sapped the economic, financial and military resources of Tipu. The cession of Baramahal, Palghat and Coorg broke down the natural barriers which offered protection to his kingdom, and the invasion of Mysore both from the east and from the west became easy. On the contrary, the invasion of the Carnatic by Tipu became very difficult owing to the loss of Baramahal, Dindigul and Salem.[3] The surrender of Dindigul and the fertile districts of the Doab deprived him of the granaries of his kingdom. The reduction of half of his kingdom, and the huge indemnity which he had to pay, disorganised his finances. With such limited resources it became difficult for him to maintain a large Europeanised army. The Treaty of Seringapatam, in reality, paved the way for his final overthrow by Wellesley.

Nevertheless, Dundas, the President of the Board of Control, and some of the military officers in the Company's service in India, did not like the peace. Dundas, who towards the end of September 1791, on hearing the news of a set-back to the Company's army by the Mysoreans, had sent orders to Cornwallis to make an "honourable

[1] Furber, *John Company at work*, p. 247.

[2] The net revenues of Malabar amounting to 25 lakhs of rupees would also be of great help to Bombay. (P.R.O., 30/11/151, Cornwallis to Dundas, March 17, 1791, ff. 113a-14a).

[3] *Ibid*.

peace" with Tipu Sultan as soon as possible, if need be, by sacrificing all the British gains in the war,[1] was no longer satisfied with the peace; he now wanted Tipu crushed for ever.[2] Medows also wanted Tipu's overthrow and the restoration of the old Raja's rule.[3] Nor was Munro satisfied with the peace; he wanted Tipu's extirpation, for he believed that "while his power remains unimpaired, so far from being able to extend our territory, we shall be perpetually in danger of losing what we have. Why then not remove, while we can, so formidable an enemy? But his system, if not broken, may in time be communicated to the successors of the Nizam, or other Moorish princes who may hereafter appear in the Deccan. If once destroyed, there is little danger of its being re-established."[4] Munro was so disappointed with the treaty that he wrote: "Everything now is done by moderation and conciliation; at this rate we shall be all Quakers in twenty years more."[5]

In reality, however, Cornwallis could not have secured better terms. He himself believed that "the destruction of Tipu's power would be desirable,"[6] but he knew that it was not possible. In fact, it appeared that the prolongation of hostilities would prove advantageous to the Sultan. It is true that Tipu had suffered severe reverses, but the fort of Seringapatam had not yet fallen, and the resistance which Cornwallis had met, and the losses which he had sustained in taking the lines and in crossing the river Cauvery,[7] had given him a foretaste of what it would be like when the fort would be attacked. Moreover, it was not certain that the allies would keep together for long. There were mutual jealousies and rivalries among the members of the coalition, and some of them were suspected by Cornwallis of actually carrying on secret correspondence with Tipu. Holkar was known to be sympathetic towards the Sultan,[8] and the early arrival of Sindhia at Poona, who looked with disfavour at the success of the allied arms, was

[1] Board's Secret Letters, i, Sept. 21, 1791, cited in Philips, *The East India Company*, p. 68, footnote 7.

[2] Furber, *Dundas*, pp. 128-9. At the begining of the war Dundas had favoured the complete extirpation of Tipu's power, "for a patched-up peace would be sad policy," (cited in Philips, p. 68, footnote 5). But now he reverted to his original view.

[3] P.R.O., 30/11/125, Medows to Cornwallis, Jan. 17, 1791, f. 35b. Medows tried to commit suicide by shooting himself. It is possible that he might have been affected by what he regarded as lenient terms granted to Tipu, but it is more likely that his attempt to take his own life was due to the shame he felt on account of his ill-managed attack on Tipu's retrenchments on the night of Feb. 6. (See A.N., C[2] 242, de Fresne to Minister, March 5, 1792, No. 68).

[4] Gleig, *Munro*, i, pp. 123-4.

[5] *Ibid.*, p. 131.

[6] Ross, Cornwallis, ii, p. 145.

[7] Parasnis, *Itihas Sangraha*, ii, Haripant to Nana; P.A.MS., No. 5303, Raymond to de Fresne, May 26, 1792.

[8] See p. 171, *supra*.

likely to introduce a disturbing element in South Indian politics. The English had not only established their military superiority in the war against Tipu, they had also dominated the peace negotiations. This had stirred up feelings of jealousy and apprehension in the minds of the Nizam, Nana and Sindhia; so they had become partial towards Tipu, and exercised pressure on the English to conclude peace.[1] Even Nana and Parashuram Bhau, who had been most inimical to the Sultan, did not want his complete extirpation.[2] It should also be remembered that war between Britain and France was imminent, and it was expected that at any moment the British troops lent by the King to the Company might be withdrawn for other battle-fields. Besides, the Directors were urging Cornwallis in every letter to make peace because of the great expenditure and the loss of the Company's trade which the war was causing.[3] In fact, if the conflict had lasted another year, it would have been difficult for the Company to sustain it, and all the business firms of Bengal would have gone bankrupt. Already, for the last six months, the Bank of Calcutta had suspended its payments, and its paper had lost 40 per cent in value.[4] And further, Cornwallis was awed by the idea of having to take possession of Seringapatam owing to the new problems of administration involved, and owing to the jealousies of the Indian powers he would have to reckon with. This had made him frequently exclaim: "Good God! what shall I do with this place?"[5]

Under these circumstances, the conclusion of peace was the best course for Cornwallis, and the terms which he had secured were the best that he could obtain. That was why he was able to write to Dundas: "We have at length concluded our Indian war handsomely, and I think as advantageously as any reasonable person could expect. We have crippled our enemy without making our friends too formidable."[6]

*Causes of Tipu's Defeat*

Tipu had carried on a gallant struggle against a powerful combination for nearly two years. He had defeated Floyd, baffled both Medows and Maxwell, and frustrated their plan for the invasion of Mysore. According to Munro, "these gentlemen themselves are as well convinced as any private in the army, how cheap Tipu held them, and

[1] A.N., C[2] 242, de Fresne to Minister, March 5, 1792, No. 68.

[2] Pol. Pro., March 21, 1792, Malet to Cornwallis, Cons. No. 6; Duff, ii, p. 215; P.R.C., iii, Nos. 344, 385.

[3] See the despatch of Sept. 21, 1791, which called the attention of Cornwallis "to the conclusion of an early peace, as alike essential to the finances and the interests of the Company."

[4] A.N., C[2] 299, de Fresne to Minister, March 1792, No. 77.

[5] Gleig, *Munro*, i, p. 131.

[6] Ross, *Cornwallis*, ii, p. 155.

how little honour he could have gained by foiling them. One, or rather two, sallied forth; and after spouting some strange, unintelligible stuff, like ancient Pistol, and the ghost of a Roman, lost their magazines by forming them in front of the army, and then spent the remaining of the campaign in running about the country after what was ludicrously called by the army the invisible power, asking, which way the bull ran?"[1]

However, with the arrival of Cornwallis in the south, the tide of war began to turn against Tipu. Cornwallis brought with him his prestige of a Governor-General and a larger and better equipped army. He possessed greater audacity, fertility of mind and power of quick decision than Medows, and he was able to provoke the Marathas to more effective action. Nevertheless, Tipu continued to fight with great courage, hitting hard and sometimes very hard. During Cornwallis's advance on Seringapatam in May 1791 Tipu displayed brilliant strategy. By hanging on the skirts of the English forces, by destroying their baggage, and by laying waste the country through which they marched, Tipu's cavalry wore them off. And then, before Seringapatam, Tipu offered such stubborn resistance that Cornwallis was compelled to retreat. In the second encounter with the Governor-General before Seringapatam, he again fought with great courage, and "defended his capital in a manner truly worthy of his father, himself, and of the nation which alone is attached to him."[2] His generals too showed great dash and resource. Fath Haidar destroyed Farid-ud-din's force and recaptured Gurramkonda, while Qamar-ud-din Khan cut off a detachment of the Marathas in Maddagiri and reoccupied Coimbatore. In February 1792, when the ring of powerful enemies was closing round the Sultan from all sides, a small body of Mysore cavalry cut off a great part of Abercromby's camp equipage, and would have captured the whole had it not been relieved by Colonel Floyd.[3] "The Colonel found him" (Abercromby), wrote Munro, "so much dismayed as if he had been surrounded by the whole Austrian army, and busy in placing an ambuscade to catch about six looties:—he must have been a simple looty that he caught..."[4]

That in spite of these achievements Tipu was defeated was due to a number of causes. He did not make any provision for the defence of his kingdom against the invasion by Cornwallis, but wasted valuable time near Pondicherry trying to enlist French support, wrongly imagining that, while he remained in the Carnatic, Cornwallis would not attempt an invasion of Mysore. He also did not properly defend Bangalore and allowed it to fall. Besides, the defences before Seringa-

[1] Gleig, *Munro*, i, p. 132.
[2] P.A.MS., No. 5303, Raymond to de Fresne, May 26, 1792.
[3] Gleig, *Munro*, i, p. 133.
[4] *Ibid.*

patam were not so well organised and fortified as they should have been.[1] He further made the mistake of not following up the success gained over Cornwallis at the battle of Arikere on May 15, 1791, when the English army was weak, exhausted and demoralised. There was yet another mistake which he committed. During Cornwallis's second march on Seringapatam, he did not offer any resistance at all. This was a wrong strategy, and its result was that the English army was able to encamp within a few miles of his capital without even firing a shot. Actually Tipu should have "left a sufficient garrison under a resolute leader for the defence of his capital and turned the bulk of his forces against the British lines of communications."[2] But instead, he put more trust on the position which he occupied before his capital and on the defences of the island and the fort of Seringapatam.

The defeat of Tipu was also due to the superiority of European science and organisation. Although Tipu had modernised his forces, they were still inferior to the English army in infantry and artillery. He had also improved, and, in some cases, rebuilt his forts with the help of his French engineers at great cost. These forts formed an important link in the chain of Mysore's defences, but they failed to resist the English whose siege guns were able to blast a way through walls however stout.

But the main cause of Tipu's defeat was that he had to fight against overwhelming odds. If he had been confronted only with the English, he would have emerged victorious. There is no doubt that they possessed a superior infantry and artillery, but this was more than balanced by his superiority in numbers, by the improvements which he had introduced in his infantry and artillery, and, above all, in excellent cavalry. Cornwallis was obliged to admit that Tipu's *looties* were "the best troops in the world, for that they were always doing something to harass their enemies."[3] In 1785-87 he had defeated a Maratha-Nizam coalition. In the Second Anglo-Mysore War, owing to the losses which they had sustained, the English had been compelled to seek peace with him. During the first phase of the Third Anglo-Mysore War also Tipu had established his superiority over the English army "the finest and best appointed that ever took field in India."[4] It was only from the time the Marathas and the Nizam took a more active part in the war that Tipu began to lose ground. Cornwallis admitted that the main cause of Floyd's retreat before Tipu and the failure of Medows to invade Mysore was that the armies

[1] A.N., C²242, de Fresne to Minister, March 5, 1792, No. 68; Fortescue, iii, p. 594.

[2] Fortescue, iii, p. 594.

[3] Gleig, *Munro*, i, p. 133.

[4] Ross, *Cornwallis*, ii, p. 52.

of the Marathas and the Nizam showed "slowness in entering Tippoo's country."[1] On the other hand, according to Munro, "Cornwallis could not have reduced Tippoo without the assistance of the Marathas."[2]

It is true that the armies of the Nizam and the Marathas were ill equipped, ill organised and ill disciplined. Nevertheless, they proved to be very useful to the English. The cavalry arm of the English army was very weak, but this deficiency was made good by the cavalry of their allies. Moreover, the armies of the Nizam and the Marathas, by creating diversions on different fronts, kept large forces of Tipu engaged which, otherwise, would have been free to concentrate against the English. Further, by occupying large parts of the Mysore kingdom, they cut off Tipu from his supplies of recruits, money and provisions. It must also be remembered that the English had at their disposal the resources of the Carnatic and Bengal which unlike Mysore did not suffer the ravages of war. They also received large supplies of men, money and material from England. To these were added large supplies of provisions obtained from the territories of the Nizam and the Marathas. Against such a combination, drawing as it did from almost limitless resources of man power and material, Tipu was at a serious disadvantage. There is no doubt that the main brunt of the war was borne by the English, but it is certain that without the timely arrival of the Marathas at Melukote, when the English army was retreating from Seringapatam in May 1791, Cornwallis would have met the fate of Baillie and Braithwaite; or at any rate "without them he could never, after falling back from Seringapatam in May, have advanced again beyond Bangalore."[3]

[1] N.A., Pol Proc., Oct. 13, 1790, Cornwallis to Malet, Oct. 11, Cons. No. 18.
[2] Gleig, *Munro*, i, p. 132.
[3] *Ibid*

CHAPTER XVII

# THE AFTERMATH OF THE WAR

After the departure of the allied armies from Seringapatam, Tipu employed himself in repairing the ravages of war, in suppressing the refractory *poligars*, and in arranging for the discharge of the large sum which still remained to be paid to the allies. He had paid one crore and ten lakhs of rupees from the treasury, but for the rest he decided, on the advice of his counsellors, that the army should give sixty lakhs as a voluntary contribution, while one crore and sixty lakhs were to be raised from the civil officers and the people of Mysore.[1] By these measures Tipu succeeded in punctually discharging all his dues to the allies. In March 1794, therefore, the hostages returned accompanied by Captain Doveton, who had been in charge of them during their stay at Madras. The Sultan moved from Seringapatam to receive them at Devanhalli, where they were formally restored by Doveton.[2] The latter and other persons who had looked after the princes were given rich presents and then dismissed. After a week, to celebrate the return of the princes, festivities were held in which Tipu conferred on his officers titles, ranks and gifts according to the services which they had rendered to him.[3]

*Suppression of rebellions*

During the Third Anglo-Mysore War, some of the *poligars* in Mysore had declared their independence, and some, who had been once dispossessed by Tipu, had recovered their territories with the support of the allies. So when the war was over, Tipu decided to crush those rebels who were still his subjects. Early in 1793, he despatched Sayyid Ghaffar against Buswapa Naik who claimed to be a relation of the *poligar* of Harpanahalli and had seized the fort of Uchangidurga.[4] But Sayyid Ghaffar having suffered a severe repulse, Qamar-ud-din Khan was sent with a large force, and on his report, a further reinforcement was sent under Khan Jahan Khan. In spite of this the garrison put up an obstinate resistance, and it was only after three months that the fort could be carried by two separate and simultaneous assaults.[5] Buswapa Naik, its chief, with

[1] Wilks, ii, p. 562.
[2] *Ibid.*, p. 594.
[3] Kirmani, p. 347.
[4] It was a strong hill-fort in Chitaldrug Dist., Mysore.
[5] Wilks, ii, pp. 590-1; Kirmani, pp. 368-9.

400 men, was taken prisoner, and the walls of the fort were razed to the ground. According to the Sultan's instructions, Qamar-ud-din, by way of example, ordered the hands and feet of some of the prisoners to be cut off, and some to be made eunuchs.[1]

After the capture of Uchangidurga, Babar Jung, the *subedar* of Harpanahalli, who had taken refuge in Chitaldrug, returned and recovered the towns of Anagondi and Kanakagiri. But the *poligar* of Kanakagiri, having pledged loyalty to the Sultan, was given back his territory, and as a mark of royal favour received a *khilat* and an elephant. Meanwhile, Sayyid Saheb had been engaged in reducing the rebels who had seized Maddagiri, Rutlengiri and other places. After a campaign of about three months these were recovered, and their chiefs had their noses and ears cut off.[2]

### *Dhoondia Waugh*

Dhoondia Waugh, a Maratha by descent, was born at Channagiri in Mysore. He served in the army of Haidar and Tipu as a horseman, but during the Third Anglo-Mysore War, he, with some of his followers, left Tipu's service, carrying off considerable booty. He proceeded to the north and took shelter under the Desai of Lakshmeshwar. After the conclusion of the war and the return of the Maratha armies, he collected a party of freebooters and began to levy contributions in the neighbourhood of Dharwar. He seized Haveri early in January 1793, then occupied Savanur and other places, and began ravaging the territories assigned to the Marathas by the Treaty of Seringapatam.[3] Elated with success, he sent to Tipu an Afghan, his agent, soliciting secret aid in return for which he promised to recover for him the whole principality of Savanur. But Tipu declined to have any truck with him.[4]

Meanwhile, Dhoondia's depredations having alarmed the Poona Government, Dhondu Pant Gokhale was sent to crush him. Dhoondia was defeated, and was in the end so hard pressed that he decided to enter Tipu's service with his whole party consisting of 200 horsemen. He arrived in the neighbourhood of Seringapatam in June 1794, and proceeded to pay his respects to the Sultan. He was received cordially and appointed to a military command. He embraced Islam and was named Shaikh Ahmad, but at his own request was called Malik Jahan Khan. Soon after, however, he incurred Tipu's displeasure and was imprisoned.[5] But he was treated well. Tipu, in fact, wanted to release him and make him an officer in his

[1] Kirmani, p. 369.
[2] *Ibid.*, pp. 369-70.
[3] Khare, ix, Nos. 3497, 3580.
[4] Wilks, ii, p. 599.
[5] Parasnis, *History of Sangli State*, pp. 24-5.

army, but Mir Sadiq dissuaded him by pointing out that Dhoondia was a dangerous man and should remain in confinement.[1] Dhoondia remained in prison until the fall of Seringapatam in 1799 when he escaped, and putting himself at the head of a band of adventurers, gave the English considerable trouble for several months. But on September 11, 1800, he was killed in an engagement with Colonel Wellesley.[2]

*Relations with the Marathas*

After the Treaty of Seringapatam Tipu wanted to be left in peace in order to devote his attention to the affairs of his kingdom which he had been compelled to neglect during the two years of war. He, therefore, desired to remain on friendly terms with his neighbours, and to settle all his disputes with them by peaceful methods. His policy was to remain neutral in the disputes between the Nizam and the Marathas, and to have nothing to do with their internal affairs.

We have seen of the devastation caused by Parashsuram Bhau's forces in Mysore during the Third Anglo-Mysore War. But even after peace was signed, the Marathas did not cease from ravaging the Mysore territories and carrying away peasants and cattle.[3] They did not evacuate Sunda, which had not been assigned to them by the Treaty of Seringapatam, and continued to occupy many villages and *taluks* belonging to Mysore.[4] Moreover, they delayed the release of Badr-uz-zaman Khan, who had been unjustly made a prisoner after the capitulation of Dharwar.[5] It was only after Cornwallis's repeated remonstrances that Badr-uz-zaman was released. But it took some more time for other controversial matters to be settled between Tipu and the Peshwa.

The settlement of these disputes was facilitated by a number of factors. Mahadji Sindhia, who arrived in Poona in June 1792 to establish his political ascendancy there, was less inimical to Tipu than Nana. In fact, for a short time before his death on February 12, 1794, he carried on friendly correspondence with the Sultan.[6] Besides, the Marathas, having obtained extensive territories from Tipu, now wanted to direct their attention to the Nizam. So long as Tipu was powerful, the Marathas did not press their demands for *chauth* and *sardeshmukhi* upon the Nizam, and twice united with

[1] Kirmani, p. 380.
[2] For more details about Dhoondia, see *History of Sangli State*, pp. 25-32, and *Bombay Gaz.*, *Dharwar*, xxii, pp. 421-5.
[3] P.R.C., iii, No. 465A.
[4] *Ibid.*
[5] *Ibid.*
[6] Duff, ii, p. 241.

him against Tipu. But now that Tipu's power was crippled, they revived their claims upon him.[1]

The result of the Maratha policy was that Tipu's relations with the Poona Government improved. Thus on the death of Mahadji Sindhia and Haripant, Tipu sent condolences to the Peshwa, and similarly the latter sent congratulations to him on the occasion of his son's marriage.[2] It was owing to the existence of cordial relations between Tipu and the Peshwa that rumours were spread that the Sultan was in league with the Marathas against the Nizam.[3] But these reports were without any foundation whatsoever. During the Maratha-Nizam conflict (1795), it was said that the Peshwa had written to Tipu to employ his troops collected at Gooty in ravaging the Hyderabad territories. But Kirkpatrick, the English agent at the Nizam's court, did not think the report to be true.[4] Rumours were also spread of an alliance between Tipu and the Marathas against the English. But these were regarded by Sir John Shore, the Governor-General, as baseless. And as regards Amrit Rao's communication to Joshua Uthoff, the Company's Assistant Resident at Poona, that Nana had received a proposition from Tipu to unite with him against the English, Shore observed: "Nothing has since occurred to corroborate that information which was, probably, invented by Amrit Rao."[5] It must be remembered that the exchange of *wakils* between Tipu and the Peshwa was only of a friendly nature and was not directed against any power. It was only when Wellesley became Governor-General and began preparations to invade Mysore, that Tipu tried to secure the military assistance of the Marathas.

*Relations with the Nizam*

But Tipu's relations with the Nizam did not improve. Like the Marathas, the Hyderabad forces also, on withdrawing from Seringapatam, devastated Mysore territories, though to a lesser extent, and continued to occupy villages belonging to Mysore to which they were not entitled by the Treaty of Seringapatam. Moreover, the Nizam tried to delay the restoration of Tipu's sons,[6] while the Kurnool question further embittered his relations with the Sultan.

Kurnool originally formed part of the kingdom of Vijayanagar. It afterwards became a province of Bijapur, and later Aurangzeb gave it to a Pathan family in lieu of military service. With the decline of the

[1] *Ibid.*, pp. 240-1.
[2] P.R.C., iv, No. 152.
[3] Wilks, ii, p. 620.
[4] P.R.C., iv, No. 188.
[5] N.A., See, Pro., Aug. 8, 1797, Shore's Minute of July 21.
[6] M.R., Mly. Cons., Jan. 14, 1794, Bengal to Madras, Dec. 1793, vol. 182A, pp. 193 *seq.*

Mughal Empire, Kurnool became a tributary of the Nizams, and it remained under them until about 1765 when Haidar Ali invaded it and compelled its ruler, Ranmust Khan, to pay him tribute and recognise his suzerainty. After the Treaty of Seringapatam, however, the Nizam revived his claim to Kurnool on the ground that it had been once under him; and when Tipu demanded his arrears of tribute from Ranmust Khan, he decided to intervene.

Shortly after the Treaty of Seringapatam was signed, the Nizam sent two persons to Fort St. George to negotiate with Tipu's *wakils* the question of Kurnool, and to secure the diplomatic, and, if necessary, military assistance of the English in the matter.[1] But Cornwallis instructed the Madras Government to "remain neutral and take no concern whatever in any negotiations upon that subject between the Nizam's deputies and Tippoo's vakeels."[2] At the same time he advised the Nizam not to concern himself with the affairs of Kurnool. Ranmust Khan, he pointed out, did not deserve any sympathy, for he had not helped the allies in the Third Anglo-Mysore War. Even when the allies had succeeded in establishing their military superiority and their victory had become certain, Ranmust Khan had not changed his attitude. He had not furnished them grain and horses, which he had promised, and had, in spite of the Nizam's remonstrances, allowed Tipu's news-writer to reside in Kurnool.[3]

As regards the Nizam's contention that Kurnool should be restored to him since it was a military fief granted by the *subedar* of the Deccan, Cornwallis was of the opinion that "the ancient but obsolete claims of the Soubah of the Deccan extend nearly over the whole southern part of the Peninsula and include the possessions of Muhammad Ali and Tippoo as well as those of the Nawab of Kurnool, but the revival and support of such dormant claims is suited only to a Government which has determined to pursue a line of ambition and conquest and is ill-adapted to the system of moderation and peace that we profess."[4] Moreover, according to the usage of the country "a tributary state is dependent on the power to which tribute is paid."[5] From the papers which Tipu had produced and from the statements of Ranmust Khan it was evident that the latter had been paying tribute to Haidar Ali and Tipu Sultan for about thirty years.[6] During all this period their right of realising tribute from Kurnool had never been disputed by the Nizam, so that, according to Cornwallis, "the Nizam's rights, whatever they were, have been for a term of twenty-five or thirty years

[1] M.R., Mly. Sundry Book, vol. 83, 1793, p. 1.
[2] *Ibid.*, Cornwallis to Madras, April 24, 1792, p. 2.
[3] *Ibid.*, Cornwallis to Kennaway, June 16, 1792, pp. 19-21.
[4] *Ibid.*, Aug. 4, 1792, pp. 75-6.
[5] *Ibid.*, Dec. 18, 1792, p. 134.
[6] *Ibid.*, pp. 75, 84.

totally and to all appearances relinquished."[1] To Mir Alam's plea that this was due to "superior force" of Tipu, Cornwallis's reply was that "the rights of sovereigns are too often decided by an appeal to force."[2]

There were other reasons, too, which proved that the Nizam had no right to demand Kurnool. Kennaway had informed Mir Alam at the Seringapatam Peace Conference (Feb-March 1792) that if vouchers were produced, the question of the Nizam's claim to Kurnool could be taken up. But Mir Alam had done nothing to assert the claim of his master.[3] Moreover, Tipu's cession by the Treaty of Seringapatam of two districts belonging to Kurnool, to which the Nizam had made no objection, proved that it was independent of the Hyderabad Government. Tipu had also included in the schedule of his possessions the *peshkush* from Kurnool. Although Mir Alam had objected to it, he had not pressed the point any further. Thus the right of Tipu to the *peshkush* of the district had not been rejected by the allies, and neither had Tipu surrendered his suzerainty over the district to any of the allies.[4] From Tipu's letter to the Nizam it appears that when Tipu's *wakils* had suggested that the *peshkush* of Kurnool should be included in the Nizam's share, Mushir-ul-mulk had stated that he did not want Kurnool, and that Tipu could keep it in his possession. Accordingly, the Nizam had been given another place instead.[5] Owing to these reasons Cornwallis entertained "great doubts of the policy and even the justice of the Nizam's interference in favour of Ranmust Khan."[6]

In spite of the discouraging attitude of Cornwallis, the Nizam did not relinquish his pretensions over the district. He proposed to Kennaway, the Company's Resident at Hyderabad, that if he were allowed to annex Kurnool he would give Ranmust Khan an equal *jagir* somewhere else. But Kennaway regarded the proposal as inadvisable, and wrote to Cornwallis that "even if Ranmust Khan agreed to this, still the position would remain unchanged, for Tippoo would consider his claims transferred from Ranmust Khan to the Nizam."[7] The Nizam, thereupon, proposed that if he secured Kurnool, he would not only pay the usual annual tribute to the Sultan, but would also discharge the arrears due to him from Ranmust Khan. In fact he was willing to become a tributary of Tipu. But he desisted from this

[1] *Ibid.*, pp. 130-4.
[2] *Ibid.*, April 12, 1793, p. 229.
[3] *Ibid.*, Kennaway to Cornwallis, June 2, 1792, pp. 3-5.
[4] *Ibid.*, Dec. 12, 1792, pp. 121-25, and Cornwallis to Nizam, April 12, 1793, p. 224.
[5] N.A., Pol. Pro., March 13, 1797, Tipu to Nizam, Cons. No. 23.
[6] M.R., Mly. Sundry Book, vol. 83, Cornwallis to Kennaway, Aug. 4, 1792, p. 76.
[7] *Ibid.*, Kennaway to Cornwallis, Sept., 14, 1792, pp. 81-3.

step because Cornwallis informed him that "if you can submit to such degradation and enter into a private agreement with Tippoo, Kurnool can never be considered by the allies in the same light as other parts of your kingdom, and we cannot guarantee attacks on Kurnool against Tippoo."[1]

Meanwhile, towards the end of 1792, Ranmust Khan died and a war of succession began between two of his sons, Azim Khan, the eldest, and Alif Khan, a younger son. On his death-bed Ranmust had appointed Alif Khan as his successor, and had advised him to pay the arrears of tribute to Tipu.[2] Owing to this Alif Khan was supported by the Sultan, while the Nizam took up the cause of Azim Khan; and when Alif Khan occupied Kurnool, the Nizam decided to use the Company's troops in favour of Azim. But as soon as Kennaway came to know of this he informed the Nizam that the English detachment could not be used for such a purpose.[3] Kennaway was also informed by Cornwallis that "as the Nizam had decided to interfere in the late succession of Ranmust Khan without waiting for my opinion, I do not find myself at liberty to support him."[4]

Owing to this unsympathetic English attitude, the Nizam's ardour for Azim cooled off, and he began negotiations with Alif Khan, who, pressed for arrears of tribute by Tipu, had sought his assistance.[5] But to this also Cornwallis objected. Nevertheless, the Nizam concluded an agreement with Alif Khan, by which the latter promised to pay him immediately fifteen lakhs of rupees as tribute, and in return receive a *jagir* of 60,000 rupees. But Kennaway denounced the agreement. In consequence, Alif Khan's agent left Hyderabad without obtaining *sanads* for Kurnool or paying the Nizam any money.[6] Meanwhile Alif Khan had been reconciled to Tipu; and having accepted his suzerainty, denounced the Nizam. The latter, thereupon, decided to send the Company's battalions to invade Kurnool. But both Cornwallis and Kennaway were against a measure that was certain to lead to a conflict with Tipu. Nor was Cornwallis prepared to countenance the annexation of Kurnool by Tipu, because it was situated near the Nizam's southern frontier and was, therefore, of strategic importance for him.[7] In consequence, while the Nizam did not succeed in establishing his suzerainty over Kurnool, Tipu also failed to annex the district, which only remained his tributary.

[1] *Ibid.*, Cornwallis to Nizam, April 12, 1793, p. 229.
[2] P.R.C., iii, No. 494.
[3] M.R., Mly. Sundry Book, vol. 83, Kennaway to Cornwallis, Dec. 12, 1792 pp. 121-2.
[4] *Ibid.*, Cornwallis to Kennaway, Dec. 27, 1792, p. 138.
[5] *Ibid.*, Jan. 12, 1793, pp. 151-3.
[6] Fraser, *The Nizam*, pp. 57-8.
[7] M.R., Mly. Sundry Book, vol. 83, Cornwallis to Kennaway, April 12, 1793, pp. 216-22.

While the controversy over the Kurnool question was going on, the Marathas invaded the Hyderabad kingdom to realise their arrears of *chauth* and *sardeshmukhi*. The Nizam advanced to offer resistance, but was defeated at Kharda in March 1795, and had to submit to an ignominious peace. These events induced the Nizam to change his hostile attitude towards Tipu, and cultivate friendly relations with him. Mir Alam, who was now his Prime Minister—Mushir-ul-mulk having been taken by the Marathas as a hostage—proposed to Kirkpatrick, the Company's Resident at Hyderabad, a triple alliance between the Nizam, Tipu and the English, and inquired that if the English did not wish to join it, whether they would have any objection to the Nizam's entering into a defensive treaty with Tipu as a safeguard against Maratha aggression.[1]

On being informed of these proposals, Shore wrote to Kirkpatrick that he was opposed to the triple alliance, because that "would be against the positive prohibition of the Statute, and a dissolution of the treaty between the Marathas, the Nizam and the Company."[2] As regards his view of an alliance between Tipu and the Nizam, Shore pointed out that Tipu would defend the Nizam only on condition that he should be allowed to recover the territories he had lost in 1792. But if this condition were agreed upon, the effect would be "a complete alteration in our political relations with the three powers, and in fact the annihilation of the triple alliance."[3] Kirkpatrick was, therefore, instructed to prevent the formation of any union between the Nizam and Tipu by convincing Mir Alam that it would prove harmful to his master. Besides, there was no necessity for such a union because the Marathas, being involved in their internal dissensions, were no longer in a position to invade the Hyderabad kingdom.[4]

But, in spite of the English advice, the Nizam made overtures to the Sultan, who responded favourably and, in 1795, sent Sukkaram Pundit to Hyderabad to discuss the question of Kurnool and negotiate an alliance with the Nizam. After sometime he deputed Qadir Husain Khan and Madina Shah as his envoys for the same purpose. But these talks proved abortive, although Imtiaz-ud-daulah, the Nizam's nephew, advised his uncle to form an alliance with Tipu, and with his help turn out the English from the Deccan.[5] Wilks's explanation that "the Nizam was ready to conclude arrangements for a perfect union of interests with Tippoo," but did not succeed because the latter refused "to exchange the pledge of the Koran," which the

[1] N.A., Sec. Proc., July 18, 1796, Cons. No. 4.
[2] *Ibid.*
[3] *Ibid.*
[4] *Ibid.*
[5] N.A., Sec. Pro., Sept. 5, 1796, Cons. No. 33.

Nizam desired, is ridiculous.[1] The negotiations seemed to have failed because of the successful intrigues of Kirkpatrick and of the Anglophile Mir Alam. Apart from this, the Nizam was never really serious in his advances to Tipu. He was only trying to use them as pressure tactics, so that the English might be compelled to enter into a defensive treaty with him. In fact, while he carried on talks with Tipu, all kinds of rumours were fabricated at his court with the object of embroiling the Company in a war with the Sultan.

*Relations with the English*

Cornwallis had humbled Tipu and crippled his power, but he was not satisfied with that. He wanted to keep the Sultan in a state of permanent isolation lest he should try to recover his lost territories. After the Treaty of Seringapatam, therefore, Cornwallis endeavoured to clarify and reduce into an explicit form those articles of the Treaty of Alliance (1790) by which the contracting parties had agreed to guarantee each other, against any future attacks of Tipu, the territories which they would acquire at the end of the war. He framed a draft treaty on these principles and transmitted it to Poona and Hyderabad.[2] The Nizam after some hesitation welcomed it, as he was anxious for security both against Tipu and the Marathas.[3] But Nana was not prepared to accept any engagements which might limit his expansionist designs; so he put forth a counter-proposal, demanding the Peshwa's right to claim *chauth* from Tipu.[4] To this both Cornwallis and the Nizam were opposed. The Governor-General informed Nana that the Company's Government "neither considers itself bound by treaty, nor will ever be induced to support any pecuniary claim of the Peshwa upon Tippoo, beyond that which was specifically mentioned in the Treaty of Seringapatam."[5] Owing to this reply of Cornwallis the talks for a guarantee treaty broke down. The Nizam was no doubt ready to conclude an alliance with the Company even without the Marathas, but Cornwallis, and after him Sir John Shore, refused since it would antagonise the Poona Government.[6]

Cornwallis's policy was to preserve the balance of power in South India. Although he was opposed to the revival of Tipu's power, he did not want its further reduction, for he regarded it as a bulwark against the ambitions of the Nizam and the Marathas. That was why he asked them to evacuate Tipu's territories which had not been

[1] Wilks, ii, p. 630.
[2] Malcolm, *Political History of India*, i, p. 121; P.R.C., ii, No. 145.
[3] Malcolm, i, p. 122.
[4] *Ibid.*, pp. 122-23.
[5] P.R.C., ii, No. 159.
[6] Malcolm, i, p. 123.

assigned to them by the Treaty of Seringapatam, and refused to support the Nizam's claim to Kurnool. Cornwallis felt that if the Nizam had his own way over the Kurnool issue, the Marathas would also be encouraged to put forth fresh claims on Tipu.[1] This would not only involve the Company in diplomatic complications, it would also in the end prove detrimental to its hegemony in India.

But while Cornwallis regarded the claims of the Marathas and the Nizam on Tipu as unjust, he did not hesitate to advance the Company's claims on him. Thus the English occupied Wynad and other places, and allowed the Raja of Coorg to retain possession of Amara and Sulya. Tipu repeatedly demanded their restoration, but without success. Although the Bombay Government admitted that Wynad and Corrumbala had not been ceded to the Company by the Sultan, it desired the Commissioners "to instruct the persons to be deputed for arbitration not to immediately disallow the Company's right to those districts, but to maintain the argument in the Company's favour and then give in, if necessary."[2] The Bombay Government thought that "the present object is not so much to set forth reasons against the Company's right to Wynad, as to be able to assign sufficient grounds of arguments to be used by our deputies."[3] Wynad was finally restored to the Sultan by Wellesley in August 1798. But this was done really to deceive Tipu and cover up the war preparations which the English were making against him.

Amara and Sulya were, however, not restored. When the Company's authorities asked for proof from the Coorg Raja regarding his claims to the districts, he made quite contradictory statements. Sometimes he said that Amara and Sulya had been in his family's possession for the last five hundred years. On other occasions he maintained that the places had been given as a gift to his ancestors by the rulers of Bednur two hundred years ago. He also stated that one of his ancestors had purchased Sulya from the Bednur Raja.[4] In several letters, which he wrote to Cornwallis, he relinquished his claim to Sulya, and yet in June 1793 he reoccupied it.[5] Tipu, on the other hand, argued that Amara and Sulya were included in the Bangalore province which had been part of Mysore for centuries.[6]

After repeated requests on Tipu's part, the Company's Government at last appointed Mahony and Uthoff as its representatives to discuss with Tipu's *wakils*, Shihab-ud-din and Mir Muhammad Ali,

[1] M.R., Mly. Sundry Book, vol. 83, Cornwallis to Kennaway, June 16, 1792, p. 20.

[2] M.R., Mal. Sec., Com. Diaries (pol.) 1798, vol. 1729, Bombay Govt. to Commissioners, July 19, 1798, pp. 361-365.

[3] *Ibid.*

[4] N.A., Pol. Pro., June 20, 1798, Cons. No. 39.

[5] *Ibid.*, No. 38.

[6] *Ibid.*, No. 36.

the question of Amara and Sulya. The meeting between the representatives of the Company and those of Tipu took place on the borders of Sulya district. The Coorg Raja failed to produce any documents, and his attitude was marked by prevarications. In consequence, the English representatives' confidence in the Raja's claims was shaken, particularly when Tipu's deputies produced documents in support of their master's claims.[1]

From the above it is clear that the districts should have been restored to the Sultan. But this was not done, and the Company's representatives came to the strange conclusion that although neither Tipu nor the Raja had established their rights, yet on Amara the Raja's claims were justified, while on Sulya Tipu's. However, since the Raja was in possession of both these places, he should continue to retain them. Just as he had rendered great service to the Company in the last war, so he would help in the next.[2] Nothing should, therefore, be done to estrange him. Since the war with Tipu was imminent, it was unnecessary to enter into any further discussion with him regarding the districts.[3]

Apart from the controversy over Wynad and Amara-Sulya, Tipu's relations with the Company ostensibly improved with the appointment of Sir John Shore as Governor-General. Thus when the Marathas attacked the Nizam, and it was rumoured that they might be joined by Tipu, Shore did not believe the news, and decided to remain neutral, pointing out that the Sultan was too occupied with his own affairs to take part in the Maratha-Nizam conflict.[4] He believed that there was no likelihood of any alliance between Tipu and the Marathas, unless the English provoked it by lending their support to the Nizam. Uthoff, the Assistant Resident at Poona, even held the view that "the present disposition of Tippoo is more favourable to us than either to Nizam Ally Khan or to the Mahrattas."[5]

But the Anglophile party at the Hyderabad court and the war mongers in the Company's service did not agree with these assessments of Shore and Uthoff, and began to spread all kinds of stories regarding Tipu's aggressive designs against the Company. War was going on between the English and the French in Europe; and since Tipu was regarded as the friend of the French, rumours were spread that he was in league with them, and having received reinforcements from France, was planning to attack the English. Arthur Wellesley, later the Duke of Wellington, who arrived in India towards the end of

[1] N.A., Pol. Pro., April 1, 1799, Cons. No. 25.
[2] *Ibid.*
[3] *Ibid.*
[4] Malcolm, *Political History of India*, i, p. 137.
[5] P.R.C., iv, No. 72; Furber, *The Private Record of an Indian Governor-Generalship*, p. 50.

1796, discredited the rumours and wrote: "People say that Tippoo Sahib has an army on foot, which I do not believe. As I have observed since my arrival here, he is a constant object of fear to the English, and whenever they want to add a colouring to a statement of danger, they find out that he has an army in motion."[1] Shore also regarded the reports as baseless, and informed Kirkpatrick that there was no truth in the arrival of French ships at Mangalore, or of ambassadors from France. Such rumours, he thought, "are fabricated for the purpose of deception or with a view to derive importance or reward."[2] Similarly, in 1797, James Stuart and Jonathan Duncan wrote from Tellicherry that there was no French authorised agent at Seringapatam now, nor had there been any lately. There was also no truth in the suggested alliance between Tipu and the French.[3] John Morris, Secretary to Captain Kirkpatrick, wrote that the report of the arrival of French armaments at Mangalore was quite baseless, and "other reports they hope of Tipu's inimical preparations will also prove false."[4] Again on July 5, 1797, Shore wrote of the intelligence which he had received regarding Tipu, that "no part of it has the character of authenticity, sufficient to entitle it to full confidence."[5] Similarly Uthoff informed Shore on September 2, 1797, that Tipu was not preparing for war against the Company, and that people were spreading alarming news.[6] To Kirkpatrick Uthoff wrote that such news were "frequently unfounded, or of their originating in misconception, selfish interestedness, or insidiousness."[7] For example, Tipu sent his agents to Hyderabad to discuss the question of Kurnool, but this "has been shown to us a secondary affair, and it has been made out that these agents have come to Hyderabad to form a confederacy against the English."[8] Early in 1798, again, Uthoff informed Kirkpatrick that for the past eighteen months all kinds of rumours had been spread about Tipu by the Hyderabad court. Tipu, Madina Shah and the French were a useful instrument for the Nizam to work upon the fears of the English, and thus secure an offensive and defensive alliance with the Company. It is true that Tipu had massed troops at Gooty, but that had been done "to enforce his claims on Kurnool, claims which neither the Company nor the Mahrattas can justly controvert or oppose." He eventually withdrew the troops, partly because of the remonstrance sent by the Nizam in the name of the allies, and parly because the stay

[1] Gleig, *British Empire in India*, iii, p. 154.
[2] N.A., Pol. Pro., May 8, 1797, Shore to Kirkpatrick, Cons. No. 72.
[3] Mal. Sec. Com. Diaries, vol. 1717, 1797, pp. 196-7.
[4] N.A., Pol. Pro. July 10, 1797, Cons. No. 41.
[5] N.A., Sec. Cons. Aug. 8, 1797, vol. v, p. 429.
[6] N.A., Pol. Pro., Oct. 6, 1797, Cons. No. 9.
[7] *Ibid.*, Oct. 20, 1797, Cons. No. 8.
[8] M.R., Mly. Cons., Jan. 23, 1798, Uthoff to Kirkpatrick, Dec. 18, 1797, vol. 232, p. 352.

of the troops at Gooty was becoming expensive.[1] Uthoff maintained that the danger to British power either separately or jointly by the French and Tipu "may be suspected of coming through some native channels, interested or insidious." Such intelligence, he thought, must be received with "considerable reservation." Addressing Kirkpatrick, Uthoff continued: "You yourself wrote about the Hyderabad court to the Governor-General on October 5, 1797, that it was a court that would not scruple, I fear, if its interests were in the least degree at stake, to take advantage of that which it is sufficiently sensible to promote its own insidious purposes." Uthoff also pointed out that rumours of danger continue to float in your quarter "notwithstanding the authentic intelligence of security to us against Tippoo and the French, through the respectable channel of the Committee of the Bombay Government. We have now to admire the stupendous superstructure that has been raised of a French embassy and thousands of French troops and on the simple circumstance of a botilla with about dozen Frenchmen on board, which happened to be alone by accident on the Malabar coast, and was compelled, from the want of the necessaries of life, to put into Mangalore, whence some of those Frenchmen have preferred throwing themselves on our mercy to remaining with their potent and faithful ally, the Sultaun."[2] Sir John Shore, who was wedded to a policy of peace, did not believe in rumours which, he thought, were fabricated to embroil the English in war with Tipu.

These rumours, though exaggerated, were not without foundation, for Tipu could not reconcile himself to his defeat, and not long after the Treaty of Seringapatam, he began to make advances to the French. In June 1792, he sent two messengers with a letter to de Fresne requesting him to convey to Louis XVI that, although he had suffered on account of his friendship for the French, he still remained as attached to them as ever.[3] As a gesture of his goodwill, he gave them permission to buy rice, cardamom and sandlewood at the current market rate, and pepper at Rs. 140 per candy, although the market price was Rs. 150 per candy.[4]

Later, in July of the same year, Tipu demanded from de Fresne 20,000 muskets in exchange for pepper, sandlewood and cardamom, and 500 recruits for Vigie's detachment. De Fresne felt his position extremely embarrassing, because he had no clear instructions from Paris as to the policy he was to follow in his dealings with Tipu. So the only alternative that remained for him was to give vague and evasive replies. At the same time, anxious to keep Tipu in good

[1] N.A., Pol. Pro., Feb. 16, 1798, Cons. No. 42.
[2] M.R., Mly. Cons., Jan. 23, 1798, vol. 232, pp. 347-9.
[3] A.N., C²299, de Fresne to Minister of Marine, June 29, 1792, No. 80.
[4] *Ibid.*, Tipu to de Fresne, arrived July 2, 1792, No. 80.

humour for the sake of French trade with his kingdom, he did not want to refuse his demands. But since he possessed neither men nor ships to carry them to Mangalore, he forwarded the Sultan's letter to the Governor of the Isle of France who was in a better position to comply with these demands. The Sultan also proposed to send an envoy to France, and later deputed Rama Rao to discuss this with de Fresne. But de Fresne, remembering the failure of the mission of 1787 and anxious not to provoke the English, discouraged the project.[1]

We have seen that in 1791 Tipu sent Leger to France with proposals for an alliance.[2] Louis XVI and his Minister of Marine, Bertrand de Moleville, were prepared to help Tipu, knowing that his overthrow would be harmful to French interests in India. But owing to the disturbed social and economic conditions in France they were helpless to do anything. Meanwhile, monarchy had been abolished and a republic proclaimed in France. Leger was sent back to India with a letter from the Executive Council addressed to Tipu, informing him that owing to the developments in France and Europe it was not possible for the French Government to enter into an alliance with him.[3]

The result of the failure of Leger's mission was that when, in 1793, hostilities started between the French and the English, and the former instigated Tipu to attack the latter, pointing out that it was a good opportunity for him to recover the territories he had lost by the Treaty of Seringapatam, he decided to remain neutral. His reply was that all his misfortunes were due to his connections with the French. They had betrayed him in 1783 by making peace with the English, leaving him alone to continue the war with them. He had then sent an embassy to France, but it led to no result. He was, therefore, not prepared to take any step against the English and enter into a treaty with the French in India unless and until the National Convention at Paris ratified it, and it was agreed that he would be informed about the peace negotiations with the English, and in the peace treaty his name would be mentioned. Since the French response to this reply was unsatisfactory, he watched with indifference the capture of Pondicherry in August 1793. In fact he did not even reply to the French commander's letter soliciting his aid.[4]

Towards the end of 1794, Lescallier, who was appointed Civil Commissioner of Pondicherry, made friendly approaches to Tipu. He deputed two agents who explained to him the significance of the French Revolution and pointed out to the great benefits that would

[1] *Ibid.*, de Fresne to Minister of Marine, July 30 1792, No. 87; *Ibid.*, Tipu to de Fresne, 4 shawwal, 1206/May 26, 1792.

[2] See *supra*, p. 185.

[3] A.N., C[2]302—1793, p. 251.

[4] P.A., MS., Nos. 2140, 2195, 2200.

accrue to him through his friendship with the new government. Tipu, in reply, while complaining of his past disappointments with the French, expressed his willingness to enter into an alliance with them and laid down the following conditions:

1. That war against the English should be started simultaneously by him and the French, and when peace was to be made he was to be informed of it, and he was also to be a party to the treaty.

2. That he should be supplied with 10,000 men (later the number was reduced to 6,000) and arms and ammunition in proportion.

3. That the conquests made on the coasts of India were to go to the French, while the conquests of inland territory were to be annexed by him.[1]

Lescallier sent Tipu's proposals to Paris along with his observations that friendship must be cultivated with Mysore, and that as soon as the French troops would set foot on the Indian soil, all Indian powers, both big and small, would join them against the English. Meanwhile, he informed the Sultan through Monneron, Deputy Extraordinary of the French Establishments in India, of a favourable response to his proposals. Monneron conferred with Tipu and drew up a draft of an offensive and defensive alliance. Its terms were: That if peace were made in Europe, Tipu was to be mentioned as an ally of France and Holland; that for every 1000 men set on the field by France, Tipu would put forth 5,000 men and would, in addition, supply them provisions. Tipu then presented his plan for driving out the English from India. The French army was to land in Tellicherry, which was to be occupied with his help. He would then proceed to conquer Pondicherry and Madras. He would keep the forts of Trichinopoly, Tanjore and Etrour and half of the Carnatic, while the rest would be annexed by the French. Bombay would be occupied by the French, while Bengal would be equally divided between them. The treaty was signed by Louis Monneron on April 17, 1796.[2]

In 1793 Tipu had refused to enter into any alliance with the French authorities in India until it was ratified by the French Government in Paris. That now he acceded to an alliance was because of his faith in the vain promises of Lescallier and Monneron. No less important was the part played by the Cossigny brothers in influencing his decisions. They sent to him exaggerated reports of their country's victories in the war against the coalition, and assured him of French assistance against the English.[3]

[1] A.N., C[2]304, from Lescallier, Oct. 16, 1794, No. 4.

[2] *Ibid.*, C[2]304 Colonies—(1794-1800)—Affaires Secret No. 95; also the same document in Archives du Ministère des Affaires Étrangères, vol. 20 (1792-1814), pp. 150 *seq.*; and Antonova, *The Struggle of Tipu Sultan against British Colonial Power*, document Nos. 3,4.

[3] *Ibid.*, documents Nos. 1, 2.

The Directory, however, while admiring Lescallier's project, rejected it, pointing out that it might be reserved for future use. Since the peace talks with the English, which had taken place in December 1796 and July 1797, had failed, the movements of the French navy were restricted, and, in consequence, it was decided not to undertake any fresh commitments in India.[1]

[1] A.N., C²304, Minister of Marine to Minister of Foreign Relations, Oct. 12, 1797.

CHAPTER XVIII

# TIPU AND WELLESLEY

During the Third Anglo-Mysore War the English had sustained great losses. After its conclusion, therefore, they needed peace in order to recuperate and consolidate their gains before embarking on fresh schemes of aggrandisement. That was why Cornwallis, during the remaining term of his office, and then Shore, who succeeded him, avoided all entanglements which might involve the Company in a conflict with the Indian powers. But Shore's too strict an adherence to a policy of peace and non-interference as laid down by the Pitts India Act of 1784 and the instructions of the Court of Directors, led to the alienation of the Nizam from the English and the increase of French influence in India. The British Government itself had, at first, favoured a policy of neutrality in the disputes of the Indian powers, but "as the troubles in Europe progressed, Dundas was becoming more and more sympathetic to a policy of aggression and aggrandizement in India."[1] So when Shore retired in March 1797, it was decided to appoint in his place a man who should follow an active policy. The choice, in the end, fell upon Richard Wellesley, Earl of Mornington, a friend of Pitt and Dundas, and an anti-Jacobin and imperialist to the core.

Thus Wellesley came to India pledged to a policy of aggression and aggrandisement. As Philips says: "Dundas encouraged Wellesley's aggressive policy in India. From the instructions he issued and from the actions and replies of Wellesley it seems likely that they had agreed, probably before Wellesley left England, that the time was ripe for an expansion of British India."[2]

The Mughal Emperor, Shah Alam II, blinded in 1788 by Ghulam Qadir, an Afghan chief, was now a prisoner in the hands of Daulat Rao Sindhia. The Rajput states to the south and west of Delhi were disunited and found it difficult to hold their own against the Maratha encroachments. Oudh, although nominally independent, was virtually controlled by the English Resident. The Raja of Travancore was a tributary of the Company, while the Nawab of Arcot was no longer "a real potentate," but "a shadow, a dream, an incubus of oppression," and his government was carried on by the English. Of the three principal Indian States of Poona, Hyderabad and Mysore,

[1] Furber, *The Private Record of an Indian Governor-Generalship*, p. 7.
[2] Philips, *East India Company*, p. 103.

the first two were in an advanced stage of decay. The Maratha confederacy was in the process of disintegration. Baji Rao II, the Peshwa, was incompetent and treacherous, while Nana had lost much of his former influence over the affairs of the Poona Government. The Nizam's kingdom, already weakened by a corrupt administration, was further enfeebled by the defeat its forces had sustained at the hands of the Marathas at Kharda.

In contrast with this picture of inefficiency, political and administrative chaos, the kingdom of Mysore was a model of efficiency and good government. Cornwallis had deprived Tipu of his treasure and of half his kingdom. Nevertheless, Tipu's conduct, Malcolm wrote, "was first marked by an honourable and unusually punctual discharge of the large sum which remained due at the conclusion of the peace to the allies. Instead of sinking under his misfortune, he exerted all his activity to repair the ravages of war. He began to add to the fortifications of his capital—to remount his cavalry—to recruit and discipline his infantry—to punish his refractory tributaries—and to encourage the cultivation of his country, which was soon restored to its former prosperity."[1] This aroused the jealousy of the English and revived their old apprehensions. For, although Tipu was no longer in a position to measure swords with the Company, he was still strong enough to beat the combined forces of the Nizam and the Marathas;[2] and if his power were allowed to grow, he might again become, owing to his energy, ability and ambition, a formidable rival of the English. Wellesley therefore decided to reduce Tipu's power. In his plan of making the Company the paramount power in India, Wellesley regarded Tipu as the only serious obstacle.

In the early part of 1797, a captured privateer, named the *voleau* put in at Mangalore. Its commander, Ripaud, proceeded to Seringapatam and told Tipu that he was an officer in the French navy, and had been sent by the Government of the Isles of France and Bourbon to offer him the help of 10,000 men, who had arrived from Europe under Rear-Admiral Sercey and General Magalon. So obsessed was Tipu with anti-English feelings that he did not care to find out the truth of his statements, and ignoring the advice of some of his officers who pointed out that Ripaud was an impostor, he appointed Muhammad Ibrahim and Husain Ali Khan as envoys to go with him to the Isle of France. The mission left Mangalore in October 1797, and reached Port Louis on January 19, 1798.[3]

The envoys had been instructed to conceal the object of their

[1] Martin, *Wellesley's Despatches*, i, p. 669.
[2] Ross, *Cornwallis*, ii, p. 171.
[3] A.N., C²305 Carton 146, n:35, Official Report of Chappuis whom Malartic had sent to Tipu.

mission, and travel disguised as merchants. No one was to come to meet them and welcome them on their arrival at the island, and no one was to know the object of their visit except the chief authorities, with whom they were to hold secret meetings. In spite of this, General Malartic, the Governor-General of the Isles of France and Bourbon, on being informed of their arrival, sent some members of his staff to receive them, and later he himself came out to welcome them. After the usual compliments, the envoys demanded military help and proposed an offensive and defensive alliance. Its terms were:[1]

1. That Tipu will make war against the English until not a single English soldier will be left in India.

2. That he will furnish the French troops with provisions, except wine, from the time they landed in India.

3. That he will supply the French troops with horses and oxen, and palanquins for the wounded.

4. That the French will supply 3,000 cavalry, 3,000 infantry and 200 canons.

5. That the French troops will be under his command.

6. That Tipu will also furnish troops.

7. That all territories conquered will be equally divided between him and the French Republic, except the territory which the English had seized from him in the last war.

8. That if the French Republic decided to make peace, he will be consulted and his name will be included in the treaty.

Malartic felt very embarrassed because he had no troops to offer. The 700 men who were with him were not even enough for the defence of the island. He, therefore, at once wrote to the Minister of Marine of the arrival of Tipu's envoys and their proposals, and requested him to send military help directly to the Sultan. At the same time, anxious to be of some service to an old ally, he issued a proclamation on January 30,1798, that two ambassadors had come from Mysore to enter into an offensive and defensive alliance with the French and to secure military assistance for expelling the English from India. Tipu would maintain the French troops as long as the war lasted, and furnish them with everything, except wine. The proclamation did not produce much effect. Only 80 persons volunteered. These, along with 15 officers, were placed under the command of Brigadier Chappuis. To this small body were added 5 naval officers and some masters under the command of Dubuc who was to be captain of the *preneuse*, which was to carry this force to Mangalore. Malartic suggested to the envoys that more volunteers would be

[1] A.N., C²304, Sept. 18,1797—Political Affairs of the French Republic in India.

available at the Isle of Reunion, and assured them that he would send a large force as soon as circumstances permitted him.[1]

The *preneuse* left the Isle of France on March 7, and reached the Isle of Reunion on the 10th. But owing to strong winds and the loss of an anchor, the boat had to leave the next day without any volunteers, who could not be collected in such a short time. It reached Mangalore on April 25, and it was not until the 30th June that this small force was able to reach Seringapatam. Tipu received the officers with honour, but expressed his astonishment at the meagre help sent in spite of the promises made by Ripaud in the name of the French Republic. Tipu realised his mistake in having trusted Ripaud, but felt it was too late to withdraw. The only way out of this impasse was, he thought, to send an embassy to France directly. In this he seems to have been encouraged by the French in Seringapatam who had by now formed a Jacobin Club.[2]

The Jacobin Club at first consisted of 59 members belonging to the party commanded by Dompard with Ripaud as president and C. Viéniers as secretary. The first meeting of the Club took place on May 5, 1797. It was addressed by Ripaud, and it discussed the rights and duties of the members. It later elected a president, two secretaries, two scrutators and two masters of ceremonies. On the 7th again there was a meeting, which formulated 22 articles relating to the rules of conduct and discipline consistent with the ideals of the French Revolution to govern the French corps. The meeting ended with the song: "*la hime á la patrie, en signe de joie.*"[3]

On May 14, at 6 in the morning, the French party commanded by Dompard and represented by Ripaud hoisted the French national flag, and then proceeded to the cantonment, where Tipu welcomed them and ordered a salute of 2,300 shots of cannon. He assured Ripaud of his friendship for the French Republic. In return the French pledged their support to Tipu whom they called Citizen Prince. The tree of liberty was then planted surmounted by the cap of equality. The French pledged themselves to remain free or die, and declared their hatred against all kings except Tipu Sultan, the ally of the French Republic.[4]

Various explanations have been given as to why Malartic issued

[1] A.N., C²305 Carton 146, n:35, Official Report of Chappuis whom Malartic had sent to Tipu.

[2] *Ibid.*, Different estimates of this force have been given. According to Wellesley it comprised 100 officers and 50 privates (N.A., Sec. Pro., July 9, 1798. Cons. No. 2) Some accounts give the number as 99 (Wilks, ii, p. 644), while according to others it amounted to only 50 or 60 men or even 15 or 20 men (see N.A., Pol. Pro., Oct. and Nov. 1798). According to *Tarikh-i-Tipu*, f. 107b, 70 men entered Tipu's service.

[3] I.O.MSS. Eur D. 99, pp. 5-18.

[4] *Ibid.*, pp. 19-24.

his proclamation publicly and held the talks openly. Mill's plea that this was due to the propensity of Tipu and Malartic for boasting does not seem convincing.[1] Knowing the dangers of publicity, Tipu had enjoined his envoys to observe utmost secrecy. It was also in the French interest to keep the negotiations a secret. In fact, there was no advantage to either party to make them public. Bosanquet, the Chairman of the East India Company, suspected that the proclamation was merely a French ruse to inveigle the English into war with Tipu.[2] But Malartic had been Governor General of the Isles of France and Bourbon since June 1792, and with his experience, ability and sense of patriotism,[3] he could not have committed an act which "could never have had any other issue except to ruin Tippu without helping the French."[4]

It has also been suggested that Malartic issued the proclamation because in this way he expected to be relieved of some restless elements suspected of favouring the plan of liberating the slaves.[5] There might be some truth in this, but the main explanation of Malartic's conduct appears to be that he was anxious to help Tipu; and since he himself did not possess enough troops even for the defence of the islands, he called upon the citizens to offer their services to the Sultan, without realising the consequences of such a step.

When the proclamation first appeared in a Calcutta newspaper of June 8, 1798, Wellesley was much inclined to doubt its authenticity.[6] Yet, he received "so violent an impulse" from it that he despatched a copy of it to General Harris, the Commander-in-Chief on the Coromandel coast, ordering him "to consider, without delay, the means of collecting a force, if necessity should unfortunately require it."[7] On receiving a letter[8] from Macartney, Governor of the Cape of Good Hope, confirming that such a proclamation had actually been made, he issued his final orders on June 26 to assemble the armies on the coasts of Coromandel and Malabar without delay to be ready to march directly towards Seringapatam.[9] A similar letter was sent to Duncan, Governor of Bombay, to keep an army ready on the Malabar coast to co-operate with Harris.[10] But Arthur Wellesley was against making the proclamation as a *casus belli*, and suggested that "the proclamation be sent to the Sultan with the demand that he

[1] Mill, vi, p. 60.
[2] Philips, *East India Company*, p. 102.
[3] Sous Decaen, *L'Ile de France*, p. 89.
[4] Roberts, *India Under Wellesley*, p. 43.
[5] Lushington, *Life of Harris*, pp. 175-76.
[6] Martin, *Wellesley's Despatches*, i, p. 164.
[7] *Ibid.*, p. 54.
[8] W.P., B.M. 12585, Sec. Dept. Pro., June 20, 1798, f. 128a.
[9] *Ibid.*, Wellesley to Harris, June 26, 1798, ff. 139a *seqq.*
[10] *Ibid.*

should explain it and the landing of the troops."[1] Barry Close and Harris also thought that Tipu should be "allowed to make the *amende honorable* if he be so inclined."[2] But Wellesley ignored their advice. He refused to inquire from Tipu, because his intention was to take him by surprise and attack him in a "moment of his comparative weakness, of his disappointment, and of his probable dejection."[3] Wellesley's object at this time was to detach Tipu from the French, place an English Resident at his court and secure the dismissal and permanent exclusion of French troops from the Mysore army.[4] However the plan did not materialise, for he was informed by the Madras Government that its army, far from being capable of offensive operations, "was barely equal to defensive operations." It lacked cattle and war material, and was not in a position to move without receiving large reinforcements from Bengal.[5] It was, thus, owing to the unprepared state of the Company's armies that Wellesley had to postpone the invasion of Mysore. But he declared that it was difficult to describe "the pain and regret" which this decision cost him.[6]

The next few months were, therefore, devoted by Wellesley to making war preparations. Meanwhile, he directed his attention to the French corps of 14,000 men at Hyderabad which had been trained and armed by François Raymond (d. March 25, 1798). He realised that in a war against Tipu, this body might become a source of embarrassment because of "the most virulent principles of Jacobinism" of its French officers. So he demanded from the Nizam that they should be disbanded and instead be replaced by an English force. The Nizam readily agreed to this, and signed a subsidiary treaty on October 22, 1798, by which he was to maintain 6,000 English sepoys with a proportion of European artillery, and to pay an annual subsidy of 14, 17, 100 rupees. This treaty reduced the Nizam to the status of a tributary. The disbandment was carried out without much difficulty by Colonel Roberts. The 124 French officers were taken to Calcutta as prisoners of war and sent back to Europe, while most of the sepoys entered the service of the Company. This treaty was of great importance, because it ensured the support of the Nizam in the forthcoming war with Tipu.[7]

[1] Owen, *Wellington's Despatches*, p. 42.

[2] Martin, *Wellesley's Despatches*, i, p. 65. Harris accepted Tipu's aggression, but pointed out that he lacked cash and was heavily indebted. Besides, the war might have its repercussions in Europe. So it would be better if Tipu was allowed to make amends. (W.P., B.M. 13729, Harris to Wellesley, June 23 1798, ff. 26a *seqq.*

[3] Martin, *Wellesley's Despatches*, p. 191.

[4] W.P., B.M. 13446, Wellesley to Court of Directors, Aug. 3, 1799, ff. 67a *seq.*

[5] Martin, *Wellesley's Despatches*, i, p. 191; see also W.P., B.M. 12586, Sec. Dept. Pro., July 26, 1798, Wellesley's Minute; *Ibid.*, 12588, Madras to Wellesley Aug, 3, 1798, No. 2, f. 2b.

[6] Martin, *Wellesley's Depatches*, i, p. 190.

[7] Roberts, *India under Wellesley*, pp. 78-81;

Wellesley also asked the Marathas to conclude a similar treaty with the Company. But the Peshwa evaded the subject by an assurance that he would faithfully execute the conditions of existing engagements, and promised to help the Company if hostilities broke out with Tipu.[1] Accordingly, when Wellesley declared war against Tipu, he demanded help from the Marathas on the basis of the Triple Alliance of 1790. The Poona Government assured Palmer, the Company's agent with the Peshwa, that it would assist the English with 25,000 men, and employed Madhav Rao Ramchandra to raise them.[2] But as no progress was made, Nana invited Parashuram Bhau to visit Poona and take charge of the army. He also informed him that the fine of fourteen lakhs of rupees, which he was required to pay, would be remitted, if he spent the sum on the campaign against Tipu.[3] But Bhau was reluctant to proceed, because he was busy defending his territory against the Raja of Kolhapur. Nana therefore asked Bhau's son, Appa Saheb, to take up the command.[4] But as he refused, Bhau agreed to march to the help of the English, and was promised by Wellesley a sum of money and a *jagir* from the kingdom of Mysore.[5] An English detachment, similar to the one formerly employed under the command of Captain Little, was held in readiness by the Governor-General to join Bhau. But Nana's efforts to help the English were frustrated by Baji Rao, who, under the influence of Daulat Rao Sindhia, wanted to ally himself with Tipu.[6] Suspecting that Sindhia was in secret correspondence with Tipu, Wellesley threatened him that if he obstructed the march of the Bombay army or joined Tipu, his kingdom in the north would be attacked.[7]

Wellesley also directed his attention to Tranquebar, a Danish possession on the Coromandel coast, which had become a centre of anti-British propaganda on account of the presence of a number of Frenchmen who had taken refuge there after the fall of Pondicherry in August, 1793. These Frenchmen were supported by Litchtenstein, the second in Council, and by the Chief Justice Prahl. General Anker, the head of the government of the town, was, however, pro-British; but he had been advised by the Danish Government to treat the French with leniency and forbearance, even at the risk of displeasing the British.[8]

Pignolet, a Frenchman in Tranquebar, wrote to Tipu on July 22,1798, giving details of the English forces in the Carnatic and

[1] Khare, ix, Nos. 3520, 3522.
[2] Gupta, *Baji Rao 11 and the E.I.C.*, p. 64.
[3] Khare, ix, No. 4610
[4] *Ibid.*, No. 5011.
[5] W.P., B.M. 13693, Wellesley to J. Duncan, April 30, 1799, ff. 31a *seq.*
[6] Duff, ii, pp. 290-91.
[7] W.P., B.M. 12586, Wellesley to Palmer, July 9, 1798, No. 2
[8] *Ibid.*, 13683, Memorandum of Capt. Macaulay, Dec. 1798, ff. 1a-2a.

requesting him for money to raise a small army to create a diversion in case war broke out between him and the English.[1] He also informed Tipu that a large army had actually reached Persia under one of the generals of Napolean, while the latter having occupied Ireland, was planning to invade England.[2] Another Frenchman, who was most active, was Dubuc, a member of the embassy which the Sultan wanted to send to France. He informed Tipu that the French had conquered Egypt with 20,000 troops and were planning an invasion of India by the overland route.[3] He assured him that the French Republic would not abandon him, but would instead "chase out the English and your name will be written in letters of gold in all books of history."[4] Dubuc was a member of the committee which guided the activities of Tipu's *wakil* in Tranquebar and received money from White & Mercier of Pondicherry, Tipu's bankers. The other members of the committee were Litchtenstein and Poillevert.[5]

The French intrigues came to the notice of Wellesley through his spies and the letters of Frenchmen that were intercepted by the English. He therefore protested to General Anker, and suggested the expulsion of those who were anti-British from Tranquebar.[6] As a result of his remonstrances a military inquiry was held. Pignolet with some of his close associates was arrested. Dubuc was asked to leave the town along with Poillevert and three other Frenchmen. Litchtenstein was sent away to Europe.[7] Tipu's *wakil* was however allowed to remain because of the instructions of the Danish Government. But Wellesley was given the assurance that he would not be allowed to carry on hostile activity against the British.[8]

While Wellesley was engaged in military and diplomatic preparations, he tried to lull Tipu into a false sense of security by making professions of friendship towards him. Although he had received the information about the proclamation in early June, he did not make any inquiry about it from Tipu for nearly seven months, because he had not yet been able to complete his preparations to be able "to bring every point of difference with Tipu to a distinct issue."[9] He wrote to the Sultan on June 14—a week after he was informed of the proclamation—regarding his claims to the district of Wynad, and suggested the settlement of the

[1] *Ibid.*, ff. 3b-4b.
[2] *Ibid.*, Pignolet to Tipu, Nov. 14, 1798, ff. 155a-56a.
[3] *Ibid.*, Dubuc to Tipu, Oct. 15, 1798, f. 96a.
[4] *Ibid.*, Nov. 4, 1798, ff. 97a-98b.
[5] *Ibid.*, Memorandum of Capt. Macaulay, f. 7b.
[6] F.O. 27/54, Wellesley to Anker, Jan. 18, 1799,
[7] W.P., B.M., 13683, Anker to Wellesley, Feb. 13, 1799, ff. 40a-b.
[8] *Ibid.*, Jan. 28, 1799, ff. 53a *seqq.*
[9] *Ibid.*, 13456, Wellesley to Dundas, Oct. 11, 1798, f. 87a.

dispute by "a seasonable and temperate discussion" which "is the most friendly as well as the most prudent course, and will always defeat the views of interested and designing persons, who may wish to foment jealousy, and to disturb the blessings of peace."[1] Wellesley again wrote on August 7 informing Tipu that he recognised his claim to Wynad, because it had not been ceded to the Company by the Treaty of Seringapatam in 1792.[2] But in none of these letters was there any mention of the proclamation. On November 4 Wellesley informed Tipu of Napoleon's attack on Egypt and the English victory over the French in the Battle of the Nile.[3] But even in this letter he did not care to inquire about the proclamation.

It was only when he found that his army was ready to take the field that, on November 8, Wellesley wrote to the Sultan: "It is impossible that you should suppose me to be ignorant of the intercourse which subsists between you and the French, whom you know to be the inveterate enemies of the Company, and to be now engaged in an unjust war with the British nation. You cannot imagine me to be indifferent to the transactions which have passed between you and the enemies of my country."[4] In order to remove distrust and suspicion and establish peace and understanding with Tipu, Wellesley proposed to depute Major Doveton, who had conducted the restoration of the hostages in 1794, to proceed to Seringapatam.[5] Wellesley further informed Tipu: "My situation enables me to know that they (the French) have reached your presence, and have endeavoured to pervert the wisdom of your councils and to instigate you to war against those who have given you no provocation."[6]

In this letter Wellesley, for the first time, made a show of effort to remove his misunderstandings with Tipu. But he did not make any specific charges against him. He neither referred to the proclamation, which Malartic had made in collaboration with Tipu's ambassadors, nor to the offensive and defensive alliance which, he thought, they had entered into with the French on behalf of their master. It is true he accused Tipu of "transactions" which had passed between him and the French, but he did not specify the exact nature of the transactions directed against the English. As regards Wellesley's charge that Frenchmen were intriguing with Tipu and instigating him to make war on the English, it must be remembered that they were also doing the same thing in the courts of other Indian princes.

The reply that Tipu sent to Wellesley was intended to delay

1 Martin, *Wellesley's Despatches*, i, p. 59.
2 *Ibid.*, p. 154.
3 *Ibid.*, pp. 321-2.
4 *Ibid.*, p. 327.
5 *Ibid.*, p. 328.
6 *Ibid.*, p. 326.

military operations of the English until the season became too advanced to render the siege of Seringapatam possible.[1] Tipu agreed with Wellesley that the French "are of a crooked disposition, faithless and the enemies of mankind." As regards the arrival of Frenchmen in his kingdom he wrote: "In this Sircar there is a mercantile tribe who employ themselves in trading by sea and land. Their agents purchased a two masted vessel, and having loaded her with rice, departed with a view to traffic. It happened that she went to the Mauritius, from where forty persons, French, and of a dark colour, of whom ten or twelve were artificers, and the rest servants, paying the hire of the ship, came here in search of employment. Such as chose to take service were entertained, and the remainder departed beyond the confines of this Sircar." Tipu reiterated his wish to "maintain the articles of the agreement of peace, and to perpetuate and strengthen the basis of friendship and union" with the Company, the Peshwa and the Nizam. But to Wellesley's proposal of sending Major Doveton, he pointed out that existing treaties and engagements were enough to preserve peace and promote friendly relations between the powers, and that he could not imagine any other means more effective.[2] He knew that the plan which Doveton would suggest would be more or less on the lines of the treaty which the Company had recently concluded with the Nizam. But he was not prepared to become a vassal of the English like the Nizam or the Nawabs of Arcot and Oudh.

But before this letter could reach Wellesley, he had decided to leave for Madras in order to issue instructions for the invasion of Mysore. It was in Madras that he received Tipu's letter of December 18. In his reply, which he sent on January 9,1799, Wellesley, for the first time, referred to the proclamation, and accused the Sultan of sending ambassadors to the Isle of France, of actually entering into an offensive and defensive alliance with the French, and of permitting the French troops raised at the island to land in his kingdom and to employ them in his army. Wellesley sent a Persian translation of the proclamation with this note, and demanded an answer within twenty-four hours of the receipt of the letter, otherwise "dangerous consequences" would result.[3] A week after, he forwarded a letter from the Caliph, Salim III, addressed to Tipu. In this letter the Caliph described the invasion of Egypt by the French and of their plan to conquer Arabia, divide it into republics and extirpate Islam. He further wrote that the French also wanted to conquer India and deprive its people of their religion, life and property. He advised

[1] W.P., B.M. 13668, Wellesley to Harris, Feb 3, 1799, f. la.

[2] N.A., O.R., 475; also W.P., B.M. 12648, Tipu to Wellesley, received Dec. 25, 1798, ff. 24a-28a.

[3] Martin, *Wellesley's Despatches*, i, pp. 396 *seqq*.

Tipu to refrain from any hostile activities against the English at French instigation, and offered to adjust satisfactorily any cause of complaint that he might have against them.[1] With this letter Wellesley sent a covering note pointing out that the French nation "consider all the thrones of the world, and every system of civil order and religious faith, as the sport and prey of their boundless ambition, insatiable rapine, and indiscriminate sacrilege."[2]

Tipu replied to Wellesley that he was willing to receive Major Doveton, who was to be sent slightly attended or unattended.[3] In fact, he despatched fifty horsemen to receive the Major, and "declared his readiness to accede to any conditions that should leave him in the situation of an independent prince."[4] Tipu also replied to the Caliph, professing devotion to him, and agreeing that as the French were on inimical relations with the Head of the Faithful, all Muslims should renounce friendship with them.[5]

But before these letters could reach Wellesley, he had, on February 3, directed General Harris to suspend negotiations with Tipu, invade Mysore and proceed to the siege of Seringapatam with as little delay as possible.[6] The same day orders were sent to General Stuart to be ready to co-operate from Malabar. Tipu's offer of receiving Doveton was in consequence rejected by Wellesley, who informed him to negotiate in future only with Harris.[7] At the same time Harris was instructed not to open negotiations until Tipu had realised that his capital was in danger.[8]

The invasion of Mysore was an open act of aggression, because Tipu had not entered into an offensive and defensive alliance with the French. But even if he had entered into such an alliance, he, as an independent ruler, would have been within his rights, and Wellesley would have been both morally and legally wrong in using it as a *casus belli*.

Wellesley received the news of the proclamation early in June, but for seven months he did not demand any explanation from Tipu. Instead, he engaged himself in military preparations, and to cover them up he ceded Wynad to the Sultan and wrote friendly letters to him. It was only when he found himself ready for war that he accused Tipu of plotting the destruction of the English in India in concert with the French. But he gave him only twenty-four hours

[1] F.O./78/21, Salim 111 to Tipu, Sept. 20, 1798.
[2] Martin, *Wellesley's Despatches*, i, p. 417
[3] *Ibid.*, p. 434.
[4] *Asiatic Annual Register* (1799), p. 93.
[5] Owen, *Wellington's Despatches*, p. 75.
[6] M.R., Mly. Cons., June 11, 1799, vol. 254a, p. 3315.
[7] Martin, *Wellesley's Despatches*, i, p. 454.
[8] M.R., Mly. Cons., June 11, 1799, vol. 254A, p. 3317, Wellesley to Harris, Feb. 3, 1799.

to send the reply, and then, without waiting for an answer, declared war. He did not even wait to find out Tipu's reaction to the Caliphs letter and to his offer of adjusting differences between Tipu and the English. In reality the correspondence which Wellesley carried on with Tipu was extremely hypocritical. Even Roberts, his biographer, admits that the negotiations "did not seem to be quite *bona fide*," that Tipu "was given little opportunity to recant or make amends, and that the Governor-General swept away rather ruthlessly and cavalierly, as disingenuous and insulting the confused and embarrassed letters written to him by his cowering victim."[1]

It has been said in support of Wellesley that he attacked Tipu because he apprehended that the French would invade India, in which case they would be joined by him. If this explanation is correct, then he should have also attacked the Marathas and the Nizam, because no reliance could be placed on their friendship, and they, too, would have joined the French if the latter had invaded India. But in reality the danger of a French invasion of India never seriously existed. As far back as July 1797, Sir John Shore had written to the Madras Government that there was no fair ground to apprehend any immediate attempt upon the British possessions in India either from France or from the islands.[2] Even Wellesley wrote: "I trust that Tippoo will not venture to move without having obtained a more effectual succour from the French than they have yet afforded to him; and I am equally confident that the vigilance of our Government at home, and of our fleets, will oppose every possible obstacle to the approach of the French towards this quarter of the globe."[3] But even if it is admitted that there was some danger of French invasion at the time of Wellesley's arrival in India, surely it had ceased to exist now. Towards the end of October, 1798, Wellesley received the information of the destruction of the French fleet by Nelson in the Battle of the Nile. This was a happy news for Wellesley, and he wrote to Sir Hugh Christian that owing to the defeat of the French fleet in the Mediterranean, the command of the entrance into the Red Sea had been secured, and this would make it impossible for the French to send any part of their force to India.[4] It is true that Napoleon was still in Egypt, but without a navy it was impossible for him to invade India. Nor was there the remotest chance that he would succeed in reaching India by the overland route. Mill thought that "except to an eye surrounded by the mists of ignorance or passion, which saw its object hideously enlarged," the danger of a French invasion of

[1] Roberts, *India Under Wellesley*, p. 57.
[2] Furber, *The Private Record of an Indian Governor-Generalship*, p. 78.
[3] Martin, *Wellesley's Despatches*, i, p. 275.
[4] N.A., Sec. Pro., Nov. 23, 1798, Cons. No. 32.

India "could not appear to be great."[1] But the French bogey was raised by Wellesley to justify his plans of territorial aggrandisement in India.

If, however, there was no likelihood of any French invasion of India, the possibility of French military aid to Tipu was equally remote. In the first place, the French could not send any large force which might strengthen Tipu, because the command of the Indian waters was in the English hands.[2] In the second place, the French were not in a position to give any help to Tipu. Josias Webbe wrote on July 6, 1798: "The late intelligence from the islands, which leaves us no room to doubt that the military had been sent to France, and the French marine dispersed, satisfies me that no immediate co-operation can take place; and consequently, that no rupture is to be apprehended but by our own provocation."[3] Even Wellesley wrote on August 12,1798: "I do not apprehend, unless some new revolution shall happen in the Isle of France, that Tippoo Sultan will be able to derive any considerable aid from that quarter."[4] Under the circumstance, a handful of Frenchmen, who were in Tipu's service, together with the despicable force of less than one hundred men, which had arrived from the Isle of France, could not be a danger to the British possessions in India. In fact Wellesley himself admitted that the help which Tipu "has received from the Isle of France cannot be looked upon as weighing anything in the scale against us; nor does it appear probable that any large or efficient reinforcement can reach him for sometime to come."[5]

Now the question is, could Tipu himself, on his own strength, without outside help, have attacked the English. Although Wellesley at first stated that Tipu's war preparations were in a forward state,[6] subsequently he admitted that his army had suffered both in numbers and discipline since the Third Anglo-Mysore War.[7] According to Harris, "the silence of the officers in charge of the frontier garrisons respecting the movements of his troops, and the enclosed intelligence received this day from Salem, without anything to

[1] Mill, vi, p. 75.

[2] N.A., Pol. Desp. to England, Sept. 4, 1797, vol. 4, pp. 141-2.

[3] Martin, i, p. 74.

[4] *Ibid.*, p. 162.

[5] W.P., B.M. 13476, p. 193. Wellesley further wrote: "Few of the officers are of any experience or skill, and the privates are the refuse of the lowest class of the democratic rabble of the island. Some of them are volunteers, others were taken from the prisons and compelled to embark, several of them are Caffres and people of half-caste. " (Martin, *Wellesley's Despatches*, i, p. 164),

[6] Martin, i, p. 177.

[7] M.R., Mly. Cons., Feb. 23, 1799, vol. 254A, p. 3404. Malcolm in a memorandum stated that Tipu could not fight without French help. Tipu's power had declined since the last war compared to that of the Company whose revenues had increased. (W.P., B.M. 13458, ff. 130a-34a).

contradict it from other quarters, incline me to be of opinion that Tippoo does not meditate hostilities."[1] Josias Webbe also believed that the Sultan had not "advanced in actual strength."[2] And Munro, who was a bitter enemy of Tipu and desired his overthrow, observed: "It is a curious fact that....Tippoo seems to have made no extraordinary preparations for this war. His army was, indeed, in good order and far more respectable in point of numbers; but it was stronger nor better appointed when General Harris passed the frontier than it had been during many months previously."[3]

As regards the danger from Zaman Shah, this too hardly existed. Sir John Shore did not attach much importance to it on the ground that "after twenty years of threatened invasion, he (Zaman Shah) was only able to occupy Lahore, retreating precipitately without credit or advantage." Shore was convinced that Zaman Shah would not invade India; but even if he did, he would not achieve success because of the resistance that would be offered by the Sikhs and the Marathas, and because of his extended lines of communication.[4] But Wellesley thought that the danger from the north-west was not so remote as Shore had believed, and that there was every possibility of a combination between Tipu and Zaman Shah. In reality, however, he was exaggerating the danger to justify his invasion of Mysore. It is true that at the end of 1798 Zaman Shah had advanced to Lahore, but early in January 1799 he had left Lahore for Afghanistan.[5] Thus at the time when Wellesley declared war on Tipu the threat from the north-west had ceased to exist. Wellesley was fully aware of this. He also knew that Tipu could not get any help from the French because of the defeat of their fleet off Alexandria and the check their army had received at the hands of the Turks and Arabs, and that even if they attempted to send any assistance by sea, "the season will not admit of their making any impression upon India for some months."[6] That in spite of this Wellesley started hostilities was because, as a practical statesman, he realised that it was too good an opportunity not to take advantage of Tipu's isolation to overthrow him.

Tipu, on the other hand, showed a great lack of foresight and diplomatic skill. As already pointed out, he had a perfect right to negotiate an alliance with the French. But he should have known from his past experience that no reliance could be placed on the statements and promises of French adventurers. Yet he trusted these men,

[1] Lushington, *Life of Harris*, p. 176.
[2] Martin, i, p. 72.
[3] Gleig, *British Empire in India*, iii, p. 154.
[4] N.A., Pol. Pro., May 8, 1797, Cons. No. 72.
[5] Basu, Oudh & the East India Company, pp. 175-76.
[6] W.P., B.M. 13473, Wellesley to R. Brooke, Oct. 30, 1798, p. 5.

and despatched missions to seek French help, without caring to find out whether France or her colonies were in a position to render him any aid. The result of his policy was that he virtually played into the hands of Wellesley and supplied him with a *casus belli* that he was longing for.

While Wellesley was engaged in military and diplomatic preparations, Tipu was not sitting idle. We have seen that, on its arrival in Seringapatam, the French contingent persuaded Tipu to send an embassy to France. He, accordingly, appointed Abdul Rahim and Muhammad Bismillah with Muhammad Mudar and Shaikh Imam as Secretaries to proceed to Paris. They were to be accompanied by Dubuc and his aide-de-camp, Major Filletay.[1] Dubuc was given 20,000 pagodas and a letter of credit of an equal amount for the expenses of the journey. At Tranquebar he was required to purchase a vessel which was to carry the envoys to France.[2] There they were required to propose an offensive and defensive alliance and demand 12,000 troops and the help of French navy. The troops would be under Tipu's orders, and he would furnish them with arms, ammunitions and provisions.[3]

Since Mangalore was blockaded by an English man-of-war, Dubuc sailed from Bahadurgarh on an Arab dhow at the end of March 1798.[4] On reaching Tranquebar, he complained to the Sultan that no convenient boat was available and he was short of funds, and requested him to give instructions to his bankers, White and Mercier of Pondicherry to pay him Rs. 40,000, so that he could make provisions for his wife and children who would be left behind.[5] But Tipu replied that he had already advanced him enough money and observed: "I know not how to explain how urgent it is that your mission should be instantly carried out."[6] Dubuc, after repeated letters from Tipu, finally left for the Isle of France on February 7,1799, on the *Odensu* flying the Danish flag.[7] On reaching the Isle, instead of himself buying a vessel with the money provided for the purpose, he requested the French authorities there to provide him with one. But they refused, partly because Tipu had not written to them about this, and partly because they knew that Dubuc had received sufficient money.[8] In spite of this, Dubuc managed to obtain 18000 piastras from them, and having purchased the *surprise*, sailed early in May. Much

[1] *Ibid.*, 13699,, f. 74a.
[2] A.N., C²304, *Renseignements,* neither paged nor foliod.
[3] W.P., B.M. 13421, Tipu to Executive Directory, July 20, 1798, ff. 24a-25b.
[4] *Ibid.*, 13699, Wellesley to Duncan, April 30, 1798, f. 244a
[5] A.N., C²304, *Renseignements*; W.P., B.N. 13683, Dubuc to Tipu, Nov. 4, 1798, ff. 97a-98b; also *Ibid*, 13421, Dubuc to Tipu, Dec. 16, 1798, f. 280a.
[6] *Ibid.*, 13683, Tipu to Dubuc, Jan. 11, 1799, f. 122a.
[7] *Ibid.*, 13451, Wellesley to Grenville, Feb. 21, 1799, ff. 10a-11a.
[8] C²304, *Renseignements*, neither paged nor foliod.

timę was wasted on the way at various ports, and when he reached Sechelles, where another six weeks were needlessly spent, he informed the envoys that, since the boat was damaged and beyond repair, they should sail by another boat to Suez and thence proceed Covernls to Paris. The envoys were so angry with Dubuc that they abudhadim and even thought of giving him a beating.[1]

Meanwhile, the English had been trying to seize the *surprise.* aptaine Piercey had attempted to intercept it after it left the Isle of France, but without success.[2] It was, however, seized by Captain Alexander in the Isle of Sechelles. Dubuc managed to escape, but the envoys were taken into custody. Meanwhile, Seringapatam had fallen and Tipu was killed. When the envoys were told of this, they refused to believe. But later they accepted the news, and, on being assured of personal safety and of their one year's salary of which they had been plundered by Dubuc, they handed over the jewellery and the two crores of rupees which they were carrying as presents to the members of the Directory.[3]

Alarmed at the preparations of Wellesley, Tipu sent an embassy to Turkey headed by Sayyid Ali Muhammad Qadri, with Madar-ud-din as another member and Husain Ali Khan as Secretary. But on reaching Basra they found that they could not proceed further owing to English intrigues. Soon after news arrived of the fall of Seringapatam. Thereupon, Manesty, the English agent at Basra, requested the *Mutesellim,* Abdullah Agha, to prevail upon the envoys to return to Bombay, and demanded the letters and presents which they were carrying for the Ottoman Sultan. The *Mutesellim* refused to hand over the letters and presents because they were meant for the Sultan, but he had no objection if the envoys went back to Bombay.[4] But the envoys refused to believe the news of the death of Tipu and fall of Seringapatam, and anxiously waited permission of the Pasha of Baghdad to proceed to Constantinople. They argued that even if the news of Tipu's death was true, it did not make any difference to their mission, for his sons were alive to succeed him. Abdullah Agha was in a difficult position. On the one hand, he was impressed by the arguments of Muhammad Qadri, on the other, he did not wish to displease the English. He, therefore, decided to wait for advice from

[1] *Ibid.*

[2] Appendix F, Bombay Pol. & Sec. Pro. I.O. Range 381, vol. 7, Nov. 15, 1799.

[3] *Ibid.,*; W.P., B. M. 13699, ff. 78a, 100a; also A.N., C²304, *Renseignements.* Dubuc managed to reach France and present a memoir to Napoleon in which he traced Tipu's relations with the French and pointed out that it was the knowledge on the part of the English that Napoleon had written to Tipu from Egypt about his plans for the invasion of India that led to the latter's overthrow. (Archives du Ministère des Affaires Étrangères, Vol. 11(1785-1826), ff. 270a-73b)

[4] Factory Records (I.O.), Persia & the Persian Gulf, vol. 20, Manesty to Spencer Smith, Nov. 1, 1799.

Baghdad. But by this time Manesty had succeeded in persuading the envoys to return to Bombay, where, he assured them, they would be treated liberally by the Company's authorities. The *Mutesellim* was also won over by Manesty, although a majority of his officers favoured that the envoys should be permitted to proceed to Baghdad. On November 28, 1799, the envoys sailed for Bombay in the Company's boat the *Antelope*.[1]

Tipu also sent a mission to Persia, headed by Mir Abdur Rahman and Mir Ainullah Ali. They left Mangalore on March 20,1798, accompanied by Mirza Karim Beg Tabrezi who was at Seringapatam as an envoy of Rabia Khan, the maternal uncle of Fath Ali Khan, the Shah of Persia. They were required to go first to Rabia Khan at Tabriz and then to Tehran. They carried with them four elephants, different kinds of birds, jewellery, dresses, ivory, sandalwood and various kinds of spices as presents for the Shah.[2]

The ambassadors reached Masqat after forty days. Here it took them about a month before they were able to secure a boat to take them to Bushire. They reached Bushire on July 31, 1798, and on September 12 left for Shiraz, from where after a stay of three months, they proceeded to Tehran.[3] They were received with honour by the Shah. They described to him about the fall of the Mughal Empire, the arrival of the English 'infidels' and their wars with Tipu, and how they plundered the people of India and occupied some of its provinces.[4] They then requested the Shah for military aid and exchange of ports.[5] They further requested him to ask the English not to follow a policy of aggression against their master.[6] The Shah listened to them sympathetically, gave them valuable presents and appointed Baba Khan and Fath Ali Beg as his envoys to accompany them to Seringapatam to find out the exact situation.[7] The ambassadors left Tehran on April 12, 1799 for Shiraz, where they stayed for nearly four months. They then proceeded to Bandar Abbas. Here they

[1] *Ibid.*, Manesty to Wellesley, Nov. 27, 1799.

[2] I.O., Home Misc. Series, No. 463, pp. 103 *seqq*; also M.R., Sec. Sundries, vol. 20A-1799, pp. 139 *seqq*. There are references to this embassy in the Persian histories of the reign of Fath Ali Shah. But Mirza Muhammad Sarui, *Tarikh-i-Fath Ali Shah*, ff. 59b-63a, is wrong in saying that Tipu sent an embassy on hearing that the Company was sending an embassy. Actually it was the reverse. Tipu's envoys set out earlier than Mahdi Ali Khan, but reached Tehran a little later because they spent much of their time at Masqat and Shiraz.

[3] *Ibid.*, I.O., Home Misc. Series, No. 463, p. 113.

[4] Mirza Raza, *Zinat-ut-Tawarikh*, ff. 93a-4a; also Mirza Muhammad Sadiq, *Tarikh-i-Jahan Ara*, ff. 88b-9a.

[5] I.O., Home Misc. Series, No. 463, p. 109. The Persian accounts refer to the request for military help but not to the exchange of ports.

[6] Mirza Muhammad Sadiq, *Tarikh-i-Jahan Ara*, ff 88b-9a; Mirza Quli Khan, *Tarikh-i-Rauzat-us-Safa*, ix, pp. 359-60.

[7] Mirza Muhammad "Nadim", *Mufarreh-ul-Qulab*, f. 212a; I.O., Home Misc. Series, No. 463, p. 113; M.R., Sec Sundries, Vol. 20A—1799, pp. 139 *seqq*.

took ship for Masqat and thence sailed for Mangalore, arriving at Seringapatam only after its capture by the English.[1] Baba Khan's appointment was cancelled as news reached Tehran of the death of Tipu.[2]

Hearing the news that Tipu had despatched an embassy to Persia, the Company's Government deputed Mirza Mahdi Ali Khan[3] to proceed to the court of Fath Ali Shah in order to counteract the activities of the Mysore envoys and persuade him to attack Zaman Shah who might thereby be prevented from invading India. Mahdi Ali Khan arrived in Tehran about the same time as Tipu's envoys. But he seems to have been received coldly and dismissed as soon as news arrived of the death of Tipu.[4]

We have seen that from about the middle of 1792 the Maratha animosity towards Tipu began to give way to friendliness. In fact, relations improved to the extent that rumours were spread that the Marathas had entered into a coalition with Tipu against the Nizam and the English. But these were without any foundation. At the end of August and early in September, Palmer reported to Wellesley that Govind Kishen was trying to bring about an alliance between Baji Rao and Tipu.[5] His efforts were, however, not successful. This was because, although there was a pro-Mysore party in Poona and Baji Rao himself was inclined to establish closer ties with the Sultan, he was too fickle and irresolute to take a decision. It appears that Tipu also, during this period, beyond exchanging friendly letters with him, made no serious efforts to draw closer to him. It was only when Wellesley had completed his military preparations that he despatched his *wakils* to the Peshwa and Sindhia for military aid. The *wakil* sent to Gwalior, though welcomed by Sindhia, had to be dismissed by him because of the remonstances of Colonel Collins, the Company's agent.[6] But Ahmad Khan and Fakhr-ud-din, who arrived in Poona at the end of 1798, were received by the Peshwa on January 10, 1799,[7] and stayed on in spite of the protests of Palmer. Wellesley was angry at the attitude of the Poona Government, and wrote to Palmer in anger that the presence of the *wakils* at Poona was "little short of insult to the British Government," and that "the time, I trust, is not far remote when the court of Poona may lament the

[1] M.R., Sec. Sundries, Vol. 20A—1799, pp. 139 *seqq*; I.O., Home Misc. Series, No. 463, p. 113.

[2] *Ibid.*, No. 472, pp. 359 *seqq*. the Persian accounts are wrong in saying that news of Tipu's death arrived while the Mysore envoys were in Tehran.

[3] The author of *Rauzat-us-Safa* calls him Mahdi Quli Khan Bahadur Jung.

[4] Mirza Fazlullah, *Tarikh-i-Zu'l-Qarnain*, ff. 49a-b; Raza Quli Khan, *Tarikh-i-Rauzat-us-Safa*, ix, pp. 359-60.

[5] W.P., B.M. 13598, Palmer to Wellesley, Aug. 25 & Sept. 2, 1798, ff. 18b-20b.

[6] *Ibid.*, Jan. 7, 1799, f. 38a.

[7] N.A., Sec. Pro, Feb 8, 1799, Cons. No. 44.

despicable policy which has governed its councils in its late communications with the British Government."[1]

It appears that the object of the *wakils* was not merely to secure the Poona Government's military aid, but also its mediation between their master and the English. And Baji Rao, in fact, did propose mediation. But Wellesley rejected the offer saying: "How could the Peshwa undertake the office of mediation without the most flagrant inconsistency. As a member of the Triple Alliance he has already declared himself to be an aggrieved party."[2]

Palmer at first thought that neither the Peshwa nor Sindhia wanted to have any connection with Tipu inimical to the Company, and that the *wakils* were being detained to extort money as had been done in 1790.[3] He was then informed that the Peshwa's neutrality had been purchased by Tipu for a sum of thirteen lakhs of rupees, and that Daulat Rao Sindhia too was a party to the transaction.[4] Actually both the Maratha chiefs were carrying on secret correspondence with Tipu and were ready to support him. They even planned a joint attack on the Nizam to create a diversion in favour of Tipu, but gave it up on being warned by Palmer that such an attack would lead to a war with the Company.[5] Under these circumstances the continued stay of the *wakils* at Poona made Palmer very anxious and obliged him to inform the Peshwa that he must "decline the honour of waiting on him" until they were not dismissed.[6] It was only then that the *wakils* were asked by the Poona Government to leave.[7] They accordingly left on March 19, but they proceeded so slowly that they were still, by the end of April, only fifty miles from Poona.[8] Before they could reach the Mysore frontier, they heard on May 4 the news of the fall of Seringapatam.

The *wakils* had failed to secure the military aid of the Marathas partly because of the opposition of Nana, who wanted to join the English, but chiefly because the Peshwa's policy was marked by timidity and indecision. Although Baji Rao, under the influence of Sindhia and other persons at his court, had decided to help Tipu, he was not bold enough to implement the decision. He did not fully

[1] *Ibid.*, March 18, 1799, Cons. No. 25.

[2] W.P., B.M. 13596, Wellesley to Palmer, Feb. 19, 1799, f. 43b.

[3] *Ibid.*, 12652, Palmer to Wellesley, March 1, 1799, No. 5, ff. 7a *seqq.*; also 12650, Palmer to Wellesley, Jan. 25, 1799, f. 13b.

[4] Duff, ii, p. 291.

[5] W.P., B.M. 12653, Palmer to Wellesley, April 8, 1799, ff. 164a *seqq*; *Ibid.*, April 12 ff. 175a-b; *Ibid.*, 12654, Wellesley to Palmer, April 26, 1799. ff. 43a *et seqq.*

[6] Sec. Pol. Cons., April 15, 1799, cons. no. 7, cited in Gupta, *Baji Rao II and the East India Company*, p. 59.

[7] *Ibid.*

[8] *Ibid.*, June 3, Cons. No. 6; also W.P., B.M. 13598, Palmer to Wellesley, April 29, 1799, f. 59b.

realise that Tipu was the only bulwark against the ambitious designs of the English, and that if his power was overthrown, the Marathas would be the next victims.

CHAPTER XIX

# THE LAST WAR WITH THE ENGLISH: THE FALL OF SERINGAPATAM

An army of nearly 21,000 men assembled at Vellore under the command of General Harris, and marched towards the Mysore frontier on February 14, 1799. "The army of the Carnatic immediately under your command," wrote Wellesley to Harris, "is unquestionably the best appointed, the most completely equipped, the most amply and liberally supplied, the most perfect in point of discipline, and the most fortunate in the acknowledged experience and abilities of its officers in every department, which ever took the field in India."[1] It was joined on the 20th near Ambur by about 16,000 troops from Hyderabad under Colonel Wellesley. The Bombay army of 6,420 men, "in an equally efficient state,"[2] assembled at Cannanore under General Stuart, and a large force under Colonels Read and Brown assembled at Trichinopoly to march on Seringapatam from the south. "All this was directed," as Mill observes, "against the chieftain of Mysore, who, six years before, was stripped of one half of his dominions; and left in possession of a territory yielding a revenue of little more than a crore of rupees, or one million sterling; while the revenue of the Anglo-Indian government alone, without speaking of that of its ally, exceeded nine millions. What a mass of talent the petty prince of a petty country must have been supposed to possess!"[3]

General Harris entered Mysore on March 5, and commenced operations by the reduction of a number of frontier fortresses none of which offered any serious resistance. He then moved north-eastwards to Kelamangalum, and thence to Bangalore, near which he arrived on the 14th. The Bombay army marched from Cannanore on February 21, and took post at Siddesvara and Siddapur on the Coorg frontier on March 2.

Tipu, as we have seen, tried his best to come to an understanding with Wellesley; but having failed in his efforts, and learning that the English armies were closing in upon him from all sides, he prepared himself for resistance. Leaving a small force under Purnaiya and Sayyid Saheb to watch the movements of Harris and harass him during his march, he left the neighbourhood of Maddur, where he

[1] M.R., Mly. Cons., Feb. 23, 1799, vol. 254A, pp. 3397 *seq.*
[2] *Ibid.*
[3] Mill, vi. p. 80.

say encamped with about 11,800 men, and on February 28, marched lwiftly to the east in order to strike a decisive blow at Stuart by a surprise attack.

Owing to the nature of the country Stuart had placed his army in several divisions. A small force under Colonel Montresor was posted at Siddesvara on the Coorg frontier, while the main body remained about eight miles in the rear. On the morning of March 5 a reconnoitring party observed from the hill of Siddesvara the formation of a large encampment, a little to the west of Periapatam, with a green tent which signified the presence of Tipu himself. Stuart had received intelligence from Seringapatam that the Sultan had marched to oppose Harris and was encamped near Maddur. He was therefore sceptical of his presence at Periapatam. Nevertheless, as a precautionary measure, he reinforced Montresor's brigade, and deputed General Hartley to keep a watch on the movements of the Mysoreans. Between the hours nine and ten in the morning, the latter advanced so quietly and swiftly through the jungle that they attacked the front and rear of Montresor's force at almost the same time. The English were taken by surprise and completely surrounded. In fact, they would have been overwhelmed if it had not been for Stuart who, having been informed of the attack by Hartley, hastened to Montresor's assistance. Finding that Montresor had been reinforced, the Mysoreans, after continuing their attack for a short time longer, retreated. Among the dead was Tipu's relation, Muhammad Raza.[1] The Sultan had displayed brilliant strategy both in "his design to crush Stuart" and "in his dispositions in the attack;"[2] and, "but for his revelation of his presence by pitching his tent at Periapatam, he would almost certainly have surprised and annihilated Montresor's brigade, and possibly also the greater part of the Bombay contingent."[3]

Tipu remained at Periapatam until March 11 and then marched to Seringapatam to refit. From there he set out to meet Harris who was advancing on his capital. Harris had left the neighbourhood of Bangalore on the 16th and had reached Kankanhalli on the 21st. He had then marched to the Maddur river, which he had reached on the 24th, and encamped on its eastern bank.

Until now Harris had met with practically no resistance. Purnaiya and Sayyid Saheb had been left by Tipu to prevent Harris's advance, but as they had entered into an understanding with the English, they remained inactive and allowed the enemy to march without any

[1] Muhammad Raza was the son of Haidar's maternal uncle, Ibrahim Saheb. He was the head of *mir miran* (*zumra*) *cutchehri* and was commonly known as Benki Nawab because of the devastation he had caused in Malabar. *Benki* means fire in Kanarese.

[2] Fortescue, iv, part 11, p. 728.

[3] Gleig, *Munro*, i, p. 217.

hindrance.[1] The English army was overloaded with equipment, carrying an enormous train of battering cannon, and provisions and stores for a campaign to be carried on without an open line communication. There were 60,000 bullocks in Harris's army and 36,000 bullocks in the Nizam's army. There were even more bullocks, camels and elephants belonging to private individuals. To all this was added a host of *bunjaras* and camp followers who outnumbered the fighting men by five to one.[2] "The whole of this gigantic mass required forage and in the first few days after entering Mysore it seemed that the task of providing would break the whole expedition down."[3] From the outset the bullocks began to die in large numbers. In consequence, by March 18, such large quantities of military stores had to be destroyed as to excite some degree of alarm.[4] Since sufficient measures had not been taken for "the orderly movement of this vast, unwieldy machine,"[5] the army's progress was very slow—it averaged about five miles a day—and several times it had to halt for a whole day. According to Harris, after he left Kelamangalum, his army "showed deficiency in the bullock department. .This deficiency crippled our movements. Our marches have been tedious and short; our progress slow and halts frequent."[6] Under the circumstance, if the Mysoreans had shown the same activity and skill which they had displayed against Cornwallis in his march on Seringapatam in May, 1791, they would have easily captured the English army's baggage and military stores, thus retarding its progress until the commencement of the rains. But the Mysore commanders, being in league with the English, did nothing to prevent their advance. During Cornwallis's first march on Seringapatam, the Mysore cavalry, by hanging on to his rear and flanks, and by destroying forage on the route, had caused the failure of his enterprise. But in the present campaign, no difficulties were created for the English, although conditions were much more favourable for the Mysoreans than before owing to the disorganised and unwieldy state of the enemy's army.

When after his return from the attack upon Stuart, Tipu left Seringapatam to meet Harris, he made his first movement on the middle road; but on hearing that the English were following the

[1] Kirmani, pp. 383-4; *Tarikh-i-Tipu*, f. 109b. See for more details at the end of this chapter. The Persian sources do not mention the presence of Sayyid Saheb, but it is clear from the English and French accounts that he had also been left by Tipu to oppose the English.

[2] Owen, *Wellington's Despatches*, p. 59; Fortescue, iv part 11, pp. 729-30

[3] Fortescue, iv, part 11, p. 730.

[4] Beatson, p. 65. According to Arthur Wellesley the failure of the bullocks increased in such an alarming manner that by the time the English army reached the neighbourhood of Bangalore, it was apprehended that it might have to take post there and defer operations to another season. (*Wellington's Despatches*, p. 61).

[5] Mill, vi, p. 83.

[6] W.P., B.M. 13727, Harris to Wellesley, April 5, 1799, f. 47b.

route via Kankanhalli, he marched to Malvalli, and on March 18 encamped on the Maddur river, where he was joined by Purnaiya and Sayyid Saheb. He occupied a commanding position which would have enabled him to prevent Harris from crossing the river. But preferring to fight in the open instead of in a woody country, he withdrew towards Malvalli. The result was that the English forces crossed the river without any difficulty. Lushington, Harris's biographer, wrote: "The efficient state of the Mysore gun cattle, and the miserable condition of the Carnatic bullock, precluded all idea of a successful pursuit of Tipu's army, and this gave him the confidence to venture upon the experiment of this battle on the highland of Malvalley, a finer field of action it would be difficult to find."[1]

After passing the river, the English encamped five miles east of Malvalli, and early next morning advanced towards it. On approaching the intended ground of encampment, they saw Tipu's army drawn up on a height. Harris's object was to avoid action and reach Seringapatam as soon as possible. But the advanced picquets being attacked by the Mysoreans and more troops being sent to their aid, a general action ensued. Tipu attacked the English right with his cavalry, which he himself led, supported by his infantry. "The charge was prepared with deliberate coolness and executed with great spirit;" nevertheless, it was repelled, although many European horsemen fell on the bayonets.[2] At the same time that Tipu's cavalry charged the English right, a large body of Mysore infantry advanced against the English left which was under Colonel Wellesley. But this attack too was repulsed. The retreating troops were pursued by Floyd's cavalry which killed many of them.[3] It now appeared that Tipu would make a stand on another height occupied by his second line, but actually that move was intended to cover the retreat. According to Arthur Wellesley, in this action Tipu's "troops behaved better than they have ever known to behave. His infantry advanced, and almost stood the charge of bayonets of the 33rd, and his cavalry rode at General Baird's European brigade. He did not support them as he ought, having drawn off his guns at the moment we made our attack, and even pushed forward these troops to cover the retreat of his guns. This is the cause of the total destruction of the troops he left behind him...."[4] Arthur Wellesley's criticism is undoubtedly correct, but

[1] Lushington, *Life of Harris*, p. 283.
[2] Wilks, ii, p. 714.
[3] Lushington, *Life of Harris*, p. 287.
[4] Owen, *Wellington's Despatches*, p. 62. Chappuis also says that Tipu's defeat was due to the wrong disposition of his army which led to the loss of 2,000 to 3,000 of his troops (A.N., C[2]305). According to Harris, Tipu lost 2,000 killed and wounded (W.P., B.M. 13727, Harris to Wellesley, April 5, 1799, ff. 48a *seqq*).

it must be remembered that Tipu's failure in the engagement was also due to the treachery of his officers. We have already seen how Purnaiya and Sayyid Saheb had conducted themselves. It was unlikely that on this occasion they should have shown any energy and enterprise. According to Kirmani, Qamar-ud-din Khan, instead of attacking the English with his cavalry, as directed by the Sultan, fell upon a body of Mysoreans and put them all into disorder.[1] Under the circumstance Tipu's defeat was inevitable.

Immediately after this action, Tipu marched in order to place himself on the rear of Harris, expecting that he would advance by the same road which had been followed by Cornwallis in 1791. But Harris, learning that forage on this road had been completely destroyed, while that on the north bank of the Cauvery was preserved by Tipu for his own army, decided to cross at the ford of Sosile, where the passage was not likely to be opposed. Besides the acquisition of cattle, forage and grain derived from this movement, it had also other advantages. It would facilitate the junction with the Bombay army, and make it easy to obtain supplies from Coorg and Baramahal. Moreover, it was felt that an attack on Seringapatam from the west would have a greater chance of success. By March 30 the whole army with its equipment had crossed the ford,[2] without meeting the least resistance. As expected, Harris found abundant forage and some draft and carriage cattle. He also found a number of slaughter cattle and sheep for the European troops and some grain for their followers,[3]

Harris left Sosile on the 1st April. On the 2nd, a favourable opportunity to attack the English presented itself to Tipu because their artillery had not yet arrived on account of bad roads. And actually Tipu decided upon an action, but cancelled it as he was told that the day was inauspicious. The result was that Harris advanced by easy marches, and, on April 7, took up his position within two miles of Seringapatam.[4]

Tipu now thought that Harris would cross into the island. He therefore prepared to prevent this, and after crossing at the ford of Arikere, took up his position near the village of Chendgal. But Harris, instead of trying to enter the island, made a circuit to the left and reached the ground occupied by Abercromby in 1792. The army took up its position about two miles from the western face of the fort. After crossing the Cauvery it had taken Harris five days to cover twenty-eight miles. His advance had been miserably slow, and yet there had been no harassment. The Mysore horse had appeared in his front,

[1] Kirmani, p. 385.
[2] M.R., Mly. Sundry Book, 109A—1709, Harris to Wellesley, April 5, 1799 pp. 85-6.
[3] W.P., B.M. 13727, Harris to Wellesley, March 31, 1799, f. 46a.
[4] A.N., C²305, Official Report of Chappuis, Carton 146, n: 35.

but had showed themselves "less active than usual in devastation."[1]

The English occupied a strong position. But there were beyond it several posts which were held by the Mysoreans and gave shelter to their rocket men who caused great annoyance to the English. On the evening of May 5 Harris sent two parties to seize the posts. The one under Colonel Shaw was to attack the post at the aqueduct which in its winding course protected much of the English front. The other party was sent under Colonel Wellesley to occupy the Sultanpet Tope. Both marched at sunset, but owing to the stiff resistance offered by the Mysoreans, and the deadly fire from the fort, the enterprise failed, and the English retreated with considerable loss. But the next morning a larger force was sent which succeeded in occupying the posts. In consequence, the English established themselves in strong positions within 1,800 yards of the fort.[2]

On the 6th Floyd set out to bring Stuart advancing from the west. On being informed of this, Tipu despatched Qamar-ud-din Khan to intercept his march and prevent the junction being effected between the two armies. But the Khan ignored Tipu's orders and remained inactive,[3] with the result that Floyd succeeded in joining the Bombay army which, having crossed the Cauvery, easily reached Seringapatam. Stuart, however, being himself short of supplies, had not brought any for the General. By the 15th it was discovered that there was also a great shortage of provisions in Harris's army. On the 18th Harris wrote to Wellesley: "This morning, on measuring the rice to ascertain the exact quantity in store, we discovered that from loss or fraud, only eighteen days' rice at half-allowance is in camp for fighting men. Unless Col. Read's *bunjaras* arrive before the 6th May, the army will be without provisions."[4] Harris further wrote: "There is plenty of provisions in the Coorga country, but we have no means to convey or escort them hither."[5] In his Diary also Harris speaks of a shortage of supplies, and says that if they did not arrive under Colonel Read by the 6th, the army would starve.[6]

This shortage of supplies compelled Harris to expedite the attack on the fort; and, according to the advice of the engineers, the north-west angle, being the weakest side, was selected for an attack. At first efforts were directed to dislodge the Mysoreans from the positions they were still holding outside the walls of the fort. The English continued to make steady progress in spite of the determined resistance

[1] Fortescue, iv, part 11, p. 734.
[2] M.R., Mly. Sundry Book, 109A, Harris to Wellesley, April 7, 1799, pp. 92-3.
[3] Kirmani, pp. 387-8; *Tarikh-i-Tipu*, ff. 110a-b.
[4] M.R., Mly. Sundry Book, 109A, Harris to Wellesley, April 16, 1799, p. 96.
[5] *Ibid.*
[6] Lushington, *Life of Harris*, p. 315; see also Wilkin, *Life of Baird*, p. 61, and Kirmani, p. 392.

of the Mysoreans. On the night of May 26 the Mysore posts were attacked and occupied after an obstinate contest which lasted nearly the whole night. This was a valuable acquisition for Harris, because it furnished the ground on which the breaching batteries were to be erected.

Meanwhile, Tipu, realising the danger to his capital, again tried for a settlement with the English. He had sent a letter to Harris on April 9, protesting against the invasion of Mysore and enclosing with it Wellesley's last letter to himself. But Harris had not given any satisfactory reply; he had only asked Tipu to refer to the letters which Wellesley had written to him. On the evening of April 20 Tipu again wrote to Harris, reiterating his desire to remain on amicable terms with the English, and proposed to send a *wakil* to negotiate a settlement.[1] Harris replied on the 22nd, transmitting the draft of a preliminary treaty which the Sultan was required to accept, if he desired peace.

Wellesley had instructed Harris on February 22 to send to the Sultan the draft (A) before opening the batteries on the fort of Seringapatam. But after opening the batteries the draft (B), which contained much harsher terms than the first, was to be sent.[2] Nevertheless, the draft of a preliminary treaty, which Harris sent to Tipu on April 22, was drawn up according to the second and severest set of terms, although the breaching batteries had not yet being erected. Tipu was required to cede one-half of his kingdom, to pay two crores of rupees as indemnity—one crore immediately and the other within six months—to surrender four of his sons and four of his generals, to be named by Harris, as hostages. These conditions should be accepted within twenty-four hours and the hostages and the money to be delivered within forty-eight hours. If Tipu did not accept them, Harris would hold himself at liberty to extend his demand even to the possession of the fort of Seringapatam, until the conclusion of the treaty of peace.[3]

Tipu considered these terms very harsh, so he turned them down. He remembered the treaty of peace which the English had imposed on him in 1792 after they had secured his sons and his money; he was certain that now he would have to submit to an even more humiliating peace, if he agreed to the English proposals. But even if Tipu had accepted them, Harris would still have broken off with him on some pretext or other, for Wellesley had instructed him that Tipu's power, should be, "if possible, utterly destroyed."[4] Thus the terms which Harris had offered to the Sultan were only intended as a cover for completing his preparations to assault the fort.

[1] M.R., Mly. Sundry Book, 109A, p. 101.
[2] M.R., Mly. Cons., Feb. 22, 1799, vol. 254A, pp. 3383-97.
[3] M.R., Mly. Sundry Book, 109A, Harris to Tipu, April 22, 1799, pp. 104-5.
[4] M.R., Mly. Cons., April 23, 1799, vol. 254A, p. 3433.

On the morning of April 28 Tipu sent another letter to Harris, signifying his intention to despatch two persons for a conference with the English representatives.[1] To this Harris replied that no modification of the draft already sent would be made; that ambassadors were, therefore, unnecessary, and would not be received unless they were accompanied by the hostages; and that only until three o'clock the next day would time be allowed for an answer.[2]

Meanwhile military operations had not been suspended. From the batteries, which began to be erected from April 28, fire was opened for effecting a breach. On May 3 a breach was caused. But although it was incomplete, Harris decided to assault at once. Indeed, he had no other alternative, for his supplies had fallen very low and his army was almost starving. Harris himself admitted to Captain Malcolm that "the European sentry over my tent is so weak from want of food and exhaustion that a sepoy can push him down."[3] The possession of Seringapatam had thus become necessary to the existence of the English army. But realising that it would not be easy for his starving troops to capture the fort, Harris sought the assistance of Mir Sadiq who, like Purnaiya and Qamar-ud-din Khan, had been for some time past carrying on correspondence with the English against his master.

On the night of May 3 some officers crossed over to the glacis, examined the breach and the manner of attacking the fort.[4] It was probably on this occasion that it was arranged between the English officers and Mir Sadiq that the assault should take place at midday. The preparations for it were completed by the next morning. About 5,000 troops, of whom three-fifths were Europeans, who were to participate in the attack, were all in the trenches by daybreak, having been sent there to disarm suspicion. As the hour approached, Mir Sadiq withdrew the troops stationed at the breach under the pretext of distributing their pay.[5] There was no one to protest against such a measure. Sayyid Ghaffar, who was very loyal to the Sultan, had been unfortunately killed by a cannon ball. Immediately after the Sayyid was killed, the traitors made a signal from the fort by

[1] M.R., Mly. Sundry Book, 109A, p. 111.

[2] *Ibid.*, p. 112.

[3] Lushington, *Life of Harris*, p. 332.

[4] Ibid., p. 325; Owen, *Wellington's Despatches*, p. 65.

[5] Kirmani, p. 390; Wilks, ii, p. 739, says that Nadim, the Commandant, made an issue of pay to some of the troops, which caused their absence at the time of the assault. Chappuis says that the troops were withdrawn under various pretexts. (C²305 Official Report of Chappuis).

See also Ahmad b. Muhammad Ali b. Muhammad Baqar, *Mirat-ul-Ahwal* (neither paged foliod). Tehran University Central Library, MS. 5716. The author arrived in India early in May 1805 and visited both north and south India. He says that a wicked Qizil-bash, evidently referring to Mir Sadiq, was responsible for the fall of Seringapatam. The traitor was killed.

holding out a white handkerchief to the English troops who were assembled in the trenches, waiting for such a signal.[1] At once the English troops moved. "From the trench to the bank of the river was but 100 yards. The river itself, rocky and varying in depth from ankle-deep to waist-deep, measured 280 yards more; beyond that again was a stone wall, then a ditch some 60 yards wide, and finally the breach."[2] Moreover, the passage was fully exposed to a heavy fire from the fort.[3] Yet a handful of men succeeded in less than seven minutes, from the period of issuing from the trenches, in planting the British flag on the summit of the breach.[4]

After capturing the breach, the English force divided itself into two columns. The right column commanded by Colonel Sherbrooke was directed to attack the southern rampart, while the left column, under Colonel Dunlop, was directed to attack the northern rampart. The officers commanding were to meet at the eastern rampart. There was no resistance to the advance of the right column. As Beatson observes: "The three cavaliers within the south face, from which it was apprehended the right attack would have received great annoyance, fortunately made no resistance. Those stupendous works were abandoned; the right attack succeeded in getting possession of them, and of the whole of the southern ramparts; and within less than an hour, arrived upon the eastern face of the fort."[5]

The left column, on the other hand, was met with severe resistance. Dunlop was disabled by a sword-cut on the wrist in a personal combat upon the breach with one of Tipu's officers, but his men succeeded in taking possession of the north-west bastion. After this, however, the resistance to the advance of the column was so stubborn that it failed to make any progress. This was because Tipu himself, having heard of the assault, had arrived to rally his troops. All the leading English officers were either killed or disabled. Lieutenant Farquhar then put himself at the head of the column, but he too was instantly killed. The loss of the English would have been still greater and they would have given way, if it had not been for some fresh troops which came to their rescue.

What happened is that, when Baird had first surmounted the breach, he had discovered a second formidable ditch full of water and

[1] Kirmani, p. 391. Magnac, a Frenchman who was in the service of Tipu, informed Dubuc that at one o'clock, on the signal given by Mir Sadiq, the assault was made. (B.N., *Nouvelle Acquisition* MSS. 9368, undated, ff. 484b-85a). Chappuis also says in his official report that Mir Sadiq gave a signal to the British troops. But according to him the time was 1-30 P.M.

[2] Fortescue, iv, part 11, p. 741. See also, I.O.MSS. Eur., F. 66, Harris to Dundas, May 15, 1799, f. 66.

[3] *Ibid.*

[4] Allan, p. 75; Beatson, p. 127; Wilks, ii, p. 743.

[5] Beatson, p. 129.

further works beyond it. These divided the outer from the inner rampart. "Good God!" the General had cried, "how shall we get over these?" Fortunately Captain Goodall with a detachment had managed to cross the inner ditch by means of a plank, and had thus got on the inner rampart.[1] On this occasion also there had been no opposition. According to Beatson, "so entirely abandoned was the inner or second rampart, and the cavalier, that a small party of only eight or ten men of his Majesty's regiment, crossing a *batardeau* in the inner ditch, a little to the right of the breach, got possession of the west cavalier."[2] The detachment had then advanced parallel to the main body of the column, and had come to the relief of the left column. The Mysoreans being exposed to the fire coming both from the inner and from the outer ramparts, became panic-stricken and fled. Major Lambton, who now took the command of the left column, pushed them to the north-eastern angle. Some escaped, but thousands were put to the sword. After the capture of the northern rampart, Lambton joined Baird near the eastern gate. Thus in one hour, with the exception of the palace, the ramparts and every part of the fortifications had been occupied by the English.[3]

Ever since the English appeared before Seringapatam, Tipu remained encamped on the ramparts varying his position according to the movements of the enemy. At first he caused a tent to be pitched on the south face; then he moved to the western angle; and finally, when the English opened their first batteries, he fixed his headquarters on the northern face in a small stone *choultry*, where he dined and slept, and from where he gave directions to his officers for the defence of the fort. On the morning of May 4 Tipu mounted his horse, and after inspecting the breach in the wall, gave instructions to the pioneers to repair it. He then went to the palace to have a bath. In the morning, the Hindu and Muslim astrologers warned him that, since it was an inauspicious day for him, he should remain with the army till the evening, and in order to avert disaster he should give alms. After his bath, therefore, he gave money and cloth to the poor who had assembled there. To the chief priest of Chennapatna, he presented an elephant, a bag of oil seeds and two hundred rupees. To the other Brahmins he gave a black bullock, a milch buffalo, a male buffalo, a black she-goat, a jacket of coarse black cloth, a cap of the same material, ninety rupees, and an iron pot filled with oil; and previous to the delivery of this last article, he held his head over the pot in order to see the reflection of his face and thereby avert

[1] Wilkin, *Life of Baird*, p. 68.

[2] Beatson, p. 129.

[3] Allan, p. 76. The author of *The Memoirs of Tippoo Sultaun*, p. 183, says that "in about half an hour the fire in the fort had entirely ceased, and the British flag was triumphantly displayed in every part of it."

misfortune.[1] He then returned to the *choultry*, and ordered his dinner. He had just begun eating when he received the news of Sayyid Ghaffar's death. Sayyid Ghaffar was in charge of the western angle of the fort, and was killed by a cannon shot while giving instructions to the pioneers to cut off the approach by the southern rampart. He was a brave and loyal officer and the Sultan was very much affected by the news of his death.[2] Tipu at once left eating, washed his hands and hastened towards the breach on horse-back.[3] But before he could reach it, the English had already hoisted their flag over it, and were advancing to seize the ramparts. However, the presence of the Sultan inspired his troops to resistance, and owing to this the enemy's left column received a set-back. But when the Mysoreans became exposed to the fire of the English detachments both from the inner and from the outer ramparts, it spread consternation among them and they fled.[4] Tipu's efforts to rally them were unsuccessful.

During the greater part of this fight Tipu had remained on foot, fighting like a common soldier. But after his troops became completely demoralised, he mounted his horse and rode to the sally-port of the water-gate. Wilks says that if Tipu wanted to escape it was easy, for the water-gate was near.[5] Beatson, on the other hand, states that the water-gate was so crowded that he could not make his way into the town.[6] But in reality the gate had been deliberately shut so that the Sultan might not be able to escape; and when he ordered the guards to open it, his order was not obeyed. Mir Nadim, the Commandant of the fort, stood on the roof of the gate, but he ignored his master.[7] Tipu then proceeded to the gate which led to the interior fortress. He had already been wounded, and before reaching the gate he received a second wound. Yet he pressed on. The English were pouring forth a destructive fire from the outer as well as from the inner ramparts on the Mysoreans who were crowding on both sides of the gate in order to escape. In attempting to pass the gateway Tipu received a third wound; he was shot through the left breast and his horse was killed under him. His attendants tried to remove him in a palanquin, but were unable to do so because the place was choked with the dead and the dying.[8] At this time Raja Khan, his personal attendant, advised

[1] Beatson, p. 162; Kirmani, p. 391.

[2] He had been an officer in the English Company's Madras army and had been taken prisoner along with Braithwaite on Feb. 18, 1782. After sometime he had been released and had entered Tipu's service.

[3] Kirmani, p. 390.

[4] Beatson, p. 130; Allan, p. 76.

[5] Wilks, ii, p. 746.

[6] Beatson, p. 164.

[7] Kirmani, pp. 391-2.

[8] Wilks, ii, pp. 746-7.

him to make himself known to the enemy. But he rejected the advice. He preferred death to falling a prisoner into the hands of the English.[1] Shortly after some English soldiers entered the gateway, and one of them seized his sword-belt which was very rich. Although half-fainting with loss of blood, he could not tolerate this insult, and seizing a sword, which lay within his reach, he made a cut at the soldier. The blow fell upon the latter's musket, so he made a second stroke at another soldier with more effect. But he was shot through the temple, and he fell dead.[2]

Meanwhile there was a shout of triumph, proclaiming that the two columns had seen each other and were about to meet. At this time the Mysoreans had become very panicky and were trying to escape from all sides. Some also tried to escape by the eastern or Bangalore Gate, but here the English troops began to massacre them, and they set fire to the gate. Large numbers perished in the fire, and those who survived fell victims to the bayonets of the enemy.[3]

After the ramparts were seized, it was decided to occupy the palace. Major Allan was, therefore, sent with a flag of truce to inform those within the palace that if they surrendered immediately their lives would be spared, but if they resisted no quarter would be given. On arriving before the palace, Allan communicated the message to the persons present on the balcony. Thereupon the Commandant, accompanied by two other men, descended by an unfinished part of the wall. Finding that they were reluctant over the question of surrender, Allan insisted on entering the palace himself and speaking to Tipu personally. Although he was told that the Sultan was not in the palace, he did not believe it, and entered by ascending the broken wall. He met the princes and asked them to open the gates. At first they refused, saying that this could not be done without the permission of their father who was not in the palace. But realising their helpless state, and after Allan had assured them of the protection of the life and honour of every one in the palace, they agreed to his proposal. When the gates were opened, Baird was already there waiting outside with a large body of troops. He did not enter, but ordered the princes to be brought to him. The princes did not wish to leave, but seeing that resistance would be useless, they came. Baird received them well, and shortly after sent them to Harris.[4]

After the princes were taken prisoners, it was decided to search

[1] Allan, p. 96; Beatson, p. 165.

[2] Beatson pp. 164-5.

[3] Fortescue, iv, part ii, p. 743. Fortescue says that the gate caught fire from some unknown cause. But in reality this must have been done by the English soldiers. According to the English accounts 10,000 Mysoreans perished in the storm. But this is an underestimate.

[4] Beatson, pp. 135-6; Allan, pp. 78-80.

Tipu in the palace where he was still supposed to be hidden. Some of the English troops entered the palace and searched it, but could not find any trace of the Sultan. The Commandant reassured the English that Tipu was not in the palace, and informed them that he had been wounded during the storm, and was lying in a gateway on the northern side of the fort. He even offered to conduct them to the spot. Major Baird and other officers accompanied him to the place which was covered with a heap of bodies, dead and wounded. With the help of a light Tipu's palanquin was found, and under it Raja Khan lay mortally wounded. It was he who pointed out the spot where Tipu had fallen. "When Tippoo was brought from under the gateway," wrote Major Allan, an eyewitness, "his eyes were open, and the body was so warm, that for a few moments Colonel Wellesley and myself were doubtful whether he was not alive; on feeling his pulse and heart, the doubt was removed. He had four wounds, three in the body, and one in the temple; the ball having entered a little above the right ear, and lodged in the cheek... His dress consisted of a jacket of fine white linen, loose drawers of flowered chintz, with a crimson cloth of silk and cotton round his waist; a handsome pouch with a red and green silk belt, hung across his shoulder; his head was uncovered, his turban being lost in the confusion of his fall; he had an amulet on his arm, but no ornament whatever... He had an appearance of dignity or perhaps of sterness in his countenance, which denoted him above the common order of people."[1] According to another observer, "the features were neither agitated by passion nor disfigured by the extinction of life—an uncommon degree of composure and serenity was spread over his face. The expression was gentle and contented. In fine, the countenance of the Sultan far from discovering any furious passions had a tranquil and courteous air for which he was distinguished when alive."[2]

The next day in the evening the funeral procession set out from the palace. The bier was borne by Tipu's personal attendants and escorted by four companies of Europeans. Prince Abdul Khaliq rode immediately behind the bier, followed by the principal officers of the court. "The streets through which the procession passed, were lined with inhabitants; many of whom prostrated themselves before the body, and expressed their grief by loud lamentations."[3] When the body reached the gate of the mausoleum at Lal Bagh, the troops presented arms, and after it was buried near the grave of Haidar Ali, 5,000 rupees were distributed among the poor who had followed the funeral procession. "To add to the solemnity of the scene, the

[1] Allan, pp. 80-1.

[2] National Library of Scotland (MS.), *Journal of the War with Tippoo*, 1799, pp. 178-79.

[3] *Ibid.*, p. 84; Beatson, p. 148.

evening closed with a most dreadful storm, attended with rain, thunder and lightning, by which two officers in the Bombay camp were killed, and many severely hurt."[1]

During the night of May 4 almost every house in the town was plundered by the English troops, a large number of buildings were set fire to, and the inhabitants were subjected to all kinds of atrocities. In fact, according to Arthur Wellesley, nothing could have exceeded what was done on that night.[2] The soldiers obtained so much booty that "every soldier had to relieve himself of the burden by throwing away a portion of it to any comrade that he could meet."[3] Jewels of the greatest value, bars of gold and silver were offered for sale by the soldiers in the camp.[4]

The soldiers also succeeded in entering the treasury in the palace, and carried away a vast amount of coin, and jewellery before they could be stopped. Among the valuables which they took away, one casket of jewels alone was worth Rs. 45,00,000. One soldier was related to have found Tipu's armlets, set with precious diamonds. He sold them to a Company's surgeon for 1,500 rupees, the surgeon sold them for a sum that brought him in £2,000 a year.[5] The plunder and rapine continued till the 6th when order was restored by Colonel Wellesley who was put in charge of Seringapatam. But in spite of these depredations there was still a priceless treasure left in the palace. There was a magnificent throne, a beautiful silver haudah, solid gold and silver plate, richly-jewelled matchlocks and swords, expensive carpets, bales of finest muslin and silk, and large quantities of jewels[6] There was also in the palace a valuable library consisting of about 2,000 volumes of Arabic, Persian, Urdu and Hindi manuscripts, dealing with History, *Fiqh*, Sufism, Medicine, *Hadis* and various other subjects.[7] A diamond star, some ornaments, and one of Tipu's swords were presented

[1] Beatson, p. 149; Allan, p. 84.

[2] Owen, *Wellesley's Despatches*, p. 771; see also Kirmani, p. 392. Kirmani says that Muslims were slaughtered, their property was looted and their women were violated. Kirmani is right, but the Hindus equally suffered. In the excitement of the moment and intoxicated with victory, the English troops could not have differentiated between Muslims and Hindus. According to Allan pp. 83-4, women of the family of Sayyid Saheb and Qamar-ud-din Khan were subjected to great indignities.

[3] Sastri, *Petrie Papers* (I.H.R.C., xviii).

[4] Owen, *Wellesley's Despatches*, p. 771.

[5] Dodwell, *The Nabobs of Madras*, p. 67.

[6] The price property found at Seringapatam consisted of specie valued at 16,74,350 star pagodas, and jewellery, gold and silver bullion valued at 25,00,000 star pagodas. In addition, there were 20 or more boxes, full of jewels, the contents of which were not valued because of the lack of experts. (W.P., B.M. 13670, f. 147a).

[7] For more details about Tipu's library, see Stewart, *A. Descriptive Catalogue of Tippoo's Oriental Library*, and *Islamic Culture*, xiv, No. 2; see also W.P., B.M 26583, ff. 34a-64b, for details of the MSS. in the library. The total number of MSS. was 1889.

to Wellesley on behalf of the English army. Another sword of Tipu was publicly presented by Harris to Baird, while the gilded tiger's head from the Sultan's throne was sent to adorn the treasures of Windsor Castle. Tipu's turban, one of his swords, and a sword of Morari Rao were sent to Cornwallis.[1] Harris received £1,42,902 from the total amount of prize-fund reckoned at £2,000,000.[2] Mir Alam was given one lakh of pagodas to be distributed among 6,000 of the Hyderabad cavalry. But both he and Nizam regarded this sum as too small compared to what the Company's troops had received, and were very dissatisfied.[3]

With the fall of Seringapatam the kingdom of Mysore lay at the feet of the English. It is true they had captured only the capital and some other minor forts, and that a large part of Mysore, including important forts like Chitaldrug and Sira, were still in the possession of the Mysoreans, but after the death of the Sultan there was no will to resistance left. Harris informed Ghulam Ali Khan, *mir sudur*, that if he helped the English in securing the surrender of Mysore forts, the Governor-General would confirm him in his *jagir* in perpetuity that he had held under Tipu and would also, in addition, grant him adequate compensation. Ghulam Ali Khan, thereupon, issued orders to the commandants to surrender their forts to the English. Gooty and Hulal alone resisted but were captured.[4] The other principal officers had already entered into secret engagements with the English, and now they formally surrendered to them. Abdul Khaliq, Tipu's second son, surrendered on the day after the fall of Seringapatam. Fath Haidar was, however, advised by Dhoondia and his father's loyal officers to continue the struggle. But deceived by the conciliatory language of Harris, and the assurances of some of his own officers that the victors would restore to him his father's kingdom, he did not take up arms, and threw himself on the mercy of the English.[5] Purnaiya was of the opinion that "Muslim interests were so much blended with every department of the State that any other arrangement could not reconcile troops and powerful class of inhabitants."[6] So he proposed that Fath Haidar should be placed on the throne of Mysore, but should be required to pay tribute to the English who should also be entitled to garrison such forts as they con-

[1] Allan, p. 101.

[2] This prize-fund also included the value of 920 pieces of ordnance, ammunition and military stores, which were at first reserved until the receipt of instructions from London, but afterwards on receipt of orders they were given to the army.

[3] M.R. Mly., Sundry Book, 109B—1799, Malcolm to Wellesley, June 14, 1799, p. 521.

[4] W.P., B.M. 13728, Harris to Wellesley, May 18, 1799, ff. 98a-b.

[5] Kirmani, pp. 394-5.

[6] M.R., Mly. Sundry Book, 109A—1799, Harris to Wellesley, May 12, 1799, pp. 130 *seqq.*

sidered strategically important. But Wellesley rejected the proposal on the ground that "such a settlement would have cherished in its bosom a restless and a powerful principle of its own dissolution."[1] Wellesley had, in fact, made up his mind, even before the invasion of Mysore, to destroy the power of Tipu and his house. There was thus no question of restoring the kingdom of Mysore to Fath Haidar. The princes were therefore given an annual allowance of 2,24,000 pagodas and sent away to reside in the fort of Vellore. After the Vellore Mutiny of 1807, in which the princes were suspected of having a hand, they were exiled to Calcutta, where some of their descendants still survive, eking out a miserable existence.

After the surrender of Tipu's sons and officers it was open to Wellesley to annex the entire Kingdom of Mysore. And nothing would have given him greater satisfaction. Moreover, he would be acting according to the wishes of Dundas who also favoured the annexation of Mysore. Having had enough experience of the evils of double government, Dundas was opposed to the restoration of the old Raja, who would be a mere cipher. He even desired that neither the Marathas nor the Nizam be given any territory. But if the Nizam insisted, he should be given cash or better still restored the Northern Cirkars.[2] Wellesley, however, could not follow such a course of action, because he knew that this "would have raised such a flame both at Hyderabad and at Poona as could hardly have been extinguished without another war."[3] He also did not want to divide the whole between the Company and the Nizam, because that would have made the latter powerful and would have aroused the jealousy of the Marathas.[4] He, therefore, decided to leave the central part of the Mysore kingdom intact and to hand it over to a descendant of the old ruling family of Mysore. The result of this would be, "as further security, to divide both at this moment and hereafter, the Hindoo and Mahomedan inhabitants of Mysore."[5] The bulk of what was left was to be divided between the Company and the Nizam, and a small portion was to be offered to the Marathas.

This was a very astute settlement, for it made the English masters of the whole kingdom of Mysore. They obtained the whole of Kanara, Wynad, Coimbatore, Dharapuram and the town and island of Seringapatam. The Nizam got the districts of Gooty and Gurram-

[1] Martin, ii, p. 36. Mir Alam and Mushir-ul-mulk were also against the restoration of Tipu's family to the throne of Mysore. (N.A., See. Pro., June 24, 1799, Cons. No. 7).

[2] W.P., B.M. 37274, Dundas to Wellesley, Oct. 9, 1799, 247a *seqq.*; also Melville Papers, National Library of Scotland, Dundas to Wellesley, Oct. 9, 1799, ff. 64a *seqq.*

[3] *Ibid.*, p. 203.

[4] *Ibid.*, pp. 36, 74.

[5] W.P., B.M. 13667, Malcolm to Wellesley, May 31, 1799, ff. 78a-b.

konda and a part of the district of Chitaldrug. The Peshwa, having refused to agree to the English terms, the districts of Sunda and Harpanahalli, which had been offered to him, were also divided between the Nizam and the Company. The Nizam, however, was not destined to enjoy his new acquisitions long, because in 1800 he ceded all these to the Company. The kingdom which was set aside for the Raja also became a British possession. Owing to the treaty which, under Wellesley's pressure, the Raja signed with the Company, he became virtually a cipher and the entire sovereignty of his country was assumed by the English. As Mill wrote: "The Raja was a species of screen, put up to hide, at once from Indian and from European eyes, the actual aggrandisement which the British territory had received."[1]

The overthrow of Tipu not only brought huge territorial gains to the English, it in fact made them "paramount in India."[2] Tipu had been the most formidable opponent whom the British ever faced in India, but now there was no one left to challenge their supremacy. While Plassey had established the Company as one of "the country powers," the fall of Seringapatam made them in fact the "Power paramount."[3] One English correspondent went even to the extent of saying that, as a result of this event, "the Empire of the East is at our feet."[4] And Scott observed: "The fall of Seringapatam, and the far more consequential fall of Tipu Sahib taken together was the greatest event that ever happened since the admission of Europeans into India."[5]

The Marathas had joined the English against Tipu in the Third Anglo-Mysore War, but they had remained neutral in the last war. They never seriously realised that the existence of Tipu was their only protection against the English designs of aggrandisement. It was only after Tipu's fall that they awoke to the gravity of the situation. When Baji Rao heard the news, he is reported to have said that Tipu's death had been to him like "the loss of his right arm."[6] Nana too was affected by the news and remarked: "Tipu is finished; the British power has increased; the whole of east India is already theirs; Poona will now be the next victim. Evil days seem to be ahead. There seems to be no escape from destiny."[7]

But these were after all the fruits of Nana's own policy.

*Causes of the Fall of Seringapatam*

The fort of Seringapatam was strongly built and possessed formid-

[1] Mill, vi, p. 116.

[2] Owen, *Wellesley's Despatches*, p. xcii.

[3] Thompson and Garratt, *Rise and Fulfilment of British Rule in India*, p. 206.

[4] Auber, *Rise and Progress of the British Power in India*, ii, p. 192.

[5] Philips, *The Correspondence of David Scott*, ii, p. 256.

[6] Home Miscellaneous Series, 574, p. 598, cited in Gupta *Baji Rao II and the East India Company*, p. 59.

[7] Cited in Sardesai, *New History of the Marathas*, iii, p. 354.

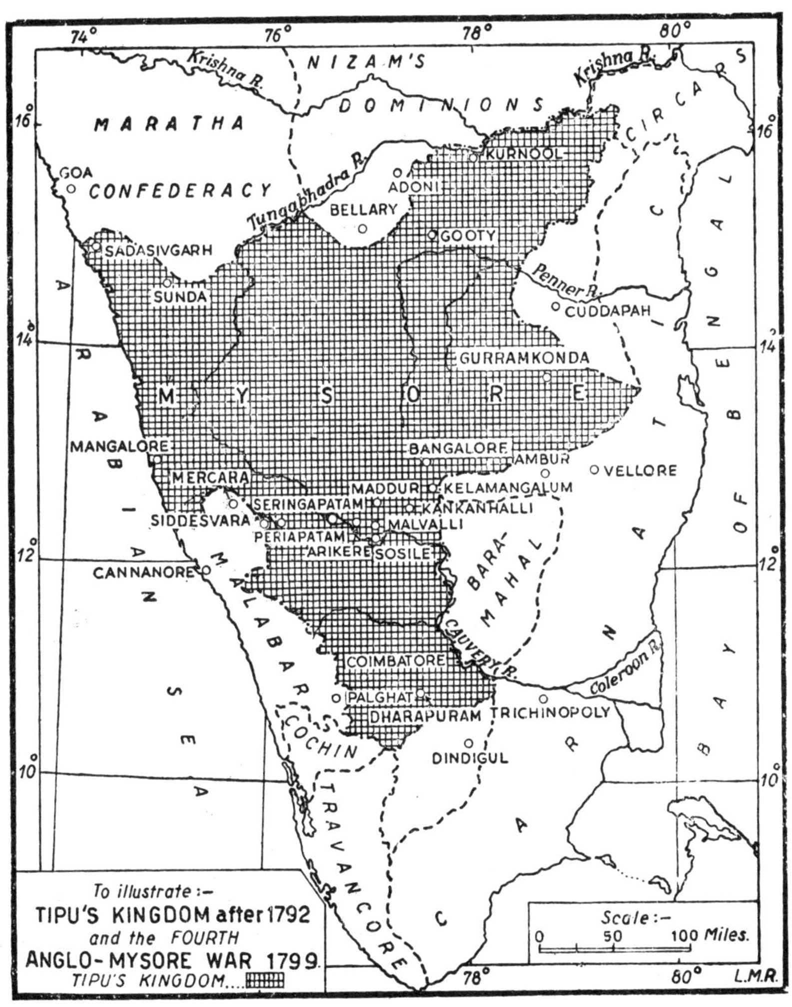

To illustrate :-
TIPU'S KINGDOM after 1792
and the FOURTH
ANGLO-MYSORE WAR 1799
TIPU'S KINGDOM....

able fortifications. It had a garrison of 21,839 men—13,739 regular infantry within and 8,100 in the entrenchments—and possessed ammunition and provisions sufficient to withstand a long siege. Since 1792 Tipu had considerably strengthened the fort to the south, east and north. To the north-west angle an entire new bastion of European construction had been added, and a new inner or second rampart having a deep ditch extending the whole length of the north face had nearly been completed. With such a large garrison and such fortifications the fort was capable of withstanding a long siege. Yet it had been seized by almost starving troops in less than two hours. This was because hardly any resistance had been offered to them. As Lushington observes: "There was nothing like that lengthened, awful and doubtful struggle for victory which had been anticipated in the storming of a fortress, whose works are, even in their ruins, still stupendous to look at."[1] Sherbrooke's troops did not encounter any opposition although, as Fortescue says, "there were strongholds which, in the hands of a few resolute men, could have wrought great havoc among them!"[2] Similarly there was no opposition to the English advance along the inner rampart. That was why the English loss had been very slight. In fact, the whole loss very little exceeded that of one of the preceding days.[3] The only troops which put up a fight were those led by Tipu in person. But they failed to turn the tide of war in their favour because, before the Sultan could reach the breach, the English had already consolidated their position on the ramparts. The reason why no resistance had been offered to the English was, as has already been pointed out,[4] that some of the Mysore officers had entered into league with them against Tipu.

We have seen that Tipu committed a tactical mistake at Malvalli. He also failed to display the same vigour and energy in opposing the march of Harris on his capital that he had done in the Third Anglo-Mysore War against Cornwallis. When the siege of Seringapatam began, then, too, he did not show any marked activity. Since the season was sufficiently advanced, he should have thrown every obstacle in order to prolong the siege. Instead there was indolence and supineness in the fort. The efforts made to stockade the breach were trifling, and no attempt was made to bring cannon to bear upon the breach. These were, indeed, serious mistakes. Yet the main cause of the fall of Seringapatam was the treachery of some of the principal Mysore officers who had entered into league with the English.[5]

[1] Lushington, *Life of Harris*, p. 441.
[2] Fortescue, iv, part ii, p. 742.
[3] Lushington, *Life of Harris*, p. 443.
[4] See pp. 313-14, 316 *supra*
[5] National Library of Scotland (MS.), *Journal of the War with Tippoo*, 1799, pp. 190-91.

Before Harris opened the campaign against Mysore, he was instructed by Wellesley to form a Commission consisting of Colonels Wellesley, Close, Agnew and Captain Malcolm, with Captain Macaulay as Secretary. The task of the Commission was to spread disaffection among Tipu's subjects and to win them over to the English side by propaganda, offers of money or territory. A large number of Mahdavis, who had been exiled by Tipu, were employed by Wellesley as irregular horse, and it was expected that they would help the Commission by their contacts with the people in Mysore.[1] The Commission was required to win over Mir Sadiq and Purnaiya, who "would become useful instruments in establishing a new government."[2] And Qamar-ud-din was to be won over by promising him the nawabship of Cuddapah.[3] The Commission was also to get in touch with the adherents of the old ruling family of Mysore. And lastly, it was required to incite the Muslim inhabitants of Mysore. This was to be done by using those passages from the Caliph's manifesto and letter to Tipu "which expose the character of the French Republic, and the outrages committed by the French against the acknowledged head of the Mohammedan church."[4]

Secret negotiations between some of Tipu's principal officers and the allies had been going on for a long time. Realising that the star of of the English was in the ascendant, and that sooner or later Tipu's power would be overthrown, they had made up their minds to come to terms with their future masters before it might be too late. According to the reports of the Company's secret agents in Mysore, in 1797 the correspondence of Mir Sadiq, Purnaiya, Qamar-ud-din Khan and that of some other officers with the English, the Nizam, and the Marathas was intercepted. The Brahmins, who were implicated in the plot, were executed, while Mir Sadiq and Purnaiya were imprisoned.[5] However, after they had retracted and pledged

[1] The Mahdavis were living in the neighbourhood of Hyderabad after being expelled by Tipu. Agreement was signed between their leader, Jafar Khan, who had been a member of the embassy that Tipu sent to Constantinople in 1786, and the Company. The latter agreed to employ him and his 200 horsemen on a monthly salary of Rs. 12,500. At the end of the war Jafar Khan and his followers would be conferred upon with marks of favour in accordance with their services. Similar terms were granted to other Mahdavi chiefs. (M.R., Mly. Cons., Feb. 21, 1799, vol. 254a, pp. 3354-60; also W.P., B.M. 13668, Kirkpatrick to Wellesley Jan. 1799, ff. 20b-22b, 23a *seqq.*

[2] W.P., B.M. 13665, Political Commission on General Harris's Campaign, f. 44a.

[3] *Ibid.*

[4] M.R., Mly. Cons., Feb. 22, 1799, vol. 254A, pp. 3334 *seqq.*

[5] N.A., Pol. Pro., July 10, 1797, Cons. Nos. 20, 24; *Ibid.*, July 17, Cons. No. 2. Since Mir Sadiq and Purnaiya had acquired considerable property, and Tipu's future was uncertain, they began intrigues with his enemies. Mir Sadiq "was made the instrument by money of effecting the escape of the raja when Cornwallis invaded Mysore." From this period onwards Mir Sadiq kept himself in touch with the English. (see W.P., M.B. 13665, Webbe to Wellesley by, f. 43a).

their loyalty to the Sultan, they were released and reinstated in their posts. Nevertheless, they did not desist from their treasonable activities. In the middle of 1798 Qamar-ud-din Khan wrote to Mushir-ul-mulk, the Nizam's Prime Minister, that he was ready to hand over Tipu to him provided he was promised the province of Cuddapah as a free gift in perpetuity. But Mushir-ul-mulk was prepared to grant him only a pension of ten lakhs of rupees annually.[1] From the subsequent events it appears that Qamar-ud-din was in the end promised the *jagir* of Gurramkonda on condition that he should help the English in an Anglo-Mysore War. As we have seen he did help them by not offering any resistance to their advance; so, after the fall of Seringapatam, he was awarded the *jagir* of Gurramkonda by the Nizam "without the least hesitation."[2]

Another person who entered into communication with the English was Shaikh Shihab-ud-din, commonly known as Sady Beherry, an influential Moplah who was Tipu's revenue officer in the Mangalore area and had acted as his representative in the demarcation of boundaries between the Mysore kingdom and the Company's territories on the west coast. He promised the English that he would promote their cause on the Malabar coast with the help of Tipu's principal officers in other parts of his kingdom, and informed them that, in future, correspondence with him was to be carried on via Coorg through Chokra Musa, a Moplah merchant of Tellicherry.[3]

The existence of traitors in Mysore was acknowledged even by Wellesley, who wrote on February 13, 1799: "I have already received intimations from various parts of his (Tipu's) dominions, and from his principal ministers and officers, which promise considerable advantage in the prosecution of hostilities against him."[4] Again, he wrote on February 22: "I have reason to believe that many of the tributaries, principal officers, and many other subjects of Tippoo Sultan, are inclined to throw off the authority of that prince, and to place themselves under the protection of the Company and their allies."[5] In the same letter he referred to "a certain secret negotiation which has been opened by Meer Allum,"[6] and about which Captain Malcolm would inform the Commission.

There is further evidence of fifth column activity inside the fort.

[1] NA., Sec. Pro., Sept. 10, 1798, Kirkpatrick to Wellesley, Aug. 7, Cons. No. 32. Kirkpatrick suspected the genuineness of the letter, but Mir Alam and Mushir-ul-mulk believed it to be genuine. See also W.P., B.M. 12588, Kirkpatrick to Wellesley, Aug. 5, 1798, No. 31 and No. 32.

[2] N.A., Sec. Pro., June 17, 1799, Cons. No. 21.

[3] W.P., B.M. 13665, Uthoff and Mahony to Wellesley, Dec. 18, 1799, ff. 17a *seqq*; also Scottish Record Office, Wellesley to Dundas, March 16, 1799, iv/249/22.

[4] Martin, *Wellesley's Despatches*, i, p. 437.

[5] *Ibid.*, p. 442.

[6] *Ibid.*, p. 446, Mir Alam was also deputed by Wellesley to win over Tipu's subjects. (N.A., Mly Cons., Feb. 22, 1799, vol. 254A, p. 3332).

According to Munro, Tipu's principal officers concealed from their master that a breach had been made. But one of his servants (probably it was Sayyid Ghaffar), impatient at hearing the false reports brought to the Sultan, informed him that a breach had been effected, and that soon it would be practicable.[1] On the morning of the day the fort was stormed, Tipu seemed to have examined the breach, but did not think that any attack would be made for a day or two, and his officers encouraged him in this belief by observing that the resources of Seringapatam were great.[2]

The folk songs called *lavanis* in Kannada refer to the conspiracy which some of the Mysore ministers had organised for the overthrow of their master.[3] The correspondence of William Petrie of the Madras Council also shows that Seringapatam fell because of fifth column activity. In a letter to a friend in England Petrie wrote: "You will hear every event and circumstance of this unparalleled war attributed to the sole cause of the invincible valour and prowess of our troops. It is natural for military men to look for no other cause. Of course this is a theme on which I am silent here and on which I shall speak and write with great caution and reserve elsewhere. I am possessed of much information on this curious edifying event, which is still lodged in my mind and from whence I may never have leisure to extract it, before many of the most important traces are erased from the tablets of my memory. But I never can forget on how many slender hairs and threads the fortune of this great event has been suspended, almost any of which breaking would have dangerously retarded, if not entirely frustrated, the grand object of the measure."[4] Petrie did not openly speak of the treachery of Mysore officers, but from his reticence, and his reference to causes other than military, it is clear that the capture of the fort was facilitated by the Mysorean support which the English had obtained. Petrie was silent over this matter because he feared that it would detract from the glory of the English achievement.

From the above analysis it is clear that the fall of Seringapatam was facilitated by a conspiracy organised by some of the chief officers of the Mysore Government in concert with the English. In fact, this was the culmination of a series of plots which had been hatched again and again for the overthrow of Haidar and Tipu. In these Maharani Lakshmi Ammanni, the widow of Krishnaraja Wodeyar, played the most conspicuous part. Ever since Haidar had captured power, she had never ceased striving for the restoration of her family

[1] Gleig, *Munro*, i, p. 217. Kirmani, p. 389, says that Tipu was not told about the breach.

[2] National Library of Scotland (MS.), *Journal of the War with Tippoo Sultan*, 1799, p. 162.

[3] Sastri, *Petrie Papers* (I.H.R.C., xviii, p. 289).

[4] *Ibid.*, 294-5.

to the throne of Mysore. After Khande Rao's attempt against Haidar had failed, she turned to the English, and sent one Srinivas Rao as her emissary to Lord Pigot, the Governor of Madras.[1] The latter promised help, but could not do anything. The negotiations were revived when Pigot was reappointed Governor of Madras. The Rani assured him through her agent, Tirumala Rao, that in return for his support she would pay one crore of rupees towards the maintenance of the Company's army, and thirty lakhs as a reward to influential persons.[2] Bur owing to the arrest and dismissal of Pigot nothing came out of the talks. The Rani, however, remained in touch with the English, and when the Second Anglo-Mysore War broke out, Tirumala Rao, on her behalf, signed with them a treaty by which they pledged themselves to restore the kingdom of Mysore to her family. Several Mysore officers, who were in communication with Tirumala Rao, also promised to help the English in overthrowing Haidar. But the Company's forces did not succeed in defeating Haidar and Tipu, while the plot to seize the capital was foiled by the vigilance of Tipu's officers, and the conspirators were hanged.[3] When the Third Anglo-Mysore War broke out the Rani revived her activities, and entered into an agreement with General Medows.[4] But her efforts bore no fruit owing to the conclusion of the Treaty of Seringapatam (1792). In 1796 she incited Sir John Shore to declare war against Tipu, because, she argued, he had entered into an alliance with the French, and she assured the English of success.[5] But Shore was too much wedded to a policy of peace to listen to such advances. When Wellesley became Governor-General she began correspondence with him through her agent, Tirumala Rao, who was also in contact with some of the Sultan's chief officers.[6] Wellesley welcomed her overtures and entered into an agreement with her and with some of the principal Mysore officers for the subversion of Tipu's power.

Tipu was quite ignorant of the existence of any conspiracy against him. A few days before the fall of Seringapatam, when he found his capital surrounded on all sides and the walls of the fort battered, he sent for Monsieur Chappuis, and asked him what course he should follow. Chappuis advised the Sultan to retire to Sira or Chitaldrug, and from there to continue the struggle against the enemy. Chappuis

[1] *Mysore Pradhans*, p. 4; see also W.P., B.M. 13665, ff. 39a-42a, for a detailed account of the intrigues of the Raja's family with the English since the time of Haidar Ali.

[2] Shama Rao, *Modern Mysore* (*From the beginning to* 1868), p. 270.

[3] See pp. 35, 74, *supra*.

[4] See p. 179 *supra;* for more details see *Mysore Pradhans*, pp. 9, 10, 30,.

[5] Shama Rao, *Modern Mysore* (*From the beginning to* 1868), p. 271.

[6] W.P., B.M. 13627, Clive to Wellesley, Nov. 29, 1798, f. 70a. Henry Wellesley to Arthur Wellesley, Aug. 7, 1801; see also Hayavadana Rao, *Mysore Gazetteer*, ii, p. 2710, for the Rani's intrigues with Wellesley.

was prepared to defend the capital provided none of the Mysore officers interfered with him. If, on the other hand, Tipu wanted to conclude peace, the Frenchmen, who were in his service, would be prepared to be delivered to the English.[1]

Tipu's reply to Chappuis's proposition of surrendering the Frenchmen to the English was that, even if his whole kingdom were devastated by the enemy, he would not betray his friends who were strangers from a distant land. As regards the other two propositions, he asked the advice of his councillors. Mir Sadiq's advice was that the French were treacherous, and that if the fort were placed in their charge, they would immediately surrender it to the English. As regards evacuating the fort, Budr-uz-zaman Khan advised the Sultan against following such a course on the ground that, if he left, the garrison would lose heart and the fort would soon fall.[2] Tipu, nevertheless, decided to evacuate. He kept his family and treasure in readiness to leave at the shortest notice. Prince Fath Haidar was posted at the Karighatta hill, and was directed to cross into Shahr Ganjam in the night and remove the family and the treasure to Chitaldrug.[3] It appears from Kirmani's account that by this time Tipu had discovered the treacherous designs of some of his officers. He therefore prepared a list of the traitors, with Mir Sadiq heading it. All these persons were to be hanged the next evening. But Mir Sadiq came to know of it, and made arrangements to surrender the fort before Tipu's orders could be carried out.[4] Further, in order to prevent Tipu from escaping, he instructed his protégé Mir Nadim, Commandant of the fort, to keep the water-gate shut.[5]

As the price of the betrayal, the Mysore officers were generously rewarded by the English. Qamar-ud-din, "who from family, as well as character and conduct, merits attention in any general agreement that is adopted,"[6] received the *jagir* of Gurramkonda, while Purnaiya, who "appears to be an able man and has hitherto been useful,"[7] was made chief minister of the new Raja. Mir Sadiq, however, did not live to enjoy the fruits of his treachery. After perpetrating the foul deed, he tried to escape and join the English. But he was killed by the

[1] Kirmani, p. 388.
[2] *Ibid*, p. 389.
[3] *Ibid.*; *Tarikh-i-Tipu*, f. 111a.
[4] Kirmani, p. 390. Kirmani says that Tipu handed over the list to Sayyid Saheb, and while the latter was reading it in an open durbar, a servant of the palace (a *farrashi*) happened to cast a glance at the name of Mir Sadiq which was at the top, and he reported this to him. Kirmani seems to be prejudiced in favour of Sayyid Saheb. It is quite possible that the latter himself sent the information to Mir Sadiq. It is strange that he should have read such an important and confidential paper in a public place.
[5] *Ibid.*, p. 390.
[6] W.P., B.M. 13667, Malcolm to Wellesley, May 31, 1799, f. 79b.
[7] *Ibid.*

Mysore soldiers, who believed that he had betrayed the Sultan. They mangled his body in a shocking manner. Even after he was buried, his body was dug up and for over two weeks it was treated with insult by men, women and children, who assembled around it and threw filth on it. Strong measures had to be taken by the English to put a stop to this. Even now people, who revere Tipu's memory, while visiting Seringapatam, throw stones towards the spot where Mir Sadiq was killed.

CHAPTER XX

# ADMINISTRATION AND ECONOMY

## *The Nature of the Government*

Tipu, like other Indian rulers, was an autocrat. It is true that he consulted his chief civil and military officers on important matters, but he was not bound by their advice, and the final decision always rested with him. He was the supreme legislative, judicial and executive authority in his kingdom. He was his own foreign minister, and personally dictated all important correspondence. He was also his own commander-in-chief. During the time of war he commanded the principal army, and the generals whom he sent to fight on different fronts, had to act according to his instructions. He constituted the highest court of appeal, and dealt out justice to rich and poor alike.

Although there were no constitutional checks on Tipu's powers, this did not mean that he was an irresponsible ruler. On the contrary he had a high sense of duty to his office, and believed that his subjects "constitute a unique trust held for God, the Real Master."[1] Owing to this belief he spared no pains to promote the welfare of his people, and was busy from morning till evening with the affairs of the State. He personally supervised every department of the Government, and endeavoured to check the laxity, oppression and speculation of his officers by inflicting upon them exemplary punishments. In the words of Mackenzie: Tipu "invigorated the whole system by principles of good government, and by an economic management of material resources to which those of any neighbouring power bore no comparison.........Checking the frauds of intermediate agents by severe and exemplary punishments, the Sultan protected the raiyats, who were chiefly of Hindu religion, from the enormities of black collectors."[2]

But Tipu not merely wanted his officers to be honest in their official dealings, he also expected from them a high moral tone in their private life. Thus when he came to know that Arshad Beg, the *faujdar* of Malabar, had illicit relations with a courtesan, he rebuked him and insisted upon his renouncing the connection. Arshad resented this interference, and decided to proceed on a pilgrimage to Mecca. On Tipu's advice, however, he gave up the idea. The courtesan, who had been imprisoned, was exiled from the town.[3]

[1] O.R. No. 16, Tipu to Nizam.
[2] Mackenzie, ii, pp. 72-3.
[3] Kirkpatrick, p. 464.

The sphere of Mysore Government's activity under Tipu was much wider than that of other Indian States. While other rulers were merely interested in establishing law and order and in defending their countries from invasion, Tipu took upon himself, in addition to these, further responsibilities. Realising that the European nations owed their greatness to commerce and industry, he undertook the role of a trader, manufacturer, banker and money-changer. In this respect he closely resembled Muhammad Ali, the founder of modern Egypt.

In his zeal to promote the welfare of his people Tipu also adopted the role of a social reformer. He banned the use of liquor and all intoxicants in his kingdom, permitting only Lallée to open a shop in the camp for the French soldiers in the Mysore army. He prohibited persons of illegitimate or slave birth from marrying into respectable families. He forbade prostitution and the employment of female slaves in domestic service, and tried to stop the practice of polyandry in Malabar and Coorg.[1] In some parts of Malabar women did not cover themselves above the waist; so Tipu decreed that no woman should go out of her house naked.[2] He abolished the custom of human sacrifice which was practised in the temple of Kali Devi near Mysore town. In order to promote the prosperity of the peasants, he instructed his district officers to enforce economy upon the villagers who were accustomed to squander away their incomes upon marriages and festivals. A village was to spend no more than one per cent of its wealth on charities and festivals.[3]

Tipu's Government was highly centralised. He sent to his provincial and district officers detailed instructions which they were required to follow. His orders were: "Act according to the instructions which have been delivered to you, and do not pursue the suggestions of your fancy." Nevertheless, sufficient powers were left to his officers, and if they followed too literally his instructions or did not act on their own responsibility, he reprimanded them.[4] Generally speaking Tipu laid down principles for their guidance, and for the rest they were to act according to their own discretion.

Tipu called his Government *Sarkar-i-Khudadad* (Government given by God).[5] But this did not mean that it was meant only for the Muslims. While the *sharia* law was applicable to the Muslims, the

[1] *Ibid.*, No. 14. see also Buchanan, ii, pp. 411-12, for details about the custom of polyandry prevalent in Malabar.

[2] Kirmani, p. 398.

[3] Crisp, *Mysorean Revenue Regulation*, p. 25.

[4] Kirkpatrick, pp. 210-11.

[5] See Kirkpatrick, Kirmani and Beatson. But it is strange that this title is nowhere found stamped except on the bindings of books in the Sultan's library. *Tarikh-i-Khudadadi* calls Tipu's Government *Ahmadi Sarkar*, while *Sultan-ut-Tawarikh* refers to it as *Sarkar-i-Asad Ilahi*. In Kirkpatrick also sometimes this last title is employed.

Hindus were governed by their own laws, which Tipu never interfered with. He gave his subjects complete freedom of worship. He respected the old traditions of Mysore, and allowed the age-long system of village *panchayats* to function without any hindrance. "The Mysore Government," wrote Munro to his father on January 17, 1790, "is the most simple and despotic monarchy in the world, in which every department, civil and military, possesses the regularity and system communicated to it by the genius of Hyder, and in which all pretensions, derived from high birth being discouraged, all independent chiefs and zamindars being subjugated or extirpated, justice severely and impartially administered, a numerous and well disciplined army kept up and almost every department of trust or consequence conferred on men raised from obscurity, gives the Government a vigour hitherto unexampled in India."[1] Similarly Moor, on the basis of personal experience, wrote: "When a person travelling through a strange country finds it well cultivated, populous with industrious inhabitants, cities newly founded, commerce extending, towns increasing, and everything flourishing so as to indicate happiness, he will naturally conclude it to be under a form of government congenial to the minds of the people. This is a picture of Tippoo's country, and this is our conclusion respecting its government."[2]

*The Central Government**

Tipu inherited a fairly efficient system of Government from his father, but owing to his zeal for innovation and improvement, he introduced considerable changes. He borrowed from the Great Mughals, and was also influenced by Western political institutions, as established by the European Companies in India. Tipu, according to Dodwell, "was the first Indian sovereign to seek to apply western methods to his administration."[3]

There were seven principal *cutchehris* (departments) at the centre. Every department had a chief, who, with his subordinate officers, constituted a Board. Thus there were seven such Boards which met separately from time to time to discuss the affairs of their respective departments. Every member recorded his views with his signature in the book of minutes which was kept in a box under the seal of the department. The decisions were taken by a majority of votes, and Tipu was kept regularly informed of the proceedings. If there was

[1] Gleig, *Munro*, i, p. 84.

[2] Moor, p. 201.

[3] Rushbrook Williams, *Great Men of India*, p. 216 (Chap. on *Tipu Sultan* by Dodwell); also A. N., C²172, Monneron to Cossigny, Sept. 14, 178b, f. 207b. Monneron also expressed similar opinion.

* See S. C. Sen Gupta, *Government and Administrative System of Tipu Sultan*, *Journal of the Dept. of Letters*, xix, xxi. (Calcutta University). I am indebted to these two articles, which, though based on published works, are very illuminating.

anything which required secrecy, the report was written by one of the members of the Board who personally delivered it to the Sultan and obtained his written opinion about the matter.[1] Sometimes the heads of various departments also met to deliberate on matters of common interest. It was Tipu's practice that whenever he wished to take a decision, he spent a whole day in deliberation. He then invited advice from his chief officers, who first discussed among themselves and then submitted their opinions in writing. It was after comparing these with his own that he issued his final orders.[2]

### *Mir Asaf Cutchehri* (*The Revenue and Finance Department*)

The head of this department was called variously *diwan, saheb diwan*,[3] *huzur diwan*[4] or *mir asaf*.[5] He was the most important officer in Tipu's Government, and, along with his five officers, who were also called *mir asafs*,[6] constituted the Central Board of Revenue and Finance. Each officer was in charge of one or two branches of the department, and under him were *sarishtadars* (Chief Accountants) and *mutasaddis* (accountants or clerks). The accounts were kept in three languages—Persian, Kanarese and Marathi.[7] Mir Sadiq was the President of the Revenue and Finance Department and was Tipu's chief *diwan*. He was not a *wazir* or Prime Minister, for there was no such office in Tipu's Government. Mir Sadiq's annual salary was 2,100 pagodas. Besides, he had a small *jagir* and was paid an annual allowance of 100 pagodas. The five officers under him received a salary of 5,460 pagodas annually.[8]

### *Mir Miran Cutchehri* (*The Military Department*)

This department was also, like others, organised into a Board. Purnaiya was the President of the Board and the head of the department. He was the chief *mir miran*, and his salary and *jagir* were equal to those of Mir Sadiq. Under him were fifteen officers who received 12,880 pagodas annually,[9] and were called *mir mirans*.[10]

[1] Kirkpatrick, Appendix E, pp. xxxiii *seqq*. These regulations were not only meant for the Commerce Department but also for other departments. See also I.O. 4685 (Persian), ff. 8a-9a, for a detailed account of how the dept. worked.

[2] Beatson, p. 157; Edmonstone, pp. 13-19, 22-3, 29; Kirkpatrick, Appendix D, p. xxix.

[3] Kirmani, pp. 280, 378, 381 *seqq*. Kirmani generally calls Mir Sadiq *diwan*.

[4] Kirkpatrick, No. 318.

[5] I.O.MSS. Eur. C. 10 p. 208. It appears that there was also a deputy *diwan*. In 1794 Ashraf Ali Khan held that post (Mly. Sundry Book. vol. 101, 1792-95, p. 112).

[6] Edmonstone, pp. 23,29.

[7] M.R., Mly. Sundry Book, vol. 101, 1792-95, p. 112.

[8] N.A., Sec. Cons., July 23, 1799, vol. viii B, pp. 1158 *seqq*.

[9] *Ibid*.

[10] Kirmani, p. 375. In 1793 Tipu conferred the title of *mir miran* on a number of officers. Sayyid Ghaffar was the first to receive this title. Muhammad Raza, Khan Jahan Khan, Purnaiya and others received it later.

*Mir Miran Cutchehri (Zumra)*

This was another department created by Tipu in 1793. It looked after the army called *zumra* which was composed of men born in Mysore. Muhammad Raza was in charge of this department, and received an annual salary of 1,050 pagodas. Besides his pay, he was given a small *jagir*. There were ten officers under him. Eight of them were paid 700 pagodas and the rest 500 pagodas each annually. Each officer had also a *jagir*.[1]

*Mir Sudur Cutchehri (The Ordnance and Garrison Department)*

The chief officers constituted a Board with one of them as the head. The department supervised the stores and the manufacture of arms and ammunition. It also looked after the proper defence of the forts in the kingdom by a regular supply of troops, provisions and war materials.[2] Further, it was in charge of the *ahsham* troops (garrisons), and kept the army accounts. Ghulam Ali Khan, who was the head of the department, was known as *mir sudur*, and was paid an annual salary of 840 pagodas. The eight officers under him were called *bakhshis*, and received 5,250 pagodas annually.[3]

*Malik-ut-Tujjar Cutchehri (The Commerce Department)*

This department looked after trade and industry and, until 1796, also the naval establishments. The head of the department with eight officers under him formed a Commercial Board.[4] Ahmed Khan was the head of the department, and received 840 pagodas annually. The six officers under him received 3,920 pagodas annually.[5]

*Mir Yam Cutchehri (The Marine Department)*

At first the marine force was placed under the Commerce Department, and its function was to conduct maritime trade. But in 1796 a separate department was formed, the chief officers of which constituted a Board of Admiralty with one of them as the head.[6] Hafiz Muhammad, who was the *mir yam*, received a salary of 630 pagodas annually. He had seven officers under him who received 3,570 pagodas annually.[7]

*Mir Khazain Cutchehri (The Treasury and Mint Department)*

The officers of this department, with one of them as the head,

[1] N.A., Sec. Cons. July 23, 1799, vol. viii B, pp. 1158 *seqq*.
[2] Kirkpatrick, Appendix, p. xiv footnote; also I.O. 4685 (Persian), f. 26b.
[3] N.A., Sec. Cons., July 23, 1799, vol. viii B, pp. 1158 *seqq*.
[4] Edmonstone, pp. 23, 29.
[5] N.A., Sec. Cons., July 23, 1799, vol. viiB, pp. 1158 *seq*.
[6] Edmonstone, pp. 16, 29; Kirkpatrick, Appendix K, p. ixvii-viii.
[7] N.A., Sec Cons., July 23, 1799, vol. viiiB, pp. 1158 *seq*. According to Kirkpatrick, p. lxxvii, the number of *mir yams* was 11.

constituted a Board. Sayyid Amin, the head of the department, was paid an annual salary of 595 pagodas, and had, in addition, a *jagir*. The seven officers under him received an annual salary of 2,730 pagodas.[1] Each officer or *darogha* was in charge of a separate department, and had assistant *daroghas* and *mutasaddis* under him.

The *tosha-khana* or treasury was the place where valuable state papers were kept. All the *hukm-namahs* and other papers bearing the seal and signature of the Sultan were deposited in a box to which the seal of the department was affixed. If required, copies of these documents could be obtained by authorised persons.[2]

The *tosha-khana*, as established by Tipu, was of two kinds—*naqdi* and *jinsi*. In the *naqdi* bullion and money were kept; while in the *jinsi* fruits, wardrobe (shawls, woollen and silk cloths), state papers and other articles were kept. It is not clear whether ordnance stores were also kept in the department.[3]

There were five mints at Seringapatam. One of them minted gold and silver coins and was within the walls of the palace. The other four minted copper coins and were outside the palace. Each was under a *darogha*, who was under the treasury department. The chief *darogha* of the treasury supplied the mints with gold, silver and copper, and after the coins had been minted, he received them and deposited them in the treasury.[4] He also kept money belonging to various departments. Thus in one instance he received orders to keep in a separate coffer, with a distinct label on it, five lakhs of rupees for the construction of a canal, and not to spend a single pie out of it for other purposes.[5]

These were the seven principal departments. But there was one other which was equally important. This was the department of Post and Intelligence under a *darogha* stationed at Seringapatam. Under him were other *daroghas* in the principal towns of the kingdom. It was an important department because, with its help, Tipu kept himself in touch with the activities of his officers both at the centre and in the provinces. The department employed the services of a large number of spies who, after collecting information, passed it on to the *daroghas*. The *daroghas* then sent the information to the capital through *harcarahs* who, sometimes, had to travel at the rate of five miles an hour.[6]

Besides these eight important departments, there were also a number of minor ones. The Public Buildings Department was under a

[1] *Ibid.*
[2] Kirkpatrick, Appendix E, p. xxxv.
[3] *Ibid.*, pp. 81-2, No. 251.
[4] *Ibid.*, Nos. 400, 416.
[5] *Ibid.*, No. 400.
[6] *Ibid.*, pp. 215-6.

*darogha*. Then there was a department which looked after slaves. There was also a department of temples which was under a manager.[1] *Keren berek* Department (The Cattle Department) was established by Chikka Devaraja Wodeyar (1673-1704) to form a breeding stud and to provide the palace with ghee and milk. It was called *bennea chaouree* or the Butter Department. Tipu first changed its name to *amrit mahal* and then to *keren berek*. It looked after the Government establishment of sheep, cows and buffaloes.[2] The finest cattle in the Mysore district, and indeed in South India, are the *amrit mahal* or the Sultan's breed, which is supposed to have been obtained by Haidar from a conquered *poligar*. The breed was maintained by Tipu with the greatest care.[3] Like his father, he also tried to improve the Mysore breed of horses. The irregular horse sprang generally from Arab sires and Maratha dames.[4]

The most important officer in the kingdom was Mir Sadiq, the *huzur diwan*. Next to him was Purnaiya, who was not only the head of the *mir miran* department, but was also a member of the *mir asaf* Board. Next came the heads of other departments and their subordinates. Besides these there were also other officers at the centre occupying responsible positions. There was the chief *peshkar* of Tipu.[5] Then there was the *arzbegi*,[6] the presenter of petitions before the Sultan. The *mir samani* looked after the Royal Household.[7] The *qiladar* of the fort of Seringapatam exercised authority over the fort administration, and looked after the political prisoners. The *kotwal* of Seringapatam was responsible for maintaining law and order at the capital. The *qazi* of Seringapatam was the chief *qazi* of the whole kingdom, and under him were the *qazis* posted in the different towns of the kingdom.

*Provincial and Local Administration*

After concluding the Treaty of Mangalore, Tipu divided his kingdom into seven *asafi tukris* or provinces. But finding that they had extensive jurisdictions, which was not conducive to good government, he increased their number to nine in 1784, and two years later to seventeen. After the conclusion of his war with the English, he again changed the provincial boundaries of his kingdom, so that in 1794 there were 37 *asafi tukris* and 1024 *amildari tukris*.[8] These con-

[1] M.A.R., 1938, pp. 123-5.
[2] Wilks, i, p. 121 footnote.
[3] Rice, *Mysore and Coorg*, ii, p. 203.
[4] *Ibid*., i, p. 166; Buchanan, i, p. 121.
[5] M.R., Mly. Sundries, vol. 106 (1799), p. 24.
[6] Kirmani, p. 379. It appears that there were two *arzbegis*, one for the day and one for the night. (I.O. Mss. Eur. C. 10 p. 210).
[7] Baramahal Recds., Section 1, p. 8.
[8] N.A., Sec. Cons., July 23, 1799, vol. viiiB, p. 980 *seq*.

stant changes must have greatly hampered the smooth working of the Government.

Each province was in charge of an *asaf* or civil governor and a *faujdar* or military governor. The *asaf* was in charge of revenue, while the *faujdar* was responsible for the maintenance of law and order, and neither was to interfere in the affairs of the other. The separation of powers was introduced in order to prevent the *asafs* or *faujdars* from becoming too powerful.[1] In some provinces there were two *asafs*, one being the senior *asaf* and the other his deputy.[2] The *asafs* had under them *mutasaddis*, *sarishtadars*, clerks, peons and copyists to help them with the administration of the province. Once a year, on the day of the *Id-ul-Fitr*, the *asafs*, accompanied by their *naibs* (deputies), were required to visit Seringapatam. On their arrival their accounts were examined and presented to the Sultan.[3] After 1799 the post of *asaf* was abolished, but that of the *faujdar* was retained.

The *tukris* were further divided into *amildari tukris* or districts. Generally an *asafi tukri* contained from twenty to thirty *amildari tukris*. And each *amildari tukri* contained from thirty to forty villages. It was under an *amil*, also called *amildar*, who had under him *tarafdars*, *sarishtadars*, clerks and peons.[4] As head of the district the *amildar's* duty was to look after the welfare of the peasants, to promote agriculture and supply the Commandants with stores and provisions.[5] They were responsible to their respective *cutchehris*, to which they sent their accounts and their collections.[6]

The villages were managed by *patels* and *shambhogs* (accountants) as under the Rajas. The *patels* were required to look after roads, to plant trees for shade on both sides of the road, to protect the villages and settle disputes between the villagers with the help of the *panchayats*.

Orders from Seringapatam were sent in three languages: Persian, Kanarese and Marathi. Every order was sent to the *asaf* who sent a copy of it to the *amildar*, and the *amildar* forwarded it to the *tarafdars* with instructions to have it notified throughout the district. The revenue accounts were made out in Kanarese by the *tarafdars* who sent them to *amildars*, in whose office they were translated into Marathi and Persian. A copy of each was retained by the *sarishtadars*, and a Persian copy was sent to the *asaf*.[7]

[1] Baramahal Recds., Section 1, p. 157; Wilks, *Report on the Interior Administration of Mysore*, p. 34.

[2] M.R., Mly. Sundry Book, vol. 109A, p. 207. According to Read there were two to four *faujdars* in some districts as checks on each other (Baramahal Recds., Sec. 1, p. 152).

[3] I.O. 4685 (Persian), f. 22b.

[4] Mack, MSS. 15-6-8 (Athavana tantria). See also Rice, *Mysore and Coorg*, i, p. 489.

[5] See Crisp, *Mysorean Revenue Regulations*, for the duties of *amils*.

[6] Baramahal Recds., Section 1, p. 8.

[7] Mack. Mss., 15-6-8 (Athavana tantria); Rice, *Mysore and Coorg*, i, p. 489.

Tipu demanded a high degree of honesty from his officers. Addressing the *amils* he told them: "Wages sufficient for your maintenance are allowed to you and to your officers. It is therefore expected that you will not be guilty of misrepresentation in any matter, whether trifling or great."........."Falsehood is an offence of the highest nature against both morality and religion."[1] On June 5, 1794, he called his *asafs* and their staff to Seringapatam, and then asked them to take an oath according to the forms of their respective religions that they would not accept bribes, but would perform their duties with honesty and integrity.[2]

Justice was administered in the villages by the *patels* with the help of the *panchayats*. In the towns, the *asafs*, *amils* and *faujdars* dealt out justice. Besides, each town had a *qazi* and a pundit who decided cases for Muslims and Hindus respectively. But in case of dissatisfaction with the judgments of these courts, an appeal could be made to the High Court at Seringapatam, which consisted of a Muslim and a Hindu judge. The Highest Court of Appeal was the Sultan himself.

The punishments inflicted upon criminals were on the whole severe. Traitors and murderers were hung on the gallows. A more common form of punishment was to drag the condemned man to death by binding his hands and feet and attaching them by a rope to the foot of an elephant. Sometimes thieves, defaulters and traitors were punished by cutting off their ears and noses and hands and feet. Sometimes they were even emasculated.[3] Government clerks were flogged for disobedience and laziness.[4]

*Revenue System*

Tipu had acquired great knowledge in revenue affairs while managing the districts of Malvalli, Konanur, Dharmapuri, Pennagaram and Tenkarai-Kottai, which his father had granted him as *jagir* in 1760, and which, under him, became prosperous. This early experience proved to him very useful when he became ruler of Mysore.[5]

Tipu's revenue system was much the same as it had been under Haidar, except that he introduced greater efficiency into it. The principle of land tenure was that a tenant and his heirs occupied land so long as they cultivated it and paid rent. But if they failed to fulfil these conditions, the Government was entitled to transfer the land

[1] Crisp, *Mysorean Revenue Regulations*, p. 89.

[2] Q.J.M.S., x, Oct. 1919.

[3] See pp. 71, 76, 271, *supra;* Punganuri, p. 35; I.O. 4685 (Persian), ff. 157a-b, 198a-b.

[4] Kirkpatrick, No. 1.

[5] See p. 8, *supra;* Baramahal Recds., Section 1, p. 145; Rice, *Mysore and Coorg*, ii, p. 247.

to other tenants.[1] The cultivators of dry lands (lands which are irrigated only by rain) paid a fixed money rent calculated to be equal to one-third of the crop; and those of wet lands (lands which are irrigated by tanks or rivers) paid in kind about one-half of the crop, but this was generally discharged in money at the average rates of the district. If the *amil* and the peasant disagreed regarding the rates, then the rent was paid in kind.[2] Wet lands were assessed at two to twelve pagodas per candy, and dry lands from two and a half to thirty pagodas per candy. Sugar-cane was taxed from sixteen to seventy-two pagodas per candy. This was the practice followed by Haidar and Tipu in the districts of Bangalore and Maddagiri. But in the Chitaldrug district ten to thirty pagodas were charged on such lands as were irrigated by wells. However, as a relief to the peasants, Tipu granted as much dry land as could be cultivated by one plough. The grain from the districts of Mysore and Seringapatam was stored at the capital.[3] In Baramahal the rent of dry land was never less than half a rupee, or more than a pagoda (about three rupees) per acre. The rent of wet land was usually four times as much. This rate of assessment was maintained by the English when the district was ceded to them in 1792.[4] In Kanara all rents were fixed in money. The rent in kind entered in the statement was not a certain proportion of the crop, but the equivalent to a certain portion of the rent in cash, which was taken to store different garrisons.[5] According to Munro, "there was no instance in which the Sircar's share was more than one-third. In many it was not one-fifth, or one-sixth, or in some not one-tenth, of the gross produce."[6]

The cultivated area was considerably enlarged under Tipu's rule. This was done by giving lands to the peasants on favourable terms. Waste lands were rent-free in the first year; in the second year they were subjected to one-fourth of the customary assessment; and in the succeeding years to the usual amount. Lands which had been lying fallow for ten years were rent-free in the first year; in the second year they were subjected to the usual assessment; and in the third year they were fully assessed. Lands which were barren, mountainous or rocky, were exempted from revenue in the first year; in the second year they were subjected to one-fourth of the customary assessment; in the third

[1] Wilks, *Report on the Interior Administration of Mysore*, art. 35.
[2] *Ibid.*, art. 45.
[3] Wilks, *Notes on Mysore*, pp. 5-7, Land in Mysore was not actually measured; it was measured by the quantity of seed grain required to sow a particular area. A candy of land was equal to a candy of seed grain sown in it. But since wet land required four times the seed grain that was sown in dry land, it meant that a candy of dry land was equal to four times as large as a candy of wet land.
[4] Gleig, *Munro*, i, pp. 204, 206.
[5] *Ibid.*, 290.
[6] *Ibid.*, 291.

year they were assessed at one-half the rate; and in the fourth year they were fully assessed. It is interesting to note that the Company's Government followed similar methods in order to extend the cultivated area.[1]

Tipu was greatly interested in encouraging the cultivation of sugar-cane, wheat and barley, and the plantation of betel-leaf, pine, saul, acacia and teak, and mango, betel-nut and sandalwood trees. The cultivation of bhang, however, was prohibited throughout the kingdom. The peasants who planted betel-nut trees were exempted from tax payment during the first five years. From the sixth year until the trees bore fruit, they were assessed at one-half the established rate. After this period they were fully assessed. The peasants who made plantations of betel-leaf were required to pay only one-half of the usual tax during the first three years. From the fourth year they had to pay at the full rate. Similar exemptions were given to those who planted coco-nut trees.[2] Tipu was also anxious to develop silk industry in Mysore, and accordingly ordered the inhabitants of Baramahal to plant mulberry trees. But unfortunately, owing to the outbreak of hostilities with the English in 1790, and because the district passed into the Company's possession, their culture was given up by the inhabitants.[3] Tipu's two gardens, both called Lal Bagh, one at Bangalore and the other at Seringapatam, were the nurseries in which seeds and saplings from various countries of the world were obtained and planted. They were divided into square plots separated by walks, both sides of which were lined with tall cypresses. The plots were filled with fruit trees and pot herbs, a separate plot being allotted to each kind of plant. The gardens contained mulberry, cotton, and indigo plants, and mango, apple, orange and guava trees. The pine and oak plants, introduced from the Cape of Good Hope, also throve.

As head of the district, the *amil* was required to develop agriculture and protect the peasants from exploitation. At the end of every year he toured the district under his charge, and examined the area under cultivation. He prepared a general statement regarding the district, giving the number of villages it contained, the area of land cultivated, and the number of peasants with their families, their castes and occupations.[4] The peasants, who were too poor to purchase ploughs, were given *taqavi* (advances of money), and measures were taken to protect them from the exploitation of the local officers and moneylenders. The *patels* were prohibited from employing peasants on their fields without paying them wages; if they defied this order, their whole produce was to be confiscated by the Government.[5] Farming

[1] Baramahal Recds., Section. 1. p. 22.
[2] Crisp, *Mysorean Revenue Regulations*, pp. 10-16.
[3] Baramahal Recds., Section IV, p. 75.
[4] Crisp, *Mysorean Revenue Regulations*, pp. 16-17
[5] *Ibid.*, pp. 2, 4.

was common, but a person could obtain only one village, and he had to give security for the full payment of his dues. The *amil* was to see that the peasants were not oppressed by the farmer. He toured the district and distributed the assessment among the peasants according to the total sum settled with the farmers.[1] Rent was to be realised by gentle methods and in three instalments a year.[2] If a peasant absconded owing to the oppression of the *amil*, the latter had to pay twenty pagodas for every plough of a rich peasant, and ten pagodas for the plough of a poor peasant. Peasants who had left the country were persuaded to return. *Amils*, *sarishtadars* and *tarafdars* were prohibited from accepting diet money from the peasants. In fact, with the exception of the Government dues, nothing was to be realised. If the peasants had any grievances against the officers it was to be inquired into.[3] If there was a failure of the crop, or there was some other reason owing to which the peasants could not pay their rents, the *amils* were required to immediately report the matter to the Sultan who, under such circumstances, invariably granted remissions. Thus, when in 1786 Tipu was marching on Adoni, the *amil* of Kodikanda represented to him that its population was very small, and asked for remissions of land-tax and other concessions to induce people to settle in the village, his request was granted and, as a result, a new suburb called the Sultan's Pettah was built.[4]

Before Tipu's rule the revenue used to be collected and sent to Seringapatam by intermediaries who were mostly *sahukars* (money-lenders) and who charged a commission for it. This was a defective system because it caused unnecessary expenditure, and at the same time encouraged the money-lenders to exploit the peasants. Tipu, therefore, abolished it, and began to employ his own revenue officers for collecting and transmitting the revenue to the capital.[5] Further, in order to "prevent speculation in the revenue line, he conceived the idea of forming an establishment for it with such rank and allowances annexed to the appointment, as would excite emulation among the people in it to recommend themselves by their zeal and rectitude of conduct."[6] But we do not know whether such an establishment was set up or not.

In 1788 Tipu directed a fresh investigation of revenue throughout his kingdom to be made by the provincial *cutchehris*.[7] On the basis

[1] *Ibid.*, pp. 5-7. In the *taluk* of Rayakottai some horsemen oppressed the peasants in the course of the Third Anglo-Mysore War. As soon as Tipu came to know of this, he at once wrote to his *asaf* to see that the peasants were protected. (I.O., 4682 (Persian), f. 30b).

[2] *Ibid.*, p. 22, 28,

[3] *Ibid.*, pp. 26-28.

[4] Mack MS. on Hindupur *taluk*, cited in *Anantapur Gazetteer*, p. 174.

[5] Baramahal Recds., Section 1, p. 151; *Ibid.*, Section VIII, pp. 46-7.

[6] *Ibid.*, p. 151. [7] *Ibid.*, p. 153.

of this survey, which was done village by village, he resumed all unauthorised *inam* lands. But the authorised grants were left in the possession of their holders, and even fresh grants were made to temples, mosques and Brahmins. Munro regarded the resumption of the *inam* lands as necessary, and wrote: "It does not appear that the Hindu princes were much more scrupulous than Tipu in resuming *inams*......for as almost every prince gave away, and none resumed, the whole country would in a short time have been converted into *inam*."[1]

Tipu abolished the custom of giving *jagirs* to his officers in lieu of salaries, which were henceforth to be paid in cash. However, some of his officers and his four eldest sons were allowed to retain their *jagirs*. Fath Haidar and Abdul Khaliq had a *jagir* of 12,000 pagodas each; Muiz-ud-din and Muin-ud-din had *jagirs* of 4,300 pagodas each. Sayyid Saheb had a *jagir* of 12,000 pagodas and Qamar-ud-din Khan's *jagir* was of 4,000 pagodas. A *jagir* of 4,000 pagodas was given to Haidar's tomb, 24,680 pagodas to Haidar's family and 46,008 pagodas to Tipu's family. The *inams* to mosques and temples amounted to 250,000 pagodas.[2]

Tipu was against the retention of *poligars* who were a threat to his power, and who, by their depredations and by constantly fighting with each other, disturbed the peace of the country. He at first annexed the territories of only those *poligars* who were disloyal to him, and left those who paid their tribute regularly and sent their quotas of troops in possession of their estates.[3] But by the end of his reign, under one pretext or another, he had deprived almost all the landlords of their hereditary possessions. However, as Wilks observed, "by means of frauds the *poligars* continued by mutual collusion of *poligar* and *amil* and Tipu was told of their elimination."[4]

Tipu's revenue policy in Malabar, owing to the peculiar conditions of the area, was very different from that he followed in the rest of his kingdom. At the time of Haidar's invasion, there was no tax on land, although a general contribution was levied which was equal to one-fifth of the gross produce. The Rajas, however, possessed considerable lands of their own and also derived income from trade and mint, fines, royalties from gold ore, elephants and elephants' teeth, teak trees and cardamom.[5] Another significant thing about Malabar was that no land survey had ever been caried out; land was usually measured by the area that was to be sown with a *poray* of rice.[6]

[1] *Ibid.*, Section V, VII, p. 101.
[2] N.A., Sec. Cons., July 23, 1799, viiiB, pp. 1174-75.
[3] Wilks, *Report on the Interior Administration of Mysore*, Art. 10-12.
[4] Wilks, *Notes on Mysore*, p. 6.
[5] Spencer, *A Report on the Administration of Malabar*, July 28, 1801, p. 2, para 7.
[6] Buchanan, ii, p. 355.

It was in 1773, when Haidar appointed Srinivas Rao Governor of Malabar, that for the first time an attempt was made to introduce a regular system of revenue administration, but without much success. Soon after Haidar's death, Tipu appointed Arshad Beg Khan Governor of Malabar, and he tried to remove the defects of the earlier assessment after the province was restored to Mysore by the English in 1784. But in spite of the vigilance of Arshad and Tipu not much was achieved, because many landlords (*jenmkars*) were able to bribe the officers and thereby got the land valued at a low rate, while the lands of those who were too poor to bribe the assessors were valued high. When Tipu heard of this he tried to remove the inequalities by ordering Ram Lingam Pillai to conduct a fresh land survey by measurement instead of by the old system.[1] Arshad also ordered a general reduction of 20 per cent tax both on wet and garden lands in south Malabar. It is difficult to say how far these orders were effectively carried out. But his settlement continued in south Malabar down to the end of the last century, and considerably influenced the settlements made by the English in north Malabar.[2]

Before the Mysorean conquest the Namboodiri Brahmins and Nairs used to lease out the greater part of their estates to farmers called *kanamdars*. But Arshad Beg made settlements with the latter by levying six-twentieth of the gross produce. His calculations were that the cultivator was to get three-twentieth of the gross produce; profits and charges of cultivation amounted to about eleven-twentieth and the remainder six-twentieth went to the Government. Arshad supposed that 1 *poray* of seed sown would on an average produce 10; out of this 5½ would go to the cultivator and 4½ to be divided between the Government and the landowners. On this produce one fanam was fixed per *poray*, of which the Government received three and the *jenmkar* 1½. This fitted in with Arshad's general assessment that 7,43,481 *porays* of seed sown were calculated to produce 2,31,481 Huns, which was nearly equivalent to the rate of 3 fanams per *poray* sown.[3]

Tipu's taxation policy regarding fruit trees, spices and vegetables was very liberal. Cash crops like cashew, cardamom, cinnamon and vegetables were exempted from taxation. But coco-nut trees which did not produce more than 10 coco-nuts were not taxed.[4]

When Haidar invaded Malabar, those Rajas who submitted and

[1] *Ibid.*, 446.

[2] Innes, *Gazetteer of the Malabar and Anjengo Dists.*, i, p. 326 (1951 ed.); Logan, i, p. 630.

[3] *Minute of Sir John Shore*, pp. 9-10; Spencer, *A Report on the Administration of Malabar*, July 28, 1801, p. 10, para 37; see also Warden, *Report on Land Tenures in Malabar*, pp. 7-8, 19.

[4] Buchanan, ii, pp. 404-05, gives the rates of taxation, but it is not clear to which period of Tipu's reign they relate.

promised to pay tribute were allowed to retain their estates.[1] Tipu continued this policy. In fact, both he and his father did not want to interfere with the local usages concerning the transfer of land, and, as Warden observed: "They did not arbitrarily move the occupants from one estate to another or oust them and place their own favourites or dependents in their place."[2] However, since many Rajas and landlords rebelled or fled the country, the Mysore Government took possession of their lands and directly entered into arrangements with the peasants. But this process does not seem to have gone very far, for, as Warden further says: "The landed property in Malabar did not sustain that violent convulsion during the Mahomedan government as the Board has been led to suppose."[3]

Tipu's income from revenue until the Treaty of Seringapatam (1792) was 68,89,893 pagodas (over two crores of rupees), including the tribute of 66,666 pagodas from Kurnool.[4] After that treaty, which deprived him of half his kingdom, his income too was reduced to about thirty-five to forty lakhs of pagodas. To make up for this loss, in 1795 he increased the assessment by 37½ per cent (30 per cent on produce and 7½ per cent as excise duty).[5] In spite of this, his income from revenue could not have reached the previous figures, although he seems to have managed his affairs sucessfully; and when Seringapatam fell, his treasury was found to have been full.

*Trade and Industry*

Few Indian rulers in the past were so much interested in the promotion of trade and industry as was Tipu Sultan. Influenced by the example of the European powers, he alone realised that a country could be great and powerful only by developing its trade and industry. Like them, therefore, he tried to promote the trade of his kingdom by establishing factories. He had two factories in Cutch which were established in 1789—one at Mundhi and the other at Mundra. They had a staff of seven *daroghas* and one hundred and fifty sepoys, and a brisk trade was carried on between Cutch and Mysore.[6]

[1] Warden, *Report on the Land Tenures in Malabar*, p. 7.

[2] *Ibid.*, p. 8.

[3] *Ibid.* Tipu granted a *jagir* to one of the young Rajas of Zamorin family for help given to Arshad Beg against the rebel Moplah Goorkul. (Spencer, *A Report on the Administration of Malabar*, July 28, 1801, p. 7, para 22).

[4] M.R., Mly. Sundries, vol. 106 (1799), Appendix 12, pp. 51 *seq.*

[5] *Ibid.*, Mly. Sundry Book, vol. 101, 1792-95, pp. 107-8. At another place Macleod says that Tipu's income was 8367549 pagodas, including the increase of 10 lakhs which he had made in 1795. (Mly. Sundry Book, 109A-1799, pp. 205-7). Read also gives the same figures. But I regard these as highly exaggerated. Macleod also says that, since 1792, Tipu's receipts were only from twenty-five to thirty-five lakhs of pagodas. But there could not have been so much difference between demands and receipts considering the strictness and efficiency of Tipu's administration.

[6] N.A., Pol. Proc., Aug. 4, 1797, Cons. No. 4.

Tipu also established one factory at Ormuz to purchase mainly pearls and the other at Jeddah.[1] Efforts were made to establish factories at Aden, Bushire and Basra, but without success. It was, however, the factory at Masqat, established in 1785,[2] that was most important, because it was through this that exports from the Mysore kingdom were distributed over the Persian Gulf, and imports from the Persian Gulf were brought into Mysore. The exports were timber, sandalwood, silk, cardamom, pepper, rice, ivory and cloth. The imports were saffron-seeds, silkworms, horses, pistachio-nuts, raisins, rock-salt, pearls, sulphur, copper, dates and coarse china-wares. The silkworms were required to develop the silk industry. Horses were meant for the army, and sulphur was imported for the manufacture of gunpowder. Among the exports rice was an important article, for whenever its export from Mangalore was withheld, it caused great hardship to the people of Oman.[3] Malabar teakwood was used in the Persian Gulf for the construction of boats, and was mostly exported from Calicut.[4] The cloth exported was of different varieties, some of which was manufactured in Mysore, while others were obtained from different parts of India.[5]

Owing to the commercial importance of Masqat, which was the chief emporium of trade between India, the Red Sea and the Persian Gulf, Tipu kept, like his father, a *wakil* there to look after his interests, and maintained friendly relations with the Imam.[6] The latter reciprocated these sentiments, and realising the dependence of Oman to rice from Mangalore and other articles from Malabar, he gave preferential treatment to Tipu's subjects at Masqat. Thus, while the Europeans had to pay a duty of 5%, the Indians 8%, and the Arabs and Persians 6½%, merchants belonging to the Mysore kingdom paid only 4%. Similar privileges were, in return, given to the Imam and his subjects at the Mysore ports.[7]

[1] Kirkpatrick, Nos. 160, 172. [2] *Selections from State Papers*, Bombay, No. cclvii.

[3] Salil b. Razik, *History of the Imams and Seyyids of Oman*, trans. G.P. Badger, pp. 170-71 & n. 1. See also this work for the relations between Haidar Ali and the Imam.

[4] Hourani, *Arab Seafaring in the Indian Ocean*, pp. 89-90; see also *Selections from the Records of the Bombay Government* (New Series), No. 24, p. 613. Nos. 159, 172, 206, 207. Since Tipu had prohibited the selling of rice to the English and Portuguese merchants, they adopted the practice of sending other merchants to Mangalore disguised as Masqat traders to purchase rice. When Tipu came to know of this, he issued orders that only those persons who had a passport or a certificate bearing the seal and signature of the *darogha* of the Mysore factory at Masqat could purchase rice in his kingdom.

[5] The different varieties of cloth are mentioned in the *Waqai-i Manazil-i Rum*. *Shila*, thin white muslin was probably obtained from Dacca. *Khadi nirmali*, a thick coarse cloth, was obtained from Nirmal, Adilabad district (Andhra Pradesh).

[6] *Selections from State Papers*, Bombay, p. 337

[7] *Waqai-i Manazil-i-Rum*, ed. Mohibbul Hasan, p. 28; see also Kirkpatrick, Tipu to Seth Mao, Jan. 6, 1786, p. 239

The organisation of the factory at Masqat was based on that of the English and French factories in India. At the head of the factory was a *darogha* (factor), and under him were *mutasaddis* (writers) and *gumashtas* (agents) and a body of troops. The buying and selling was done either directly by the *darogha* himself or through a broker. Tipu's chief broker at Masqat and Bushire was Seth Mao. At Basra, his chief broker was Abdullah, a Jew and a confidant of the *Mutesellim*.[1] Tipu maintained a brisk correspondence with the *darogha* at Masqat, giving him detailed instructions about buying and selling transactions and various other matters relating to trade and organisation of the factory. In one of the letters, for example, he informs Mir Kazim, his *darogha* at Masqat, that the pearls which he has purchased are expensive, and that he should buy them at a cheaper rate from Bahrain. He further tells him that since the price of sandalwood and pepper is low at Masqat, they must not be sold until the rates become favourable. The *darogha* is asked to send ten shipwrights for the construction of dhows.[2] In a subsequent letter the Sultan fixes the price at which sandalwood is to be sold. The first quality is to be sold at 120 pagodas per candy; the second at 100 pagodas per candy; the third at 90 pagodas per candy; and the fourth quality at 80 pagodas per candy.[3] In another letter the Sultan instructs the *darogha* to obtain silkworms and their eggs from Qishm Island and send them to Seringapatam, including a few men acquainted with the art of rearing them.[4] Similarly, there are letters in which the *darogha* is ordered to buy saffron-seeds and sulphur from Persia and date-palms from Masqat. Furthermore, he is required to send pearl divers from Bahrain to help establishing a pearl-fishery on the Malabar coast.[5]

No figures are available of the volume of Mysore exports to and imports from the Persian Gulf. From the letter of a broker at Masqat, addressed to the Governor of Bombay, it appears that about five or six vessels, laden with goods, arrived annually at Masqat under Tipu's colours.[6] In addition, there were a large number of smaller vessels and dhows and dinghies belonging to Indian and Arab merchants, which plied between the Malabar coast and the Persian Gulf. That this trade must have been considerable is evident from the fact that Tipu sold all cardamom to the Arabian coast.[7]

The extent of Tipu's interest in trade is evident from the fact that he tried to open commercial relations with Pegu, and sent Muhammad

[1] In the *Waqai* the names of these brokers is constantly mentioned. See for Abdullah and other brokers *Waqai*, Appendix B, s.v.

[2] Kirkpatrick, No. 200

[3] *Ibid.*, No. 122

[4] *Ibid.*, No. 155

[5] *Ibid.*, No. 258

[6] *Selections from State Papers*, Bombay, No. cclvii, p. 337.

[7] Van Lohuizen, *The Dutch E.I.C. and Mysore*, p. 142.

Qasim and Muhammad Ibrahim as his envoys to its Raja.[1] Embassies, as we have seen, were despatched to France, Turkey and Iran in order to develop the trade of his country. Trade relations were also established with China; and since the Chinese merchants were reluctant to visit the Malabar coast owing to the fear of pirates, Tipu issued instructions to his officers to bring the Chinese vessels under the protection of Mysore convoys.[2] Armenian merchants, being regarded as good businessmen, were encouraged to settle in Mysore, and were provided with suitable places of residence. They were given full freedom to buy and sell and to import articles duty free.[3] Tipu, however, placed great restrictions on the trade of the European Companies with Malabar. In consequence, the trade of the English settlement of Tellicherry and the French settlement of Mahé declined.

But while permitting private enterprise, Tipu became the chief merchant of his country, and established State monopoly of gold ore, tobacco, sandalwood, precious metals, elephants, coco-nut and black pepper. Timber was also a monopoly, the owners of forests being given three rupees a candy. The income from forests in Malabar was 30,000 pagodas. But it must be remembered that the monopoly of timber was only confined to teakwood; merchants were allowed to deal freely in ebony and other kinds of wood. Calicut was the centre of timber trade. From there some teakwood was sent to Mangalore, where it was used to build vessels for Tipu. The rest was sold to the Indian, Arab and European merchants. At first a Moplah was in charge of cutting teakwood trees, but later a Brahmin was appointed in his place.[4] By Tipu's orders Raja Ramchandra established in every *taluk* State shops which did business in gold, silver, cloth and other articles.[5] Furthermore, the Sultan tried to abolish the local bankers and take over himself the functions of remittance and exchange.

The great interest which Tipu took in the trade and commerce of his kingdom is evident from the two very detailed regulations that he issued—one on March 25, 1793, and the other on April 2, 1794. These were meant for his nine officers, the *malik-ut-tujjars*, who were at the head of the Commerce Department. They were to look after shipping and factories, and to see that elephants and various articles, such as silk and cotton cloth, sandalwood, pepper, cardamom, rice, gold, silver and sulphur were available for export. They were to make purchases through the *asafs*, and pay the same duty on exports as the private merchants. They were to encourage foreign merchants to

[1] Kirkpatrick, No. 211
[2] Ibid., Appendix E, p. xxxvii.
[3] *Ibid.*, No. 425
[4] Malabar Sec. Com. Diaries (Revenue), Aug. 31 to Sept. 26, 1797, Vol. 1710, pp. 89, 236, 238; *Ibid.*, Jan. 17, 1799, pp. 90, 94; Forest Recds., Vol. 2408, p. 33.
[5] Kirkpatrick, No. 98.

settle in Mysore. Able and trustworthy *gumashtas* and *mutasaddis* were to be appointed in the factories both at home and abroad. The *gumashtas* were to be experienced enough to keep accounts properly and be able to prevent fraud and embezzlement. The heads of the Commerce Department and the officers under them were to pledge themselves according to the forms of their respective religions that they would discharge their duties honestly. In case any officer should behave dishonestly, the others should together expose the offender to shame and disgrace, and report him to the Sultan so that he might be given suitable punishment. The department was also directed to establish factories in foreign countries by securing the permission of their rulers. The factories were to buy the rare products of those countries for sending them to Mysore, and in return to sell the products of Mysore. There were to be thirty factories in Mysore and seventeen in the rest of India and outside.[1] But Tipu could not succeed in his object; he was only able to establish a few factories. After the fall of Seringapatam the factories in Cutch and at Masqat remained subordinate to the Mysore Government owing to a misunderstanding on the part of Lovett. But by the end of 1800, they were closed down, and the employees were ordered to return to Mysore.[2]

To interest his subjects in trade and commerce, Tipu established a trading company. Every one was welcome to buy shares in it. Any one who deposited five to five hundred rupees was entitled to a profit of fifty per cent at the end of the year. For a deposit of five hundred to five thousand rupees, the profit was twenty-five per cent; and over the deposits of five thousand, it was twelve per cent. In case any shareholder wanted to sell off his shares, he was to be given back his principal together with the profits. High dividends were paid to persons investing small amounts in order to encourage the small investor.[3]

For developing industry in Mysore, Tipu secured the services of French artisans and workmen who were sent to him by Louis XVI. He also employed French adventurers, English deserters and prisoners of war for the purpose. As we have seen, he wrote to the Ottoman Sultan to send him craftsmen who could help in the development of industries in his kingdom.

Tipu established various types of factories at Seringapatam, Chitaldrug, Bangalore and Bednur which employed European and Indian workmen, and manufactured scissors, hour-glasses, pocket-knives, guns, muskets, powder, paper, watches and cutlery. A French artist had prepared an engine, driven by water, for boring cannon.[4] The

[1] *Ibid.*, Appendix E, pp. xxxiii-xxxv, xliii; I.O. 4685 (Persian), ff. 11a-19a.
[2] I.O. Home Misc. Series, No. 475, pp. 355-58, 360-63.
[3] *Ibid.*, p. xliv; I.O. 4685 (Persian), ff. 20a-b.
[4] Buchanan, i, p. 70; A.N., c²172, Monneron to Cossigny, Sept. 14, 1786, f. 208a.

ammunition factories at Bednur produced 20,000 muskets and guns every year, and made the Sultan, according to his claim, self-sufficient in arms.[1] There was a big paper-mill in the fort of Seringapatam.[2] In the stone-quarries near the capital stones were cut into various shapes. The gunpowder manufactured in Mysore was of a better quality than that manufactured even by the English.[3] At Chennapatna glassware were made. The place was also famous for steel wire of musical instruments which was sent to different parts of India. Besides, very fine sugar was produced at Chennapatna, but the process was kept a secret.[4] The sugar candy made at Chickballapur was of a very superior quality, and clayed sugar was very white and fine. The process of its manufacture was introduced by Tipu and was kept a secret.[5] In the Devanhalli *taluk* sugar of a superior quality was manufactured with the help of the Chinese brought over for the purpose by Tipu's orders.[6] Weavers of Bangalore made very fine and rich cloth, but after the fall of Seringapatam in 1799 the industry declined because of the lack of patronage.[7] Silk industry was developed in Mysore by obtaining silkworms from Bengal and Masqat, and by encouraging the plantation of mulberry trees. Efforts were also made to establish a pearl-fishery on the Malabar coast, and for this pearl-divers were brought over from Masqat.

### *The Fighting Forces*

Tipu possessed a regular, standing army which was better equipped, better disciplined and more used to war than that of the Nizam or the Marathas. According to Campbell, "Tippoo is an active, ambitious and enterprising prince whose troops are in higher order than the force of any Asiatic State we are acquainted with."[8] Similarly, William Macleod observed: "Tippoo is the only prince who has persevered in disciplining and arranging his army after a regular plan. In this respect he is perfectly unprejudiced and ready to adopt any change which may serve for the improvement of his troops."[9] A French officer testified that Tipu's "artillery is in very good order and well served, his troops are inured to the hardships of war, and they are the best paid and best disciplined among the princes of India. He has become redoubtable to the English, and the troops

[1] A.N., C²172, Tipu to Cossigny, July 5, 1786, ff. 45a *seq.*
[2] *Asiatic Annual Register*, (1799), p. 243.
[3] *Ibid.*,
[4] Buchanan, i, pp. 147 *seq.*
[5] *Ibid.*, p. 340.
[6] Rice, *Mysore and Coorg.*, ii, p. 56.
[7] Buchanan, i, pp. 203 *seq.*
[8] Cornwallis Papers, P.R.O., 30/11/118, Campbell to Cornwallis, May, 1787, f. 88b.
[9] Mly. Sundry Book, vol. 101 (1792-95), p. 93.

of the Suba or the Mahrattas are not in a state to fight them."[1]

Tipu's regular cavalry was armed with carbines and swords, but did not wear any particular dress.[2] His cavalry wore no martingals, and this was a distinction by which the English could recognise them from the cavalry of the Nizam and the Marathas.[3] Tipu's irregular horse were by far the most useful troops. They could undergo all kinds of privations, and having more experience than the regular forces, were less apprehensive of danger and more capable of taking advantage of the enemy.[4] Tipu's infantry was armed, like the European troops, with muskets and bayonets which were manufactured in his own kingdom after the French models. He possessed large quantities of English and French arms, but he generally gave preference to the things made in Mysore, though they were not always so good. His field-guns were also generally cast in Mysore with the help of French artificers, and being larger than those of the English, and having a much longer range, had a great effect in action. This gave both Haidar and Tipu considerable advantage over the English in cannonades. The infantry was disciplined after the European manner with Persian words of command. Its dress consisted of a jacket of cotton of a mixed purple colour, with spots in imitation of those of a tiger, red or yellow turban, and short, loose trousers.[5] The greater part of the infantry in peace time was cantoned on the island of Seringapatam; while the cavalry was stationed as near the capital as it was convenient to secure forage. Tipu regarded it as a bad policy to trust any large body of his troops to be absent from his own immediate inspection, and seldom allowed the same officers to remain long in command of the same men.[6] He enforced strict military discipline, and orders were issued that any one who attempted to desert or to run away during an engagement was to be shot.[7] For the payment of salaries, Tipu's month varied between 36,[8] 45, 50 and even 60 days.[9]

Tipu retained the entire patronage of the army in his own hands,

[1] P.A. MS., No. 1337; See also A.N., C²172, Monneron to Cossigny, Sept. 14, 1786, ff. 207a-b. Monneron thought that Tipu's artillery was superior to that of even the Europeans, not to speak of the artillery of the Indian powers. Conway, Governor of Pondicherry, also spoke highly of Tipu's artillery, and stated that 40,000 bullocks were employed to drag the cannons. (A.N., C²184, *Colonies*, Conway to de la Luzerne, Feb. 6, 1788, f. 33a).

[2] Mly. Sundry Book, vol. 101 (1792-95), p. 111.

[3] P.R.C., iii, Nos. 311, 314.

[4] Mly. Sundry Book, vol. 101, p. 100.

[5] *Ibid.*, p. 110, W. P., B. M. 13659, pp. 79-85. (I.H.R.C., xix, pp. 134-38.)

[6] M.R., Mly. Sundry Book, vol. 101, p. 93.

[7] Shushtari, *Fath-ul-Mujahidin*, f. 36b. Monneron also spoke of strict discipline in Tipu's army. (See A.N., C²172, Monneron to Cossigny, Sept. 14, 1786, f. 207b. See also p. 349, *supra*, for the descipline in Tipu's army.

[8] *Waqai*, ed. Mohibbul Hasan, p. 68.

[9] A.N., C²172, Monneron to Cossigny, Sept. 14, 1786, f. 207a; C²184, *Colonies*, Conway to de la Luzerne, Feb. 6, 1788, f. 32b.

and being constantly with it both in peace and in war, his presence created a spirit of emulation which did not exist in the armies of other Indian rulers. His army was not modelled on a feudal basis, and this was a great source of its strength.[1] He obtained recruits for his army not only from Mysore but also from the neighbouring kingdoms. The families of the soldiers had to reside either at Seringapatam or Bangalore or at Bednur.[2] The soldiers recruited in Mysore were called *zumra*, and were given green turbans with a reddish border; while those recruited from outside the kingdom were called *ghair zumra*, and their turbans were wholly green.[3] Tipu exempted Brahmins, *darweshes* and merchants from military service. Among the Hindus only the Rajputs and the Marathas were enlisted, while among the Muslims the recruitment of Shaikhs, Sayyids, Mughals and Pathans was encouraged.[4]

During the early period of Tipu's rule the Mysore army was divided into *cushoons*, *risalas* and *juqs*. Each *cushoon* was commanded by a *sipahdar*, and had a *bakhshi* and *mutasaddis* attached to it. At the head of each *risala* was a *risaldar*, and at the head of each *juq* was a *juqdar*. Next in rank were the *sarkheils*, the *jamadars*, the *dafadars* and the *yazakdars*.[5]

The duty of the *sipahdar* was to look after the conduct of the officers and men belonging to his *cushoon*. He was empowered to promote the *juqdars* and other junior officers to higher ranks as well as to punish them. In the latter case they were to be tried by a court-martial. But if a *risaldar* deserved punishment or reward, his case was to be reported to the Sultan. The *sipahdar*, with the *bakhshi* and the *mutasaddis*, were required to take the muster-roll of the troops once every month, and inspect their firelocks and accoutrements. He was then to submit a report conjointly with the *bakhshi*. He was to see that his *cushoon* was well supplied with arms and ammunition, that guns were kept clean, and that parade was regularly held. If he was faced with some difficulty, he was to consult the *risaldars*, and take their opinions in writing. If their views differed from his own, the decision was to be taken by mutual agreement.[6] The duty of the *bakhshi* was to prepare a statement of the salary of the troops of his *cushoon* at the end of every month, and after obtaining the money from Seringapatam, to distribute it on the first of every month in the presence of the *sipahdar*.[7] The duty of the *risaldar* was to hold the parade of the troops of his *risala* every day of the week, except on

[1] W. P., B. M. 13659.
[2] Shushtari, *Fath-ul-Mujahidin*, f. 60b.
[3] I.O. MSS. Eur. C.10, p. 224; Mly. Sundry Book, vol. 102b (1796-97). p. 572
[4] Mack. MSS., I.O. NO. 46, p. 129; Mly. Sundry Book, vol, 102B, p, 572.
[5] Shushtari, *Fath-ul-Mujahidin*, f. 71a.
[6] *Ibid.*, ff. 60b-61b..
[7] *Ibid.*, f. 62b.

Thursday which was to be a holiday.[1] Another important officer in the army was the *saryasaqchi*. His duty was to visit his *risala* everyday in order to find out the condition of the army, and submit a report first to the *sipahdar*, then to the *jaish cutchehri* of the *huzur*, and finally to the Sultan. The duty of the *yasaqchi* was to keep the *risaldar* and the *sipahdar* in touch with the troops. He was to wander about the *risala* and find out the condition of the soldiers and their equipment, and then to report to the *risaldar* and the *sipahdar*. He was also to carry the orders of the commanders to their subordinates in the time of war. Further, he was to be present at the time of the parade of the troops and to see that it was done properly. If he merited advancement, he was promoted to the position of a *juqdar;* but if he deserved punishment he was degraded to the rank of a *sarkheil*.[2]

After sometime Tipu reorganised his army. As a result, the *bakhshi*, who had formerly occupied the position of merely a Paymaster, now became the most important officer in the army. The *askar* (regular horse) was divided into *cutchehris* (brigades). There were four such *cutchehris*. Each *cutchehri* was divided into five *mokums* (regiments). The number in each *cutchehri* or *mokum* was not fixed. The commander of a *cutchehri* was called *bakhshi*, that of a *mokum* was known as *mokumdar*. The *mokum* was divided into four *risalas* (squadrons), each having a *risaldar* as commander. The *risala* was further divided into *yaz* (troops) each having a *yazakdar* (captain) at its head, and under him were *sarkheils* (subalterns), havaldars and sepoys.[3]

The *silhadar* (irregular horse) was not formed into corps, and each officer commanding a party made such arrangements as he thought proper. Although the irregular horse was very useful, it was without any discipline. The horses of the regular cavalry were the property of the Government, at whose expense the soldiers were clothed and armed. But the horses of the irregular cavalry belonged to the commander or the horsemen, and the Government paid a regular monthly salary to their owners. If the horse was killed on service the Government paid its price. Half of the plunder obtained by the regular cavalry was regarded as the property of the Government. The rest was distributed among the soldiers.[4]

The *jaish* (infantry) was divided into four *cutchehris* (brigades). Each *cutchehri* consisted of six *cushoons* (regiments). Each *cushoon* was divided into *juqs* (companies). Each *cutchehri* was commanded by a *bakhshi* who was provided with accountants and a number of assistants. At the head of a *cushoon* was a *sipahdar* (commandant). Each

[1] *Ibid.*, f. 63a-b.
[2] *Ibid.*, ff. 62a, 63a.
[3] M.R., My. Sundry Book, vol. 101, p. 101; W. P., B. M. 13659.
[4] Martin, *Wellesley's Despatches*, Appendix C, p. 653; Mly. Sundry Book, vol. 101, p. 94.

*risala* was commanded by a *risaldar*. At the head of a *juq* was a *juqdar* (captain), who had under him *sarkheils* (subalterns), *jamadars* and privates.[1] Each *cushoon* had an establishment of rocketmen under a *juqdar*, and an establishment of gunners under a *subedar*, including lascars for drawing the guns. The number of guns attached to each *cushoon* depended upon the strength of the corps and the nature of the service, and accordingly varied from one to five guns. Each *cushoon* had a red, triangular standard, with a green border and pendants to distinguish the corps.

The general administration of the army was carried on by the *mir miran* department. After the Treaty of Seringapatam (1792) a separate department was formed to look after the troops recruited from among the inhabitants of the Mysore kingdom. The *mir sudur* department was responsible for inspecting the defences of the forts and for supplying them with provisions, war materials and troops.[2] But so far as matters relating to military policy were concerned, these were decided by the Sultan himself who was his own commander-in-chief.

The strength of Tipu's army was not fixed, but varied in accordance with his military requirements and resources. According to Alexander Read, Tipu's military strength on the eve of the Third Anglo-Mysore War was 3,000 regular cavalry, 5,000 irregular cavalry, 3,000 *looties*, 48,000 regular infantry, 10,000 *asad-ilahis*, 60,000 peons armed with matchlocks and swords, and 3,000 pikemen.[3] In the Third Anglo-Mysore War Tipu's army consisted of 18,000 cavalry and 50,000 regular infantry. The 1,00,000 irregular infantry was employed to garrison the forts and assist in the collection of revenue.[4] But owing to the Treaty of Seringapatam (1792), which deprived Tipu of half his kingdom, he was compelled to reduce his armed forces. Thus, the Mysore army in 1793 consisted of 7,000 regular cavalry, 6,000 irregular cavalry, 30,000 regular infantry, 5,300 revenue peons, 36,000 *cundachars* and 2,000 artillery.[5] During the next year it was further reduced to 6,450 regular horse, 7,500 irregular horse, 360 independent horse, 23,800 infantry, 3,500 artillery including rocketeers, and 12,000 constituting the garrisons of Seringapatam, Bednur, Chitaldrug and other places. The total expense of maintaining the army as it stood in 1794 amounted to 24,30,186 pagodas, excluding the expense to maintain the garrisons of different forts which was

[1] *Ibid.*, p. 101; W. P., B. M. 13659.

[2] See p. 334, *supra*.

[3] I.O. MS. No. 46, pp. 134-35. But according to the W. P., B. M. 13659, the army in 1790 consisted of 45,000 regular infantry and 20,000 cavalry. exclusive of irregular peons or *cundachars*. Tipu continued Haidar's system of forming the prisoners of wars into separate battalions. Haidar had called them *chelas*, but Tipu gave them the name of *asad-ilahi* or *ahmadi* troops.

[4] Dirom, p. 249.

[5] W. P., B. M. 13659.

5,70,331 pagodas.[1] Tipu's army in July 1798 numbered 6,000 regular horse, 7,000 irregular horse, 30,000 regular infantry, 4,000 *ahmadi* or *asad-ilahi* troops, 1,500 pikemen, 8,000 peons and 6,000 pioneers.[2] Tipu's French force consisted of 4 officers, 40 privates (Europeans), and 350 half-castes and Caffres belonging to Lallée's party. Those that had arrived from the Isle of France in April consisted of 6 officers, 50 Privates (Europeans) and 100 half-castes and Caffres.[3] Although Tipu was accused by Wellesley of aggressive designs, it is clear from Macleod's statement that his army, at the time of the issue of the last pay prior to December 1798, was less than it had been in July of the same year. The infantry numbered 22,375 including 3,828 comprising the garrison of Seringapatam, but excluding the other garrisons and the new levies. The regular cavalry was only 2,662, and the irregular cavalry 7,087.[4] It was only when Wellesley had completed his war preparations that the Sultan also increased his forces; and on the eve of the Fourth Anglo-Mysore War he had 3,502 regular horse, 9,392 irregular horse, 23,483 regular infantry, 6,209 regular militia and 4,747 matchlockmen and peons.[5]

The French in Tipu's army were never so important as they were in the armies of the Nizam and Sindhia. Perron had created a force of 8,000 cavalry and 2,000 infantry, and had acquired great influence over Sindhia who had, in fact, no control either over him or over his regular troops. Similarly, Raymond, who had created a disciplined army of 14,000 men, was very influential with the Nizam. But the French officers in Tipu's service always remained his servants and never became his masters. His French corps in the Third Anglo-Mysore War consisted of 350 men and was commanded by Lallée. After the death of Lallée in 1791, Vigie was entrusted with the command. In 1794 the French corps consisted of only about 20 Europeans, among whom were some Swiss and 200 Indian Christians.[6] When Vigie died in 1794, M. Question succeeded him. On the fall of Seringapatam the French corps had only 4 officers and 45 non-commissioned officers and privates. In addition, there were several deserters from the English army who had entered Tipu's service, but their number is not known.[7]

*The Navy*.

Haidar Ali had twice attempted to build a navy. His first attempt

[1] M.R., Mly. Sundry Book, vol. 101, pp. 101-107.
[2] W. P., B. M. 13458, f. 119a
[3] *Ibid.*, f. 119b. See also pp. 288-89 and footnote 2.
[4] M.R., Mly. Sundry Book, vol. 102B, pp. 567 *seqq.*
[5] Owen, *Wellington's despatches*, p. 60.
[6] P.A. MS., No. 2140; M.R., Mly. Sundry Book, vol. 101, p. 111.
[7] *Ibid.*, vol. 109A, pp. 199-201, 202-3, Harris to Wellesley, May 22, 1799.

had failed because, in 1768, Stannett, his naval commander, had gone over to the English, taking with him a number of ships. In spite of this loss, Haidar had again built a fleet with the help of European technicians. But this time it had been crippled by Sir Edward Hughes, who had entered Mangalore in 1780, and destroyed a number of vessels lying at anchor.

When Tipu succeeded his father, he did not try to replace the navy destroyed by the English, because he was more interested in strengthening his land forces. He, no doubt, possessed a number of men-of-war, both large and small, but these were only meant to protect merchantmen from the attacks of pirates, and were not in a position, either from the point of view of numbers or equipment, to make a stand against the English navy. It was because of this that the Mysore navy played a very inglorious role in the Third Anglo-Mysore War, and the English easily occupied Tipu's Malabar possessions. Even the Maratha navy was able to capture the Mysore ports in the Karwar district.

It was only towards the last few years of his reign that Tipu directed his attention to the building of a navy. In 1796 he organised a Board of Admiralty under a *mir yam*, who had under him 30 *mir bahrs* or commanders of the fleet, assisted by a *mirzai daftar*, a *mutasaddi* and a large staff. These *mir yams* were to reside at the sea-ports. The navy was to consist of 22 line-of-battleships and 20 large frigates. The line-of-battleships were divided into first and second class, mounting 72 and 62 guns respectively; while the frigates were to carry 46 guns. For the construction of the ships, three dockyards were established—one at Mangalore, the other at Wajidabad near Merjan and the third at Molidabad. Each was under the supervision of two *mir yams*. Teakwood was cut in the Malabar forests, and sent to the dockyards from Calicut. The models of the vessels were supplied by the Sultan himself.[1] The whole scheme was undertaken with great zeal, but owing to the capture of Seringapatam it could not be realised.

The following is the list of shipping found in the Mysore ports of Mangalore, Cundapur and Tadri after the fall of Tipu.[2]

At Mangalore

| afloat | |
|---|---|
| 1 ship | 104ft by 27ft |
| 1 grab snow | 112ft by 24ft |
| 1 gallivat | 70ft by 16ft |
| 1 new ship | 112ft by 32ft |

[1] Kirkpatrick, Appendix K, pp. lxxix *seqq*. According to Kirkpatrick the number of *malik-ut-tujjars* was 9; see also I.O. 4685 (Persian), f. 6b.

[2] I.O., Home Misc. Series, Vol. 457, pp. 240-43.

In the marine yard

| | |
|---|---|
| 1 ship | 120ft by 40ft |
| 1 snow | |
| 1 grab | 65ft long |
| 1 gallivat | 78ft by 18ft |
| 3 gallivats | 60 to 70ft by 14 to 15 |
| 1 large luggage boat | |

In addition to these there were a number of large and small boats.

At Cundapur

| | |
|---|---|
| 1 large dow | |
| 1 snow | 60ft by 20ft |
| 3 gallivats and 3 small boats | |

At Tadri

3 ships, the largest measuring 110 ft.
2nd ship measuring 105ft.
3rd ship measuring 95ft.
5 gallivats and 2 large boats ready to be launched.

All these were well proportioned and their workmanship was good.

CHAPTER XXI

# STATE AND RELIGION

Tipu's policy towards his non-Muslim subjects has been variously estimated. Kirkpatrick calls Tipu "the intolerant bigot or the furious fanatic."[1] Wilks, in his *History of Mysore*, describes stories of forcible conversions, mass circumcisions, the destruction of temples and the confiscation of temple lands, and arrives at the conclusion that Tipu was "an intolerant bigot", and "in an age when persecution survived only in history renewed its worst terrors."[2] Some modern historians like Roberts and Sardesai also hold similar views. Surendranath Sen, on the other hand, is of the opinion that Tipu was not a bigot, and where he made forcible conversions to Islam, his motive was political and not religious.[3] Dodwell agrees with this view, and observes: "In fact a rational consideration of his career shows him not the bigoted tyrant of tradition, but an active, enterprising man, moving in a world in which new forces had recently been let loose, forces beyond his control and to some extent beyond his comprehension."[4]

In this chapter, an attempt has been made to show that Tipu was not a bigot but an enlightened ruler who raised Hindus to high positions in his Government, granted them complete freedom of worship, conferred grants on temples and Brahmins, gave money for the consecration of images, and on one occasion even ordered the building of a temple. There is no doubt that he sometimes ill-treated his non-Muslim subjects, but this was not due to their religion; it was because they were guilty of disloyalty. He, like his father Haidar Ali, kept religion and politics apart and rarely permitted his personal beliefs to influence his administrative policies. He treated his Muslim subjects with equal harshness when they were guilty of disloyalty or treason.

Haidar Ali had appointed Hindus to posts of responsibility in the State. Tipu followed the policy of his father. Thus Purnaiya held the very important post of *mir asaf*, while Krishna Rao was the Treasurer. Shamaiya Iyengar was the Minister of Post and Police, and his brother Ranga Iyengar and Narsinga Rao held high positions at Seringapatam. Srinivas Rao and Appaji Ram were Tipu's chief

[1] Kirkpatrick, p. x.
[2] Wilks, ii, p. 766.
[3] Sen, *Studies in Indian History*, pp. 166-67.
[4] Rushbrook Williams, *Great Men of India*, (Chapter on *Tipu Sultan* by Dodwell) p. 217.

confidants, and were sent on important diplomatic missions. Mool Chand and Sujan Rai were his chief agents at the Mughal court.[1] The Sultan also placed great trust in Naik Rao and Naik Sangana.[2] His chief *peshkar*, Suba Rao, was a Hindu.[3] Narasaiya, one of his *munshis*, was also a Hindu.[4] Nagappaya, a Brahmin, was appointed *faujdar* of Coorg.[5] A Brahmin was given the exclusive privilege of cutting the timber forests in Malabar.[6] Another Brahmin was appointed *asaf* of Coimbatore and afterwards of Palghat;[7] and many of Tipu's *amils* and revenue officers were Hindus. In the army also Hindus held responsible positions. Hari Singh was the *risaldar* of the irregular horse.[8] Sripat Rao was appointed with Roshan Khan to reduce the rebellious Nairs.[9] Sivaji, a Maratha, held the command of 3,000 horse, and fought bravely when Bangalore was besieged by Cornwallis in 1791.[10] A Brahmin named Rama Rao also served as commander of cavalry.[11]

In 1916 Rao Bahadur K. Narsimhachar, the then Director of Archaeology in Mysore, discovered a bundle of letters[12] in the temple of Sringeri.[13] They were addressed by Tipu to the Abbot of the place, and they throw a flood of light on his religious policy. It appears from the letters that in 1791 some Maratha horsemen under Raghunath Rao Patwardhan raided Sringeri, killed and wounded many people there, including many Brahmins, plundered the monastery of all its valuable property, and committed the sacrilege of displacing the sacred image of the goddess Sarada. Owing to this the Swami was obliged to leave the place, and began to live at Karakala. He informed Tipu about the Maratha raid, and asked his help for consecrating the image of the goddess. Tipu felt both indignant and grieved at the news, and replied: "People who have sinned against such a holy place are sure to suffer the consequences of their misdeeds at no distant date

[1] Kirkpatrick, No. 73; another *wakil* at Delhi was Mukand Rao. (see p. 129, *supra*).

[2] Punganuri, pp. 42, 47. [3] See p. 257, *supra*,

[4] M.A.R., 1916, p. 75.

[5] *Tarikh-i-Coorg*, f. 27a.

[6] Mal. Sec. Com., vol. 1716, Jan. 1799, p. 94.

[7] *Malabar Commission, First Commissioner's Diaries*, vol. ii, No. 1663, p. 223.

[8] Kirmani, p. 279.

[9] *Ibid*., p. 275.

[10] Hamid Khan, f. 78a.

[11] Rice, *Mysore and Coorg*, i, p. 299.

[12] M.A.R., 1916, pp. 10-11 73-76; See also Sen, *Studies in Indian History*, pp. 155-69. There are thirty records of Tipu's reign. With the exception of one, all are in the possession of the Sringeri Math. They range in date from 1791 to 1798, and are dated according to the *mauludi* era, but side by side, in most cases, the corresponding Hindu dates are also given.

[13] The village of Sringeri is situated below a hill on the left bank of the Tunga, and is the chief of the four places where in the eighth century Sankaracharya established maths or monasteries. The Abbot of the temple is looked upon with great reverence by the Hindus all over India.

in this Kali age in accordance with the verse: *Hasadhbih kriyate karma rudadbhir anubhuyate*" (People do evil deeds smiling but will suffer the consequences weeping). Treachery to the gurus will result in the destruction of the line of descent. At the same time Tipu immediately ordered his *asaf* of Bednur to supply the Swami with 200 rahatis (fanams) in cash, 200 rahatis worth of grains and other articles, if required, for the consecration of the goddess Sarada. He then wrote to the Swami requesting him to "pray for the increase of our prosperity, and the destruction of our enemies" after consecrating the goddess and feeding the Brahmins. After the idol was installed, Tipu received *prasada* and shawls, and in return sent cloth and a bodice for the goddess and a pair of shawls for the Swami.

In another letter Tipu acknowledges the receipt of the details of expenditure to be incurred for the *sata-chandi-japa* and *sahasra-chandi-japa* ceremonies, expresses pleasure at the news that these ceremonies will be performed for the welfare of the country and the destruction of its enemies, intimates that orders have been sent to his officers to go to Sringeri and provide everything necessary for the ceremonies, and requests the Swami to have the ceremonies performed, to make money gifts to the Brahmins engaged, and to feed one thousand Brahmins every day. In a subsequent letter of the same year, he expresses pleasure at hearing that the ceremony of *sahasra-chandi-japa* had commenced. There are two other records of this period. From one it appears that Tipu instructed his *asaf* of Bednur to send a palanquin for the goddess; and from the other, that a fine palanquin had been despatched for the Swami's use. In a letter of 1792, Tipu informs the Swami of having sent a pair of *chauris* with silver handles for his use.

All these letters are "couched in respectful language and breathe a spirit of reverence for the holy personages." They clearly expose the absurdity of the view that Tipu was a bigot and persecuted his Hindu subjects. For if he had been a fanatic, he would never have called a Hindu priest "*jagadguru*"; nor would he have ever supplied the Swami with money and materials for the reconsecration of an idol and the performance of Hindu religious ceremonies.

It might be argued that Tipu displayed generosity towards the Swami and the temple because he was anxious to conciliate his Hindu subjects and secure their whole-hearted support at a time when he was beset by his enemies on all sides. But it must be remembered that his interest in the temple and friendship for the Swami were not confined merely to the war period, but lasted down to the fall of Seringapatam. He continued to write to the Swami inquiring about his health, and occasionally sent him shawls and valuable clothes for the goddess. In a letter of 1793, when the Sultan was at peace with his enemies, after acknowledging the receipt of the Swami's letter who had gone on pilgrimage, he wrote: "You are the *jagadguru.* You are always performing penance in order that the whole world may prosper, and the people may be happy. Please pray to God for the increase of our prosperity. In whatever country holy personages like yourself may reside, that country will flourish with good showers and crops." If Tipu had been a fanatic Muslim he would never have addressed a Hindu priest in such a language; nor would he have ever believed in, and encouraged, forms of worship abhorrent to his religion.

Moreover, Tipu did not confine his patronage only to the Sringeri temple; he extended it to the other temples of the kingdom as well. From the inscriptions on four silver cups, a silver plate and a silver spittoon belonging to the Lakshmikanta temple in the village of Kalale in Nanjangud *taluk*, it appears that the vessels were presents from Tipu.[1] Similarly, at Melukote, the Narayanasvami temple possesses some jewels, and gold and silver vessels with inscriptions telling that they were presents from Tipu.[2] Tipu also gave to this temple in 1785 twelve elephants[3] and in 1786 a kettledrum.[4] A jewelled cup, set with five kinds of precious stones at the bottom, in the Srikanthesvara temple at Nanjangud was a present from *Tipu Sultana Padasa.*[5] Seven silver cups and a silver camphor-burner in the Ranganatha temple at Seringapatam bear inscriptions stating that these articles were the gifts of *Tippu Sultana Pachchha.*[6] And at Nanjangud in the Nanjandesvara temple there is a greenish jadite *linga* called *pachcha* or *padshah linga* which is said to have been installed by Tipu's orders.[7]

Tipu has been accused of having carried out the wholesale expropriation of lands belonging to the temples and Brahmins of his kingdom. In fact, what he did was to resume only the unauthorised grants, but those for which proper *sanads* from the previous rulers existed were left in the possession of their owners. In many cases Tipu himself made fresh grants of land and money to Brahmins and temples. Thus, according to a Marathi *sanad* issued by him to his *amildar*, Konappa, the Swami of Pushpagiri Math was allowed to enjoy the revenues of Thongapalli and Gollapalli villages.[8] He also made a grant of Kothanuthala, a village in Cuddapah District, to one Ramachar for performing *puja* in the Anjaneyasvami temple of

[1] M.A.R., 1917, p. 59.
[2] *Ibid.*, pp. 21, 37.
[3] *Epigraphica Carnatica*, iii, Sr. 77.
[4] M.A.R., 1916, p. 39.
[5] *Ibid.*, 1912, pp. 23,40.
[6] *Ibid.*, p. 58.
[7] *Ibid.*, 1940, p. 26.
[8] Local Recds., iv, p. 434, cited in *Tipu's Endowments to Hindu Institutions*, I.H.C., 1944, p. 416.

Ganjikota.[1] Similarly he assigned lands to a number of Brahmins in the Kamalapura *taluk*.[2] In 1794 he granted to a Brahmin named Maharaj Haripa an *inam* in the Manjarabad *taluk*.[3] A Sanskrit verse in Kanarese script records that Tipu granted lands to the temples and Brahmins on the banks of the Tungabhadra.[4] Lands were also assigned by him for the feeding of the Brahmin travellers. He issued orders to Haradasiyah, his *amildar* of the Baramahal, to resume all grants except the *Devadayam* and the *Brahamadayam* (endowments to temples and Brahmins).[5] In 1794 he conferred a hereditary pension of ten pagodas annually on Narasimha Joshi, a Brahmin of Dharmapuri.[6]

Tipu allowed the Hindus complete freedom of worship. The magnificent temple of Sri Ranganatha is situated within the fort of Seringapatam, about one hundred yards west of the palace from where the Sultan used to listen daily to the ringing of the temple bells and to the hymns of the Brahmin priests. Yet he never interfered with these. The Narasimha and the Gangadharesvara are the other two big temples inside the fort and near the palace. But neither in these temples nor in the thousands of others which were scattered throughout his kingdom, Tipu ever prevented Hindus from worshipping. On the contrary, in many cases, he gave the Brahmins money to perform their religious ceremonies. We have seen how he instructed his officers to supply the Swami of the Sringeri Math with all articles necessary for the performance of *sahasra-chandi-japa*. Similarly he gave an allowance to two pagodas at Rayakottai. Their priests possessed by him *sanads* which they produced before Munro in 1793, requesting him to continue the grant without which they would not be able to perform religious ceremonies.[7] Money was distributed to both Hindus and Muslims on the occasion of their religious festivals. According to a *sanad*, Tipu ordered the continuation of the usual worship of Venkatachalapali temple, and the restoration of the discontinued *puja* of Anjaneyasvami temple at Pullivendla in the Cuddapah district.[8] In one instance he even ordered the construction of a temple. When Haidar had invaded the Carnatic in 1780, he had laid the foundation of a Gopur temple in Conjeeveram, but he could not complete it. When Tipu visited the town during the

[1] Local Recds., iv, p. 434.
[2] *Ibid.*, ii, pp. 294-95.
[3] *Epigraphica Carnatica*, vol. v, part 1, Mj. 25, p. 268.
[4] Local Recds., xxiv, p. 16, cited in I.H.C., 1944, p. 417.
[5] Bàramahal Recds, Section v, p. 39, 116. See Subbaraya Chetty, *New Light on Tipu Sultan*, pp. 89-91, for more examples of grants which Tipu made to the Brahmins.
[6] Baramahal Recds., Section xviii, p. 98.
[7] *Ibid.*, Section xxii, p. 8.
[8] Local Recds., iv, p. 280, cited in I.H.C., 1944, p. 417.

Third Anglo-Mysore War, he made a grant of 10,000 huns towards the construction of the temple. And during his stay there he participated in the celebrations of the chariot festival, and bore the cost of the fireworks on the occasion.[1]

In a *sanad* in the possession of the Parakalla Math at Mysore, Tipu appears in the capacity of a mediator between two sects of Hindus who were wrangling with each other about the recitation of certain invocatory verses in the temple of Melukote. The *sanad* was issued by Tipu, and is written in Kanarese. It has a seal above in Persian characters with the name of Tipu Sultan, and is addressed to the manager of the department of temples in the State. It is stated in the *sanad* that since Anche Shamaiya, an officer under Tipu, was violating the old usage in the temple at Melukote regarding the use of invocatory verses, it was ordered that both forms of invocation should be used. Further, the manager of the department of temples was ordered to be fair to both the Vadagalai and Tenkalai sects which used the above invocation, and to remove the image of a saint of the Tenkalai sect to its original place at Melukote.[2]

Now if Tipu was not a bigot but an enlightened and tolerant ruler, how is it that he issued orders for the forcible conversions of Hindus in Coorg and Malabar to Islam? The true explanation appears to be that he did this not due to religious but to political motives. He regarded conversion as a form of punishment which he inflicted on such of his non-Muslim subjects as were guilty of repeated rebellion. Accordingly, he issued instructions to his officers that if the people of Coorg and Malabar did not give up their refractory conduct they should be proselytised. In one of his letters to Cossigny, he confesses that he converted Nairs to Islam "as a punishment to their rebellion", and that they deserved this punishment because "they rebelled six times and six times I forgave them."[3] Tipu expected that by these threats and examples he would be able to reduce the Coorgs and Nairs to obedience.

It is difficult to say how many inhabitants of Coorg and Malabar were forcibly made Muslims. The English versions cannot be regarded as authentic, because they were, for the most part, intended to malign Tipu and serve as propaganda against him. Nor should any reliance be placed on Muslim accounts which, in their anxiety to represent the Sultan as a champion of Islam, also have a tendency to exaggerate, distort, and falisify. They are intended to create effect, to surround

[1] Khare, viii, No. 3286.

[2] M.A.R., 1938, pp. 123-25.

[3] A.N., C[2]172, Tipu to Cossigny, March 3, 1788, f. 35a; *Sultan-ut-Tawarikh*, ff. 47, 51; *Tarikh-i-Khudadadi*, pp. 55, 61-2; see also Sen, *Studies in Indian History*, pp. 166-67, for a discussion of this question. Sen agrees that Tipu "regarded conversion as an extreme form of punishment."

Tipu with a religious halo and exalt him to the position of a religious hero. Thus, for example, the *Sultan-ut-Tawarikh* says that the Sultan converted 70,000 Hindus to Islam in Coorg.[1] But this is an absurd statement, because at that time the whole population of Coorg was much below this figure.[2] Besides, according to Ramchandra Rao "Punganuri", only 500 men, women and children were converted, and sent in groups to Seringapatam, Bangalore and other forts.[3] On the other hand Moor, who discusses different aspects of Tipu's policy, says nothing about his religious persecutions in Coorg.

It is usually forgotten while assessing Tipu's religious policy that some of the conversions were voluntary. Thus, for example, Ranga Nair, one of the Coorg leaders, who had escaped returned on Tipu's invitation and embraced Islam.[4] Similarly, there were other rebels who changed their religion to please the Sultan. The latter welcomed their conversion hoping that in this way they would lose their influence over their followers, and thus cease to be dangerous. It is not unlikely that he might have even offered them inducements to become Muslims. But this is quite different from the traditional picture of Tipu painted by some writers in which he is represented as being perpetually engaged in making wholesale conversions of Hindus, and massacring those who refused to accept Islam.

We should also remember that, except for Coorg and Malabar, Tipu did not adopt the policy of proselytisation in other parts of his kingdom, for the rebellions there were few and far between. Even in Malabar, it is significant to note, Tipu did not give up his patronage of Brahmins and temples. In 1789, when he marched towards the Travancore lines, he stayed at Trichur from the 14th to the 29th December, and borrowed from the temple of Vadakkunnathan vessels for cooking food for his army. On leaving Trichur, he not only returned the vessels to the temple but presented it a large bronze lamp.[5] He also gave grants of lands to temples and Brahmins in other parts of Malabar. The following is the list of such grants:[6]—

[1] *Sultan-ut-Tawarikh*, pp. 47, 51; *Tarikh-i-Khudadadi*, pp. 55, 61-2.

[2] See p. 79 footnote 4, *supra*.

[3] Punganuri, p. 37.

[4] Kirmani, p. 298. Some of the Yeravas and Holeyas, who formed a majority of Coorg's population, must have also embraced Islam, because they were enslaved and looked upon with contempt by the Kodagas, the ruling class. The same thing applies to the low caste people of Malabar who must have taken advantage of this opportunity to embrace Islam and thereby raise their social status.

[5] This information has been very kindly supplied to me by Prof. Mohideen Shah, Dean of the Faculty of Arts, Calicut University, who has published a paper entitled "Mysore rulers and Trichur", based on the temple records, in a special number of the Malyalam Daily "*The Light*" of April 26, 1969.

[6] I am grateful to Dr. C. K. Kareem, State Editor, Kerala Gazetteers, for sending me these details.

1. To Mannur temple in Chelambra Amsom, Ernad *taluk*, 70.42 acres of wet land and 3.29 acres of garden land.

2. To Tiruvanchikulam Siva temple in Vailattur Amsom, Ponnani *taluk*, 208.82 acres of wet land and 3.29 acres of garden land.

3. To Guruvayoor temple in Guruvayoor Amsom, Ponnani *taluk*, 46.02 acres of wet land and 458.32 acres of garden land.

4. Trikkantiyur Vettakkorumakankavu temple in Kasba Amsom, Calicut *taluk*, 122.70 acres of wet land and 73.36 acres of garden land.

5. To Kattumadathil Srikumaran (Namboodiripad), in Kadikad Amsom, Ponnani *taluk*, 27.97 acres of wet land and 6.91 acres of garden land.

6. To Trikkandiyur Samooham temple in Trikkandiyur Amsom, Ponnani *taluk*, 20.63 acres of wet land and .41 acres of garden land.

7. To Naduvil Madathil Tirumumbu in Trichur, 40.26 acres of wet land, 22.13 acres of garden land and 4.17 acres of dry land.

Thus we see that Tipu appointed Hindus to high posts, conferred gifts and grants on temples and Brahmins, installed idols, gave money for, and believed in the efficacy of, Hindu religious ceremonies, and never interfered with the magnificent temples scattered throughout his kingdom. It is, therefore, incredible that a ruler who showed such tolerance and generosity, and who had such eclectic beliefs could ever have been guilty of religious persecutions of Hindus.

Tipu has also been accused of having indulged in the religious persecution of his Christian subjects. But no reliable evidence exists to support this view. Tipu's attitude towards the Christians also was determined not by religious but by political considerations. He treated the Christians generously; and it was only when they were guilty of treason that he punished them.

During the Second Anglo-Mysore War the Kanara Christians, who were Mysore subjects, rendered valuable help to the English. When Matthews invaded the west coast, they acted as spies and guides and helped him in the conquest of Mangalore and the province of Bednur,[1] and about thirty-five Christians, who were in the Mysore army, deserted and entered his service.[2] Moreover, the Kanara Christians also gave the English financial assistance. Thus, in a letter which Matthews wrote just before the fall of Bednur, he mentioned that he had borrowed 33,000 rupees from the Kanara Christians, and requested that any one who happened to read the letter should make the fact known to the President and Council in any of the Presidencies.[3]

[1] Pissurlencar, *Antigualhas*, fasc., ii, No. 77; W. P., B.M. 37274, pp. 33-4; see also A.N., C[2] 172, Monneron to Cossigny, Sept. 14, 1786, ff. 201a *seq.*

[2] Cited in Saldhana, *The Captivity of Canara Christians under Tipu*, p. 18, footnote b.

[3] *The Captivity, Sufferings and Escape of James Scurry*, pp. 99-100 footnote.

When the Mysoreans besieged Mangalore, the Kanara Christians secretly helped Campbell, and entered into league with Qasim Ali and Muhammad Ali, who had formed a plot with the English for Tipu's overthrow.[1] Even Father Don Joaquim de Miranda, the head of the Mount Marian Seminary, supplied the English garrison with 1,000 bags of rice.[2] But, in spite of this, Tipu pardoned him, received him with respect, issued orders that no one should molest him, and on his mediation released 150 Christians.[3] Nevertheless, when Cossigny withdrew from the Mysore army, because an armistice had been signed between the English and the French, the Father gave him refuge and showed the way to the coast.[4]

It was owing to these reasons that the Christians were punished by Tipu. Father Joaquim was imprisoned in a fortress, and after a trial by a tribunal, he was exiled along with the whole Christian colony of Mount Marian to Cochin;[5] some of the Kanara Christians were exiled to Goa; while others were sent as prisoners to Seringapatam and Chitaldrug; and one Christian, who was an accomplice of Muhammad Ali and Qasim Ali, was hanged.[6] It is, however, difficult to estimate the number of men affected by Tipu's decrees. In one of the letters addressed to the Secretary of State by the Viceroy of Goa the number placed is 20,000;[7] but in a subsequent letter it is mentioned that 40,000 Christians were expelled by Tipu;[8] while according to another version, about 30,000 men are said to have been exiled.[9] Wilks's statement, however, that 60,000 were banished appears to be grossly exaggerated. Later, owing to the efforts of Pierre Monneron, the French envoy in Seringapatam, Tipu allowed Father Joaquim to return to his Convent at Mangalore, and with him many persons belonging to his Congregation also returned.[10]

As regards the charge that Tipu made forcible conversions of Christians to Islam, no reliable evidence exists to support such a view. Some, no doubt, accepted Islam. But this they did voluntarily in

[1] Pissurlencar, *Antigualhas*, fasc., ii, No. 79.
[2] *Ibid.*
[3] I.O., Portug. Recds., *Conselho Ultramarinho*, Vol. 2, part 2, letter from Father of Mt. Marian to Viceroy, pp. 571-73. It seems that de Morlat also interceded with Tipu on behalf of the Father. (*Ibid.*, Document 8, de Morlat to Felicis and Ramos Nobre Monrao, Oct, 17, 1783, pp. 432-33).
[4] Pissurlencar, *Antigualhas*, fasc. ii, No. 79; A. N., C[2] 172, Instructions by Cossigny to Monneron, ff. 197a *seq.*
[5] Pissurlencar, *Antigualhas*, fasc. ii, No, 79; I.O. Portug. Recds., *Conselho Ultramarinho*, Vol. 2, part 2, Father Joaquim to Viceroy, pp. 575-78. Father Joaquim also says that 40,000 Christians were exiled. (Ibid., pp. 582-83).
[6] Pissulencar, *Antigualhas*, fasc., ii, No. 79.
[7] Ibid., No. 77.
[8] Ibid., No. 81.
[9] Ibid., No. 80.
[10] A.N., C[2]172, Instructions by Cossigny to Monneron, Feb. 2, 1786, ff. 199a-200a.

order to escape the boredom of prison life. After they were released, they were given responsible posts in the palace and in the army. A large number, however, remained imprisoned in Seringapatam and Chitaldrug and were allowed to retain their religion. This is clear from the fact that, in 1789, Tipu sent an embassy to the Viceroy and Archbishop of Goa requesting them to send priests to the Christians who had neglected their religious duties owing to their captivity. He even promised to build their churches which had been destroyed.[1] Many priests were released, and allowed to proceed to Goa unmolested either because they asked forgiveness, or because the Viceroy of Goa interceded on their behalf.

But it should not be supposed that all Christians suffered at the hands of Tipu. It was in reality only the Kanara Christians who were harshly dealt with. They consisted for the most part of emigrants from Goa, and being under the ecclesiastical jurisdiction of the Archbishop of Goa, were not trusted by Tipu, since his relations with the Portuguese were not cordial. Besides, they had been repeatedly guilty of disloyalty to the Mysore Government. Haidar had treated them generously, and yet they had helped the English in the conquest of Mangalore in 1768.[2] Under Tipu also they committed treason; so they were exiled, since their presence endangered the security of the State. The Syrian Christians were, however, treated well by Tipu. Similarly, he encouraged the Armenian merchants to come and settle in Mysore, and all kinds of facilities were given to them.[3] Moreover, there were a number of Christians in his army who were given complete freedom of worship. Even the Kanara Christians, who had been guilty of disloyalty, were allowed to reside in his kingdom provided they paid compensation for the loss of three crores of rupees which they had caused him by helping the English in the conquest of Mangalore. Fresh emigrants from Goa were also allowed to settle on condition that they agreed to abide by the laws of Mysore.[4] These facts show that Tipu's attitude towards the Christians in his kingdom was determined not by religious but by political considerations. The Kanara Christians were punished not because they were Christians but because they were traitors. And there is no reason to suppose that if they had remained loyal to the Sultan, they would still have been persecuted.

Tipu's attitude towards the Mahdavis was also determined by political and not by religious considerations. While he was at Devan-

[1] Saldanha, *The Captivity of Canara Christians under Tipu*, pp. 29-30.

[2] See for more details regarding Haidar and the Malabar Christians, Moraes, *Muslim Rulers of Mysore and their Christian Subjects*, pp. 443-45 (I.H.C., 1944).

[3] Kirkpatrick, No. 425.

[4] Pissurlencar, *Antigualhas*, fasc., ii, No. 75, Tipu to the Viceroy of Goa., March 24, 1784.

halli celebrating the return of the hostage princes from Madras, the Mahdavis made preparations to perform their particular form of worship on the night of Ramazan 27, 1208 A.H./April 28,1794.[1] The Sultan did not object to this, for he had always granted them complete freedom of worship and belief; but, since they were in the habit of praying very loudly, which was likely to disturb other Muslims in the army engaged in prayers and thus lead to trouble, he sent Mir Sadiq, his *diwan*, to ask their chiefs to tell their followers not to pray within the camp, but at some distance away, where they would be provided with tents and other facilities. The chiefs agreed to this, but during the night about 3,000 of the Mahdavis began to celebrate their rites. Tipu woke up, and for this act of defiance, the next morning, he ordered the imprisonment of two of their chiefs, Mahtab Khan and Alam Khan, and exiled not only the Mahdavis in the army, but all the followers of the sect from his kingdom. The only exception was made in the case of Sayyid Muhammad Khan whom Tipu greatly respected. In spite of this Sayyid Muhammad made up his mind to escape with his family from Mysore. But Tipu came to know of this; so, on his return to Seringapatam, he ordered him into confinement from which he was only released after its capture by the English in 1799. Mahtab Khan and Alam Khan were, however, released by Tipu in 1795.[2]

The question is why did Tipu inflict such heavy punishment merely for an act of disobedience? Besides, why should he have to banish all the Mahdavis for the fault of a few? The reason seems to be that he had begun to suspect them of treason; and the act of defiance on the night of the 27th Ramazan confirmed him of his suspicions. And since they were a united, well-knit community, whose members he could no longer trust, he exiled all of them from his kingdom. It is difficult to say whether these suspicions were justified—although from the way the Mahdavis were easily won over by the English, it appears that his suspicions were not altogether baseless—or they were, as Kirmani thinks, the result of Mir Sadiq's intrigues,[3] the consequences of their exile proved to be unfortunate, for, on the eve of the Fourth Anglo-Mysore War, the exiled Mahdavis joined the English and played an important role in the overthrow of Tipu.

[1] The night of 27 Ramazan, called in Arabic *Laylat al-Qadr* and in Persian *Shab-i-Qadr* is of great religious significance to the Muslims, because on this day, while he was engaged in meditation within a little cave on a hill outside Mecca, the Prophet Muhammad received his first revelation. During the night of that day, therefore, the Muslims engage themselves in prayers. The Mahdavis also pray, and in addition perform *zikr*.

[2] Wilks, ii, pp. 597-98.

[3] Kirmani, pp. 378-79; see also Sayyid Aziz, *Mashahir-i-Mahdavi*, i, pp. 96-100.

## CHAPTER XXII

# REVIEW AND CONCLUSIONS

Few Indian rulers have been so much maligned and misrepresented as Tipu Sultan. His memory, as Thompson and Garratt observe, "has been stereotyped into a monster pure and simple."[1] As early as 1794 Moor wrote: "Of late years, indeed, our language has been ransacked for terms in which well disposed persons were desirous to express their detestation of his name and character; vocabularies of vile epithets have been exhausted, and doubtless many have lamented that the English language is not copious enough to furnish terms of obloquy sufficiently expressive of the ignominy wherewith they in justice deem his memory deserves to be branded."[2] After Tipu's death Beatson, Kirkpatrick and Wilks vied with each other in their campaign of vilifying the Sultan, and their statements were blindly accepted by subsequent historians, both English and Indian.

The reasons why Tipu was reviled are not far to seek. Englishmen were prejudiced against him because they regarded him as their most formidable rival and an inveterate enemy, and because, unlike other Indian rulers, he refused to become a tributary of the English Company. Many of the atrocities of which he has been accused were fabricated either by persons embittered and angry on account of the defeats which they had sustained at his hands, or by the prisoners of war who had suffered punishments which they thought they did not deserve. He was also misrepresented by those who were anxious to justify the wars of aggression which the Company's Government had waged against him. Moreover, his achievements were belittled and his character blackened in order that the people of Mysore might forget him and rally round the Raja, thus helping in the consolidation of the new regime.

Tipu was, however, not regarded by all his contemporaries, nor by all the subsequent writers as a wicked, tyrannical and worthless ruler. According to a French officer, "Tipu made the cultivator happy, and protected the Indian merchant."[3] Even Englishmen, when they were not swayed by political motives and passions, held a

[1] Thompson and Garratt, *Rise and Fulfilment of British Rule in India*, p. 206.
[2] Moor, p. 193.
[3] P.A.MS., No. 1337. The letter is addressed to the Minister of Marine and Colonies, 1790.

favourable view of Tipu's character and administration. Thus, on hearing the news of Haidar's death, Macartney, the Governor of Madras, wrote: "The youthful and spirited heir of Hydar, without the odium of his vices and his tyranny, may succeed to that power and that ambition which have been so prejudicial to the Company's tranquility and welfare."[1] Two months later, he again wrote: "The accounts which I have been able to procure of the disposition and sentiments of Tippoo Sahib, concur in attributing to him a more humane and civilised character than that of his father Hydar Ali."[2] And Dundas, who was an implacable enemy of Tipu, observed that after the fall of Haidar the Mysore power would have been overthrown "if Tippoo Sultan had not inherited his father's abilities and vigour."[3] In February 1790, an Englishman wrote from India to a member of the British Parliament: "Tippoo is not only superior in enterprise to all the monarchs of the East, but many of the features of his character might be exhibited in the picture of an Achilles."[4] Moor, Dirom, Mackenzie and Sir John Shore also acknowledged that Tipu was a lenient and indulgent master, an able and popular ruler who promoted the well-being of his people. Even Rennell, who was very hostile to the Sultan, admitted that he possessed "great qualities of war and finance."[5] Mill, who was not entirely able to shake off his British bias, declared that "as a domestic ruler he sustains an advantageous comparison with the greatest princes of the East," and that his country was "the best cultivated and its population the most flourishing in India."[6] In recent years also, as a result of a more objective study of Tipu, similar opinions have been expressed, although there are still some writers who prefer to repeat *ad nauseam* the views of Wilks and Kirkpatrick.

Tipu had a dignified appearance. He was of a brown complexion, and had small delicate hands and feet, an aquiline nose, lustrous eyes and a short, thick neck. He had splendid health and with years his royal person assumed greater amplitude.[7] He wore no beard, but, unlike his father, retained his eyebrows, eyelashes and moustache.

Tipu dressed simply but elegantly, and enjoined simplicity on his courtiers as well. That was why he banished from his court long robes and trailing drawers.[8] But on his journeys he wore a coat of golden

[1] Mly. Cons., Dec. 14, 1782, vol. 84A, p. 3901, Minute of the Committee.
[2] *Ibid.*, Feb. 11, 1783, vol 86A, p. 608, President's Minute.
[3] Scottish Record office, iv/33/9-1792.
[4] *A letter to a Member of Parliament*, p. 10.
[5] Rennell, *Memoirs*, p. cxxxix.
[6] Mill, vi, p. 105.
[7] Beatson, p. 152.
[8] Kirmani, p. 398. Beatson, p. 153; Wilks, ii, p. 761.

cloth with a red tiger-streak embroidered on it.[1] He was also dressed richly when he attended the durbar. But, unlike other Indian princes, he did not wear any jewellery. He ate simple food, taking only two meals a day, in the company of his chief officers, courtiers and two or three of his sons. During his repasts he was fond of reading books on history, tradition, religion and biography. He also heard stories and anecdotes from his courtiers, but he did not like coarse jests.[2] His energy and activity were astonishing. He worked hard for sixteen hours a day, occupying himself with the minutest details of administration and leaving very little time for pastimes. However, for a diversion, he sometimes witnessed dancing.[3]

Tipu left his bed an hour before daybreak. After a bath, he performed his morning prayers and read the Quran. He then took some exercise[4] and dressed himself. With a rosary in his hand and wearing a small Burhanpur turban, a fine white gown having a diamond button, a shirt with a broach of copper and gold to fasten it, short drawers in the procket of which was a European watch, and leather shoes with iron spurs, he proceeded to the presence chamber, where he gave audience to his chief civil and military officers.[5] He then inspected the *jamadar-khana*, where the jewellery, plate, fruits and other articles were kept. After making inquiries and giving instructions to the *daroghas* of different establishments, he returned to the presence chamber, where he learnt from the astrologers about his stars, and got himself shaved.[6] At nine o'clock he took his breakfast with two or three of his sons and some of his officers. During this meal, which consisted of nuts, almonds, fruit, jelly and milk, he talked about his past wars and his future plans. And this was the time when he dictated important letters to his secretaries.[7]

After breakfast Tipu dressed himself in rich clothes. He wore a red or purple or pale crimson green turban wrought with the threads of gold. It was tied in a circular form, and had a diamond plume with fine tufts on either side. His frock was of fine white cloth and tight, with the sleeves drawn up in plaits. It was short in the waist, had long skirts, and was fastened at the chest by a diamond button. On his loins he had a gold bordered kerchief. On the finger of his right hand he wore a diamond ring or one set with ruby or emerald,

[1] Kirmani, p. 398.
[2] *Ibid.*,
[3] A.N., $C^2$172, Monneron to Cossigny, Sept. 14, 1786, f. 207a; Kirmani, p. 398.
[4] According to I.O.MSS. Eur. C. 10 p. 205, after his exercise, Tipu took light breakfast consisting of cooked brains of male sparrows.
[5] I.O.MSS. Eur. c. 10, p. 205.
[6] *Ibid.*, p. 206; see also Beatson, p. 159.
[7] I.O.MSS. Eur. C. 10, p. 208; Beatson, pp. 159-60.

varying every day in colour according to the course of the seven stars.[1]

When Tipu entered the hall of public audience, the two *arzbegis* (Masters of Requests), Masters of Ceremonies and the chief civil and military officers made their obeisance. Then the postmaster delivered a bag full of petitions and letters, and the heads of departments informed the Sultan of the news which they had.[2] In front of the throne sat the chief heads of departments and his Persian, Kanarese, Telugu and Marathi secretaries, to whom he dictated letters. He also went through the accounts of different departments for each month and despatched other affairs.[3]

About three o'clock the Sultan rose from the audience and retired to the bed chamber. Here he performed his prayers. He then went out to inspect the foundry and manufacturies and reviewed the troops. He also examined, when the repairs of the fort of Seringapatam were going on, the progress of the works. He returned to the palace an hour after sunset through the bazaar.[4]

On reaching the palace he received reports from the different departments and the news of the day. At the same time he issued instructions, dictated letters and answered petitions. He generally passed the evening with his three eldest sons, some principal officers, a *qazi*, and his principal *munshi*, Habibullah. All of them had dinner with him. Tipu's conversation was very lively, entertaining and instructive. During his meal he discussed on learned and religious subjects with those who were present. He also sometimes recited passages and verses from the works of great historians and poets. After dinner he dismissed the company, and strolled for some time alone. Then he lay down in his bed, and read books on religion or history until he fell asleep.[5]

Haidar Ali wanted Tipu to be married to the daughter of the late Imam Saheb Bakhshi, a Navayet. But Tipu's mother and other ladies in the palace were opposed to this, and desired the prince to marry Ruqayya Banu, the daughter of Lala Mian and sister of Burhan-ud-din. In the end Tipu was married to both girls the same night in the same year in 1774.[6] Ruqayya Banu died on the day after the English stormed Tipu's position before Seringapatam in February 1792. After three years, in 1795, Tipu married Khadija Zaman Begum, the daughter of Sayyid Saheb. In 1797 a son was born to her, but after a few days both mother and child died.[7]

[1] I.O.MSS. Eur. C. 10, p. 207.
[2] *Ibid.*, pp. 209-10.
[3] *Ibid.*, pp. 212, 215-16.
[4] *Ibid.*, p. 221.
[5] Beatson, p. 160-61.
[6] Kirmani, p. 155.
[7] *Ibid.*, pp. 377-78. Miles in his translation of Kirmani's history says that a daughter was born to her.

Kirmani does not refer to any other marriage. Arthur Wellesley also says that at the time of the fall of Seringapatam Tipu had only one wife called Sultan Begum Saheb or Padshah Begum, who was the daughter of Imam Saheb Bakhshi and sister of Ghulam Husain Khan, known as the Pondicherry Nawab, a descendant of Chanda Saheb.[1] But Marriott, who was in charge of the palace in Seringapatam in July 1800, adds the name of Buranti Begum as another wife of Tipu. She was the daughter of Mir Muhammad Pasand Beg, a nobleman of Delhi, and her mother's father was Sayyid Muhammad Khan, once a *subedar* of Kashmir.[2] Roshani Begum, the mother of Fath Haidar, Tipu's eldest son, is regarded by Wellesley as a concubine. But the prince claimed that his mother was the principal wife (*khas mahal*) of his father.[3]

How many concubines Tipu had is difficult to say. Kirmani, Mackenzie, Dirom, Beatson and other contemporary accounts do not mention of any concubine. In fact, according to them, the Sultan led a strictly moral life. But both Arthur Wellesley and Marriott say that there were 193 concubines of the first rank and one hundred slave women in Tipu's *mahal*.[4] But in another place Marriott does not refer to any concubine.[5] It must be remembered that to Europeans every woman in the palace appeared to be a concubine. They did not realise that most of them served as nurses, cooks, seamstresses, teachers, maid-servants, char women and in other capacities.

Tipu was survived by twelve sons, namely, Fath Haidar, Muin-ud-din Sultan, Abdul Khaliq Sultan, Muiz-ud-din Sultan, Muhammad Subhan Sultan, Shukrullah Sultan, Ghulam Ahmad Sultan, Ghulam Muhammad Sultan, Sarwar-ud-din Sultan, Muhammad Yasin Sultan, Jamal-ud-din Sultan and Munir-ud-din Sultan.[6] According to Kirmani Tipu left behind only one daughter who was married to Husain Ali Khan.[7] But Arthur Wellesley gives the names of four daughters[8] and Marriott of eight.[9]

Tipu was affectionate by nature. He gave his sons proper educa-

[1] M. R., Mly. Cons., Sept. 4, 1799, A. Wellesley to Mornington, Aug. 19, vol. 257b, p. 5868; I.O., Home Misc. No. 461, Marriott to Webbe, July 2,1800, p. 172.

[2] *Ibid.*, p. 173.

[3] M. R., Mly., Cons., Dec. 19,1799, Doveton to Col. Wilks, Nov. 30, 1799, vol. 261a, p. 7513.

[4] M. R., Mly. Cons., Sept. 4, 1799, p. 5868. Marriott says that there were in the palace a number of slave girls purchased from Constantinople and Georgia (I.O., Home Misc., No. 416, Marriott to Webbe, July 2,1800, p. 170).

[5] *Ibid.*, p. 176.

[6] Kirmani, p. 395; M. R., Mly. Cons., Sept. 4, 1799, vol. 257b, p. 5868.

[7] Kirmani, p. 395.

[8] M. R., Mly. Cons., Sept. 4, 1799, vol 257b, p. 5868.

[9] I. O., Home Misc., 508, pp. 280-82, Marriott to the Vellore Mutiny Commission of Enquiry, Aug. 8, 1806; *Ibid.*, No. 461, f. 280b, Marriott to Webbe, July 2, 1800.

tion and training.[1] Two or three of the princes always dined with him, and listened to the illuminating discussions that took place on the occasion. It was the measure of his love for his children that in 1792 he agreed to the cession of Coorg and did not resume hostilities, lest any harm should come to the two princes who were in the English camp as hostages. He was also kind towards his half-witted brother, Abdul Karim, although the latter had allowed himself to be used at the time of Haidar's death by persons who wanted to exclude him from the succession. Tipu held his mother in high esteem, and always spoke with tenderness and respect of his father, and tried to follow in his footsteps in matters of State policy.

Another admirable trait in his character was his devotion to those whom he regarded as his friends. Thus, when the English proposed in 1783, as one of the conditions of peace, the surrender of the French who were fighting on his side, he rejected the proposal on the ground that he was pledged to protect them and would not do anything against his honour.[2] Again in 1799, when the fall of Seringapatam was imminent and Chappuis suggested that, if the Sultan wished to conclude peace, the Frenchmen in his service would have no objection to being delivered over to the English, he rejected the advice, saying that, under no circumstance whatsoever, he would betray his friends.[3]

Tipu was very considerate towards his officers. The letters which he wrote to them were couched in affectionate terms.[4] He was very solicitous for their health, and if he heard of their illness, he prescribed medicines for them.[5] His most trusted officer was his brother-in-law, Burhan-ud-din, who was killed at Satyamangalam in 1790. He also placed great confidence in Sayyid Ghaffar, Sayyid Hamid and Muhammad Raza, all of whom remained loyal to him till the end. Other persons whom he consulted were Purnaiya, Badr-uz-zaman Khan and Mir Sadiq. They remained loyal to the Sultan till the peace of Seringapatam, but after that they were bought off by the English. However, with the exception of a few men at the top, the majority of his servants, high or low, were always faithful to him.

Tipu was a good rider, and despised the use of a palanquin, which he regarded as fit only for women and invalids.[6] He was a skilful

[1] See p. 256, *supra*, for the impression created by the hostage princes on Cornwallis and others in the English camp in 1792.

[2] See p. 57, *supra*.

[3] See p. 328, *supra*.

[4] See Kirkpatrick, for letters addressed to Qamar-ud-din Khan and Burhan-ud-din.

[5] Kirkpatrick, No. 115. There are many other letters which show that Tipu was solicitous for the health of his officers and clerks to whom he prescribed medicines, if he was informed of their illness.

[6] Beatson, p. 153; Wilks, ii, p. 761.

marksman and was fond of the chase, particularly of hunting antelopes with the leopards who were specially trained for this. A large tract of land to the south-west of Seringapatam called the *Rumna* was reserved for this purpose.[1] Tipu possessed great personal courage. He was an able general and a gallant soldier as is evident from the numerous wars he fought against the English, the Nizam and the Marathas. His personal valour, fearlessness in danger and perseverance inspired his troops with confidence and enthusiasm. He was very solicitous for his army, and wrote to his military commanders to look after the wounded, and give the soldiers rest after a long march.[2] If they fell in battle *inams* were granted to their relatives. But these were discontinued if the relatives or dependents could provide for themselves. Sometimes, however, the pensions were hereditary.[3] Owing to these reasons he was extremely popular with his army. Dirom testifies to the fidelity of the Mysore troops to Tipu.[4] Even Wilks admits that the army remained loyal to the Sultan till the last.[5] According to Moor there were "such instances of attachment and fidelity as excite our admiration, and perhaps can scarcely be equalled. Without attempting to draw a comparison that might have an invidious appearance, let it be asked, what troops, under such highly disadvantageous circumstances, would have shown attachment superior to those of Tippoo?" Moor further observed: "When we see troops, after being continually beaten for two years, fight as well at the end as at the beginning of the war, we must surely allow it to proceed from something superior to a blind obedience to commands, without admitting loyalty and attachment to the commander, to have any share in stimulating them to their duty."[6]

Tipu was not only popular with the army and the officers, but also with his subjects. Mackenzie, who was with the English armies during the Third Anglo-Mysore War, wrote: "Nor have we to boast of many instances when his people were induced by our flattering prospects of success to throw his yoke and shelter themselves under the benign influence of Christian rulers."[7] Similarly Moor testified: "We have reason to suppose his subjects to be as happy as those of any other sovereign; for we do not recollect to have heard any complaints or murmurings among them, although had causes existed, no time could have been more favourable for their utterance, because the enemies of Tipu were in power, and would have been gratified by an

[1] Milfred Archer, *Tippoo's Tiger*, pp. 6-7.
[2] Kirkpatrick, No. 101.
[3] Baramahal Recds., Section 4, p. 98.
[4] Dirom, p. 249.
[5] Wilks, ii, p. 762.
[6] Moor, p. 197.
[7] Mackenzie, ii, p. 72.

aspersion of his character. The inhabitants of the conquered countries submitted with apparent resignation to the direction of their conquerors, but by no means as if relieved from an oppressive yoke in their former Government; on the contrary, no sooner did an opportunity offer, than they scouted their new masters, and gladly returned to their loyalty again."[1] Even now the people of Mysore speak of Tipu with tenderness, in spite of the ceaseless propaganda carried on for the last one hundred and fifty years to efface his memory.

Tipu's contemporaries, both friends and foes, are almost unanimous in their verdict that he was proud, vain and imperious.[2] But it should not be forgotten that these defects were natural to a person born to the purple, conscious of his own abilities, and possessing a large and prosperous kingdom and the finest army in India. But, in spite of his pride and imperiousness, he was, as a rule, gentle and amiable, and was aroused to anger only when there was sufficient cause for it. But within a pleasant exterior, he concealed a grim determination, constancy of purpose and great self-confidence which remained unaffected by failures, hardships and humiliations. Yet, with these qualities he did not combine a ruthless and cruel disposition. He never enjoyed killing or torturing people, or watching their death-agonies. He punished only such persons as were dangerous to him or to the State. At the same time there are instances when he showed clemency towards his enemies, if they submitted and promised to be loyal to him. Sometimes the clemency was misplaced, as in the case of Mir Sadiq, Purnaiya and Qamar-ud-din Khan who had been guilty of treason, and yet were pardoned and reinstated. He, however, never showed mercy to those who were guilty of prolonged opposition to his will or of repeated treachery. The punishments inflicted on such persons were very severe. But this was because the modes of punishment then prevalent in India were of an appalling kind.

Another trait in his character was his great ambition. But this did not so much consist in making new conquests as in retaining the kingdom which he had inherited from his father, in making it powerful and prosperous and earning a name for himself so that posterity would remember him. This does not mean that he believed in pacifism. On the contrary, if an opportunity had presented itself he would not have hesitated to extend his territories.[3] But the wars which he waged were none of his own making; they were fought in self-

[1] Moor, p. 202.

[2] I.O. MSS. Eur. C. 10, p. 205; A.N.C²172, Cossigny to Minister of Marine, Jan. 20, 1786, f. 23a; also Bib. Nation. MS., Française, *Nouvelle Acquisition* No. 9368 de Morlat to Suffren, Feb. 1783, ff. 469b-470b.

[3] See Moor, p. 193, for this aspect of Tipu's character; also A.N., C²172, Monneron to Cossigny, Sept. 14, 1786, f. 208a.

defence. He was more interested in the arts of peace than in the arts of war. He was a great soldier, but he was a much greater administrator; and it was upon the work which he did in this capacity that his chief title to fame and greatness should rest.

In every quality required for civil and military administration, in imagination and initiative, in capacity for hard work and minute attention to detail, Tipu ranks among the greatest rulers India has produced. No doubt he made mistakes, for example, he repeatedly altered his provincial boundaries and reduced his cavalry. Sometimes his officers did not carry out his orders. There were also not enough men to sympathise with and carry out his schemes. Nevertheless, he succeeded in establishing a strong Government and in promoting the well-being of his people. By exhortations, punishments and personal inspections, he corrected abuses in administration and suppressed peculation. He developed agriculture, promoted trade and industry, built roads, confiscated unauthorised grants and generally eliminated intermediaries. Munro and Read, who were in charge of the districts which formerly belonged to Mysore, although very critical of Tipu's administration, frequently allude to it in laudatory terms. Similarly, Dirom found in the years 1790-92 Tipu's kingdom "full of inhabitants, and apparently cultivated to the utmost extent of which the soil was capable; while the discipline and fidelity of his troops in the field, until their last overthrow, were testimonies, equally strong, of the excellent regulations which existed in his army. His government, though strict and arbitary, was the despotism of a politic and able sovereign."[1] Dirom further observed that on account of Tipu's "wise resolutions, his country is much improved and highly cultivated, far more so than the Niẓam's, his people seem to be happy and much at their case, while those of others are oppressed on all hands."[2]

It is sometimes maintained that the defeat which Tipu sustained in the Third Anglo-Mysore war, permanently weakened his Government and ruined his country. In reality, however, with extraordinary speed the devastation and disorganisation wrought by the war was repaired, so that his Government soon became strong and efficient, and his country prosperous. Sir John Shore admitted: "We know by experience his abilities—he has confidants and advisers, but no ministers, and inspects, superintends, and regulates himself all the details of his government......the peasantry of his dominions are protected, and their labours encouraged and rewarded."[3] When the English conquered Mysore in 1799, they were surprised at the

[1] Dirom, p. 249.
[2] I.O. MSS. Eur. F. 76. It is neither paged nor folied,
[3] Malcolm, *History of India*, ii, Appendix ii, pp. lx-ixi

flourishing condition of the country.[1] These verdicts recorded by men, whose normal sympathies were "pre-eminently British," clearly show that it was owing to the "unusual sources of internal strength," which Tipu possessed, that he was able to withstand "the impact of three desperate wars with a European power without distintegration."[2]

Tipu "had a spirit of innovation and curiosity recalling Akbar's; a new calendar, new scale of weights and measures, new coinage, occupied his energy."[3] It is true that the changes which he sometimes introduced were unnecessary. But for the most part his innovations were intended to improve the administration and the condition of the people. He abolished the Muslim calendar with its lunar years, because it was administratively inconvenient, and introduced, instead, a calendar based on luni-solar years. The new coins which he introduced are of exquisite beauty. He banned prostitution[4] and the use of intoxicants, because he felt these were harmful to his people. He was the first ruler in the East who endeavoured to apply Western methods to his administration, and who was not suspicious of Western science[5], which he applied to improve his country's defences and economic condition. He engaged Frenchmen, English prisoners of war and European deserters to train his army, to organise his arsenals and to introduce European arts and crafts and mode of production in his country. He himself used the articles manufactured in Mysore, and enjoined his officers to do the same in order to encourage home industries. In all this he was anticipating the policy of self-sufficiency which modern States are following. Realising the importance of trade and commerce, he assumed the role of chief merchant of his kingdom, established factories both at home and abroad, and opened trade relations with a number of foreign countries.

Tipu was the first Indian to think of sending his son to Europe for education. In 1788, Tipu's ambassadors to Louis XVI informedt he French Government that their master desired that one of his sons received education in Paris. The French authorities approved of the idea, but suggested that it would be better if, before leaving for France or in the course of his journey, the prince could learn to read and write French, learn a little calculus and some arithmetic.

[1] Owen, *Wellington's Despatches*, p. xxvi.

[2] Roberts, *India Under Wellesley*, p. 60.

[3] Thompson and Garratt, *Rise and Fulfilment of British Rule in India*, p. 206.

[4] Tipu made it known to his people that he would defray the marriage expenses, as prescribed by their respective castes, of all those who were desirous of marrying, but could not do so owing to financial difficulties (I.O. Mack. MSS., No. 46, p. 122).

[5] Tipu requested Cossigny, the Governor of Pondicherry, to obtain for him one telescope, thermometers, and 2 barometers. (A.N., C[2]236, Cossigny to Minister of Marine, May 4, 1786, No. 35).

It would not be difficult to find in India a French teacher for this purpose. The expenses of the prince's education in Paris, amounting to about Rs. 40,000 or 50,000 annually, would have to be borne by the Sultan. Expenses could be reduced to half this amount, if the prince did not live in luxury.[1] Tipu's plan, it seems, did not materialise because soon after the Third Anglo-Mysore War broke out, and as a result of the Treaty of Seringapatam, which ended the war, he had to give two of his sons as hostages to the English.

Tipu was a Sunni Muslim with leanings towards Shiism. He was sincerely religious, and named his kingdom *Saltanat-i-Khudadad* (God-Given State). He prayed five times a day, kept the *Ramazan* fasts, and throughout the day carried a rosary in his hand. He had great reverence for Ali, and inscribed on his weapons *Asadullah-ul-Ghalib*, one of Ali's titles.[2] He also revered the other Shia Imams, and named many of the coins after them. The manuscripts of his library had the names of Fatima, Hasan and Husain stamped on them. The ambassadors he sent to Constantinople were instructed by him to give offerings on his behalf to the tombs of Ali and Husain at Najaf and Karbala; and they were to ask the Caliph's permission for constructing a canal from the Euphrates to Najaf where there was a great shortage of water.[3]

Tipu was deeply interested in Sufism, and under his patronage a number of books were written on it. Like his father, he revered saints and conferred grants on their tombs. He also held the Hindu sadhus, saints and gods in great respect. Further, like his father, he was extremely superstitious, and believed that the performance of certain ceremonies could avert misfortune. Everyday he consulted the astrologers attached to his court about his stars. He fed Brahmins, bore the expenses of Hindu religious ceremonies performed to invoke success for his arms. On every Saturday, without fail, according to the advice of the astrologers, he made an offering to the seven stars of seven different kinds of grain, of an iron pan full of sesame oil, of a blue cap and coat and one black sheep and some money. All these articles were distributed among the Brahmins and the poor.[4]

To a man who possessed such eclectic beliefs and was so catholic in his outlook, it would be a mistake to attribute either religious fanati-

[1] A.N., C²189, de la Luzerne to Conway, Oct. 12, 1788, f. 360a; also *Ibid.*, Minute of the letter to Ruffin, the French Government's interpreter of Oriental languages, f. 361a.

[2] Beatson, p. 155.

[3] Hikmet Bayur, *Maysor Sultani Tipu Ile Osmanli Padisah Larindan* 1. *Abdulhamid VE* 111. *Selim Arasindaki Mektuplasma*, Letter No. 4; see also *Hukm-namah*, R.A.S.B. MSS. No. 1677; and *Waqai*, p. 48.

[4] I.O.MSS. Eur. C.10, p. 206; see p. 315 *supra*, for the ceremonies which Tipu performed on the morning of May 4, 1799, before the fall of Seringapatam.

cism or religious motives to his actions. If he crushed the Hindu Coorgs and Nairs, he did not spare the Muslim Moplahs. His conversion of some Coorgs and Nairs was not due to religious but to political motives. He had warned them several times that they should remain peaceful. But they ignored his warnings and repeatedly rebelled. He therefore converted them as a warning to others.

In his relations with both Indian and foreign powers also Tipu, like his father, was not influenced by religious considerations. He sent embassies to Persia, Afghanistan and Oman to obtain military aid or promote commercial relations. He sent a mission to Contantinople for military and commercial reasons as well as to legalise his position as ruler of Mysore, because he had failed to secure confirmation of the title from the Mughal Emperor. He made war on the Muslim rulers of Savanur, Kurnool, Adoni, Hyderabad and the Carnatic just as he fought against the Marathas and the Raja of Travancore.

However, although religious considerations did not influence his State policy, Tipu did not hesitate to exploit religion if it served his purpose. Thus, in his efforts to win over the Nizam against the English, he appealed to his religion, pointing out that for the good of the Muslims they should forget their past differences and unite against the common enemy. Similarly, in order to obtain the support of the Ottoman Sultan, he tried to excite his religious sentiments by dwelling on the atrocities which the English were committing on the Muslims in India. Where these religious appeals were ineffective, as in the case of the French, he made appeals to their self-interest, stressing the danger to which they were all exposed by British designs of aggrandisement. The same appeal he made to the Marathas; but, in addition, he tried to arouse their patriotic feelings.

Tipu, like most autocrats, enjoyed flattery and the poems written by his court poets to celebrate his victories were full of praises of the most fulsome kind. But he had a cultured mind. He was very versatile and could talk on all kinds of subjects. He could speak Kanarese and Hindustani, but he mostly talked in Persian which he wrote with ease.[1] He was interested in science, medicine, music, astrology and engineering, but theology and Sufism were his favourite subjects. Poets and learned men adorned his court, and he was fond of discussing with them various topics. He was greatly interested in calligraphy, and a treatise in Persian named *Risala dar Khatt-i-Tarz-i-Muhammadi* on the rules of calligraphy invented by him exists.[2] He also wrote a book on astrology named *Zabarjad*.[3] Besides, no less than forty-five books on subjects like Sufism, music, history, medicine, military

[1] Michaud, i, p. 83, says that Tipu was able to speak several European languages.

[2] *Islamic Culture*, xiv, No. 2, p. 151.

[3] *Ibid.*, p. 152.

science, law and *hadis* were either composed or translated from other languages under his direction and patronage. Tipu had a fine library consisting of 2,000 volumes of Arabic, Persian, Turkish, Urdu and Hindi manuscrips, dealing with music, *hadis*, law, Sufism, Hinduism, history, philosophy, medicine, grammar, astrology, military science, poetry and mathematics. The volumes, which were bound at Seringapatam, bear the names of God, Muhammad, his daughter Fatima, and her sons, Hasan and Husain in the medallion on the middle of the covers; and the names of the first four Caliphs on the four corners. At the top is stamped *Sarkar-i-Khudadad*, and at the bottom *Allah Kafi* (God is sufficient). Some of the bindings also bear the impression of Tipu's private signet.[1]

After the fall of Seringapatam, the library was presented, with the exception of a few manuscrips selected for the Asiatic Society of Bengal (now Asiatic Society, Calcutta) and for the Universities of Oxford and Cambridge, to the East India Company. Wellesley transferred all the manuscripts to the Fort William College founded in 1800. After the abolition of the College in 1830, the manuscripts were presented to the libraries in India and England.

Tipu possessed great artistic taste. He adorned his currency with the finest calligraphic designs; and his double-rupee is more attractive than any coin ever struck in India. He was a patron of music, and often witnessed dancing. It was under his direction that a book on the music of Mysore named *Mufarreh-ul-Qulub* was written by Hasan Ali "*Izzat*" in 1785.[2] The books in his library were richly adorned and beautifully illuminated. His throne was of considerable beauty and magnificence. It was supported by a wooden tiger, standing erect, covered with gold. It had an octagonal frame, eight feet by five, surrounded by a low railing on which were ten small tiger heads made of gold and beautifully inlaid with precious stones. The ascent to the throne was by small silver steps on each side. The canopy was made of wood, covered with a thin sheet of the purest gold, and decorated with a fringe of pearls strung on threads of gold. The *huma*, of the size of a small pigeon, was placed on the top of the canopy, and fluttered over the Sultan's head. It was formed of gold and was entirely covered with precious stones. It was valued at 1600 guineas in India.[3]

Tipu had great fondness for architecture. Haidar had built a small summer resort called Darya Daulat on the southern bank of the river Cauvery, midway between the Lal Bagh and the fort of Seringapatam.

[1] Stewart, *A Descriptive Catalogue of Tippoo's Oriental Library*, p. v; According to W. P., B.M. 26583, 1889 books were presented to the Asiatic Society of Bengal and the Fort William Library.

[2] *Islamic Culture*, xiv, No. 2, p. 158. Another work, *Jalwa Nama*, containing a series of nuptial songs, celebrating the various stages of the wedding feast, was written by Tipu's orders. (*Ibid.*, p. 160).

[3] Beatson, p. 154 footnote.

It became a favourite resort of Tipu who made additions to it. It is a picturesque building, and its striking feature is the painted walls. "The lavish decorations, which cover every inch of wall from first to last, from top to bottom, recall the palaces of Ispahan."[1] The walls inside are covered with richly painted arabesques, while outside are a series of frescoes representing the triumphs of Tipu over the English. Inside the fort Tipu had built a palace, but it no longer exists. It was a small, unpretentious building from the outside, but was very magnificent from the inside.[2] Close to the eastern or Bangalore gate stands the mosque built by Tipu in 1787. It is a fine structure, its two beautiful minarets combining majesty with grace. At the extreme end of the island is the beautiful mausoleum of Haidar built by Tipu, who also was buried there. It is a square building, surmounted by a dome and supported by polished black marble columns. The palace in the Bangalore fort was begun by Haidar in 1781 and completed by Tipu in 1791. The building was in the style of Darya Daulat and was very magnificent. According to Mackenzie, this palace was, "if we except the palaces of Agra and Delhi, the most airy and elegant in the East."[3] Both Haidar and Tipu were very much influenced by the Mughal buildings erected at Sira by Dilawar Khan, its Mughal Governor.

Tipu was the pioneer of road building in Malabar. Before his time the common form of conveyance was by boat, which was also the chief mode of transporting goods from one place to another. Porters were also employed to carry goods. It was however Tipu who, for the first time, introduced the wheeled traffic.[4] In the words of Major Dow, one of the Joint Commissioners for Malabar, "Tipu projected, and in great part finished an extensive chain of roads that connected all the principal places of Malabar and pervaded the wildest parts of the country."[5] Tipu built roads in other parts of his kingdom as well. The best known road associated with his name ran through the wild, broken country on the left bank of the Cauvery to the west of the Hosur and Dharmapuri *taluks*.[6] He also built a superb road connecting the different parts of the Dharmapuri *taluk*. "It is still marked at intervals by the remains of superb avenues and of the rough stone causeway which served as its foundation."[7] Another important road constructed by the Sultan was that connecting Krishnagiri with Budikottai.[8] To make travelling easy he constructed in Malabar

[1] Rees, *The Duke of Clarence in South India*, p. 81.
[2] Buchanan, i, p. 69.
[3] Mackenzie, ii, p. 46.
[4] *Gazet., of the Malabar and Anjengo Dists.*, i, p. 268; Buchanan, 11, p. 434.
[5] *Gazet., of the Malabar and Anjengo Dists.*, i, p. 268. Innes gives details of the roads constructed by Tipu, (*Ibid.*, pp. 268-69')
[6] *Gazet., Salem Dist.*, vol. i, part i, p. 194.
[7] *Ibid.*, vol. i, part ii, p. 191.
[8] *Ibid.*, vol. i, part i, p. 194.

inns, which had never existed before, and brought Hindus from Mysore to run them.[1]

Another form of public work in which Tipu took special interest was irrigation. In 1797 he constructed a few miles west of Seringapatam a dam across the Cauvery with an embankment seventy feet high.[2] In Daroji there is a big tank which was also constructed by the Sultan. It possesses a huge embankment some two and a half miles long, and in places forty-five feet high.[3] Another large tank known as Moti Talab, which had been built by the Hoyesalas, was reset and repaired by him.[4] He also encouraged his subjects to make tanks by giving them lands for the purpose, and conferring on them *jagirs* when the work was finished. They were required to keep them in good condition, but if they were unable to do so owing to the lack of funds, the Government helped them. The *amils* were provided with a large staff whose duty was to keep the tanks and channels in a proper state of repair.[5]

Tipu has been criticised for his anti-English policy, for his failure to win the Marathas and the Nizam over to his side, and for cultivating the friendship of the French. But on closer analysis these criticisms would be found to be unjust. It is true that Tipu was against the English but this was due to the fact that, in spite of his desire to live at peace with them, they were hostile towards him. No sooner the Treaty of Mangalore was signed than they began to intrigue with the Nizam and the Peshwa against him. In 1786 Macpherson, in violation of that treaty, decided to send military help to the Marathas and the Nizam who had invaded Mysore. Although later, Cornwallis withdrew the offer of aid lest it should involve the Company in a war with Tipu and the French for which it was not prepared, his attitude towards the Sultan did not become friendly. On the contrary he began to incite the Nizam and the Marathas against him; and in 1789, in violation of the Company's previous treaties with Haidar and Tipu, he wrote a letter to the Nizam assuring him his support in the conquest of Mysore.[6] The cause of English hostility towards Tipu was that he was not prepared to become a tributary of the Company. Besides, they regarded him as an obstacle to their ambitions, because he was "unquestionably the most powerful of all the native princes of Hindustan,"[7] and they feared that "his steadiness in establishing that system of Government and discipline in his army, which have raised him above the

[1] Buchanan, ii, 413, pp. 427.

[2] *Epigraphica Carnatica*, iii, Sr. 17.

[3] *Bellary Dist*, *Gazet.*, p. 258. The tank was completely destroyed in 1851 by a great flood but was rebuilt in 1853 by the Collector of the district.

[4] M.A.R., 1939, p. 28.

[5] Baramahal Recds, Section 1, p. 180; Crisp, *Mysorean Revenue Regulations*, p. 20.

[6] See Chapter x, *supra*.

[7] Rennell, Memoirs, p. cxxxix.

other princes in India, cannot fail to make him every day more formidable."[1] That was why Cornwallis attacked him and deprived him of half his kingdom. But the English were not satisfied with this: they wanted his complete extirpation. As Munro wrote on September 21,1798: "Our first care ought to be directed to the total subversion of Tippoo. After becoming masters of Seringapatam and Bangalore, we should find no great difficulty in advancing to the Kistna, when favoured by wars and revolutions in the neighbouring States; and such occasions will seldom be wanting, for there is no government among them that has consistency enough to deserve the name."[2]

The Nizam and the Marathas also were hostile towards Tipu. They were jealous and afraid of his abilities, and were anxious to recover the territories which Haidar had conquered from them. In 1780 the Marathas had recognised Haidar's sovereignty over the districts south of the Krishna, and yet, soon after, they began to demand their restoration. If Haidar had not died in 1782, the Marathas would have sooner or later made war on him. In fact, while he was still alive, they had entered into a treaty with the English for the invasion of Mysore, but owing to their internal dissensions they were powerless to act. When Tipu became ruler they demanded the territories from him. Tipu was anxious to live at peace with them provided they did not interfere in his internal affairs and left him in possession of the kingdom he had inherited from his father. But the Marathas, ignoring their previous treaties, supported the chief of Nargund, who was his tributary, and invaded Mysore. To win their friendship he ceded to them Nargund, Kittur and Badami. Yet, in 1790, in violation of the treaty of 1787, they joined the coalition organised by the English against him. He again tried his best to establish friendly relations with them by warning them that it was not he but the English who was their real enemy. He told them that the English had come to India as traders, but taking advantage of the break-up of the Mughal Empire and of the dissensions of the Indian princes, they had succeeded in carving out a kingdom for themselves, and were now aiming at the conquest of the whole country. But his warnings fell on deaf ears. The Indian rulers were totally blind to the realities of the situation. They were too interested in securing immediate gains to think of the ultimate effects of their policy. They imagined that they could best serve their interests by allying themselves with the English against Tipu. But, in reality, by pursuing this policy they were paving the way for their own downfall.

It is only when this background is clearly visualised that the reasons

[1] I.O., Mack, MSS., No. 46, p. 137.
[2] Gleig, *Munro*, i, p. 203.

why Tipu sought the alliance of the French, and sent embassies to France and Turkey can be properly appreciated. Finding himself completely isolated, and surrounded on all sides by enemies, he tried to seek an alliance with the French, for whom he had inherited a tradition of friendship from his father, and therefore sent embassies to France. Ignorant of the social, political and economic conditions in that country, he was certain that owing to their rivalry with the English, they would help him. But although they raised his hopes, they never came to his assistance in the hour of his need, partly because of the internal troubles at home, and partly because their policy in India lacked boldness and foresight. He sent ambassadors to Turkey to secure the Caliph's alliance and to request him to mediate in settling his differences with the English. But the Ottoman Sultan too, like the French, owing to his pre-occupations and commitments in Europe, could not do anything. To break the ring of his enemies, Tipu had, at one time, even decided to send an embassy to England in order to inform the English King of the intrigues which the Company's servants in India were carrying on against him.

Tipu was, however, not the only ruler to seek help from foreign countries. Haidar Ali had twice sent missions to Persia, and had once even obtained one thousand Persian troops.[1] The Peshwa Raghunath Rao had also sent an agent to England to secure the friendship of the English Government against his rivals.[2] In 1786 the Poona Government wanted to send an embassy to the Isle of France.[3] Further, not all the missions which Tipu sent abroad had political objects in view. The embassies he sent to Persia, Masqat and Pegu were intended to promote his country's trade. Even the ambassadors who went to France and Turkey were directed to establish commercial relations between Mysore and those countries and to obtain from there technicians to develop industries in his kingdom. The envoys to Turkey had an additional object in view. They were required to secure the recognition of Tipu's title to the throne of Mysore from the Ottoman Caliph.

The missions which Tipu sent to foreign countries were able to achieve some of these aims. They succeeded in promoting commercial relations with the Persian Gulf area, and secured for him an investiture which legalised his status. They also obtained technicians for introducing industries in Mysore. As against these advantages must be set the increasing hostility of the English which these missions earned for Tipu and which ultimately led to his overthrow. But it can be argued that, since the English were not prepared to see an

[1] See p. 129 and footnote 7, *supra*.
[2] See p. 116 footnote 1, *supra*.
[3] A.N., C²127, Cossigny to Minister, Jan. 20, 1786, f. 142a.

independent and powerful kingdom of Mysore, they would have, sooner or later, found some other *casus belli*, though it is possible that if he had not sent an embassy to the Isle of France, he might have secured some breathing space.

Tipu has also been criticised for having allowed his cavalry, which was a "terror of Madras," to decay, and for having given up his father's mode of warfare. This criticism is justified, but it is wrong to say that this was the "principal reason" of his fall.[1]

In 1780 Haidar's cavalry numbered 34,000 and his infantry 15,000.[2] But Tipu,by 1790, had increased his infantry to 50,000, while he had reduced his cavalry to 20,000.[3] This was a wrong policy. He should have improved his infantry but not at the cost of the cavalry, which had made Haidar so successful in his wars against the English. He did not realise that he would never be able to make his infantry as strong as that of the English, because of his inability to keep pace with the constant improvements that were being introduced in Europe. Nevertheless, the changes Tipu brought about did not impair the strength of his army which, on the contrary, became very formidable. This was partly because of the improvements which he had effected in his infantry and artillery, and partly because the reduction in cavalry had not been considerable. Moreover, although he began to make increasing use of his infantry, he did not give up Haidar's mode of warfare. In fact, it was because both his infantry and cavalry played their distinctive and proper role that he was able to gain victory over the Maratha-Nizam coalition, and to carry on a gallant struggle for nearly two years against an Anglo-Nizam-Maratha confederacy. Thus in his war with the Marathas, although it was mainly due to his superior infantry and artillery that he defeated them, his cavalry too rendered great help by harassing the enemy and cutting off his supplies. The success which he gained over Medows was entirely due to the efficient use which he made of his cavalry. But when Cornwallis advanced on Seringapatam in May 1791, it was the co-ordination of the Mysore cavalry and infantry that checked his further advance at Arikere and forced him to retreat. When Cornwallis again marched on Seringapatam, Tipu failed to make proper use of his cavalry; but his numerous infantry offered such stubborn resistance before the capital that the Governor-General was compelled to make peace. The main cause of Tipu's defeat in this war was that the English were assisted by the Nizam and the Marathas.[4]

[1] Fortescue, iv, part ii, p. 745.

[2] Wilks, i, p. 812 footnote.

[3] See p. 351, *supra*. According to de Souillac Tipu reduced his cavalry from 30,000 to 14,000 or 15,000. (A.N., $C^2$169, from de Souillac, Sept. 15, 1785, No. 15, f. 48b).

[4] This has been discussed at the end of chapter xvi.

After the Treaty of Seringapatam, which deprived Tipu of half his kingdom, he was compelled to reduce his army. But the mistake which he made was that he not only reduced his infantry but also his cavalry. The result was that, although he was still strong enough to beat the combined forces of the Nizam and the Marathas,[1] he could no longer confront the English. Having reduced his infantry, which was now inferior to that of the English both in numbers and equipment,[2] he should have improved his cavalry which, according to Arthur Wellesley, was "the best of the kind in the world."[3]

Another mistake which he committed was that he did not make proper use of whatever cavalry he possessed. He failed to see that "his true advantage against the British lay in superior mobility." He did not employ his cavalry to devastate Baramahal which would have rendered the problem of supplies difficult for the English. He offered no check to Harris's advance by destroying forage and harassing the English troops. He fought what Fortescue calls "a campaign of walls and ditches." He placed too much reliance on the defences of the fort of Seringapatam, hoping that these would enable him to hold out until the English would be compelled to raise the siege owing to the want of provisions or the approach of the monsoon, when the Cauvery would be flooded and make siege operations impracticable.

But although Tipu committed these mistakes, it should be remembered that his defeat was also facilitated by the treachery of his officers who, as we have seen, did not care to impede the advance of the English forces, and finally brought about the surrender of the fort of Seringapatam. But for their attitude, the resistance against the enemy would have been much more stubborn and prolonged. It is also necessary to point out to those who argue that if Tipu had retained Haidar's military organisation and mode of fighting he would not have been defeated, that conditions in 1790 and 1799 had considerably changed since 1767 and 1780, and that Haidar never fought under such unfavourable circumstances as Tipu did. In the first place, he was never without allies in his wars against the English; nor did he have to fight against any coalitions. In the First Anglo-Mysore War he had the support of the Nizam. In the Second Anglo-Mysore War he was allied with the French, and had the further advantage that, while the Nizam was neutral, the Marathas were also engaged in hostilities against the English. Tipu, on the contrary, had

[1] Ross, *Cornwallis*, ii, p. 171; M.R., Mly. Sundry Book, vol. 101, p. 109

[2] Tipu's total of actual fighting men was about 29,000 (*Gleig*, *Munro*, i, p. 215), while the English forces numbered about 42,000, including the Hyderabad contingent. Besides, the English could obtain more troops, if required, from the Presidencies.

[3] Owen, *Wellington's Despatches*, p. 62.

to confront alone, first, an Anglo-Maratha-Nizam coalition and then an Anglo-Nizam coalition. In the second place, when Haidar fought against the English they had no cavalry. But in the Third Anglo-Mysore War they were supplied with cavalry by the Nizam and the Marathas. And by the time of the last Anglo-Mysore War, the English had themselves developed the cavalry arm which considerably reduced the effectiveness of Tipu's cavalry.[1] Moreover, Cornwallis, realising that the Mysore light horse was "superlatively excellent for the purposes of partisan warfare," and that "to fight against such an enemy was to court disaster", no sooner took command than "he made concentration the keynote of the campaign."[2] These tactics, which were later followed by Harris, made the Mysore irregular cavalry much less useful than it had been under Haidar. Furthermore, the proportion of Haidar's troops to those of the Company had been four to one.[3] But the proportion of Tipu's forces to those of the Company in the Third Ango-Mysore War was less than two to one. The Treaty of Seringapatam reduced Tipu's power, while it increased that of the Company. In consequence, in the Fourth Anglo-Mysore War Tipu's forces were outnumbered by the English, who were also better equipped. It was owing to this superiority of the English forces in numbers, equipment, resources and strategy that Tipu's operations in his last war were not characterised, save for his march against Stuart, by the same dash and brilliance which he had displayed in his previous wars.

In addition to these, another factor which had a decisive influence in the Third and Fourth Anglo-Mysore wars was the change in the Company's organisation. Until 1784 this had been very weak. But the Pitt's India Act and the supplementary acts introduced considerable changes. Formerly the Governor-General had been at the mercy of his council, but now he was entrusted with supreme authority. The conflict between the civil and military authorities had formerly marred the progress of wars. But this was ended by the union in the same hands of the offices of the Governor-General and the Commander-in-Chief. Moreover, formerly the authorities in Bombay and Madras had defied the Governor-General in the conduct of external affairs, but now he was given complete authority over the subordinate Governments. The result of these changes was that both Cornwallis and Wellesley were able to carry on war against Tipu much more vigorously than Hastings had ever been able to do against Haidar.

The Pitt's India Act introduced another change. Until 1784 the Home Government had only occasionally intervened in the affairs of

[1] In this war the English had 4,400 cavalry, besides 9,621 horses supplied by the Nizam.

[2] Fortescue, iii, p. 609.

[3] Sinha, *Haidar Ali*, p. 260 (1949).

the Company, but henceforth it established its full control. This was all the more necessary, because the Company was to serve as the instrument of national policy in order to compensate the loss of the American colonies. The result was that, while Haidar had fought only against the English Company, Tipu had to contend with "the English Government and the East India Company combined, the resources of both of which were clubbed to provide for the war."[1] Moreover, it should not be forgotten that Tipu was fighting a people who were disciplined, united, self-confident and led by the middle class. They were also technically most advanced and possessed great resources. On the other hand, India was feudal, caste-ridden and demoralised, having no unity, no national consciousness and no common purpose.

In spite of these drawbacks, if Tipu had been joined by the Nizam and the Marathas he would have succeeded in defeating the English. But they refused to unite with him; instead they allied themselves with his enemies. Thus it was due to their help which Cornwallis received that he was able to defeat Tipu. This defeat was very decisive because it crippled Tipu, and paved the way for his final overthrow by Wellesley. It is true that in 1799 the Marathas did not help the English, but neither did they join Tipu. Maratha neutrality would have been useful to the Sultan in 1790, but now what he required most was their military assistance. The French also, as in 1790, failed to render him any aid. On the other hand the English were again assisted by the Nizam. Once more, therefore, Tipu had to confront his enemies single-handed. But while his armies and resources had become reduced, the English possessed larger and better equipped forces and greater resources than ever before. Under the circumstance his defeat was inevitable, and even if Haidar had been in his place, he too would have been overwhelmed. No doubt Tipu could have saved himself if he had agreed to become a vassal of the English Company. But he was too independent, too proud, able and energetic to accept such a position. The result was that he lost his life and his throne, and with him ended his dynasty.

[1] Mill, v, 326.

# APPENDICES

## APPENDIX A

## TIPU AND THE PORTUGUESE

Haidar Ali had tried to cultivate friendly relations with the Portuguese in India in order to secure their military help against the English and the Marathas. But they not only ignored his overtures, they even helped the English in the conquest of Mangalore in 1768, and, later, attempted to seize Sadasivgarh which was in his possession.[1] In spite of this Haidar did not interfere with their trade with Mangalore. It was only in 1776, when the Portuguese refused an offensive alliance proposed by him on the ground that relations between them and the English were very cordial in Europe, that he revoked all the commercial privileges which they had been enjoying in his kingdom.[2]

On Haidar's death, the Portuguese Viceroy wrote to Tipu a letter of condolence, at the same time congratulating him on his accession, and requesting him to restore the trade facilities in Mysore which had been cancelled by Haidar.[3] But meanwhile, Mathews invaded the west coast, and Tipu's Roman Catholic subjects gave him both financial and military help in the conquest of Mangalore and other places.[4] They again helped the English when Mangalore was besieged by Tipu. The Roman Catholics being under the ecclesiastical jurisdiction of the Archbishop of Goa, Tipu was convinced that they were acting under orders from the Portuguese Government. He therefore punished them and refused to lift the ban on the Portuguese trade with his kingdom.[5]

In spite of this, Tipu's correspondence with the Viceroy of Goa was very cordial. At the latter's request the Sultan released the Fathers and some Christians, who had been guilty of treason, and allowed the Portuguese to trade with Mangalore in all articles except rice which he needed for his army.[6] Tipu, like his father, was anxious to cultivate friendly relations with the Portuguese in order to secure their alliance

[1] It is a village in the Karwar *taluk* of North Kanara Dist., Bombay, situated on the west coast about four miles from Karwar. It is called Piro by the Portuguese, because it has a domed tomb of a Muslim *pir* (saint) built in it.

[2] Sinha, *Haidar Ali*, pp. 156-59 (1949).

[3] Pissurlencar, *Antigualhas*, fasc., ii, No. 72.

[4] See pp. 364-66, *supra*.

[5] Pissurlencar, *Antigualhas*, fasc., ii, Nos. 77, 88.

[6] *Ibid.*, Nos. 79, 81.

against his enemies and, in return, was prepared to grant them all the commercial privileges which they had formerly enjoyed in his kingdom. But the Portuguese did not want to ally themselves with him owing to their friendship with the English. Besides, they were anxious to capture Sadasivgarh, and were reluctant to help a power which they regarded as dangerous to the security of Goa. So when the Marathas proposed an offensive and defensive alliance against Tipu they readily accepted it with minor modifications. The following are the main clauses of the treaty proposed by the Marathas along with the replies of the Portuguese:[1]

1. The Peshwa thinks of destroying Tipu, and in this the Portuguese should help him. As far as possible no peace will be made with Tipu, but if there is no alternative, and hostilities cease, the Portuguese will not think that the Marathas had broken the treaty.

The Portuguese are ready to ally themselves with the Peshwa.

2. While the Marathas will advance southward into Tipu's territory, the Portuguese will operate against him on the sea-coast.

The Portuguese agree to this.

3. After the war is over the Peshwa will pay to the Portuguese all the expenses incurred by them. In return the Portuguese will hand over to him all their conquests.

The Portuguese do not want any money. Instead, they will prefer to retain Sunda and some other territory which the Peshwa may like to give them.

4. If on the conclusion of peace the Peshwa receives any war indemnity from Tipu, he will pay to the Portuguese all the expenses incurred by them in the campaign, and will prevail on Tipu to cede to them a part of the territories occupied by them.

If the Peshwa receives war indemnity, and in return restores the territories conquered from Tipu, the Portuguese will also do the same. But they will get from the Peshwa a part of the money which he receives from Tipu.

5. In case the Peshwa does not receive any money, the Portuguese will not demand any war expenses from him.

The Portuguese agree to this, but they will not restore the territories conquered by them unless the Peshwa demands from them such a sacrifice.

6. After the peace is concluded, if Tipu breaks it by attacking the Portuguese, the Peshwa will help them.

The Portugese accept this.

7. In the territories annexed by the Marathas, the Peshwa will confirm the commercial privileges which the Portuguese had formerly enjoyed.

[1] Pissurlencar, *Antigualhas*, fasc, ii, No. 90.

8. Hindus will not be converted to Christianity in the Portuguese kingdom; nor will cow slaughter or the destruction of temples be allowed. In return the Peshwa promises to prevent the Muslims in his army from converting Christians to Islam.

The Portuguese will not compel either Brahmins or Muslims to become Christians. Nor will cows be slaughtered unless they belong to the Christians.

9. If there is an engagement between the Mysore and Maratha navy, the Portuguese will help the latter.

The Portuguese agree to this.

10. After seizing Tipu's territories and punishing him, the fortresses of Sadasivgarh and Ximpim and their adjoining lands will be left in the possession of the Portuguese.

The Portuguese accept this.

Although this treaty was never ratified, and the Portuguese did not give any military help to the Peshwa, Tipu's relations with them remained estranged. When the Third Anglo-Mysore War broke out, the Portuguese, thinking that this would lead to the overthrow of Tipu, occupied Sadasivgarh on June 30, 1791.[1] However, to their great disappointment, his power was not destroyed, and after concluding peace with the English, he demanded the restoration of Sadasivgarh. The Portuguese authorities in Goa realised that if they refused to comply with his wishes it might lead to war, which would be not only expensive but disastrous, for Tipu by preventing the export of rice from Mangalore would be able to starve Goa. So they decided to hand over Sadasivagarh to him, on condition that the Portuguese be allowed to trade with the Mysore kingdom.[2] After the place was restored to the Mysoreans, Tipu issued instructions to his officers that all Mysore ports should be opened to the Portuguese merchants, who should also be permitted to export rice from Mangalore at reduced rates.[3] He in return wanted to establish a commercial house in Goa, but the Portuguese authorities did not comply with his wishes, because they were afraid that this would make the English angry.[4] In spite of this, henceforth Tipu's relations with the Portuguese remained cordial.

[1] *Ibid.*, No. 101

[2] *Ibid.*, Nos. 102-04; I.O. Portug. Recds., *Conselho Ultramarinho*, Vol. 3, part 2, Bundle 68. No. 35, Francisco da Cunha e Meneses to Martinho de Mello e Castro, March 10, 1793, pp. 720-23.

[3] Pissurlencar, *Antigualhas*, fasc., ii, No. 109; I.O. Portug. Recds., *Conselho Ultramarinho*, Vol. 3, part 3, Bundle 68, No. 35, Francisco da Cunha e Meneses to Martinho de Mello e Castro, March 10, 1793, pp. 723 *seq.*

[4] *Ibid.*

## APPENDIX B

# TIPU AND HIS ENGLISH PRISONERS OF WAR

It has been generally held that Tipu's treatment of his English prisoners of war was not only severe but cruel and barbarous. Thus Thompson and Garratt observe: "His letters to commandants besieging forts would instruct them to offer quarter and, when quarter had been accepted, butcher everyone irrespective of age and sex. It was impossible to ascertain what captives he held; and as a preliminary, when war broke out, he would murder any who still survived."[1] According to Bowring, after the Treaty of Mangalore, "a great majority of those who had suffered imprisonment had either perished from the hardships they endured, or had met violent death at the hands of Tipu's executioners."[2]

These conclusions are extremely prejudiced and one-sided. For, both as a prince and as a ruler, Tipu was always kind towards his prisoners of war, except when he was given serious cause to act harshly. When Haidar routed the English forces under Baillie in 1780, "several officers were also carried to Tippoo, who treated them with great humanity. He invited them into his tent, gave them biscuits, and to each five pagodas. One of the gentlemen, Captain Monteinth, who was a married man, expressed an earnest desire of sending a letter to his wife at Madras with which Tipu readily complied."[3] Similarly, when some of the officers of Braithwaite's detachment fell into the hands of Tipu on February 18, 1782, "he paid them every attention that was necessary. He not only furnished them with clothes and money, but at the same time gave strict orders to all his keeladars to be attentive to them during their march to Hyder's army, who was lying at Conjeveram."[4]

When Tipu became ruler of Mysore his attitude towards the prisoners of war did not change. One of the captives himself testified that "the gentlemen confined at Bangalore were not only permitted to purchase every article they wanted, but, during the latter part of their confinement, they were allowed to visit each other in their different prisons."[5] Sayyid Ibrahim, Tipu's Commandant of Bangalore who was in charge of these prisoners, treated them so well that, when

[1] Thompson and Garratt, *Rise and Fulfilment of British Rule in India*. p. 176.
[2] Bowring, *Haidar Ali and Tipu Sultan*, p. 130; also Wilks, ii, p. 271.
[3] Lawrence, *Captives of Tipu Sultan*, p. 102.
[4] *Ibid.*, p. 126.
[5] *Ibid.*, p. 168.

he died, Lord Clive, the Governor of Madras, ordered a mausoleum to be erected over his grave to perpetuate his memory.[1] Qamar-ud-din Khan also paid great attention to the prisoners in his charge.[2] Captain Nash and Lieutenant Chalmers, who had been taken prisoners at Coimbatore in 1791, had nothing to complain of, for they had been treated humanely, and when they were released, they appeared healthy and cheerful.[3]

In spite of these instances it should not be taken for granted that the prisoners were always treated well and were happy. In fact, their lot depended on the man in charge. Consequently at some places they were better off than at others. Thus, "the officers who were left wounded at Bednur were much better used than at any other place. They were permitted to keep all their clothes, doolies, cots, chairs, tables, knives, forks and other articles. They were indulged in the free use of pen, ink and paper....."[4] In other places, if the officer was corrupt or of hard disposition, there were cases of maltreatment. But whenever Tipu came to know of this, either through his spies or through the Company's authorities, he reprimanded the officers and enjoined them to treat the prisoners well and look after their welfare.[5]

It has been generally held that Matthews and Baillie, along with other English officers, were mercilessly murdered by Tipu's orders.[6] There is, however, no foundation at all for such a belief. Braithwaite, who was for sometime confined at Seringapatam, wrote to Macartney, the Governor of Madras, that the rumours of the English officers having been murdered were untrue, and that he had thoroughly investigated the matter. "Baillie", he observed, "had died of an ordinary bilious complaint under which he languished for months and from which probably he might have recovered if he had medical assistance." As regards General Matthews, Braithwaite wrote that he had been confined in an airy, pleasant place, had two European servants with him and a low caste cook. He had been provided with a table, a bed, chairs, knives and forks. He had also been supplied with liquor and sugar, and had been given some money. In short, he had been made to feel very comfortable. But he did not deserve this treatment and soon brought trouble on himself. Being very fretful in his temper, one day he gave away a pagoda in front of the *jamadar* of his guards who reported it to the Commandant. Tipu's officers came and took away all the money, amounting to one thousand pagodas, which was part of the Bednur treasure appropriated by

[1] M.A.R., 1925-6, p. 9.
[2] Mly. Sundry Book, vol. 60A, Major Lysaght to Qamar-ud-din, Nov. 27, 1783, p. 139.
[3] Dirom, p. 190.
[4] Lawrence, *Captives of Tipu Sultan*, p. 168.
[5] M.R., Mly. Sundry Book, vol. 60A, p. 219.
[6] Wilks, ii, p. 217. This news appeared in a Bengal newspaper of the period.

Matthews in violation of the terms of the capitulation. Soon after, he beat his own servant, who was therefore taken away from him. As he was found talking a great deal with his English servants, he was suspected of some conspiracy, so they were also removed from him and his ration was cut down. And when he beat one of his guards, he was put in irons. After this Matthews laid himself upon his bed, never spoke to any one and did not eat anything except some dry rice, and died on the 6th September, on the 7th day after he had been put in irons.[1]

There were, however, occasions when Tipu was unable to show his usual clemency towards his English prisoners and was obliged to treat them harshly. When, for example, they attempted to escape or mutinied, organised conspiracies against him or behaved mischievously in other ways, they were severely dealt with. The prisoners would sometimes circumcise dogs and run them through the streets of Seringapatam, thus offending the religious susceptibilities of the Muslims.[2] On one occasion, during a Muharram night, one of the prisoners stole out of the prison and robbed the *tazias* of the offerings.[3] On another occasion they were privy to a conspiracy headed by Shamaiya, Ranga Iyenger and other important Mysore officers with a view to restoring the Hindu family to the throne of Mysore.[4] Nor was it unusual for the prisoners to carry on secret correspondence among themselves or with their own Government. Several times they attempted to escape, and in some cases they were successful. The result was that those who were left behind were naturally looked upon with suspicion. It was owing to these reasons that Tipu was sometimes compelled to treat the prisoners harshly, for any indulgence to them would have undermined the basis of his power. But the punishments, though severe, were not barbarous, which "is a very different thing from the deliberate massacre of prisoners with which contemporary English opinion charged Tipu Sultan. No evidence survives which confirms that opinion."[5]

Nor is there any truth in the statement that Tipu did not release all the English prisoners of war after the conclusion of the Treaties of

[1] N.A., Sec. Pro., Nov. 1, 1784. Macartney accepted this account and observed: "We have now the strongest reason to believe, from the circumstantial narrative delivered by Col. Braithwaite, that General Matthews was not murdered. In respect to other gentlemen, we have no possible information concerning their deaths, and are not warranted, however strong our suspicions may be, in charging Tippoo with the guilt of murdering them." (Macartney Papers, Bodleian MS. Eng. hist. C. 79, Macartney to Hastings, Oct. 29, 1784).

[2] Lawrence, *Captives of Tipu Sultan*, p. 12.

[3] Bristow, *A Narrative of the Sufferings of Bristow*, p. 45.

[4] *Ibid., p.* 32; Lawrence, *Captives of Tipu Sultan*, p. 140.

[5] Rushbrook Williams, *Great Men of India*, p. 215 (Chap. on *Tipu Sultan* by Dodwell). Mill, vi, p. 106, says: "Of his cruelties we have heard the more, because our own countrymen were among the victims of it."

Mangalore and Seringapatam. There were 4,261 prisoners with him at the time when the Armistice of Mangalore was signed on August 2, 1783. All these were sent to Vellore after the conclusion of the Treaty of Mangalore.[1] Similarly, the prisoners taken in the course of the Third Anglo-Mysore War were released, otherwise Tipu's two sons, who were with the English as hostages, would not have been restored. In spite of this the English were not satisfied, because they wanted every Englishman in Mysore to be sent away. But some of the prisoners themselves were reluctant to return to Madras for they had entered Tipu's service. There were also some deserters in Mysore who could not be classed as prisoners of war. Desertion in the English and French armies was a common thing. In fact, "the commonest crime, after drunkenness, was desertion."[2] These men who had deserted and entered Tipu's service did not wish to go back, because "the penalty of desertion was no longer a mere return to the boredom of a familiar garrison, but at least the cat, and often the firing party or the gallows."[3] Of course, Tipu himself did not insist that they should go back, since they were useful to him as artificers. Besides, Macartney, the Governor of Madras, had agreed that neither the Company would surrender those Mysore subjects who might have taken refuge in Tellicherry, nor would it demand the return of its deserters who might be unwilling to return to its service.[4]

Tipu has also been accused of having forcibly converted the prisoners to Islam. But this again is a false charge. Those who became Muslims did so willingly. They changed their religion for the sake of rewards or for securing their liberty from the boredom of prison life. Tipu being anxious to recruit Englishmen as artificers in equipping, or as instructors in training, his army, his officers were ready to offer inducements to those ready to embrace Islam and enter his service. In this way alone, he thought, Englishmen would not leave Mysore. But as Dodwell observes, "there is no reason to believe that there were any converts other than those who elected thus to purchase their freedom."[5]

[1] M.R., Mly. Count. Corresp., vol. 33B, No. 124, Tipu to Governor, June 28, 1784. p. 294. Tipu maintained that he had two receipts under the seal of the Governor, acknowledging that he had received the prisoners; see also Mly. Desp. to England, 1782-83, vol. 18, pp. 160-61. According to Macartney also Tipu released the same number of prisoners i.e. 1,200 Europeans and about 3,000 sepoys. (Macartney Papers, Bodleian MS. Eng. hist. C. 106, Macartney to Sullivan, May 1, 1784, f. 17a).

[2] Dodwell, *The Nabobs of Madras*, p. 25.

[3] *Ibid.*, p. 86.

[4] M.R., Mly. Cons., Oct. 6, 1783, vol. 93A, p. 4332.

[5] Rushbrook Williams, *Great Men of India*, p. 215 (Chap. on *Tipu Sultan* by Dodwell).

APPENDIX C

# COINAGE

The coins of Tipu are to be found in far greater variety and number than those of his father; and, according to Henderson, "many of the gold and silver pieces afford indisputable testimony to the decorative value of the Arabic script, and it may be doubted if any coin more attractive in this respect than Tipu's double-rupee has ever been struck in India."[1] Tipu issued his coins in gold, silver and copper from twelve mints at Seringapatam, Bednur, Gooty, Bangalore, Chitaldrug, Calicut, Satyamangalam, Dindigul, Gurramkonda, Dharwar, Mysore, and Ferokh or Farokhabad.

Owing to his war with the English, Tipu issued but few coins in the first year of his reign, and these only from Seringapatam and Bednur mints. In the fifth year all the mints were in operation, except the Calicut mint whose place was taken by the one at Ferokh. From the tenth year of his reign coins were only issued from the Seringapatam, Bednur and Gooty mints.

It is interesting to note that Tipu's own name is not to be found on any of his coins. Nor do they bear the name of the reigning Mughal Emperor, Shah Alam II, whom Tipu did not regard as his sovereign. But the initial letter of his father's name 'H' is frequently met with on the gold and silver issues. They also sometimes bear inscriptions like "the religion of Ahmad is illumined in the world by the victory of Haidar. He is the Sultan, the Unique, the Just."

The coins issued during the first four years of Tipu's reign bear the *hijra* date; the numerals, as usual, reading from left to right, while those from the fifth year to the end of the reign are dated in accordance with Tipu's *maulудi* era, and the figures read from right to left. The coins of the fourth year are dated 1200 A.H., while those of the fifth year bear the date 5121 (1215 A.M.). From Tipu's own coins it appears that he ascended the throne on May 4,1783.

Sometime after the introduction of the *maulудi* era, Tipu invented names for his coins, on the reverse of which they are usually inscribed. The gold and silver coins are called after the Prophet, the first two Caliphs and the twelve Shia Imams. The copper coins, with the single exception of the double-paisa which is called after the third Caliph,

[1] Henderson, *The Coins of Haidar Ali and Tipu Sultan*, p. vii; see also for a study of Tipu's coins, Taylor, *The Coins of Tipu Sultan;* and *Indian Antiquary*, vol. xviii.

bear the Arabic or persian names of stars. But it must be remembered that the coin-names first appear on the gold and silver coins in or after 1216, while in the case of the copper coins, with the exception of the double-paisa which bears the name of Osman as early as 1218, the names do not appear till 1221. But strangely enough no name is found inscribed on Tipu's gold fanams.

*The Gold Coins*

The Muhar or *ahmadi* was called after Ahmad, which is one of the names of the Prophet Muhammad. The average weight of the *ahmadi* is 211 grains and is equal to four pagodas.

The half-Muhar or *sadiqi* was called after the first Caliph, Abu Bakr Siddiq, and after Jafar-i-Sadiq, the sixth Shia Imam. The average weight of the *sadiqi* is 106 grains and is equal to two pagodas.

The quarter-Muhar or *faruqi* was called after Omar, the second Caliph. Faruqi is also known as Sultan pagoda. Its average weight is 52½ grains and is equal to 3½Rs.

The lowest denomination of Tipu's gold coin is called fanam. To this Tipu is said to have given the name of rahati. Its average weight is 5 to 6 grains that is 1/10 of a pagoda. The fanam had considerable circulation in South India in spite of its small size.

The *ahmadi* was struck at Seringapatam and Bednur mints, while the *sadiqi* was struck only at Seringapatam. But none of these coins was extensively issued. Pagodas and fanams were much more common. The pagodas were coined at Seringapatam, Bednur and Dharwar, while the fanams were struck at Calicut, Ferokh, Dindigul, Bednur, Dharwar and Seringapatam.

*The Silver Coins*

The double-rupee or *haidari* was called after Ali. Its average weight is 352 to 355 grains.

The rupee or *imami* was called after the twelve Imams of the Shias. Its average weight is 175 to 178 grains.

The half-rupee or *abidi* was called after the fourth Imam. Its average weight is 87 grains.

The quarter-rupee or *baqiri* was called after the fifth Imam. Its average weight is 43 grains.

One-eighth rupee or *jafari* was called after the sixth Imam. Its average weight is 20 grains.

One-sixteenth rupee or *kazimi* was called after the seventh Imam. Its average weight is 10 grains.

One-thirty-second rupee or *khizri* was called after Khizr, the Prophet. Its average weight is 5 grains. This is the smallest of Tipu's coins.

These were the seven varieties of silver coins issued by Tipu. The double-rupee was struck at Seringapatam, Bednur and Calicut. The rupee was struck at Seringapatam, Bednur and Dharwar. The half-rupee was struck at Seringapatam and Bednur, while the quarter of a rupee was issued only from Seringapatam.

*The Copper Coins*

The double-paisa or *osmani* was called after the third Caliph, Osman. The name *osmani* is used from 1218-1221, but after 1221 it is called *mushtari* (Jupiter). It weighs from 331 to 351 grains. The paisa was called *zohra* (Venus). Its average weight is 174 grains. The half-paisa was called *bahram* (Mars). Its average weight is 87 grains.

The quarter-paisa was called *akhtar* (star). Its average weight is 42 grains. The one-eighth-paisa was called *qutub* (Poll Star). Its average weight is 18 grains.

The copper coins were issued by Tipu from all his twelve mints. The copper coins, unlike the gold and silver coins, invariably bear on the obverse a figure of an elephant, generally fully caparisoned, in different poses. Haidar had introduced the figure of an elephant towards the close of his reign because it is generally associated in India with royalty. Tipu, like his father, continued to use it on his copper coins.

APPENDIX D

# CALENDAR

Tipu instituted a new calendar sometime between January and June 1784, because the *hijra* years being lunar years of twelve lunar months each were administratively inconvenient. But the new era which he introduced consisted of twelve luni-solar years of twelve lunar months. In both the eras the year consisted of 354 days. But while in the Muslim year the shortage of eleven days as compared with the solar year was not regularised, Tipu adopted the principle of intercalary months in order to make his calendar agree with the solar year. This method was borrowed from the Hindu calendar. But whereas in the latter the extra month followed the normal month, it came first in Tipu's calendar. The following were the names of the months of Tipu's calendar: *ahmadi, bahari, jafari, darai, hashimi, wasii, zabarjadi, haidari, tului, yusufi, aizdi, bayazi.* The first, fourth, fifth, eighth, ninth and eleventh months consisted of 29 days each, the rest were of 30 days each. The first name was called after one of the names of the Prophet; *haidari* was called after Ali or after Haidar, Tipu's father; *bahari,* referred to spring (*bahar*); while *hashimi* was derived from the name of Hashim, the ancestor of the Prophet Muhammad. The other names had no significance, except that the initial letter of each month denoted its place in the calendar according to the *abjad* system, which assigned a certain numerical power to every letter in the alphabet. But since there was no letter to express either 11 or 12, the first two letters of *aizdi* and *bayazi* were added together to denote that they were the 11th and 12th months respectively.

The names given to the years of the cycle were also formed on the *abjad* system of notation, with the exception of the first two years which were named Ahad and Ahmed after God and the Prophet. The rest of the names merely signified the order of each year in the cycle, which was obtained by adding together the numerical powers of the different letters composing the name. Tipu's calendar, too, like the Hindu era, had a cycle of sixty years.

Tipu introduced a second reform of the calendar in 1787. But this change did not go beyond the substitution of new names to the months and years. But the names were assigned not in accordance with the *abjad* system, but on the basis of the *abtath* notation;[1] and

[1] See Taylor, *The Coins of Tipu Sultan,* pp. 16-18 for the value of each Arabic letter in the *abjad* and *abtath* systems.

like the old indicated the order of the year and the month by virtue of their numerical power. The names of Tipu's new months were: *ahmadi, bahari, taqi, samari, jafari, haidari, khusravi, dini, zakri, rahmani, razi and rabbani.* The number of days which each month contained were the same as in the former case and, similarly, as there is no letter to express either 11 or 12, the 11th and 12th months were indicated by the addition of the first two letters of the respective names.

Tipu called the new era *mauludi*,[1] and dated it from the spiritual birth of the Prophet instead of from his flight (*hijra*). The *hijra* era begins from 622 A.D., while the Prophet first announced himself as the Messenger of God in about 609 A.D. The *mauludi* era, therefore, began some thirteen years prior to the *hijra* era.

Tipu's State papers, coins and many of the contemporary works written by his courtiers are dated according to the new calendar introduced by Tipu. A knowledge of this is therefore necessary to a student of his reign.

[1] Kirmani, p. 328, calls it *muhammadi* era. See also *Islamic Culture*, vol. xiv. No. 2, pp. 161-64 for a discussion of the *mauludi* era.

APPENDIX E

# BIBLIOGRAPHY

## I. Original Sources

### *A. Contemporary Works (Persian)*

*Nishan-i-Haidari* by Husain Ali Khan Kirmani, R.A.S.B. MS. 200- Edition: Bombay 1307/1890. Translated into English by Colonel W. Miles in two volumes as (a) *The History of Hyder Naik... Nawab of the Karnatic Balaghaut*. London 1842. (b) *The History of the Reign of Tipu Sultan, being a continuation of the Neshan-i-Hyduri*. London 1864. The translation is not reliable. The Bombay edition has, therefore, been utilized and has been checked with the R.A.S.B.MS. Kirmani was Tipu's courtier, and had also been in the service of Haidar Ali. After the fall of Seringapatam he became a pensioner of the English, and wrote his work under their patronage in Calcutta. He is, therefore, biased in their favour. Besides, his dates are usually wrong; he does not give the sequence of events correctly, and furnishes very scanty information regarding Tipu's administration, his army, and the condition of the people under his rule. Furthermore, although his delineation of Tipu's character is on the whole sympathetic, being himself a fanatic, he represents the Sultan also as a bigot whose every action was determined by his religion, and whose life mission was to spread Islam by the sword. But in spite of these defects, *Nishan-i-Haidari* is very valuable, because it is written by one who knew both Haidar and Tipu intimately, and is the only extant contemporary history which gives a detailed account, and covers the full period of their reigns.

*Tarikh-i-Tipu Sultan*. Author not known. I.O.MS., 5F.3057 (Mackenzie Collection). It is a short history of Mysore from 1713 to 1799 but it bears no title. It gives few dates, describes the events sometimes in wrong sequence, and contains hardly any information regarding the administration of Mysore. Nevertheless, the work is very useful, having been written with a balanced judgement and impartiality. It ends on a note of praise for the English for having displayed justice and generosity towards the members of Tipu's family after the fall of Seringapatam.

*A Persian MS. History of Mysore* described by A. Qadir Sarwari in the Mysore University Journal (New Series), V, No. 1, pp. 23-40, appears to be a summarised version of the India Office MS. The former contains 51 folios, the latter 112 folios.

*Sultan-ut-Tawarikh*. Author not known. I.O.MS. 521, and Government Oriental MSS. Library, Madras, MS. 288. I have used the latter manuscript. Wilks and Kirkpatrick say that its author was Zain-ul-Abidin Shushtari. But there is no mention of this in the work itself. Besides, if Shushtari had been its author, there is no reason why this fact should have been concealed. However, it must have been written by some one intimately connected with the Sultan, because some of the passages in it, as the author says, were dictated by Tipu himself (f. 8b). Folios 9 at the beginning and 81 towards the end describe Tipu's ancestors in a very sketchy manner. The rest of the work deals with the Sultan's reign from his accession to the rebellion in Malabar in 1789. But it does not assign dates, nor does it mention the attack on Nargund and Kittur by the Mysoreans. Although the events of the Maratha-Mysore war (1785-87) have been graphically described, the military operations of the Marathas have been ignored. But in spite of these defects the work contains useful information. (Some of the criticism made below against the *Tarikh-i-Khudadadi* is also applicable to the *Sultan-ut-Tawarikh*.

*Tarikh-i-Khudadadi*. Author not known. I.O.MS. 2990. It is defective at both ends. It abruptly begins with the siege of Bednur, and ends after giving the first article of the treaty signed between Tipu and the Marathas (1787). It has been regarded by Kirkpatrick as Tipu's autobiography. But a study of it shows that this is an incorrect view, for it is almost a verbatim copy of *Sultan-ut-Tawarikh* written in the first person. If the Sultan had been its author he would have at least made some reference to his personal life, his courtiers and his subjects. Being interested in the study of history and biography, he must have read *Tukuk-i-Jahangiri*, *Babar-namah*, and other similar works. Yet, unlike these, the *Tarikh* does not describe anything except the dull, unedifying events of Tipu's campaign against "the unworthy and accursed infidels". Nor does it give the sequence of events correctly, nor assigns any dates to events. At the same time it makes a number of incorrect statements. It says that the English *wakils* were delayed in their journey from Madras to Mangalore for six months, and that it was after two months of bargaining that at last the Treaty of Mangalore was signed (p. 27). Actually it took the Commissioners four months to reach Mangalore, and the treaty was signed only a month after their arrival there. If Tipu had been the author of the *Tarikh*, he would not have, owing to his great love of detail, made these mistakes.

The *Tarikh* also suffers from other serious defects. The attack on the forts of Nargund and Kittur have not been mentioned. Similarly many of the events of the Maratha-Mysore War have not been described. On the other hand, sometimes incidents have been narrated which never happened. Thus the *Tarikh* says that at the time of signing the Treaty of Mangalore, "the Commissioners stood with their heads uncovered and the treaty in their hands for two hours, using every form of flattery and supplication to induce his compliance." Further, it says that, after releasing the prisoners of war in 1785, Tipu supplied them with asses belonging to salt merchants; and it was on their backs that they marched in procession through Mysore to the derision of its inhabitants and entered Madras (p. 42). The Maratha chiefs have also been, similarly, represented as being greatly anxious to conclude peace with Tipu in 1787. They are said to have made humiliating protestations, admitted their mistake in bringing about the war, and pleaded before the Sultan to conclude peace by pitying the unworthy Peshwa who stood in the place of a son to him. (pp. 88-89).

It might be argued that Tipu misrepresented facts because of his propensity for boasting. But even if we admit that Tipu was boastful, and therefore indulged in exaggerations, there is no reason why he should have written of things which never happened. He knew that his autobiography would be read by people after him, and his forgeries would only discredit him.

The picture of Tipu which emerges from a study of the *Tarikh* is that of a religious maniac who was perpetually engaged in killing non-Muslims, or forcibly converting them to Islam. But as we have already seen, this is an absolutely false picture of the Sultan. Besides, the *Tarikh* abounds with indecent and impolite words and phrases. Tipu's enemies are always described as "unworthy". Tukoji Holkar is referred to as holding a "superior rank among the worthless chiefs of his people". Coorgs are called "bastards and whoresons". The Nizam and the Peshwa are mentioned as "the two bastards". Tipu was very cultured and polite, and he could not have expressed himself in such an unrefined language. Some of the passages in the *Sultan-ut-Tawarikh* are said to have been dictated by Tipu. But there his enemies have not been called by vile epithets. It is, therefore, incredible that he should have lost all sense of decorum while writing his so-called life. No one has ever written an autobiography to misrepresent himself, but the *Tarikh* is for the most part an indictment of the rule and character of its author.

*Tarikh-i-Hamid Khan* by Hamid Khan. Bankipur MS. 619. Hamid Khan was the *mir munshi* of George Cherry, Cornwallis's private secretary, and accompanied the Governor-General in his campaign against Tipu (1791-92). His work describes the full history of Haidar, and of Tipu until the Treaty of Seringapatam (1792). Nearly half the work is devoted to the family, early life and reign of Haidar; but the information regarding these matters is not always reliable. The events of the first ten years of Tipu's reign have been described briefly and not always correctly. It is really the history of the Third Anglo-Mysore War, particularly the military operations of Cornwallis, which have been described accurately and elaborately. These descriptions, which he wrote from personal experience and observation, are useful in correcting and supplementing the accounts of the war given by the English and Indian writers. (See for more details my article, *Tarikh-i-Hamid Khan* in I.H.R.C., xxiii, p. 13-15).

*Tarikh-i-Coorg* by Husain Khan Lohani. R.A.S.B.MS. 201. Husain Khan Lohani was a *munshi* of Maharaja Vira Rajendra Wodeyar (1789-1834), and it was at the latter's request that he translated from the original Kanarese his history of the Rajas of Coorg from A.H. 1047/1637-38 to A.H. 1222/1807. The work is biased against Tipu and is partial to the English. Yet it contains useful information. It describes in detail the conquest of Coorg by Haidar, the attempts of Tipu to crush the rebellions of its inhabitants and of the assistance which the Vir Raja rendered to the English in their wars against Tipu. Further, it relates how Abercromby persuaded Cornwallis to include Coorg as part of the English share in the list of districts demanded from Tipu at the peace conference at Seringapatam (February—March 1792).

*Waqai-i-Manazil-i-Rum*. R.A.S.B.MS. 1678. This is the diary of the embassy despatched by Tipu to Constantinople in 1786. It was written by Khwaja Abdul Qadir, secretary to the embassy. It is dated according to the *maula̤di* era, although sometimes the *hijra* dates are also given. It gives very graphic accounts of the places the ambassadors visited, and the people they came across in the course of their journey. It is evident from the diary that one of the chief objects of the mission was to promote the trade of Mysore and to obtain commercial privileges in Masqat, Persia and the Ottoman Empire. However, as the diary was kept only up to 19 Rabi-ul-Awwal, 1201/January 9, 1787, while the ambassadors were still at Basra, their journey to and reception at Constantinople and other matters connected with their mission have not been described. It is only incidentally from a letter of Ali Raja of Cannanore addressed to Tipu and appended at the end of the manuscript that we know that the ambassadors proceeded from Constantinople to Suez and then to Jeddah, Mecca and Medina. After performing their pilgrimage they returned to Mangalore.

*Fath-ul-Mujahidin* by Zain-ul-Abidin Shushtari. R.A.S.B.MS. 1669. Zain-ul-Abidin was the brother of Mir Alam. He left Hyderabad at an early age, entered Haidar's service, and finally became a courtier of Tipu. He wrote this work at the Sultan's request. It does not give the strength of the Mysore army, but deals with its rules and regulations and its organisation. Its importance lies in the fact that it is the only work in Persian which deals with Tipu's military administration, and supplements the information obtained from the English sources.

*Hadiqat-ul-Alam* by Mir Alam. Hyderabad 1266 A.H./1850 A.D. Abul Qasim Musawi Shushtari surnamed Mir Alam was of Persian origin. He enjoyed great confidence of the Nizam who entrusted him with important diplomatic missions. But in reality he was an English agent. He was instrumental in establishing an alliance between the Nizam and the English in 1790, and played an important part in bringing about the downfall of Tipu. For his services he was given a pension of Rs. 24,000 a year by the English. (Briggs, *The Nizam*. p. 139.) He was appointed Prime Minister by the Nizam in 1803.

*Hadiqat-ul-Alam* is a history of the Qutub Shahs and the Nizams in two volumes. The second volume ends in 1799 with the fall of Seringapatam. It is an important source for the Maratha-Mysore War (1785-87), and for the part played by the Nizam's troops in the Third Anglo-Mysore War. But since Mir Alam was an English protégé, his work is very much prejudiced against Tipu, and does not describe things discreditable to his masters.

*Hukm-namah*, R.A.S.B.MS. 1677. This contains the instructions given by Tipu to his ambassadors who were sent to Turkey, and were to proceed from there to France and then to England. This embassy did not go beyond Constantinople, and a separate mission was despatched to France. But to this also probably the same instructions were given. *Hukm-namah*, No. 1676 contains instructions to the ambassadors regarding the talks which they were to have with the French authorities at Paris. There are many other *Hukum-namahs* of Tipu in the R.A.S.B. Library, but they contain very little useful information.

*Mirat-ul-Ahwal* by Ahmad b. Muhammad Ali b. Muhammad Baqar. Central Library, Tehran University MS. 5716. Ahmad arrived in India early in May 1805 and visited both northern and southern India. He refers to the treachery of Mir Sadiq about which he must have heard during his stay in Hyderabad.

*Tarikh-i-Fath Ali Shah* by Mirza Muhammad Sarui. B.M.MS. Add. 7665.

*Zinat-ut-Tawarikh* by a number of people, principally Mirza Raza "Banda" Tabrizi and Mirza Abdul Karim Ishtihardi. B.M.MS. Add. 23527; *Mufarrih-ul-Qulub* by Mirza Muhammad "Nadim" Barfurushi. B.M.MS. Add. 3449; *Tarikh-i-Jahan Ara* by Mirza Muhammad Sadiq "Huma" Marwazi. R.A.S., vol. i, MS. 153; *Tarikh-i-Zulqarnain* by Mirza Fazlullah "Khawari" Shirazi. B.M. MS. OR. 3527. Among these works, which give a brief description of Tipu's embassy to Fath Ali Shah Qachar, Mirza Fazlullah's account is more coherent and reliable than those of other historians of Fath Ali Shah's reign.

B. *Contemporary Works* (*non-Persian*)

Allan, A. *An Account of the Campaign in Mysore* (1799). Calcutta 1912.

Bristow, J. *A Narrative of the Sufferings of James Bristow Written by Himself*. Calcutta 1792.

Beatson, A. *A View of the Origin and Conduct of the War with Tippoo Sultan*. London 1800.

Campbell, J. *Memoir of the Life and Character of the Lieut.-Colonel John Campbell*. Edinburgh 1836.

Dirom, Major. *A Narrative of the Campaign in India Which Terminated the War with Tippoo Sultan in* 1792. London 1794.

Crisp, B. *The Mysorean Revenue Regulations*. Calcutta 1792.

Druon, H. *Les Française dans l'Inde*. Paris 1886.

Fullarton, W. *A View of the English Interests in India*. Madras 1867.

*Haidarnama*. A Kanarese MS. published in the Mysore Archaeological Report 1930.

Law de Lauristan, *État Politique de l' Inde en* 1777. Pondichery 1913.

Mackenzie, R. *A Sketch of the War with Tippoo Sultaun*. 2 vols. Calcutta 1793-94.

Malcolm, J. *The Political History of India*. 2 vols. London 1826.

Mautort, L.F. *Mémoires* (1752-1802). Paris 1895. The writer served under Bussy during the Second Anglo-Mysore War.

Michaud, J. *Histoire des Progrés et la Chute de l'Empire de Mysore sous les Regnes d'Hyder-Ally et Tippoo-Saib*. 2 vols. Paris 1801.

Moor, E. *A Narrative of the Operations of Captain Little's Detachment, and of the Mahratta Army Commanded by Purseram Bhow*. London 1794.

Moris, H. *Journal de Bord du Bailli de Suffren dans l'Inde* 1781-84. Paris 1888.

Munro, I. *A Narrative of the Military Operations on the Coromandel Coast*, 1780-84. London 1789.

Oakes, H. *An Authentic Narrative of the Treatment of the English who were taken Prisoners on the Reduction of Bednore by Tippoo Sahib.* London 1785.

Punganuri, Ramchandra R. *Memoirs of Hyder and Tippoo*. (Translated by C. P. Brown.) Madras 1849.

Rennell, J. *Marches of the British Armies in India during the Campaigns of* 1790 *and* 1791. London 1792.

Salmond, J. *A Review of the Origin, Progress, and Result of the Decisive War with Tippoo Sultan in Mysore*. London 1800.

Scurry, J. *The Captivity, Sufferings and Escape of James Scurry Written by Himself*. London 1824.

C. *Records (unpublished)*

*National Archives of India*

(*a*) Secret Proceedings, 1780-1799.

(*b*) Political Proceedings, 1790-1799.

(*c*) Original Records, 1783-1799, contain original letters in Persian and Marathi addressed by Tipu and other Indian rulers to the Governor-General. They also include some of the corre pondence between Tipu, the Nizam and the Marathas.

*Madras Government Records Office*

(*a*) Military Consultations, 1782-99.

(*b*) Military Country Correspondence. Vols. 32-42.

(*c*) Military Despatches to Court, 1783-90, contain despatches sent by the Madras Government.

(*d*) Secret Despatches from England, 1785-91, contain despatches sent to the Governor-General in Council.

(*e*) Political Despatches to England, 1791-98, contain despatches sent by the Madras Government.

(*f*) Madras Secret Consultations contain information not only regarding diplomatic and military affairs, but also regarding Tipu's administration. Vols. V (1797), VI (1798), VIII B (1799) are very important.

(*g*) Military Sundry Books.

   (*i*) Vols. 60A-60B (1783), 61 (1784) deal with the activities of the Commissioners appointed by the Madras Government in 1783 to proceed to Mangalore and negotiate peace with Tipu. They throw interesting light on Tipu's attitude towards the English prisoners of war and the Commissioners.

(*ii*) Vol. 66 (1785) contains the letter which Fullarton wrote to the Governor of Madras. It describes the military operations of the Second Anglo-Mysore War, and suggests plans for the invasion of Mysore.

(*iii*) Vols. 109A-109B contain Harris's letters to Wellesley describing the English campaign in Mysore and the fall of Seringapatam. They also give useful information regarding Tipu's income, the war material which the English obtained in Seringapatam, and other matters relating to Mysore.

(*h*) Military Sundry Books.

(*i*) No. 83 (1793) relates to correspondence regarding the Nizam's claim to Kurnool.

(*ii*) No. 101 (1792-95) contains a description of Tipu's army in October 1794 and of his civil administration by William Macleod.

(*i*) Military Sundries.

(*i*) Vol. 106 contains the journal written by Kennaway of the different conferences held with Tipu's *wakils* from February 14 to the end of March 1792 to conclude the Treaty of Seringapatam.

(*ii*) Vol. 107 (1799) contains the letter from the Governor of Tranquebar to the Governor-General regarding Mons. Dubuc. It also contains an abstract of Tipu's income in 1798.

(*iii*) Vols. 109A-109B contain useful information regarding the Fourth Anglo-Mysore War, and other matters after the fall of Seringapatam.

(*iv*) Vol. 102B contains a description of Tipu's military strength in December 1798 by William Macleod.

(*j*) The following volumes are mainly useful for Malabar affairs:

(*i*) Cochin Commissioner's Diary. Vols. 2032-2034.

(*ii*) Collectorate Records (Revenue). Vols. 2211, 2246-48.

(*iii*) Factory Records: Tellicherry (*a*) Diaries (*b*) General.

(*iv*) Forest Records. Vol. 2408.

(*v*) Government Committee Diaries. Vols. 2135-39, 2146, 2147, 2150-53, 2156

(*vi*) Malabar Commission, First Commissioner's Diaries. Vols. I-II. Nos. 1660, 1663.

(*vii*) Malabar Commission, Supervisor's Diaries (Revenue). Vol. 19. No. 2050.

(*viii*) Malabar Commission, Supervisor's Diaries (Political). Vol. 31. No. 2062.
(*ix*) Malabar Commission, Supervisor's Diaries (Public). Vol. 20. No. 2041.
(*x*) Malabar Records, Supervisor's Diaries. Vol. 201. No. 2053.
(*xi*) Malabar Commission, Joint Commissioner's Report. Vol. 13. No. 1676.
(*xii*) Malabar Secret Committee Diaries (Revenue). Vols. 1710, 1716.
(*xiii*) Tellicherry Factory Records. Vol. 38. No. 1503.

*India Office Library Manuscripts* (English)
(*a*) MS. No. 46, contains the report of Captain Read from January 1787 to August 1790. He was appointed by Cornwallis to do espionage work is Mysore.
(*b*) Qasim, Munshi M. *An Account of Tipu Sultan's Court.* No MSS. recorded. English translation I.O. MSS Eur. C. 10.
(*c*) Peixoto, *History of Nawab Haidar Ali Khan Bahadur*, Ed. Charles Philips Brown. I.O. MSS. Eur. D. 295.
(*d*) Proceedings of a Jacobin Club at Seringapatam. I.O.MS. Eur. 99.
(*e*) Letters to Dundas. MSS. Eur. F. 66.
(*f*) Wellesley to Dundas. MSS. Eur. D. 587.
(*g*) Journal of Military Events during 1790-91 by Major Dirom. MSS. Eur. F. 76.
(*h*) Wellesley to Scott. MSS. Eur. D. 588-89.
(*i*) Mss. Eur. D. 607 and E. 196.
(*j*) Two Ordinances of Tipu. MSS. Mar. C. 33
(*k*) MSS. Eur. D. 562/18.
(*l*) Mss. from the Ames Library of South Asia, Minnosota, U.S.A., I.O. Reel Nos. 607, 643, 648-50, 759-80. These contain the correspondence of Macartney, Wellesley and Dundas.
(*m*) Factory Records: Persia and the Persian Gulf, No. 18.
Political and Secret Department Records:
(*n*) Bengal Secret Letters, vol. i, (Jan. 1778-Aug. 1794).
(*o*) Secret Letters from Fort St. George, vol. i (Sept. 1784-Oct. 3, 1796); vol. ii (Jan. 19, 1797-Oct. 6, 1803).
(*p*) Secret Despatches to Bengal (1788-1803).
(*q*) Secret Committee of the E.I.C. to the Governor-General, June 18,1798.
(*r*) Secret Letters Received from Madras (1788-1803).
(*s*) Home Miscellaneous Series, Nos. 293, 460-61, 463, 472, 475 and Vols. 85, 248, 457, 508.

*Persian Documents*

(*a*) No. 4682 contains Tipu's letters to his officers.
(*b*) No. 4684 deals with Tipu's administration.
(*c*) No. 4685 deals with the civil and military administration and commercial policy of Tipu.

*India Office Portuguese Records*

*Conselho Ultramarinho*, vol. 2 part 1 (trans.), vol 2 part 2 (trans.), vol. 3 part 2 (trans.). These volumes deal with the relations of the Portuguese with Haidar and Tipu.

*British Museum*

Wellesley Papers, Additional MSS. 12585-88 12606, 12610, 12648, 12650, 12652-54, 13421, 13423, 13446-48, 13451, 13456, 13458, 13473, 13476, 13482, 13596, 13598, 13621, 13627, 13653, 13665, 13667, 13670, 13683, 13693, 13699, 13710, 13727-29, 13788, 26583, 37274-76, 37278-79.

Macartney Papers, MSS. 22, 452.

*Public Record Office*, *London*

F.O. 78/7-1786; F.O. 78/8-1787; F.O. 78/9-1788, contain despatches of Sir Robert Ainslie, British Ambassador in Constantinople, to Carmathian, the British Foreign Secretary, regarding the activities of Tipu's envoys to the Ottoman Sultan.

F.O. 78/20-1798; F.O. 78/21-1798, contain correspondence of the Ottoman Sultan with Tipu.

F.O. 27/28-1787-88; F.O. 27/29-1788; F.O. 27/30-1788; F.O. 63/11-1788, contain letters of Lord Dorset, the British Ambassador in Paris, addressed to Carmathian regarding Tipu's envoys sent to the court of Louis XVI.

Cornwallis Papers: 30/11/112; 30/11/114; 30/11/115; 30/11/116; 30/11/117; 30/11/118; 30/11/125; 30/11/134; 30/11/150; 30/11/151; 30/11/152.

*Journal de Paris*, June 30, 1788, No. 182.

Extract of a letter written from Marseilles on June 14, 1788, pp. 794-95.

*Bodleian*, Oxford

Macartney Papers, MS. Engl. Hist. C. 74, 77-9, 91-3, 104-05, 107-08.

*Scottish Record Office*

(*i*) Letters addressed by Wellesley and other officers of the E.I.C. in India to Dundas: IV/33/9; IV/249/20; IV/

249/22; IV/250/34; IV/250/37; IV/250/37; IV/250/38; IV/431/9. In addition to these the following in Section IV are also of interest: 46, 69, 70, 87, 99, 101, 104-05, 114, 118, 132, 163, 216, 230-31, 364, 381, 384, 401, 432, 527. Nos. 249-50 of Section IV cover the correspondence between Wellesley and Dundas.

*Other Private Papers*

(*i*) Letters sent to Gen. Alexander Ross, colleague and friend of Lord Cornwallis (1784-1825). (British Records Association, No. 833.)

(*ii*) Records of Major Gen. Sir Archibald Campbell while Chief Engineer and Governor and Commander-in-Chief of Madras, 1769-89. (Campbell of Inverneill, Nos. 1-19).

(*iii*) Letters of Dundas, Sir Robert Abercromby, etc. (Hamilton Bruce, Nos. 104, 208.)

(*iv*) Letters from Norman Macleod to Lt. Gen. Fraser, M.P., describing the war in India against Haidar Ali and the French, 782. (Macpherson of Cluny No. 908.)

(*v*) Letters from Capt. Andrew Macpherson and Capt. (later Col.) John McIntyre to Col. Allan Macpherson of Blairgowrie, 1785-1802. (Macpherson of Cluny, Nos. 913, 917.)

(*vi*) Letters from Alexander Macpherson to Col. Duncan Macpherson of Cluny describing operations against Tipu in South India, 1790-91. (Macpherson of Cluny, No. 929.)

(*vii*) MS. and printed papers concerning the last Anglo-Mysore War, 1799. (Dalhousie, Sect. 5, No. 1.)

In these documents there is constant reference to Tipu's threat for an invasion of Travancore, but there is no mention of the Raja's plan for the purchase of Ayicotta and Cranganur.

*National Library of Scotland*

(*i*) Melville Papers: Nos. 1060, 1062, 3385, 3387.

(*ii*) *Journal of the War with Tippoo*, 1799. (MS.)

(*iii*) *Memoir of the Life and Principal Transactions of Tippoo Sultan by a Maratha Sardar*, Eng. trans. (MS). It was written after Tipu's death. It is full of inaccuracies.

*Pondicherry Archives*

The documents in the Pondicherry Archives contain valuable information regarding Tipu's relations with the French and the French policy in India. But unfortunately there are no records throwing light on Tipu's relations with the French during the years 1797-99. The Pondicherry records have now been removed to Paris.

*Archives Nationales, Paris*

*Catalogues des Manuscrits Conserves aux Archives Nationales*. Paris 1892.

2769 (T, 15267) *Memoire sur l'Inde*, 1788, No. 6. It describes how the English can be overthrown by the French with Tipu's support.

2903 (AF, LV, 1686, 5 dossier).

2909 (AF, LV, 1686, 5 dossier).

Series B, Nos, 214, 224. Registre Colonies. In other documents of this series there is no useful material on Tipu.

Series $C^2$ Colonies Nos. 62-5, 69, 93-4, 117, 155, 163, 165-67, 169, 172, 174, 176, 179-81, 184, 187, 189, 191, 233-34, 236-40, 242, 265-66, 291, 295-96, 299, 301-02, 304-05.

Series $C^4$ Colonies, Nos. 55, 58, 66-7, 73, 79, 84, 89, 95, 102-04, 112-13.

*Archives Nationales, Affaires Étrangères*

Series $B^1$, Nos. 176-77, Correspondance Consulaire, Baghdad (1776-86; 1787-91); No. 197, Bassorah (1743-91; No. 448, Constantinople (1787-90).

*Archives du Ministère des Affaires Étrangères, Paris*

Vol. 11 (1785-1826), Memoir presented to the First Consul by Dubuc, as to how the English could be overthrown by the French with Tipu's support. (ff. 270a-73b.)

Vol. 18 (1784-86), Monneron to Cossigny, Sept. 14, 1786, describes the relations between Tipu and the French 282a *seqq.*

Vol. 20 (1785-1814), ff. 176a *seqq.*, gives the terms of alliance proposed by Tipu. Trans. from Persian and signed by Monneron at Seringapatam, 17th April, 1796; ff. 220a-23a, Memoir relating to a military expedition in India by Cossigny. This plan was presented by Cossigny to Napoleon.

Vol. 178—Turqui, refers to the embassy which Tipu sent to Constantinople.

*Bibliotheque Nationale*, MS. française, Nouvelle Acquisition, Nos. 9368, 9373. The remaining documents bearing on Tipu are the same as in the Archives Nationales.

*Mackenzie Manuscripts*

These are in Tamil, Telugu and Kanarese, and contain useful information about Tipu's administration and campaigns.

*Haidar Kaifyat* (Kanarese)

MSS. Nos. (*a*) 18-15-15. (*b*) 18-15-7.

*Karnataka Rajakkal Savistara Charitam* (Tamil)
MSS. Nos. (*a*) 17-5-11. (*b*) 17-5-25. (*c*) 17-5-34. (*d*) 15-3-1. (*e*) 15-3-2. (*f*) 15-3-9. (*g*) 15-3-11 to 15-3-13. (*h*) 15-3-17. (*i*) 15-3-19. (*j*) 15-3-27 to 15-3-31. (*k*) 15-3-36 to 15-3-43. (*l*) 15-3-47 to 15-3-52. (*m*) 15-3-57. (*n*) 15-3-65. (*o*) 15-3-46. (*p*) 15-4-20. (*q*) 15-4-13. (*r*) 15-4-10. (*s*) 15-6-8.

*Kaifyat of Hanumangundam Zamindars* (Telugu)
MSS. Nos. (*a*) 15-4-36. (*b*) 15-3-27.

D. *Records* (*Published*)

(*i*) *English*

Aitchison, C. U. *A Collection of Treaties, Engagements and Sanads*. Vols. VI, IX. Calcutta 1909.

Antonova, K. *The Struggle of Tipu Sultan against British Colonial Power* (*New Archive Documents*). Moscow 1962.

Baramahal Records, Section I-IV, XV-XVIII, XXII.

Baramahal Records, No. XLVII, Agrahara, 1793-98.

*Calendar of Persian Correspondence*. Vols. VI-X. Delhi 1938-59.

Cobbett, W. *Parliamentary History of England*. Vol. XXVIII. London 1816

Forrest, W. G. *Selections from the State Papers Preserved in the Bombay Secretariat*. Home Series. Vol. II. Bombay 1887.

—*Selections from the State Papers Preserved in the Bombay Secretariat*. Maratha Series. Vol. I. Bombay 1885.

—*Selections from the State Papers Preserved in the Foreign Department of the Government of India*, 1782-85. 3 vols. Calcutta 1890.

Furber, H. *The Private Record of an Indian Governor-Generalship* (1793-98). *The Correspondence of Sir John Shore with Henry Dundas*. Harvard University Press. 1933.

Gleig, G. R. *The Life of Sir Thomas Munro*. Vols. I-II. London 1830.

Gurwood, J. *The Despatches of the Duke of Wellington*. 3 vols. Calcutta 1840.

Kirkpatrick, W. *Select Letters of Tippoo Sultan*. London 1811. These letters contain useful information, but they must be used carefully. Kirkpatrick was very prejudiced against Tipu, as is evident from his comments on each letter. While translating the original letters from Persian into English, he never cared to sift the genuine from the spurious. It is not unlikely that he might have himself forged some letters to damage Tipu's reputation.

Malabar Secret Commission Diaries (Public). Vol. 1697.

Malabar Secret Commission Diaries (Political). Vols. 1727-35, 1800.

Malabar Secret Commission (Correspondence). Vols. 1895-96.

Martin, R. M. *Despatches, Minutes and Correspondence of the Marquess Wellesley*. 5 vols. London 1836-37.

*Minute of the Governor-General Sir John Shore on the General and Supplementary Reports of the Joint Commissioners on the State and Condition of Malabar*, 1792-93. Madras 1879.

Owen, S. J. *A Selection from the Despatches...relating to India of the Duke of Wellington*, Oxford 1880.

—*A Selection from the Despatches of the Marquess Wellesley*, Oxford 1877.

Philips, C. H. *The Correspondence of David Scott*—(1787-1805). 2 vols. London 1951.

*Poona Residency Correspondence*, Vols. II-VI, VIII. Bombay, 1936-43.

Ray, H. C. *Some India Office Letters of the Reign of Tipu Sultan*. Calcutta 1941.

*Report of a Joint Commission from Bengal and Bombay Appointed to Inspect into the Condition of Malabar in* 1792 *and* 1793. Madras 1862.

Ross, C. *Correspondence of Charles, First Marquis Cornwallis*. 3 vols. London 1859.

Spencer, J., Smell, J., and Walker, A. *Report on the Administration of Malabar*—1801. Calcutta 1910.

Warden, T. *Report on Land Tenures in Malabar*—1815. Calicut 1916.

—*Report on the Revenue System in Malabar*—1813. Calicut 1916.

—*Report on the Land Assessment in Malabar*—1815. Calicut 1916.

Wilks, M. *Report on the Interior Administration, Resources and Expenditure of the Government of Mysore under the System prescribed by the Order of the Governor-General in Council, dated* 4th September, 1799. Bangalore 1864.

—*Notes on Mysore*. Bangalore 1864.

(*ii*) *Marathi*

Khare, V. W. *Aitihasik Lekha Sangraha*. Vols. VII-XI.

Parasnis, D. B. *Itihas Sangraha*. Vols. I-III, VI.

Rajwade, V. K. *Itihas Sangraha*. Vols. XIX-XX.

—*Aitihasik Sadhane*, Vol. VII.

(*iii*) *French*

Gaudart, E. *Catalogue des Manuscrits des Anciennes Archives de l'Inde Française*. Tome I, Pondichéry 1690-1789. Tome II, Pondichéry 1789-1815. Pondichéry 1942. Tome V, Mahé et Logis de Calicut des Surate 1739-1808. Pondichéry 1934. Tome VI, Yanaon, Muzulipatam et diverses localites 1669-1793. Pondichéry 1935.

Martineau, A. *Lettres et Conventions des Gouverneurs de Pondichéry avec*

*les divers Princes Indiens de* 1666 *à* 1793. Pondichéry 1911-14.
——*Journal de Bussy*. Pondichéry 1932.

(*iv*) *Dutch*

Selections from the Records of the Madras Government. Dutch Records Nos. I-V. Madras 1907.

(*a*) No. I. *Memoir on the Malabar Coast* by J. V. Stein Van Gollenesse composed in 1743.

(*b*) No. II. *Memoir* written in 1781 by Adriaan Moens, Governor and Director of the Malabar Coast, for his successor.

(*c*) No. III. *Memoir* of Commandeur Frederik Cunes delivered to his successor Caspar De Jong on December 31, 1756.

(*d*) No. IV. *Memoir* of Commandeur John Gerard Van Angelbeek delivered to his successor J. L. Spall in 1793.

(*e*) No. V. *Historical Account of Haidar Ali Khan.*

(*f*) Record No. 13. Madras 1911. This contains an English translation of Records Nos. I and II.

The importance of the Dutch Records is that they throw light on the affair of Cranganur and Ayicotta and on the relations of the Dutch with Haidar and Tipu.

(*v*) *Portuguese*

Pissurlencar, P.S. *Antigualhas. Estudos e Documentos sobre a Historia dos Portugueses na India*. Vol. I, fasc. II. This volume contains useful information regarding Tipu's relations with the Portuguese and the Christians of Kanara.

(*vi*) *Ottoman Archives*

Hikmet Bayur, *Maysor Sultani Tipu Ile Osmanli Padisah Larindan I. Abdulhamid VE III. Selim Arasindaki Mektuplasma*. Ankara 1948. This contains the correspondence between Tipu and the Ottoman Sultans, Abdul Hamid I and Salim III. There are seven photographic copies of the original letters along with their translations in Turkish by Mr. Hikmet Bayur. Many of the facts mentioned in these letters are contained in the R.A.S.B. MS. 1677.

## II. Secondary Works

Archer, Mrs. M. *Tippoo's Tiger*. London 1959

*Authentic Memoirs of Tippoo Sultaun by an Officer of the East India Service.* Calcutta 1819.

*The Asiatic Annual Register for the Year* 1799. London 1801.

Auber, P. *Rise and Progress of the British Power in India*. 2 vols. London 1837.

Basu, P. *Oudh and the East India Company.* Lucknow 1943.

Beveridge, H. *A Comprehensive History of India*, Vol. II. London 1867.

Bowring, L. B. *Haidar Ali and Tipu Sultan* (Rulers of India Series). Oxford 1893.

Briggs, H. G. *The Nizam: His History and Relations with the British Government.* 2 vols. London 1861.

Buchanan, H. F. *A Journey from Madras through the Countries of Mysore, Canara, Malabar*....3 vols. London 1807.

Cadell, P. *History of the Bombay Army.* London 1937.

Campbell, J. *An Account of the Gallant Defence made at Mangalore.* 1786.

Cunat. Ch. *Histoire du Bailli de Suffren.* Rennes 1852.

Dasgupta, A. P. *The Central Authority in British India*, 1874-84. Calcutta University 1931.

——*Studies in the History of the British in India.* Calcutta University 1942.

Davies, F. S. *Cochin, British and Indian*, London 1923.

Day, F. *The Land of the Permauls or Cochin, its Past and Present.* Madras 1863.

Decaen, S. *L'Isle de France.* Paris 1901.

Dodwell, H. H. *The Nabobs of Madras.* London 1926.

——*Cambridge History of India*, Vol. V. Cambridge 1929.

Duff, G. *History of the Mahrattas.* S. M. Edwardes, 2 vols. O.U. Press 1921.

Fortescue, J. W. *History of the British Army.* Vol. III. London 1911. Vol. IV, Part II. London 1915.

Forrest, Denys, *Tiger of Mysore—The life and death of Tipu Sultan.* London 1970.

Fraser, H. *Our Faithful Ally, the Nizam.* London 1865.

Furber, T. *John Company at Work.* Cambridge 1948.

Glachant, R. *Histoire de l'Inde des Française.* Paris 1965.

Gleig, G. R. *British Empire in India*, Vol. III. London 1835.

Gupta, P. C. *Baji Rao II and the East India Company* (1796-1818). O.U. Press 1939.

Hatalkar, V. G. *Relations between the French and the Marathas.* Bombay 1958.

Hatton, W. H. *Marquis Wellesley*, Oxford 1893.

Henderson, J. R. *The Coins of Haidar Ali and Tipu Sultan.* Madras 1921.

Herman, L. *Histoire de la Rivalité des Française et des Anglais dans l'Inde.* Paris 1852.

Hollingberry, W. *History of Nizam Ally Khaun.* Calcutta 1805.

*Imperial Gazetteer* (1909).

Joshi, V. V. *Clash of Three Empires.* Allahabad 1941.

Kincaid, C. A. and Parasnis, D. B. *A History of the Maratha People.* Vol. III. O.U. Press 1925.

Labornadie, Marguerite, V. *La Revolutions et les Etablissements Française dans l'Inde* (1790-93). Pairis 1930.

Lawrence, A. W. *Captives of Tipu Sultan*. London 1929.

Logan, W. *Malabar*. 2 vols. Madras 1887.

Lohuizen, J. Van, *The Dutch East India Company and Mysore*. 1961.

Longford, Elizabeth, *The years of the Sword*. London 1969.

Lovat-Fraser, J. A. *Henry Dundas, Viscount Melville*. London 1916.

Love, H.D. *Vestiges of Old Madras*, Vol. III. London 1913.

Lushington, S. R. *Life of General Lord Harris*. London 1840.

Malcolm. J. *A sketch of the Political History of India*. London 1811.

Mahmud Khan Mahmud. *Tarikh-i-Sultanat-i-Khudadad* (in Urdu). Bangalore 1939.

Matheson, C. *Life of Henry Dundas*. London 1933

*Madras and Bombay District Gazetteers*.

Malleson, G.B. *Final French Struggles in India and on the Indian Seas*. London 1878.

——*Seringapatam, Past and Present*. Madras 1876.

Martineau, A. *Bussy in the Deccan*. Translated by Dr. Miss Cammiade. Pondichery 1941.

——*Bussy et l'Inde Française*. Paris 1935.

Mill, J. *History of British India*. Ed. H. H. Wilson. Vols. III-VI. London 1848.

Menon, S. *A History of Travancore from the Earliest Times*. Madras 1878.

Moegling, H. *Coorg Memoirs*. Bangalore 1850.

Munro, I., *Gazetteer of the Malabar and Anjengo Districts*. 2 vols. Madras 1906.

*Mysore Gazetteer*. Vols. II-V. Ed. by C. Hayavadana Rao. Bangalore 1930.

Nair, G. *The Mappilas of Malabar*. Calicut 1922.

Pannikar, K. M. *Malabar and the Dutch*. Bombay 1931.

Parasnis, D. B. *History of the Sangli State*. Bombay 1917.

Philips, C. H. *The East India Company* 1784-1834. Manchester 1940.

Shama Rao. *Modern Mysore* (*From the beginning to* 1868). Bangalore 1936.

Rapson, E. J. *The Struggle between England and France for Supremacy in India*. London 1887.

Raza Quli Khan, *Ranzat-us-Safa*, vol. IX. Iran 1338.

Rice, L. *Mysore and Coorg*. 3 vols. Bangalore 1876-78.

——*Epigraphica Carnatica*. Vols. III-IX.

Roberts, P. E. *India under Wellesley*. London 1961.

Sachot, O. *La France et l'Empire des Indes*. Paris 1887.

Saldanha, S. N. *The Captivity of Canara Christians under Tippu in* 1784. Mangalore 1933.

Sardesai, G. S. *New History of the Marathas*. Vol. III. Bombay 1948.
Sayyid Abdul Aziz Mahdavi, *Mashahir-i-Mahdaviya*, Vol. 1, (in Urdu) Bangalore 1369 A. H.
Sen, S. N. *Studies in India History*. Calcutta University 1930.
Sen, S. P. *The French in India* 1763-1816. Calcutta 1958.
Sheik Ali, B. *English Relations with Haidar Ali*. Mysore 1963.
Sinha, N. K. *Haidar Ali*. Vol. I. Calcutta 1941. Complete Second Ed. 1949.
Stewart, C. *Memoirs of Hyder Aly Khan and his Son Tippoo Sultan (in a Descriptive Catalogue of the Oriental Library of the Late Tippoo Sultan)*. Cambridge 1809.
Sutton-Keir, W. S. *The Marquess Cornwallis*. Oxford 1890.
Tantet, M. V. *L'Ambassade de Tippou-Sahib à Paris en* 1788. Paris 1899.
Taylor, G. P. *The Coins of Tipu Sultan*. Oxford 1914.
Thompson, E. and Garratt, G. T. *Rise and Fulfilment of British Rule in India*. London 1934.
Thornton, E. *A History of the British Empire in India*. Vols. II-III. London 1842.
Weber, H. *La Compagnie Française des Indes* (1604-1895). Paris 1904.
Wilkin, W. H. *The Life of Sir David Baird*. London 1912.
Wilks, M. *Historical Sketches of the South of India in an Attempt to Trace the History of Mysore*. Ed. M. Hammick, 2 vols. Mysore 1930.
Williams, R. *Great Men of India*. Chapter on *Tipu Sultan* by H. H. Dodwell.
Wilson, W. J. *History of the Madras Army*. Vols. I-II. Madras 1882.

## III. Journals and Reports

*Annual Reports of the Mysore Archaeological Department*
*Bengal: Past & Present*
*Epigraphica Carnatica*
*Islamic Culture*
*Indian Antiquary*
*Journal of Indian History*
*Journal of the Department of Letters*, Calcutta University
*Mysore University Journal*
*Proceedings of the Indian Historical Records Commission*
*Proceedings of the Indian History Congress*
*Quarterly Journal of Mythic Society*. Bangalore

# INDEX

# ERRATA AND ADDENDA

page 44, note 7, *for* 20 *read* 18.

page 46, note 2, *for* 28 *read* 26.

page 49, note 2, *for* Francaise *read* Française *and the same elsewhere.*

page 72, note 6, *for* 71-2, *read* 62-3.

page 75, line 14, *for* Pollilure *read* Pollilore.

page 77, lines 8 and 17, *for* Nayak *read* Naik.

page 108, note 1, line 3, *for* 9 *read* 7.

page 137, note 1, line 2, *add :* According to Alexander Read's report from Mysore the Caliph acceded to Tipu's proposals and sent him 100 Turkish soldiers. (1.0. Mack. MSS., No. 46, p. 99).

page 184, line 29, *for* Tiagarh, *read* Tiagar *and the same elsewhere.*

page 301, line 4, *for* Covernls *read* overland; line 5, *for* abudhadim *read* abused him; and line 7, *for* aptaine *read* Captain.

map to face page 88, *for* Shirhatthi *read* Shirhatti.

map to face page 194, *for* Muddagiri *read* Maddagiri; *for* Tirruvannamalai *read* Tiruvannamalai; and *for* Vipeen I *read* Vypin I.

map to face page 320, *for* Penner R. *read* Pennar R.